The Civil War Reminiscences of General Basil W. Duke, C.S.A.

The Civil War Reminiscences of General Basil W. Duke, C.S.A.

New Introduction by James A. Ramage

First Cooper Square Press edition 2001

This Cooper Square Press paperback edition of *The Civil War Reminiscences of General Basil W. Duke, C.S.A.* is an unabridged republication of the work originally published as *Reminiscences of General Basil W. Duke, C.S.A.* in New York in 1911, and here supplemented with a new introduction by James A. Ramage.

New introduction copyright © 2001 by James A. Ramage

All rights reserved.
No part of this book may be reproduced in any form or by any electronic or mechanical means, including information storage and retrieval systems, without written permission from the publisher, except by a reviewer who may quote passages in a review.

Published by Cooper Square Press
An Imprint of the Rowman & Littlefield Publishing Group
150 Fifth Avenue, Suite 817
New York, New York 10011

Distributed by National Book Network

Library of Congress Cataloging-in-Publication Data

Duke, Basil Wilson, 1838-1916.
  The Civil War reminiscences of General Basil W. Duke, C.S.A. / Basil Duke.
    p. cm.
  Originally published: Garden City, N.Y.: Doubleday, Page, 1911.
  ISBN 0-8154-1174-X (pbk. : alk. paper)
    1. United States—History—Civil War, 1861-1865—Campaigns. 2. United States—History—Civil War, 1861-1865—Personal narratives. 3. Duke, Basil Wilson, 1838-1916. 4. Generals—Confederate States of America—Biography. I. Title.

E470.D89 2001
973.7'82—dc21

                                2001042206

∞™ The paper used in this publication meets the minimum requirements of American National Standard for Information Sciences—Permanence of Paper for Printed Library Materials, ANSI/NISO Z39.48-1992.
Manufactured in the United States of America.

To the memory of my beloved wife
HENRIETTA MORGAN DUKE
this volume is affectionately dedicated

CONTENTS

INTRODUCTION   xiii

CHAPTER I

The political and social conditions existing in both sections which induced Civil Strife — The militant character of the American people which made compromise impossible — The various manifestations of this feeling and its many phases — The filibustering expeditions — The American volunteer, his aptitude for military service and the readiness with which he acquires the instruction and habits of a soldier.   3

CHAPTER II

The Bluegrass region of Kentucky — Its topography and the character of the soil — Its ante-bellum social life — The old-fashioned barbecue shooting match — The breeding of the thoroughbred and love of the race-horse — The recollections of early youth still haunting old age.................................   19

CHAPTER III

Outbreak of the Civil War — Political sentiment in Missouri — Struggle for control — Blair and his Wide-Awakes — Organization of the Minute Men — Raising the Southern flag — Lyon — Governor Jackson requests President Davis to furnish arms for capture of St. Louis arsenal — I am sent on this secret mission — The *Swan* carries arms from New Orleans to St. Louis — Vigilance committee thinks me a Federal spy — Am threatened with hanging — The *Swan* safely reaches St. Louis and arms successfully distributed — Capture of General Frost's command by Lyon — Alarm at Jefferson City — Burning of bridges — Preparations made to resist attack — I am informed that I have been indicted by the Federal Grand Jury — Armistice concluded between Generals Price and Harney — I go to Kentucky to be married — Return to Missouri but take service with General Hardee's forces at Pocahontas, Ark. — The Shamrock Guards — Receive my first lessons in scouting — General Hardee is ordered to Kentucky and I go there also — Attempt to reach Lexington to see my wife, but am intercepted — Stampede at Elizabethtown — I escape capture by the generous aid of a Federal colonel, afterward an associate justice of the Supreme Court...................................   32

CHAPTER IV

Gen. M. Jeff Thompson, of Missouri — I visit his camp to obtain recruits from his brigade of Missouri State Guards for the Confederate service — A brief conversation with him induces me to leave without an effort to recruit — His headquarters at Memphis and his canoe fleet — A review of his brigade by some English officers and the sequel — "Camp Boone" visited by a commissioner sent from Hopkinsville, Ky. — What he didn't tell those who sent him, when he returned — The relations which existed between Morgan's men and Wolford's — How Major Coffee observed his parole, and how it resulted in a visit to Richmond — The extraordinary gift of speech of "Captain Sam"— How it gained him victory in political discussion and caused other wagon trains to give his the right of way — He comes to grief before a court martial — How soldiers liked strong drink and how cavalrymen procured it — How I got into trouble by trying to prevent them.. 79

CHAPTER V

Gen. Albert Sidney Johnston — His early service in the United States Army — Resigns and goes to Texas at the date of the Texan struggle for independence — Is appointed Commander of the Texan Army — Duel with Gen. Felix Houston — Service in the struggle — Life in Texas — Reënters the United States Army — Service in the Mexican War — Commands the expedition sent to Utah when the Mormons threaten revolt — His exalted character — Instances of his influence and control over all who approached him — His conduct and death at Shiloh.. 100

CHAPTER VI

Irregular warfare and its usually relentless ferocity — Guerillas and bushwhackers — Champe Ferguson and "Tinker" Dave Beattie — Morgan's use of the telegraph in war — Ellsworth, his success as an operator — How he ran a foot race with a jockey "up"— "Parson" Wynne, who condemned "horse pressing" but thought a "compulsory" trade sometimes excusable — Profanity; how General de Polignac expressed his inability to understand camp slang, and how another Frenchman expressed his admiration of Forrest — Major John S. Throckmorton, of Kentucky.. 120

CHAPTER VII

Gen. Roger W. Hanson — His service in Mexico with Gen. John S. Williams, and how the record subsequently figured in a political canvass — His service in the Confederate Army and death at the Battle of Murfreesboro — Gen. Humphrey Marshall, his ability and eccentricities — How Mr. Davis utilized one of his infirmities — George W. Johnson, first Provisional Governor of Kentucky during the Civil War — His heroic death at Shiloh — Col. George St. Leger Grenfell — His early life as a soldier of fortune — Subsequent service in the English Army — Service with Morgan — Takes part in effort to release Confederate prisoners at Chicago — Is arrested, tried and convicted, and drowned in an attempt to escape from the Dry Tortugas — Col. J. Stoddard Johnston — His gallant and efficient service — He issues proclamations in Kentucky and, fleeing from arrest, mistakes friends for Yankees.... 138

CONTENTS

CHAPTER VIII

The *Vidette*, a periodical which appeared between "raids"— Sport in the army, horse racing, cock fighting and cards — a Gander-pulling at Christmas — Mumble-peg under fire — The Civil War in Shelbyville — Captain Armstrong's company and Captain Armstrong's uniform — A new way to repel cavalry — The effect of Captain Armstrong's uniform on his own men — An optical illusion, I mistake a boy on a pony for a warrior on a charger — A camp under snow...... 160

CHAPTER IX

Gen. John C. Breckinridge — His military service and capacity — Conduct at Shiloh, Chickamauga, and with the Army of Northern Virginia — Conduct in independent command — Battle of Baton Rouge — Battle of New Market — Defence of the Department of South-western Virginia — Battle of Saltville — Drives the enemy out of Bull's Gap and routs him — Combat at Marion — Is appointed Secretary of War.. 176

CHAPTER X

Gen. William Preston — His ante-bellum career as member of Congress and minister to Mexico — Part taken in the political agitation of 1861 — Enters the Confederate Army — Serves on Albert Sidney Johnston's staff at Shiloh — Promoted to brigadier and then to major general — Splendid conduct at Murfreesboro and Chickamauga — Appointed minister to Mexico — Meeting with the bandit chief Cortinas — Life in Kentucky after the war........................ 195

CHAPTER XI

The negro in the South before and during the war — Slavery in its economic and political aspects — General treatment of the negroes, and relations between master and slave — Character of the negro and plantation life — Hog-killing times and Christmas — Negro humour, his superstition, "spirits and witches"— The "Old Mammy," and the coloured "Boss" — Effect upon the negro of enlistment in the army and emancipation... 223

CHAPTER XII

Superstition and lack of superstition among the soldiers of the Civil War — A certain belief in "luck," in omens and presentiments — Incidents of warfare which do not go into history — Tragedy harsher than battle, courts martial, and executions — An ideal encampment and a sudden summons to leave it.................................. 243

CHAPTER XIII

Southern hospitality during the war — Depreciation of Confederate money — High prices and small returns — A big game of poker — How a Tennessee cavalryman "belted" the wrong horse — Major "Dick" McCann; his adventures and eccentricities.......................... 258

CHAPTER XIV

An examination of the muster rolls recalls many memories — How "Tom" Boss took charge of a steamboat pilot — How the volunteer soldier sometimes managed to "get away" with his officers — The debatable ground — How an honest farmer found it impossible to distinguish between Yankees and rebels and was fleeced by both — How "Bob" McWilliams acquired several bouquets and a good pair of breeches — That malarial and melancholy ditty, "Lorena" — The question of horseflesh — The practical manner in which a pedigree was disproven — General Morgan's favourite steeds, "Black Bess" and the "Bay Glencoe"— The Confederate epic, "I Lay Ten Dollars Down.".. 272

CHAPTER XV

General Braxton Bragg — His conduct at Shiloh — His campaign in Kentucky in 1862 — The possibilities of that campaign — Its admirable conception, feeble execution, and ultimate failure — Unusually favourable strategic opportunities neglected — Failure to concentrate and fight between Green River and Louisville permits Buell to march to Louisville unmolested — Failure to concentrate at Perryville — Battle of Perryville — Declines battle at Harrodsburg and retreats from Kentucky — Battle of Murfreesboro — Operations preceding Battle of Chickamauga — Chickamauga, Chattanooga, and Missionary Ridge — Resigns command of the Army of Tennessee — Is made inspector general of the Confederacy... 297

CHAPTER XVI

Jefferson Davis, President of the Confederacy — His character and conduct the subjects of much misconception by friends and foes alike — One whom history will vindicate — Lieutenant General Nathan Bedford Forrest — His post-bellum life — Quells a bully — Affair with General Kilpatrick — The hope of universal peace — Arbitration or preparation... 339

CHAPTER XVII

Prison life — Devices employed by the captives to alleviate the woes of bondage — I am taken from the Ohio Penitentiary by a Federal officer, whose kindness to me gets him into some trouble — Fifty of us are sent from Fort Delaware to be placed under fire of Confederate batteries at Charleston — We remain three weeks on the brig *Dragoon* under the guns of the frigate *Wabash* — Fishing for sharks and discussing exchange — Exchange at last — Hospitably entertained at Charleston — When the bombardment is renewed, I am badly scared by our own guns — Rejoin my wife and little ones................. 361

CONTENTS   xi

CHAPTER XVIII

Consternation caused by news of Gen. Lee's surrender — Confederate troops in South-western Virginia seek to join Gen. Joseph E. Johnston in North Carolina — We march through the mountain passes — Skirmishing on mule-back — Five Confederate cavalry brigades escort Mr. Davis and his cabinet from Charlotte, N. C., to Washington, Ga. — Gen. Breckinridge, as Secretary of War commands escort — At Abbeville, Mr. Davis holds a council composed of the commanders of the five brigades — I am put in charge of the treasure brought from Richmond; it occasions me much care and concern! — Part of it is paid to the troops; I turn over the residue to the acting treasurer of the Confederacy and hear a touching homily on the evils wrought by gold — At Washington, Ga., Mr. Davis leaves us, ostensibly to escape — Final surrender and general parole — Experience of Confederate soldiers after surrender — How they made their way to their homes — My own experience in that regard... 380

CHAPTER XIX

Social and political changes effected in the South by the war — Material damage wrought — Effect of emancipation upon the negro — Influences which induced unrest and agitation; lack of regular judicial administration; political graft; the Carpet-bagger and the Scallawag — Reconstruction — The Union League and the Ku-Klux Klan — Political conditions in Kentucky at the close of the war — Attitude of the Southern whites toward the negroes................................ 400

CHAPTER XX

Religious sentiment in army life — The "Exaggerated Ego"; some instances of it — A Kentucky apology — Some giants I have known — "Baby" Bates and Fish Cook — How Cook defeated a Bill for the "better regulation of Shows and Circuses," requiring them to have their performances comply fully with advertisement, but thereby accomplished his own political ruin... 416

CHAPTER XXI

An anecdote of Gen. John C. Breckinridge's early political career — The old time joint political discussion — One in which several distinguished gentlemen participated, but which became "personal" and serious consequences were threatened — The erroneous idea formerly prevalent in both the North and the South that the people of the two sections were utterly unlike — Some differences induced by environment; in the main all native-born white Americans much alike — The Southerner in fiction little like the Southerner in fact — Similarity between the Kentuckian and the Tennesseean — A question of "Civilization" which might have produced friction — An orator who wouldn't be called to order... 436

CHAPTER XXII

The years between the Fall of the Confederacy and the establishment of the New Order — The struggle in the South for social and material reorganization — Talk of exodus to foreign lands; but few go away and nearly all go to work — The women of the South and the "Daughters of the Confederacy" — Cessation of duelling in the South, and how it was discouraged in Kentucky — The last affair of honour in which I took part — "Lawlessness" in the South only a manifestation of the same spirit prevailing generally in the whole country — The "Unreconstructed Rebel" — Kentucky politics and politicians of the postbellum period — Unfortunate prevalence of partisan spirit 459

CHAPTER XXIII

My life in Louisville — The kind of place it is, and why I like it — A brief sketch of its past history and some guarded remarks about its present population — The people I have known in Louisville; some famous journalists, lawyers, judges, physicians, and preachers, and some others who ought to have been famous — The Filson Club and the Salmagundi Club — The sort of philosophy age should cultivate...... 489

INTRODUCTION TO THE COOPER SQUARE PRESS EDITION

No Southerner was more dedicated to the Confederacy than General Basil W. Duke, who first achieved world fame as colonel and second-in-command of General John Hunt Morgan's Raiders. Before the Civil War even began, Duke employed violence to take Missouri out of the Union, and he was one of the last to surrender at the war's end.

Duke was one of the most handsome men in either army—he appeared intelligent, self-confident, and competent for any challenge. He was twenty-two years old when the war began, and he moved with athletic strength and grace. He had dark hair and vigilant eagle eyes that seemed to look within a man's soul and perceive his thoughts. With his trim regulation uniform and sparkling cavalry accoutrements, Duke looked the essence of a spit-and-polish officer. Cool in times of crisis, he loved fighting and had a gentle way of giving orders that enabled him to discipline volunteers while retaining their friendship.

Born on May 28, 1838, in Scott County, Kentucky, Duke attended Georgetown College and Centre College and studied law at Transylvania University. In 1858 he moved to St. Louis and began practicing law. On June 18, 1861, he married John Hunt Morgan's sister, Henrietta Hunt Morgan, with whom he had seven children.

In *Reminiscences*, first published in 1911, Duke relates his role in the coming of the Civil War in Missouri, and recounts in detail his combat experiences, the atmosphere in camp, and life as a soldier and as a prisoner-of-war.

Duke first attempted to force Missouri to secede by proposing that the pro-South "Minute Men" militia goad the pro-Union "Wide-Awake" home guards into a fight. Duke and his men raised a secession flag on the courthouse in St. Louis, and he hoped that a riot would ensue so that during the fighting the Minute Men could capture the federal arsenal, the largest in a slave state. But pro-South Governor Claiborne F. Jackson rejected such aggression, and instead sent Captain Duke and another man on a secret mission to obtain artillery from President Jefferson Davis and the new Confederate government. Duke smuggled four cannon through enemy lines, but the stronger Union militia in St. Louis quickly captured them. Confederate forces withdrew to southern Missouri, and Duke served for a few weeks, scouting and raiding along the front toward St. Louis.

He then attempted to recruit a Missouri-based cavalry company, but finding it difficult, crossed the Mississippi River to try his luck in Kentucky. Instead he joined the Confederate forces defending southern Kentucky and began raiding behind enemy lines with the cavalry company of John Hunt Morgan, his brother-in-law from Lexington. On October 27, 1861, he mustered in as Morgan's first lieutenant. Rising to brigade commander with the rank of colonel, Duke played a key role in Morgan's achievements as "guerrilla par excellence" of the Confederacy, as the model for the Partisan Ranger Act (which authorized President Davis to commission units of Partisan Rangers for detached guerrilla operations), and as a romantic folk hero of the Southern people.

Duke was wounded or incarcerated several times during the war. His shoulders and back were injured while leading a frontal assault at Shiloh, and on December 29, 1862, shrapnel struck him in the head during a skirmish on Rolling Fork River near Elizabethtown, Kentucky. He was captured while leading a rearguard action at Buffington Island, Ohio, on July 19, 1863, and held at Johnson's Island, the Ohio State Penitentiary, Camp Chase, and Fort Delaware.

Rumors in the Union army declared that Duke was the life and soul behind all of Morgan's movements. When Duke was captured on the Great Raid in Ohio in July 1863, the *New York Times* declared that the renowned "BASIL DUKE" had "planned all the campaigning which MORGAN has executed. He is a military genius of no ordinary kind, and his loss is a heavy one to the guerrilla enterprise of the rebels." Morgan agreed that Duke was wise in counsel and gallant in the field and reported, "His services have ever been invaluable to me."

Duke, however, denied that he was in charge, and in the present book describes an incident that provides an inside view of how he related to Morgan. On the Cave City Raid in May 1862, Morgan's raiders captured Union Major W. A. Coffee and paroled him, which meant that he was to go home and to refrain from fighting until exchanged. Instead, Coffee passed through the lines, showed up at Morgan's camp in Knoxville, and volunteered to spend his parole as a prisoner-of-war. When Department Commander General Edmund Kirby Smith suggested sending Coffee to prison in Richmond, Morgan told Duke that he planned to violate orders and dispatch Coffee to Kentucky on a good horse with an escort. Duke gently pointed out that such action might ruin Morgan's career and suggested meeting with Coffee to discuss the matter. Coffee said that he appreciated the favor, but preferred to go to Richmond rather than get Morgan courtmartialed. Thus, Morgan obeyed orders and sent Coffee to Richmond, where he was treated well and soon exchanged. This type of interaction occurred many times; Duke acted as a restraining influence on Morgan and, with regard to the men, took charge of their discipline. Duke said that for him, when Morgan was killed on September 4, 1864, the chivalry and glory of the war disappeared.

After Morgan's death, Duke was promoted to brevet brigadier general and took command of Morgan's division. When General Robert E. Lee surrendered, Duke and some of his men escorted Jefferson Davis during his flight from Richmond.

A significant portion of Duke's postwar *Reminiscences* is devoted to vivid descriptions and evaluations of fellow Confederate commanders. He observed Western Departmental Commander General Albert Sidney Johnston several times and reported that his majestic appearance and manner impressed everyone who came into his presence. One day when Duke was waiting alone in a room at headquarters, Johnston suddenly walked in and Duke, awe-inspired, was speechless. Twice Johnston attempted friendly banter, but all Duke could do was bow in silence. Finally, Johnston bowed elegantly and left as Duke silently bowed once again.

Duke greatly admired Johnston's "unhesitating promptness" in withdrawing from Kentucky and Nashville and in seizing the initiative and surprising U. S. Grant's army at Shiloh. He concluded that Johnston was "a great man" and speculated that if he had not been killed the first day at Shiloh, he would have won the battle and reoccupied Tennessee and Kentucky.

P. G. T. Beauregard succeeded Johnston, and on June 27, 1862, Braxton Bragg took command of the Army of Tennessee. Duke declared that Bragg was an effective subordinate general, but failed to inspire confidence as a commander. Indeed, Bragg was so sullen and gloomy in manner and appearance that Duke found him repellant and enveloped in an atmosphere of failure. He was timid in execution and afraid to fight. With the benefit of hindsight, Duke wrote that in the 1862 Kentucky invasion Bragg should have fallen back on Nashville and gone on the defensive as soon as Don Carlos Buell's army marched into Kentucky. Duke felt that Bragg should have attacked Buell at Munfordville—an opinion that still stands strongly in Civil War historiography today. Duke also contended that when Bragg failed to take the offensive in Munfordville and allowed Buell to march to Louisville in safety, Bragg lost the initiative, and thus the campaign.

Duke saw General Nathan Bedford Forrest while the latter commanded the rearguard during the Confederate withdrawal from Nashville. He wrote that Forrest's resolute face seemed to cause all who gazed upon it to submit to his will, and praised his tall, powerful form towering above the mob, which, even in its most furious moments, gave way before him. He described the famous interview between Morgan and Forrest when the latter explained the key to success in his Murfreesboro Raid: "I just took the shortcut and got there first with the most men." Duke became even more well-acquainted with Forrest after the war and related how they were on the same train on the way to the 1868 Democratic convention in New York when a bully rushed onto the train to give Forrest a thrashing. Forrest stood up and said, "I am Forrest. What do you want?" Immediately, the bully turned, rushed out of the car, and disappeared. Later, challenging a political opponent to a duel, Forrest requested that Duke serve as his second, and asked him to persuade the man to fight on horseback with sabers.

Reminiscences is rife with anecdotes about the many colorful characters whom Duke encountered in his travails. Tom Boss, one of Morgan's Men, invariably raided with an axe strapped to his back. During a mounted melee a Union captain struck Tom on the head with a saber. Tom grabbed the officer's throat with his left hand, and axed open the man's skull with his right.

Soldier of fortune Colonel George St. Leger Grenfell, a bold and impressive Englishman, carried a large, keen-edged knife. When a bone felon (an infected or abscessed joint) developed on the forefinger of his left hand and surgeons refused to amputate it, Grenfell spread his hand on a chopping block and cut off the finger himself.

Parson Wynne gave lengthy discourses against the impressment of horses, and castigated his friend Dan Ray and others for stealing them. One day when Wynne's own horse was injured and a civilian appeared riding a fine horse, Parson unhesitantly impressed the animal. He explained to Dan that in this case it was not horse-pressing but a "compulsory" and "necessary" trade.

Colonel J. Stoddard Johnston, an editor of *The Louisville Courier-Journal* after the war, was one of the most loquacious men whom Duke met. He joined the Confederate army in 1862 and, arriving one night within Confederate lines after an arduous journey, fell into a sound sleep. Duke and others decided to play a practical joke on him. They dressed a tall, red-bearded Rebel unfamiliar to Johnston in a Union blue overcoat and stood him at the foot of the bed. Johnston awakened and, assuming that he had been captured, let out a roar, launching into a lengthy explication of how he was an innocent, loyal man, a peaceful farmer from Indiana. Then, after the laughter subsided, Johnston grinned and claimed that he had known from the beginning that it was a ruse, and had played along solely for the men's enjoyment.

Duke herein recalls how two guards of the New Madrid Vigilance Committee captured him during his attempt to smuggle four cannons from Baton Rouge to St. Louis. Duke stood before them in the bar of the wharf-boat; two other men guarded the doors with cocked pistols. "We think that you are a Yankee spy," said the Chairman of the Committee, "and if we become satisfied that you are one we are going to hang you." Duke calmly bargained for a twenty-four-hour delay and assured them that, within that time, the steamboat *Swan* would arrive with the cannon as proof of his dedication to the Rebellion.

Later, as a scout for Confederate forces in southern Missouri, he was delivering an official message to civilian Cagey Graham one night, and announced himself with a loud voice as he approached Graham's house. The next morning at breakfast Graham's son Bill told Duke that he had been on guard in the woods near the house when Duke arrived. "When you rode up to the house and hollered out like you did," Bill said, "I concluded you didn't mean no harm. If you had hitched your horse out in the brush and prowled around on foot, I'd have let you have both barrels of my shotgun."

Duke also tells how he quelled a drunken free-for-all one morning in camp, describes his intense feelings in having to order a deserter shot by a firing squad, and recalls fishing for sharks as a prisoner-of-war on a transport ship at Hilton Head.

Moving to Louisville in 1868, Duke was active in public life and was one of the city's most respected leaders. He was elected as a Democrat to the Kentucky House of Representatives in 1869 and, from 1875 to 1880, was the commonwealth's attorney for the Fifth Judicial District.

After the Civil War the Louisville and Nashville Railroad rapidly expanded into the first major railway in the South. By 1880 L&N tracks extended through the northern Alabama iron-and-coal region and reached New Orleans, Mobile, and Pensacola. In order to communicate effectively with Southern state legislators and local leaders, the L&N employed Duke as its chief counsel and lobbyist. For over twenty years Duke served as the symbol of the L&N, and—with his stylish beard, gentlemanly manner, magnetic charm, and integrity—won friends and influenced politicians.

He was made a charter member of the Filson Club Historical Society in 1884. First President Rueben Durrett introduced him to President Theodore Roosevelt, who appointed Duke in 1901 as commissioner for Shiloh National Park. He edited *Southern Bivouac* magazine from 1885 to 1887, and in 1895 published *History of the Bank of Kentucky, 1792–1895*. He was active in veterans' organizations and in demand as a speaker. In April 1914 he spoke at the monthly Filson Club meeting on his recollections of the Battle of Shiloh. He died after surgery in New York City on September 16, 1916, and was buried in the Hunt-Morgan family plot in Lexington Cemetery.

INTRODUCTION   xix

Duke's purpose in writing most of the twenty-three essays in this book was to entertain the readers of *Home and Farm*, a Louisville publication. He had no thought of publishing the articles as a book, but later agreed in response to popular demand. He had written *A History of Morgan's Cavalry* in 1867, respected today as one of the most accurate and fascinating books of the Civil War. Both that work and *Reminiscences* are factually reliable and frequently quoted by contemporary scholars. Duke's writing captured the spirit of the times.

Historically, one of *Reminiscences*'s most lasting values is that Duke candidly and openly expressed his opinions on Reconstruction and, in so doing, articulated the mind of white Southern business leaders of his era. Duke believed that the L&N properly encouraged industrial development, but was convinced that progress could be made only through the restoration and continuation of white supremacy. For historians and readers today, this book provides a voice for that view. Duke's prejudiced opinions of slavery and African Americans in the Reconstruction era are valuable reminders of how far history and society have advanced since 1911.

In his time, however, Duke's interpretations prevailed among scholars, and this book reflects the scholarship of Ulrich B. Phillips, a native of Georgia who earned his Ph.D. in history at Columbia University in 1902. Phillips was teaching at the University of Michigan in 1918 when he published *American Negro Slavery*, the standard study of the time. Phillips described African American slaves as inferior, childlike, docile, and content in bondage. He declared that African Americans were fortunate to have the plantation as a training school for vocational skills and for education in democracy.

Today, after fifty years of revision, this view has been completely overturned, and historians emphasize that under the surface slave plantations seethed with discontent. Slaves resisted in many ways, including violent uprisings (planned and actual), sabotage, and escaping to freedom in Canada and in the free states.

Another influence on Duke was William A. Dunning, a mentor of Phillips at Columbia, who concluded that Reconstruction was a disaster in that unscrupulous carpetbaggers used ignorant and childlike freedmen to gain power and to plunder state treasuries.

Today, historians stress the active role of freedmen in Reconstruction and the political, social, and economic progress achieved by blacks. Public schools were established, churches and religious societies were organized, and freedmen agitated for the right to vote as well as for political and civil rights. Reconstruction was a time of progress, and the Fourteenth Amendment, though almost immediately besieged by racist or reactionary opponents, served as a legal foundation for the Civil Rights movement. But neither Dunning nor Phillips, and therefore Duke, shared this view.

James A. Ramage
Highland Heights, Kentucky
May 2001

James A. Ramage, author of *Gray Ghost: The Life of Col. John Singleton Mosby* and *Rebel Raider: The Life of General John Hunt Morgan,* is Regents Professor of History at Northern Kentucky University. He lives in Cold Spring, Kentucky.

The Civil War Reminiscences of General Basil W. Duke, C.S.A.

CHAPTER I

THE reminiscences contained in this volume, of the Civil War and the period just preceding it, were, most of them, written for the *Home and Farm*, of Louisville, and with no thought at first of their publication other than in that paper. They are compiled and published in more permanent form in deference to the wishes of a number of those who read them when they originally appeared.

They can scarcely be regarded as positive contributions to the history, so much as attempts to describe incidents characteristic of the period and its potential thought and feeling; but may help to illustrate some things which graver historical recital will expound when the time has come to construct the fabric of history with the material provided by the chroniclers. In writing them I had chiefly in mind the experiences of the soldier, the atmosphere of the camp, the gossip of the bivouac.

The history of no period can be justly written — certainly the character and meaning of no struggle which is in effect a social or political revolution can be correctly and graphically portrayed — unless the conditions of the times, the habits of thought then prevailing, and the predominant sentiment which influenced or incited popular action, be taken into account.

To no important and striking epoch of modern history is this rule of historical narration more applicable than to our great civil conflict — "the war between the states." For the treatment of this subject an abundance of the material ordinarily employed in historical composition has already been supplied. The "historical facts" have, in so far as such a thing is possible, been ascertained and agreed on. The writers on both sides of the controversy have been industrious in proclaiming all that investigation or research could procure. No document or declaration, perhaps, of the kind usually termed historical, has been overlooked; and ingenious use has been made of the results so obtained, in support of each contention.

The record has been so often quoted that the average reader may be excused some impatience if more than mere reference to it be attempted; and the arguments, pro and con, have become tedious from frequent repetition. We are familiar with all that has been or can be said in defence of the effort made by the South for separate and independent governmental existence, and with all that has been asserted in justification of the action taken by the North to maintain the integrity of the Union. We know why the people of the one section believed secession to be the unpardonable political sin; and why the people of the other regarded coercion as a brutal crime, not only against the American idea that all governments derive their just powers from the consent of the governed, but against the liberty it has been the chief purpose of our institutions to protect. Every "intelligent school-boy" in the South knows that the Southern people held that the Federal Constitution and the "more perfect union" that instrument was intended to construct was a compact formed between sovereign, equal, and independent states, and were absolutely convinced that the parties to such a contract had the right, for any reason in their own discretion sufficient, to withdraw from it. Every boy in the North who has read a school history understands that the men who fought "to preserve the life of the Nation" believed the Union was not only of superior sanctity to any other institution of human creation, but that it was meant to be indissoluble and perpetual. The technical contentions and data on which they are founded are all on file for the use of the future historian; nor can he, nor need he, add anything to either.

Likewise, every cause or provocation which conduced to incite the conflict has received as thorough discussion and as equally clear exposition. No statement now made could present more forcibly than has been done the chief issue of the fierce debate, or show more plainly how the persistent agitation of the question of slavery, in its varied phases, inflamed sectional passion and resentment, and suggested to the disputants the thought that it could be settled only by civil war.

No amount of dissertation could make us understand more distinctly that a few men in the North sought the abolition of slavery, at any cost, for the sake of humanity; that others thought it not in accord with the spirit of the age and an economic mistake; and a still greater number objected for political and commercial reasons to its introduction into territories which would soon become states.

We shall never comprehend more perfectly the irritation with which the South regarded what it deemed unjust interference with an institution in which immense proprietary interests were involved; and which was recognized and guaranteed protection by every muniment that had given the Union claim to respect, and the government — the product of that Union — title to demand allegiances. We know, as well as we shall ever know, that the resentment burned hotter because the Southern people felt that they were not responsible for the existence of slavery, and that it had been unloaded on them by the communities whence came the clamour for its abolition.

We know that the South dreaded with reason, as subsequent experience demonstrated, the effect of sudden and arbitrary emancipation, and believed it would be compelled, by an overwhelming free-soil majority, if the slave-holding states remained in the Union.

Both sections were alarmed. The one feared an unrestricted extension of slavery into the public domain; the other feared its abolition. The South saw safety only in secession. The North believed that, with the dissolution of the Union, permanent peace upon this continent would be impossible. There was assuredly an intelligible apprehension, if not a sufficient *casus belli*, on both sides.

Nevertheless, it will always be more or less a matter of wonder that, serious as was the dispute, it could not have been adjusted without resort to arms. At this date, and to the generation born since the close of the war, it is doubtless incomprehensible that a people descended from the same ancestry; speaking the same language; inheriting the same patriotic traditions; entertaining, in the main, identical ideas regarding the purpose of political institutions and the functions of government, and cherishing a similar hope for the happiness and glory of the country in which they lived — should have obstinately rejected compromise and insisted upon war. Even the veteran of that war, now distant from the influences which induced it, must remember with some bewilderment, and marvel mildly, at least, when he recalls the irresistible impulse which urged him into the fight.

The population of the United States is to-day nearly thrice as numerous and distinctly less homogeneous than it was in 1861. The area covered by the states which now compose the Union is greater, the interests represented more diversified than then. Consequently it might be thought that occasion for dangerous dispute and the occurrence of internecine altercation is more to be apprehended now than at that date. Happily, no sectional difference — the most potent incentive to such quarrel — exists, although we can see how trouble might come in other ways. Yet no man fears that popular discontent, however extensive; political or factional dissension, however bitter; or even the most extreme phase of social reform or experiment — will ever receive such general and formidable expression. There may be frequent exhibitions in future American history of sporadic revolt and partial insurrection, but it is not at all probable that this country will again witness another domestic disturbance of like magnitude.

One very excellent reason why more caution will be observed hereafter, in this respect, than was exercised by the men of 1861 is at once suggested. The experience and stern teachings of that former four years of devastating strife will long linger in the national memory and serve as wholesome warning. But, independently of this consideration, it is not difficult to explain why the generation by which that war was waged was more willing and more apt for such ultimate measures than any subsequent generation would or could be.

The temper of the people at that date and their racial traditions inclined them more readily to such action. The bulk of the white population was still of British ancestry. The Celtic and Dutch settlers of earliest arrival in the country had become commingled and closely identified with that element. Each of these stocks had inherited a jealous regard for personal liberty and popular rights, and a disposition to maintain them.

Moreover, there was more leisure and a greater inclination to consider such matters then than now; and questions which were topics of great doubt and discussion then were very effectually determined afterward by the logic of the sword.

The attention of men at that time was not directed to so many subjects as the crowded conditions of to-day make necessary; but those which were considered produced a profounder impression.

It should be taken into account that modern commercialism, while it breeds bickerings in smaller affairs, induces a conservative feeling in respect of public and governmental conduct. Popular grievances have multiplied with the increase of population and the vast heterogeneous immigration of the past thirty or forty years; but their very frequency and diversity prevent any large class or number of people from enlisting in their advocacy. It is much easier to inaugurate a strike or establish a boycott than to organize the extensive and determined resistance which would amount to civil war.

More than anything else, however, which made war possible was the aggressive, assertive spirit and war-like temper characteristic, at that period, of the people of the whole country. This disposition had been developed and cultivated by the conditions of previous American life — had been an almost habitual feature of that life — since the days when the first settlers fought for their homes with the savage. It had become instinctive, and was under no such restraints, when the sectional contention culminated in hostilities, as are now felt.

We can scarcely conceive, as we reason and feel about such matters now, that any provocation, any form of persuasion, could "fire the Southern heart" or reconcile the Northern mind to so desperate a remedy. But those who knew the people of fifty years ago, when these questions so fraught with passion and perplexity were urged, can understand how — after the failure of other methods — the solution was attempted by force.

The earliest settlers of this continent were taught, as I have said, to consider constant warfare the normal condition of American life. The same racial education and habit of thought continued throughout the colonial period, and were intensified by the passionate vicissitudes of the Revolutionary War. The spirit so bred remained as a characteristic trait of the American people until the Civil War finally furnished it full opportunity and scope for exercise, and, it is to be hoped. gave it also in large measure, its quietus.

The English armies in the French and Indian wars waged previously to the separation of the colonies from Great Britain consisted more largely of colonial contingents — "provincial militia" — than of British regular troops: and the alacrity with which these unprofessional, but by no means unskilled or inefficient, fighters responded to every call made on them evinced their love of warfare quite as thoroughly as their conduct in the field demonstrated their aptitude for it. Taught from their boyhood indifference to danger, habituated to combat, inured to hardships and fatigue, and enjoying the excitement of the campaign and battle very much as they did that of the chase, little training was needed to make them soldiers. So it was that in Braddock's disastrous defeat, after his regulars were almost destroyed, the American riflemen saved the remnant of his army. In all of the greater battles fought with the Indians, when the latter, under French tuition and suggestion, had learned how to coalesce and join forces, the colonial militia did the fighting.

Nearly every colonist of military age served in the "rangers," the volunteer force which guarded the frontiers against Indian incursions. The term survived to be applied to the daring riders who on the Texas border drove back Mexican banditti and met the raids of the Lipan and Comanche. Some of the most picturesque figures among the heroes of the Revolution were conspicuous as officers in this body before winning later and wider fame: notably Putnam, Stark, and Ethan Allen; and Marion, Sumter, and others who won subsequent distinction and performed similar service in the South.

The troops enlisted in the continental line proved equal — even in the use of the bayonet — on more than one occasion — to the best of the English infantry regiments. "Light Horse Harry" Lee and Col. William Washington organized a cavalry which held its own with the famous legion of Tarleton.

But it was by the irregulars that the war-like temper of the American was best illustrated in the war for American independence. It is not too much to say that, notwithstanding an occasional panic to which undisciplined troops are always subject, the greater number of decisive successes was achieved by them. The victory of King's Mountain, which many historians consider as, more than any other, the pivotal event of the war, was won by the frontier backwoods riflemen under the leadership of Shelby, Campbell, and Sevier. In this battle, men who had no previous military training in the ordinary acceptation of the term, and officered by captains untaught save by experience in Indian warfare, defeated and well-nigh annihilated a picked body of British regulars.*

The settlement of Kentucky and Tennessee, accomplished only after years of dire and incessant contest with the savage tribes from whom the white man wrested those fertile regions; the acquisition of the great Northwestern territory and its subsequent settlement; and that of Alabama and Mississippi — all done at the cost of hard fighting and lavish bloodshed — yet further accustomed this martial population to appeal to force and arms as the first as well as last resort. More than that, these constant territorial accessions and the elation born of success taught the habit of conquest and an adventurous spirit which thought everything possible to daring and effort.

As each successive generation came on the stage it received its lesson, and fresh stimulus was given this appetite for war. When the American settlers in Texas, aided by their sympathetic countrymen, who eagerly embraced the inviting opportunity, had thrown off the Mexican yoke, and after the consequent war with Mexico, this feeling, perhaps, reached its acme; but there was no diminution of it as late as 1861.

The disposition to acquire territory, inherited from his Anglo-Saxon ancestor — than whom, since the Roman, the world has seen no more inveterate "land-grabber" — enhanced the American's love of combat, or, rather, became identified with it; because in almost every case of such acquisition he had to fight for what he got. I think that this combative feeling entered into his

---

*The term "militia" is used so loosely and applied so indifferently to troops serving under dissimilar conditions and often altogether unequal in respect of equipment, training, and consequent efficiency, that it has become confusing. The efficiency of a militia depends in no slight degree upon the readiness with which it may be summoned and the period for which it may be kept in the field. A militia which is or can be called into service infrequently and only for a few weeks, and receives no instruction in the interim, will necessarily be less efficient than one of which longer, more frequent and more arduous service is demanded. It is certainly an egregious error to confound the American militia man, as some European writers constantly do, with the American volunteer soldier enlisted for "three years, or the war."

The immediate moral effect upon the man, of enlistment for a definite term and the realization that he must serve during that period, is of itself considerable.

The meaning of Washington's oft-quoted criticism of the militia is frequently misunderstood. He had in mind the colonial militia whose members were bound to no definite term of service, under little obligation to serve at all, and were always returned to their ordinary avocations after very brief service. While such troops might at times fight well, little dependence could, of course, be placed in them for the purposes of a protracted campaign. On the other hand the regiments of the continental line on which he so thoroughly relied, and which he termed "regulars," were the exact equivalent of the volunteers of the Civil War.

every idea of public duty. Patriotism and pugnacity became, in popular estimation, synonymous virtues. A man was not thought to love his country or to take a proper interest in the welfare of his immediate community if he was not willing, indeed anxious, to fight in any quarrel in which either might be involved.

Whenever an international misunderstanding occurred, or sectional debate grew bitter, statesmen and orators came forward with militant suggestions, certain to receive abundant popular endorsement. Every striking phrase which voiced such sentiment, whether directed against opponents abroad or at home — "Fifty-four forty, or fight," in a dispute about a boundary; "Tear down the flaunting lie," if the issue was domestic — became a motto and slogan for thousands. When a people are in that temper they are ripe for strife.

But the most remarkable expression of this spirit of adventure and combativeness was that furnished by the "filibustering" expeditions undertaken between the years 1849 and 1860. These expeditions were in no sense piratical or purely for plunder, as many people have supposed, although ultimate profit in the shape of allotment of lands and lucrative employment was, doubtless, expected by many who enlisted in them. That they were *per se* lawless, in the strictest construction of public policy and canon, goes without saying. But they were in accord with the spirit of the times, in America at least, and certainly intended to establish a better social and governmental condition than they assailed. As has been said especially of the three expeditions made by Narciso Lopez in the effort to free Cuba, they "were movements in the interest of humanity. They were not for plunder and spoils, but for the freedom of human beings from the galling yoke of tyranny."

Col. R. T. Durrett, in his introduction to the exceedingly interesting contribution to the Filson Club publications entitled "Lopez's Expeditions to Cuba," written by Mr. A. C. Quisenberry, claims that these expeditions were by no means exceptional or *sui generis*, and names Cortez, Miranda, Aaron Burr, and Gen. Sam Houston as having been, before the date of which I write, "the four principal filibusters in the Western world. Two were successful and two were failures."

Of the latter attempts of this nature, the principal, indeed the only, ones worthy of record were those of Lopez and those subsequently undertaken by Gen. William Walker, "the gray-eyed man of destiny" and most eccentric and "all-around" soldier of fortune.

Walker made an expedition into Lower California in October, 1853, "annexed" Sonora — by proclamation — and was captured at San Diego. He went to Nicaragua in June, 1855, won and occupied a considerable part of that country, made war, as a Nicaraguan executive and "patriot," with Costa Rica, and executed a native general for "treason." He was elected President, and his government was recognized by President Pierce; but unfortunately he clashed with the on-coming "commercialism" of the near future. Confiscating some of the property of the Vanderbilt Steamship Company, in his need of revenue, that soulless corporation turned against him, and a United States naval officer arrested and bore him "in exile" from his adopted land. Nevertheless, in 1860, he made an expedition to Honduras, and was captured and shot by the native authorities at Truxillo.

The young men recruited in the United States for these expeditions were, as a rule, of good birth, good education, and unimpeachable honour and integrity. They were urged, perhaps, by some surviving impulse derived from the old Scandinavian strain — the same Viking instinct which impelled Raleigh, Drake, and Hawkins, and which to-day seduces the Briton, so "respectable" when at home, into amateur interference with quarrels in which he has no conceivable interest, and causes him to "pot" people who never did him or his forbears the least injury.

An incident of the third and last expedition of Lopez — the "Bahia Honda" expedition, as it was termed — excited at the time intense feeling throughout the United States, and will, perhaps, never be forgotten in Kentucky. No story in American annals possesses a more pathetic and heroic interest. The second, or "Cardenas," expedition had been partially successful, and Lopez was encouraged to attempt another in the following year, 1851. In August of that year he disembarked a force of four hundred and fifty-three men at the village of Morillas, in Bahia Honda harbour, seventy miles from Havana. He expected a larger body of troops, which he had recruited principally in Kentucky, to follow and reinforce him. Before transportation could be furnished them, however, the expedition had ended in disaster, and Lopez himself had died on the scaffold.

Among the officers who accompanied Lopez on the *Pampero* — the steamer which bore the ill-fated expedition — was Col. William Logan Crittenden, a young Kentuckian and graduate of West Point, who had served gallantly in the Mexican War and had resigned his commission in the Army of the United States that he might devote his best efforts to the cause of the oppressed people of Cuba. He was the great-grandson of Benjamin Logan — with the exception of Boone only, the most famous and the ablest of the Kentucky pioneers. He was a grandson of Col. John Allen, who commanded a regiment of Kentuckians and was killed in the battle of the River Raisin; and was a nephew of John J. Crittenden, so long the worthy colleague and peer of Henry Clay in the Senate. Young Crittenden was noted, even in that day of reckless daring, for undaunted courage, but his amiable disposition and attractive manner had won him greater favour. There can be no doubt that he was animated solely by love of liberty and hatred of oppression.

The *Pampero* was sighted from Havana, and a Spanish warship, *Pizarro*, immediately went in pursuit of her. The *Pampero* ran upon a reef in Bahia Honda harbour, and it was with great difficulty that the troops could be landed. The first boats which approached shore were fired upon by the Creoles, from whom Lopez had expected welcome and support. Lopez pressed on a short distance into the interior, leaving Crittenden with a small detachment at Murillos to guard the stores. Eight hundred Spanish troops were landed from the *Pizarro*, which followed and defeated Lopez. Crittenden embarked with his party in four small fishing boats, hoping to make his way to Key West or Yucatan. He was overtaken by the Spanish steamer *Habanero* and surrendered to the officer commanding her on condition that the lives of himself and men should be spared and that they should be treated as prisoners of war. The captain general of Cuba, when the prisoners were brought to Havana, refused to recognize the terms upon which they had surrendered and ordered them to be instantly tried by a drumhead court-martial. They were all — Crittenden and his fifty comrades — sentenced to be shot. The execution of the sentence was delayed for thirty minutes that they might write to their friends. The following letter was written by Crittenden to Dr. Lucien Henseley, of Frankfort, Ky.:

Ship of War *Esperanza*, Aug. 16, 1851.

DEAR LUCIEN: In half an hour I, with fifty others, am to be shot. We were in small boats. General Lopez separated the balance of the command from me. I had with me about 100. Was attacked by two battalion infantry and one company of horse. The odds were too great, and, strange to tell, I was not furnished with one single musket cartridge. Lopez did not get any artillery. I have not the heart to write any of my family. If the truth ever comes out, you will find that I did my duty and have the confidence of every man with me. We had retired from the field and were going to the sea and were overtaken by the Spanish steamer *Habanero* and captured. Tell General Houston that his nephew got separated from me on the thirteenth day of the fight and I have not seen him since. He may have straggled off and joined Lopez, who advanced rapidly into the interior. My people, however, were entirely surrounded on every side. We saw that we had been deceived grossly and were making for the United States when taken. During my short sojourn in this island I have not met a single patriot. We landed some forty or fifty miles to the westward of this, and I am sure that in that part of the island Lopez has no friends. When I was attacked Lopez was only three miles off. If he had not been deceiving us as to the state of things he would have fallen back with his forces and made fight.

I am requested to get you to tell Mr. Green of the custom-house that his brother shares my fate. Victor Ker is also with me; so also Stanford. I recollect no other of your acquaintance present. I will die like a man. My heart has not failed me yet, nor do I believe it will. Communicate with my family. Tell my friend on Philippa Street that I had better have been persuaded to stay; that I have not forgotten him and will not in the moment of death. This is an incoherent letter, but the circumstances must excuse me. My hands are swollen to double their thickness, resulting from having been too tightly corded for the last eighteen hours. Write to Whistlar; let him write to my mother. I am afraid that the news will break her heart. My heart beats warmly toward her now. Farewell. My love to all my family. I am sorry that I die owing a cent, but it is inevitable. Yours, strong in heart. W. L. CRITTENDEN.

When the half-hour of respite had expired the prisoners were taken to Castle Atares, in the immediate vicinity of Havana, and were shot on the slope of the hill in front of the fortification.

Crittenden was shot first. Mr. Quisenberry says:

"One of the rabble pushed through the line of soldiers and rushed up to Crittenden and pulled his beard. The gallant Kentuckian, with the utmost coolness, spat in the coward's face.

He refused to kneel or to be blindfolded, saying in a clear, ringing voice: 'A Kentuckian kneels to none except his God, and always dies facing his enemy.'"

The wonderful material progress of the past fifty years has been scarcely so remarkable as has been the alteration in thought and sentiment along the lines I have indicated. We are now almost as far removed, in this regard, from the immediate antebellum generation as it was from the day of the Spanish conquistador or the early English explorer.

A notable trait of the period and a natural result of this racial experience was the sanguine, unlimited self-reliance of the American, especially in the matter of what he could do in war and battle.

Those who are old enough to remember the immediate antebellum period may recall as vividly as anything which characterized it, the confidence with which both sides believed that the issue of the conflict would be in accord with their wishes.

The people of the South, especially those of an age to serve in the army, affected to believe, and many of them did believe, that "one Southerner could whip five Yankees." On the other hand, while the faith of the Yankee in his individual prowess and invincibility was not so arrogant, he was nevertheless quite convinced that one Yankee would be able to give a good account of himself in a fight with one Southerner. He also relied, and, as the result showed, with reason, upon the superior numbers the North could put into the field, the overwhelming superior resources of the national government and its ability to furnish all the means necessary to prosecute war successfully.

He cherished another belief, not so well founded — *viz.*, that the Southern man, although a daring and dashing fighter, lacked endurance and would not be able to stand the strain of protracted warfare and its concomitant toils and privations. It was abundantly proven that this idea was a mistaken one, as much so as the whimsical Southern notion that the Northern man lacked courage. It was amply demonstrated that fortitude and pluck, stamina and combativeness, were qualities common to both.

This fact, very important to be considered then, but unfortunately not sooner realized, and never, it is to be hoped, to be forgotten, was first discovered at the battle of Shiloh and the military operations immediately preceding it; but was incontestably established by the tremendous efforts subsequently made, and the fearful decimation suffered by the combatants in both hosts, in many an arduous campaign and on innumerable stricken fields, ghastly with carnage.

The native-born Americans of the respective armies were so nearly akin in blood, descended, as they were, from practically the same racial stocks, that there could be, of course, little difference between them in inherent qualities; although immediate environment and social training might produce an apparent dissimilarity. In respect of aptitude for military service — that is to say, when they first entered the ranks — the youth of the Southern, Western, and border states were unquestionably superior to those from the North-eastern states. They were more habituated to an active out-of-door life, and more inured, therefore, to the exposure and physical exertion which military service demands than were those who had pursued more sedentary occupations. They were nearly all of them expert horsemen and marksmen, and, accustomed to hunt and live in the woods, were already initiated in the life of the camp.

Among the Southern troops some of the young fellows from the cities seemed, during the first months of service, to take more kindly to the camp and campaigning than even the hardiest of their rural brethren, who had known only the life of the farm. This was doubtless because the former were already habituated to irregular hours and eating and sleeping when most convenient. The country boy could endure fatigue, but not, at first, the lack of his rest and meals at due time.

The number of those, reared altogether in the country, who had escaped the usual diseases of infancy was surprising, and they were generally afflicted with them after getting into camp.

Brief time was required, however, to cause these minor differences to disappear and make the native-born soldiers of both armies alike in all essential respects; and, when equally well disciplined and commanded, all fought with equal daring and tenacity.

Military writers will eventually agree, I think, that the American volunteer can be made a veteran in briefer time than such change can be wrought in men of any other nationality; and when he becomes a veteran, no soldier is more apt and resourceful, bolder, or less susceptible to panic.

Many declarations of the belief so fondly cherished of the invincibility of the Southerner and the incapacity of the Northern man to match him in battle will be remembered, and some good stories of how the Southerner frankly expressed his subsequent disillusion in this respect have been told. Every one has heard of the explanation of such extravagant utterance made by the man who, having been red-hot for secession and fight before the war, kept discreetly in the rear after it commenced and became an unconditional supporter of every obnoxious measure to which the South was subjected during the reconstruction period. He was making a speech at that date, and some one in the crowd shouted the question:

"Didn't you say in 1860, on this very spot, that we could whip the Yankees with popguns?"

"I did," replied the unabashed demagogue, "and I think so still. But, d — n 'em, they wouldn't fight us that way."

Some two or three years previous to the beginning of actual hostilities, and while the whole country was convulsed with the agitation which induced the conflict, I heard this idea of the Northern man's lack of courage or combativeness very earnestly denied, and in a way which made a strong impression on my mind. It was at a political meeting held at Lexington, Ky., which was addressed by a number of distinguished gentlemen. At that time men of all political parties in Kentucky, with scarce an exception, entertained strong pro-slavery sentiments. The probability of armed conflict between the sections was freely discussed by the speakers who addressed this meeting, and all announced that, in such event, they would take part with the South, and their belief that the South would be victorious. In the audience, listening intently to all that was said, was the Hon. Thomas Francis Marshall, the most brilliant orator Kentucky has produced, and one of the strongest intellects this country has known. When those regularly on the programme had concluded, the crowd called vociferously for Marshall, and he took the stand.

He gave little attention to the topics which had been chiefly discussed by the speakers who had preceded him, except to combat in brief terms certain contentions that he esteemed peculiarly sophistical or obnoxious, but addressed himself, as if with prophetic instinct, to what had been said concerning the sectional controversy and a possible separation of the states. He especially insisted that the opinion expressed by some of those who had spoken, that there might be a peaceable dissolution of the Union, was fallacious. Such a thing, he said, as disunion without war was impossible; the idea was sheer lunacy. He maintained that the people of the North and East would regard an effort to dissolve the Union and establish another and separate government on this continent as the declaration of a war which might be continued for generations; that no matter what technical right the South might show to take such action, or whatever cause of complaint she might have, those people would never consent to disunion and would oppose its attempt by force. Moreover, the people of the North-west would fight rather than suffer the mouth of the Mississippi to be controlled by a government in which they had no share, and those everywhere who wished a great and powerful national government and the development and material prosperity of the country would resist national disintegration to the bitter end. "The foundations of this Union," he said, "were laid in the blood of the sires of the Revolution; and if the structure shall be destroyed its fragments will be drenched with the blood of their descendants."

An attempt to dissolve the Union meant inevitable war — fierce, desolating strife — with consequences, perhaps, even more terrible than bloodshed.

He warned his hearers not to be misled into believing that in such a contest they would meet antagonists who would flinch from the deadliest grip of battle.

"You are all bred from the same stock, that stubborn British blood which, once aroused, maintains the struggle until strength and hope are utterly exhausted. I see before me young men who, if that war comes, will certainly be in it, and on their account, if for naught else, I would not have it come; above all else I exhort you not to underrate those with whom you will have to fight." He quoted the tribute which Edmund Burke rendered the people of the New England colonies — those hardy mariners who "vexed every sea with their fisheries," who cast the net and drew the line on the coasts of Greenland and struck the sperm whale among the isles of the Pacific.

"You young fellows," he said, "think the Yankee won't fight. Well, he doesn't always fight upon the same provocation and exactly in the same fashion that you do. If a man calls a Southern boy a liar, that man or that boy must die. Give a Kentuckian a mint julep and a pistol and he'll fight the devil. A Yankee doesn't often fight about a punctillio, nor does he fight duels. But you get in between him and a cod fishery, or you try to take away from him a barrel of molasses, and he'll give you h — ll.

"I thoroughly appreciate and justly value Southern courage and prowess. Every drop of blood in my veins is Southern. I am proud of the record the South has won for valour. But I pray — although I am not among those whose prayers 'avail much' — that the people of the South shall never display that valiant spirit in conflict with those of kindred blood and the same resolute temper, and which, however it terminate, will cause the world to shudder."

I thought of that speech very often while that conflict was in progress, and realized the truth of its predictions.

Whatever may be the ultimate verdict of history upon the merit of the controversy or in justification or censure of the resulting strife, there is little doubt that it will exonerate the men on both sides who fought in the ranks and gave their breasts to the battle.

As in all such struggles, they were impelled by mingled motives and feelings they themselves could scarcely have defined. But with far the greater number the dominant incentive was a devotion to their homes and their people — an unselfish wish to discharge what they esteemed a patriotic duty.

CHAPTER II

I WAS born and reared in the Bluegrass region of Kentucky. It is widely and justly celebrated for its beauty and fertility. It is the settled conviction of those who were born or who dwell there that the sun in its orbit and the stars in their courses look on no land so favoured and generous; and this belief is largely shared by Kentuckians who live in other parts of the state. A quasi-dissenting opinion is sometimes expressed regarding its superiority in general crops over the best of the central and South-western counties and the corn-raising alluvial Ohio River bottoms; but its unrivalled excellence in all else is admitted.

A Kentuckian may listen to argument and permit discussion of every other matter but this. He may modify certain very stubborn social opinions — prejudices, his critics call them; he may realign his religious views and denominational relations. He is generally inclined, indeed, to exchange the tenets taught him by his mother for those, if variant, entertained by his wife. He has been known — more frequently in quite recent years — to alter his political affiliations, and even entertain some doubt of the infallibility of his political traditions; for he is not altogether a bigot, except in matters connected with the soil. But only in the hallucinations of some strange form of insanity could he believe that Kentucky is not the fairest land the Creator has made, and the Bluegrass region its paradise.

Before the white man saw and coveted this land, its bounteous promise had irresistibly attracted aboriginal admirers. The red tribes which dwelt north of the Ohio and their fierce rivals of the same hue and race who inhabited territory south of the Cumberland fought many and bloody battles for its possession. Then, and ever since, the spell of the lovely landscape has fascinated all who have beheld it. La Salle, gazing from his canoe as he floated down the Ohio to its falls upon the rich verdure and entrancing scenery of its southern shores, christened the great stream "La

Belle Riviere." Findlay and Boone from the mountain peaks looked on the valleys in their virgin beauty. Returning from this pilgrimage into the wilderness, the glowing narrative of what they had seen urged hundreds of daring adventurers to enter and wrest it from the savage. After its partial settlement, an old pioneer preacher, having in an earnest sermon informed his hearers of the punishment to be visited on the wicked and unrepentant in the next world, but wishing to also fitly depict the happiness awaiting the righteous, concluded a fervent description of such future bliss with the declaration, "And, oh, my brethren, heaven is a Kentucky of a place."

While yet beautiful, the Bluegrass country has lost some of the charm which made it so attractive forty or fifty years ago. So many of its groves have been given to the plough, so many noble trees, which added a certain dignity as well as beauty to the landscape, have been felled, that its aspect, save in a few localities, has been materially changed. This alteration has doubtless been of commercial advantage, but at the cost of a sad sacrifice of the picturesque. The tobacco fields which yield large profits — when the night rider permits them to be worked — are not nearly so pleasing to the eye as were the stately forest growth they have replaced.

In the immediate ante-bellum period, this region was in the acme of its loveliness. Then, so to speak, the charm of nature was blended in just degree with the grace of cultivation, making the picture perfect. The original dense and far-stretching forests, thinned but not destroyed by the axe, had been succeeded by woodland pastures in which the savage majesty of the wilderness was softened to a milder glory by the sunlight admitted into the glades. But thousands of mighty trees — survivors, perhaps, of the time when the pioneer first came and the Indian yet lingered — still stood like huge sentinels guarding the olden character of the soil. Between and in vivid contrast with the woodlands, stretched broad fields of tasselled maize and other cereals, of tufted hemp, and meadows where grazed the lordly horses and cattle which were then, as now, the pride of the Kentucky breeder. Over woodland and meadow was spread the bright green mantle of the bluegrass, from which the region takes its name.

The beauty of this country is much enhanced by its peculiar topography. It is neither hilly nor level but undulates in all directions in a succession of wide "swells," rising to no great height, the depression of the intervening ground being so gradual that it rarely gives the impression of a valley. This formation very little diminishes the extent of the vista, while it presents every feature of the prospect to the eye. It may be purely fancy, but I think that this was more noticeable at the date of which I speak than it is now.

The only needful provision of nature which this region may be said to lack — more particularly that part of it lying between the little Licking River on the north and the Kentucky on the south — is an adequate water supply. Sometimes, in periods of extreme drought, this want is seriously felt, especially for live stock. Although a native of the Bluegrass and well acquainted with all of it, I did not thoroughly realize its deficiency in this respect until I traversed it with considerable bodies of cavalry during the Civil War. We found more difficulty in procuring water for our horses on the march than we had ever experienced in Tennessee and northern Alabama. Nevertheless, several minor streams — creeks — flow through this part of the country, some of them, like the North and the South Elkhorn, very beautiful and furnishing abundant water even for milling purposes. There are also many springs, of pure and deliciously cool water, whence issue small brooks; but while these generally furnish water for household use, few are large enough to provide for the multitude of deep-drinking live stock of all kinds bred there.

The country for some miles about Georgetown, in Scott County, was then the fairest and most typical spot of the Bluegrass. It is yet, despite the fact that it has been subjected to some extent to the general desecration of timber destruction and tobacco planting. I am a native of that locality, and my testimony therefore is competent and impartial. I will also state that it has never been disputed by any one whose opinion in such matters I have had reason to respect. Georgetown was one of the earliest settlements made in Kentucky. A small station was established there in October, 1775, induced, perhaps, by the unusually large and fine spring which gushes in generous volume from a ledge of rocks near where the stockade was erected. The first settlers called it the "Royal Spring." The name originally given the settlement was "McLellan's Fort," in honour of its founder. In 1776 it was attacked by the Indians, but offered a successful resistance and was not afterward seriously threatened. Tradition, however, long preserved fragmentary accounts of thrilling adventures supposed to have occurred in the vicinity during the long, dark period of warfare with the red savage. The numerous specimens found of flint arrow heads and spear points, such as the Indians are said to have used before the coming of the whites, would indicate that this locality had been a favourite hunting ground of the Indians and, perhaps, the scene of fierce battles.

Be that as it may, it is certain that in this region, known now as the Bluegrass, was waged the most desperate and protracted struggle with the original occupants of the soil which is recorded in the history of Western settlement; by far the fiercest in the history of Kentucky, for it was here that actual settlement was first attempted.

Boonesboro, upon its verge, was more than once besieged by the most redoubtable of the Shawnee and Piankeshaw warriors, aided, in one instance, by French allies, and as often repulsed the assailants. Harrodsburg and Logan's Fort had each an almost similar experience. Ruddle's and Martin's Stations, on the Licking, were assaulted by combined Indian and English forces. The heroic defence of Bryan's Station, situated not far from Lexington, is famous in the annals of Indian warfare; and the bloody battle of the Blue Licks has scarcely a parallel in such strife for the daring with which the settlers attacked a much more numerous body of their savage enemies, and the tragic disaster they sustained.

The pioneers had all been long gathered to their fathers, when I, then a child, first heard old men of the succeeding generation, tell strange tales of these combats and of the atrocity of the red demons, learned from those who had witnessed them. I do not know to what extent — if any — these narrations may have been embellished. A more recent and thorough acquaintance with the character of war stories induces me to believe that they may not have been related with the most scrupulous adherence to accuracy; and I used to listen to some marvellous and appalling narrations along this line. While immensely impressed and somewhat frightened by the dangers of battle and the ferocity of the combatants as they were painted in these recitals, I could not, boy-like, help secretly hoping that I might, some day, see similar scenes — with some of the details, such as scalping and torture, omitted — reënacted on the same soil. I lived to partially realize the wish, and to regret its fulfilment.

I remember more particularly one of these stories, perhaps because it differed altogether in kind from the others, and served to illustrate the justice of a remark that I once heard from a Texas frontiersman, to the effect that "After all said, Injuns is partly human."

According to this story, as it was told me, an old pioneer and Indian fighter, of whose name I can only remember that he was called "Captain Billy," lived in his old age somewhere between Lexington and Maysville. In the "dark and bloody" days, when Kentucky was constantly menaced with Indian raids and massacres, he had, so ran the story, for some inexplicable reason, rendered friendly service to a Shawnee brave, giving him, when wounded, shelter and protection. What might equally excite incredulity — for few people who have had dealings with the "wild" Indian believe him capable of such sentiment — this Indian cherished a grateful remembrance of the kindness, and the two became close and warm friends.

After the terrible hostilities had ceased and, with security, a more pacific feeling prevailed, the Indian was accustomed, once every year, to visit his white comrade at his home in Kentucky. Captain Billy was always glad to receive him and usually made him stay for several days. This was kept up until both had attained a very great age. I should say that, after the whites had learned to tolerate his presence, the Indian was also given the title of captain. When the friends met they would cordially shake hands with the usual salutation of "howdy," and would then sit for hours in solemn unbroken silence, exchanging, perhaps, less than a dozen words during the entire visit. The Indian, except when at meals, incessantly smoked his pipe, and Captain Billy as inveterately chewed tobacco.

One day two or three neighbours of Captain Billy dropped in to see him, but in a short time were forced to practise the same reticence, simply because he wouldn't talk. At length the Indian seemed suddenly smitten with a realization of the humour of the situation, and — an unusual thing in one of his race — broke into a loud and prolonged fit of laughter. When his paroxysm of uncouth mirth had partially subsided, seeing a look of astonishment and inquiry on the faces of the others, he condescended to explain:

"Ole Cap'en Smokepipe," he said, "come to see Ole Cap'en Chawterbac; have heap fun."

There are many legends current in this region regarding events of later date than those of the pioneer period — legends which deal with achievements of which Kentuckians are proud and embalming names which they revere. I love best, however, to recall the ordinary incidents associated with my boyhood memories and the scenes with which I was then familiar.

The rural life of central Kentucky, in the twenty or thirty years preceding the Civil War, was extremely pleasant, and while simple and unostentatious, had some social features peculiarly attractive. The Bluegrass farmers were a robust and well-to-do generation; very much inclined to enjoy creature comforts, and well supplied with them; fond, also, of good company and hail fellowship. Their farms yielded them abundant provisions for home consumption, and generally a handsome revenue in addition. As people so situated usually are, they were hospitable, and liberal in all matters save, perhaps a few cherished opinions.

The peculiar "institution" furnished a domestic service which was of great assistance in such functions, for the negro, in "slave times," seemed intuitively to comprehend and vastly like the duties of hospitality, and was always ready and untiring in his efforts to care for a guest and vicariously play the part of host.

In this respect, life in Kentucky at that date much resembled what it was in Virginia, Tennessee, and other Southern states. Much time was given to visiting and mutual entertainment among neighbours and friends. Nearly all of the farmers were amply provided with the kind of transportation then in common use and most favoured. They had carriages and wheeled vehicles of all sorts and sizes, but the favourite method of getting about was on horseback. Usually each member of the family claimed his or her especial "riding" horse — as was then the term for the saddler; and they not only rode to church and town, and on short visits, but sometimes made journeys of many miles on horseback. Gen. John B. Castleman, in one of his articles on the American saddle horse, graphically refers to the preference prevailing at that period for the saddle. He says that two acquaintances might meet in Lexington on county court day. "Tom," one would inquire, "is Andy Gorham in town to-day?"

"Yes," Tom would answer. "I haven't seen him, but I saw his horse standing at the hitching rack a little while ago."

I recall no recollection of my early boyhood with keener relish than that of the old-fashioned "barbecue." I do not mean the big political meetings that were so designated, where the candidates and orators of one or the other party would hold forth to sympathetic and applauding crowds. Those which I have in mind were much smaller, but far more agreeable occasions, when the residents of some particular locality — immediate neighbours — would assemble purely for social converse and enjoyment, and more than forty or fifty people seldom attended. It used to be said that a gathering of this kind was not much favoured by any one who sought distinction either as orator or raconteur. The size of the audience was discouraging, inasmuch as "it was too small for a speech and too large for an anecdote."

Saturday was the day usually selected for these barbecues, and they were always held in a woodland pasture and near some cool spring and brook. Everybody who attended was expected to come early in the morning, and the roasting of the meat and preparation of the "burgoo" began at or before daybreak. In pits previously dug for such purposes, large fires — preferably of hickory — would be started and allowed to burn for some hours before those charged with the duty of roasting or "barbecuing" the meat commenced their task. In order that this work, which demanded careful and skilful attention, might be properly done, it was necessary that the sides of the pit should become as hot as the lid of an oven, and its bottom — the flames of the fire having subsided — should be filled with a mass of glowing embers. Then carcasses of sheep and half-grown pigs, suitably dressed and skewered with long, stout sticks, were placed over the pits and the beds of hot coals, remaining until done to a turn. Of course the most judicious supervision had to be exercised, that the fire should be kept hot, but not allowed to rise in flame which could scorch the meat, and that the meat should be turned and basted at proper intervals. It can be well understood that those upon whom this important responsibility was imposed, claimed autocratic authority and brooked no interference. The meat so cooked had a delicious flavour.

As for the "burgoo," no description can give one who has never tasted it an idea of its luscious excellence, when it has been made by a real expert.

I believe that this dish is made now very much as it was then, but I do not find it now nearly so palatable. While termed a soup, it had more the consistency of a stew and was composed of a number of savoury ingredients. Several kinds of vegetables — corn and tomatoes being the staple ones — with beef, mutton, sometimes a small piece of pork, and chickens, were put together in kettles and boiled slowly and thoroughly until the various materials had become blended into a culinary product of perfect and exquisite flavour. It was highly seasoned, of course, with salt and pepper, and served in new tin cups. Gastronomic authorities averred that its taste was impaired, if served in any other way. Young squirrels were considered to be a valuable addition to the receipt, and the part assigned the boys in the preparation of the banquet was to procure the squirrels. Starting out in the early summer morning, while the dew yet glistened on the grass, and the gleaming sun, just risen, lighted up the green wood with his first slanting rays, we rarely failed to secure a full bag of this game. At that hour the little gray gossips were much in evidence, chasing about among the trees, leaping from one swaying bough to another, and chattering until the welkin rang with their small but shrill clamour.

The principal and most popular feature of these gatherings was the "shooting match." As I first remember them, and for some years thereafter, these contests were conducted entirely with the old "squirrel rifle," which, with the exception that the percussion lock had been substituted for the flint, was much the same kind of piece as that used by the pioneers and early hunters. Its small calibre and the light bullet it carried peculiarly adapted it to squirrel shooting, for which it was eventually almost solely used; but in the hands of the pioneer, it brought down larger game, deer, bear, and quite often the Indian.

I do not know what was the extreme effective range of this rifle. I should think not much more than two hundred yards. Nevertheless, in all of the battles with the Indians, it did efficient service, and its deadly accuracy was demonstrated at New Orleans, when Packenham's regulars fell in heaps before the breastworks of cotton bales, manned by the Kentucky and Tennessee riflemen who were armed with this weapon. The stories told of the marksmanship of Boone, Kenton, and their confreres sound almost as marvellous as those related of the English bowmen — the feats of archery performed by Robin Hood and Will Scarlet. Of course, the men whom I saw use the rifle, at the time of which I write, were tyros compared with these heroes of tradition; nevertheless, they could do some fairly good shooting.

The distance usually chosen for these contests was sixty yards, which may appear insignificant to those accustomed to modern arms. But the range of the old-fashioned rifle was short, and the marksmen fired "off-hand," that is to say, without a rest. The target was a wide, thick plank, on which was tacked a circular piece of white paper a little larger than a silver dollar. In the centre of this paper a black spot, about the size of a 25-cent piece, was painted. Two lines were drawn across this black spot, intersecting each other at right angles. The point of their intersection was considered the exact centre of the target. I have more than once seen five or six out of perhaps a dozen competitors put their bullets in the white paper, and one or two, in the same match, hit the black spot. I can recall no instance when I saw any one "cut the cross," that is to say, hit the exact centre. Although jollity and merriment were prevalent at these meetings, they were never riotous or disorderly, and good humour always obtained. Much drinking was neither encouraged nor tolerated;

but a reasonable quantity of "Old Crow," the most famous whiskey ever made in Kentucky, was supplied and used in moderation. The presence of the older men — the patriarchs and nestors of the community — was a certain restraint on the younger. These old gentlemen sat in the shade, waited on by darkies sedulously attentive to their comforts. They watched the sports with unabated interest, talked about "early times" in Kentucky, occasionally offered a sage political opinion or prediction, and gave wise advice to the little boys — reverently listened to and immediately forgotten. If a dispute arose among the marksmen difficult to settle, it was referred to them as a court of last resort.

Sometimes a reverend gentleman — usually the pastor of some neighbouring church — would come to these barbecues, and he invariably received the profoundest respect and deference. No matter what the provocation, the most impetuous forbore to swear if he was supposed to be within ear-shot — unless, indeed, in a very subdued tone; and it was considered very bad form to imbibe ardent spirits, while he was on the ground, without getting behind a tree. These gentlemen were entitled to such consideration. They were good men, of edifying conversation and exemplary conduct. This was especially true of one preacher who was a frequent attendant on such occasions. I do not remember to what denomination he belonged. I never heard him mention such matters, but he always took part in the shooting matches, and could hit the black as often as any one.

The "Sport of Kings," however, was the one which beyond all others fascinated the people of whom I write. The love of the thoroughbred horse is instinctive with the Kentuckian. So soon as it was discovered that no pasturage was so nutritious as that of certain sections of Kentucky, and especially of the region which in this regard has become so famous that it is believed the grass and water of no other soil produces such bone and flesh as does that underlying the blue limestone — the farmer of the Bluegrass turned his attention to stock raising, and made the breeding of the thoroughbred — the race-horse — a specialty. Inheriting this predilection from his Virginia ancestry, he procured the first of the strain he afterward so greatly improved from the mother state; but when the region was quickly recognized as, par excellence, the congenial habitat of the blooded horse, the finest and fleetest specimens from other parts of the continent were brought to Kentucky, and their progeny soon outclassed all that had been previously reared in America.

Some envious satirist once said that the "First citizen of Kentucky is always a horse." While this statement is conceived in a spirit of malicious criticism, it must be admitted that if the thoroughbred or the saddle horse could be taught to vote, *viva voce* or by ballot, many Kentuckians would be willing to concede him constitutional and statutory right to attain that exalted eminence.

Race meetings were held in Kentucky early in the last century. Nearly every town in the Bluegrass had its race course, and the interest in racing was intense and pervaded all classes. The descendants of Diomed, and of his famous son, Sir Archy, of Medley, Fearnought, and Priam contended with the get of less celebrated sires.

At a later day Lexington became the racing as it is now the breeding centre. Short races, and the racing of two-year-olds were not then in favour. Four and two miles were the favourite distances. While these contests did not furnish such exhibitions of speed as have been more recently witnessed, they were surer tests of courage and endurance. Frequent importations of English stallions continued to improve the blood. Glencoe, Yorkshire, Leamington, and Lexington — native born and chief of all — were recognized as the monarchs of the stud.

In course of time larger stakes and purses were offered, and the breeding of the thoroughbred became a profitable industry. The large racing stables, however, so common in recent years, were not then in existence. The wealthy farmers, who were the principal patrons of the sport, raced colts of their own breeding, and the hope of victory was a stronger incentive than any desire of gain. The trainers and jockeys at that time were almost always negroes, and although not so intelligent and competent as their Caucasian successors in the same vocations, they were perhaps more trustworthy. Loyalty to the interest of their masters, and pride in their equine wards, made them proof against the seductive wiles of the bookmaker.

At one time "match races," in which two famous racers would be pitted against each other — something never seen now — were quite popular. A Kentucky horse would be matched against one from another state, and large sums were often wagered on the result.

It cannot be doubted that racing as then practised tended to improve the general breed of horses. The blood of the thoroughbred benefits that of any stock with which it is mingled. He has inherited from his Arab ancestor the potency with which he reproduces his own distinctive traits, and impresses them durably on even the inferior strains with which his own is blended. To the large infusion of this blood in the horses which it used may be, in great measure, attributed the excellent service rendered by the Southern cavalry during the Civil War and the extraordinary marches it performed.

The last decade of their ante-bellum history must always be regarded by the people of the South and of Kentucky with a peculiar interest. A revolution was impending which was to destroy the old order, and inaugurate another that to them would appear like a new world. Dimly discerning, but not entirely conscious of what was coming, they were thrilled with a feeling of mingled expectancy and apprehension. In Kentucky, where there was earnest debate over action which in the extreme South was already regarded as pre-determined, popular opinion was divided. There were many able men in Kentucky at that date, although some of the greatest had recently passed away. Eminent divines spoke from her pulpits, and eloquent orators and advocates on the stump and in the forum. Mr. Clay had just died and to his overweening influence had succeeded the extraordinary personal popularity of John C. Breckinridge. Mr. Crittenden, on the verge of the grave, was yet active in his public efforts, and even those who would not heed his counsel loved and respected him.

It is the proverbial inclination of old age to regard the past with an appreciation it cannot accord the present. In the winter of life we do not find the bloom and aroma that we perceived in its spring and summer. Looking back upon that period, through the glamour in which an old man views the scenes and events of his youth, I may be pardoned for believing that, in some respects, it was better and happier than the one in which we are living.

The Kentuckians of fifty years ago, with all their faults, were a virile generation, somewhat over-passionate, and perhaps unduly inclined to submit their differences to the trial by combat, but loving fair play and hating cowardly or cruel injustice.

Whether the "old" Kentucky was, or was not, better than the Kentucky of to-day — and it is just as well not to discuss that question — something of her former glory and prestige, as well as interest and beauty, seems lacking. The land has undergone a metamorphosis, and "the tender grace of a day that is dead" can never return.

CHAPTER III

AT THE beginning of the Civil War I was a citizen of Missouri and resident of St. Louis, and first did service in the cause of the South, or, as our opponents termed it, gave aid to the rebellion, in that city. If I had needed other excuse for such action than the approval of my own judgment and conscience, I might have found it in the character of my associates; for no men were ever influenced by sincerer convictions or impelled by more unselfish motives. I may add with pardonable pride that many of my comrades of that period, the majority of whom were very young men, subsequently won enviable reputation in the Confederate army; but the daring courage and adventurous spirit which distinguished them as soldiers were never more conspicuously shown than in that exciting novitiate in St. Louis.

While political sentiment in Missouri was greatly divided on the issues presented in the Presidential campaign of 1860, the great bulk of her people, although there were among them few "original secessionists," to use the term then in vogue, were heartily in sympathy with the South. Of the Presidential candidates, Douglas, Breckinridge, and Bell, received 148,489 votes, as against only 17,028 cast for Lincoln; and much the larger part of the number first mentioned ultimately became ardent, if not open and active, supporters of the Confederacy. The Republican party of Missouri was confined almost entirely to St. Louis, but was strong and aggressive in the city; and the initial struggle between the warring political elements, when, after Lincoln's election, the real and sterner conflict began, was decided there.

It is not my purpose to attempt an extended account or discussion of the political situation then existing in Missouri, but merely to relate my own personal experiences. Yet these can scarcely be described intelligibly without some brief narration of the more important events with which they were connected.

In January, 1861, the General Assembly of Missouri passed an act providing for an election during the following month of members of a convention which should consider the future relations to exist between the government of the United States and the people of the State of Missouri; that is to say, which should determine whether the state should remain in the Union or secede.

By this measure the issue was sharply and suddenly defined — too promptly and positively, indeed, to permit any chance for success for the hopes and plans of the extreme Southern and states' rights men; because the greater number of those who were Southern in sentiment were not yet reconciled to the thought of disunion, or prepared to take action which would almost inevitably precipitate strife and bloodshed. Nothing demonstrates this more clearly than the fact that very many prominent Missourians who were subsequently leaders in the councils of the South and among the most distinguished soldiers of the Confederacy — Gen. Sterling Price was of the number — took strong ground in the canvass preceding the election of its members and in the convention itself, in advocacy of the Union and opposition to secession. Price was chosen president of the convention because he was considered the most earnest and, perhaps, the ablest exponent of such views. No one should have been surprised, therefore, although many were, when the convention decided that Missouri should remain in the Union.

But while the greater number of the Southern sympathizers, and especially those of such age and prominence as entitled them to aspire to seats in the convention, were thus conservative, there were a few influential men among the recognized political leaders of the state who desired that Missouri should make common cause with her Southern sisters and share the fate of their people; and the very young men of both wings of the Democratic party and of those who voted for Bell and Everett were, with few exceptions, determined to take the part of the South. Some of these youths had listened with little patience to any suggestion of a dissolution of the Union until it became apparent that coercion of the seceding states would be attempted. But they believed that coercion was more to be condemned than secession, and they were resolved to side with their kinsmen of the South, whether right or wrong. Additional confidence and stimulus was given this element by the knowledge that Gov. Claiborne F. Jackson cordially entertained the same sentiment and would urge action in conformity with it.

Governor Jackson had been elected as the regular Democratic nominee; that is to say, as the representative of the Douglas wing of the party. He had always been an ardent and uncompromising "states' rights" man, but was not, in the strict acceptation of the term, a secessionist; nor had he, I believe, ever contemplated with favour the idea that Missouri should withdraw from the Union until after Lincoln's election to the Presidency and the threat of forcible interference with the states which proposed to secede. He was a man of strong sense and strong character, more vehement than cautious, notwithstanding his training as a politician, generous and magnetic and capable of both feeling and attracting warm personal friendship. Immediately upon the passage of the act providing for the convention, he had publicly and frankly announced his opinions and his desire that Missouri should be committed to the Southern movement.

While the canvass preceding the election of the members of the convention may not have been so conducted elsewhere in the state, it immediately assumed in St. Louis the character of a struggle between the "unconditional Union men" on the one side and those who were equally as determined that Missouri should take side with the South on the other. The Union men had certain advantages in such a controversy, especially when it was so suddenly presented. They would have at their back, so soon as Mr. Lincoln was inaugurated, the power of the national government, and already had the aid which hopes and fears thus excited could afford. A more potent factor was their attitude as the advocates of established conditions and apparent conservators of law and order. They could appeal to all who dreaded change and uncertain and, perhaps dangerous, experiment. Many who believed that the rights of the Southern states and of Missouri were menaced by the policy proclaimed by the leaders of the Republican party nevertheless shrank from the idea of revolution and were unwilling to countenance action not clearly sanctioned by legal authority.

Sympathy and sentiment inclined them in one direction; mental habit and fear of the unknown and untried held them to the existing status.

No matter what provocation might be given they could not consent to break the peace. Even the leaders of that element which had reached the conclusion that Missouri should join her Southern sisters and that the convention ought so to declare, were affected by this predisposition. With the exception of Governor Jackson and a very few others, they hesitated to adopt the only policy which could accomplish their wishes. "Willing to wound," they were yet "afraid to strike." Only those whose youth and lack of influence precluded their leadership eagerly counselled and prepared to attempt the sort of action which might achieve success.

In the unconditional Union ranks were many men of ability, whose opinions and example had great weight in the community, but two men dominated their councils and controlled their conduct. These were Francis P. Blair, the acknowledged leader of the Republican party of Missouri, and Capt. Nathaniel Lyon, of the regular army, who had been recently ordered to duty at St. Louis. Lyon was, in his own way, a man of as much capacity as Blair, fully as energetic, and as quick to decide and execute, with a will as strong but even more relentless; and absolutely fanatical and indifferent concerning the means he employed to accomplish what he deemed a proper end.

Blair, recognizing from the first that the political situation must be eventually determined by the strong hand and by force, had early gone to work to organize a military body similar in many respects to the state guard, but over which the state authorities should have no control; which should, indeed, if the occasion arose, set at defiance the authority of the state government.

Lyon, thoroughly in accord with such a plan, gave it his hearty support, and aided to make this body more efficient in drill and equipment. It was composed principally of Germans. It numbered originally about eight hundred men, and took the name of the "wide-awakes." It subsequently grew to be several thousand strong. This force was the more readily recruited and organized, because contributions of money for that purpose were liberally furnished in St. Louis and probably from the East, and Lyon promised to provide, and ultimately did provide it with arms from the St. Louis arsenal.

It is almost impossible to estimate how vastly the chances of Southern success would have been augmented had Missouri been permitted to take her place in the Southern column. I was convinced then, and believe now, that it would have eliminated all danger of failure. Her warlike population, which could so readily and promptly be converted into an efficient soldiery, would have, in that event, furnished a much larger and more formidable contingent to the Confederate cause than it did; while the number furnished the Federal army would have been greatly minimized. The strategic situation of Missouri, so to speak, as part of the Confederacy, would have been of incalculable advantage as an obstacle to invasion of the South along some of the lines by which invasion was subsequently most successfully attempted. Lying along the flank of the Western loyal states, and occupied by adequate Confederate forces, she would have so threatened Illinois and even more eastern territory as to effectually hinder any enterprise which might have stripped that region of troops; and armies would have been required to defend it against the invasions made from Missouri. When we remember what efforts the Federals were compelled to make to overrun and subjugate Missouri after she had been practically disarmed and shackled by her own people, we can form some idea of the difficulties that would have been encountered in expelling from her limits the hosts they would have found there, had she, in the very beginning, been enrolled as a Confederate state. Meanwhile the South, so far exempt from the havoc and demoralization of warfare on her own soil, could have faced her foes on more equal terms along the border. But important as was the acquisition of Missouri to the Confederacy, the possession of St. Louis was scarcely less so. There were in the city abundant supplies of all kinds necessary to the conduct of military operations. To hold St. Louis was well-nigh equivalent to the complete control of the immense shipping of the great river, at least to the fleet of steam-boats which habitually harboured there; and this would not only have enabled supplies to be distributed to all points of the South where they were most needed, but would have effectually prevented the occupation and control of the lower Mississippi waters by the Federal gunboats.

But if the possession of Missouri and the city of St. Louis was important to ultimate Confederate success, the seizure of the St. Louis arsenal was a matter of vital and immediate necessity. That arsenal contained sixty thousand stand of small arms, thirty-five or forty pieces of artillery, and a vast store of ammunition and military equipments. An almost invincible force could have been promptly armed from this source, and such a force would have been at once recruited; for with the capture of the arsenal by the secessionists all doubt and vacillation would have disappeared from their ranks. It would have assured the most timid and hesitant, and have been the signal for an instant and overwhelming uprising, both in St. Louis and the state, in behalf of the Southern cause. Such an evidence of purpose and of capacity to deal practically with the situation would have settled in advance the questions which the convention had been called to determine. The earnest and resolute men on both sides thoroughly realized this, and to seize or defend the arsenal became the watchwords of all who really "meant business."

Unfortunately for the hopes of the Southern men in St. Louis, however salutary such policy may have proven for the future of the country, their leaders temporized. They admitted the extreme importance of capturing the arsenal, but insisted that it ought not to be attempted until after the convention had acted. This counsel seemed fatuous to the younger men, who thought that something should be done to influence the election of the delegates and the decision of the convention, and believed that, as matters were being handled, the game was going against them. They resolved, therefore, to make an organization of their own, with a view to prompt and decisive measures, and also as an offset to Blair's "Wide Awakes," who soon became exceedingly insolent and aggressive. This movement was inaugurated, as I remember, by Colton Greene, James R. Shaler, Rock Champion, Overton W. Barrett, Samuel Farrington, James Quinlan, Arthur McCoy, and myself. Greene was subsequently a brigadier-general in the Confederate service.

Shaler was one of the bravest and most efficient colonels whom Missouri gave to the South. Barrett served gallantly and with distinction, and Champion, Farrington, and McCoy, after winning the highest reputation for courage and fidelity, died under the Southern flag.

This organization was designated the "Minute Men," and was of a semi-political and military character. We made no secret of the organization or of our purpose, but openly proclaimed both. It grew to be about four hundred strong, and was divided into five companies, commanded by Greene, Shaler, Barrett, Hubbard, and myself, which subsequently composed a battalion of the state guard, of which Shaler was elected major. The chief and primary object of this organization was the capture of the arsenal. We were handicapped, however, not only by the scruples and remonstrances of the older and more conservative men, but by the difficulty of procuring arms. The muster-roll of the Minute Men could have been increased to a much larger number, but we wished to enlist only the kind of material which could be relied on for any service and in any emergency, and no more than we could arm in some fashion. We had no funds with which to purchase arms, and those fitted for the use of soldiers were not to be easily gotten even with money. During February we secured some sixty or seventy old muskets, but armed the greater number with revolvers and shot-guns, which were indeed better weapons for street fighting.

No opportunity for such demonstration as we wished to make was afforded until the convention, having first assembled at Jefferson City, adjourned to meet in St. Louis on the 4th of March. We resolved to utilize that occasion in such wise as to bring matters, if possible, to a crisis and incite the popular outbreak during which we might find means to execute our project. We wished also to act before the Republican national administration — just about to be inaugurated — might interfere.

The measures taken seem almost ludicrous in the narration, but they were the only kind we could employ, and were really better calculated, in the then excited condition of the public mind, than any others to precipitate the collision we desired without becoming ourselves actually the aggressors. By virtue of my position as chairman of the "Military Committee of the Minute Men," I had charge of the headquarters, which were established in the old Berthold mansion, one of the early Creole houses of St. Louis; I was also empowered — so far as the Minute Men could give me authority — to inaugurate and direct such enterprises as that which I am about to describe. I called the committee together on the night of the 3d of March, and, after a brief consultation, we decided to display on the succeeding day such unmistakable symbols of secession and evidence of an actively rebellious disposition as would be a plain defiance to the Union sentiment and challenge to the Wide Awakes. We accordingly improvised two secession flags. The South had not then adopted a banner, so we were obliged to exercise our imaginations to a rather painful extent in order to devise a fit emblem. We knew, however, that nothing which floated over the Minute Men's headquarters could be possibly misconstrued, and we blazoned on both flags every conceivable thing that was suggestive of a Southern meaning. Champion and Quinlan undertook to place one of these flags on the very summit of the court-house dome, and did so at great risk to neck and limb. The other was hung out from the front porch of the headquarters.

I summoned fifty or sixty of our most determined and reckless followers, put the muskets in their hands — they were also provided with revolvers — and told them they would be required to remain on duty not only that night, but as long as might be necessary. They were more than willing to do so. I, of course, stayed with them in command. Among other implements of defence, we had a small swivel, which, loaded with a number of musket balls and a double handful of ten-penny nails, was planted to command the front door, and was to be fired only in event that the door was forced. Early the next morning, when our ensigns were observed, an extraordinary commotion began in the immediate neighbourhood and soon extended over the entire city. The flag on the court-house was at once removed. We had expected this and could not have prevented it.

Then a large and angry crowd collected in front of the headquarters and demanded the removal of the flag there. When no response was made, some of the boldest climbed up on the porch with threats of tearing it down. They were thrown back on the pavement beneath, but none were seriously injured, although much discouraged. I cautioned my men not to fire unless they themselves were fired on.

The Wide Awakes sprang to arms, but showed no haste to attack. We received notice that they had assembled and formed and were coming. Their drums were loudly in evidence. While unwilling to fire on the mob without the amplest provocation, we were determined to fire on the Wide Awakes so soon as they were in sight; for after the repeated threats they had uttered, their appearance at such a time would have been an unmistakable demonstration of hostility. Frost's brigade of state militia, as fine a body of the kind as I ever saw and exceedingly well armed, drilled, and disciplined, was ordered under arms to assist the police in keeping the peace. This force was about seven hundred strong, and would have cheerfully sided with us had the Wide Awakes and the mob attacked. With such other aid as would have been rendered under the excitement of conflict, we could certainly have taken the arsenal in the mêlée and before the affair ended.

General Frost came to the headquarters and said that he thought we had been imprudent, but that he would advise no concession to the demands of the mob. He also said that the militia would endeavour to keep the peace and prevent aggression by either side. Soon afterward I was visited by a deputation composed of the Hon. O. D. Filley, the mayor, Col. Samuel Churchill, and Messrs. Thomas S. Snead, James Lucas, and Ferdinand Kennett. I knew these gentlemen well and held them in the highest respect, as did all the community. Mr. Snead, afterward chief of staff to General Price, and Colonel Churchill did not seem to be especially desirous that the flag should be removed, although they advised it. Mr. Kennett, perhaps to the surprise of his colleagues, offered what might have been termed a minority report, or dissenting opinion. "Duke," he said, "I rather think you acted like a fool when you hung out that flag, but you'll act like a coward if you take it down." The mayor and Mr. Lucas very earnestly requested me to have it taken down. They called my attention, although I had already observed it, to the violent excitement and resentment which its display had occasioned, urged that the feelings of the

Union men ought to be respected, and that nothing should be done, during a period of such political passion, to offend or anger any class of citizens. I temperately and respectfully represented that the Union men ought not to be so sensitive. I pointed out that a convention was, at that very hour, sitting in St. Louis to discuss and decide whether Missouri should remain in the Union or secede. I suggested that the question, therefore, was one on which a citizen had a right to take either side; and that each side had an equal right to exhibit its insignia, and in any way or by any device define its contention. "There is not a man among us, Mr. Mayor," I said, "who would think of protesting against the display of the stars and stripes; why, therefore, should the Union men object to our floating a Southern banner?"

He said he couldn't explain it, but that the Union men certainly were objecting, and that he would be greatly pleased if I would remove the objection and permit the crowd, which was constantly growing larger and more noisy, to disperse. Champion then suggested that the mayor should call on his fire department and turn out the engines to throw water on the crowd, which he, Champion, thought would certainly cause it to disperse; but for some reason the mayor would not consent to do that. I finally said that I would very gladly do anything — except the specific thing asked — to help him allay the tumult, and suggested that if he or Mr. Lucas would make a speech to the crowd much might be accomplished. Mr. Lucas accordingly climbed into a small donkey cart belonging to an Italian fruit seller, which had somehow become wedged into the press, and began an impressive address, imploring the people to be calm and to go home. But the donkey, suddenly taking fright either at the eloquence of the orator or at the shouts of the crowd, kicked and plunged violently and tried to run away, so that Mr. Lucas was prevented from fully presenting his case.

Several abortive rushes were afterward made by the mob, and one or two more serious demonstrations, easily repulsed, however, and with little damage to either faction; and then our friends began to rapidly assemble. After some rough and tumble fighting in the streets it became apparent that our side was the stronger.

But the opportunity we had hoped and striven for did not occur; and we could not afford to attack the arsenal without having been ourselves assailed. Our instructions were explicit to commit no aggressive act. On more than one other occasion it became manifest that in the event of actual collision the Southern sentiment would be thoroughly aroused and would predominate; but as time wore on our opponents made more complete preparation, while we made little, if any.

This fatal policy of irresolution and delay continued until Mr. Lincoln issued his proclamation calling for troops to suppress the rebellion; and although our people were then, at last, awakened, it was too late to recover from the effects of previous procrastination. The legislature was in session during the greater part of the winter, and until March 28th, but although strongly Southern in feeling and composition, it was affected by the same indecision and lethargy which had paralyzed our efforts in St. Louis. It passed high-sounding resolutions, but did little else, and even refused to permit the governor to call out the militia. Bills were introduced providing for the better organization and armament of the state guard, but were not pressed to passage. On March 23d, however, a bill was passed to create a Board of Police Commissioners for St. Louis, by which the control of the police force was taken from the mayor, who was a Republican. It authorized the governor to appoint four commissioners, who, with the mayor — ex officio a member of the board — should have absolute control of the police of the city, of the sheriff's officers and of all conservators of the peace, both in the city and county. The passage of this bill two months earlier might have shaped the political situation very differently; but at so late a date it had little effect.

When it became a law the governor appointed as commissioners: Charles McLaren, John A. Brownlee, James H. Carlisle, and myself. All were Southern in sentiment. My appointment was severely censured, ostensibly because of my youth, but really because of my connection with the Minute Men, which made it peculiarly offensive to Unionists of all shades of opinions. I had not asked the position, and, telling the governor that I did not wish him to be criticised on my account, requested him to appoint some one else. He answered that he did not care a cent for the criticism, and that if I didn't accept he would leave the place vacant.

It finally became apparent that the Southern party must either adopt and promptly execute decisive and practically effective measures, or publicly abandon all purpose or pretence of maintaining the authority of the state in matters wherein Blair and Lyon had determined to interfere. Before the capture of Fort Sumter by the Confederates and Mr. Lincoln's call for troops to suppress the rebellion, Governor Jackson made up his mind that the seizure of the arsenal should be attempted at the earliest possible date. During all this delay, however, the garrison of the arsenal had been considerably strengthened, and the number of the Wide Awakes very greatly increased. Lyon's efforts had also resulted in their better organization and in furnishing them with excellent rifles issued from the arsenal. The Union leaders estimated that they could, at this date, put six or seven thousand well-armed and equipped troops in the field, as against less than one thousand two hundred on the other side.

Governor Jackson had never been a soldier, and was totally devoid of military experience. He relied for advice in such matters on General Frost, who was a graduate of West Point, and had served for several years in the regular army. General Frost was well versed in his profession, had much technical knowledge, and was undoubtedly a man of personal courage. He advised a course, however, which, under the circumstances, rendered success almost impossible. Although he must have known that he could not possibly muster an armed and organized force one fifth as strong as that which would oppose him, he advised the governor to order a formal encampment of the state guard in the environs of St. Louis, send South for heavy guns, and proceed to attempt the capture of the arsenal by slow and regular approaches; by siege operations, indeed. It seems almost incredible that any one could have supposed it to be possible to capture the arsenal, defended as it was, and considering the disparity of forces, except by a sudden *coup de main*, and unexpected reckless rush. Yet the plan I have described was the one resolved on. The governor, therefore, directed that the state guard should assemble on May 3d at a designated spot near the city limits and remain in encampment for a week. He despatched Capt. Cotton Greene and myself to Montgomery, Ala., with letters to President Davis requesting him to furnish us with the sort of cannon described in another paper prepared by General Frost.

Such action, when he had men like Blair and Lyon to deal with, was almost equivalent to a specific declaration not only of his plan, but of how he was going to execute it. This ostentatious assemblage of the state guard at St. Louis could mean only one purpose; and while the mission on which Greene and I were sent was, of course, intended to be kept secret, our very absence, at such a time, was certain to excite suspicion and inquiry.

We started on April 6th and proceeded via Cairo to Memphis, thence via Chattanooga to Montgomery. I remember that as we stood on the platform at Corinth, where our train had stopped for a few minutes, and gazed on the dense forest and thick undergrowth which fringed the railroad — it has since been almost entirely cleared away — I remarked, "If we ever get the Yankees down here, we'll pepper them." "If the Yankees ever get this far down," responded Greene, "we may as well quit." Neither of us had the faintest premonition of the future. In less than one year from that date I passed in the immediate vicinity of Corinth, en route to the field of Shiloh, and the war lasted three years longer.

When we reached Montgomery we sent our credentials to President Davis and he received us at a meeting of his cabinet. We were questioned very closely about the conditions in St. Louis and Missouri, but only Mr. Benjamin, who, if I remember correctly, was then secretary of war, seemed to consider the matter serious or at all difficult. The others were inclined to entertain a roseate view of the situation, not only in our region, but everywhere else. The President very cheerfully granted Governor Jackson's request, and gave us an order on the commandant of the arsenal at Baton Rouge for the guns specified in the list prepared by General Frost. We proceeded immediately to New Orleans, and then to Baton Rouge. I shall never forget the scenes I witnessed in Louisiana while on that mission. Every one anticipated war but believed it would be brief, and there seemed to be a universal feeling of confidence and elation. A great number of military companies had been recruited, but regimental and brigade organizations had not yet been completed, and each company wore its own peculiar garb. The streets of New Orleans were thronged during the day and the theatres crowded at night with a multitude of young fellows clad in an infinite variety of brilliant uniforms; and as we ascended the river to Baton Rouge we could see everywhere along the coast squads of volunteers drilling among the orange trees. The first sight that met our eyes, when we landed at Baton Rouge, was a company of "*chasseurs*" habited in vivid green, no member of which spoke English or appeared to care a continental what was going to happen.

Having procured, on our order to the commandant of the arsenal, two twelve-pound howitzers, two thirty-two pound siege guns, some five hundred muskets, and a quantity of ammunition, we returned to New Orleans to make arrangements for their transportation to St. Louis, and for that purpose chartered the steam-boat *Swan*. The guns and ammunition, packed in such wise as to conceal, as much as possible their real character, were taken on at Baton Rouge. Greene took charge of the boat, while I went in advance by rail to Cairo, which in the meantime had been occupied by Federal troops, to reconnoitre and ascertain what would be the danger of detection or delay. I found a large force of soldiers at Cairo; but they were not so vigilant or suspicious of visitors within their lines as the troops on both sides became at a later period. An incident happened immediately upon my arrival which I found at the moment only amusing, but had reason afterward to consider fortunate.

The first man I saw as I stepped into the hotel was a particular friend from St. Louis — Mr. James Casey — one of the truest, warmest-hearted men I ever knew. He was a brother-in-law, by the way, of Gen. Ulysses Grant. Grant, when President, appointed him Surveyor of the Port at New Orleans, but at this date "Jim" was a strong secessionist. His look of amazement and dismay, when he caught sight of me, was almost too much for my gravity. Although I knew him to be both shrewd and cautious, I was apprehensive that he might say something imprudent; so I approached him and said: "You don't remember me, Mr. Casey, but I am John White. I live in your native town in Union County, Kentucky." "I'm very glad to see you, Mr. White," he responded. "Come up stairs to my room." We went to his room; he locked the door and asked me why in the name of heaven I had come to Cairo. He said that the rumour was current in St. Louis that Greene and I had gone South on some embassy, and that Blair would be on the lookout for us. "Well," I said "he won't be looking for me here." Casey replied that among the officers in Cairo were a number of St. Louisians, some of whom would probably recognize me. I said I would get away as soon as possible, but must first ascertain what sort of inspection was made of north-bound boats, and also write or telegraph Frost. "You will be arrested," he said, "if you either attempt to write or wire." "Then you must send a letter for me," I said. He assured me that he would do so, by a friend who was a river pilot just about to leave for St. Louis. I subsequently learned that the letter was duly delivered. I then went to the wharf-boat and witnessed an inspection of one or two cargoes. The careless and imperfect manner in which it was conducted convinced me that there would be little risk of detection, and that the *Swan* and her freight could pass in safety.

I therefore promptly departed for New Madrid, the point at which it had been agreed that I should meet the *Swan* as she came up the river. Here I came near being involved in quite serious trouble. I had to remain at this little place two or three days before the boat arrived, and was, of course, the object of much curiosity, as a stranger always is in a very small town. I did not realize, as I should have done, the importance of returning consistent answers to the questions propounded me, but whenever any one expressed a desire to know my reason for coming, I gave an explanation, the first that came to me, ingenious enough, perhaps, but generally totally at variance with other responses. Indeed, discretion is something which the majority of mankind only acquire by experience. I subsequently had occasion to regret very much my lack of caution and fertility of invention.

On the second night that I was at New Madrid, fearing that the *Swan* might arrive during the night and that I might fail to learn it, I concluded to change my quarters from the small hotel at which I had stopped, to the wharf-boat. I should say in explanation, that in ante-bellum days, old, dismantled steam-boats were frequently used as wharf-boats and the former state-rooms were rudely fitted up for the accommodation of guests, although meals were not furnished. Quite a large old boat was used for this purpose at New Madrid at the date that I made this visit. I engaged one of the state-rooms and, instructing the wharf master to awaken me if the *Swan* came, slipped off my coat and shoes and laid down. I could not, however, go to sleep, and was pleased when a man came to my room about ten o'clock. He said that some of my acquaintances were in the bar-room and wished to see me. I, of course, suspected no danger, and immediately arose, put on my shoes, and leaving my revolver where I had placed it, under the pillow, proceeded to join my friends, as I supposed them to be. When I passed the door which opened from the saloon into the bar-room I saw a man standing by it with a cocked pistol in his hand. Glancing toward the other door I saw a man, similarly armed, there also.

I at once realized that I was in the hands of a vigilance committee and, in the phrase of that day, "suspected of being a suspicious character." It was by no means a pleasant situation; my hair bristled and I was fairly chilled. It was fortunate, perhaps, that I had left my revolver in the state-room, for in the excitement and consternation I felt, I might have attempted to use it, in which event I would certainly have been killed. The committee, six or seven in number, were seated just in front of the bar. I was not invited to take a seat and remained standing.

There was perfect silence for perhaps a minute, by which time I had recovered my composure.

"I understand, gentlemen," I said, that you sent for me to pass a social evening with you, but you evidently had some other reason. I shall be glad to know what you wish and your purpose."

The chairman was an elderly man, rather deaf. I heartily wished before he stopped talking that he had been born dumb.

"Mr. Duke," he said, "you came here from Cairo, which is occupied by Yankee soldiers. You have told three or four different stories to account for your presence here, and they can't all be true. We think that you are a Yankee spy, and if we become satisfied that you are one we are going to hang you."

I frankly admitted that none of the explanations of my visit to New Madrid, previously given, were correct; and then gave them the real reason, telling them of the instructions I had received from Governor Jackson and how far they had already been carried into effect.

I further told them that I was hourly expecting the arrival of the *Swan*.

"Now, gentlemen," I said, "you can readily understand why in previous conversations I was unwilling to make this statement. If my real business had transpired the object of my mission might have been defeated. I would not be thus frank with you now if my life were not threatened, and also if I did not believe you to be Southern men. But if you are really Southern men, as you claim to be, you will help instead of hanging me."

The chairman remarked that this was very pretty talk, but that he did not credit a word of it. "A fellow will say almost anything to save his life, and you acknowledge that you have already lied to us." He repeated his belief that I was a spy.

I answered, rather indignantly, that there was nothing at New Madrid to invite the visit of a spy. "I have already told you," I said, "that the *Swan* will soon be here. You know her captain. If he doesn't verify what I have told you, why hang me. You can easily guard me and prevent my escape. Even if I should get free I couldn't reach Cairo if you tried to prevent me. At least give me twenty-four hours to prove the truth of my story. If the *Swan* does not reach here by that time, act as you please."

The chairman was still obdurate. He insisted that they could not afford to take any risk and that I ought to be put out of the way. So far no other member of the committee had uttered a word, but all had remained, in appearance, as stolid as statues. Now, however, one of them spoke up very emphatically. His name, I think, was Louis Walters. He was about thirty years of age, a very handsome man, and six feet two or three inches in height. During my brief stay in the town I had seen more of him than of any one else. He suddenly sprang to his feet, with blazing eyes and his grip on a revolver, and delivered what I thought to be the finest speech I had ever heard. "I believe," he said, "everything this young fellow now tells us. I can perfectly comprehend why he at first attempted to deceive us. He would have been a fool and false to his trust if he had dropped an intimation why he came here or said anything which might induce suspicion of his real purpose. At any rate, it would be plain murder to hang a man who offers to furnish, in a few hours, proof of his innocence — evidence which we will be compelled to believe. He must have the twenty-four hours he asks, and more, if necessary. No one is more determined than myself to execute the proper work of this committee, but before you shall hang a man without giving him a chance you must first kill me."

It was perhaps imprudent and not in the best taste, but I could not refrain from expressing my hearty approval of these remarks. There was an immediate and general endorsement — with the exception of the chairman — of the position taken by Walters; and it was determined that I should be kept under guard, but treated kindly, pending the arrival of the *Swan*. The committee remained on the wharf-boat about an hour longer, but that time was devoted to convivial enjoyment, and even the chairman tried to be agreeable. I returned to my quarters, but the two men who had acted as guards while my examination was being conducted, were detailed to watch each door of the state-room. They remained outside, however, in order not to disturb my sleep.

Early next morning I was awakened by a noisy and angry colloquy going on in the saloon, just in front of my door. Some one was fiercely threatening the guard for refusing him entrance to my room. I thought I recognized the voice, and on looking out, found that I was not mistaken. The angry man was Doctor Leonard, a friend of mine, who lived in New Madrid, but frequently visited St. Louis. I had inquired for him immediately on reaching the place, and learned that he was absent on professional business. He was also a member of the vigilance committee, and having gotten home that morning, was told what had been done with me. His indignation was extreme, and he expressed a strong desire to shoot the chairman, which would have been, of course, out of order. He started instantly for the wharf-boat to offer me aid and consolation. I was very glad to see him, but had some difficulty in reducing him to a quiet state of mind and pacific disposition. He said that he had not "helped to organize the —— committee for the purpose of hanging his own friends."

I finally persuaded him not to attempt my rescue by force, but to propose to the committee that I should be released upon his becoming responsible for my return to custody if it should be necessary. He easily effected such an arrangement, and I was permitted to go at large in his company. Late that afternoon the *Swan* arrived, and I lost no time in getting aboard of her.

The *Swan* had already lost some time, and her captain was determined to make it up, appreciating as thoroughly as Greene and I did, that events were moving too rapidly to permit of his boat going slow. He entered heartily into the spirit of the enterprise, for he was a gallant man and his sympathies were cordially with us. Even the crew, although, of course, not informed of the nature of the cargo on board, and the necessity of getting it to port as speedily as possible, seemed to realize that something unusual was to be done, and shared our excitement as the big boat, with her furnaces crammed full, the smoke roaring out of her funnels, and the steam hissing and snapping from her escape pipes, flew along at a racing rate. We reached Cairo about ten o'clock at night, but did not venture to run past without landing. The inspection, as I had anticipated, was careless, and nothing was detected.

We reached St. Louis on the morning of May 9th and turned over the guns and munitions to Major Shaler, sent by General Frost to receive and take them to Camp Jackson. Blair and Lyon were doubtless almost immediately informed in some way of their arrival and the disposition made of them, for the latter promptly prepared to seize them.

On the evening of the 9th the board of police commissioners became convinced, by a report of the chief of police, that a movement against the camp was imminent. The chief reported that the regiments into which the Wide Awake companies had been organized were mustering at their respective points of rendezvous, and that ammunition had been distributed to them; also, that a number of horses had been taken into the arsenal for the purpose, he thought, of moving artillery. I went to the camp that night, notified General Frost of this information, and urged him to prepare for an attack, which I believed would be delivered early the next morning. He, however, did not apprehend such danger or was unwilling to make any disposition to meet it. I saw him again about seven o'clock in the morning, but could learn nothing whatever of his intentions. As my rank in the state guard was only that of captain, he felt, perhaps, that there was no reason why he should inform me of his plans. But I was also a police commissioner, and had been deputed by the board to confer with him on their behalf. I soon became convinced that he had not decided on any line of action.

Greene and I, therefore, determined to proceed at once to Jefferson City, whither we had to go, at any rate, to make our report to the governor. When we got there, we procured an interview as soon as possible with him, taking Mr. Snead and Colonel Churchill, who was state senator from St. Louis, with us. We described to Governor Jackson the situation, as we understood it, and ventured to express the opinion that General Frost ought not to await attack in his camp, but that he ought either to assume the offensive himself or retreat to some point not so easy of reach by his enemy. While we were discussing this matter, news was received that Lyon had delivered his blow and that Frost's entire command had been surrendered.

The strength of the state guard at Camp Jackson was not more than seven or eight hundred men, and it was attacked by, perhaps, seven thousand. It probably could not have offered successful resistance after it was surrounded, but it was not permitted to attempt resistance. As the prisoners were being marched to the city, their captors, angered by the taunts and reproaches of the spectators, fired on the crowd, killing and wounding twenty-eight people.

The excitement in St. Louis was, of course, intense, and it was not less so in Jefferson City. The legislature was in special session, the governor having called it to assemble on May 2d. When it heard of the capture of Camp Jackson and the slaughter of the citizens, it passed the military bill and other measures which should have been adopted long before. A rumour came that Blair and Lyon were marching on the capital, and I was sent that night to burn the bridge over the Osage River, and Rock Champion to burn that which spanned the Gasconade. Champion and Farrington, then lieutenants in Shaler's battalion — composed of the Minute Men — had been sent to Jefferson City a few days previously with details from their respective companies, and consequently, like Greene and myself, escaped the fate of our comrades at Camp Jackson. During the following week Captain Joseph Kelly came from St. Louis with his company of more than a hundred young Irishmen. It was an exceptionally fine body of men; intelligent, educated, spirited young fellows, every one of whom held an excellent business position in the city. Yet, without an exception or the least hesitation, they committed themselves to the cause, and all, save those who fell in battle, served honourably to the close of the war. They also, by some good fortune, had happened not to be in Camp Jackson when it was taken.

In a few days nearly one thousand militia were assembled at the capital, armed generally with hunting rifles. The greater part of them were encamped in the fair grounds and placed under the command of Captain Kelly. He was a veteran of the English army, a good soldier, and a brave and excellent man. I have always remembered him with the kindest feeling, not only because of his sterling character, but because he gave me my first lessons in discipline. I soon had cause to learn that he was something of a martinet, and would brook slackness or negligence in none about him. He very often made me officer of the day, and required me to accompany him every night in making the grand rounds. It was in the performance of this duty that I had occasion to note particularly and somewhat nervously the kind of arms with which the militia were provided; for every sentry would cock his rifle, set the hair-trigger, and draw a bead on any one who approached his post. This was quite discouraging to me and other officers, and made Kelly very angry. We anticipated no attack at that time, and enforced strict sentry duty merely as a matter of training. The men grumbled a good deal when Captain Kelly, finding it impossible altogether to correct this unpleasant habit, at length required them to stand guard without arms.

Many of the previously "unconditional Union" men, some of them very prominent, were converted into implacable secessionists by the events which had occurred at St. Louis. Most conspicuous among them was Sterling Price. He announced his adherence to the Southern cause and tendered his services to the state of Missouri. He had served with distinction in the Mexican War, and Governor Jackson promptly appointed him major-general of the state guard, under the provisions of the military bill, which gave him command of all of the troops which Missouri might put into the field.

General Price's record in the Confederate army is so familiar to his countrymen that it would be almost presumptuous in me to testify to its excellence; but it is impossible for any one who knew him personally to mention his name without some tribute to his exceeding kindness of heart and grandeur of character. He impressed all who approached him with the conviction that he was a good, as well as a great, man. Col. Thomas L. Snead, of whom I have more than once spoken, became, as chief of staff to General Price, as well known by the Missourians and almost as much beloved as his commander. His faithful and valuable services in that capacity are best attested by the deeds of the splendid soldiery in whose organization and training he so greatly assisted. Col. Richard T. Morrison, another personal friend of mine, at that time in Jefferson City, was immediately placed on General Price's staff and served with him during the entire war. Colonel Morrison was a true man and a delightful, although, sometimes with those he disliked, a rather dangerous companion. A certain haughty grace of manner and a strain of reckless, but chivalric, courage, which he had frequently displayed in the duelling, ante-bellum days, had earned him among his associates the sobriquet of "Athos," Dumas's famous mousquetaire.

John S. Marmaduke, who rose to be a general and won an excellent reputation in the Confederate army, and who, after the close of the war, was governor of Missouri, had resigned his commission in the old army and had come to Jefferson City to offer his sword to Missouri. Richard Weightman and

Alexander E. Steen were there with the same purpose; both were brave and excellent officers, but Weightman was killed not long afterward.

Among other celebrities there, of whom I saw a great deal and whose society I much enjoyed, were state Senator Thomas A. Harris and the irrepressible M. Jeff Thompson. Harris was appointed to the command of one of the military districts into which the state was divided under the military bill, with the rank of brigadier-general. Such justice has been done his military record by no less a personage than General Grant, in the latter's own memoirs, that I need not enlarge upon it. He did not, however, remain long in the field, but served Missouri even more efficiently in the Confederate congress. Thompson was also appointed brigadier-general and assigned to command. He never obtained Confederate rank, I believe, but served actively and efficiently throughout the war. Among the numerous visitors attracted to Jefferson City at that period and who thronged the hotel lobbies, opinion was divided as to which of the two, General Harris or General Thompson, was the more brilliant and instructive conversationalist or greater man.

General Thompson was inclined to believe that he was. General Harris did not agree with him.

The Hon. Nat Claiborne, one of the most effective popular speakers I have ever heard, was then a member of the Legislature of Missouri. He had made a decided hit at the Charleston convention by a speech in which he seconded the nomination of Douglas, and his speeches during the Presidential canvass which followed were exceptionally eloquent. My own high opinion, however, of his extraordinary power in that respect was in great measure induced by a speech which he made directly to me, when he brought me the order to burn the bridge over the Osage River. He was accompanied by two or three other legislators, and all were full of fervid patriotism and something else equally as potent. He delivered the order in a fiery oration which made me feel as if I would like to burn every bridge on the continent.

Two other men, J. Proctor Knott and George Vest, occupied official station at that time at Jefferson City, and were exceedingly influential in shaping events, and both subsequently achieved enviable national reputation. Knott was the attorney-general of Missouri, and Vest was a state senator. Both were comparatively young, scarcely past thirty, but were already recognized as men of far more than ordinary capacity, indeed, of brilliant talent.

The anticipations then formed of their future were abundantly realized after the close of the war, when Knott was ranked by common consent with the ablest debaters in the lower house of congress and Vest was admitted to be one of the foremost members of the senate.

Cotton Greene, my colleague in the mission to Montgomery, was busily employed in the camps as drill master and assistant in the organization of the militia; and then followed General Price and Governor Jackson from Jefferson City to serve gallantly to the close of the war. I never knew a better man or more thorough gentleman. He was unusually cultured and intelligent, and was the soul of honour. Our friendship continued until his death, and I shall remember it with pleasure while I live.

But it was fated that even yet there should be delay — that hesitating policy which was always so harmful to the South. Upon the advice of many of his own friends and at the invitation of General Harney, the Federal commander of the district, General Price consented to meet Harney at St. Louis on May 21st, with the view of coming to some agreement which might prevent armed collision. In the conference which ensued, General Price undertook to maintain order in Missouri on condition that General Harney would refrain from military operations within the limits of the state. General Harney was unquestionably sincere in this agreement, and, if permitted, would have faithfully observed it. This agreement was undoubtedly a grave mistake on the part of the Southern men, for the slightest reflection might have convinced them that it was one which would not be maintained. The Federal government, having determined on the policy of coercion, could not afford to respect it; and when General Price virtually disbanded his troops, under its terms, he surrendered a great advantage, never to be fully recovered, and immensely increased the subsequent task of assembling an army. Blair and Lyon were absolutely opposed to the agreement, and immediately made efforts for Harney's removal. They were successful, and Lyon was appointed in his stead. He at once, without scruple or explanation, abrogated the agreement and began active military operations.

General Price had, in the meantime, ordered the state troops assembled at Jefferson City to return to their respective military districts, to be organized there under the new military law. Governor Jackson consented to the agreement with extreme reluctance, but approved it because, like General Price, he wished to avert bloodshed if possible, and he did not anticipate the indecent haste, if not, indeed, flagrant violation of good faith, with which it was repudiated.

It was apparent that, under this arrangement, active hostilities in Missouri would be indefinitely postponed; so I asked and obtained leave of absence. I was very anxious to go to Kentucky, for I was soon to be married to one of her most beautiful daughters; and as the date of that event approached, I felt a less acute interest in the military situation and heard with more patience suggestions of an armistice. Before leaving, however, I wished to make a brief visit to St. Louis to settle my affairs there. My friends in Jefferson City remonstrated strongly against such a step on my part, declaring that I would certainly be arrested, and a cousin of mine in St. Louis, when he learned of my purpose, came post-haste to dissuade me.

I was very unwilling to be dissuaded. As other men equally involved, I thought, with myself in all that had occurred, had recently returned to St. Louis without molestation, I saw no reason why I should not be permitted to do so. On the day that I proposed to go, some of my friends were discussing the matter with me in a room of one of the hotels, and still urging me to abandon the intention, when a message came to me to the effect that some one in the hall wished to see me. I stepped out to find the party who wanted me, and a bright, alert-looking young fellow, with red hair, was designated as that individual.

I should say in explanation of what passed between this gentleman and myself that one of my warmest friends in St. Louis was a young lawyer, a few years my senior, named Asa Jones, who had been appointed United States district attorney for Missouri, just after Mr. Lincoln's inauguration. He was a native of Vermont, but although an ardent Republican and unconditional Union man, his closest personal friends were among the Southerners, who all appreciated his generous and manly nature.

When I accosted the young man pointed out as the one who wished to see me, and whom I had never seen before, he inquired: "Are you Captain Basil Duke?" Having assured him that I was, I asked his name.

"Never mind my name," he responded, "it's better that you shouldn't know it. But I bring you a message from Asa Jones. He has heard that you are about to return to St. Louis and has sent me to tell you not to do so; for he knows that if you come you will have serious trouble. The Federal grand jury has indicted you for treason, and if you are arrested you will be convicted on evidence of having brought the guns from Baton Rouge. He would extremely dislike to prosecute you, and he wishes you to promise that you won't come."

This was definite and very "striking" information, and at once decided me to abandon my purpose.

"Very well," I said. "Thank Asa for me and tell him I won't come."

"I'm glad to hear it," he replied. "I'll go straight back and report to Jones, and on his account you must forget what I've told you."

I immediately rejoined my friends, and after some further conversation announced that I was much impressed by what they had said and that, after reflecting upon the reasons they had advanced, had concluded not to go to St. Louis. They were much pleased and declared that they had from the first believed that I would eventually listen to reason.

On the following day I set out for Kentucky.

General Harney was removed from Federal command in Missouri on May 30, 1861, and Lyon was appointed in his stead. The latter promptly evinced his disposition to repudiate the terms of the Price-Harney agreement and resume hostilities. In order definitely to ascertain what he might expect in this regard, Governor Jackson, with General Price and other gentlemen, visited St. Louis and held a conference with Lyon and some of his officers on June 11th. Lyon clearly and with almost brutal frankness informed the representatives of Missouri that the state must choose between immediate and complete submission or war.

Instantly upon his return to Jefferson City, Governor Jackson issued a proclamation in which he announced the rejection by the Federal authorities of every proposition contemplating a peaceable adjustment of the questions which had excited so much discussion and feeling; declared that the dangers which threatened Missouri could be averted only by an appeal to arms, and called into the field fifty thousand state troops. On July 13th he personally joined at Booneville some three hundred or four hundred men, who were the first to respond to this call. He was attacked there on June 15th by Lyon and forced to retreat into south-western Missouri. A series of active operations and small combats ensued, culminating in the sharp battle and decisive Confederate victory of Wilson's Creek. Price and McCullough having united their forces near the Arkansas border, moved in the direction of Springfield, Mo., and near that place encountered and defeated Lyon, who lost his life in the battle.

In the latter part of June Gen. William J. Hardee, then brigadier-general in the Confederate army, had been ordered to take command of "that portion of Arkansas lying west of the White and Black Rivers and north of the Arkansas River, to the Missouri line." On July 15th, following, all the troops then recruited in Arkansas for the service of the state were formally transferred to the service of the Confederate States, and General Hardee assumed command of the district assigned him July 22d with headquarters at Pittman's Ferry. He had four or five regiments of infantry, two battalions of cavalry, and three batteries of artillery, in all between four and five thousand men. These troops were all at first encamped at Pocahontas, Ark., but a considerable number of them were in the early part of August moved to Greenville, Mo.

I was at that date returning from Kentucky, and on my way to rejoin the Missouri troops under Price. Taking that route as the shortest and surest one by which I might reach General Price, wherever he might be, I arrived at Pittman's Ferry shortly before General Hardee moved thence to Greenville.

I found very few there whom I had previously known, but among them was John S. Marmaduke, who was then serving as Hardee's chief of staff, and very busily employed in drilling and disciplining the new troops. He had excellent material to handle and was rapidly getting them in shape. When I informed him of my purpose to rejoin General Price, he advised me against any attempt to do so at that time. He said that I would find it more difficult than I supposed; and that while travelling between the respective commands of Hardee and Price, both of which might soon be actively engaged in offensive operations, I would probably altogether miss opportunities of witnessing service I would much like to see. He offered, although I was not then enrolled in the Confederate service, to obtain for me some position under General Hardee, corresponding with my rank in the state service. I at once took his advice, the more readily because he gave me to understand that General Hardee was desirous of attempting a movement upon St. Louis, in which his own forces and those of Price and Pillow might be combined. In a day or two Marmaduke fulfilled his promise to "take care" of me, by introducing me to Colonel, afterward Major-general, Thomas C. Hindman, who was then in command of the Second Arkansas Regiment of Infantry. This regiment was so large, having seventeen companies in it, that it was popularly termed Hindman's "Legion." Colonel Hindman, feeling, doubtless, that because of the unusual strength of his regiment he needed and was entitled to something more than the regular regimental staff, invited me to serve with him as volunteer aide, and I gladly accepted. I am not sure that my services were of any value, but he certainly kept me constantly and actively employed, which was his custom with every one, not sparing himself.

Hindman had been a successful politician, and was in congress at the breaking out of the war. He was a forcible and attractive speaker, and, indeed, a really able man. His energy was extraordinary, and his temper as impetuous as his courage. While arbitrary and imperious in his dealings with those who opposed him, or whom he deemed his enemies, he was much admired and liked by his friends. At the time of which I speak he was very popular with the Arkansas troops, and his influence over them was greater, perhaps, than that of any other officer.

The camps at Pittman's Ferry and Pocahontas were scourged by the usual diseases to which raw troops are liable, and measles, especially, raged with extreme virulence and counted its victims by scores. The march to Greenville was of great benefit to the troops, not only by removing them to a healthier locality, but because of the diversion it effected from unpleasant and melancholy scenes to more wholesome and agreeable surroundings. It was made through a densely wooded country and over rugged roads, which for two or three days severely tested the endurance of men unaccustomed to moving in large bodies and close order, but the experience was just what they needed, and their new encampments were all the more welcome because of it.

Soon after reaching Greenville, the adjutant of Hindman's regiment was taken sick and I was temporarily assigned to that position. I found it not altogether a sinecure, as one incident in which I participated will illustrate. There was a company in the "Legion" composed entirely of Irish, which, in accordance with a custom very prevalent at the time, had been given an appellation distinct from its regimental designation, *viz.*, the "Shamrock guards." It numbered more than eighty men, and was officered entirely by Irishmen. The captain and first lieutenant had been railroad contractors, and the men, having all worked under them, were pretty thoroughly under their control. The other two lieutenants and the non-commissioned officers were younger, less experienced, and not so well known to the men and could exercise, consequently, less authority over them. The Shamrocks, with some five or six other companies of Hindman's regiment, were encamped in a large apple orchard near the town, and one morning word was brought to the colonel's headquarters that the company was on a big drunk. It was reported that they were not only fighting among themselves, but had declared war against all who might approach them, and had gotten completely beyond control.

This news was the more disquieting because the captain and first lieutenant were both absent on leave. Colonel Hindman instructed me to go instantly to the scene of disturbance and promptly restore order. I did not feel an implicit confidence in my ability to execute the mission, but was consoled by the reflection that I was well known to the Shamrocks and on exceedingly good terms with them. While big muscular men, and capable of the hardest labour, they were poor pedestrians, and on the march from Pocahontas to Greenville had suffered more from fatigue and sore feet than any of the other troops. During that march I had more than once assisted every man in the company, perhaps, by permitting him, when lagging weary and crippled in the rear, to ride my horse until he caught up with his comrades; and I knew that I had gained their gratitude and good-will. Yet when I reached the ground where I was to tackle the Shamrocks, I saw a sight which sorely tried my nerves and somewhat shook my resolution. All the company except the two lieutenants and the non-commissioned officers were in liquor. Thirty-five or forty were roaring drunk and fighting like tigers. They had not taken the trouble to pair off, but were engaged in a free fight, each man for his own hand and hitting at any head he saw. Fortunately they were not using weapons, but were, nevertheless, inflicting on each other considerable damage. The others were looking on with approbation, and occasionally furnishing a fresh combatant. The lieutenants and non-commissioned officers were striving conscientiously but ineffectually to stop the fray, and when I got there were almost in a state of collapse. Their efforts for peace met with fierce resentment, and they had been beaten until they were as limp as wet rags, and their faces looked like raw steaks dripping with blood. I was at first inclined to call on some of the other companies of the regiment to quell the riot, but, as outside interference might have induced subsequent jealousy and bad feeling, I thought it better to recognize the principle of home-rule and require the Shamrocks to police themselves. Moreover, the Arkansas boys, if roughly handled, might have used weapons. I therefore ordered the partially sober men, who were the more numerous, to arrest the disorderly ones. They showed such reluctance to obey, not wishing to stop a beautiful fight, that I found it necessary to set the example. I did so very unwillingly, for I knew that such a pounding as had been given the officers would quickly extinguish me. I immediately discovered, however, to my great satisfaction, that even the drunkest and most furious would not strike me. Either my rank protected me, or, as I rather believe, they remembered my previous good offices. At any rate, they simply shoved me aside when I would catch hold of them and continued to batter each other. Becoming as bold as a lion when I found that I was in no danger, I rushed into the midst of the mêlée and imperatively commanded the bystanders to follow and assist me. When these saw I was in earnest they obeyed. But the fighters showed them no such consideration as they had extended me. On the contrary, they turned in a body on the interlopers, and that once quiet and smiling orchard was converted into a seeming pandemonium, and the tumult of battle and bloody murther rose to the startled skies.

But after a few minutes of hard struggle, during which I prudently withdrew to the outside of the ring, numbers prevailed and the rioters were overpowered. Then arose the question what should be done with the offenders. Very little respect was paid to my opinions or wishes in the matter. The constabulary force had lost all their former sympathy with the fighters, and were so angry because of the trouble given them and the punches they had received that they thought only of revenge and future security. It was unanimously resolved that the culprits should be bucked and gagged. I had a soft spot in my heart for the Shamrocks, and notwithstanding the fact that I was compelled to approve the sentence, I pleaded that they should be gagged with corn-cobs instead of bayonets. The suggestion elicited a storm of dissent. "Just listen to that," said one fellow. "Did ye ever hear the like? Gag them big flannel-mouths with corn-cobs. Begorra, he'll be tellin' us next to wash their throats wid buttermilk."

"Yu're a good mon, adjutant," said another, "but yu're too tindher-hearted. Thim divils wud mind a corn-cob no more'n a pig wud a sthraw. The boy'nit's the thing for thim to chaw on."

So a bayonet was crammed into each guilty mouth, and having been also "bucked," that is, tied up knees to chin, they were left as the sergeant expressed it, "To go to shlape paycably in the sun." In a few hours they were all sober and nearly as good as new. No unpleasant feeling remained, and except for the black eyes and bruises no one could have guessed that anything had happened to the Shamrocks.

About the middle of August we got the news of the victory won over Lyon by Price and McCullough, and it lost nothing in the telling. The troops at Greenville were greatly elated by it and spurred to such emulation that they thought and talked of nothing but marching against the enemy and early battle. It was expected that General Price would immediately press forward into central Missouri and to the Missouri River — as he did — and General Hardee was very desirous of advancing on St. Louis if he could secure the coöperation of General Pillow and of the Missouri state troops in his vicinity, commanded by General Thompson.

The situation seemed propitious for offensive operations on the part of the Confederates. The defeated army of Lyon was in full and disorderly retreat. The respective forces of Hardee, Pillow, and Thompson were so located that coöperation and junction between them would be easy; and a rapid march would take them to the immediate vicinity of St. Louis sooner than those fleeing from the disaster at Wilson's Creek could arrive to assist in the defence of that city. Combined they would probably out-number the other Federal troops on which Frèmont relied to hold St. Louis, and were certainly better prepared for battle.

When my temporary service as adjutant of Hindman's regiment terminated on the return of Lieutenant Patterson, I sought and obtained permission from General Hardee to do scouting duty. I was very desirous to procure command of a body of cavalry strong enough to attack and capture the garrison at the bridge over the Meramee, near St. Louis, so soon as the forward movement should commence. After its destruction it would be difficult, if not impossible, for the Federals to reinforce Ironton, the then terminus of the Iron Mountain railroad, and the road to St. Louis would be open and clear of obstacles. I was sent on missions which took me far to the front, and I prized these opportunities more highly because I was thus enabled to get a good knowledge of the country the army would traverse if advance was determined upon. I learned at this time my first lessons in scouting and outpost duty, rudimentary compared with those I afterward received under Morgan, but nevertheless valuable.

Two young friends of mine from St. Louis, White Kennett and Harry Churchill, were respectively captain and first lieutenant of a small company of cavalry which belonged to the Missouri State guard but was then unattached and virtually acting independently. The boys of this little squad were well armed and mounted, roved at will and lived on the fat of the land. As their movements were generally along the same lines with my own, I accompanied them on many of their excursions. Their service was neither arduous nor "bloody." There was not a great deal of fighting done anywhere at that date, but it was bold and interesting. Kennett and Churchill at least kept their eyes open and discovered a good deal worth reporting to headquarters, and as they were often in close proximity to the camps of the enemy, they occasionally took prisoners or made more valuable captures.

I had one experience while engaged in this sort of duty which I remember vividly, trivial as it may seem. On one occasion General Hardee ordered me to go to Frederickton, a little town a few miles from Ironton, and, as nearly as my memory serves me, some fifty or sixty miles from Greenville, to communicate certain instruction to parties there and bring back information which they were expected to furnish. It was more than an ordinary day's ride, and although I made an early start from Greenville, I was, at nightfall, still a considerable distance from my destination. That country was then quite thinly peopled. The houses were far apart and dense woods stretched for miles in every direction. I was alone, and, as I rode along the deserted, dusty country road I could not prevent my imagination from strongly asserting itself and suggesting that all sorts of prospective dangers might be lurking in the thickets on either side. The very fact that the moon shone brightly rather added to my discomfort, for I fancied I could see things moving in the shadows.

At intervals, among the usual noises of the night, I heard sounds which I listened to with anything but pleasure. I had heard these sounds more than once before when riding through this region at night. I had supposed them to be the cries of hounds running at large, and hunting without a master, but those, professing to be informed, told me that they were the howls of wolves chasing deer. On former occasions, as I had never seen the wolves and had been surrounded by companions, I had given the matter little concern; but now I listened with an apprehension which was heightened by the fear with which my horse evidently heard the melancholy music. I was really in no danger, for if these brutes ever attack man under any circumstances, they would, at any rate, not have done so at that time of the year. But the thing was unpleasant and set my nerves on edge, so that whenever an owl hooted, or a wild hog scared by my approach dashed through the brush with sudden grunt, I too, very nearly went off in a panic.

About ten o'clock, a late hour for the country people, I reached a house which, with its premises, answered in appearance to the description I had been given of the place where I had been advised to stop for the night. The house was a little back from the road, but with no yard or fence in front of it. I rode up to it and found the door closed and no lights showing; the inmates had long been asleep. I shouted at the top of my voice, but for some minutes received no answer. At length the door was pushed partially open, a man looked out cautiously and gruffly asked what I wanted. I told him that I wished to get lodging until morning. He suggested that I look for it farther on. I declared that I couldn't think of doing that.

"Well, stranger," he said, "I ain't in the habit of turnin' folks off, but in these times I don't like to let in them I don't know."

"Isn't this Cagey Graham's house?" I responded. "I was told to ask for him."

"What in the — do you want with Cagey Graham?" he inquired with considerable emphasis. I had been informed that Cagey Graham was an old farmer of that "neck of the woods," quite a leading man in his neighbourhood and a red-hot rebel. I felt pretty sure that I was at the right place, and thought it best to speak plainly, so I told him that I was just from Greenville and bearer of despatches from General Hardee to parties in Frederickton. I added something which was not strictly accurate, but ought to have been so, I said that General Hardee, Colonel Hindman and, indeed, all of the Confederate officers at Greenville, had particularly requested me to see Cagey

Graham, learn from him all that was going on, and find out what he thought ought to be done. He was so much mollified by this statement that he stepped out of the house and admitted that he was Cagey Graham.

After ascertaining that I was entirely alone, he said that I might stay all night. He directed me where to stable and feed my horse, and gave the welcome information that I should have something to eat myself. When I returned from the stable I saw, although he treated me hospitably, that his doubts were not entirely resolved, and he was not convinced that I was what I represented myself to be until I had answered satisfactorily a number of inquiries. Fortunately I knew all of the cavalry men, Confederate and state guard, with whom he, too, was personally acquainted, and who had passed through that part of the country. When I finished supper he gave me a bed in an adjoining room and bade me good night. Just as I was dropping off to sleep my slumber was postponed by the sound of the opening of the front door and the entrance of some one. To the old man's quick challenge of "who's that?" the new comer answered, "Bill," and proceeded in turn to inquire, "Who's that man who came in here a while back?" I listened with a good deal of interest while the old man vouched for me.

"He's all right," he said. "He knows Kennett and Churchill and Borland's men. He's one of Hardee's people himself. Thar ain't no trouble 'bout him."

The other did not seem to be perfectly assured, but saying: "Well, I'll see him in the mornin'," let the subject drop.

Early the next morning old Cagey called me to breakfast. Two or three men beside himself were seated at the table, and looked at me rather suspiciously. One of them, a good-looking, powerfully built young fellow of about twenty, was introduced to me by the old man as "My son Bill."

When Bill spoke I recognized the voice which had so particularly inquired about me during the night. At first his demeanour was sullen, almost surly, but after talking with him a short time it underwent a sudden and agreeable change. He smiled in a genial and encouraging fashion. "Why, captain," he said, "I didn't know you at first, but I've jest placed you," I expressed my gratification to learn that such was the fact, and he continued:

"I belong to Kennett's company, and I recollect seeing you being along with us two or three times. I'm powerful glad I didn't shoot you last night."

I assured him that his satisfaction in that regard could certainly not be so great as my own, but begged to know why it was he had harboured any thought of shooting me. He explained that the people who lived in the neighbourhood and his father, especially, had recently been annoyed and harassed by a band of men who differed with them politically, and expressed such difference of opinion in a very objectionable manner. These fellows, he said, who dwelt within the Federal lines, were in the habit of making nocturnal incursions into the vicinage, driving off stock, occasionally sacking a house, and altogether behaving in a way that he thought was "ridiculous." He was approaching his father's house the last night just as I did so. Hearing me coming, he had slipped into the woods, and when I passed followed me. He was ignorant of my purpose and of whether I was or was not one of the marauders, and was willing to give me the benefit of the doubt.

"When you rode up to the house and hollered out like you did, I concluded you didn't mean no harm. If you had hitched your horse out in the bresh and prowled around on foot," he said, "I'd have let you have both barrels of my shot-gun."

I was profoundly grateful to the Providence which had inspired me to ride up to the house and "holler."

While this region, at the time of which I write, was sparsely settled, remote from any large commercial point and not easy of access, it was prosperous and its people were well-to-do. The country was wild and somewhat rugged, but in certain localities well cultivated and fruitful. The peach orchards, I remember, were exceptionally fine, and much enjoyed by roving cavalrymen; and the "square meals" were excellent.

There were very many gallant men in the little army then encamped at Greenville, nearly all of whom became in a brief time excellent soldiers; and among the officers several attained just distinction. I first saw and made the acquaintance there of two, who were subsequently ranked only a little below the ablest and most famous of the Confederate leaders. These two were Hardee and Cleburne.

General Hardee was a thoroughly educated and exceedingly accomplished soldier. No one in the old army, perhaps, was more perfectly versed in either the more important or the minutest details of professional knowledge. I believe that it is admitted that he had no superior as a corps commander, and his capacity for handling troops on the battle field and his skill as a tactician were unsurpassed. I have frequently heard it stated that he was offered the command of the Army of Tennessee when Bragg was removed, and that Hood was not appointed, until after his declination. I don't know whether this be true or not, but if it be, I am sure that he was influenced by undue modesty. My estimate of him may be enhanced by gratitude for kindness received at his hands, but I believe that he possessed almost every quality which is necessary to make an able general, unless it may have been self-confidence. His grasp of a strategic question or situation was clear and comprehensive, and as an army leader he was prompt, bold, and alert. I have sometimes heard General Hardee characterized as a martinet. This is not just to him. He believed in careful discipline and was sometimes strict in enforcing its essentials. But he was never harsh, and was not only solicitous for the comfort of his men, but entertained the kindest feeling for them. He was a handsome man of very striking figure, and extremely courteous and pleasant in manner.

Gen. Patrick R. Cleburne has been sometimes termed the Stonewall Jackson of the West, and, while it cannot be claimed that he possessed the genius of Jackson, the appellation is unquestionably extremely apposite. He had the same dauntless temper and patient, unflagging energy, the same conscientious, almost fanatical devotion to duty, and an equally combative inclination as a soldier. At Greenville he was the colonel of the First, afterward, I think, designated as the Fifteenth Arkansas Infantry. I cannot remember that I ever saw an officer who was so industrious and persistent in his efforts properly to drill and instruct the men under his command. He took great interest in everything connected with tactics, and personally taught it all, and was occupied from morning until night in superintending squad, company, and battalion drill, guard mounting, inspection and, indeed, everything mentioned in the books or that he could conceive of. I have seen him during the hottest hours of the hottest days in August instruct squad after squad in the bayonet exercise until I wondered how any human frame could endure the fatigue that his exertions must have induced. He was unlike Stonewall Jackson in one particular; when angered, annoyed or astonished, he would swear, and, although his oaths were brief, they were intensely energetic. His speech ordinarily had little of the Irish accent, and was slow, clear, and precise, but in his moments of excitement or dissent the brogue became broad and strong.

A member of the company he commanded as captain before he was elected colonel, told me of an amusing instance of this peculiarity. It occurred the first time that all the companies composing the regiment were assembled for battalion drill. Cleburne had up to that date studied assiduously everything about company drill, but had not read further. The tactical instructor of the regiment on that occasion gave some order to be found only in the pages devoted to movements performed in battalion drill, accompanying it with the explanation of how it was to be executed and the corresponding order each captain should give his company. Cleburne gave the required order in a loud, resonant tone, and then muttered in a growl, which was heard by every man in his own ranks, "There's no such dom'd evolution in the buk."

He was extremely temperate and simple in his mode of life, reserved and studious; and was an ardent botanist. No braver or more resolute man ever lived, but he was warm-hearted and generous to a degree and devoted in his friendships. He was skilful, I believe, in the use of all arms, but was extraordinarily so with the pistol. A remarkable and very tragic incident illustrative of his perfect command of this weapon occurred while the troops were encamped at Greenville. Cleburne's headquarters were in the court-house of the little place, and he used one of the rooms in the building as an office and also sleeping room. One day a lieutenant of the Missouri State guard came to Greenville with a small detail of men, escorting some Federal prisoners whom they had captured near Ironton. After taking the prisoners, this party had marched continuously for two or three days and nights, and were, of course, very much exhausted and in a very nervous condition when they reached Greenville. The prisoners and the guard were also quartered in the courthouse, and late that night the lieutenant, dreaming that the prisoners were escaping, sprang up and yelled in the wildest excitement, arousing, of course, every one in the building, and creating a wild uproar and confusion. The guard and other soldiers who were in the house, unable to recognize each other in the dark, began fighting among themselves. The somnambulist, still madly shouting, rushed past Cleburne's room, the door of which was open. As the man sped by, Cleburne, believing him to be one of the prisoners attempting to escape, seized his revolver, which was under his pillow, fired and inflicted a fatal wound. For a man just aroused from sleep to make such a shot, hitting a mark presented to his vision for only a fraction of a second, was certainly extraordinary. The poor fellow who was shot survived only an hour or two, but with his dying breath exonerated Cleburne of all blame. Cleburne was sorely grieved by this unfortunate occurrence, and some of his friends have told me that he never recovered from the remorse it occasioned.

His subsequent brilliant career in the Confederate service and his heroic death at the bloody battle of Franklin are so well known that I need not comment on them. He is entitled to high place among the heroes whose memory the South loves to honour.

General Hardee's desire to march on St. Louis was never realized. The plan was abandoned not, I think, because Hardee would not have been able to secure such coöperation of the commands of Pillow and Thompson with his own as would have insured its success, but because the authorities at Richmond deemed it better to concentrate all available forces in that quarter in Kentucky. Hardee was therefore ordered to Bowling Green, where the headquarters of Gen. Albert Sidney Johnston's department had been established, and took with him to that point the greater part of the troops which had been under his command in south-western Missouri. From that date until the close of the war Missouri was constantly and more perfectly in the Federal grasp than was even Kentucky, although her territory, like that of Kentucky, was frequently penetrated by Confederate raids and incursions.

The partisan cavalry operations conducted by Marmaduke and Shelby in Missouri were very similar to those of Morgan in Kentucky and directed to much the same purposes. The border and guerilla warfare there was quite as fierce and bloody, and productive of more intense and enduring resentment; and, as in Kentucky, there were countless skirmishes fought in which many lives were lost, which have never been recorded and have been even nameless.

When General Hardee received his orders to proceed to Bowling Green, he apprised me of them and very kindly advised me to give up all idea of rejoining General Price, and to go immediately to Kentucky and endeavour to recruit such a cavalry command there as I had hoped to raise in Missouri. He gave me a letter to General Buckner, with whom I was not then personally acquainted, and promised me all the aid in his power when he reached Bowling Green.

He was very partial to this use of cavalry and was an intelligent, firm believer in its efficacy. He became an ardent friend and advocate of Morgan, so soon as the latter began to develop his remarkable efficiency in this service, warmly encouraged and commended him, and constantly urged his promotion.

I reached Nashville on the same day that Gen. Albert Sidney Johnston arrived there on his way to Bowling Green and then saw that great man for the first time. I saw him more than once afterward, but never without being impressed by the majesty of his appearance and manner, which was inexpressibly striking and affected all who approached his presence. Troops were hastening to Bowling Green from every point whence they could be drawn, but, as was soon demonstrated, in no such number as was necessary to maintain the line which General Johnston wished to hold. The little town, however, was so crowded with staff officers and gentry who sported flashy uniforms, and its environs so completely covered with encampments, the long lines of tents stretching in every direction, that to the inexperienced — and we were all without experience then — a vast host seemed to be assembled.

My friend, Captain Kennett, had accompanied me from Missouri with a purpose which to those who do not remember the conditions of that period can scarcely be made comprehensible.

Like myself, he was a young husband and very much pained by his enforced separation from his wife and the difficulty of writing or hearing from her. While in Missouri, although never over one hundred miles from St. Louis, he had found it impossible to send a letter or receive one through the lines, so he determined to go to Louisville, at any risk of capture, whence he could correspond with Mrs. Kennett in the full assurance, at least, of mail facilities. We proceeded together to Bowling Green and thence to Munfordsville, where the Second Kentucky Infantry, under Col. Roger W. Hanson, was posted in the extreme advance of the army. It was my wish to get to Lexington, and Kennett's, as I have said, to reach Louisville, but the southern end of the railroad had ceased operations any farther than Munfordsville, with the Confederate occupation of that point, and it was very difficult to procure any means of transportation. We found three or four well-known merchants of Louisville, who had made a flying visit to Nashville on the eve of this sudden development of the military situation, and, having gotten as far back on their way home as Munfordsville, were stranded there like ourselves. Finally, after diligent inquiry and effort, we secured a large, covered road wagon with its team and engaged it to carry the whole outfit, mercantile and military, to Elizabethtown. It was a weary mode of progression and far less comfortable than a march along the same road on horseback would have been, but after a long night of jolts and cramps we arrived at Elizabethtown about ten o'clock of a bright Sabbath morning.

The population of the town and the adjacent country was in a state of great excitement. Information had been received that a large body of Federal troops had started the day previous from Louisville southward, and a party of citizens — Southern sympathizers — had burned a small bridge, or culvert, eight or ten miles north of Elizabethtown with a view of impeding its progress. It very materially impeded our progress also, inasmuch as it considerably interrupted rail communication with all territory beyond Elizabethtown. Kennett and I, after much discussion, effected an arrangement with a livery-stable keeper who agreed to hire us, at an exorbitant price, a conveyance to take us to Bardstown, whence we might make our way, as chance aided us, to our respective destinations. He was an exceedingly pious man, however, and would not consent to send out his teams on Sunday, so we were compelled to wait until the next day.

There was a large crowd of people in town. Some who had come to attend services in the various churches, but much the greater number had been attracted by the desire to hear the news and talk about matters of much more moment and interest than their usual topics of conversation. Without an exception the crowd was Southern in sentiment, and many of the younger men loudly declared their intention to enlist in the Confederate army "so soon as Buckner came." Encouraged by the prevalence of a feeling so much in unison with our own, we made no secret of our own proclivities and recent antecedents. Learning that we were just from a region where war was being waged, a host of eager auditors pressed around us, listening with insatiable curiosity and touching confidence to everything we chose to tell. I must admit that we described incidents of our service in Missouri in such wise that other eye-witnesses of the same events might have had difficulty in identifying them; and I should regret extremely to be held responsible now for many very startling statements which I made then. It occurred to me that I could find no better occasion to recruit the cavalry command I had been so anxious to raise, and Kennett, from a feeling of comradeship, heartily seconded my efforts.

One quite serious difficulty presented itself upon the very threshold of my enterprise. While nearly every man to whom I mentioned the matter wished to enter the Confederate army a clear majority wanted to be captains, and would consent to go to war on no other terms. I represented, as well as I could, that a company or squadron composed exclusively of officers would be rather anomalous, and might be thrown into confusion by some unusual or unexpected exigency, but my arguments were not received with favour. I found an ally, however, in the county judge, in front of whose office the most important deliberations were conducted. He was a sensible, hard-headed old gentleman, extremely incredulous upon most subjects, but such a red-hot rebel that he would believe almost anything told him on the Southern side. He had consequently been very much impressed by our stories, and was anxious to render any assistance he could to warriors of so much experience. Ascertaining the deep interest he felt in driving the Yankees out of Kentucky, I had already suggested to him a plan of campaign with the capture of Louisville as its ultimate object, to be inaugurated so soon as the two companies absolutely essential to its success could be recruited and organized. I frankly admitted it would be inexcusable audacity to attempt this movement with a less force than two full companies, for it was credibly reported that a body of Federal troops, four thousand strong, was already on the march between Louisville and Elizabethtown. It was commanded by Sherman, but the people of Kentucky had never heard of Sherman, and they believed it to be commanded by Rousseau, of whom they had heard a great deal. The details of this plan — that is to say, what we termed such — had been submitted to the judge, and he had entirely approved them. He, therefore, strongly espoused our side, and finally, late in the afternoon, had overcome all opposition and persuaded the most ambitious and recalcitrant to enlist as privates. I was much elated, but just as I began to prepare a muster-roll an ominous and appalling sound came rolling down the long street, at one end of which we were assembled. It was the hoarse, threatening rattle of a drum, and every man knew at once that the Yankees were upon us. Almost immediately a fleeing figure appeared flashing like a meteor from the same direction, each throbbing drum note behind seeming to impel it to additional speed. I can see that earnest, rapid man with mental vision to-day almost as plainly as I actually saw him then. He wore a pink and blue striped swallow-tailed jeans coat and baggy breeches, and as he whizzed down the pike his loose shoes clattered like castanets. It was hard to understand how a pair of eyes could protrude as his did, and yet remain in their sockets. I am not sure that such was his name, but some one remarked, "Thar comes Ab Jenkins." He was the harbinger of dismay, and, as he drew near, sent his voice before him in wild warning, "Save yourselves, gentlemen, Rouser's in town."

I have rarely witnessed such a stampede as then ensued, and never one more excusable. The bravest men may be pardoned for demoralization and panic if they are not only surprised, but attacked before they are enlisted. The men who were to compose the two companies were so promptly and completely scattered that they were never gotten together again. The judge made a dash for a horse which was hitched near by. The bridle was knotted tightly to the post — a pernicious practice, for no man can say when it may be necessary to use a horse in a hurry. Unable to untie the knot as rapidly as the emergency demanded, the judge solved the problem by cutting the reins, and, mounting, fled in hot haste across the creek, descending one bluff bank and leaping to the top of another. He seemed to be simultaneously on both sides of the creek and splashing through it, darting across like a scared black snake gliding over a ditch.

There was a general disposition to leave town and "take to the woods," in which Kennett and I, with better reason than the others, heartily shared; so, after having made a hasty visit to the hotel to recover our slender baggage, but more especially certain incriminatory papers which were among our effects, we started out on a small country road running in an easterly direction from Elizabethtown, and, before dark, reached a house the very look of which was redolent of hospitality. It was the residence of old Major English, one of the finest, kindest gentlemen in Kentucky. He cheerfully granted our request to be permitted to stay all night, and, as we were not long in discovering his sentiments, we frankly confessed our own. On the next morning, against the old gentleman's strong protest, who had begun to feel a deep interest in our safety, we returned to the town. We encountered a good many soldiers, but were in no wise molested. When we asked the liveryman, however, to let us have the conveyance for which we had contracted we found that he was obstinately determined to rue the bargain. He was greatly alarmed by the advent of the Federals and feared to have dealings with unknown parties who might be rebels in disguise. It was in vain that we assured him that we were inoffensive citizens. In the heat of reply and refusal he even forgot his religion and said: "I don't care a d — n who you are, I'm going to take no chances." Kennett was about to indulge in an angry remonstrance, but it occurred to me that our deliverances of the previous afternoon might have gained general circulation, and I thought it best to let the matter drop.

We then concluded that we would walk along the railroad track until we reached some point where we might catch a train. Quite a number of the troops were bivouacked on both sides of the road, and we were compelled to pass through them. I cautioned Kennett not to call me by name or do anything which might especially attract attention. I had learned that there were several Kentucky regiments in this force — many of the men from central Kentucky — and among these it was extremely probable that there would be some who knew me. We got through safely, and, although occasionally "guyed," no one halted us. I believed that the danger was past, but reckoned a little too hastily. Just as we drew near the entrance to the tunnel at Muldraugh's Hill, two miles north of Elizabethtown, a hand-car with several Federal officers upon it, overtook us. We stepped aside to let it pass, and I pulled my hat-brim over my face to avoid possible recognition. But Kennett, moved by an impulse of pure mischief, called out, "Won't you let us ride with you, gentlemen? We are very foot-sore and tired." I forgot my caution, threw back my hat, and looked up just as the car came alongside, and realized that I was face to face with three or four men with whom I was well, and had previously been quite pleasantly, acquainted. Among them were Col. George Jouett, afterward killed at Perryville, and Colonel subsequently, Gen. John M. Harlan, since one of the most distinguished of the associate justices of the Supreme Court of the United States. I was immediately recognized, and my name was called by two or three of them, accompanied with expressions of surprise at my presence in that locality. They also imperatively ordered me to surrender. I tried to seem astonished and look as if it was a case of mistaken identity, but was very much puzzled about what I should do. Greatly to my wonder and relief, however, the car, instead of being stopped, rolled on into the tunnel. When I saw this I hurriedly bade Kennett good-bye, sprang up the side of the cut, which was neither steep nor very high at the point where I happened to be, and made off at a full speed through a field of standing corn. By the time that the hand-car with its occupants had returned to the spot I had so rapidly evacuated, I was beyond immediate pursuit.

It was not until after the close of the war that I learned how and by whom my escape had been aided. I related this incident to a gentleman in Lexington and noticed that he listened with some amusement, as well as interest. When I had finished my story he informed me that he had heard it before. "John Harlan told me of it," he said, "just after it happened, and it is to him that you are indebted for your good fortune in getting off as well as you did." When Judge Harlan recognized me it at once occurred to him that I was trying to make my way to Lexington to see my wife; but he also realized that if captured I would be in great peril of being tried and punished as a spy. I was dressed in citizen's clothing and within the Federal lines on no ostensible military business. Under ordinary circumstances, he would have taken me without hesitation, but was unwilling that I should be put to death for an offence of which he believed me innocent. So he quietly placed his foot under the brake, and the efforts of his companions failed to stop the car. Judge Harlan's foot, like everything in his make-up, mental, moral, and physical, is constructed on a liberal, indeed, a grand scale, and might affect the motion of a passenger coach, not to mention a hand-car. It was an exceedingly generous and kindly act, and I, of course, can never know exactly how deeply I am indebted to him.

Feeling that any further effort to reach Lexington at that time would be futile, I turned southward again, to get back as speedily as possible into Confederate territory. My immediate safety also concerned me, for I had reason to expect that an effort to find and capture me would be promptly made. After a wide and toilsome détour about Elizabethtown, traversing the most obscure and difficult paths and keeping as closely as possible under cover, I at length, just at nightfall, came to the turnpike south of the town and farther out than I supposed the pickets would be posted. I was worn down with fatigue and applied at the first house to which I came for shelter and supper. The owner, a tall, raw-boned man, with a keen, good-humoured face, smiled quizzically when he noticed my jaded and travel-stained appearance, but asked no questions. He gave me something to eat and showed me to a room. "You'll be safe here to-night," he said, "but you'd better get away before daybreak." Sure enough, he had me up and started me off at a very early hour the next morning. I learned afterward that my kind-hearted host was the only Union man in that neighbourhood, and that he had strongly suspected me of being a rebel, but it was his instinct to help any one who was in need. I afterward had the opportunity to requite, to some extent, his good services.

After another long tramp, I was gratified late in the afternoon by the sight of our outpost videttes.

Not long afterward Capt. John H. Morgan came with his company, the Lexington Rifles. I enlisted in it and was elected first lieutenant. My sporadic service ceased, and I served until the close of the war in a more regular fashion.

CHAPTER IV

WHO of the Missourians who served in the Confederate army — indeed of all that gallant host which fought in the Trans-Mississippi department — and what man among those who endured a term of imprisonment at Fort Delaware does not remember Gen. M. Jeff Thompson?

At the beginning of the unpleasantness the general, who had long been a citizen of Missouri, was appointed a brigadier-general in the state guard of Missouri; and, although he served with Confederate troops bravely and efficiently to the close of the war, he never, I believe, held rank in the Confederate army. He was an extremely eccentric, although really able man, and his sharp sayings and curious adventures would fill a volume.

My acquaintance began with him at Jefferson City at the incipiency of the troubles in Missouri, but I saw a great deal of him at other periods.

During the summer of 1861, and while I was myself a member of the Missouri state guard, for it was before any part of Morgan's command had been organized, indeed before the greater number of the men who subsequently composed it had been enlisted, I had an experience with General Thompson which I have often remembered, if not with satisfaction, at least with amusement. General Hardee was then at Pocahontas, Ark., near the Missouri line, with seven thousand or eight thousand men, and was contemplating an advance on St. Louis.

Returning from Kentucky, I found it more difficult to reach General Price's command, which was in south-western Missouri, than I had supposed it would be, and was easily induced by Colonel, afterward Gen. John S. Marmaduke, and other friends whom I found there, to sojourn at Pocahontas and witness the projected movement on St. Louis. I was immediately put on service, instructed first to report to Colonel Hindman and perform whatever duty that energetic officer might assign me, and subsequently given a *quasi* position on General Hardee's staff. I was charged in this latter capacity to accompany most of the scouting expeditions and keep General Hardee informed regarding the conditions obtaining in our front. After some two or three weeks' experience in this service, and having become pretty thoroughly acquainted with the situation, I asked General Hardee to permit me to undertake a certain expedition. I wanted to burn the Meramee Bridge on the Iron Mountain Railroad, about twenty miles from St. Louis, and guarded only by a small garrison. The general was perfectly willing that I should undertake it, but there were obstacles in the way that even his authority could not remove. I requested that two companies of cavalry should be placed under my command for the purpose of the expedition. The colonels did not fancy this, and the captains of the companies very naturally objected to serving under a man younger than, and quite as inexperienced as, themselves, and who, also, held only militia rank while they had Confederate commissions. So while various excuses were made, the result was that every application I made for the troops was defeated. General Hardee at length suggested that I go to work and recruit two companies of my own; and, inasmuch as he desired to send despatches to General Thompson, who was encamped about eighty miles distant in south-eastern Missouri, he further suggested that I should bear the despatches and endeavour to induce two companies of the militia under General Thompson to enter the Confederate service. He kindly promised that if I succeeded he would see that the companies would be properly and amply equipped. I was greatly rejoiced and gladly started on the mission. In two days I was in General Jeff Thompson's camp and duly delivered the despatches. I employed the next day in a sort of inspection, preliminary to the execution of the principal object I had in view. General Thompson had under his command nearly three thousand men, and splendid fellows they were. They afterward belonged to that contingent which Missouri furnished the Confederate army, and which on so many bloody fields sustained the reputation of their state and added lustre to the Confederate glory. But at this time, while anxious to fight for the South, they entertained a strange repugnance to enlisting in the Confederate army. They wished to preserve their status as state militia.

After a day or two I formally declared my wishes to General Thompson and asked his permission to recruit such men as he might be willing to have go. He answered very cordially that he had no objection at all, and that I had his full leave to take all the men I could persuade to enlist. But he said that it would be not only a difficult task but a dangerous one.

"Now there was a fellow here the other day," he said, "from Arkansas, on the same mission. He also was ignorant of the prejudice the men feel against quitting the service of the state and entering that of the Confederacy, and he wasn't as prudent as you have been. He didn't first come and consult with me, but went to work his own way. The result was that he hadn't been talking more than half an hour when the whole camp rose on him and ran him into the swamp. He got away by the skin of his teeth, but they fired at him by platoons, and chased him God knows how far. I don't know what's become of him. I haven't heard from him for two days, but from the report of the rate at which he was then going I'm inclined to think that if he hasn't been killed he must be somewhere in Texas by this time.

"However, I wouldn't discourage you for the world. I like your patriotic spirit and want to help you if I can. Let me beg you, however, to be discreet. When you get ready to talk to these fellows have your horse where you can reach him handy.

"And, by the way, I'll tell you what I'll do. On some pretext or another I'll get the men down to one end of the camp, so that after you have made your proposition they'll have to go back some distance for their guns, and you can get a good start. Keep a close watch out for the camp guards, however, and steer clear of the pickets. Then, if your horse don't fail you, it's possible you may get away. When would you like to make your speech? Will to-morrow be soon enough?"

I told General Thompson that upon reflection it seemed to me that I had better let the matter drop. It was really wrong to deprive him and the State of Missouri of such soldiers. I thanked him for his hospitable reception.

"But, general," I said, "I hope you won't mention this conversation to any one while I'm in your camp. I'm a modest man and dislike to attract any particular or pointed attention to myself. Moreover, I've become satisfied that I couldn't make a success as a recruiting officer. So, instead of making a speech to your men to-morrow, I'll take leave as soon after an early breakfast as possible."

For some months before the evacuation of Memphis, General Thompson, although his bailiwick was yet in south-eastern Missouri, made his personal headquarters in that city, and shone with even more than the usual effulgence of the state guard brigadier, who, amenable to no particular authority, demeaned himself as if he were clad with it all. His brigade was encamped some twenty-five or thirty miles above Memphis, on the western side of the river, and while passing the night in the city he punctually visited his camp every day. He had organized what he called a "canoe fleet," and by some means had gotten possession of a small tug boat, which he termed his "flag-ship." He would steam up the river every morning, drill his troops and attend to the policing and care of his camp all day — for he was a careful and efficient officer — and return to Memphis in the evening in time to patronize the theatres and other places of amusement. Attended by a numerous and very "gay" staff, riding a spotted stallion which he called Sardanapalus, with a gigantic and truculent-looking Canadian Indian who answered to the name of Ajax, for his orderly, General Thompson and his train were always in evidence and the objects of ever-curious observation. Ajax habitually wore a gorgeous suit of black velvet, a headdress of eagle feathers, and a belt with imitation scalp locks dangling from it. It was a favourite trick of the general to have Ajax enter the theatre, when it happened to be especially crowded, and, with hurried mien, hand him a despatch. Then the general would spring to his feet and dash for the door, followed by his staff. On two or three such occasions the audience became greatly excited, thinking that General Thompson had received stirring news from "the front" and expecting to hear of immediate battle. After frequent repetition, however, people placed another construction upon this conduct, and actually came to the conclusion that it was a device by which general and staff could conveniently get out for "another drink"; and quite often irreverent voices would shout: "General, take one for me."

During this time some English military officers came to Memphis and expressed a desire to visit the encampments in that vicinity, and see something of the Confederate soldiery. General Thompson at once took charge of them. He hád much to say about the excellence of his own command; and asserted that, state troops though they were, and therefore comparatively inadequately equipped, his fellows were by far the best soldiers in point of instruction and discipline in the West. He invited the Englishmen to satisfy themselves of the accuracy of his statement by ocular proofs, and appointed a date, at their suggestion, when they should inspect his brigade. On the day before this inspection he sent staff officers to the camp with orders to have the men practise all night forming by companies, in front of their respective grounds.

He had informed the Englishmen, however, that he intended to surprise the camp, so that they might perceive the ease and rapidity with which his men could perform impromptu evolutions; and hinted that lack of time and of suitable ground in the vicinity was all that prevented him from putting up a brigade drill better than any they had ever witnessed in Hyde Park or on the Champ de Mars.

But he had one company, known as "The Dunklin County Dead Shots," which was commanded by an ex-sheriff, an excellent officer in some respects, but who could never acquire the least smattering of drill, and always persisted in substituting his own very peculiar phraseology for the proper words of command. General Thompson, fearing some solecism on the part of this officer, had strictly enjoined that he and his company should be sent, on the day of inspection, "seven miles" out into the swamp, and on no account to be allowed to return until the parade was over.

On the appointed morning the "flag-ship" steamed away from Memphis with the military tourists on board, and in due time arrived at the encampment. The party disembarked, and, approaching the sentries, were duly saluted, the guard was turned out, drums were beaten and all seemed well. As they walked leisurely through the lanes of tents the companies sprang to arms and formed like clockwork. Some of the men were pale and somewhat fatigued from having gone through with the same thing all night; but, of course, the strangers detected nothing suspicious. The programme worked like a charm. The visitors were profuse of compliments, which Jeff received modestly, but with an air of conscious desert. The inspection was nearly concluded, and success seemed certain, when suddenly a mighty and appalling voice arose which smote the Englishmen with amazement and General Thompson with consternation. The order to remove the ex-sheriff and his company had been forgotten or neglected. There he stood, as they passed around a clump of bushes, standing on a stump in all the majesty of command. He waved a hickory rammer around his head and shouted in tones that would have drowned a steam whistle: "Oh, yes! Oh, yes! Oh, yes! All you Dunklin Dead Shots fall into li-on on the end of this log, tell the gin'ral and them Britishers passes."

Some of my readers will doubtless remember that in the summer of 1861, before hostilities had fairly commenced in Tennessee, or war had taken definite shape in that region, a rendezvous for the Kentuckians who wished to join the Confederate army was established at a point not far distant from Nashville, on the Kentucky and Tennessee line. This place of refuge and enlistment was named "Camp Boone," and men were assembled and recruited there who subsequently became attached to the regiments which composed the Kentucky Infantry, better known as the "Orphan Brigade," so justly famous in Confederate history.

Colonel, afterward General, Loyd Tighlman, a former officer of the regular army, was in command of this camp, and from him the "boys" received their first and most salutary lessons in discipline.

Of course a great deal of interest and curiosity about this camp was immediately aroused in all the surrounding country. The number, the condition, and the purpose of the force collected there were matters of constant and excited speculation, and were vastly exaggerated in popular rumour. The general consensus of opinion was to the effect that it was an army several thousand strong of veteran soldiers — how they had become veterans no one stopped to consider — splendidly armed and equipped, which in due time would over-run Kentucky, capture Cincinnati and then make a "flank movement" on Washington City. Finally the Southern sympathizers of Hopkinsville, Ky., determined to positively ascertain what was there and what was going to be done; wishing to lend such assistance as they could if an effort to occupy Kentucky with Confederate troops was intended.

They held a meeting and selected one of their number to proceed to Camp Boone and obtain the information desired. The name of this gentleman was Scott, one of the best and most respected citizens of Hopkinsville and a very intelligent man, but, like every one else at that time, totally ignorant of all military matters. Mr. Scott reported to Colonel Tighlman, who received him quite cordially and showed him everything that was to be seen in the camp. There were about seven hundred men there, armed with one hundred and fifty flint-lock muskets. The largest body of soldiers Scott had ever previously seen was the Clarksville guards. On the 4th of July last past he had witnessed that gallant corps — sixty-five strong, not counting the captain — march down the streets of Clarksville in serried column, with two drummers and a bandy-legged fifer playing alternately "Stump-tailed Dolly" and the "Girl I Left Behind Me." So when he saw these seven hundred men together Scott thought that the beneficent heavens had been fairly raining Confederate soldiers; and the fact that nearly three fourths of them were unarmed was a little matter which he totally overlooked. He was greatly impressed and elated with this formidable array, for he was an ardent rebel. Colonel Tighlman, however, enjoined on him the necessity of the utmost caution, and reticence. "More wars have been lost, Mr. Scott," said Tighlman, "by loose and indiscreet talk than by all other causes combined, therefore while I'll let you see and hear everything, I must request you to disclose nothing that you learn here to any one."

Scott gave the required promise, and when he returned home would tell nothing. The committee which had sent him, begged with tears in their eyes, that the information he was despatched to obtain might be given them, but he was obdurate. "No, gentlemen," he said, "I can't tell you. Colonel Tighlman and I agreed that it wouldn't be safe to let any one else know what he and I know." So the committee was worse off than if it had never sent an agent to Camp Boone at all.

Finally some one suggested that a particular friend and former partner in business of Scott should be sent for. This gentleman was supposed to have great influence with him, and it was thought that if any one could extract the much-wanted story John J. Fisher was the man to do it. A telegram was rushed to Fisher at Louisville and he came post haste to Hopkinsville. When informed of what he was expected to do, he became as eager as any of the others, and tackled Scott without delay; but Scott, although with obvious reluctance and sorrow, refused also to confide in him. At length, however, apparently moved by Fisher's pleading entreaties, Scott said that if Fisher would meet him that afternoon at six o'clock at a certain point on the Cadiz road, about a mile from town, he would tell him "something." Fisher was at the appointed spot an hour ahead of time, and, just at six o'clock, Scott arrived. He took Fisher off into the woods, at least one hundred yards from the road, and backed him up behind a big tree. Then he said, with great solemnity:

"John J. Fisher! I've known you for more than forty years, and I'd tell you things that I wouldn't tell any other livin' man: but there are some things I can't even tell you. But I'll say this much to you: If old Abe Lincoln had seen what I saw down at Camp Boone he'd 'a' thought he had a mighty heavy contract on his hands."

The attitude which the soldiers of Morgan's command and those of some of the Kentucky Federal cavalry regiments held toward each other during the greater part of the Civil War, was of a kind which would have been termed by martinets "highly" irregular and prejudicial, if not to efficiency, at least to all military etiquette. Indeed, every one cognizant of these relations was compelled to admit that they were unusual and peculiar, and could have obtained in the volunteer service only.

This was especially the case with regard to the Second Kentucky Cavalry, C. S. A., of which regiment Morgan was the first colonel, and the First Kentucky Cavalry, U. S. A., which Col. Frank Wolford so long and gallantly commanded. The "differences" between the men of these two very active bodies of "light horse," like those of Gabriel and Lucifer in Byron's "Vision of Judgment," were "purely political," and did not seem to affect their personal and "social" relations in the least.

Morgan's regiment was recruited principally from the Bluegrass region and central Kentucky. Wolford's principally from south-western Kentucky; and each was composed of material very similar in character — reckless, dare-devil youngsters, always eager for adventure and excitement, who if they had not "charity for all," certainly bore little "malice to none." These two regiments made each other's acquaintance at a very early period of the war — an acquaintance which continued with scarcely any intermission until the close of the Ohio raid. They fought frequently, for as they were engaged in the same sort of service, reconnoitring and scouting in front of their respective armies, they often came in collision. Their combats were sharp and closely contested, but the prisoners taken on either side were always treated with the utmost kindness and consideration, until a strange sort of friendship grew up between them.

Between Morgan and Wolford especially there was a warm and mutual regard. In our numerous encounters with him "Old Frank" was more than once wounded, as much to our regret perhaps as his own. When Morgan was captured in Ohio, Wolford, who had been foremost, indefatigable in his pursuit, made every effort to have him paroled and exchanged, and on more than one occasion was involved in quarrels with the angry crowds which threatened Morgan on his way to prison.

One of the majors of Wolford's regiment was W. A. Coffee. In appearance he was a typical Kentuckian of the older generation, considerably over six feet in height and of massive, well-proportioned figure. His broad, good-humoured face was constantly irradiated with smiles, which on the slightest provocation developed into explosive and contagious laughter. He was a brave, generous, and thoroughly true man.

On May 5, 1862, Morgan's command, then about three hundred strong, was attacked by a brigade of Federal cavalry under General Dumont, at Lebanon, Tenn., and badly cut up. In this engagement Wolford was seriously wounded. Morgan lost, besides killed and wounded, more than one hundred prisoners, but rallying the remnant of his command, set out in a day or two for Kentucky, with the hope of rescuing the men who had been captured. He intercepted and seized a north-bound train on the Louisville & Nashville Railroad near Cave City, Ky., expecting to find his men on it. In this, he was disappointed, but found it laden with a number of Federal officers and soldiers of different regiments.

None of these, save one, offered resistance, but he ensconced near the door of one of the coaches, delivered a warm fire on the assailants until his two revolvers were exhausted. Then, as the bullets were splintering the wood-work and smashing the glass about his head, the door was thrown open and out stepped Major Coffee on the platform. With a shout of laughter he called out:

"Stop firing, boys! I'm out of ammunition and have concluded to quit."

The prisoners, including Coffee, were paroled, but with the understanding that if not exchanged within a certain period they would report to Morgan within the Confederate lines.

The Federal authorities, however, refused to recognize any such obligation, and directed all those so paroled to immediately report for duty to their respective commands. All, with the exception of Coffee, did so. He declared that, while his services, and his life, if necessary, were due the government under whose flag he had enlisted, his word was his own and he would not break it. He accordingly made his way through the lines and reported to Morgan at Knoxville as prisoner. Such conduct was of course, very highly appreciated and applauded by us, and made Coffee as popular with the other Southern soldiers there as with Morgan's men. He was permitted absolute freedom of movement, and Colonel Morgan had him as his guest at the hotel, where he, Morgan, was quartered during our sojourn at Knoxville. The gallant major conducted himself much as if he had forgotten that he was an enemy and had become one of us.

After a week or ten days, however, Gen. Kirby Smith, who was then in command of that department, with his headquarters at Knoxville, sent for Colonel Morgan to talk with him about Coffee. The general said that he was much pleased with the manner in which Coffee had behaved, and desired to show him every courtesy and indulgence. But he did not think that the perfect liberty allowed him and the free and easy way in which matters, however confidential, were discussed in his presence, exactly accorded with military usage and the treatment a prisoner should receive even when on parole. It was his intention, therefore, he said, to send the major to Richmond to be disposed of by the authorities there. Morgan remonstrated, but without avail. General Smith promised kind treatment on the way to Richmond, and until Coffee was out of his hands, and also that he would exert himself to procure favour for him afterward.

Morgan returned from the interview in a state of great indignation. He summoned me at once to confer about a plan he was already formulating for Coffee's benefit. He declared that it was shameful that a man who had behaved so honourably should be sent to prison, and proposed to despatch him "on a good horse," and with a reliable escort to Kentucky.

"Coffee is my prisoner," he said, "and I have a right to dispose of him as I think best."

I ventured a mild dissent from this view of the case, and opposed his plan for other reasons. I insisted that every one at Richmond would be just as favourably impressed by Coffee's conduct as the people of Knoxville had been, and that he would not be sent to prison, but that he would certainly be exchanged. I pointed out that what he proposed to do would be a grave breach of discipline and might lead to his dismissal from the service; but it was difficult to persuade him that what he wished to do in the matter could be so characterized. Finally I suggested that we should consult Coffee himself and learn what he thought of it.

We accordingly laid the matter before him. He listened attentively and then remarked emphatically:

"Colonel Morgan, if I consent to what you propose, it may result in your being court-martialed, and I'll never let a friend get into trouble on my account if I can prevent it. Moreover, I don't think I'll be sent to Libby Prison. I believe I will be exchanged, and I'd like to go to Richmond and see the sights there."

This closed the debate and Coffee was sent to Richmond. General Smith wrote strongly to the authorities in his behalf, and Morgan wrote his friends to render all possible help. He remained in Richmond for several days, receiving every attention during that time, and was then sent North, and on special exchange.

Some months after the close of the war I was in New York, and one evening, at a hotel much frequented by Southerners and Kentuckians, I heard a howl of recognition, and, turning to see who it was, fell into the arms of Coffee. After some general conversation I inquired about his visit to Richmond.

"It was the greatest event of my life," he said, "I can never forget the kindness shown me, and the only thing to mar my pleasure was that I couldn't conscientiously be a rebel."

Modern English and American literature has furnished abundant example of that sort of humour which quaint and exaggerated language, independent of the idea it may express, usually furnishes; and the story is rendered amusing either by the peculiar dialect in which it is related or by the big words and pompous phrases which the narrator is made to employ, most often entirely out of place, but all the more ludicrous and delightful for that reason. From Shakespeare's time to that of Artemus Ward and Petroleum V. Nasby a host of readers have been entertained by these sapient solecisms, and we find them refreshing, whether uttered by Dogberry, Sarah Gamp, Mrs. Partington, or more recent and obscure enunciators of such pleasant nonsense.

Very many men entirely unknown to fame, either in fact or fiction, have excelled in this regard; every reader of these lines can doubtless recall some such character. I have known quite a number of them, but one especially, with whom I became acquainted in the army, could have held his own, I believe, in grandiloquent and platitudinous speech with the most accomplished masters of the art. It was not because he used such remarkably big words or used them always inappropriately. Indeed, his language generally aptly conveyed his meaning; but he would announce the baldest propositions and communicate the most ordinary information in an ornate, oracular way and in diction so impressive that his comrades around the camp fires often heard him with a kind of awe. He had, too, an apparently polite but disagreeably frank manner of resenting any difference of opinion that would overawe all but the most audacious and veteran disputants. He had practised law for some years, and thereby enlarged both his vocabulary and his assurance.

While only an enlisted man, his having been detailed as forage master of his regiment caused him to be dubbed "captain," and he was called "for short" "Captain Sam."

I listened on one occasion with much edification to an exceedingly able debate which he conducted with an orator (a good deal of his own style) in respect to the most politic method which the Southern states might have adopted in their withdrawal from the Union.

The other party to the discussion was a planter who lived in the neighbourhood of the camp, and had come to it to visit certain acquaintances. None of the captain's comrades would have ventured to tackle him, but the stranger, who was an oracle and a "power" in his community, rushed in where soldiers "feared to tread." As well as I can now remember, this gentleman, with fluent and amazing eloquence and a logic which was entirely convincing to himself, contended that the Southern states should not have seceded after the fashion which they followed in that regard, but should have adopted the plan of "coöperation." Captain Sam, on the contrary, insisted that the method adopted, of each state separately seceding with a magnanimous disregard of concerted action and consequences, was not only in consonance with political ethics, but was right as a matter of expediency.

The subject was treated in a wonderful and exhaustive style on both sides. In the long run, however, the stranger's enthusiasm and vehement delivery were completely borne down by the captain's steady, undisturbed and unruffled utterance. Captain Sam never permitted himself to become excited or hurried. His calm, concentrated, conclusive talk always bored into the matter in controversy like an augur. He went at the most difficult topic like an anaconda swallowing a goat, never losing confidence or slackening effort because either of hide or horn. Finally his opponent, losing temper, shouted a savage remonstrance.

"By blank, captain," he said, "you don't give me any chance at all to present my side of the question. You talk all the time yourself. You won't let another man slip in a word edgewise. If you just let me have the floor for five minutes I'll absolutely demolish every position you've taken. I'll convince even you, sir, that your arguments are conceived in ignorance and absurdity, and are dangerous and debauching to the best interests of the Confederacy. Now give me a chance."

"I'll do it," responded the captain in his serenest tones and with a pitying smile. "I'll give you the floor. Go on, sir: go on and say your d — dest. I'll listen to you in profound silence and with supreme contempt."

For some reason this remark closed the discussion.

I have said that Captain Sam was forage master of the regiment to which he belonged, and in his opinion this was an office not only of unusual importance but considerable dignity; and when he was riding at the head of his train of wagons in search of fodder, no commander-in-chief ever "felt his oats" more sensibly. Once, when traversing a very muddy country road, he encountered a similar train of some Mississippi regiment, moving in an opposite direction. On such a road no one liked to yield the right of way, for it might involve the ditching of the wagons. Captain Sam, impressed with the idea, of course, that everybody should give way to him, without saying a word, waved his hand in quite an autocratic manner to the opposing forage master as a signal that he should clear the track. The Captain wore a very tall and slick silk hat, which was not military in appearance, but, as he thought, suggested authority, and he was sufficiently full of good liquor to cause his naturally protuberant eyeballs to bulge more than ordinarily. The other forage master was, like many Mississippians, choleric and impatient of dictation, and he got mad.

"You blamed old red-faced, pop-eyed, high-hatted idiot!" he shouted: "What do you mean by shaking your fist at me?"

"I wish you," said the captain with perfect composure, "to evacuate the highway."

"The — you do; who are you anyways?"

"This is Colonel Blank's train," said the captain.

"Well, are you Colonel Blank?"

"No," responded Captain Sam. "I'm not exactly or personally Colonel Blank. But for the purposes of this case, and to make you give me the track, I'm him constructively and *quod hoc*. I'm his *alter ego* and principal auxiliary."

The Mississippian's anger subsided, such diction was too much for him; he sidetracked his train and the captain's moved majestically on.

But, despite his remarkable gift of speech, he finally came to grief because his conduct was not equally as exceptional. Like a multitude of other great men, he succumbed to the temptations of graft. At the beginning of the war the supply of quinine in the South was scanty, and as it was esteemed one of the most necessary medicines for the diseases most prevalent in that region strenuous efforts were made to obtain and preserve it. While Gen. Albert Sidney Johnston's army was at Bowling Green the surgeon of Captain Sam's regiment had providently procured a considerable quantity of this much-valued remedy, packed in small china jars, and had jealously hoarded it for future use. He had little occasion to employ it for some time, the health of the regiment remaining unusually good; but when he finally had need for it he found, to his consternation, that much the greater part of it had disappeared.

An investigation was immediately instituted, and it was ascertained that Captain Sam, "not having the fear of God before his eyes, but moved and instigated thereto by the devil" in the shape of a country doctor, had disposed of the quinine for his own personal gain. The jars containing the drug had been deposited in one of the wagons under the captain's charge and he had sold most of it to a practising physician in a small village in Tennessee. Jim Ball, the driver of the wagon, and another man had witnessed the transaction. Without the captain's being aware of it, they had seen him in close consultation with the doctor; had witnessed them both go to the wagon in which the quinine was stored and the captain take thence a number of the jars; had seen the doctor place money in the captain's hands, put the jars in a basket and go off with them. Ball was a taciturn man, and had not thought it necessary previously to report the matter, but when inquiry about it was made he and his comrade told all that they had seen.

The colonel was extremely indignant, and at once ordered Captain Sam to be brought before a regimental court-martial, and Ball and the other man testified to the facts as above narrated. There seemed to be no defence or hope of acquittal, but the captain was dead game and didn't quit worth a cent.

He demanded permission to cross-examine Ball, which was, of course, allowed.

"Mr. Ball," he commenced, "you've testified in this case pretty spontaneously and obnoxious to me; now I wish to ascertain if you have any real knowledge of the subject about which you've discoursed so liberally. Do you know what quinine exactly is?"

"I never said I did," answered Ball, "but —— "

"Hold on now. Don't get off the path. Do you know whether quinine is the residuum of the calcined bark of the chincony tree or whether it's made from the ashes of mullein stalks? Now do you?"

"No," said Ball, "I don't know nothin' about that, but I seen you —— "

"Stop, Mr. Ball. Please return categorical and applicable answers to my interrogatories. I will ask you again if you are acquainted with quinine? Do you understand its constituent elements? Do you know its hygenic and symptomatic effects upon the human system? Can you recognize quinine when you see it? Would you know it if you should meet it on the pike? Could you distinguish it by mere inspection from an equal amount of flour or a corresponding proportion of magnesia? Could you now?"

"Maybe I couldn't, and I don't care a d — n if I can't," blurted out Ball, who had begun to lose his temper and his awe of the court, "but I seen you take them jars, which you said had quinine in 'em, out of the wagon and hand 'em to that doctor, and I seen him pay you and walk off with 'em."

The captain strove hard, but vainly, to interrupt this outburst, and when Ball ceased he addressed himself to the court with an air of absolute confidence.

"Gentlemen, you cannot help perceiving how utterly obtuse and inconsequential is this testimony. Manifestly this witness hasn't the remotest conception of what he is talking about. He don't know quinine from one of the ten commandments. Surely you wouldn't convict a dog that bays the moon on such evidence, far less a Confederate soldier and a forage master."

The hard-hearted court did convict him, however, and inflicted what he characterized as a "cruel, unusual, unconstitutional, and unparalleled punishment."

One of the most important matters an officer commanding troops in the field has to consider is how to prevent their too free and frequent use of liquor. It is a more difficult task with cavalry than with infantry, because it is impossible to enforce strict discipline with the former when engaged in active service, and not nearly so easy to keep them closely in camp.

It should not be inferred from this statement that the soldiers of the Civil War — the volunteers — were habitually intemperate and addicted to the inordinate use of strong drink whenever they could procure it. It was not the liquor that they liked so much, as the frolic. They were nearly all of them quite young, had led sober lives before they enlisted in the army, and with few exceptions, did so after their term of service was over.

Nor were they accustomed to indulge such tastes when seriously employed. When a campaign was in active conduct, or battle was imminent, they seemed to care little or at least much less, for liquor. Even the cavalry man when scouting, was lively and skirmishes frequent, partially forgot his thirst. But when matters were monotonous, when the men were subjected to the tedium and inaction of the camp, they were very apt to seek the excitement, otherwise lacking, in the stimulating influence of the canteen. In common, perhaps, with all other cavalry officers, I had a rather large experience in this respect, and, while often greatly annoyed by it, was sometimes compelled to admire the ingenuity displayed in the practice. The expedients resorted to to procure whiskey and to smuggle it into camp were numerous and difficult of detection.

My first positive dealings with the "liquor question" came near getting me into serious trouble, not withstanding the rectitude of my purpose. It was when Morgan's squadron was encamped at Bowling Green, Ky., in November, 1861. For some weeks previous we had been scouting north of the Green River, and the service was so constant and exciting that, as I have before intimated, the "boys" had evinced little desire for intoxicants. But when we lay in camp near Bowling Green for ten days or two weeks, with little employment except drill and camp police duty, the craving was strongly developed and flagrant cases were reported. It was some time before I could discover where the men were able to get liquor so readily and in such abundance, as they were certainly obtaining it. I at length ascertained that they got it from a store at a railroad station about a mile from the camp.

I remonstrated with the proprietor and requested him not to sell liquor to soldiers, at least to the men of Morgan's squadron. He promised me that he would not do so in the future. His business in this line, however, was too extensive and profitable to be lightly relinquished and made him unscrupulous about keeping such pledges. Or it may be that, dealing as he was with a multitude of soldiers — for crowds of customers came from many other camps — he could not well distinguish Morgan's men from the others. At any rate it was not long before matters were as bad as ever, and I had unmistakable evidence that the liquor came from the same source.

It occurred to me, then, that the evil could be cured only by drastic and heroic remedies, and I immediately, unfortunately, without giving thought to the probable consequences, proceeded to apply them. I determined to seize all the liquor in the store and keep it under guard as long as we remained in that vicinity, and then return it to the owner. Some one suggested that such a move on the part of an officer so subordinate in authority might be regarded more as a breach of discipline than as the just exercise of police power, so I concluded to conceal, as far as possible, the identity of all concerned in the affair. A very excellent man and good soldier named John Sisson was then forage master of the squadron. He was afterward a captain in the Ninth Tennessee Cavalry. I instructed him to select a detail of five or six men, who, like himself, never drank, and who, I believed, would not be recognized by the proprietor of the store, and taking two wagons, go to the store and bring away all of the liquor which might be there. An order was written out for Sisson, representing that he was a provost marshal and empowered to do everything in that vicinity which might be conducive to order, discipline, and good conduct. He arrayed himself in resplendent garb, principally consisting of a red sash and two enormous plumes, and with four pistols and two sabres buckled around his waist, presented himself late one afternoon at the store. Dismayed by his appearance and the documents which he produced, the owner capitulated at once, and Sisson brought off a load of liquors of various kinds in each wagon, which was stored in two large tents.

But then real trouble began. It was impossible, of course, to conceal from the men the fact that all this liquor was in camp, and equally so to prevent them, in some way, getting at it. The guard about the tents where it was stored was doubled and trebled but without avail; sometimes the guard exhibited suspicious symptoms of having tampered with the stuff they were posted to protect.

One day a man named Roberts, who was a brave and, when sober, good soldier, but a devil incarnate when drunk, was brought to the guard tent in a state of howling intoxication. As he invariably attacked every one who came near him when in that condition, he was bound hand and foot, and even then it was dangerous to approach him.

Shortly after his arrest and incarceration, the orderly sergeant of one of the companies reported to me that a member of his company had refused to serve on picket duty although it was his regular turn to be detailed. I knew the man well, and knew him to be worthless as a soldier, although not a bad fellow otherwise. The sergeant suspected that his refusal was because of the fact that the videttes, at the point to which he was to have been sent, had been fired upon the night before. I had him brought to me, and he made to me the same positive declination to go on duty which had previously been made to the sergeant.

"Very well, then," I said. "You will go to the guard tent."

He signified a decided preference for that assignment to standing picket, and walked off with a very satisfied air. I felt quite sure that had he known who was to be his companion in confinement he would not have so cheerfully accepted his punishment. The guard tent was a large, commodious "Sibley," and "Ben," as the last mentioned offender was named and generally addressed, was inducted into it without ceremony, and the opening tightly strapped. A good many men gathered about the tent, for all felt sure that Roberts would instantly attack any one who entered it, and that, bound as he was, would be formidable. They were not disappointed. In a few seconds a sound of struggling could be heard within the tent and the sides of it bulged as if some one was running rapidly about in there; soon afterward agonizing cries for help were heard from Ben. I was inclined at first to give no heed to them, but they became so vociferous being accompanied by asseverations that Roberts was devouring him, "biting his leg off," that I thought it best to investigate. When several of us entered we found Ben prostrate and Roberts fastened upon him like a bulldog, with his teeth firmly gripping the fleshy part of his thigh. Ben was a fat, clumsy creature, and Roberts had rolled after him until in the limited space in which the encounter took place, Ben had lost his footing and the other immediately nipped him. It was with some difficulty that we pulled Roberts off and released his victim. So soon as I thought Ben had somewhat recovered from this exciting adventure, I sent for him and asked if he had changed his mind and would consent to do picket duty. He answered firmly that he was still of the same mind and wouldn't stand picket.

"Very well then," I said. "You must go back to the guard tent."

"My God, adjutant!" he howled, perfectly aghast. "You are not going to put me in the tent again with that mad dog, that cannibal?"

I assured him that I would certainly do so unless he performed his fair share of duty. He pondered the matter for awhile and then ruefully consented to go with the detail. A few minutes afterward I saw him ride away with the others, having a large wet rag bound around his leg and sitting sideways on his saddle.

After several other episodes of somewhat like nature, manifestly due to the vicinity of the whiskey, I greatly regretted my action in bringing it to the camp, but I soon had cause for serious apprehension. The owner of the liquor, notwithstanding our strategic efforts to deceive him, strongly suspected who were the parties who had bereft him of his goods, and when he reported his loss at headquarters also declared his suspicions. General Johnston was extremely indignant. He had no idea, of course, why the liquor had been seized, and even had he been properly informed would doubtless have disapproved of so summary a procedure. But believing, as he had reason to do, that it was sheer, plain robbery, he determined to make a terrible example of the guilty ones.

One night about nine o'clock, captain, afterward Col. R. C. Morgan then on Breckinridge's staff came in haste to our camp with an unpleasant piece of news: General Johnson had instructed General Breckinridge to investigate the matter and arrest the author of the "unparalleled outrage," if discovered. Breckinridge had ordered Capt. Keene Richards, another of his staff, to proceed to our camp and make a thorough search. Richards had given Morgan a quiet tip to the effect that he would not start immediately on the mission, but Morgan did immediately set out on his errand.

Upon receipt of this information no time was lost, and we proceeded to get rid of the liquor much more expeditiously and with less ceremony than we had procured it. Sisson hitched up his wagons and loaded them in exceedingly short order and drove out into a thick woods about half a mile from camp, where he remained until after midnight. He then drove down to the store and quietly discharged his cargo in front of it, where it was found next morning by the proprietor. Some twenty minutes after Sisson's departure, Captain Richards rode up and gravely informed Captain Morgan and myself of the charges against us, and stated that he must thoroughly search our premises. We felt very much hurt, of course, at such an accusation, but gave all the aid we could in his work. He carefully looked through the commissary tents and every other, and in every place where anything might be hidden. Some of the men, in their zeal to show that he had been misinformed, turned out their pockets, and none of them had either bottle or barrel concealed about their persons.

The matter was dropped when Captain Richards made his report, but it was a lesson to me not to attempt measures of that sort again. At any rate, while in such close proximity to army headquarters.

CHAPTER V

IT WOULD be difficult to induce the people of the South to admit that any other man — even another of their own most revered heroes — is worthy to be ranked on the same level with General Lee. But if any of the great men of the Confederacy shall, in the estimation of his countrymen or by the verdict of history, be accorded that extraordinary eminence, it will be, I believe, Albert Sidney Johnston. Not that the fame of the one is commensurate with that of the other. Men of action must be judged chiefly by their records, and no record of the Civil War, on either side, can bear comparison with that of General Lee.

General Johnston's Confederate career was brief, closed by a premature but glorious death before opportunity was afforded him to prove by actual performance all of what he might be capable, and to earn the recognition which can be justly given only to accomplished work.

General Lee's record was not only well-nigh unexampled as a master of offenso-defensive warfare and remarkable in all respects, but it was complete. He served with active, incessant effort from the inception to the close of the struggle. His name was identified with its every phase and vicissitude. His influence and leadership were felt and acknowledged wherever the Confederate banner waved and Confederate soldiers fought. He became the idol of the Southern armies and the Southern people. In the latter days of the war the Confederate soldiers everywhere looked to him for inspiration. Whether battling and starving in Tennessee and Georgia, in Lousiana, or Arkansas; whether raiding in Kentucky or holding the shattered forts of the Coast and the Gulf against the storm of shell poured upon them from the monitors, they spoke his name as a talisman when hope was failing and disaster seemed irremediable, and believed that he would turn the tide of adverse fortune and save the cause for which we strove. This invincible faith in him was as strong among troops who never saw or directly served under him, as with that band of heroes whom he immediately commanded, and who had been taught it by the many victories they had won under his eye.

General Johnston was not accorded this universal sympathy, confidence, and admiration. Indeed it was the lot of no man to receive such endorsement at the date when he met death on the field of Shiloh. On the contrary, he had been the recipient in larger measure, than any other Confederate general, perhaps, of that criticism which, in the earlier days of the war, spared no commander who did not accomplish extraordinary results with altogether inadequate means — criticism from which even General Lee was not entirely exempt in his earlier command — and his retreat from Kentucky, although perfectly justified by the strategic situation and necessitated by military circumstances utterly beyond his control, subjected him to censure as bitter as it was unjust. One of the most unmistakable evidences of his capacity was the fact that he succeeded in so brief a time and under arduous difficulties, in completely reversing public opinion and recovering the enthusiastic support of those previously estranged; and this was not merely a compassionate sentiment evoked by his heroic death, but a real conviction that he was equal to the situation, which became general so soon as he concentrated at Corinth and advanced to attack Grant at Pittsburg Landing.

Nor is it his least claim to magnanimity and moral grandeur that he neither resented criticism which he knew to be undeserved, nor was deterred by it from deliberate adherence to what he believed the wisest policy.

It is generally conceded that the one campaign which General Johnston conducted during the Civil War, and the one battle that he fought, should rank him very high as a commander. In the estimation of many competent military critics, neither was excelled in the operations of the entire war upon either side. He was forced to abandon the line he at first attempted to hold in Kentucky because of the immense numerical superiority and better equipment of the Federal forces marshalled to assault it; but he acted with unhesitating promptness, instantly realizing the nature and full scope of the situation, and as instantly proceeding to meet it, quitting Bowling Green without a moment's delay, evacuating Nashville, marching across and out of Tennessee, rousing meanwhile a roar of popular indignation by his apparent sacrifice of all he was expected to defend. By this rapidity of movement, however, he effected a concentration of all forces at his command, of every available man, at the point which it was most important to protect, in the vicinity where he might hope to deliver battle with best hope of success, and at a time when successful battle would recover all he had relinquished — certainly all this proves him to have possessed strategic ability of the highest order. Nor can it be denied that the disposition of his troops preceding his attack at Shiloh and the successful progress of the attack until he was killed, entitled him to be considered an unusually skilful tactician. Most assuredly his conduct both of the campaign and the battle conclusively demonstrated that he had in rare measure that most essential quality of the great captain — prompt, unflinching decision.

In no campaign in the West during the war was the initiative taken upon the Confederate side anything like so boldly and pressed so vigorously and with such promise of a success that would have given decisive results. It is almost impossible to doubt that had General Johnston survived, the Confederate victory of the first day at Shiloh would have been complete. In that event we may claim that the recovery of Tennessee and Kentucky and the Confederate occupation of all that territory would have certainly followed.

A general who could plan and successfully execute one such campaign might surely be expected, with opportunity, to accomplish other things of like nature; and we are justified, therefore, in believing that had General Johnston lived to the close of the war his Confederate record would have been inferior to none.

Moreover, it should be remembered that while Shiloh was a drawn battle, the campaign, beginning with the retreat from Bowling Green, must be regarded as a successful one; although not nearly so much so, of course, as it would have been after complete victory at Shiloh. The plan of Federal invasion — of which the capture of Forts Donelson and Henry were the initial steps, and the concentration of all the troops under

Grant, soon to be joined by those under Buell, at Pittsburg Landing was the most important preparatory measure — was thoroughly disconcerted, indeed thwarted, by Johnston's rapid concentration at Corinth and subsequent attack at Shiloh. This plan contemplated the occupation of Corinth during the month of April, 1862, as early in the month as practicable, and, if possible, before any Confederate force had reached there. If any such force had gotten there it was to be beaten by the combined armies of Grant and Buell.

Corinth was located at the intersection of the Memphis and Charleston and Mobile and Ohio Railroads, and these two railroads controlled almost the entire transportation of the South, from the Mississippi River to the Atlantic coast, and from the Tennessee River to the Gulf. Had the plan been carried out as originally projected, and as soon, the fall of the Confederacy would have occurred perhaps within a few months thereafter. If the Federal commanders had gotten to Corinth before the Confederates, preventing Johnston from effecting a junction of the troops under his immediate command with those under Beauregard and Polk, or if he had been attacked immediately after such junction by the overwhelmingly superior forces of Grant and Buell combined, the result in either event would have been almost certainly fatal to his army and to the Confederacy. His early divination of the intentions of his antagonists, quick decision, and prompt action parried the danger. By concentrating so speedily that he was able to fight Grant singly and defeat him, and striking so soon as he got within reach of his enemy, he so crippled the army of invasion as to delay its march until ampler preparation to meet it could be made, one of the two important railway lines was prevented from falling into its hands, and the immediate and extensive occupation of Southern territory, which had seemed imminent, was no longer threatened.

No one, however, can form a just estimate of General Johnston as a soldier without some knowledge of his service in the old army, nor understand how great a man he was, except from the testimony of those who knew him in his private life.

Gen. Albert Sidney Johnston was born in Mason County, Ky., February 2d, 1803. He was appointed to West Point in

1822, and was graduated in 1826. His room mate and most intimate friend at the academy was Gen. Leonidas Polk, and the devoted friendship which existed until his death between himself and Jefferson Davis began there.

In July, 1826, immediately after his graduation, he was commissioned brevet second lieutenant in the Second Infantry, and was assigned to duty in the field. It may be mentioned as indicative of his soldierly disposition and inclination to really earnest professional work, that he declined an offer soon afterward made him to serve on the staff of General Scott, then commander-in-chief of the army. The offer was a flattering one, as such positions, when given very young officers, were confined to those of excellent repute and promise, and afforded opportunity for rapid promotion, as well as social advantages generally much desired. His service was active and constant. He was instrumental in bringing to conclusion the trouble with the Winnebagoes in 1827, and shortly afterward he took part in the Black Hawk War, in which the band of that celebrated warrior, the war chief of the fierce tribe of Sacs, was exterminated. General Johnston served during this campaign as assistant adjutant-general to the commander, General Atkinson.

In April, 1834, he resigned his commission in the army. He was induced to do this by the failing health of his wife, to whom he was tenderly attached and to whose care he wished to devote his entire time and strength. His solicitude, however, was unavailing, and she died in the following year.

He was a poor man; he had, of course, saved little out of his meagre pay as a lieutenant, and he had given every cent of his share of the property inherited from his father to the support of his sisters. It was necessary that he should immediately go to work to maintain the two little children whom his deceased wife had left him. It seems that he hesitated for a time between Kentucky and Louisiana when looking for a location and a point where he could hope to secure profitable occupation, but finally determined to buy a plantation in Texas. He was doubtless attracted there by his sympathy with the struggle the gallant settlers were making against the tyranny of Mexico, whose yoke they had just thrown off. The battle of San Jacinto, fought a few months after Texas had declared her independence, had conclusively demonstrated the superiority in the field of the imperfectly organized and undisciplined Americans to even the best of the Mexican regular troops commanded by the ablest of their generals. But the Mexican government would listen to no proposition for an honourable and satisfactory peace, and, while making no further actual demonstration, still maintained a hostile and threatening attitude. This, of course, necessitated a constant state of preparation for defence upon the part of the Texans, and the republic was compelled to keep an army — a small, but very gallant one — in the field.

General Johnston arrived in Texas shortly after the battle of San Jacinto was fought, and when another and early Mexican invasion was expected. He naturally offered his military services to the republic, and as his reputation as an officer had preceded him and he also bore the highest testimonials from his former comrades and commanders, they were gladly accepted. He was appointed adjutant-general of the Texan army by General Rusk, who was commanding it during the temporary absence of Gen. Sam Houston, and on the same day, the 5th of August, 1836, he was appointed colonel in the regular army and adjutant-general of the republic. His success in organizing and disciplining the troops received the highest commendations upon all sides; but the government soon felt the need of his services at the capital, and he was summoned thither by an order from the Hon. John A. Wharton, secretary of war, of date September 17, 1836. He remained in the performance of this duty, until he was appointed senior brigadier-general of the army, and virtually in command of it, and he assumed command on the 31st of January, 1837.

The acceptance of this position involved him in serious trouble and came near costing him his life. Besides Gen. Sam Houston, there was another distinguished man of that name then playing a conspicuous part in Texas, *viz.*, Gen. Felix Houston. Shortly after the battle of San Jacinto, General Rusk, who was commanding the army during the absence of Gen. Sam Houston, had in turn turned over the command to Felix Houston, a very gallant but extremely ambitious man, and of an arbitrary disposition. Having already distinguished himself as a general officer, and having been recommended by Rusk for the position, he had reason to expect the promotion which was given General Johnston. Instead, however, he was given the subordinate rank of junior brigadier. Gen. Felix Houston was a native of Kentucky, as was General Johnston, but, unlike the latter, was a man of unreasonable and overbearing temper. He was a man of prepossessing appearance and demeanour; tall, finely formed, quite handsome, and with a manner amiable and attractive to all save those who opposed his purposes or aspirations. He was also a fluent and impressive speaker. He had served longer with the Texan army than had General Johnston, was much better known to the troops, and, at that time, far more popular with them. He fiercely resented the seniority of rank accorded General Johnston, and immediately made it a personal matter. His action in this regard was typical of the times, and the challenge he sent General Johnston was illustrative of the follies — as we would now deem them — which were frequent with the high-mettled and unrestrained spirits of a region just thrown open to settlement and civilization. He expressed the highest esteem for the character and repute of the man with whom he sought mortal conflict; no champion of ancient chivalry could have couched his defiance in more courteous language, but claimed that, under the attendant circumstances, General Johnston's appointment over him was a personal reflection upon him and an insult he could not brook, and he therefore demanded satisfaction.

At a later date and under other conditions, it would have perhaps been General Johnston's inclination and duty to decline the challenge. But he knew that if he did so he would forfeit the confidence of the army and absolutely lose all control over it. The hot-blooded, adventurous and fearless young fellows who filled its ranks — the "*tumultuario*," as Santa Anna termed them, of the Mississippi Valley — esteemed and valued personal prowess and a perfect readiness to meet danger in any form above every other quality, and would never have forgiven or obeyed an officer who refused such an offer of combat. He, therefore, promptly accepted the challenge and indicated an early hour of the next day for the meeting. His son, Col. William Preston Johnston, in his very interesting book, the "Life of Gen. Albert Sidney Johnston," gives a circumstantial and graphic account of this affair, which I shall abbreviate.

General Houston was an almost unequalled shot with the pistol. General Johnston, on the contrary, while skilful in the use of other weapons, especially the rifle, had very little practice with the pistol. Nevertheless, he selected pistols as the weapons with which the duel should be fought, although his friends urged him to choose another with which he might have a better chance. He seemed determined to prove — if he must fight — that no man could be more indifferent to danger. The duel was fought in the presence of a good many spectators, to which neither party objected. Colonel Johnston says: "The contest, though deadly in intention, was chiefly one for the moral control of these very men; and their presence, therefore, was equally desired by the antagonists."

Although the very reverse of sensational or theatrical in his nature or manner, General Johnston did a thing on this occasion which was unusual in such affairs, and which seemed to savour of a seeking after dramatic effect. It was the only occasion of his life, perhaps, in which he departed from perfect simplicity; but it was evidently done with a view of exhibiting his willingness to incur any personal hazard and to emphasize the evidence of it he was compelled to give.

"General Houston, according to the custom of practised duellists, who wish to present as inconspicuous a mark as possible to the aim of an opponent, closely buttoned his coat as he took his position, General Johnston, on the contrary, laid aside his coat and vest, and bound his sash around his waist, thus offering his body, clad in a white shirt, as an almost certain target. When Houston perceived this, not wishing to be outdone in audacity, he somewhat angrily followed his example."

General Johnston knew his opponent's skill with the pistol, and was fully aware that if opportunity was given him to take deliberate aim the result to himself would almost certainly be fatal. He determined therefore to "draw" Houston's fire. The hair trigger of the old-fashioned duelling pistol was so sensitive that, if the finger touched it, the involuntary contraction induced by the report of another pistol was almost sure to cause a premature discharge. Johnston, therefore, when the word was given, fired just as he saw Houston raise his pistol, and thus drew his fire before he could catch an accurate aim. He repeated this five times with the same result, much to Houston's discomfiture, whose reputation as a "dead shot" was at stake. One of Johnston's shots grazed Houston's ear, and the latter long afterward said that he had not desired to kill his opponent, but that this "close call" admonished him that he must take care of himself. At the sixth shot his skill asserted itself, and General Johnston fell with a severe wound in the hip.

Houston, who, with all his faults, was a man of generous nature, was stricken with remorse and expressed his keen regret for what had happened, sending word to General Johnston that he would cheerfully serve under him. He would not receive the congratulations of his friends and admirers who flocked around him on his way from the ground, and always afterward spoke of General Johnston as "the coolest and bravest man" he had ever known, and became his staunch supporter. The effect of the duel was to establish General Johnston firmly in the confidence and regard of his troops. His recovery was slow and he suffered much pain. He was unable to mount his horse for many weeks, but at no time, even when confined to his bed, did he relinquish his command or fail to perform his official duties. It was the more necessary that he should remain at his post because of the attitude of the Mexican government. It became apparent that the republic was in danger of attack from this power, both by land and sea.

The ports of the little republic were blockaded and severe loss inflicted by the capture of vessels and supplies. It is estimated that in March, 1857, eight thousand Mexican troops were collected along the Rio Grande for another invasion of Texas, and the Indians, who were intensely hostile to the American settlers, were incited to every species of outrage. General Johnston's little army, at no time exceeding two thousand men, was kept in constant position and readiness to meet the invasion; and the very small force of cavalry under his command was kept actively employed in observing and skirmishing with the enemy. The invasion was fortunately prevented by internal dissensions in Mexico, which induced the recall of the troops threatening Texas. But the Indian troubles fomented by Mexican intrigues grew worse and were kept up for some years. A long standing quarrel with the Cherokees and certain other confederated tribes culminated in the battle of the Neches, fought July 16, 1829. General Johnston was at this date secretary of war, having been at length forced by the painful consequences of his wound to relinquish the active command of the army. Nevertheless, although Gen. K. H. Douglass was commanding the troops, General Johnston was upon the field advising with and assisting him. The victory of the whites was complete, the Indians sustained heavy loss, and, in that quarter, gave little further trouble. But the Comanches and other bands on the southern and western borders continued their depredations and outrages.

General Johnston resigned his place as secretary of war in March, and with it all participation in public life until after the admission of Texas into the Union. At the beginning of the war between the United States and Mexico, he was appointed to the command of one of the Texan volunteer regiments, enlisted for six months, and subsequently was assigned to duty as inspector-general of Butler's division, in which capacity he served until after the battle of Monterey. He was in all of the five days of hot fighting in the assault on that city, and was especially complimented upon his conduct. He returned to Texas before the conclusion of the war, and at the urgent solicitation of his wife — he had married again in 1843 — bought a plantation in Brazoria County, Tex., and settled there with the intention of making it his permanent home, and its cultivation his future occupation.

General Johnston's family, when he settled in Brazoria County upon his plantation, known as China Grove, "consisted of his wife and infant son, a negro man and his wife, and two negro boys and a girl." He had few neighbours, as this region was then very sparsely inhabited, only one near him, Col. Warren D. Hall, who had been one of Austin's colonists, and had taken a prominent part in the earlier revolutionary movements. His companionship and that of his wife, a devoted friend of Mrs. Johnston, was almost the sole society the family had for three years. During that time General Johnston laboured hard upon his farm. Each year he raised "a crop of Indian corn for bread for his family and forage for his work animals; a crop of cotton for the purchase of supplies; and an ample supply of all sorts of vegetables." Much of this was due to the toil of his own hands. His son, speaking of this period of life, which was patriarchal in its simplicity, says:

"I remember that some years after, when he had changed his occupation, a wealthy and cultivated friend with whom we were dining, very ingeniously maintained the theory that manual labour unfitted a man for the higher grades of thought and spheres of action. 'What you say,' replied General Johnston, 'seems very plausible, but self-love forbids me to agree with you. I have ploughed and planted and gathered the harvest. The spade, the hoe, the plough, and the axe are familiar to my hands, and that not for recreation, but for bread.'"

He was appointed paymaster in the United States army, October 31, 1849. The appointment gave him the nominal rank of major, but conferred no authority or command. It necessitated, however, much travelling, and upon the frontiers of Texas, where his duties were performed, a good deal of arduous work, not unaccompanied with danger. He accepted the office only because he hoped it would assist him ultimately to enter the line.

In 1853 he sold his plantation, which he had greatly improved, upon terms which enabled him to discharge his entire indebtedness; but, by a curious freak of fortune, he had no sooner obtained relief from a condition which had long oppressed him than he was confronted with another which threatened him even more seriously. He discovered that some one was systematically plundering the government funds placed in his charge. His accounts were kept very carefully, and he could detect almost the exact dates at which the money was taken, although he failed for some months to catch the thief. As much as $1,700 were stolen from the fund in 1853. He made no report of these losses to the government, but bore them himself; thereby forfeiting the almost entire benefit of his meagre salary, besides being harassed with the constant fear that the robberies might eventually amount to sums so large that he would not be able to replace them. All efforts to discover the perpetrator of the thefts was for a long time unavailing, although every device and the utmost vigilance were employed; but in 1855 they were brought home to a negro servant of General Johnston, who had been for years in constant attendance upon him, was a great favourite and implicitly trusted. Indignation against the negro was strongly aroused among all who had known of these peculations, and there was a general clamour for his exemplary punishment. General Johnston was urged to compel him to reveal the names of his accomplices, as it was believed that other parties had incited him to the thefts. General Johnston would not listen to this suggestion. "Evidence so obtained," he said, "is worthless. Besides the whipping will not restore what is lost; and it will not benefit the negro whom a lifetime of kind treatment has not made honest. It would be a mere act of revenge to which I cannot consent." His friends, however, insisted that the negro should be sold so that the proceeds of the sale might in part replace the money he had stolen. General Johnston agreed to do this, permitting the negro to select his new master, but informing the purchaser of the crime he had committed.

In 1855 he at last obtained the preferment he had so long desired and so greatly deserved. His friend and warm admirer, Jefferson Davis, was at that time secretary of war, and principally through his influence, although at the earnest solicitation of many other eminent men, General Johnston was appointed colonel of the Second Regiment of dragoons, U. S. A., which had just been created by act of congress. His most formidable competitor for this much coveted position was the justly celebrated Ben McCulloch, of Texas. The Second Dragoons was an exceedingly fine regiment, and the most famous, perhaps, that has ever been in the regular army of the United States. No regiment in any army was ever better officered than it was at the date of its organization, and until the beginning of the Civil War. Robert E. Lee was its lieutenant-colonel. Wm. J. Hardee and George H. Thomas — whose splendid records on different and opposing sides in the great struggle are so well known — were appointed its majors. Among its captains who rose to high rank and won renown in the Confederate service were E. Kirby Smith, Earl Van Dorn, and N. G. Evans; those of like grade who obtained exalted position in the Union ranks were J. N. Palmer, George Stoneman, and R. W. Johnson. Among the lieutenants who obtained the rank of general in the Confederate army were John B. Hood, Charles W. Field, and Charles Phifer. Perhaps in no modern army have so many distinguished soldiers held commissions in any one regiment.

The Second Dragoons seemed to be a favourite corps from the date of its creation, and was recruited with enlistments of the very best material within an unusually brief period. It was almost immediately ordered upon active service, and was constantly employed for two years upon the frontiers of Texas against the Indians. In a series of arduous campaigns and hotly contested and successful combats — eleven of which received complimentary mention in one general order — it fully justified the high expectations which had been entertained of its prowess.

In 1857 the troubles with Mormon settlements in Utah, which had long been a cause of apprehension to the government of the United States and of indignation to the people, reached a point which demanded actual and very nearly armed interference. After repeated and brutal outrages committed against the emigrants travelling from the older states to the Pacific Coast and insolent refusal upon the part of the Mormons to make redress or even promise future forbearance, the latter at length threatened open rebellion. The prophet and his priests incited them to every conceivable crime provided it was done at the expense of the "Gentiles," and preached the duty of resistance to the authority of the United States Government if exerted to protect its citizens. Some of my readers will probably remember the terrible massacre at Mountain Meadows in Utah perpetrated in September, 1857, by a band of the "Danites" or "Destroying Angels," acting, as was afterward clearly proven, by the orders of Brigham Young and his chief councillors. These ruffians attacked an emigrant train of one hundred and thirty-five in number and murdered every man and woman in it, only sparing seventeen small children.

In a state of conditions like this it became necessary to do something more than merely remonstrate. A strong body of regular troops, consisting of Colonel Johnston's regiment of cavalry, two regiments of infantry, and two batteries of artillery, with supplies for two thousand five hundred men, was ordered to proceed to Utah and occupy Salt Lake City. General Harney was at first indicated as the commander of this expedition, but before the march began Colonel Johnston was placed in command of it.

The difficulties and dangers attending this expedition consisted chiefly in the immense distances which had to be traversed through a wilderness as yet barely explored — part of it a desert — and the fact that the troops were exposed to the terrible rigours of a winter upon the bleak plains.

The Mormons proved to be as cowardly as they were cruel; they blustered and menaced, and Brigham Young assured his followers that divine protection would be given them and the divine wrath be visited on their enemies. He said, in allusion to the report soon afterward confirmed, that President Buchanan had removed him: "I am and will be governor and no power can hinder it until the Lord Almighty says, 'Brigham, you need not be governor any longer.' Come on with your thousand of illegally ordered troops and I will promise you in the name of Israel's God that you shall melt away as snow before a July's sun." But it was easier and safer to massacre helpless emigrants than to oppose an army of disciplined and veteran troops under a resolute commander, so the "saints" listened to reason and abandoned all thought of armed resistance. The Hon. Alfred Cumming, of Georgia, who had been appointed governor of Utah after President Buchanan removed Young, accompanied and was escorted by the troops. He reached Salt Lake City on April 18, 1858, and was shortly afterward inaugurated. The United States Commissioners, the Hon. L. W. Powell and Maj. Ben McCulloch, arrived on June 7th, received Brigham Young's formal submission and issued the President's proclamation of general amnesty.

For his services in this campaign Colonel Johnston was made brevet brigadier-general. He remained in Utah nearly two years, and was then assigned to the command of the Department of the Pacific, with headquarters at San Francisco. He was serving in this capacity when the war between the states began, and resigned his commission in the army of the United States, April 10, 1861, to offer his sword to the Confederacy.

Many of us can still remember the thrill of interest we felt when we heard that he was riding with a few companions across the continent to do battle for the South; our fear that he would be intercepted and made prisoner, and our joy when we learned of his safe arrival. It is said that President Davis was not aware that he had arrived in Richmond when he made his first call at the Executive Mansion. Mr. Davis heard his step on the stairway and exclaimed "That is Sidney Johnston's step. Bring him up."

Every account which has been furnished of the public and private life of Albert Sidney Johnston evinces the extraordinary impression he produced upon his contemporaries, and all that we know of him from memoir, reminiscence, the personal tributes of his most intimate acquaintances, and official testimony, warrants the belief that he was a great man. There was in his nature a stalwart manliness, a moral grandeur, shaping his action in every situation, and which, totally without harsh or imperious assertion, yet dominated, or at least largely influenced, all who approached him. Very many testimonials from those who came personally in contact with him prove how generally this influence was felt and acknowledged. His manner and bearing, while kind and courteous, were inexpressibly majestic, and seemed the unmistakable index of a lofty character. He exercised control and leadership without effort, and under all circumstances displayed the inborn faculty of command. It served him with all kinds and classes of men — the rough frontiersmen and even the wild Comanches instantly recognized his superiority.

Much of this power to impress those of his own rank and condition in life was due, undoubtedly, to the exalted sentiment expressed on all occasions in his language and demeanour, and before which a meaner feeling was abashed. His friend and comrade of the old army, Captain Eaton, relates this circumstance, which occurred during the Black Hawk War:

"On the same campaign an incident happened, illustrating Lieutenant Johnston's keen sense of propriety, his respect for female virtue, and his power of rebuke. One evening, as a group of officers were talking in the tent of one of them, a Lieutenant ——, who was of a coarse and vulgar nature, and who was eventually dismissed from the service, said he did not believe in female virtue. Lieutenant Johnston at once arose and said: 'Mr.——, you have a mother, and, I believe, a sister.' He made no other remark: but the rebuke silenced Lieutenant ——, and, vulgar as he was, he hung his head in shame and confusion. I never knew a man who could give a rebuke with more crushing effect than Albert Sidney Johnston."

Col. Samuel Churchill, of St. Louis, who knew him extremely well, told me of an instance showing how happily General Johnston could deal with men not usually supposed to be amenable to such influence; and the Colonel stated that while it surprised it also greatly amused him. He said that upon one occasion General Johnston himself, and two or three other friends were on a steam-boat en route from St. Louis to New Orleans. When only a short distance from St. Louis one of the party was taken sick and soon developed unmistakable symptoms of small-pox. The nature of his malady was concealed as carefully as possible from the passengers and crew, but the officers of the boat were of course immediately informed of it. It was thought best that he should be as speedily as practicable transferred to some steamer returning to St. Louis, not only that he might at once receive proper treatment, but because in the long trip to New Orleans the danger of contagion to others would be greatly increased. But the difficulty of procuring passage for him on another boat at once suggested itself; its officers would certainly be very loath to receive such a passenger.

Steam-boat men in those days were a very autocratic kind of gentry and not easily induced to consent to anything they did not wish to do. It was agreed, however, that the attempt should be made. In a little while a boat coming up stream was sighted. The captain of the south-bound steamer declared, however, that there would be no use in trying the experiment in that case. "I recognize that boat," he said, giving her name, "and old John —— commands her. He's the roughest man on the river, and he'll swear the scalps off our heads if we propose such a thing to him."

"Oh, no," said General Johnston, very quietly. "I'll arrange the matter with him. You get your gang-plank ready, signal the other boat and make preparations to take the patient on board of her without delay." His directions were obeyed, and as soon as the boats were alongside and the plank connected them, General Johnston crossed it and stepped up to the redoubtable captain, who was standing on the lower deck waiting to know what was wanted. "Captain," he said, saluting him politely and speaking in a matter of fact way, "I am Colonel Johnston, of the United States army. A friend of mine on our boat was taken ill with small-pox just after we left St. Louis and I've come to ask you to take him back there. Please have a state-room prepared for him and I shall send him on board."

All those who were in the secret had collected to witness the anticipated stormy scene, Colonel Churchill, who, also, knew the fierce river despot that his friend was bearding, being present. All expected an explosion which would wreck the surroundings, and perhaps turn back the tide of the Mississippi. But to their infinite astonishment, the captain, after scanning the general from head to foot and looking him a few seconds in the eye, answered, "All right, sir! Bring your man aboard. I'll get a room ready for him; but tell them who bring him to say blamed little about it." Then turning to a few of his own people who were listening in open-mouthed amazement, he added with a growl like that of a grizzly, "And if any of you d—d whelps chirp about this, I'll break his neck with a capstan bar and then fling him in the river."

Some very able and distinguished men served upon General Johnston's staff and were closely in his confidence during the campaign which preceded the battle of Shiloh; such men as Col. H. P. Brewster, of Texas; Governor, afterward United States Senator, Isham G. Harris, of Tennessee; the poet soldier, Theodore O'Hara, and Col. Robert W. Johnson and Maj. D. M. Haydon, of Kentucky; and first, perhaps, of all of these strong men and splendid gentlemen, William Preston, General Johnston's brother-in-law, who has been termed "the last of the cavaliers." Some of them had known him for many years. Some knew him only in those last months of his life, but all had learned to feel for him a devoted friendship and loyalty; all warmly testified to the grandeur and majesty of his character, and the dignity and fortitude with which he bore himself in the ordeal to which he was subjected. Preston won distinction in many ways, in congressional and diplomatic service, in social life and in the field. He was a man of wide and varied culture, and his knowledge of men was shrewd and extensive. His estimate or opinion, therefore, of any man he knew well was valuable, and apt to be just. His admiration for General Johnston was extreme. He ranked him very high, and told me that he had observed, from his earliest acquaintance with him, that extraordinary personal influence he could exert, and of which he had witnessed many instances.

I had myself a somewhat curious experience of this power of his, in the only interview, if it could be termed such, that I ever had with General Johnston. My regard and admiration for him had been taught me from infancy. He and my father had known each other intimately from their earliest boyhood and had been warm friends until the latter's death. I had never seen him, however, until he came to take command of the army in Kentucky, and was, of course, entirely unknown to him. His face and figure became very familiar to the troops serving under him, for he visited the camps frequently, and was active in inspection and all such duties. It was easy to single him out from the crowd, no matter by how many he might be surrounded; and I often noted how completely his striking appearance and commanding demeanour seemed to make men, who would have been imposing in any other presence, shrink into ordinary humanity when contrasted with him. I never saw him without hoping that I would sometime have an opportunity to make myself known to him as the son of his old friend.

Such an opportunity finally occurred, but I signally failed to utilize it. I had occasion, during the winter that the army lay around Bowling Green, to visit his headquarters; I was then adjutant of Morgan's squadron, and had been sent to see an officer of General Johnston's staff on some business. While seated in one of the rooms of the headquarters, before a comfortable fire, awaiting the coming of the officer I wished to see, the door was suddenly opened and General Johnston entered. He seemed disappointed at not finding some one for whom he was looking, but spoke to me very courteously.

Here was my chance — but in that noble and almost awe-inspiring presence, I found it impossible to execute my purpose, and verily believe lost, temporarily, all power of speech. I arose from my chair, and, without a word, bowed profoundly. He returned my bow as politely as if a general officer had been before him — although I am sure he took me for a courier — and said, "Keep your seat, sir, I see that you have been riding in the rain and cold." I felt as if I could have picked up a shell about to burst more readily than I could have resumed my chair while he was standing, so, still silent, I simply bowed again. He repeated, very kindly, "Sit down, my son. Don't mind me. Sit and warm yourself." I bowed the third time without speaking. He evidently realized my feeling and that I would never consent to be seated while he was present. After a moment, he smiled, as if greatly amused, made me the most magnificent bow I ever saw and walked out of the room.

When it was too late I, of course, heartily regretted and reproached myself for my lack of courage. His manner and speech were so kind and considerate that I felt assured he would have given me a cordial greeting if I had introduced myself, as I had originally intended to do.

Deeply as we had reason to deplore General Johnston's death when it deprived the South of his sword, his countrymen do not now altogether regret it; for no more striking and splendid incident is recorded in the pages of Confederate glory, and none that Confederate soldiers can remember with juster and profounder pride. He, the commander-in-chief, died literally at the head and in the front of his army. After leading his men in the fiercest storm of battle and making them invincible by his inspiration and example, he fell amid the thunder of the strife and in the very moment of victory. The wound of which he died was not necessarily fatal; if it had received proper attention it would not have been even serious. An artery of his right leg was torn by a minie ball, but his life could have been saved if any one had been with him to apply the simplest means of arresting the hemorrhage. He had despatched all the members of his staff in different directions with important orders, and he, his mind occupied with the conduct of the battle, gave no heed to his hurt, was perhaps not aware of it. The absence of his surgeon, Dr. David W. Yandell, at the critical moment was due to General Johnston's own positive orders, and the nature of these instructions, and the fact that they probably occasioned his death, seem in perfect keeping with the exalted character of the man. His son thus tells the story:

"Dr. D. W. Yandell had attended his person during most of the morning, but finding a large number of wounded men, including many Federals, at one point, General Johnston ordered Yandell to stop there, establish a hospital, and give them his services. He said to Yandell, "These men were our enemies a moment ago; they are prisoners now; take care of them."

"Dr. Yandell remonstrated against leaving him, but he was peremptory, and the doctor began his work. He saw General Johnston no more. Had Yandell remained with him, he would have had little difficulty with the wound. It was this act of unselfish charity which cost him his life."

CHAPTER VI

THE French have a term which happily describes the service performed by partisan troops or the somewhat irregular operations of small detachments, as contradistinguished from the movements of large armies and war, conducted on a grand scale. They term the former "The Little War." But there has always prevailed during prolonged and bitterly contested national or internecine strife another sort of conflict still, wilder, and fiercer, altogether outside of the pale of legitimate warfare and unrecognized by its rules and regulations. Sometimes this private and lawless violence is directed purely to rapine, as gangs of marauders often hover in the vicinity of armies and infest war-stricken territory; more frequently it is an attempt to wreak revenge for some of the many wrongs and hardships which legitimate warfare, however mercifully commanding generals may seek to prosecute it, invariably inflicts on non-combatants. In the latter case the citizen, without assuming the duties of the soldier, does even bloodier work, and becomes the more ferocious fighter.

In Europe, of course, during the mediæval period, and especially while the feudal system was still in force, when all social life, it might be said, was one cruel, and almost continuous strife, these conditions were chronic and nearly universal; for then the transition from the peasant to the soldier, and from either to the bandit was easy. As the proverb of the times put it, when a man's house was burned he became soldier or brigand.

But at a yet later date these same conditions were the invariable concomitants of warfare, and were widely prevalent in every war waged in Europe from the inception of what may be termed modern civilization down to our own era. Perhaps the savage, sustained, and inexorable armed resistance of the Spanish guerillas to the armies of Napoleon — a resistance far braver and more effective than any offered by the regular Spanish troops — furnishes the most memorable example in modern history of how an aroused, although unorganized, populace can sometimes fight; but the terrible devastation and oppression wrought in the Napoleonic wars everywhere on the continent, and the hatred and resentment so engendered, induced, although not to so great an extent, similar reprisals from every maltreated people.

Numerous instances in our own Civil War prove how history repeats itself in this as in all other respects; although it should be said that with us, on both sides, many of those, who, properly speaking, were "non-combatants," yet arrogated belligerent rights, were induced to do so as much by an excess of political zeal as because of actual injury. In the South and in the border states, where war was actively waged, this form of protest against invasion was common, and it became more general and gradually acquired something like organization in proportion to the duration of armed occupation or frequency of hostile incursion. It would doubtless have been manifest in the Northern states also, had they, too, been held or traversed for any considerable period by hostile forces. In the more Southern states, those which peculiarly constituted Confederate territory, the men who conducted this irregular warfare, were almost always Southern in sentiment. But, with few exceptions, they were in Kentucky and Tennessee mountains "Union men." They belonged, as a rule, to that part of the population which had never been in sympathy with their slave-holding neighbours, and abhorred the "rebellion," not so much because they thought it wrong, but because it had been inaugurated by a class with which they had never been in friendly accord.

The specific appellation by which these gentry were known was "bushwhacker," bestowed, doubtless because of their predilection for lurking in ambush and firing on their enemies from hiding places more or less secure. The bushwhacker, however, although probably quite similar in character and methods to the Spanish guerilla, should not be confounded with those whom we termed "guerillas" in our war. The latter designation was applied to men who, having deserted from one or the other army, had then resorted to unqualified brigandage — their hand, like Ishmael's, being "against all other men."

Nor again should either the guerilla or bushwhacker be confounded with the "home guard." The home guard organizations, both of the North and the South, although their regular members were not enlisted in the armies nor required to perform service, were yet recognized by law, and were indeed part of the militia forces of the states wherein they were formed. They were organized and armed, as their name indicates, for the protection of the localities where they resided, so far as their efforts were adequate to its protection.

These bushwhackers were capable of making themselves exceedingly disagreeable. Large districts of country were sometimes so infested by them that only strong bodies or troops could pass with any sort of security. It was almost certain death to an enemy, or even a man whom they suspected of enmity, to fall into their hands. They rarely gave quarter or showed mercy. They could not, of course, make head in the open against any force of regular and trained soldiers unless it were greatly their inferior in numbers; but fighting, as I have said, from ambush and under close cover, they were dangerous foes, even for the best troops, on their own chosen ground. They understood the war of the forest and the fastness, of the rock and the mountain, as well as did the red savages who were their predecessors in territory and temper. The cavalry of the Army of Tennessee, and especially Morgan's command, had an extensive and varied experience with them. When in our expeditions into Kentucky we were required to march through any region where they harboured we received abundant attention from them. In the counties of Tennessee lying along the upper Cumberland, our pickets and scouting parties had greatly more trouble with them than with the outlying Federal cavalry. In the latter part of the war when I was serving in West Virginia, and the small brigade I commanded drew its forage from Johnson County in east Tennessee, I was compelled to make strong detatchments from it to protect the foragers from the bushwhackers with which that locality was swarming. During General Bragg's retreat from Kentucky, in October, 1862, his march through the mountains to Cumberland Gap was greatly harassed by them. They collected in considerable numbers and fired from every point of vantage upon his column, inflicting smart loss, but doing some service by minimizing straggling. With much difficulty Bragg finally captured sixteen of them, whom he immediately hung up on the side of the road "by way of encouraging the others." The most redoubtable leader of these fierce people in Tennessee was "Tinker Dave Beattie." This man was bold, astute, ferocious, and unrelenting in purpose and hatred. He had drawn to himself a large following, over which his control was as absolute as any ever exercised by one of the old Scottish Highland chieftains over his clan.

The most celebrated and successful exponent of this irregular warfare, on the Southern side, was Champe Ferguson, a native of Clinton County, Ky. Ferguson could hardly be called a bushwhacker, although in his methods he much resembled them. He had a company of men, and very daring fighters they were, too, who, although not enlisted in the Confederate service, were intensely attached to Ferguson and sworn to aid the Southern cause by some sort of obligation which they apparently deemed as binding and inviolable us any oath of military allegiance. While Ferguson undertook many expeditions on his own private account and acknowledged no obedience to Confederate orders generally, he nevertheless served frequently with the Confederate cavalry commands, particularly Morgan's, and not only did good service, but for the time being strictly obeyed commands and abstained from evil practices. Although I had often before heard of him I saw him for the first time when we were just starting on the July raid into Kentucky, 1862. I utilized the first convenient occasion which occurred to impress upon him the necessity of observing — while with us — the rules of civilized warfare, and that he must not attempt to kill prisoners.

"I have nothing to do or say," I told him, "about the prisoners you take on your own independent expeditions against your private enemies, but you musn't kill prisoners taken by us."

"Why, Colonel Duke," he answered, "I've got sense. I know it ain't looked on as right to treat reg'lar soldiers tuk in battle in that way. Besides, I don't want to do it. I haven't got no feeling agin these Yankee soldiers, except that they are wrong, and oughtn't to come down here and fight our people. I won't tech them; but when I catches any of them hounds I've got good cause to kill, I'm goin' to kill 'em."

I repeated my previous declaration that I had no right to

interfere or advise regarding that matter; and then, wishing to satisfy some curiosity I entertained on the subject, said:

"Champe, how many men have you killed?"

He responded with some feeling: "I ain't killed nigh as many men as they say I have; folks has lied about me powerful. I ain't killed but thirty-two men since this war commenced."

The war had then lasted about eighteen months. He added to the number quite largely after that, but just before the close of the war he lost the notched stick on which he kept his count, and died in ignorance of the exact total.

Ferguson's intense hostility to the parties to whom he alluded as his personal enemies was due to the maltreatment of his wife and daughter by them at the very beginning of the war. Certain of his Union neighbours, who, perhaps, also had a grudge against him, for he was a man well calculated to arouse such feeling, visited his house during his absence and brutally whipped the women. He proceeded to hunt and kill every man engaged in this outrage, and, having acquired the habit of so dealing with that sort of people, never gave it up.

He was a rough-looking man but of striking and rather prepossessing appearance, more than six feet in height and very powerfully built. His complexion was florid, and his hair jet-black, crowning his head with thick curls. He had one peculliarity of feature which I remember to have seen in only two or three other men, and each of these was, like himself, a man of despotic will and fearless, ferocious temper. The pupil and iris of the eye were of nearly the same colour, and, except to the closest inspection, seemed perfectly blended. His personal adventures, combats, and encounters were innumerable. Some of his escapes, when assailed by great odds, were almost incredible and could be explained only by his great bodily strength, activity, adroitness in the use of his weapons and savage energy. One of his most formidable enemies, a man little inferior to himself in the qualities I have described as characterizing Ferguson, was a mountaineer named Elam Huddlestone, chief of a noted gang of bushwhackers. Huddlestone and Ferguson sought each other with inveterate animosity, and had several indecisive encounters. Finally, on one occasion, during the December raid into Kentucky, Ferguson obtained certain information of where

Huddlestone could be found that same night, and immediately started, with two or three of his most determined followers, and the fixed resolution that the feud should be ended then and there with the death of one of them.

They reached the house about midnight and approached it cautiously; but one of Huddlestone's men, stationed in the garret, and evidently instructed to be on watch, discovered them and fired. Ferguson's followers returned the fire but Ferguson himself sprang quickly and savagely against the door, burst it open and bounded into the house. Huddlestone and one of his band had been asleep before the fire and were just rising from the floor when Ferguson entered. He threw himself upon them, and after a short but desperate fight, killed both with his knife. I shall never forget how that terrible weapon looked when Ferguson showed it to me the next day and related the story I have just repeated. I had been severely wounded in the head a few days previously, was still faint and sick from the wound, and the sight of that knife, still covered with clotted blood, thoroughly nauseated me.

Ferguson's last exploit would have gotten him into serious trouble with the Confederate authorities if it had not occurred just before the close of the war. Among a number of wounded men, both Federal and Confederate, who were lying in hospital in south-western Virginia, was a Lieutenant-colonel Smith, a Federal officer, whose death Ferguson had sworn in retaliation for the death of his friend, Major Bledsoe, who had been killed by Smith after he had been made prisoner. Ferguson broke into the hospital, overpowered the guard and shot Smith in his bed. Orders were immediately issued for his arrest and trial, but hostilities ceased and Confederate authority was at an end before he could be found.

Instead of leaving the country or remaining in hiding after the close of the war, Ferguson, with that strange recklessness which characterized such men, returned to Sparta, Tennessee, which he had claimed for some years as his residence, and lived there openly and apparently with no apprehension. It is even asserted that he obtained a parole, such as was given the Confederate soldiers after final surrender. But he was in a few months arrested by the Federal authorities for the murder of Smith, tried by court-martial, convicted and executed.

Among the many novel and original methods, and, I think I can justly claim, improvements, which Gen. John H. Morgan introduced into modern warfare, that from which he obtained perhaps the most satisfactory results was his use of the telegraph. Not even the complete system of railroad wrecking, in which he was the pioneer, and by which his operations on the enemy's lines of communication were rendered so successful, more thoroughly aided his own enterprises, although of more benefit to the armies with which his cavalry was serving. He was the first officer who conceived the idea of employing the telegraph to procure information of what his enemy was doing or purposed to do, and to mislead him in regard to his own movements.

Very soon after he began to recruit and organize his command, he secured the services of a skilful telegraphic operator, a Canadian by birth, but who had lived in the South for several years just preceding the war. This man, George A. Ellsworth, became quite famous for his peculiar exploits in his own line, and was indeed remarkably adroit and capable in everything connected with his vocation and the uses to which he was required to apply his art. He was furnished with the necessary instruments and material for his work, which an assistant always carried and had ready for use; and sometimes on his motion, but most usually under General Morgan's immediate direction, he "milked the wires" in a marvellous way. This sort of thing appealed, of course, strongly to the imagination of the soldiers, and Ellsworth, better known by his sobriquet of "Lightning," became very popular.

He would frequently attach his wire to the main telegraph line, at some convenient spot where there was no fear of interruption, and take off the messages passing between various points on the line, reading them by the click of the instrument. But when it was decided to procure fuller or more definite information, or to send messages intended to mislead, it was necessary to take possession of some telegraph office, and seize and hold prisoner the regular operator until the work was accomplished and to prevent his giving the alarm. Ellsworth would, in such case, take the chair, personate his captive, and carry on brisk conversations with his brother-artists who happend to be on duty at the points with which he wished to hold communication. His success in dealing with those upon whom he would attempt this deception, and especially after it had become generally known that he was accustomed to practise such artifices, was extraordinary. His personal acquaintance with the operators employed at that time in Kentucky and Tennessee, and with the habits of the brotherhood — who seemed to be all inveterate gossips, constantly chatting with one another over the wires when not seriously employed — and his intimate knowledge of everything connected with the business, generally enabled him to escape detection. On more than one occasion I have seen him allay suspicion, even when it was thoroughly aroused, answering, with apparently careless merriment or irresistible simplicity, every question propounded to test his identity.

"You are Ellsworth," once said an irate operator — another Canuck, by the way — "and you d — d bloke, you can't make a fool of me."

"The Almighty has spared me that trouble," retorted "Lightning." "But don't you know, you Canadian ass, that Ellsworth is sick at Knoxville?"

Then ensued a long and angry colloquy, in the course of which, however, Ellsworth succeeded in imbuing his skeptical auditor with the very belief he had intended from the first to induce.

He would sometimes on such occasions compel the captured operator to telegraph at his dictation, meanwhile observing very carefully the man's manner of working the instrument. Then having apparently caught his style or "handwriting," he would take the instrument himself.

Ellsworth's greatest triumphs, with the exception of those achieved during the Ohio raid, were on the first or "July raid" into Kentucky in 1862. His despatches, purporting to come from the regular operators, of course, sent from Midway and Georgetown, thoroughly confused the Federal commanders at Lexington, Frankfort and Paris, and sent them moving in all directions save the one they should have pursued in order to encounter Morgan, while the latter, with one fourth of their number, was resting at

Georgetown, in easy reach of each hostile force. At Somerset, just before leaving Kentucky, Ellsworth was considerate enough to offer some excellent advice to the telegraph operators in Kentucky, and yet some of them characterized it as an impertinence. He issued the following document, which the wires carried all over the state:

Headquarters Telegraph Department of Kentucky, Confederate States of America — General Order No. 1.— When an operator is positively informed that the enemy is marching on his station he will immediately proceed to destroy the telegraphic instruments and all material in his charge. Such instances of carelessness as were exhibited on the part of the operators at Lebanon, Midway and Georgetown will be severely dealt with. By order of
G. A. ELLSWORTH,
Gen'l Military Supt. C. S. Telegraphic Dept.

But, shrewd and capable as was Ellsworth in his business, and although he was also a bright man in conversation, he was wofully obtuse, and even stupid, in many matters. He was the victim of innumerable practical jokes, some of them rather cruel. He was a vain and boastful fellow, and, being well built and muscular, posed as an athlete. He especially prided himself on his prowess as a sprinter, and never tired of vaunting his fleetness of foot. "The boys" of the Second Kentucky Cavalry at length resolved that he should make an exhibition of his capacity in this respect. They found another fellow, who likewise claimed to be a swift runner, and negotiated a match between him and Ellsworth.

"Lightning" at first acceded very willingly to the proposition. But Jeff Sterritt, who was the chief promoter of the race, insisted that each contestant should carry a rider. Ellsworth demurred to this, but his objections were overborne by the clamour of the Bluegrass Kentuckians, who declared that it was absurd to have a race without jockeys; and his opponent, who was in the joke, swore that he wouldn't run unless he had a jockey up to pilot him. This opinion was so unanimous that Ellsworth was finally forced to yield. The two men of least weight in the regiment were indicated as riders, and Jeff Sterritt was selected to ride Ellsworth. Sterritt surreptitiously buckled on a pair of Texas spurs, with long and exceeding keen rowels, and when the signal to start was given plunged them into his mount. Ellsworth was naturally disgusted at such treatment, and for awhile sulked and refused to go. But as Sterritt continued to ply the spurs, he thought better of the matter and stretched away with an amazing burst of speed. He not only overtook and passed his antagonist and beat him out many lengths, but ran forty yards beyond the goal before he could be pulled up. Yet for all the rough fun his comrades used to have at his expense, old "Lightning" was loved by them for many excellent and genuine traits, and when he died, some three years ago, he was sincerely lamented.

One of the best known and most liked men in Gen. John H. Morgan's command was Parson Wynne. He was not only an excellent soldier, but a pious and good man, and justly exercised a great influence over his comrades. Nevertheless, with all his many good qualities he was rather irritable and extremely stubborn in the maintenance and assertion of his opinions. No more aggressive and tenacious disputant ever discussed the resolutions of '98, or knocked a man down for not properly discerning the difference between secession and coöperation. His sincerity only made him the more obstinate.

On account of his extensive acquaintance in Kentucky and thorough knowledge of the country, as well as his uncommon nerve and acuteness, General Morgan frequently despatched him on secret missions into the state to obtain information not only necessary for the guidance of his own movements, but important for the use of the army. On these expeditions he was generally accompanied by Dan Ray, a gallant soldier, quite as nervy and intelligent as the parson, but the soul of good-humour. Dan never indulged in discussion except to stir up the parson and gratify his own fun-loving disposition.

One day they were riding together somewhere in southern Kentucky, when the conversation turned on a practice very prevalent in the cavalry, and, it must be confessed, carried to the fullest extent in Morgan's command. They fell to discussing the practice of impressing horses for cavalry use. Dan excused, and even mildly advocated, the practice, on the ground that it was a "military necessity," but admitted that it was sometimes abused.

The parson condemned it *in toto*. He would not admit that it could be defended or excused for any reason. He declared that he prayed daily that his comrades might be forgiven for this sin, but intimated in strong terms that he didn't believe they would be, and concluded by denouncing it as a national crime which would bring about, if anything could, the fall of the Confederacy. Finding that the parson was warming up almost to the fighting point, Ray prudently let the matter drop.

On the next day the parson found it necessary to have his horse shod, and the clumsy smith pricked one hoof so badly that in a few hours the animal became dead lame. Under the circumstances this was a serious matter, and the parson and Dan both grew anxious and apprehensive. Just as they had about determined to retrace their steps to a point where the parson might procure a remount, which would have involved an unfortunate delay, a well-to-dolooking man came riding down the road on a remarkably fine horse. The sight of such a horse might well make a cavalry man covetous, and reduce any scruple he might have had to zero. The parson looked, longed, and let go all hold on his scruples. He felt it was predestined that he should have that horse.

He gracefully initiated the "trade" he had determined on by saying:

"That's a mighty likely horse you're riding, sir — a mighty likely animal."

"Yes," was the response, "he's a right peart nag."

"Sound, too, ain't he? Nothing the matter with him?"

"Well, stranger, he's sound from his eyes to his hocks. Thar ain't a soft spot in him."

"This is a good chunk of a horse, too," said the parson, pointing to his own. "He's by Denmark. His dam was by Drennon, out of a Whip mare. He can go all the gaits when he's right, but a fool of a blacksmith pricked him this morning."

"Pull his shoes off and let him stand in wet grass."

"I haven't the time, I am engaged on public service and must get on rapidly, so I am compelled to ask you to swap horses. You have leisure and seem to be an intelligent man, and you can doctor this horse."

"The h — l you say. Well, stranger, you're the drunkest man to hide it so well I ever see."

"Don't use profane language in my presence," shouted the parson, "but help me shift saddles. You're getting much the best of the trade. There isn't such a fox-trotter and single footed racker as my horse — or rather your horse, for he's yours now — in Kentucky. Don't multiply words," he continued, as the other party to the "swap" still feebly protested, "but climb down. Your horse there needs attention; take him and attend to him." And the parson enforced obedience by the production of an army Colt. The trade was concluded. The parson mounted his new steed, and the pair pushed on. After riding some miles in silence, Ray soberly remarked:

"Parson, I have been pondering over what you said yesterday about horse-pressing, and I've about concluded you were right. I am satisfied that it can't be defended, and —— "

"Dan Ray!" broke in the parson quietly, but with significant emphasis, "I don't care to hear you discuss a matter you can't understand. Your mind hasn't been trained to draw nice distinctions. That matter awhile back wasn't properly a case of horse-pressing at all. It was a compulsory trade, rendered necessary by the unsettled condition of the country and the times, and because the laws regulating the making and enforcement of contracts are rather silent just now. I could demonstrate this without the slightest difficulty to any man accustomed to logical discussion; but if you ever allude to it again, I'll hang in your wool."

We will all agree that profanity is not only an unprofitable, but a very shocking vice, and its indulgence, even under extreme provocation, should always be censured. Nevertheless we cannot help feeling that this censure should be somewhat milder in some cases than in others. Indeed we have all known men in whom if we could not pardon the habit we have felt very much inclined to condone it. This is especially the case with our foreign-born citizens, who frequently swear energetically without meaning any harm. With them it seems to be a mere colloquial variation, having more of sound than significance, and used in speech as an exclamation point is used in print. It is said that strangers in any country pick up the oaths in use among its people more readily than any other part of the language, from which it might be argued that objectionable as it is, swearing comes by nature and is common to all humanity.

Doubtless many of my Confederate readers will remember General de Polignac, a gallant and accomplished Frenchman, who, during the entire Civil War, served the South as faithfully as any of her native sons. He belonged to the princely family of that name, one of the noblest and most distinguished in the history of France, and it certainly never furnished a braver or more creditable representative. But, while the general spoke English fluently, and, in his unimpassioned moments, with absolute propriety, he was addicted, when excited, to a multitude of imprecatory ejaculations. In plain truth, he would "swear like a trooper."

"After one or two years of service the soldiers invented, or adopted, certain expressions and forms of speech which sounded strange in the ears of the uninitiated. A peculiar slang of the camp came into vogue which, in many respects, largely superseded the proper and more decorous terms. It became the custom, for instance, to designate a battalion or brigade as "an outfit," a "layout" or a "shebang."

The story goes that on one occasion, when Polignac, before his promotion to brigadier, was commanding a regiment in Mouton's Louisiana brigade, and, during a somewhat prolonged absence of General Mouton, commanding the brigade itself, he had an interview with a soldier in which his own proficiency in profanity and this slang of the camp, just mentioned, both came strongly to the front. A handsome, bright-eyed Creole lad came to his headquarters one morning, and, duly saluting, said: "Colonel! I have been off on a two-weeks' furlough and am just back. I belong to Colonel Censer's 'layout,' but don't know where it is. Will you please tell me where it is?"

"Colonel Censer's what?" shouted Polignac, his eyes bulging with amazement.

"To Colonel Censer's 'layout,'" repeated the boy. "You know it; it belongs to your 'shebang.'"

"Well, d — n my eyes to ze deep blue h — l," groaned Polignac. "I have been militaire all my life. I was educate for ze army. I have hear of ze compagnie, ze battalion, ze regiment, ze brigade, ze division and ze army corps, but blank,

blank, blank, my soul to blank eef evair I hear of ze 'layout' or ze 'shebang' before."

Some twenty years ago two French military officers came to this country, and whatever may have been the principal object of their mission, they seemed chiefly interested in procuring information, as full and detailed as possible, regarding the cavalry operations of our Civil War, and especially the character of service performed by Morgan and Forrest. As they were themselves cavalry men, this interest in their own particular branch of the service was quite natural. They were evidently thoroughly taught in their profession, and men of experience, as well as of more than ordinary capacity. The senior of the two in rank as well as years, Colonel de Kerbrecht, had long served in the Chasseurs D'Afrique, the most celebrated cavalry corps in the French army, and the other, Captain de la Cher, was an officer of the Third Dragoons, and had served on the staff of Marshal Bazaine. Among those from whom they sought the information they desired was myself, and they plied me with eager and intelligent questions concerning my experiences under General Morgan. They wanted to know all about the organization and armament of his command; about the nature of its drill and discipline; about Morgan's methods of marching, scouting, picketing and fighting, and above all were profoundly interested in the strategy and conduct of the raid. They were thoroughly convinced that the new methods and uses of cavalry would supersede the old, and that the sabre as the cavalry arm par excellence must give way to the rifle and revolver. They expressed the hope that a cavalry corps, modelled on those commanded by Morgan and Forrest, and adapted to just such work as they performed, would be organized for the French army.

After I had answered categorically their queries regarding Morgan's service, they asked me to tell them something about Forrest. I said that my knowledge of what he had done was not personal and direct, but I had gotten it at second-hand; nevertheless, I thought I might furnish them a little information about General Forrest's campaigns of the kind they wished. I then proceeded to give them an account, as well as I could, of Forrest's famous battle with Sturgess at Tishomingo Creek. I did not seek to embellish the real story — that could scarcely be done — but I certainly tried to do it justice. I should mention the fact just here, that Colonel Kerbrecht did not speak or understand English. De la Cher spoke it quite fluently; and inasmuch as the kind of French I speak is for some reason altogether unintelligible to a Frenchman, De la Cher would translate my narrative, as I proceeded, to his countryman.

As I have said, I tried justly to describe that remarkable combat, and how Forrest, with vastly inferior numbers, came down like a cyclone on his enemy and annihilated him. At any rate, there was that in the story which appealed to the gallant Frenchmen. When I finished, the old chasseur rose to his feet, stretched both arms above his head, and with, perhaps, the only two words of our language that he knew, testified to the prowess of Bedford Forrest:

"Sapristi," he exclaimed, "G — d d — n!"

In the immediate ante-bellum period and during the war, no man, perhaps, not in public station, was more widely known in Kentucky and throughout the South than Maj. John S. Throckmorton. He was much liked and respected, but especially attracted attention and was the subject of frequent comment because of his eccentricities. Absolutely frank, truthful and honourable, he had the confidence of all who knew him; warm-hearted and ever ready to do a kindly or generous act, he had many friends; but his irascible temper, the readiness with which he became irritated upon the slightest and sometimes upon no apparent, provocation, almost exceeded belief. He was a handsome man, powerfully and gracefully formed, and in manner, when not angered or excited, polite and pleasant. Some of his younger acquaintances would occasionally, in a spirit of mischief, take advantage of this infirmity and kindle his quick, inflammable disposition, which it was easy to do, by some remark that, however harmless in itself, aroused an unpleasant memory, or which he might deem irrelevant. But it behooved the man trying such an experiment to assume the most innocent tone and demeanour and avoid all appearance of intentional offence; for if he believed that offence was intended, he was quite sure to express resentment, not merely in words, but in very strenuous fashion.

Major Throckmorton — I give him the title he subsequently

acquired — was among those who first went South from Kentucky to escape arrest because of avowed Southern sympathies, and to follow the fortunes of the Confederacy. He soon after became attached to the "Provisional Government of Kentucky," organized at Russellville on November 13, 1861, by the convention which passed resolutions declaring that Kentucky would withdraw from the Union and seek admission into the Confederacy. The gentlemen who took this action were not strong enough to maintain it upon the territory of their own state, so that, with the officials of the provisional government, they were, with few exceptions, compelled to join the exodus southward of which I have just spoken. I do not remember in what capacity Throckmorton served this state government, but a few months later — after the battle of Shiloh, where the heroic provisional governor, George W. Johnson, fell fighting in the ranks of one of the Kentucky regiments — he was commissioned as major in the Confederate army and assigned to duty in the commissary department.

I shall never forget my first meeting with him after he had "come South." It was just after his connection with the provisional government. I met him on the road in charge of the provisional wagon train; he was looking out, I believe, for a suitable site where the government might encamp. I had been on a scout with a small party and was returning to the vicinity of Bowling Green when I encountered him. I had known him intimately and pleasantly for several years, was very glad to see him, and gave him a hearty greeting which he returned as cordially. Yet I had not talked with him five minutes before I had quite innocently incurred his displeasure, which he expressed in his usual vigorous way. He was riding an old brown horse; not such a steed, in any respect, as a Kentuckian of his station and regard for handsome equipment should have bestridden, and peculiarly noticeable because of an abnormally long and pendulous lower lip. I had never seen such a feature in any specimen of the equine species. It hung down several inches, disclosing the animal's lower teeth, and twitching in a melancholy, protesting sort of fashion. My attention was, of course, attracted by such a spectacle, and I incautiously remarked on it.

"John," I said, "I never in my life saw such a lip as that horse of yours has."

He flared up at once.

"What in the hades is that to you," he shouted. "What have you got to do with it? Am I responsible for his lip? Did I make it? Every blamed fool I meet has something to say about this horse's lip. I believe there are more blamed fools in this army around Bowling Green — especially among the Kentucky troops — than anywhere else in the world."

I hastened to offer profuse and ample apologies, but for a time unsuccessfully. He insisted that I should not mention the subject. "You've got too much lip yourself," he said.

I finally placated him, and we conversed amicably for ten or twelve minutes, and he then said that he must rejoin his train, and rode off. I started in the opposite direction, but in a few seconds I heard him loudly call me. I turned and saw that he had halted and faced about.

"See here," he said, "I've thought this thing over, and have come to the conclusion that I ought to shoot the next man who alludes to this horse's lip. So you be careful not to say anything more about it."

I assured him that I would dismiss the matter entirely from my mind and never again refer to it.

Major Throckmorton had rented a house in Bowling Green, where he and two of his closest friends kept bachelors' hall, and they were living very comfortably indeed. These two gentlemen, Messrs. Oscar Murray and George Grey, were from Louisville, as was the major, and had "refugeed" thence for reasons similar to those which had induced his departure. They were liberal and hospitable in their housekeeping, and were, of course, often visited by their Kentucky friends.

It happened that on Thanksgiving Day of that year General, then Captain Morgan, and myself had ridden early in the morning a considerable distance from our camp on some errand, and returning about noon and finding ourselves in the vicinity of the major's quarters, it occurred to us that we could not do better than call on him, feeling sure that our friends would have on that day an unusually good dinner.

I should explain that, while the sincerest friendship existed between Murray and Throckmorton, which had begun when they were boys and continued throughout their lives, they would often engage in hot debates and "fall out," that is to say, the major would fall out with Murray. These quarrels were never serious; but sometimes they would not speak to each other for a week or more. Then they would become reconciled and their relations would be perfectly harmonious again. We were not aware of it, of course, but our visit occurred while one of these domestic "differences" was pending.

After joining our hosts in a toddy brewed of excellent whiskey, we sat down to a table bountifully spread. A large, beautifully roasted turkey was in front of Major Throckmorton, and Murray was prepared to carve and dispense slices of an excellent ham.

"Captain Morgan," said the major, "will you have some of this turkey?"

Captain Morgan expressed a perfect willingness to accept some.

"Lieutenant Duke," he said, "will you take some?"

I answered promptly "yes." The same question was asked of Mr. Grey, with the same result. Then the major looked up solemnly at the ceiling and remarked in a courteous but chilly tone: "If any one else at this table wants turkey, he can send up his plate," whereupon Mr. Murray's plate was forwarded. Mr. Murray then proceeded to distribute the ham in the same fashion, asking each one, except the major, if he wished a slice of it, concluding by addressing the ceiling with the same formula; and the major's plate was "sent" for ham.

Oscar Murray, although then nearly forty-five years of age, shortly afterward enlisted as a private in Morgan's squadron of cavalry, and served gallantly to the close of the war, sustaining all the toils and hardships of camp and raid as cheerfully as his younger and more vigorous comrades.

Major Throckmorton made an excellent commissary of subsistence, when commissioned and assigned to that duty, although he seasoned the rations he issued with much spicy language. A report was current at one time that General Bragg had threatened to have him shot for some peculiarly independent action — which the fierce old martinet chose to term insubordination — but I think it was merely a "camp rumour."

He lived for several years after the close of the war, becoming more eccentric in temper than ever, but retaining the respect and esteem of his friends to the last.

CHAPTER VII

ONE of the most remarkable men who served in the Confederate army was Gen. Roger W. Hanson, of Kentucky. No officer was more liked and respected by the Kentucky soldiers, or possessed more thoroughly the confidence of his superiors in command. His career previous to the war had been an exceedingly interesting, indeed, in some ways, an erratic one; but in the wildest escapades of his hot and heady youth he retained the regard of his people, and received that indulgence which even the staid citizen extends such offences when he knows the trespasser to be honourable and high-minded. When a very young man he served with distinction in the Mexican War as first lieutenant in the company of Capt. John S. Williams. Williams also became a brigadier-general in the Confederate service, and was an active and excellent officer.

When Hanson returned from Mexico he soon took a leading position at the bar of central Kentucky, and became quite famous, if not successful, as a politician in that region. His early manhood had been so much occupied with more attractive pursuits, that he had not profited, as he might have done, by the educational advantages offered him; but his mind, although unused to the discipline of study, mastered all that it grappled with. Friends and opponents agreed in pronouncing him one of the most effective speakers in the state. While his reading of law was not extensive, he seemed intuitively to comprehend the principles of the science. His vigorous native intellect and acute perception, made him formidable even when lacking professional information. His ideas were always clearly defined and his mind was never in a mist. He had an extraordinary insight into character, and a most remarkable faculty of accurate observation and life-like reproduction, especially of ludicrous traits and incidents. His command of humorous, graphic, and forcible expression was almost unequalled. Hanson had many noble traits of character, was brave, candid, and truthful, and sincerely scorned dissimulation or pretense of any kind.

His personal appearance was singular and striking. In stature, below the medium height, his form was strong and massive but ungraceful. His keen gray eyes and florid complexion indicated a sanguine temperament, and every feature of his face was expressive of energy and determination. A wound received in a duel had shortened one leg, giving him a peculiar jerky gait.

Shortly after the close of the Mexican War, Hanson ran for the legislature against his former comrade and commander, Williams. Both were popular, and Williams was nearly Hanson's equal as a stump speaker. Aware that the support given either because of "military record" would be chiefly accorded the superior in rank, Hanson sought rather to depreciate than exalt the merit in that regard that each might have justly claimed; and especially ridiculed the sobriquet of Cerro Gordo, which had been conferred on Williams because of his conduct in the battle of that name. Williams, on the other hand, discussed such topics with the serious tone of one who expected them to win votes.

Williams asserted that he had captured two six-pounder brass guns at Cerro Gordo. Hanson denied that the pieces had been taken in battle, and declared that Williams, assisted by a big Irishman, had fished them out of a bayou, into which they had been thrown by the Mexicans on their retreat. He gave an extremely picturesque account of how Williams "dived" for them. He also furnished a description of the charge up the hill on the enemy's breastworks, which differed *in toto* from that given by Williams.

"Fellow-citizens," he said, with his hands upon his hips and displaying his rotund and bulky figure to the best advantage, "inasmuch as I have never been active and fleet of foot, I was the last man to reach the top of the hill in that charge — except my captain. But when we fell back I was the first man — except Captain Williams — to get back to the spot whence we started. You will scarcely believe it, but before I ran down that hill I was six feet three inches in height, and as slender as an eagle's talon in the waist; yet, in striving to keep up with my captain, I jumped so far and lit so hard that I was stove up into the figure that you now see."

One incident of this canvass was told me by General Williams himself, and I was not more amused by the story than by the grave manner with which the general related it. Although many years had elapsed, his resentment had evidently not cooled. "Hanson," he said, "had been treating me in anything but a respectable fashion during the entire canvass, and had used language which was very irritating, but which I permitted to pass unnoticed, as I did not think it dignified to give way to anger. My friends, however, finally told me that I must resent it; that further submission to such affronts would injure me. So I made up my mind to summarily stop it upon the first occasion. But, knowing that Hanson was always ready to fight, and would probably resort to violent measures when I denounced him, I went to our next meeting well armed. This debate was to take place at a school-house standing in a small bluegrass pasture and on a gentle hill, at the foot of which was a fine spring of water. The house was crowded and people were congregated about the doors and windows to hear the speeches. I spoke first, and, informing the audience that I would no longer submit to Mr. Hanson's offensive language and manner, proceeded to give him a merciless tongue-lashing.

"Hanson at first seemed surprised and quite indignant. I thought, indeed, that he and his friends, immediately about him, would then and there force a personal encounter on me and those who were prepared to sustain me. He did not do so, however, but in a few minutes left the house, beckoning to his especial coterie to follow him. I saw them go toward the spring, and believed that they meant to take a drink all around, get their weapons ready and return for business. In a short time they did return; but to my intense astonishment showed no disposition to attack me, although I had not concluded my denunciation. Hanson, himself, looked as mild and demure as a reformed gambler, and the others were trying to do the same. I could not imagine what he was after.

"When I concluded, he took the stand, and there was another surprise for me. He began to speak in a quiet, deprecatory way, utterly unlike his usual style, and his voice seemed to tremble with emotion. 'Fellow-citizens,' he said, 'the words and the conduct of Captain Williams to-day have occasioned me great pain, and, also, no little amazement. He knows that, notwithstanding our political differences and rivalry, I feel for him the strongest and warmest personal friendship, as well as that sort of regard which should always obtain between men who have been comrades in arms. It is true that I have sometimes indulged in little, harmless pleasantries, some trivial jocularity at his expense, but never to the extent, I trust, of seeming even to derogate from the high respect in which I hold him.'"

At this point the general interrupted his narrative to exclaim: "Did you ever hear of such hypocrisy? After deluging me with his blackguardly ridicule throughout the entire preceding canvass, to speak of it as 'trivial jocularity'?"

Then he went on with Hanson's speech!

"'But, fellow-citizens, while I did not at first comprehend the meaning of this strange conduct, the true reason for it, after a little reflection, is apparent to me. The arrogant confidence with which Captain Williams entered this canvass has been rudely shaken. He has discovered that his popularity is not so great and his success not so sure as he had fondly supposed. He has discovered that he is every day losing friends upon whose support he had relied. Indeed, he sees defeat staring him in the face, and in his fury and disappointment at such impending humiliation, he is willing to thrust a quarrel upon me, and, if necessary, slay me. "Yes," he said, and pretended to snivel and wipe his eyes; 'yes, fellow-citizens, in his desperation, my old commander even seeks my life. But greatly as his conduct has distressed me, I must, in justice to myself, call your attention to one impression, industriously circulated to my prejudice, which it completely dissipates. It has been asserted that my opponent represents the law and order, moral, and God-fearing people of this community, while I, on the contrary, am the candidate of the less respectable and more reckless element.' With that," said Williams, "he pulled off his coat and vest and pranced around the platform to show that he was unarmed. He even opened his shirt front and turned his breeches pockets wrong side out, and demanded that a committee consisting of my friends should search him. 'And now,' he thundered, 'I challenge my opponent to follow my example.'

"Why, blank it," said the general, "I couldn't afford to do that. Two big pistols and a bowie-knife as long as a scythe blade were buckled around me, and I couldn't call his raise. Hanson guessed," he continued, "so soon as I began to roast him that I was armed. When he went to the spring he probably divested himself of his own weapons — the unreliable wretch — and caught me in a trap that I had really set myself." It was a hot and close contest. Williams won by a majority of only six votes.

Hanson succeeded Gen. John C. Breckinridge in command of the Kentucky infantry, or "Orphan" brigade, as it was popularly designated. He was, in all respects, an exceptionally fine officer, and was a strict and very careful disciplinarian, although somewhat eccentric in his methods. He used to visit the guard house — which he generally kept pretty full of offenders — nearly every morning, and rigidly catechize the inmates, much to their discomfiture, concerning their delinquencies. Once, believing that many complaints of illness were subterfuges on the part of lazy fellows to escape performance of duty, he issued an order that "there should be only two sick men at one time in each company."

He was mortally wounded in the battle of Murfreesboro, gallantly leading his brigade.

A decidedly interesting figure in Kentucky history, in his day and generation, although neither very prominent nor influential, was Gen. Humphrey Marshall, second of that name in the annals of the commonwealth.

It may sound paradoxical, yet it may justly be said, I think, that, while he typified the traits of a large number of his countrymen, he resembled no other individual. Much like the average man in the ordinary emotions of humanity, he was, in his methods of manifesting them and in the impression he produced on other people, utterly unlike any one else. Nor was it so much because he was eccentric, as because, so to speak, he was "in a class by himself." Chief Justice Robertson might have described him as "*Sui generis* and altogether anomalous." He recalled the image of Falstaff in that worthy's best vein, not only because of his obesity and inclination to self-indulgence, his keen acumen and shrewd humour, his manner of mingled swagger and candour, but also in his singular originality of thought and speech: nor was the fat, jolly knight of the Cheapside taverns more witty either in criticism of what others might do, or in excuse of slack performance on his own part.

Intellectually he was a superior, indeed, in many respects, a man of unusual ability. He was a ripe and astute lawyer and a politician of broad views and extensive information, and was surpassed in forensic capacity by few of his contemporaries. He ranked high at the Kentucky bar, and was esteemed one of the ablest debaters in the lower house of congress, in which body he served four terms. He also acquitted himself creditably as Minister to China during Mr. Fillmore's administration.

A graduate of West Point, he was no doubt in his early life a good soldier; at any rate, as colonel of a cavalry regiment in the Mexican War, he earned that reputation. As brigadier-general in the Confederate army he attained no special distinction, nor was he very actively employed. This was perhaps due, more than anything else, to physical incapacity. He was enormously corpulent, weighing nearly three hundred pounds, and consequently unfitted for active command in the field, especially in a mountainous region like eastern Kentucky, where he was stationed during the entire period of his service. He ate frequent and prodigious meals, although quite temperate in the use of liquor; and this inordinate consumption of food was of itself sufficient to incapacitate him for the duties and efforts of an arduous campaign. It also induced a curious condition of mind or body — a peculiar something which would frequently and suddenly assail him, and which he seemed unable to resist. He would fall asleep while in the midst of a conversation, and sometimes when on his feet. On such occasions, however, he would retain an erect position, although with eyes closed, snoring audibly, and exhibiting every evidence of slumber for several minutes. Then awakening and appearing to be conscious of all that had transpired during his brief sleep, he would resume the subject he had been discussing at the moment the drowsy god overcame him, and even answer remarks addressed him while apparently asleep.

An amusing instance is related of how President Davis took advantage of this peculiarity of General Marshall to escape, making what might have proven an unpleasant if not embarrassing avowal. Mr. Davis had removed him from command of the Department of Eastern Kentucky, without stating any particular reason for so doing; whereupon the general betook himself post-haste to Richmond, to ask an explanation of such action, and obtain, if possible, a revocation of the order and reinstatement in his former command. Mr. Davis knew him quite well and liked him, as indeed did almost every one who knew him.

Marshall repaired to the executive office, requested an interview, which was immediately granted, and proceeded to state his case, trusting that he would speedily convince the President that his removal had been a grave mistake. That he might have documentary proof to sustain his contention that his military administration had been without fault, he brought his order book along with him; and read numerous letters and orders therefrom in the course of his argument. Mr. Davis was very busy, but feeling constrained to treat his visitor courteously, listened with as much patience as he could muster.

Finally becoming interested in some letter Marshall had read, Mr. Davis requested permission to read it over himself, and took the book for that purpose. When he had finished reading and was prepared to return the book, he discovered that Marshall, who was occupying an extremely comfortable chair — was fast asleep. Mr. Davis was careful not to awaken him, but resumed his own work.

After sleeping fifteen or twenty minutes Marshall roused up and began again with his statement. But the President now knew how to handle him, and in the course of a few minutes again asked leave to look at the book. He had scarcely gotten it into his hands before Marshall was in the Land of Nod once more.

It is said that this programme was pursued for two or three days, until Marshall, despairing of finishing his argument, ceased all efforts to do so, and the President was spared the necessity of making a disagreeable explanation.

To Gen. William Preston, who was one of his warmest friends, Marshall's peculiarities furnished inexhaustible amusement,

Preston never wearied of describing a visit he once made him at his headquarters in the Kentucky mountains. Preston had great difficulty in getting to Marshall's camp, which was pitched in a very out of the way place. Marshall was at that time very apprehensive of being superseded, and was constantly expecting that some officer of superior rank would be sent to take command over him. So when Preston asked why he had posted his troops in a spot so much out of the line of usual travel, he answered that it was "for strategic reasons."

"Why," said Preston, "are you so much afraid of the Yankees as that?"

"It isn't the Yankees I'm trying to avoid," replied Marshall. "I'm dodging Confederate major-generals."

Preston subsequently expressed surprise that Marshall wished to remain anywhere in the mountains.

"You know," he said, "that these people here are inveterate Union men and very wild and savage, and much given to shooting from ambush at those who don't agree with them in politics. Of course, they will wish to shoot you; and they will be apt to recognize you, and cannot easily miss you, on account of your unusual size."

Marshall looked very grave and seemed much troubled for a while after Preston had expressed this opinion. Finally, however, his face lighted up, and he said, with a sly twinkle of the eye: "Preston, I know how to fool these bushwhackers and protect myself."

"How will you do it?" inquired Preston. "I'll surround myself with fat staff officers," replied the corpulent chieftain, perfectly willing to sacrifice his entire staff in obedience to the first law of nature.

With all of his strong sense and somewhat caustic humour, a certain simplicity characterized, at times, his utterances, which was extremely entertaining. He was a devout believer in spiritual manifestations, and a frequent attendant of the seances where such believers met and indulged their inclination for the marvellous. He was generally accompanied on such occasions by a friend, himself an excellent lawyer and very nearly Marshall's equal intellectually, and quite as devout a spiritualist. This gentleman had a voice which, naturally about as devoid of melody as a voice could well be, had been injured rather than improved by cultivation.

Nevertheless, when the efforts of the medium to invoke any expression or recognition from the invisible visitants supposed to be hovering in the vicinity, failed of effect, he would sing; fondly supposing that the spirits could be attracted by music of the right sort. He knew only two songs, and sang both to much the same air. It was his theory that good and pious spirits were summoned when he gave out, "Am I a Soldier of the Cross," and that if there were any disreputable spirits around, "Shinbone Alley" would fetch them.

One night, after he had repeated each song several times, there was a full and sufficient response and a most candid communication was received. Whereupon General Marshall remarked, sotto voce, to the man sitting next him in the circle: "The spirits seem to like Tom's singing. That would indicate that however intelligent and accomplished they may be in other respects, they are d — d poor judges of vocalism."

On another occasion, having dropped some remark which, he was gravely assured, the spirits would deem offensive, he formally and seriously apologized to "all spirits that might be present"; and declared that he wouldn't wound the feelings of any respectable spirit for the world.

It is to be regretted that no spoken or written production of Humphrey Marshall has been preserved; but he was indolent, averse to systematic labour, and utterly careless about such record; and his memory will survive only in tradition.

The memory of George W. Johnson, the first provisional governor of Kentucky, should be preserved and revered by all those who sympathized with the cause for which he died, and all who honour the most exalted type of Southern manhood. While his connection with the fortunes of the Confederacy was brief, and not of such nature as to attract especial historic mention, it was to those who knew the man, the nobility of his character, and the purity and sincerity of his motives — who knew also the circumstances under which it was formed — exceedingly interesting, rendered more so by its early and tragic conclusion.

He was a native of Scott County, Ky., and one of the

most popular representatives of a large and influential family of his own name. He was well known not only in the immediate community in which he resided, but throughout the state. A true, brave, honest man, exhibiting in his every word and act the staunchest and most virile qualities; a gentleman in the best and completest meaning of the term, cultured, amiable, and generous, he was universally liked and respected.

Possessed of an ample fortune and with leisure to indulge every wish and taste, devoted to his wife and children, beloved by his friends, susceptible by temperament to every rational pleasure, and ever desirous of making those about him happy, he was peculiarly adapted to enjoy in the fullest measure that idyllic life of the wealthy Virginia and Kentucky planter of the ante-bellum days, and there seemed to be something unusually pathetic in the sudden fate which removed him from it.

Among the pleasantest recollections of my boyhood are the visits I used to make his home, one of the most beautiful in the finest part of the lovely bluegrass country. He was accustomed to dispense a hospitality rarely equalled even in that region and period, and his manly form, courteous manner, and kindly face made it doubly attractive.

The young people were especially devoted to him. Among other attractions to them were two or three unusually large ponds stocked with fish. To the youth of the neighbourhood these were irresistibly alluring and they flocked there from all the country around. These sheets of water were kept in good condition by Mr. Johnson more for the pleasure of his youthful friends, whom he numbered by the score, than for his own use, and they were given the largest liberty to fish and bathe.

In this delightful home, surrounded by his friends, he lived until nearly fifty years of age without a trouble or care to disturb the tranquil tenor of a life passed in good and charitable work, and then, at the call of what he esteemed an imperative duty, sacrificed every personal interest in behalf of the cause to which he felt that he owed every thing.

Mr. Johnson had, from his earliest manhood, taken an earnest and active part in politics, but while repeatedly solicited to accept office, had invariably declined to do so. An ardent Democrat, he had been as instrumental, perhaps, as any man in

Kentucky, in converting the state to Democracy after its long domination by the old Whig party. His high character and earnest purpose, as well as his zeal and undaunted determination, united to more than ordinary ability, at once gained him leadership in the Democratic ranks, and no one's influence was more thoroughly recognized in the councils of the party, or more potent.

He was offered by acclamation the nomination for lieutenant-governor, and also for congress, when the election to either position would have been assured and easy; but he declined both proffers, not because he was averse to public service or indifferent to popular favour, but because he had no ambition for official preferment, and wisely chose the quiet and comfort of a private life in which he was as much or more honoured than he could have been in any public station. He was an earnest and effective speaker, with that sort of eloquence which attends courage, sincerity, and absolute conviction. So lovable and affectionate was his nature that even in that fiercely partisan period many of his political opponents were his warmest personal friends.

Although a states' rights Democrat of the strictest sect, he, like the great majority of Kentuckians, had little sympathy with the theory of secession, and listened with no favour to any such suggestion until it became apparent that the long and bitter controversy between the sections would culminate in armed conflict. Then without hesitation he took the part of the South.

On August 18, 1861, a meeting was held in Scott County, Ky., of a number of prominent Democrats; and after a full discussion of the situation, it was determined to send commissioners to Washington and to Richmond, with a view of ascertaining, if possible, whether the neutrality of Kentucky would be respected by both sides. Upon the recommendation of this conference, Governor Magoffin appointed Frank K. Hunt and W. A. Dudley, of Lexington, both Union men, as commissioners to Washington, and George W. Johnson, commissioner to Richmond.

In the letter which President Davis sent in response to that written him by Governor Magoffin, and borne by Mr. Johnson, appears the following language, which certainly very logically and properly summed up the situation:

> The government of the Confederate states has not only respected most scrupulously the neutrality of Kentucky, but has continued to maintain the friendly relation of trade and intercourse which it has suspended with the people of the United States generally. In view of the history of the past, it can scarcely be necessary to assure your excellency that the government of the Confederate states will continue to respect the neutrality of Kentucky so long as her people will maintain it themselves. But neutrality, to be entitled to respect, must be strictly maintained by both parties; or if the door be opened on the one side to aggression of one of the belligerent parties upon the other, it ought not to be shut to the assailed when they seek to enter it for purposes of self-defence.

Mr. Lincoln replied that he did not believe that it was "the popular wish of Kentucky that the Federal force already there should be removed, and with this impression I must decline to remove it."

This declaration made it plain to men of all shades of political opinion in Kentucky that the occupation of the state by Federal troops would be continued, and that their number would be increased, not only to completely suppress any sentiment in favour of the Confederacy and action taken in that behalf, but in order to make Kentucky a base of military operations against the states farther south. In a very short time after this declaration by Mr. Lincoln, numerous arrests were made of Kentuckians of known Southern sympathies, or of prominent men who ventured even to question the legality of the aggressive acts committed by the Union leaders.

George W. Johnson was one of the first and boldest to denounce such tyranny. He escaped arrest only by quitting his home and seeking the Tennessee border within a few hours before the soldiers who were ordered to make him prisoner arrived at his house.

On the 18th of November, 1861, a Sovereignty Convention was held at Russellville, Kentucky, composed of delegates from sixty-five counties of the state. It adopted an ordinance of secession and a provisional form of state government. George W. Johnson was elected governor.

This state government so organized, did not, of course, establish itself permanently within the limits of the state, or remain here very long, but of necessity followed the movements of the Confederate army under the command of Gen. Albert Sidney Johnston. All of its officials were present at the battle of Shiloh. Governor Johnson determined to take personal part in the conflict and volunteered to serve as an aide on the staff of Col. R. P. Trabue, who commanded a brigade composed in great part of Kentucky troops. His horse was killed under him early in the day, and, procuring a musket, he then attached himself to Capt. Ben Monroe's company "E" of the Fourth Kentucky infantry, and fought on foot in the front of the battle until he received his fatal wound. In the long and stubborn fighting when this brigade was engaged with heavy forces of the enemy and where it lost so heavily, Governor Johnson was one of the victims. His body was pierced by a musket ball, disabling him and inflicting a mortal wound. He lived, however, until the next day, lying upon the spot where he fell: in the rush and tumult of battle the wounded had not been removed. He was there recognized, shortly before his death, by General McCook, of the Federal army, who had become acquainted with him at the Democratic convention held at Charleston the previous year, and, like all who ever met him, had conceived for him a strong friendship. General McCook caused him to be removed to one of the boats lying at the landing and tenderly cared for, but his hurt was beyond surgical aid, and in a short time he died.

A braver, nobler, more patriotic spirit never ascended to Heaven.

I saw, some days since, an article in which reference was made to an officer whom I knew very well, and who was certainly one of the most picturesque figures of the Civil War. This was Col. George St. Leger Grenfell, an Englishman who came to America in the spring of 1862 for the purpose of serving in the Confederate army.

He brought letters of introduction to General Lee, and when he explained the kind of service to which he had been most accustomed, and which he would like to follow here, the general sent him to Morgan, with the request that he be given every opportunity to gratify his rather extraordinary appetite for hazardous adventure.

Morgan fell in love with him at first sight, and immediately took him upon his staff. He became assistant adjutant-general of the brigade which was afterward organized, but left us before the organization of the division.

His previous career had been remarkable, and, indeed, romantic; and, as he related it, as he did to me, when we had become well acquainted, I thought I had never heard or read anything more interesting in its way. His eldest brother, who was much older than himself, had been an officer in the English army, and had served under Wellington in the latter part of the war in Spain. Wellington, as is well known, was a severe and uncompromising disciplinarian; and in warfare like that which was then being waged in the peninsula, when it was as important to conciliate the native population as to keep his army in condition, he seems to have been unusually strict. At a time when rations were very meager, young Grenfell's servant took a kid from a Spanish peasant for his master's mess. The Spaniard complained, and Welling ascertaining that Grenfell had been the beneficiary of the loot had him court-martialled. This was a matter of so much mortification to his father that the old gentleman refused to permit his younger son, George St. Leger, to enter the English army. This lad, however, feeling an irresistible inclination toward a military life, quitted home at an early age and enlisted in a French cavalry corps in Algeria. He served in some of the bloodiest battles of that period when France was establishing her rule in northern Africa. At the expiration of his term of enlistment, however, having become, in a manner, naturalized, he concluded to try civil life among the Moors and became a resident and citizen of the City of Tangiers. Although not a convert to the faith of Mahomet, he was quite willing, with a broad cosmopolitan view of social matters, to conform to the prevalent customs of the community in which he dwelt, and accordingly became connected by marriage with a number of the first and most influential families of the place. When, subsequently, the French attacked and bombarded the town, he assisted in its defence, and the battery he commanded inflicted a good deal of damage on the besiegers.

Although he had been discharged from the French service several years previously, the French, very illogically, chose to regard him as a deserter and threatened him with military punishment. Escaping their clutches, however, he made his way to Abd-El-Kader, the Kabyle leader, and remained for more than four years with that celebrated chieftain, for whom he expressed the warmest admiration.

After Abd-El-Kader's final surrender he quitted Algeria, but still continued the career of a soldier of fortune. He fought the Riffe pirates off the coast of Morocco, and then served with Garibaldi in South America. Finally, tiring of this irregular and barbarous strife, and desirous of "settling down" to a more Christian and civilized kind of warfare, he returned home and sought and obtained a commission in the English service. He fought in India during the greater part of the Sepoy rebellion, and then in the Crimean war, attaining the rank of lieutenant-colonel.

When the Civil War in this country began, he found it utterly impossible to deny himself such an excellent opportunity for occupation and excitement in his favourite vocation, and, resigning his commission, came over here. Inasmuch as he sympathized thoroughly with the South, he at once espoused the Confederate cause.

When he joined Morgan he was nearly sixty years old, but showed no sign of age or failing physical powers; indeed, he seemed to be in the full vigour of manhood. The description in "Ivanhoe" of the personal appearance of the Templar, Brian de Bois Guilbert, would serve quite accurately for him. He was tall, erect, and of thoroughly military bearing. His frame was spare, but sinewy and athletic, and he preserved the activity of youth. His bold, aquiline features were scorched by the Eastern sun to a swarthy hue, and his face, while handsome, wore always a defiant and sometimes fierce expression.

He proved an exceeding efficient officer, energetic and constant in his attention to duty. His great experience in a service somewhat similar to ours — he always said the Confederate cavalry raids reminded him of the expeditions made by Abd-El-Kader into the territory held by the French — was of benefit when he acted as Morgan's chief of staff. His gallantry in battle was superb. I shall never forget the first time I witnessed his conduct in this respect. It was at Tompkinsville, the first fight Morgan made on his July raid into Kentucky. Gano had gone to the rear of the enemy with his Texans; a Georgia battalion of cavalry which was with us under Col. Archibald Hunt, who was mortally wounded in the action, was charging in excellent style on the left, and my regiment was pressing hard on the right. I did not permit it to open fire until we were within sixty yards of the enemy, and just at that moment Grenfell spurred his horse forward between the two lines, risking the fire of both, leaped a low fence behind which the enemy were lying, and began slashing at them right and left with his sabre.

It was because of something which occurred in this fight that a rather curious point of military ethics was raised. Major Jordan, of Wyncoop's regiment of Pennsylvania cavalry, was wounded and captured by a part of Gano's squadron. By the way, he behaved very courageously. Just after the fight was over he was brought to Morgan, and immediately preferred a complaint against his captors that they "had violated the rules of civilized warfare." "In what respect," said Morgan. "Why, they fired on me and my men with double-barrelled shot-guns, loaded with buckshot."

Gano's men were much surprised by this accusation, not because it wasn't true, but rather because it was. "D — n the Yanks," they said; "do they expect us to load our guns with bird shot?"

The stories that might be told illustrative of Grenfell's reckless eccentricity would fill a book, and nearly every man who knew him has an especial one to tell. I shall relate only one. During Bragg's campaign in Kentucky and for, perhaps, a month after we returned to Tennessee, he suffered severely from a bone felon on the forefinger of his left hand. He tried to have the surgeons amputate the finger, but, to his disgust and anger, they all refused to do so, saying that while the recovery would be tedious, it was sure. Finally he determined to perform the operation himself, and placing his finger on a block he chopped it off with a keen-edged knife which he habitually carried.

On the day afterward he had occasion to thrash his landlord on account of some misunderstanding, and also to chastise a brother Englishman about a mule. Notwithstanding his disabled left hand, he accomplished both transactions with one fist and without the use of weapons.

After he left Morgan's command, General Bragg made him inspector of all the cavalry of his army, which position he held for two or three months, and then, going east, served for a short time with the Army of Northern Virginia. In the latter part of 1863, he concluded to seek other fields of adventure; and, as he had never regularly enlisted in the Confederate army, had no difficulty in leaving.

He went into the Northern states, wishing to see something of them before returning to England, and in Chicago met with Captains Castleman and Hines of Morgan's command, who were there planning the release of the Confederate prisoners in Camp Douglas. He knew them both very well, of course, and so soon as he learned what they were doing volunteered to assist. The hazard of such an enterprise irresistibly appealed to him.

Unfortunately the plot was discovered, and Grenfell was arrested and tried by court-martial. He narrowly escaped a death sentence, but received one nearly as severe, and which eventually resulted in his death. He was sent to the terrible prison of the Dry Tortugas for life. After remaining there six or eight months, he attempted, with three or four others, to escape in an open boat. Just after they had put out to sea, a tremendous storm arose, and as none of the party was ever heard of again, it is supposed that all were lost.

His old comrades of the Morgan command still warmly remember him.

Few officers were better and more favourably known to the Kentucky troops than Col. J. Stoddard Johnston and no staff officer in the Army of Tennessee, perhaps, won a juster reputation for gallant and efficient conduct; none certainly was more popular. He served successively on the staff of General Bragg, and as chief of staff to General Breckinridge and then to General Echols, and all of them bore testimony to his capacity to furnish judicious counsel, as well as render valuable service on the field and in the office. A nephew of Albert Sidney Johnston, it was to be expected indeed that he should evince military aptitude and an inclination toward a martial career.

It is not, however, of Colonel Johnston's service in the army that I propose to tell, but of some incidents with which he was connected just before it began, and of his introduction to military life. He did not enter the Confederate service during the first year of the war because his presence was imperatively required at home. His father-in-law, George W. Johnson, had been elected provisional governor of Kentucky in pursuance of the programme by which it was attempted to make her a Confederate state, and every Kentucky Confederate must remember his heroic death at Shiloh, where he fell, musket in hand, fighting in the ranks of one of the Kentucky infantry regiments. Both of Governor Johnson's sons had enlisted at an early date, so that the only male member of the family who could remain and care for it was Colonel Johnston. He suceeded in doing so for the first twelve months, despite his decided and well known Southern proclivities, and his frank expression of them, but finally fate and his convictions led him into the Southern ranks.

While he was still occupying the position of "armed neutrality," Morgan made his first raid into Kentucky and reached Georgetown in Scott county, near which place Colonel Johnston was then living. He was the acknowledged leader and mentor of the Southern sympathizers in that locality; they were guided entirely by his advice, and their policy, so far as they had one, was shaped by him. They had already suffered considerably at the hands of the provost-marshals appointed for that region, numerous arrests had been made, and several of the more prominent rebels had been sent to Northern prisons; and a feeling of great uneasiness and apprehension was, of course, prevailing among those who were as yet unmolested. There was, therefore, a general and very natural disposition to reap every possible advantage from the presence of General Morgan and his command in their midst, and every one looked to Colonel Johnston to devise the best method by which it might be done.

The colonel fully appreciated the necessity of accomplishing what was expected of him, and felt also that his reputation was at stake. So he straightway prepared for General Morgan's signature one of the most impressive proclamations probably ever issued, and which General Morgan, of course, readily agreed to adopt and promulge. In this document Colonel Johnston stated, or had General Morgan state, that "the present occupation of Kentucky by the Confederate forces will be permanent," and that, by a prompt and graceful evacuation of her territory the Federal authorities might avert the unnecessary effusion of blood. They were, therefore, fraternally invited to adopt this wise and beneficent course; and Colonel Johnston, that is to say, General Morgan, on his part promised to use his victory mildly, to be just, moderate, and humane in his treatment of all Union men, to respect their rights in every particular and make no retaliatory arrests because of the previous imprisonment of Southern sympathizers. The proclamation pointed out clearly and with irrefutable logic the absolute certainty of speedy Confederate success, and with unusual eloquence urged the propriety of submitting to the inevitable and accepting a situation that no human effort could prevent.

General Morgan duly signed this paper and did all in his power to give it wide circulation.

But in the course of three or four days after it was issued, a practical contradiction of some of its provisions became necessary. Although Morgan had been uniformly successful, he found himself encompassed by a host of enemies, forces vastly superior numerically, to his own. The objects of the raid had also been accomplished; so instead of waiting until the enemy should accept the advice tendered him in the proclamation; viz., to "promptly evacuate the state," he concluded to do so himself and return with all possible celerity to Dixie.

This necessitated the promulgation of another proclamation which should explain, although, of course, not retract, the first one. But Colonel Johnston was equal to the occasion. He immediately prepared a second and even more powerful statement, in which General Morgan quite frankly admitted that because of the receipt of very important information from General Bragg, which he had not anticipated, his presence was imperatively required in Tennessee, and that the permanent occupation of Kentucky by the Confederate forces "must therefore be postponed for a brief period," at the proper time, however, it would be taken up again just where it had been left off, and the whole programme as previously indicated would be faithfully performed.

In the meantime he trusted that all parties would remember the generous and benevolent policy to which he had pledged himself in the first proclamation, and that such recollection would inure to the benefit of his friends, and insure them clement treatment. He felt it his duty, however, to say very plainly, that if this was not done, and any Southern sympathizer was in any manner molested, the bitterest reprisals would be instituted.

Not only would Union men be arrested and incarcerated in retaliation, but the Federal evacuation of Kentucky, instead of being permitted in a peaceable and bloodless fashion, would be harassed by angry and resentful Confederates until the line of retreat would be marked with gore in a way that would make the footprints of the American army at Valley Forge seem a mere faint and colourless trail in comparison. Colonel Johnston, and vicariously, General Morgan, appeared to entertain a profound personal feeling in this matter of arrest and imprisonment, and the proclamation unmistakably indicated it. The colonel had been for some time quietly making his preparations to go south and join the army, but the discovery by the enemy — the Yanks always found out everything — that he was the author of the proclamation, hastened his departure.

Soon after Morgan's departure, therefore, the colonel followed. The excitement created by the raid had not yet subsided, and the suspicion with which all nomadic strangers were regarded at that period was stronger than ever in the region through which he had to pass, and which was inhabitated by people almost entirely Union in sentiment. The Federal cavalry also traversed all that country, stopping every wayfarer they met and asking very inconvenient questions. So that Colonel Johnston found that he must be abnormally wary and circumspect, and that "Eternal vigilance was the price of liberty."

He had as travelling companion and guide a man named Parker — Bill Parker — who was one of General Bragg's spies, and, in that capacity, was often sent into Kentucky. The Colonel knew Bill's employment, but he also knew his antebellum reputation, which was exceedingly unsavoury, and that spies sometimes did business on both sides. Consequently, he was never free of the fear of betrayal, and while looking out for the Yankees, never failed to keep a "weather eye" on Bill. They got along very well, however. The colonel sometimes represented himself as a cattle buyer, and on other occasions told a pathetic story of how he was on his way south, with the hope of reclaiming a wayward and misguided younger brother who had run away to the Confederate army. Parker could play many parts. He frequently prayed and exhorted; and, when he got into congenial company, drank and gambled. Finally they reached that region of Tennessee in which Morgan's command was then stationed and stopped for the night at Sparta, at the house of Colonel Debrell. Parker learned from the family that the Confederates were encamped in the immediate vicinity, but did not impart that information to Johnston, who retired to bed under the impression that he was still surrounded by enemies. News of their arrival was shortly brought to our camp, and Col. W. C. P. Breckinridge, Captain Jennings, and myself at once proceeded to call on them, to welcome Johnston to the Confederacy, and also hoping to receive some message from our families.

When we reached the house they were both, of course, fast asleep, thoroughly exhausted by their long and arduous journey. We awakened Parker first. So soon as he was completely aroused and had answered a few questions, he said: "Gentlemen, Stoddard Johnston is upstairs, and he don't know that he's safe and among friends. He thinks the Yankees are all around here, and you can have a power of fun out of him."

I should state that while Colonel Johnston knew Breckinridge and myself intimately, he had never seen Jennings. Jennings was a tall and very imposing-looking man, with a full, long, red beard, which swept down to his waist, and was wearing on that occasion the blue uniform coat of a Federal officer.

Parker asked if Johnston knew Jennings, and, when told that he did not, suggested that we should repair to his room, awaken him and pass off Jennings as a Yankee captain who had come to arrest him. It was a mean thing to do, but rough jokes are the fashion in war times, and we all agreed to it. We found Johnston sleeping the sleep, if not of the just, at least of the very weary, and made our arrangements without disturbing him. We stationed Jennings at the foot of the bed so that Johnston's eyes should fall upon him immediately on being aroused and placed the candles so that their light should shine full on the blue coat and red beard. The others kept out of sight. When the tableau was prepared one of the party shook Johnston roughly and, in a gruff voice, demanded that he give an account of himself. He sat up in bed slowly and rubbed his eyes, but when he caught sight of Jennings, who was frowning ominously, he uttered a hoarse roar and became as alert as a nighthawk. And he at once determined on his course.

"But half awakened yet
Sprang in his mind the momentary wit."

"Gentlemen," he said, "I fear that you are about to make a fearful mistake. You are about to arrest an innocent and a loyal man. Do not be deceived by anything that man Parker tells you. He is utterly unworthy of credit and belief, and talks too much anyhow. I am a quiet, inoffensive farmer from Indiana, and ——"

Here there was a general burst of laughter, and Breckinridge and I made our appearance. He gazed in astonishment for a moment and then gave a wide grin of relief.

"Oh, you rascals," he said, "you thought you were playing a good joke on me, but I understood it all the time. I fooled you completely. I told Parker yesterday that when I got here I was going to work something of this kind on you."

CHAPTER VIII

SOME of those, who, during the Civil War, were residents of central Kentucky or middle Tennessee, may remember the *Vidette*, a so-called newspaper as always of unique appearance and altogether original management. It came out during the years 1862 and 1863, at irregular intervals, but always simultaneously with the presence of Morgan's command in the locality where it happened to be published. It had no fixed place of publication, but was nomadic, for the reason that certain members of Morgan's command printed, edited, and issued it, only when there came a lull in the more serious business in which they were engaged, and they were so fortunate as to procure the means and material necessary to the make-up of this quasi-periodical.

As might have been expected in an experiment of this nature — an attempt to run a newspaper upon partisan cavalry lines — the circulation was uncertain and limited, and entirely unsuccessful, of course, from a commercial standpoint. It nevertheless afforded great entertainment to its publishers and their comrades, and also to the country people in the vicinity of the little towns in which it was successively printed. The cavalry and their rustic friends expected its appearance with great interest and pleasure. The townspeople, on the other hand — regarded it with a good-natured indifference, such as became those who were in closer touch with the world and knew more of what was going on in it.

Its publication was suggested by some of our fellows having found, in a deserted building in Hartsville, Tenn., upon our first visit to that delightful place, a printing press and a lot of type, the property of a gentleman who had, just previously to the breaking out of the war, been the proprietor and publisher of the Hartsville *Weekly* — I forget the rest — but it was said to have been a very lively and able paper. Inasmuch as this journalist was an ardent patriot, and of a disposition even more bellicose than literary, he had, at the first tap of the drum, abandoned his business, his sanctum, and the tools of this trade to whomsoever might choose to become his successor — indeed, without giving a thought to what became of them — and enlisted in the Confederate army. He was carrying a musket in a Tennessee infantry regiment and still pouring hot shot into the Yankees, in a way, perhaps, more unpleasant to them than his former scathing editorial attacks could have been, even had these terrible invectives been read beyond the confines of Sumner County.

Gordon E. Niles, the then acting adjutant of the Second Kentucky Cavalry, was a practical printer and newspaper man. He was a native of New York State, and at the time the "unpleasantness" culminated was conducting a paper at Lockport, N. Y. But he was an uncompromising states' rights Democrat and ardently sympathized with the South. He was also as impetuous as he was brave and sincere, so at the earliest opportunity he made his way to the Confederacy and joined Morgan. When Niles saw the press and type his professional instinct urged him to utilize them, and as there were five or six printers in the regiment he had no difficulty in organizing a good working force. There was some difficulty in regard to the editorial staff — that is to say, in keeping it within due limits — as a large number of brilliant and ambitious young writers wished to be on it, and all of them wanted to write the leading articles.

The chief trouble Niles had, and after him his successors, was to procure ink and paper. There was a great scarcity of paper in the South, and that which was to be had in the small towns was so coarse and inferior as scarcely to deserve the term. It was not easy to distinguish a large sheet of it from one side of a gunny bag. Such paper as could be gotten was also of every conceivable colour except white. Some of it exhibited a decided hue of one tint, some of another. So that the *Vidette* presented an exceedingly variegated and attractive aspect and its columns were full of colour.

Niles, poor fellow, did not long survive the inauguration of the enterprise in which he felt so much interest. He was killed soon afterward before the Stockade at Edgefield Junction, pierced with five balls. He was suceeded as editor-in-chief by Captain, afterward Col. Robert A. Alston.

Alston had peculiar views about how to run a paper which

hardly accorded with those now in vogue. He adhered very closely to fact, it is true, when publishing anything of practical importance to the command — general orders, etc. — but in other matters he seemed to think that facts were impedimental if not misleading. He indulged in pleasing prognostications of certain success and profound and instructive speculations concerning the national future of the Confederacy, and the influence of the South would exert upon the history of the world. All of this accorded with the hopes and confident expectations of his readers. So the tone of the *Vidette* never admitting the possibility of disaster and frequently announcing Confederate victories even before they occurred, made it a very popular journal with those who habitually received it.

The topics which received most attention in this little paper were those, of course, more directly relating to the cavalry service, and especially the movements of our own command. The events of our marches, raids, scouts, and combats were duly chronicled; every incident of interest, in short, of campaigning experience, of personal adventure and personal prowess was narrated. The operations of the contending armies and the conduct of the commanders on both sides were freely discussed and criticized; and marvellously original plans of campaigns were suggested and explained with a strategic ability which, strange to say, never obtained recognition.

No one could read the *Vidette* without becoming impressed with its generous desire to give sound, wholesome advice to Federal as well as Confederate authorities. It evinced a singularly honest and impartial inclination in this respect, which did its managers great credit. This spirit was well illustrated by an exceedingly profound article upon the removal of General Buell from command of the Federal army in Tennessee just after the conclusion of Bragg's invasion of Kentucky. The writer pointed out, with great power and perspicuity, how ill-advised was the action of Mr. Lincoln in this regard, and demonstrated the evil results to the cause of the Union which would certainly follow. It was couched in a tone of indignant remonstrance that might have induced the belief that it was written by some staff officer of Buell, but for the fact that, in conclusion, the writer urged upon Mr. Davis the propriety of removing General Bragg.

It must be admitted that in political discussion the editors of the *Vidette* adopted a style more caustic and acrimonious, and sometimes employed language more virulent than was exactly in accordance with the demands of an austere taste. But it must be remembered that it is the fashion of the camp to speak candidly, and the writers were generally in haste and had little time to select discreet and temperate phraseology.

Inasmuch as, for reasons that can be well understood, the *Vidette* had no exchange list, there can be scarcely a doubt that the great dailies of the North rarely, if ever, had an opportunity to examine its columns. This, perhaps, spared those papers some pangs; it may even have been that it prevented Horace Greeley from calling those in charge of the *Vidette* "liars and villains." Prentice, on one occasion, excited by a proclamation from General Morgan threatening retaliation for certain conduct on the part of the Federal cavalry, and which was published in the *Vidette*, resorted to the use of language as strong and as unceremonious as that employed by the parties he was denouncing. His feeling was perhaps aggravated by the fact that a copy of this issue was smuggled to him through the lines; and he saw himself referred to as the probable instigator of the outrages for which reprisal was threatened.

I can remember no other instance in which the existence of the *Vidette* was recognized by its more noted contemporaries. I am inclined to believe that none of them was aware of how greatly journalism was being enriched and benefited by its contributions.

There was not much of what is technically termed "sport" in the army. The life of the soldier was both strenuous and simple, and little time was given or opportunity afforded for amusement; although the boys were strangely contented with their tough work and hard fare, and inclined to be jolly under circumstances that the civilian would scarcely suppose likely to induce such feeling. I remember being much impressed with a story told me in the winter of '62-'63, which curiously illustrated their propensity to find fun in even painful situations. One of my couriers had paid a visit to Manchester, Tennessee, where the "Orphan" brigade was then encamped, to see a brother who belonged to Capt. John H. Weller's company of the Kentucky infantry.

When he returned, I questioned him about what he had seen and learned, being, of course, interested in all that concerned my Kentucky brethren. He gave me a very succinct account of the condition of affairs in the brigade, and when I asked if the boys were in good spirits, answered; "Oh, the best in the world, sir. I never seen men enjoy themselves more. While I was there I seen 'em pull Captain Weller's tooth — he'd been havin' the toothache bad; it was a big jaw-tooth and awful hard to git out. They set him straddle of a log and two men held his arms while Bill Smith yanked at the tooth with a bullet mould."

"Well," I said, "I can't understand what there was in that to cause men to enjoy themselves."

"Oh, no, of course not, sir; not just in that. But when Bill histed him off of the log and drug him ten feet before the tooth come, he made a face and spit out a howl what would have made a dog laugh."

With the cavalry, when idle in camp, horse-racing was much in vogue, although, of course, strictly against orders, and therefore carried on clandestinely as a rule. Inasmuch, however, as it was inhibited, not upon moral grounds, or because it was prejudical to discipline, but in order that the horses might be kept in serviceable condition, it was in some cases, at least, connived at when no such result was likely to follow. Some of the regiments were the proud stockholders of very fleet ponies, which, when occasion offered, were matched against one another. Such events were very exciting, and large sums in Confederate money usually changed hands when they came off. Cock-fighting was a more favourite pastime with the infantry, and had the advantage that a beaten competitor could be utilized to improve the scanty Confederate ration. Cards, of course, were in general use among the soldiers of every branch of the service, and it was astonishing how long a pack would last, perhaps because more tenderly handled, and the men played on blankets instead of tables.

The most diverting and comical sight I ever witnessed during the war in the way of sport, however, was a gander-pulling conducted by the men of Morgan's squadron, on Christmas Day, 1861. It was an event of stirring interest and drew crowds of spectators from all the neighbouring commands. A stalwart, middle-aged gander, with a neck as stringy and tough as a piece of commissary beef, was suspended head down from a swinging limb. The contestants, eight or ten in number, put up a silver dollar each, and were entitled to pull in turn until some one of them should jerk off the bird's head, the winner of course, to receive the entire amount put up. They were mounted and required to ride at full gallop under the gander, snatching at him as they went by. They were prohibited by the rules of the game from halting or even slackening speed as they passed, and to enforce this regulation two men provided with stout, long, black-snake whips stood at each side of the path and belaboured his horse if any rider evinced the least inclination to go slow.

The gander dodged with wonderful adroitness, which made it extremely difficult to get hold of him, and as his neck was well soaped, it was almost impossible to maintain a grip upon it after it was obtained. After many unsuccessful efforts, the contestants began to lose temper under the laughter and jeers of the spectators. At length one big fellow came to a dead stop at the tree, and seizing the gander's neck with both hands, deliberately strove to twist it off. The whip bearers lashed his horse soundly, but gripping the horse, which was small and scarcely stronger than himself, tightly with his knees, the rider, notwithstanding the animal's plunges, held him firmly to the spot, and retained his grasp on the gander. There was at once a loud protest from the competitors and the by-standers, and many cries of foul; the offender gave no heed and still hung on. He might have succeeded in wringing off the gander's head but for something which effectually diverted his attention, and which, whether accidental or intentional, was well calculated to have that effect. It is to be expected, of course, that the nether garments of a cavalry man in active service will wear somewhat thin in the seat, and this was especially the matter with that big fellow's breeches.

By an unusually violent plunge he was suddenly thrown forward in a horizontal position along his horse's back, completely exposing that part of his anatomy which should have been protected by his saddle. Just then a whip lash descended with the full force of the muscular arm which plied it on the thinnest, most threadbare spot in his pantaloons. It must have been imagination, but, I really thought that I could see smoke rising under the stripe. The injured man instantly let go his hold of the gander and clasped both hands on the afflicted region, swearing to make the earth rumble and the air grow hazy. In a frenzy of rage he leaped to the ground and rushed upon his assailant, bent on dire revenge. For a short time it seemed a sure thing that some other neck than that of the gander's would be broken, and a large detail was required and actively employed to restrain the smarting and infuriated cavalier from bloodshed, but he was finally pacified by permission to take the purse. After this incident all parties agreed that gander pulling was a cruel and indecorous game, and the gander's head was chopped off with an axe.

The most remarkable instance I can remember of a game of any kind played under fire, was something I witnessed in November, 1864. Gen. John C. Breckinridge, then in command of the Department of South-western Virginia, had moved from Abingdon into east Tennessee for the purpose of obtaining at least brief command of a considerable portion of that fertile territory whence rich supplies might be drawn. He attacked General Gillem, who held the strong position of Bull's Gap with a force larger than that with which Breckinridge assailed it. My brigade was in advance, and I was ordered to attack and drive in a strong Federal detachment formed in front of the gap, when I came up, and to keep control of the field until the rest of our command arrived. I followed instructions, and after forcing the enemy into their fortifications, aligned my brigade in front of them, making the men lie down to avoid, as well as possible, the effect of the artillery fire, which the enemy opened on us.

The shells were bursting just over my line, but too high in the air to do much damage. As I lay flat on my back, presenting the least target I could and watching the shells explode, I noticed that at one point of the line, about thirty yards from where I was, they seemed, at each successive discharge to burst closer to the ground. There was a small bushy tree at this point, and near by it sat a Tennesseean, named McElroy, an excellent soldier. He was playing mumblepeg and methodically going through with all the devices of that old game, giving no heed to what was going on around him. Just as he had reached the point where the player takes the blade of his knife in his teeth, and, tossing it in the air, seeks to stick it in the ground near the peg, a shell burst immediately over him. What seemed to be a great ball of fire fell from it, striking McElroy on the neck and shoulders, and instantly he was enveloped in flames.

I supposed that he had been torn into fragments, but when, with two or three of my staff, I reached the spot to which we at once rushed to ascertain his condition and assist him if possible, we found him alive, but writhing and shrieking in an agony of pain. He cried out to me: "Oh, general, for God's sake put out this fire." We tore his clothing from him, scorching our hands in doing so, and it off came as easily as charred paper would have done. But, strange to say, he was not at all mutilated; no fragment of iron had stricken him, but he was horribly burned from his neck to his heels, and when he finally recovered he was wealed with ghastly scars. I saw him for the first time in many years at the Confederate Veterans' reunion at Louisville in June, 1905. He was hale and hearty and still "full of fight," but I scarcely think he would be willing to face another incendiary shell.

I have rarely heard with more interest the recital of any historical event than that of the "Civil War in Shelbyville." "Dick Owens," who related it to me, so styled it because the "fighting was entirely between home folks," and was also of a perfectly mild and innocuous character — such as, Dick said, that of a civil war ought to be, although it is generally otherwise.

Mr. Owens did not witness the scenes he was so fond of depicting. At the date of their occurrence he was carrying a musket in the ranks of the Army of Northern Virginia and an active participant in war of quite another kind.

But warmly interested in all that concerned his native town, he informed himself of such war legends as were current there upon his return from the field, and was wont to narrate the incidents on which they were founded, more accurately, he declared, and more vividly, all admitted, than those who were present and saw them.

Shelbyville, Kentucky, is one of the prettiest and most

attractive places — as every one knows — in the state. It is situated in a fertile and beautiful region, and has been noted since its earliest settlement for the intelligence, hospitality, and sterling worth of its population. Like nearly every community in Kentucky, the town and the county of Shelby, of which it is the county seat, furnished a fair quota of soldiers to both armies — Federal and Confederate — but at no time during the war did the troops of either, with the exception, perhaps, of an occasional small squad of cavalry, approach that locality with hostile intent or in any wise disturb its peace. Nevertheless it had its share of false alarms and was often agitated by rumours of impending invasion. This anticipation of belligerent horrors was, doubtless, well nigh as unpleasant as the reality. I shall endeavour to describe what occurred on one such occasion as nearly as possible as it was told to me.

While all quiet citizens deprecated the advent of military visitors of any character, resistance was, of course, never contemplated except when they were Confederates. "Home guard" companies had been organized all over the state, which were expected, in the absence of Federal troops, to defend their respective districts from "rebel" intrusion.

One such had been formed in Shelby County, and as the greater number of its members lived in Shelbyville the captain was chosen from among the citizens of the town. Although an ardent and uncompromising Union man, he was liked by his fellow-citizens of Southern proclivities and was disposed to use his influence to aid them when in trouble because of a too free expression of opinion. Independently of many other good reasons for his election to this exalted and responsible position, he was the proprietor and keeper of the hotel — a house which furnished excellent entertainment both of food and drink — and he was therefore sure to be in frequent contact with the majority, if not with all, of his company; and by ringing the bell by which the hours of meals were announced he could, if necessity required, conveniently and promptly assemble them.

The company had its due complement of officers, but in addition thereto the principal physician of Shelbyville was made the military adviser of the captain; not, as Dick Owens rather flippantly suggested, because he was supposed to have professional knowledge of every method of inflicting death, but really because he was a profound military student and had read everything about the Mexican War and the heroes of the Revolution.

Not only did Captain Armstrong conscientiously appreciate the importance of the duties which he had assumed, but his good wife likewise did. She was determined that her husband should be attired, when on duty, in a manner befitting his rank — in a uniform which should inspire his followers with confidence and his enemies with terror.

She was ignorant of what the United States army regulations prescribed in the matter of uniform; indeed, had not even a general acquaintance with the subject of military dress, but believed, and justly, that ingenuity could be made to supply the lack of knowledge. So she devised and caused to be constructed the most brilliant outfit that warrior ever wore. From the cap, which was shaped like a turban, to the gaiters, every garment and article of equipment was of a different and intensely vivid hue. The captain's portly figure—and he was unusually stout, although not tall — was resplendent in red, blue, and yellow. No chieftain, not even a Scotch Highlander, could have presented a more variegated garb to the critical eye of a sharp-shooter.

He was a proud and pleased man when this uniform was shown him. His disposition was kind and peaceable; he had never borne malice against any one, had never wished to harm even the enemies of his flag. But now he panted for combat, even if it should be accompanied with bloodshed; for he wanted to wear the uniform, but was resolved to don it only on great and serious occasions. At length the opportunity occurred.

When Morgan made his raid into central Kentucky, in the summer of 1862, the impression seemed to prevail that he was ubiquitous. It was reported that he was in or marching upon every part of the country at the same time. In every vicinage his coming was hoped by friends or feared by foes.

Early one morning the rumour came that he was rapidly approaching Shelbyville. He was really a long distance away and moving in another direction; but the report was credited and the excitement was in proportion. The bell was rung, and the home guards turned out to do or die.

There had been an understanding that the company, whenever convened for the defence of the town, should meet on the main street in front of the court-house. So almost before the brazen clangour of the tocsin had ceased, the men were at the rendezvous, anxious that fortune might turn aside the assailant, but solemnly resolved to face the worst. When the captain arrived, however, and they for the first time saw him in his uniform, all doubt and fear gave way to an unqualified anticipation of victory. After a few brave words of encouragement to their comrades, the captain and the military adviser seated themselves in the middle of the street on chairs which were brought from the hotel for their accommodation, and as the sun was beginning to send down a shower of fiery rays, the captain hoisted a large green umbrella, completing his assortment of the primary colours.

The rest of the company sat on the curb-stones on both sides of the street and awaited, as comfortably as was possible under the circumstances, the approach of the enemy. Numerous reports of his proximity and bad conduct were brought in during the morning, and about ten o'clock a courier came with the news that Morgan had sacked and burned Mt. Eden, a little hamlet about eight miles from Shelbyville, had slain all the men, and carried off the women and children into captivity. He was now marching, said the courier, straight upon Shelbyville. This was a striking example of Morgan's celerity of movement, inasmuch as at nine o'clock on the same morning he was certainly at Versailles, more than thirty miles distant.

Before the excitement created by this news had in any degree subsided, a horseman came from the same direction at a rapid gallop. He was a wild-looking fellow, and while flourishing a pistol about his head, was uttering loud shouts in which could be distinguished only the words, "Morgan" and "here he comes." This was another home-guard courier, primed with the report that Morgan was just about to enter the town; but as he was thoroughly disguised in drink, his comrades failed to recognize him. Indeed, on account of his reckless demeanour they took him to be one of Morgan's advance videttes. So when he came dashing down upon them at full speed, every one of the company, except the captain, hunted shelter of some kind, and the military adviser formed behind a tree-box.

Then it was that Captain Armstrong displayed the coolness and ready resource of a born commander. He did not rise from his chair until the rushing horse was almost upon him, and when he did so, presented the umbrella in front and directly in the animal's face. This method of "receiving cavalry" proved as effective as it was novel. The horse stopped short, and the rider was shot over his head, falling at the captain's feet with a howl of terror. His evident fright partially restored the courage of the men he had nearly stampeded, and they rushed upon him from all directions. The tall form of the military adviser emerged from the safe side of the tree-box and his voice rang out above the tumult.

"Kill him," he shouted. "Slay him where he lies. Never let him leave this spot alive." The courier, who, of course, had no idea of the mistake under which his friends were labouring, believed that they were going to put him to death because he was the bearer of bad news, as the monarchs of antiquity used to treat the messengers of evil tidings. Consequently he yelled a lusty protest.

"Good Lord, men," he said, "what do you want to kill me for? How kin I help Morgan from comin' here, if he has a mind to?" His life was spared, but the demoralization his story created when he recovered breath to tell it, was irremediable. All discipline was destroyed, and every man spoke as freely as if in a mass convention. Finally, in the multitude of conflicting suggestions, one seemed to be received with favour.

"I'll jest tell you what's the matter, Cap," said its propounder, "the trouble is this here ain't a good position. They kin come in on us here from too many points. I move that we go to the end of town whar we can't be surrounded, and when them blamed rebels come we kin fall back on Clay village."

"I second the motion," shouted the first corporal. "We kin die for our country jest as well in the edge of town as we kin at the court-house."

The motion carried itself, and every one started for the "edge of town." Just as they reached it, however, they found themselves confronted with a body of armed men hurrying forward on foot, but whether friends or enemies they could not determine. Both parties halted, uncertain what to do. But when Captain Armstrong pressed to the front of his lines and was about to give the order to fire, the other fellows, so soon as they caught sight of him, broke and fled with every evidence of consternation. It was soon discovered that they were also home guards coming from the country precincts to reinforce their friends in town; but, when first questioned, they gave the most confused and incoherent explanation of their panic. No man could assign any intelligible reason for it, until Captain Armstrong had reached the point where the fugitives had been induced to halt and parley. Then their officer spoke for them all.

"Thar's the explanation," he said emphatically. "We didn't know Captain Armstrong in that rig, and any man in sech a rig could skeer anybody what didn't know him out of the county. Me and my men jined this business expectin' to fight human bein's, but we didn't take no contract to tackle a rainbow or a rory borealis."

On one occasion in the latter part of September, 1862, during General Bragg's occupation of Kentucky, I experienced a surprise stranger than ever happened to me before or afterward. I was on my way from Cynthiana to Lexington, and was riding with a single companion — Sam Murrell, my chief of couriers — along the turnpike, then an almost unequalled road, which extends between the two towns, when the incident occurred.

About four o'clock in the afternoon we had reached a point, about five miles from Lexington, whence the pike stretched straight in front of us for perhaps six or seven hundred yards, running between two beautiful woodland pastures. I was well acquainted with the region, but had never seen it look so lovely nor had I ever gazed on it with so much pleasure. Under the bright sunlight the great trees reared their stately trunks and widely branching limbs in what seemed more than usual majesty, and the dense foliage with which they were yet clad, stirred by a slight breeze, showed every shade of green. So far as I could see on either hand, the blue grass, still retaining despite the past summer's heat its freshest and richest hue, gave each undulating hill and verdant hollow some peculiar charm. The white pike appeared in the slanting sunbeams like a broad band of silver. The whole scene glowed with beauty.

As we rode slowly along in silent contemplation of this spectacle, a gate, about two hundred yards in front of us, and opening upon the pike from the woodland upon our left, swung open and the figure, seemingly, of a very large man mounted on a very big horse, came out upon the road. Neither Murrell nor I had caught sight of this horseman previously to his advent through the gate, and we could not understand how, in the open glades of the pasture, he could have escaped our observation. His sudden and unexpected appearance, therefore, seemed rather mysterious, and attracted an attention we might not otherwise have given him. He wore a slouched black hat, and a short jacket, the colour of which we could not discern; and, as he sat on his horse in erect and military fashion, and was alert and confident in bearing, we took him to be a soldier, probably a Confederate cavalry man. His conduct, however, soon induced us to change this opinion, and suspect him of being a Yankee, and perhaps a spy.

He halted for a moment, after coming fairly in view, as if undetermined in which direction to proceed, and then, apparently alarmed at seeing us, made off up the road at top speed. We had watched him closely, and when he thus took flight, of course we gave chase. Having swift horses, we rapidly gained on him, but neither our calls to him to stop nor our threats to shoot if he did not had any effect. He neither checked his speed in the least nor even turned his head. We had drawn our pistols and in a few moments more might have fired, when what seemed a marvellous transformation happened. We had gotten within fifty or sixty feet of him, when suddenly, in the twinkling of an eye, man and horse, which had appeared just before of colossal size, dwindled to the dimensions of a boy of fifteen, and a black pony, a little larger than a Shetland. Some curious mirage effect of sun or atmosphere had wrought the previous deception. We stared in astonishment and could scarcely believe our eyes. When the little fellow — he was one of the handsomest boys I had ever seen — looked up at me with a frank, happy smile, perfectly fearless although confronted by two armed strangers, I felt really abashed. I glanced at the pistol I was holding with a sensation of shame, succeeded by one of horror as I reflected that I might have fired upon him.

"Bub," I said, "why did you run away when you saw us?"

"Oh, I didn't see you or think about you at all," he replied. "I always run Mollie" — that was the pony's name — "up this stretch of pike when I'm coming home from school."

His face seemed familiar, although I was confident that I had never before seen him. But Murrell, who had been regarding him intently, asked: "Are you not a brother of Capt. John B. Castleman?"

"Yes," he said, "I'm his youngest brother. My name's George, and I'm going to join his company."

He was as good as his word. His three brothers were in the Confederate army, two of them in the Second Kentucky Cavalry, which I then commanded. He was the youngest child and his mother's darling, but sore as was the trial she had to let him go. She knew that it was merely a matter of time — his going to the army — and thought it best that he should go in the care of his brothers. So in a few days he, too, was enlisted in the Second Kentucky and a member of his brother John's company. He immediately became a great favourite in the regiment, and especially so with Lieut.-Col. John B. Hutchinson, who had detailed him as his orderly. George's duties in this exalted station, however, were merely nominal, for Hutchinson's big, good-humoured darky servant obeyed with alacrity his master's orders to pay especial attention to the comfort of the "orderly."

In the subsequent retreat from Kentucky I had another encounter with him, less startling but more amusing than our first meeting. On the afternoon of October 24th, Morgan's command encamped at Greenville, in western Kentucky, and during the night there was a heavy fall of snow. The men were not provided with tents, but were, at that time, well supplied with blankets and gum cloths, and wrapping themselves well in these were as comfortable as they would have been under shelter. Indeed, so protected, the covering of snow only made them sleep the warmer. I was then suffering from a severe cold and threatened with pneumonia, and by the surgeon's advice had slept in a house instead of in camp. I rode out early in the morning to the camp of the Second Kentucky, and had some difficulty in finding any one except the camp guards. Inasmuch as we proposed to let them rest that day, the men had not yet arisen, and the level field in which they were encamped was marked by a great number of white mounds, under each of which lay one or more sleepers. The field really looked like a graveyard enshrouded with snow.

"Which is Colonel Hutchinson's mound?" I asked of one of the sentries, after having admired the scene for a few minutes.

"There it is," he answered, pointing to an unusually large one. I made my way to it as carefully as I could on horseback, and shouted Hutchinson's name at the top of my voice. What followed made me think of the resurrection. On all sides and throughout the encampment the mounds opened, and men sprang up, as one may imagine the dead will rise from their graves on the last day. Hutchinson was a tall and extremely powerful man, and he loomed up bearing George in his arms, as easily as if he were an infant. It seemed to me that, having been so suddenly awakened, he thought the camp was attacked, and was preparing to at least secure his orderly from capture. When he recognized me he burst into a loud shout of laughter and let the boy drop. George immediately addressed himself to me with his usual courtesy.

"I'm glad to see you at our headquarters, colonel," he said; "but we can't offer you much of a breakfast this morning."

CHAPTER IX

I HAVE always believed that Gen. John C. Breckinridge's capacity as a soldier was not fully appreciated by his Southern countrymen, much as they loved and respected him, and, indeed, by none save those who, serving immediately with or under him, had the best opportunity of correctly estimating it. His ability as a statesman, his political astuteness, and extraordinary power as an orator were universally recognized and acknowledged, and it may be because of that — because he had exhibited so conspicuously the talents which make a man eminent and distinguished in civil affairs — that due credit was not given him for the talent he undoubtedly had for war. At any rate, while his reputation in the Confederate army was good, and he was ranked among the best of those who held high but subordinate rank, it was not what I think it should have been. Nature had endowed him very generously in all respects, giving him an unusually handsome and commanding presence, a rare and most persuasive eloquence, and a manner singularly attractive. With extremely brilliant qualities, he possessed also a profound sagacity — a judgment acute and seldom at fault in any matter upon which he was adequately informed; but I am of the opinion, as were many others who knew him intimately, that he had in even greater degree than those mental characteristics for which he is best remembered, the military aptitude and soldierly instincts which, trained and well directed, make the successful captain.

His first experience of military life was in the war with Mexico, when he was major of the Third Kentucky Volunteer Infantry. He saw very little service in that war; was, I believe, in no battle, and, if such campaigning as he then shared contributed in any way toward making him the great soldier he afterward became, such educational advantage was not apparent.

In 1860 he was the choice of the Southern states for Presidential nominee, and he firmly believed, after he had accepted this distinction and the confidence they had given him, that his best efforts and his life, if need be, must be devoted to their people. In October, 1861, he announced his resignation of the seat he held in the United States Senate, and declared that he would irrevocably unite his fortunes with those of the Confederacy. His previous prominence and extreme popularity, not only with the Kentuckians, but with the entire Southern soldiery and the Southern people, of course, claimed recognition, and he was immediately commissioned a brigadier-general. His record thenceforth and during the entire period of the war, when his opportunities and the character of the service to which he was assigned are considered, are surpassed only by that of the men who are ranked at the very summit of Confederate effort and achievement.

He commanded the reserve at Shiloh, a post of great importance and responsibility. In that hot and rapidly conducted battle the reserve was soon called out, and Breckinridge's division was in action and engaged in fierce combat as early as twelve o'clock of the first day. During the rest of the battle it was constantly and actively employed upon the front, and when the army withdrew toward Corinth covered its retreat.

This was the first real battle which General Breckinridge had ever witnessed, but his conduct was like that of a veteran, and he received from his superiors the highest commendation. Very soon afterward, on the 14th of April, 1862, he was made a major-general.

In the following June he was ordered with his division to Vicksburg, won the fight at Baton Rouge, and occupied Port Hudson. His assignment to duty in Mississippi at this period prevented his accompanying the Army of Tennessee into Kentucky when Bragg entered the state in September, 1862; and when his presence and influence with the people, and doubtless, too, his advice, would have greatly benefited the Confederate cause. Returning to Tennessee with the troops he had taken to Vicksburg, he arrived at Murfreesboro at a critical moment. Bragg had commenced his retreat from Kentucky, marching out through Cumberland Gap. It was his purpose to reach and occupy the fertile region of middle Tennessee. The Federal army was pressing southward with all speed through Kentucky, having the same objective in view. A great strategic game was being played, and for an important stake. The first of the two hosts which attained the goal in force would win. If Bragg should be first upon the ground, he could overcome the garrison of eight or ten thousand men left at Nashville when Buell had followed him into Kentucky, capture that city, and recover much of the territory evacuated after the disaster of Fort Donelson.

If, on the contrary, his opponent should anticipate him, not only would Nashville remain in Federal possession, but the Federal army, if promptly massed, might prevent Confederate entrance into any part of the coveted territory and shut Bragg up in east Tennessee. The Federal army was moving by the shorter route, and was much better provided with transportation. It marched with celerity, while the progress of the Confederates through the rugged country which they were compelled to traverse was necessarily dilatory. At any rate Rosecrans reached Nashville — or the head of his column arrived there — while Bragg was yet far to the east. There can be no doubt that Breckinridge's presence at Murfreesboro prevented an immediate Federal advance to that point. The force under his command was scarcely four thousand strong; but he handled it so boldly and skilfully that the enemy was impressed with the idea that caution was necessary, and made little progress beyond Nashville, giving Bragg opportunity to reach Murfreesboro and occupy the adjacent territory.

General Breckinridge's name will always be associated with the battle of Murfreesboro because of the charge made there by his division. It was unsuccessful, for the position attacked was exceedingly strong and defended by a much larger number of the enemy. Nor was his assault supported by a demonstration upon any other part of the Confederate line. It was made with the utmost gallantry upon the part of his troops, and with heavy loss in killed and wounded.

At the battle of Chickamauga, Breckinridge's division was in the army corps commanded by D. H. Hill, and was very hotly engaged, especially on the morning of September 20th, the second day of the battle. He succeeded General Hill in command of the corps, and served in that capacity at Missionary Ridge. He had previously been sent to Chickamauga to reinforce the troops with which Gen. Joseph E. Johnston was operating in Mississippi, seeking to relieve Vicksburg, and repelled the Federal attack at Jackson. In May, 1864, he was transferred to Virginia, won the battle of New Market, took part in the battle of Cold Harbor, where he served immediately under the eye of General Lee, coöperated with General Early in driving Hunter from the Shenandoah Valley, and made the campaign in Maryland, successfully fighting the battle of Monocacy. No officer in the Confederate army, perhaps, experienced a service more varied or extending over a wider extent of territory, and very few witnessed and participated in fiercer conflicts; but in this war upon a large scale no opportunity was offered him for independent command, and to exhibit the qualities which so well fitted him for it. It was in minor and apparently less important operations that such chance was afforded him, and I shall endeavour to justify the opinion I have expressed of his unusual capacity by reference to some of those in which I believe he displayed it.

The capture of New Orleans, the fall of Memphis and the evacuation of Fort Pillow seemed to open the way for the coöoperation of the Federal fleets upon both the lower and upper Mississippi, and the Federal authorities were preparing vigorously to prosecute plans for the control of the great river through its entire length. The consummation of such purpose would necessarily be detrimental in the extreme to the Confederacy in many respects. All communication would be permanently severed between Confederate territory situated respectively on the eastern and western banks of the river, and the invasion of each facilitated. Vicksburg was the only point on the Mississippi of strategic importance — the only one, indeed, where preparations to obstruct the passage of armed hostile flotillas had been made — yet remaining in Confederate possession. It was strongly fortified, and troops were hurried to its defence. Gen. Earl van Dorn assumed command there and of the department on June 27, 1862.

The siege of the place had already begun and it was threatened by a strong army and formidable fleet.

But it was apparent that if safe and easy communication — or, indeed, any at all — was to be maintained between the Confederate forces occupying the territory upon both sides of the river, some other point besides Vicksburg and lower down, must also be held and fortified, in order that a sufficient distance should be protected from the patrolling Federal gunboats and kept free for Confederate use. It was likewise very important to maintain control of the navigation of Red river, and prevent molestation of craft plying between ports on that stream and Vicksburg, because Van Dorn expected to procure supplies for the garrison chiefly from that region.

Baton Rouge had been occupied by a Federal force sent from New Orleans and variously estimated as being from thirty-five hundred to five thousand strong. It was accompanied by a small flotilla of gun-boats. This advance to Baton Rouge was not only a menace to Vicksburg, but, inasmuch as the town is no great distance from the mouth of the Red river, it threatened serious danger to the Confederate use of that stream as well as to the proposed establishment of the additional fortress intended to hold the Federal fleets in check. General van Dorn therefore promptly determined to drive back the troops already at Baton Rouge, before they were reinforced, and immediately thereafter occupy and fortify Port Hudson in accordance with the plan previously mentioned. General Breckinridge had been sent to Mississippi with his division shortly after the battle of Shiloh, and was at Vicksburg when General van Dorn resolved to attack the troops at Baton Rouge, and he was selected to command the expedition.

He began his march on the 27th of July, "with," he states in his report, "somewhat less than four thousand men," and proceeded by rail to Tangipahva, fifty-five miles from Baton Rouge. He arrived at the Comite River, ten miles from Baton Rouge, on the 4th of August; and leaving camp at eleven o'clock that night, reached the vicinity of the enemy at daybreak the next morning, August 5th. By sickness and the casualties of his very severe march, the force with which he started had been greatly depleted, and he went into action with an effective strength of only twenty-six hundred men. He had two batteries of artillery, Cobb's and Hudson's.

The Federal force consisted of six regiments of infantry — Fourteenth Maine, Seventh Vermont, Ninth Connecticut, Twenty-first Indiana, Fourth Wisconsin, and Sixth Michigan, one company of cavalry, and three batteries of artillery.

General Breckinridge, anticipating that he would be numerically inferior to his antagonist at the moment of encounter, had stipulated that the Confederate ram, *Arkansas*, should be sent to coöperate with him, and, by engaging the three gun-boats relieve him of their fire.

Directions to this effect were given, but the machinery of the *Arkansas* became in some way disabled. She failed to reach Baton Rouge, and was burned by her crew to prevent her falling into the hands of the enemy. General Breckinridge attacked in a single line with reserves at intervals. The enemy received this onset in two lines, effectively aided by the three batteries. The fighting was hot, close, and stubborn. The Confederates made several assaults before they were successful, but at length drove the enemy out of their encampments and completely from the field. Gen. Benjamin Butler, writing a report of this battle, to which he was no nearer than New Orleans, claims that Breckinridge was repulsed — a curious statement to make when he admits that the Federals were forced to leave the ground and abandon their camps to the Confederates. General Breckinridge remained in possession of the field for some hours after the conclusion of the fight, and then fell back one mile to obtain water, his men having had none since leaving the Comite River on the previous night. The absence of the *Arkansas* also contributed to prevent his pursuing his victory, as his troops had suffered severely from the fire of the fleet in the latter part of the engagement. He destroyed the tents and camp equipage, and, lacking transportation for their removal, the greater part of the captured stores. The Confederate loss in killed and wounded was four hundred and sixty-seven, that of the Federals three hundred and eighty-three. Many officers fell. The Federals lost one general officer killed, General Williams, and two Confederate generals, Helm and Clark, were wounded.

The enemy retreated from Baton Rouge to New Orleans, and within two or three days after the battle General Breckinridge occupied Port Hudson, which was subsequently rendered almost as strong a fortified place as Vicksburg. The objects of the expedition were completely carried out.

In February, 1864, General Breckinridge was assigned to the command of the Department of South-western Virginia. A very extensive territory was included in this department, the possession and use of which was of extreme importance to the Confederacy, not only because it still furnished supplies to the Army of Northern Virginia, but because, and especially after the occupation of east Tennessee by the Federals, its maintenance was essential to the protection of Richmond upon that flank. If it, in turn, passed into the possession of the enemy, it would be impossible for General Lee's army to hold the ground, the defence of which was so vital. The department was very vulnerable and accessible to attack from many directions. Col. J. Stoddard Johnston says in the "Confederate Military History," Vol. IX., Kentucky: "It had been the graveyard of Confederate generals as far as their reputations were concerned, owing to the fact that, with a front of nearly three hundred miles open to invasions of the enemy by routes impossible to guard, whenever it was invaded, blame fell upon the commanding general and his prestige was destroyed. It came near being the ruin of General Lee, while Floyd, Loring, and a number of others were in turn retired and their future usefulness destroyed."

General Breckinridge experienced in full measure the perils and difficulties of this ardous position, but he came out of the ordeal with increased reputation. While strict watch and ward was necessary throughout the whole department, it was of chief importance to protect the lead mines in Wythe County, whence came the principal supply of that article for the armies of the Confederacy, and the salt works at Saltville, which furnished salt for the entire South, east of the Mississippi.

On May 5th, and when he was threatened with a hostile demonstration from the Kanawha Valley, General Breckinridge received a despatch from General Lee, informing him that a strong force under Siegel was marching to break the line of railroad connecting the department with Richmond. Siegel was moving up the Shenandoah Valley, and his objective point was supposed to be Staunton. General Lee therefore, directed Breckinridge to proceed immediately with all the troops he could muster to the defence of that place. Breckinridge moved forth with two brigades of infantry, making a long and toilsome march over a mountainous region and arriving at Staunton on May 11th. He called out the militia reserves of Augusta County, a small and not very effective auxiliary detachment; and also summoned into the field a body of soldiers, of whom no one until then had expected actual service, but by whom it was rendered not only as gallantly, but as efficiently, as picked veterans of the Army of Northern Virginia could have performed the same work. This was the cadet corps of the Virginia Military Institute, a battalion two hundred and twenty-five strong, composed of boys from fourteen to sixteen years of age.

It was supposed, and perhaps such was General Lee's expectation, that Breckinridge would await Siegel at Staunton, and having fortified as well as he could, endeavour to repulse him there. But with the true military instinct, he determined to press upon his enemy with all possible celerity and obtain the double advantage of attack and surprise. The fact that Siegel outnumbered him nearly two to one, confirmed him in this resolution; for he felt that he must meet numerical superiority with moral effect, encourage his own troops by a bold offensive and impress his adversary with exaggerated ideas of his strength. Accordingly, on the 13th, he led his little army, in all thirty-five hundred or thirty-six hundred strong, to meet Siegel who was advancing, and some forty or fifty miles distant. On the evening of the 14th, when within nine miles of New Market, he learned that Siegel was encamped in the vicinity of that place. The succeeding night was stormy, but he moved at one o'clock, and at daylight reached New Market, on the southern side of the town. It was Sunday, May 15th, when he formed for battle, and his line was in motion little more than a mile from Siegel's camp before the latter knew of his presence or that any formidable force had been interposed between him and the object of his expedition. Siegel, who had earned, by the rapidity of his movements, the sobriquet of "The Flying Dutchman," had been outmarched, and was already half beaten.

Attacking with vigour and immediately, Breckinridge drove his opponent from the inception of the battle, and by noon Siegel had fallen back some distance beyond New Market. He then assumed a position of considerable strength on the crest of a hill, the approach to which was over gently sloping and entirely open ground, where the attacking troops were perfectly exposed to his fire. But the Confederate onset was resistless. Breckinridge, wishing to speedily utilize his entire force, which, as I have said, was greatly inferior numerically to that of the enemy, formed only one line with no reserve. His flanks, however, were well protected, the right by a morass and the left by the steep bank of the Shenandoah. He was enabled to select an excellent position for his artillery, which, although a little in front of his line before it advanced, was safe, and with the guns so placed, opened the battle effectively.

General Breckinridge was naturally reluctant to permit the cadets to go into action, and proposed to employ them as a guard for his train. But the brave little fellows would listen with no patience to any disposition which might keep them out of the fight and their expostulations finally overcame the resolution of their commander. He consented to let them "go in" and gave them the post of honour, placing them in the centre between the two brigades, and directed the entire line to dress on them. Not only did their splendid drill and discipline justify this compliment, but no troops ever behaved with calmer or more daring courage. The fire from the ten pieces of Confederate artillery not only shook Siegel's first line, but threw his second line and reserves into confusion. He attempted to remedy this disorder by using his cavalry, but it was easily repulsed. The Confederate advance, although made under a heavy and scathing fire, was spirited and rapid, and was never checked. Siegel's entire array went to pieces under the first assault, and fled from the field, leaving three or four hundred prisoners in the hands of the Confederates. He crossed a stream, a few miles from the battle field, and, burning the bridge, effectually prevented pursuit. He continued his retreat without a halt to the Federal lines. The loss upon the Confederate side was not severe, but fell more heavily on the cadets, in proportion to their numbers, than on the other troops engaged.

By this victory, General Breckinridge saved not only the department he was commanding, but the Army of Northern Virginia from a grave disaster.

GENERAL BASIL W. DUKE 185

After the battle of New Market, General Breckinridge was ordered to the Army of Northern Virginia, serving with that army first about Richmond and then in a command of a corps under Early until the later part of September, 1864, when he was again assigned to the command of the Department of Southwestern Virginia. He had barely reached Abingdon, where the headquarters of the department were made, when he was compelled to strain to the utmost every means at his disposal to repel one of the most formidable incursions ever attempted into that territory. Burbridge was advancing with a strong column from Kentucky, while Generals Gillem and Ammen simultaneously advanced from east Tennessee. Either attacking force considerably exceeded in numerical strength the total number of troops which General Breckinridge could assemble for defence. The opportune arrival, however, almost at the moment of encounter, of Gen. John S. Williams, with twenty-five hundred men, enabled so strong a resistance to be offered by the Confederates that the enemy was compelled to retreat without accomplishing any success or doing damage to either the salt works or the lead mines, and a severe defeat was inflicted upon him at Saltville.

But it seemed fated that this department should have no respite and should be constantly in danger. General Williams had entered on his return from a raid into Tennessee, made with General Wheeler's corps, and the troops he brought with him, and which had chiefly contributed to the victory at Saltville, were required immediately afterward to rejoin the command to which they properly belonged. Of the troops regularly assigned to the defence of the department, two brigades, Giltner's and Cosby's, had been ordered, just after the repulse of Burbridge, to the Valley of Virginia. General Breckinridge could muster, after these detachments had been made, only two brigades of cavalry. Vaughn's and Duke's, one small brigade of infantry — North Carolina reserves — some five hundred dismounted men and convalescents from various commands and ten or twelve pieces of artillery. His total strength was about twenty-eight hundred men for the defence of a department threatened upon all sides.

In November information was received that Burbridge and

Stoneman were preparing to again attack from Kentucky, with, perhaps, larger forces than had taken part in the invasion of the preceding month, and the enemy in east Tennessee assumed the offensive very actively. General Vaughn, supported by Palmer's infantry brigade — North Carolina reserves — was attacked by General Gillem near Russellville and defeated, with the loss of four or five guns.

It was necessary to retrieve this disaster, and important to cripple, if possible, the Federal forces in east Tennessee before those coming from Kentucky made their appearance. Leaving, therefore, only a few scouts and picket guards at other points, General Breckinridge moved with every available man to attack Gillem at Bull's Gap, where the latter had established himself after his defeat of Vaughn.

The roads were in very bad condition, and as the dismounted men and the artillery, Page's battery of six pieces, were required to march eighty or ninety miles to the objective point, several days elapsed before the entire force was concentrated. All, however, except the infantry brigade, were in front of the enemy's position late on the afternoon of the 24th of November. General Vaughn's brigade was sent to the rear of Bull's Gap, and other troops which had arrived were posted in front. My brigade was hotly engaged with the enemy, who came out in pretty strong force to reconnoitre, until some time after night had fallen, and all of the troops bivouacked in line. General Breckinridge had made up his mind to attack at daybreak the next morning, and his determination to do so was not altered by the fact that the infantry had not even then arrived. It was a resolution audacious almost to rashness, for the position was very strong and the enemy outnumbered us by at least five hundred men.

Vaughn, whose brigade was about one thousand strong, was ordered to attack the position in the rear. Col. George Crittenden with the artillery, supported by about two hundred men, was instructed to make a demonstration directly in front of the gap, where the railroad enters it, and he did so with such boldness that the demonstration was well nigh equivalent to an attack. Some two or three hundred men were similarly employed upon the left, and Breckinridge hoped that Gillem's attention would be diverted from the right, where he meant to make his real assault and endeavour to force an entrance.

I was in command of the five hundred men indicated for this purpose, and, having to make a considerable détour in order to reach the point where the assault was to be delivered, began my march while it was yet dark. At this point the wide, deep, and precipitous ravines, which on this side skirt the hills which the Gap penetrates, are crossed by two spurs or ridges connecting the ground held by the enemy with that upon which I was approaching. These ridges are fifty or sixty yards in width, some two hundred and fifty yards apart, and with sides going almost sheer downward. General Breckinridge accompanied my column and was immediately on the firing line during the succeeding combat. It became sufficiently light to clearly distinguish objects at some distance when we had gotten within perhaps a quarter of a mile of the point for which we were making, and we were suddenly aware of the presence of two hundred or three hundred Federal troops, just on the opposite brink of one of the ravines, and which was eighty or ninety yards wide. We were marching close to the other side, so that a very slight, although impassable distance, separated us. The temptation, even with veteran soldiers, to fire upon an enemy so near at hand and in plain sight, is almost irresistible; yet neither Federals nor Confederates yielded to it. We knew it would be a mere waste of time and ammunition to open fire then, and pressed on with all possible speed to gain the ridges which bridged the gulf. The other fellows evidently comprehended our object, and seemed to think that it was wiser to hasten there and assist in our repulse than to attempt a fight where it was impossible to come to close quarters. So we moved along on the different sides of the ravine in the same direction, Yanks and Johnny Rebs exchanging gibes and taunts, but not a single shot.

About the same time we heard Page's guns open on our left and the fire of the line supporting him, answered by the enemy's artillery in the gap. Earthworks had been erected across the two ridges along which we meant to attack, and in the rear of each a fort had been constructed and so placed that the fire from the two or three pieces mounted in each, commanded the ridges equally with the musketry fire from the earthworks. Anticipating, perhaps, that this would be the point selected for real assault the position was strongly manned, and as we reached it was reinforced by the body of troops which had escorted our approach.

As quickly as possible, I disposed my command for attack. I directed Colonel Ward, with a part of the men, to follow the ridge farther to the right, while with the remainder I advanced upon the other. We each pressed forward rapidly, encountering a fire from both small arms and artillery, which completely swept the ground and was very severe in its effect. Colonel Ward carried the work on the ridge, where he attacked, but could not hold it. The men under my immediate command got within thirty or forty feet of the other works, but the heavy and concentrated fire then checked them. We remained, renewing our efforts, for an hour, but without avail. The enemy seemed to have discovered that the demonstrations made elsewhere were not serious, or, at least, dangerous; and massed against us. I never witnessed a more perfect exhibition of courage and resolution upon the part of troops than was shown by those I commanded on that occasion, or more conspicuous examples of personal gallantry. We were finally obliged to retire, with a loss of nearly one third the entire force in killed and wounded. We came back leisurely, bringing off our wounded, and the enemy attempted no pursuit. All of the other troops engaged were, of course, also withdrawn and concentrated in front of, that is to say, south of the gap.

General Breckinridge, although much disappointed by this failure, was by no means disheartened or inclined to abandon the field without further and vigorous effort. The arrival that afternoon of the infantry, between four and five hundred strong, under Colonel Palmer, encouraged him to immediately renew the offensive, and elated the other commands with the hope that they might be enabled to avenge their discomfiture in the morning. It was decided that the entire force should at once take position on the railroad in the rear of Bull's Gap and cut off Gillem from communication with Knoxville and other points in east Tennessee, occupied by Federal garrisons. Breckinridge believed that this would oblige Gillem to evacuate his strong position in the Gap, and perhaps force him to accept battle in the open. Calling in, therefore, all outlying detachments except the absolutely necessary scouting parties, he marched at ten o'clock that night through Taylor's Gap, three miles west of Bull's Gap, expecting to reach his destination by daylight.

The cavalry commands were in the front of the column, the infantry, dismounted men, and artillery bringing up the rear.

Just as our advance emerged from the narrow pass we had traversed, our scouts brought the information that Gillem also was moving; he had quitted his fortified post in the gap and was marching in the direction of Knoxville. He had perhaps, taken alarm at the attack made on that day, and, aware of the arrival of our infantry, the strength of which he no doubt exaggerated, feared a more dangerous assault on the morrow. This was welcome news. An opportunity was offered not only of attacking the enemy in the open field, but of taking him in flank and by surprise. It was at once utilized. The two cavalry brigades dashed forward and in two or three miles came upon the enemy at Russellville, striking the column squarely in flank, driving it in confusion, and cutting off one regiment. The wagon train was in front and desperate efforts were made to protect it. Our infantry was never able to get sufficiently near to take part in the fight, nor, on account of the rapidity of the action and pursuit, could our artillery, although the enemy used his at times with some effect. The combat continued for several hours, a succession of hot encounters and retreats upon the part of the Federals. A brilliant moon arose, flooding the landscape with light and plainly showing the lines of the combatants. At Morristown the enemy was reinforced by a fresh regiment brought by rail and made his last and most determined stand. When this was broken, he gave way in complete rout. We had followed and fought him until five o'clock in the morning for nearly twenty miles. More than a hundred wagons were captured, six pieces of artillery and many prisoners.

Gillem halted with the remnant of his command at Strawberry Plains, and taking position on the western bank of the river and holding the long railroad bridge, was enabled to prevent our crossing for two or three days. During this time a constant skirmish, so far as artillery and musketry fire across the stream might be so termed, was kept up, and then, General Breckinridge getting a part of his command over the river by a distant ford, so alarmed Gillem that he retreated to Knoxville.

General Breckinridge's crushing defeat and rout of Gillem seemed, for a short time, to have frustrated coöperation from east Tennessee with the movement which he apprehended from Kentucky, and to have completely accomplished to that extent the plan he had formed for the defence of his department. But the adverse fortune with which the Confederacy had always to contend prevailed in this instance also. Breckinridge had to deal with adversaries vastly his superior in resources, and who could bide their time. Had Burbridge and Stoneman invaded South-western Virginia at the date when, according to credible information, he had reason to expect it, he could have met them with the entire force at his disposal without concerning himself about foes coming from any other quarter. As it was the danger was only delayed. The movement from Kentucky, which we had anticipated would be made about December 1st, was postponed, doubtless because of the repulse of the east Tennessee contingent, until the middle of that month. By that date another formidable invading force had been organized and was pressed in from east Tennessee, and the original programme was vigorously conducted. The irruption from east Tennessee came with such celerity that General Vaughn's brigade was cut off, and Palmer's brigade of infantry could not be gotten from Asheville. But for the opportune return from the valley of Cosby and Glitner, Breckinridge would have had no troops with which to confront Burbridge and Stoneman except my brigade and a few dismounted men. As it was he was seeking to oppose more than seven thousand men with less than twelve hundred. He concentrated at Saltville for the protection of the salt works there, but as this left every other point at the mercy of the enemy, he soon resolved, with his usual daring, to come out and seek battle. He met the full force of the enemy at Marion and held it in check for nearly two days, retiring unpursued only after the Federals had ceased to attack. This was one of the most remarkable combats I ever witnessed, and it seemed almost incredible that a body of troops, numerically so inferior to their antagonists as were the Confederates, could so long have withstood their assault in the open field; for the Federal onset was determined and frequently repeated, and the fighting was at close quarters. In front of one part of our line which I was holding with less than three hundred men, one hundred and eighty-seven dead bodies were counted which had fallen by our fire.

Notwithstanding that we had held him at bay at Marion, the greatly numerical superiority of the enemy enabled him to send a force to Saltville sufficient to overpower the very scanty garrison which had been left there, and capture the place. He remained, however, only a day or two and did no serious damage. The weather became intensely cold and this, with the difficulty of procuring supplies, hastened the return of the Federal forces to Kentucky. I followed them with a small detachment to the Kentucky line, a little more than fifty miles from Saltville. The suffering among the men of my command was severe, but not to compare with that which the Federal soldiers endured, although they were very much better clothed and equipped. I could not have imagined anything so dreadful as I witnessed on that march, and can hardly believe that the most terrible scenes of the retreat from Moscow exceeded its horrors. The road was strewn with rifles, cartridge boxes, and baggage of all kinds, abandoned by the enemy, and two or three pieces of artillery, with their caissons, had been burned. But the really horrid and painful sight was that of the dead or disabled men and horses. Hundreds of men lay along the road side, their limbs literally rotted with the cold, and in many cases amputation had been attempted to relieve, but had only aggravated, their agony. The spectacle exhibited by the dead and dying horses almost baffles description. Maj. W. J. Davis, of my staff, wrote some years ago a very vivid account of what he saw on this march, and I reproduce it as being in perfect accord with my own recollection:

"We pursued. As we ascended the steep mountain road leading from Saltville, the cold intensified so as to test the greatest power of endurance. Men beat their breasts to promote a more vigorous circulation, or, dismounting, limped on benumbed feet beside their hobbling horses. The necks, breasts and forelegs of the horses were covered with clinging sheets of frozen breath or blood that had oozed from the fissures in their swollen nostrils. Often their lips were sealed by the frost to the steel bits, or protruded livid and rugged with icicles of blood. Soon we met indications of the still greater suffering of our foes. Horses dead from cold were seen along the road, frozen stiff in every imaginable attitude; some leaned against the perpendicular cliff on the right, with legs swollen to an enormous size and split open to the bone from knee to hoof; some knelt with muzzles cemented to the hard earth by blood; others lay prone but with heads upraised. I saw two — mates, perhaps — which, in the agony or final dissolution, apparently had touched lips in mutual osculation, and stood with their mouths glued together by the killing frost.

"The march of the Federal cavalry was marked by dead horses. These corpses actually impeded our pursuit; sometimes six or eight lay in one heap; once I counted two hundred in one mile. . . . You may think the sight of hundreds of horses, dead, as I have said, horrible; what think you — you have never seen war, but have read of its 'pomp and pride and circumstance,' and perchance have glorified the butchery of it — what think you of men lying on bed or floor, some of them in the article of death, frozen, as were their dumb beasts by the road side? The hands of some of these gallant men were so swollen they looked like boxing gloves, and they were cracked with bleeding fissures a quarter of an inch wide. Their legs, from which pantaloons had been ripped, looked as if affected by elephantiasis; their feet, from which boots had been cut, were a shapeless mass; legs and feet seemed red like the shells of boiled lobsters and were split into bloody cracks like the hands."

The harm done by this raid to the Department of Southwestern Virginia was scarcely commensurate with the loss sustained by the enemy. The salt works and the works at the lead mines were injured, but not to such an extent that they might not have been readily repaired, for the labour of destruction was very hastily and imperfectly performed. The most serious loss was that of the stores burned at Bristol and Abingdon, for they were sorely needed and it was almost impossible to replace them. The fall of the Confederacy, however, came so soon thereafter that the misfortune was not felt as might otherwise have been.

After this General Breckinridge was appointed secretary of war and his service in the field was definitely terminated. All of those who served with General Breckinridge in any such capacity as enabled them to form an accurate opinion of his work will, I believe, agree with me in my estimate of him as a soldier. He had unquestionably a remarkable sagacity in all matters pertaining to actual warfare, a rare military aptitude. His courage and resolution were superb. I have never, I think, witnessed an indifference to danger so absolutely calm and imperturbable as I have seen him display under very extraordinary exposure to personal peril. His chief defect as a soldier — and, perhaps, as a civilian — was a strange indolence or apathy which at times assailed him. He illustrated in his official conduct the difference between energy and persistent industry. When thoroughly aroused he acted with tremendous vigour, as well as indomitable decision; but he needed to be spurred to action, and without some special incentive was often listless and lethargic. Nature seemed to have formed him to deal with emergencies. He rose to his full stature only in the midst of danger and disaster, and was at his best when the occasion seemed desperate.

It may seem hardly appropriate, in a sketch intended to portray General Breckinridge's qualities as a soldier, to allude to his characteristics as an orator; but it is difficult to speak of him at all without some mention of his extraordinary capacity in this respect. Indeed his influence with the men he commanded was largely aided by the powerful effect of his eloquence. He had every attribute of the orator. In stature he was above the medium height, and appeared when speaking to dilate to yet larger proportions, while his manly, well-moulded figure was at such times especially graceful. His manner was dignified and majestic, his voice resonant and sympathetic, and his delivery the perfection of elocutionary skill. His diction was remarkably lucid and illustrative, without much of what might have been termed rhetoric. I never heard him, without thinking of Macaulay's description of the younger Pitt; the same command of impressive, felicitous language, and succession of stately sentences glowing with the sentiment which most directly appealed to his auditors.

Along with his stronger and more virile qualities, not less

conspicious was an exceeding amiability of temper and an admirable self-control. I never saw a man more loath to give or take offence, or one so patient with the, perhaps, over-zealous suggestions of younger subordinates, and the occasional petulance which seems an inevitable concomitant of volunteer military service. His overmastering ability and strength of character enabled him to always command easily, but he never exerted his authority harshly, and was apparently often reluctant to exert it at all.

Brave, magnanimous, capable, and devoted, he received from his comrades, associates, and followers in the service he rendered the South and his native state an unusual share of love and admiration, and their descendants should hold his memory in honour and affection.

CHAPTER X

OF THE five major-generals commissioned from Kentucky in the Confederate army, that one, next to John C. Breckinridge, who had achieved most distinction before the war, and who performed a greater share of gallant and intrepid service during the war, was Gen. William Preston; and he will appear in the history of his day and time as one of its most attractive, although not among its most prominent, figures.

His reputation will not rest so much upon a display of military capacity, although he was a capable, efficient, and faithful officer, as upon ability evinced in other directions. He was so brilliant, so accomplished in many ways, and so chivalric in nature; his name was connected with so much that attracted public attention, with so many events of historic interest and with so many events of historic interest in both his military and civil life; and he acquitted himself so admirably in every situation — that he will be awarded a conspicuous place in the Confederate Pantheon and will be remembered by the people of the South and of his native state.

Some one termed him "The last of the cavaliers," and the designation was not inaptly bestowed. He was not only absolutely true to principle and conviction, but a strong strain of romantic sentiment pervaded his character, making him sensitive to everything he regarded as an obligation, either of honour or friendship. He had rather more respect, I think, for his own word solemnly pledged, than for a statute duly enacted. He was thoroughly brave, and, although not fond of adventure or addicted to seeking it, liked the hazard and excitment of battle. His talents and his training were better adapted to success in civil affairs, but his tastes and inclinations were decidedly military. The peculiar tone and éclat of army life attracted him. Discipline elsewhere might have been irksome to him, but he appreciated and approved of it in the camp, even when required himself to submit to its restraint.

General Preston had received a careful and thorough academic education, which he supplemented by constant and assiduous self-instruction. He read widely and profoundly considered all the information so acquired. His habit of thought was close and scholarly and his faculty of clear and forcible expression remarkable. These gifts enabled him to become very popular as a public speaker, and, combined with unusual wit, a keen sense of humour and appreciation of the ludicrous, and an exceedingly kindly and courteous temper, made him an entertaining and delightful companion. His conversation was occasionally rather more ornate and didactic than some people altogether fancied, but was eloquent and enlivened by an exhaustless flow of illustration and anecdote.

In personal appearance he was unusually imposing; his face strikingly handsome, with strong aquiline features, and his form tall, large, and commanding. His manner, rather, I think, because of his vigorous physique and sanguine, decided temperament, than because he was unduly proud or arbitrary in disposition, gave a certain impression of hauteur. For, while, in the best sense of the term, he was an aristocrat, no one was, in the most essential respect, more thoroughly democratic; no one judged and esteemed men more entirely for their personal worth, regardless of adventitious surroundings. His own estimate of how people regarded him, whether accurate or not, was suggestive. He used to say that he had many friends among the rich and exalted in station, and was almost universally liked by the poor and humble, but that he had never succeeded in especially commending himself to "the great, 'respectable' middle class."

General Preston was graduated from the law class of Harvard in 1838, and immediately began the practice of law in his native city of Louisville. Like nearly all of the young men at the bar in Kentucky at that time, he took an active interest in politics, being then an ardent Whig, and was elected to the lower house of the legislature in 1851. He had previously served in the war with Mexico as lieutenant-colonel of the Fourth Kentucky Volunteer Regiment of infantry, and also for a short time on the staff of Gen. Winfield Scott. In 1852 he was elected to congress, filling out an unexpired term, caused by the resignation of

Humphrey Marshall. He was elected to congress the second time, but was beaten by Marshall for the term commencing March 3d, 1855. At that date the old Whig party had become entirely disintegrated, and the American, or Know-Nothing party, as it was nicknamed, had arisen upon its ruins. A man like Preston could have no sympathy with the intolerant and proscriptive policies advocated by the Know-Nothings, and he was especially disgusted by the revolting ruffianism incited by its leaders and practised in some of the larger cities. One of the most terrible examples of this brutality — the massacre of a number of unoffending citizens, merely because they attempted to vote in opposition to the Know-Nothing candidates — occurred in Louisville, and that day, so damaging to the good name of the city, has since been known in its annals as "Bloody Monday."

Preston, from that time and until his death, acted with the Democratic party, and was elected to the convention which nominated James Buchanan as candidate for President and John C. Breckinridge for vice-president. He had been conspicuous for his ability, and had achieved more than ordinary reputation during his congressional service, which he fully maintained upon the floor of the convention, and in the canvass which ensued; so prominently commanding the attention and approbation of his political associates that his appointment by Mr. Buchanan as minister to Spain was generally commended.

No American, perhaps, who has ever been given such a mission, was better adapted to satisfy the country to which he was accredited. He was acquainted with the language which, in brief time, he learned to speak fluently, was familiar with Spanish literature and history, and could thoroughly understand and sympathize with the character of a people, who, with all their faults, are proud, high-strung, loyal to their code of right and duty, and devotedly patriotic; who in their decadent civilization have still felt the impulse of that ancient chivalry which had expelled the Moor, discovered and begun the colonization of the new world, and for a time made their country the dominant European power. He admired the romantic and punctilious spirit and bold temper of the Spaniard as exhibited both by noble and peasant, and there was much in him that appealed to them. His presence and bearing resembled our conception of what might have been that of the hidalgo of the sixteenth century, and he could feel, although he might not think, like a knight of the conquest. He became extremely popular with all classes in Madrid, and if there had been anything of importance then for American diplomacy to effect, he would doubtless have successfully accomplished it. He did perfectly all that there was then to do; that is, to impress the Spaniards with a most favourable idea of the American.

Among the many reminiscences he related of his Spanish experience, I remember one more particularly because it was illustrative of his own most marked traits of character. It seems that a colonel of the English army, travelling with his wife in Spain, was sojourning for a time at one of the principal hotels of Madrid. One morning at breakfast a Spanish gentleman, seated just opposite the English couple at the same table, began, after he had concluded his meal, to smoke a cigarette. The Englishman, in a very surly tone and peremptory manner, bade him desist. The Spaniard was a native of a certain province — the name of which I have forgotten — the inhabitants of which were noted for their independent spirit, and cool, reckless courage. Preston said they were termed "the Gascons of Spain." The little Don — he was about half the size of the Englishman — made answer to this request in very cool and deliberate fashion. He said that he was indulging in a practice which was common and not considered objectionable in Spain, and that it was more reasonable for strangers to tolerate the customs of a country than to expect its inhabitants to forego them.

"Moreover," he said, "while the smoke of my cigarette may be offensive to you, the tone of your request is exceedingly offensive to me; nor do you prefer it in behalf of the lady, in which event I might grant it, but you insist upon it for your own convenience, with which I am not at all concerned."

The Englishman replied with hot words, and after a short altercation leaned over the table and slapped the Spaniard's face. The other, without showing the least excitement, remarked:

"Señor, it is not one of our customs to exchange fisticuffs, and besides, if you have forgotten the presence of a lady, I have not. But you have offered me an insult which can only be expiated by blood. I will send a friend to you and will expect you to grant me a meeting."

So the colonel, in an hour or two, received a visit from another Spanish gentleman who bore a cartel. In the meantime the colonel had repented his loss of temper and his act, and, while no doubt possessing a due share of his national courage, was greatly averse to duelling. It was no longer a British "custom," and he ran the risk of forfeiting his commission if he fought one. He offered to apologize, but was politely informed that no apology would be received for such an affront, and that he would be publicly proclaimed a coward if he declined to fight. That also might mean the loss of his position in the army.

In this dilemma he thought of the English ambassador, and called on him for advice and assistance. The ambassador, between whom and Preston there was a close intimacy, in turn asked the aid of the latter, as one better acquainted with the laws of the duello than himself, and likely to have more influence with the belligerent Spaniards.

Preston at first declined to take part in the affair, declaring that the colonel, having given such provocation, ought to fight; but was finally induced by the solicitations of his friend to make an effort to settle the difficulty.

He accordingly called on the challenger, by whom he was received with great courtesy and assurances of the most distinguished consideration, and presented the matter with which he was charged. He apologized for what he admitted might seem an interference in an affair with which he had no personal or immediate concern; but explained how he had consented to undertake such a mission, saying that if such intervention was not deemed proper, he would proceed no further. The Spaniard replied that he regarded the interest which Señor Preston might take in any affair with which he was connected an honour, and begged that the señor would feel no hesitation in discussing it.

General Preston began by declaring his perfect understanding and approval of the Spaniard's desire to obtain satisfaction. With his own people, he said, duelling was recognized and frequent, and that he would himself, if necessary, resort to that method of obtaining redress for insult or outrage. But, grave as was the affront, in this instance, it was yet a case, he thought, in which an apology might be accepted. He then explained that if the Englishman fought, he would be dismissed from the army and lose his only means of support, and finished by an appeal to the generosity of a Spanish gentleman to make some concession under the circumstances. The Spaniard regarded him intently for a few moments, and then said:

"Señor Preston, I will ask you frankly what you would do in a like case, and I know that you will give me a candid answer."

"I would act, señor," responded the general, "just as I have urged you to do. I will never ask any gentleman to do that which I would not do myself."

"With that assurance," said the *preux* chevalier, "I will grant your request and accept an apology; and the Señor Englishman may rest satisfied that I shall no more remember the blow he inflicted than I would the kick of an ass."

General Preston's mission terminated, and he returned to America a few months before the breaking out of the Civil War, and when the excitement consequent upon its anticipation was at the highest pitch.

Upon his return home Preston found himself and those with whom he proposed to act confronted with conditions more serious, perhaps, than he had anticipated. He had no doubt been kept informed, during his absence, of current events and the trend of political sentiment as publicly expressed. But in such a crisis, events sometimes move more rapidly than they can be exactly recorded, or, their significance be apprehended except by those immediately in touch with them; and political sentiment, as it is preparing to take shape in action, may develop at a rate with which the ordinary forms of public expression can scarcely keep pace.

In common with all intelligent observers who lived south of Mason and Dixon's line, and who were acquainted with the views and feelings of the Southern people, he was prepared for an exhibition upon their part of strong and earnest evidences of disappointment and indignation at the election of Mr. Lincoln, and realized that it would be regarded in like manner by the people of Kentucky. He probably did not immediately realize, however, the extent to which such resentment would be carried. While he had been cognizant, previously to his departure upon his mission, of the rapid growth of sectional differences and estrangement and the increasing bitterness of sectional feeling, he could not understand, when removed from participation in the debate, so well as could those daily engaged in it, how swiftly the quarrel was approaching actual and open hostilities.

At the date of his return, the incessant agitation of the slavery question, in all of its phases, had gotten beyond the region of mere political controversy, and was threatening practical and dangerous results. The mere theoretical discussion of the introduction of slavery into the territories had, for some years, greatly excited the public mind; but when it was actually attempted and real strife occurred along the Kansas border, when armed collisions betweed the pro-slavery and free-soil settlers and their respective allies became frequent, the feeling all over the country passed beyond control. Closely following these exasperating troubles in Kansas came the audacious and insolent enterprise of John Brown, at Harper's Ferry, intended, apparently, to challenge and arouse the most serious apprehension of every slave-holding community; and the Southern people were excited almost to frenzy. Had a period of two or three years intervened between this incident and the opening of the Presidential contest of 1860, during which (by some miraculous dispensation) the dispute might have been suspended and less sensational conditions have prevailed, it is barely conceivable that the great civil conflict might have been averted. But the Presidential campaign began almost immediately afterward; all of these irritating events were made prominent issues, and gave a more offensive and dangerous significance to the election of a Republican candidate, and destiny seemed to inhibit a peaceable adjustment.

Preston was not, in the phraseology of that time, an "original secessionist," nor did he regard with favour, or except as a last resort, any policy or line of action which contemplated a dissolution of the Union. Reared in the Whig party and under the the tutelage of Mr. Clay, he had been taught to believe that the Union was chiefly instrumental to the material prosperity of the states which composed it, and almost essential to the preservation of peace among their people. His mental inclination, his intellectual preference, was for national unity and greatness, and opposed to territorial disintegration and consequent diminution of the strength and dignity of government. But, above all, he was a Southern man by blood and by social ties and traditions.

It should be borne in mind that, at that date, sectional influence was more potent than now, and, with the exception of Massachusetts, perhaps, more strongly and generally recognized in the South than in the North. Upon the absorbing issue which had induced the controversy and was threatening disunion, he sincerely agreed and sided warmly with his immediate countrymen. Few men, at that day, in the South — or, indeed, in the North — gave much consideration to the abstract proposition whether slavery was or was not morally justifiable. They were more concerned with its social and economic features — with conditions which might make the negro who was here to stay, not only a useful but an always harmless element of their population. Nor were the Southern people responsible for the existence of slavery upon this continent, and scarcely so for its presence among themselves. The animus and methods with which it was assailed were virulent and injurious to every Southern interest; and the South objected to being made a scape-goat for the national sin and the "dreadful example" condemned by recent New England morality.

Thoroughly Southern in sympathy and profoundly convinced of the danger with which his section was menaced; resenting in common with every man in his position and who felt as he did, the unjust criticism of the Southern attitude with which the Northern press and pulpit resounded, and which the Northern public seemed to generally endorse, it is not surprising that the instinct and sentiment of the man overcame the effect of his political education. Little chance or time was afforded him for mature or dispassionate reflection upon the situation after his return to Kentucky, for the speedy march of events was pressing all men to a determination, and he was not one to hesitate or be slow in forming a resolution.

All hope of compromise or harmonious adjustment of the sectional troubles, or of delay of Southern effort for separation and independent government, which might have been entertained after the election of Mr. Lincoln, was quickly proved fallacious. The secession of South Carolina in less than a month after the Presidential election, followed by that of Mississippi, Alabama, and Georgia, in less than another month, and the absolute certainty, so far as such a thing could be within human prevision, that seven other Southern States would secede, conclusively demonstrated that the process of attempted national disruption was inaugurated in earnest and would be prosecuted with unflinching purpose. Either similar action on the part of the border slave-holding states, or a prompt and unmistakable declaration of determined adhesion to the Union, might then have been reasonably expected.

But while popular feeling was, as I have said, at the highest tension, and individuals everywhere were taking sides, the men in Maryland, Missouri, and Kentucky — with few exceptions — who were in a position to formulate and direct public conduct, seemed only anxious to confuse and divide public opinion. In Kentucky and Missouri these leaders, either because of timidity or lack of honest conviction, counselled and acted with a duplicity which paralyzed anything like concerted action by the people. The great majority of men in these states, either of those who stood loyally for the Union or those who, with equal sincerity, desired to take part with the South — and those especially who subsequently enlisted and fought in either army — were ready to back their sentiments by definite and appropriate public action. But no opportunity to do so was given them; and these states, after drifting aimlessly in the political storm, remained in the Union, not so much by the choice of their people, as because of a policy which permitted them no decision.

The Kentuckians who enlisted in the Confederate army have sometimes been taunted with the suggestions that the defence offered for the conduct of the men from the seceded states who fought to dismember the Union, cannot be urged for them. To those who can be satisfied with specious reasoning, the point may seem — or, rather, sound — to be well taken. But it has no real force, even as a technical criticism. As a matter of fact, the only action taken to ascertain the choice and will of the people of Kentucky, as to whether they would remain in the Union or take part with the South, was that had at the convention held at Russellville November 18, 1861.

That assembly was not provided for, it is true, by act of the legislature, but was a popular convention, called together as such bodies are customarily summoned. It was composed of more than two hundred delegates, sent from sixty-five counties, a very considerable majority of the counties of the state. It passed an ordinance of secession, adopted a provisional form of state government, and elected a provisional governor and other officers. Its assembling and procedure lacked official initiation and sanction, and may be termed irregular; but its determination was a better warrant of what the people of Kentucky desired to do than was ever given on the other side. Indeed, from the standpoint of the unconditional and uncompromising Unionist — the man who believed that the Union was legally, morally and altogether indestructible — the action of the Russellville convention was quite as authoritative and conclusive as that taken by any state which maintained its attitude of secession during the four years of the war; for, according to this creed, no state once admitted into the Union could ever by any method or possibility get out again. It is scarcely necessary to comment upon the fallacy and injustice of this criticism of the Kentucky Confederates. If the attempt was, as claimed by those who inaugurated it, a legitimate and rightful effort for separate government undetaken by states which had as good right to withdraw from the Union as they had to assist in framing it, then a Kentuckian, like the native of any other country, could without question become a citizen of the Confederacy. If the attempt was merely revolutionary — one form of exercise of that right — the citizens of the states which adopted ordinances of secession in a more formal manner had no more excuse for their action than had the Kentuckians who joined them in the effort for independence.

Moreover, while in pursuance of the theory on which it was projected and because of practical necessity the movement proceeded by separate state action, it was, as I have said, sectional in its impulse and character. It gained recruits, not so much because of solicitude for the interest of some particular state, as by reason of regard for the entire region whose interests were identical and whose welfare seemed at stake. The Kentuckians who entered the Confederate service honestly believed, and I think with reason, that a large majority of the people of their state, sympathized with and wished the success of the Southern effort, and expected that, if the Confederacy was established, Kentucky would become a member of it. Many, also, who deprecated secession, nevertheless thought coercion a far graver crime; and while not willing to assist aggression were willing to fight to repel it. I have always believed that if Virginia — whose example was always influential with Kentucky — had seceded at an earlier date, and certainly, if Tennessee, which did not secede until June 8, 1861, had acted more promptly, Kentucky would have formally and with practical unanimity united her fortunes with those of the Southern states. Her unmistakable expression of this sentiment after the close of the war justifies this belief.

It was by such considerations that Preston's conduct was controlled. He discerned with clear sagacity the true meaning of events, and understood not only that no offer of peaceable arbitrament could dissuade the people of the Southern states from the course on which they had determined, but also that the Northern people would do their utmost to prevent its consummation. He saw that war was inevitable and resolved to fight for the South.

It would seem that it should have been evident to all who had reached the same conclusion, that they could succeed only by rejecting every suggestion of compromise, in respect of state action, and by a prompt and aggressive policy. It was possible to array Kentucky on the side of the South and enable her to render the Confederacy efficient support only by anticipating the action to prevent just such a contingency which the Federal government would assuredly undertake. Nevertheless many of the recognized leaders of the Southern movement in Kentucky hesitated, consented to fatal delays, and encouraged the idea of "neutrality," until the people became so possessed with it that all active and resolute effort — any concerted, popular effort or programme, which promised a reasonable hope of success — was no longer possible.

Preston was not one of those who either doubt or temporize

and of all of the public men of the state his counsel and utterances were perhaps the frankest and most decided. I once heard the style and effect of the speeches which he delivered during the period, when these questions were matters of frequent and excited discussion, graphically and no doubt quite correctly described. An auditor of one of them, made at a large public meeting held at Lexington, said that a number of popular orators addressed the meeting, and all were listened to with earnest attention. None, however, produced a real impression until Preston spoke. In burning words and unequivocal terms he urged his hearers to help their brothers of the South. "Then," said the narrator, "the crowd went wild, and every man in it wanted to be a brigadier-general in the Confederate army."

The zeal and candour with which he expressed his convictions failed to induce the organized effort which he hoped, but undoubtedly contributed very greatly to stimulate enlistments from Kentucky in the cause of the South. The imminent danger of arrest, however, compelled him to leave his home at Lexington early in September, 1861, and evading, with some difficulty, his would-be captors, he made his way to Bowling Green which the advance of the Confederate forces just entering Kentucky had occupied.

Bowling Green was occupied by the Confederate troops on the 18th of September, 1861. The force which first entered was about forty-five hundred strong and was under the immediate command of Gen. Simon B. Buckner. Buckner had been offered a commission as brigadier-general in the Federal army, which position he declined. The same rank had also been subsequently tendered him in the Confederate service. This he also declined because of the then declared neutrality of his state. But when later it became apparent that all hope of peaceable settlement must be abandoned, he offered his sword to the Confederacy. Gen. Albert Sidney Johnston at once placed him in command of the troops which were to be moved into Kentucky and recommended his appointment as brigadier-general, which suggestion President Davis promptly adopted.

The sovereignty convention held at Russellville, Ky., November 18th, of which I have already made mention, after adopting an ordinance of secession, appointed three commissioners,

Henry C. Burnett, William E. Simms, and William Preston, with instructions to proceed to Richmond, notify the Confederate government of the action taken by Kentucky, and ask that she should be recognized as a Confederate state. Accordingly, on the 10th of December, 1861, the congress passed an act admitting Kentucky as a member of the Confederacy.

Preston immediately returned to Bowling Green and received his commission as colonel in the Confederate army, with an appointment upon the staff of his brother-in-law, General Johnston. This position was, of course, very gratifying to him personally, and, admitted as he was to the full confidence of such a chief, was greatly to be desired. A close and devoted friendship had obtained between them for many years, founded on mutual esteem and admiration, and when General Johnston received his fatal wound on the field of Shiloh, he died in Preston's arms.

Preston was commissioned a brigadier-general April 14, 1862, and served at Vicksburg, and subsequently in middle Tennessee taking part also in Bragg's campaign into Kentucky, in the autumn of that year. He served with distinguished gallantry at Murfreesboro, in which battle his brigade was in Breckinridge's division, and was hotly engaged, bearing its full share of the terrible work done by that division in its bloody charge of Friday, January 2d, upon the Federal left wing. In April, 1863, he was sent to relieve Gen. Humphrey Marshall of the command previously held by the latter in South-western Virginia, and remained in that district for some months, commanding a part of General Buckner's army entrusted with the defence of east Tennessee.

Preston's high reputation as a soldier rests more than anything else in his military career upon his conduct at Chickamauga. That battle was one of the fiercest and bloodiest fought during the war; and had complete instead of partial success attended the Confederate effort made there — had the victory, undoubtedly achieved, been instantly appreciated by the Confederate commander and energetically improved — it would, perhaps, have been the most important and valuable in results to the Confederate cause of them all.

General Bragg had fallen back after the battle of Murfreesboro about forty miles and had established his army at Manchester.

Shelbyville and Tullahoma, where it remained for five months, still holding a large share of middle Tennessee, and occupying with its cavalry much of the fertile territory to the west and north of its position. It was greatly reduced, however, during May by detachments sent to Mississippi, while the army of Rosecrans confronting it was heavily reinforced. When, therefore, the latter indicated, in June, an intention to asssume the offensive, the situation became so hazardous that retreat to the farther side of the Tennessee river was unavoidable. Bragg accordingly quitted Tullahoma on June 30, 1863, and marching for Chattanooga reached that point on July 7th. Rosecrans did not press the retreat, nor for some weeks did he evince any disposition to pursue.

Bragg fortified Chattanooga, and strove diligently to collect all forces available within his own department and which could be procured from other quarters. He knew that he must win the battle which was impending, or lose east Tennessee and northern Georgia as well as forfeit hope of recovering the territory already abandoned. General Buckner came to Chattanooga from Knoxville in the latter part of August, with the brigades of Gracie, Trigg, and Kelly. These were placed under the command of General Preston, and with some troops which he had brought from South-western Virginia, composed a division not numerically strong, but in other respects exceptionally good. Buckner was given a corps composed of this division, and that of Gen. A. P. Stewart. Breckinridge returned with his division at about the same date and Longstreet came with two divisions of the Army of Northern Virginia, but did not arrive until just before the battle. When the moment of combat was at hand, Bragg was at the head of an army which, although still numerically inferior to that of his opponent, was unsurpassed in spirit and prowess.

Rosecrans began his movement southward on the 16th of August. Demonstrating in front of Chattanooga with Crittenden's corps, he crossed the Tennessee with the main body of his army and marched up Will's valley on the western flank of Lookout Mountain, in the direction of Rome, and threatening Bragg's communications. Bragg was not strong enough, especially as Longstreet had not yet reached him, to meet this movement and, at the same time, hold Chattanooga. He accordingly evacuated that place on the 8th of September, which was immediately occupied by the Federal force which was threatening it. Rosecrans was deceived into the belief that the Confedcrate army was in full retreat on Rome and manœuvred accordingly; Crittenden pressed on from Chattanooga toward Dalton to menace Bragg's rear and rejoin the main body of the Federal army somewhere in that vicinity. Bragg, however, halted and took position in the vicinity of Lafayette, and behind the Chickamauga River, about twenty or twenty-five miles south of Chattanooga. It was his plan — and an extremely well conceived one — to strike his enemy in detail.

Before Rosecrans had ascertained that he was in error regarding Bragg's retreat to Rome, the three corps of his army had become widely separated; McCook was well on his way to Rome, Thomas was moving into the main pass of Lookout Mountain and toward Lafayette, where Bragg was eagerly awaiting him, and Crittenden was still in the vicinity of Chattanooga. The two wings of the Federal army were more than forty miles distant from each other, with Bragg's entire force virtually between them. Rosecrans was saved from a crushing disaster more by accident and good luck than by skill; yet it must be conceded that he acted promptly and decisively. McCook and Thomas were hurried back, and the Federal army was gotten together again on the 17th.

Bragg, having failed to strike either Thomas or Crittenden separately, moved toward Chattanooga with the hope of cutting Rosecrans off from that place, but was prevented by the rapid marching of Thomas. On the 18th the two armies were concentrated and front to front for battle, although the Chickamauga still separated them. Bragg had intended to cross the river early in the morning of the 18th, but bad roads and the persistent resistance of the enemy, delayed the movement, and it was not begun until late that afternoon, nor completed until the morning of the 20th, although the battle commenced and progressed with fury on the 19th.

Even were I sufficiently familiar with the story of this memorable conflict to give it accurately and in detail, I would not, in this connection, attempt to do so. It is my purpose only briefly to describe the part taken in it by General Preston. Every one at all acquainted with the history of our Civil War has doubtless some general idea of how this battle was fought. They know that Bragg marshalled his army in the dense thickets and along the banks of the little stream of Chickamauga, with Polk commanding its right wing and Longstreet its left; that, pursuing his usual battle tactics, he proposed to pivot on his left and swing his long line on the enemy in a great wheel directed from his right. They know that while the first day was principally employed on both sides in getting the troops into position, it was yet a day of fierce and stubborn fighting, scarcely less deadly than the tremendous combat which ensued. They know how the repeated attacks from the Confederate right, on the second day, were met by the tenacious resistance of Thomas; but that Rosecrans was compelled to reinforce that wing to such extent as to fatally weaken his centre and right; how Longstreet and Buckner massed in the afternoon on the Confederate left, swept the Federal right wing in utter confusion from the field, and wheeling upon the centre shattered that in turn. As night fell Thomas also withdrew, and the Confederates were left masters of the sternly contested ground that was drenched with the bravest blood of each army.

Chickamauga must always be remembered by the Kentucky Confederates with peculiar interest. Almost every Kentucky organization in the Confederate service was represented on that field. The "Orphan" brigade was there, and added to its already enviable reputation. The remnant of Morgan's division was there, fighting, as if by an instinct which directed them to seek appropriate leadership, under Forrest. Hood, Longstreet's gallant lieutenant, was a native Kentuckian. Buckner and Breckinridge were conspicuous among those intrusted with important command and distinguished for efficient conduct. Many Kentuckians fell; among them Gen. Ben Hardin Helm, than whom no man more loved and no braver or more accomplished soldier served under the Southern banner, and Maj. Rice E. Graves, the famous young artillerist, whose skill and dashing courage was recognized by all the Army of Tennesseee.

Preston's division was in Buckner's corps on the Confederate left, resting on the Chickamauga near Lee and Gordon's Mill.

It was attacked and hotly engaged on the 19th, but repulsed the enemy with smart loss, and participated on the afternoon of the 20th in the heavy fighting which resulted in the complete defeat and rout of the Federal forces upon that part of the field. Frequent and complimentary mention is made in the various Confederate accounts of the battle of the service rendered by Preston toward its close, when the reiterated and vigorous assaults made on Thomas had uncovered the Chattanooga road, and well-nigh driven him from his position. Rosecrans was compelled to support him with troops which were greatly needed in other quarters. Longstreet, utilizing his opportunity struck and crushed the Federal right, and, pressing his advantage swept down the line toward the Federal centre and left. This movement completed the defeat of the enemy and no Confederate division commander contributed more to its successful result than Preston. He renewed the attack, previously unsuccessful on the hills near the Snodgrass house, where Granger and Steedman were making a resolute stand to protect the Federal retreat and prevent the rout which it in large measure became. They were strongly posted and well provided with artillery and had repulsed more than one onset.

Preston had been ordered to support Hindman and McLaws, but ascertaining that he could take the enemy in flank by moving along a certain ravine did so upon his own responsibility. The movement was no less intelligent than bold, and Preston, after bloody and desperate work on both sides, dislodged the Federals from the position and drove them from the field. His division fired, perhaps, the last shots of the battle after the night had fallen.

Preston did not win his victory without cost; one of his regiments — the Sixty-third Tennessee of Gracie's brigade — lost in killed and wounded two hundred and two out of an aggregate effective of four hundred and four. He inflicted severe loss on the enemy, and captured the Eighty-ninth Ohio, the Twenty-second Michigan and part of the Twenty-first Ohio regiments.

There can be little doubt that had General Bragg, after the extraordinary success on his left, pressed straight after the fleeing enemy into Chattanooga, he would have so crippled the army of Rosecrans that it would have been forced to an immediate retreat on Nashville, and, perhaps, could not have safely reached that point. As it was, he rested at Missionary Ridge, in front of an enemy speedily reorganized and in a few weeks reinforced into overwhelming strength, while his own army was being depleted instead of strengthened. At the first hostile advance he was driven away and the gallant Army of Tennessee was destined thenceforth to strive with heroism never surpassed for victory almost impossible.

Preston's active military service virtually terminated with the battle of Chickamauga. Soon afterward, and before the battle of Missionary Ridge, he was replaced in command of the department of South-western Virginia, where he remained, however, only a few months. Early in 1864, he was assigned to duty in the trans-Mississippi, although he did not receive his commission as major-general until later.

At that date it seemed probable that the affairs of Mexico were about to become closely involved with those of the Confederacy, and that an alliance between the two governments, mutually beneficial, might be effected. At any rate, Mr. Davis and his advisers were of opinion that a competent diplomatic representative, one capable of so shaping the situation that it might be of advantage to Confederate interests, should be on the ground ready to utilize any opportunity. Maximilian had been made titular Emperor of Mexico chiefly by French influence, and, while perhaps acceptable to the more intelligent and conservative elements of the population, was maintained in his position almost entirely by French aid and protection. This attempt to establish an autocratic power upon American soil and place a European prince upon the throne induced strong resentment and earnest, even angry, protest upon the part of the people and government of the United States. It seemed probable, indeed, that if France persisted in this scheme of Mexican empire, war between her and the United States might result; or that, at any rate, France might conclude to recognize the independence of the Confederacy and perhaps, in some way, furnish substantial aid. In any aspect of the case it was clearly the policy of the Confederate authorities to cultivate a friendly understanding and feeling with the newly inaugurated ruler of Mexico. General Preston was sent as minister to Mexico early in 1865 with some such purpose as I have indicated.

His mission was not only tentative and dubious of result, but was somewhat difficult of accomplishment in the mere matter of reaching his destination. It was undertaken at the time that the irregular and desultory but fierce warfare waged between the soldiers of Maximilian and the recalcitrant native population was at its worst. The insurgent Mexicans, lacking the means and organization to collect and operate in bodies of any considerable strength, were scattered through the country more particularly along the northern frontier. All of these bands were guerilla in their character and most of those who composed them were banditti. The imperial troops were also divided into small detachments for the purpose of more convenient operation and active pursuit; and differed little from the men with whom they were contending in their conduct toward the peaceable inhabitants — if there were any such. With such conditions prevailing, strangers travelling through that region were naturally regarded with suspicion by both parties and were in no little danger. It was in such a "zone of hostilities" that Preston found himself when, after traversing Texas with a small escort he crossed the Rio Grande.

He used to relate one incident of this march which seemed to have greatly amused him. Among the members of his escort was a young cavalry officer, who had served gallantly in the army of the trans-Mississippi, but, ambitious of diplomatic distinction and preferment, had gladly accepted General Preston's invitation to accompany him on this mission. Just before entering Mexican territory this gentleman had procured at some point accessible to the blockade runners, a very beautiful pair of boots, articles then extremely scarce in the Confederacy. He prized them the more because they had flaming red tops, ornamented with showy tassels. On the second or third day after passing the Rio Grande, Preston's party was halted by a much larger body of Mexicans, who announced that they were part of the command of General Cortinas, and said that the Americans must go with them to the camp of that officer, which was not far distant. As no attempt was made to disarm the escort, and refusal would have been ill-advised, General Preston at once replied that he would be very glad to wait upon General Cortinas, and the two parties proceeded accordingly to the camp. It seems that, on that day, the band of Cortinas had been engaged in a skirmish with a body of the Imperialists, and had taken several French prisoners, all of whom were executed. As they rode into the camp they saw, suspended to a tree and with his throat cut from ear to ear, the body of a French officer. This was very shocking; but even more unpleasant to the young man who had obtained the boots was the fact that the dead man had on a pair exactly like them, with equally gorgeous red tops. He reached, at once, the conclusion that the officer had been butchered because of the boots, and anticipated a like fate for himself.

Cortinas received the party courteously, but expressed a desire to know the reason of their coming, and hinted that something might be expected in the way of compensation for his good offices. General Preston did not feel obliged to inform the guerrilla chief that he was on his way to open negotiations with Maximilian, and simply said that many people might be compelled to abandon their homes in the Confederacy and seek refuge in Mexico, and that he was visiting the country in advance to learn where and upon what terms they would be permitted to establish their settlements. He added that he was prepared to pay a reasonable sum for a guarantee from all molestation, if General Cortinas could furnish it. Cortinas answered that he could make an arrangement to that effect which would be binding on his own side, and a bargain was struck on better terms than Preston had expected. Cortinas then gave orders that his guests should be properly entertained; but the young man with the boots had unaccountably disappeared. After diligent search, however, he was discovered in a thick clump of bushes, apparently in the agonies of cramp colic. But he had pulled off and hidden his boots. Cortinas was much diverted when the cause of the young fellow's apprehension was explained, and requested Preston to assure him that no one in his band should take liberties with either his boots or his throat.

Upon his arrival at the City of Mexico, General Preston found little in the situation that was encouraging. Those who were advising Maximilian had little time or inclination to consider any matter not immediately connected with local affairs. It was apparent, also, that the policy of the *de facto* Mexican government in any matter of importance would be dictated by France. In a short time therefore he sailed for Europe, perhaps in order to ascertain if anything might be accomplished by application to those who were really potential. Any definite plan, however, which may have been contemplated was frustrated by the desperate fortunes of the Confederacy. He was in England when he learned of the surrender of the Confederate armies and the dissolution of his government. In a few months thereafter he returned to his home in Kentucky.

Fortunately, his estate had not been much impaired during his absence. It was of such nature and so situated that it was not injuriously affected by the four years of warfare, so disastrous to the greater number of those who had served the Confederacy. He was able, therefore, to enjoy very much the same social life he had led in ante-bellum days, and continue the amenities in which he excelled, and without which existence to him would doubtless have been very distasteful. He was a generous host to his less fortunate comrades, and a kind friend, always evincing the warmest interest in their welfare and all that concerned them. He sometimes, too, gave very excellent advice. One of his oldest friends, and a companion in arms in the Mexican War, Gen. John S. Williams, came on one occasion to consult him as to whether he (Williams) should accept the agency of a life insurance company, with a good salary, which had been offered him. Williams had once been in affluent circumstances, but the close of the war found him without a penny. He liked the salary well enough, but thought the employment rather undignified for one so distinguished as himself.

"Now, my dear fellow," said Preston, "don't hesitate. Accept the position at once, and especially the salary. A man situated as you are, and who has served his country so well, should be willing to do anything that pays well, provided it isn't indictable."

But while his property was not diminished in value, much of it was in such shape that he became necessarily involved in extensive litigation. He did not regret, but rather enjoyed this, for it gave him employment, and he, in great measure, managed his own lawsuits; disproving, by the way, the old adage, that "A man who is his own lawyer has a fool for a client," for he was almost invariably successful. His interest in public affairs, however, was unabated, and he took an active and important part in the effort to rescue the state from the dangerous civil dissension which threatened her peace and prosperity after the close of the war, and which was successfully consummated in 1867.

In the states which had constituted the Confederacy, that element of the population which adhered to the Union was scanty in numbers and, as a rule, not very respectable in either intelligence or character. The great majority of the better class of people in those states, whether rich or poor, and almost every man of repute, had been intensely Southern in feeling and with few exceptions had served in the Confederate army. Consequently when the effort for Southern independence failed, that class was universally under suspicion and political disability; it was not only disfranchised, but completely without representation and support both at home and in Congress. During the period when there was virtually no local civil government in any Southern state, and later when the reconstruction measures were in effect, no Southern white, not absolutely alien in sympathy and malignant in feeling to almost every other white person in the community in which he lived, was permitted to hold any official position or perform any official act. Those who were invested with such authority claimed the widest latitude in its exercise and were held to no responsibility. How that authority was abused may therefore be imagined when it is remembered that the "scalawag" hated the "rebel" with an inveterate rancour, and the "carper-bagger" was unwilling to diminish his own importance and profit by any concession to those under the ban.

But in Kentucky the difference of opinion upon questions connected with the war and the resulting division in sentiment pervaded the entire population, comparatively unaffected by the controlling considerations which had operated to make the South so nearly unanimous. Antecedent views and relations seemed to have little effect. Some of the largest slave-holders were the most determined opponents of secession. Men between whom not only the closest personal friendship and community of interest but a perfect agreement on all political questions had prevously existed, separated and were arrayed against each other on this. Stranger still, men who had always previously been in opposing political camps, suddenly found themselves ranked together. Ardent Whigs, who had contemplated with favour schemes of "gradual emancipation," became intense Southern sympathizers; fire-eating Democrats, who had denounced any suggestion that slavery should be confined to the territory where it was already recognized, as an abolition device, became unconditional Unionists. The cleavage followed no definite line. Families were divided, son against father, brother against brother. On more than one field Kentuckians fell in fratricidal combat, and the best blood of the state was freely given upon both sides in the quarrel.

Quite naturally, therefore, the animosities engendered by the war were not so unrelenting in Kentucky as in the states where no such incentives to reconciliation existed. Mutual respect and the inclination bred of close social relations made possible a coalition between a great number of those who had stood in opposing ranks. Many of them resumed their former friendly relations immediately upon the close of hostilities. The same was true of many who had enlisted in either army, but whom the war had estranged.

The Union men who entertained this feeling exceeded in number those who were malignant, and in the last year of the war the resentment of the radical minority was directed against them more bitterly, if possible, than against men of avowed Southern proclivities.

Of the hundreds of citizens arrested by Burbridge and imprisoned or banished, many were Union men. Some of those he shot or hanged without trial, in alleged retaliation for guerilla outrages, if not undoubtedly "loyal," were at least not open and undisguised Southern sympathizers. It is said that an eminent divine, who was the most prominent and the ablest leader of the extreme element, advised that all who were suspected should be dealt with alike, pleasantly suggesting that "if there are any among them who are not rebels at heart, God will take care of them."

Col. Frank Wolford, famous among the Kentuckians who

served in the Federal cavalry, was placed under arrest and threatened with court-martial for having in a public speech "spoken disrespectfully of the administration" that is to say having deprecated the enlistment of negro soldiers. Col. R. T. Jacob, another gallant Federal officer, was arrested for some similiar offence, although at the time lieutenant-governor of the state, and sent into the Confederate lines. A policy of intimidation was inaugurated more for the purpose of coercing conservative Union men into silence and submission than to punish or overawe the disloyal.

Fortunately the conservative Union men were in control of the state government and had the nerve and sense to thoroughly utilize that advantage. They welcomed the Kentuckians who returned home from service in the Confederate army, not only as men who ought to be restored to all rights of citizenship, but as allies from whom assistance might be expected. All disabilities which had been imposed upon them by state legislation were repealed, and every assurance given that no man should be molested for past political conduct. Gov. Thomas E. Bramlette, in a special message to the legislature, on December 9, 1865, recommended the enactment of a law granting pardon for all belligerent acts committed within the territory of Kentucky which might be construed as acts of treason against the state; and a measure to that effect was promptly passed and approved.

A little later an amnesty measure more general and even more complete was enacted, and one of incalculable benefit as preventing prosecutions of both Confederate and Federal soldiers from which bitter and dangerous feeling would have resulted. Upon the governor's recommendation the legislature passed "An act to quiet all disturbances growing out of the late rebellion." It provided, "That no officer or soldier of the United States or of the so-called Confederate states, and no person acting in conjunction with or coöperating with any one of them, or with the authorities of either government, shall be held responsible, criminally or civilly, in the courts of this state, for any act done during the late rebellion by command of and under colour of, military authority." It was declared, "That for the purposes of this act the rebellion shall be deemed to have commenced on the 1st day of May, A.D. 1861, and to have terminated on the 1st day of October, A.D. 1865." This measure certainly very largely contributed to the accomplishment of its declared purpose "of giving tranquillity to the state."

While Kentucky had not been exempt from the experiences of actual warfare — indeed, had witnessed, on a small scale, a great many of its attendant evils — her territory had not been occupied by the contending forces in large numbers for any considerable period, and had, in a large measure, therefore, escaped the ravages of war. But although spared the devastation of the conflict, her people shared its passions, and had reason to congratulate themselves that the leading men of the state, ignoring past differences, were practically united in the desire to appease resentment and effect a complete amnesty if not entire reconciliation. Kentucky's previous attitude of obedience to Federal authority and adherence to the Union, whether correctly or not representing the real and general sentiment of her people, made it difficult to subject her to the same treatment which, maintained for so many years after the termination of armed resistance, very nearly destroyed the political existence of the Southern states. There can be no doubt that the extremists of the Republican party, especially after Mr. Lincoln's benevolent and restraining influence was removed, wished to include Kentucky in the programme of proscription intended for all who felt sympathy for the South and disapproved of the radical policy. Slight pretext would have sufficed to cause these men to visit on Kentucky all the calamities with which they scourged the South; they would, had occasion offered, have inflicted upon her negro domination, the greed and gripe of the carpet-bagger and the other features of "reconstruction"— that terrible aftermath of civil strife — which wrought more injury to some of the Southern states than was done by war itself. Had the situation in Kentucky been other than it was, she might have been compelled to pass through much the same experience and wait as long for the restoration of better feeling and normal conditions. Had those who were in control of the state government been in accord with the fiercer element of the Republican party—that element which, led by Thaddeus Stevens, completely dominated congress — an excuse would probably have been found to deal with her after the same methods so relentlessly applied in the South.

The commanders of the military forces still stationed in Kentucky and the officials of the Freedman's Bureau acted in a manner that seemed deliberately intended to provoke some outbreak which might be construed as necessitating the employment of repressive measures, and a small minority of the Union men encouraged such conduct. But the state officials, a decided majority of both houses of the legislature, and by far the greater number of those who had been staunch Unionists through the war, regarded with no favour a course so abhorrent to the mass of their fellow-citizens. The so nearly equal division of sentiment, which at the beginning of the war seemed to be something to be deplored, proved in this crisis her best protection against the dangers which were threatening every former slave-holding community.

The Southern sympathizers and the returned Confederates were of course inclined to act in unison and did so. All of them appreciated the generosity as well as wisdom of this policy, and understood the propriety of aiding it to the utmost. Notwithstanding its numerical superiority in the state, the conservative Union element might have been intimidated by threats of violence and defeated in the election of 1865 and 1866 had not the Federal soldiers, who shared this sentiment, been reinforced at the polls by the Confederates; and the conservatives were maintained in power. The disposition upon the part of the Confederates themselves to seek office, quite natural, perhaps, when they found themselves so popular with the majority of the people, was subordinated to the main and most important purpose of consolidating all the elements opposed to the radical programme into one strong party.

No man was more earnest and effective in this work than General Preston. His previous acquaintance with the public men of the state of all parties, and the high estimate in which he was held by his immediate comrades and political associates, qualified him better than any other man, in the absence of John C. Breckinridge, to bring about a thorough and cordial understanding among those whom it was necessary to enlist and combine for such a purpose. All reposed confidence in his ability, public spirit, and fidelity to principle, and no one knew better how to appeal to Kentuckians who loved their state and desired its peace and prosperity.

In August, 1867, the Democratic party, as it was entitled — in reality an organization composed of men of all shades of political opinion, yet who were resolved upon absolute and general amnesty, and entire oblivion of every thing which might disturb harmonious citizenship — nominated as its candidate for governor John S. Helm, a man whose high character and recognized patriotism was a guarantee that such policy would be faithfully observed. He was elected over two competitors, representing every element of opposition, by an immense plurality, and Kentucky was rescued from all danger of political proscription and any resultant trouble.

With the exception of one term in the legislature, which he accepted at the urgent solicitation of his fellow-citizens of Lexington, at a time when his services were especially needed, General Preston never again held or asked office. He cared no longer, indeed, for official preferment. But his influence in the councils of his party was felt so long as he lived, and was always wisely exercised; and no one was more earnestly concerned for the welfare and complete enfranchisement of the Southern people.

His warm and consistent support of Tilden, of whom he was an intimate friend and ardent admirer, was largely induced by his belief that the policy of that statesman toward the South would be not only just, but generous. He advocated an endorsement of Tilden by the Kentucky state convention, and as delegate to the Democratic national convention, in 1880, earnestly urged his renomination for the Presidency. Tilden's broad culture and acute political understanding appealed strongly to his intellectual sympathies, and the action of the convention grievously disappointed him. This was his last active participation in politics, although his advice was frequently sought and generally heeded.

General Preston retained until his death the esteem and admiration of the public and the sincere affection of his intimate associates. To the last he was an exemplar of the conduct and the characteristics which had been most respected in his youth.

In his exalted idea of what was due both to and from a gentleman, and his punctilious insistence on the observance of the same rule by others, he was, perhaps, more a representative of an order that had passed away, than of the society which knew him in his later years.

CHAPTER XI

ANY attempt to describe the social conditions prevailing in Kentucky and the South before the Civil War — that epoch which, like a cataclysm, divided the old order from the new — without mention of the negro as he was before he became a freedman, must necessarily be incomplete.

The "negro question" as we have to deal with it to-day is altogether unlike what it was when it conduced so largely to that strife. Quite as perplexing, although, we hope, not nearly so dangerous, it is presented in a totally different aspect. Then it was a sectional issue, now it is a national problem. When the maintenance or the extension of slavery was the subject of dispute, the negro, as an individual, a personality, was a factor hardly taken into account. The institution of slavery as it affected the interests or might shape the future of the white race — as it might operate to open territory to occupation entirely by slave-holding or by non-slave-holding populations — was almost exclusively considered in the discussion. The small minority which regarded it purely from a philanthropic point of view was eloquent and insistent but, until debate was succeeded by actual combat, was heard with little favour or patience by the other disputants.

So long as slavery existed it was impossible to consider the racial question except in its economic phases, or as it appealed to the more benevolent instincts of humanity. The negro might be treated humanely or cruelly, his master might be kindly and considerate or harsh and unfeeling, nevertheless, as he concerned the public and from every social and political standpoint, he was regarded simply as a chattel.

The great change wrought in this respect by the enfranchisement of the black man and his elevation to the rank of citizen and voter has also utterly changed not only his former relations with the Southern whites, but the feeling with which the white people everywhere regarded him. He has unquestionably gained much along certain lines, but he has lost much along others. With the independent action, free choice of employers, and control of his own labour now permitted him, his condition has, of course, been greatly improved. Yet we may doubt if even the better opportunity which all this affords, and the respect which must be accorded a freedman, entirely compensates for the lack of the tolerance and indulgence which was formerly extended him. The advance made by many of the race in education and general intelligence has been extraordinary. But a much greater number have not so advanced, while they have retrograded in morality and integrity. The political rights granted the negro have done him little benefit. Suffrage was given him suddenly and before he was in any wise prepared to judiciously or safely exercise it. With no previous training, hereditary or individual, he was entrusted with powers on the proper use of which good government depends, and was expected to use them wisely — something the Anglo-Saxon, with eight hundred years of racial experience, has scarcely yet learned to do.

The negro's incapacity properly to perform the duties thus thrust upon him was, however, nowhere accepted as an excuse for their mal-performance. Many of those who professed themselves his friends, and perhaps desired to aid him, seemed to think that, when he had been given the ballot, ample provision had been made for his material welfare. It is not surprising that he also should have fallen into that way of thinking, and, like many white men, have reached the conclusion that the best use that could be made of a vote was to sell it. In the Southern states where, during the reconstruction period, the negro became the dangerous tool of certain thoroughly unscrupulous white politicians, negro suffrage wrought well-nigh irretrievable disaster. So menaced, such a people wasted little time in inquiring whether the evil inflicted on them was induced by ignorance or malice, but sought and applied remedies sharp, drastic, and decisive. The result is epitomized in one of Private John Allen's best stories.

A certain candidate, he said, told an old negro, whose support he was soliciting, that his opponent had declared that a "nigger had no more right to vote than a mule." "Now, Uncle Lige," he asked, "what do you think of that?"

"Well, master," Uncle Lige answered, "I don't know whether a nigger ain't got no more right to vote den a mule or not. But I know he ain't got much more chanst to vote den a mule."

The "wards of the nation" had reason at one time to regret that their tutors had included politics in the curriculum adopted for their instruction; but the matter became alarming when the example so furnished was copied in localities and under circumstances where no conceivable excuse for such policy was offered, and it became the practice to "count out" white as well as black men.

But I wish to describe the negro as I knew him *au naturel*, so to speak; as I remember him before and during the war, and antecedent to the time when freedom had transformed and politics had demoralized him.

I have little personal knowledge of the conditions of slavery as it existed in the extreme Southern states nor of the character and habits of the negroes employed upon the large sugar and cotton plantations. From what I have been told by those who were better informed, I am of the opinion that the servitude there was sterner and less relieved by the ameliorating features which in the border slave states contributed to mitigate its harshness. In the far South and on the very large plantations, where the slaves were counted by the score, the proprietors and masters were absent from their homes during a considerable part of each year; and, even when present, saw little of the slaves, leaving their care and management almost entirely to the overseers. The labour upon these plantations was also more severe, constant, and exhausting than upon the farms in the states with more temperate climates and where cereal crops were chiefly grown. Under such conditions the negro's standard, both of intelligence and character, was necessarily lower than it was in the communities where circumstances permitted a treatment more favourable to his comfort and improvement. Furthermore, the frequent importation into that region of the more vicious negroes from the border states, sold to work on the plantation as a punishment for incorrigibly bad conduct, was a constant cause of demoralization to those among whom they were sent.

With all this, however, the stories told by Northern ante

bellum writers of the brutal usage of the slaves in those states were grossly exaggerated; and it may be confidently asserted that in all cases wherein they were treated with unreasonable severity the indignation of the majority of the whites of the community was emphatically and practically exhibited toward the offenders.

In Kentucky, Virginia, Tennessee, and Missouri, in all of which states I had ample opportunity of becoming personally and accurately acquainted with the methods by which the master managed his slaves, and how the white population felt and acted toward the black, I can conscientiously testify to the kindness and consideration which the latter almost invariably received. It must be remembered that the people of the states in which slavery existed at the date when the question of its abolition or restriction was first seriously agitated, were responsible, in far less degree, for its establishment on this continent than were those who had become their censors. They had taken little, if any, part in the "slave trade," the original introduction of the negro into this country, and the imposition of his servile condition. A very considerable number of the negroes held in bondage in the South were descendants of slaves brought to New England years previously, and employed in Northern and Eastern states, until their labour ceased to be so profitable there, and then sold into communities where it commanded a premium. I mention this oft-recited and well-established fact, not as an historical gibe, or in the spirit of *tu quoque* contention, but because it serves, I think, to strongly rebut the presumption of deliberate inhumanity or conscious wrong-doing on the part of the Southern slaveholder, and affords reason, therefore, for the supposition that he would have been disposed to mitigate, rather than aggravate, a condition so unfortunate.

No argument would be accepted to-day in excuse or palliation of involuntary servitude. No plea in justification of the holding in bondage of a man of any race or colour would be listened to. Yet it may be readily understood that at a time when this form of slavery — which not long before had been universally sanctioned and was not yet generally condemned — seemed to the people of certain localities to furnish the kind of labour best adapted to their wants, they should have, without scruple, employed it. But, although slave labour was greatly desired and sought by the people of the South, and was esteemed by them to be the most valuable, they at no time, as I have said, participated in or approved the slave-trade. While willing to buy and employ negroes already in slavery, and whose manumission was impracticable, they had never countenanced the importation of the native Africans for that purpose, and were among those who most earnestly demanded the suppression of the practice.

There may seem, and be, little theoretical difference between the crime of inaugurating and that of accepting and maintaining slavery, but when the manners and the opinions of the age are considered, it is not difficult to believe that the man who erred in the latter respect might be less cruel and more humane than he who made the system, with all of its attendant evils, possible. Such, at least, was the sincere conviction of the slaveholders of the South. They honestly believed that they were guiltless, but realized their duty to make the condition of the negro better. With rare exceptions they strove to do this. It would be palpably unjust to censure a man who commits an act not accounted wrong by the code and civilization of the age in which he lives, so severely as it would be proper to visit it on the man who does the same thing after a more advanced and enlightened sentiment has branded it as a crime. In process of time, perhaps, war for any provocation — warfare between rival nations and antagonistic peoples — will come to be regarded as the direst crime that can be perpetrated against humanity. But so long as it is recognized as the *ultima ratio regum;* as it is esteemed justifiable in cases of last resort, only a visionary dreamer will hold the soldier who slays a foe in battle to be as criminal or as wicked as the homicide who takes life for personal animosity or gain. The man who does a wrong ignorantly or not in violation of the code of ethics he has been taught, is neither morally so bad nor necessarily so depraved as the man who sins consciously and in defiance of the law he knows. Even when he errs much good may be expected of him.

A great number of the slaves held in Georgia and the Carolinas at the date of the Civil War, and a yet greater proportion of those in Virginia, Kentucky, and Tennessee, had been inherited by their owners. They and their ancestors had belonged to the same families for two, three, or more generations. For these "family negroes" the masters entertained not only a warm interest but real attachment, and this sentiment influenced the master's treatment of other negroes who bore to him no such relation.

But for other reasons, chiefly the economic one, the slaveholder was disposed to treat his negroes considerately. If a mule valued at $150 was worth caring for, there was a similar and stronger inducement to care for a slave worth from $800 to $1,000, and some pains would be taken to keep him in good health and serviceable condition. A selfish concern, therefore, as well as a certain sentimental regard, operated to protect the negro, in a great measure, from wanton injury or abuse. I think this was more particularly the case in the border states where the blacks were not so numerous. No individual slaveholder in the Bluegrass region of Kentucky, in which I was reared, held at any time a considerable number of slaves, but many of the farmers there owned six, eight, or ten.

Two of my uncles, with whom I passed much of my boyhood after the death of my parents, were the largest slaveholders whom I knew in that country. Each of them had a farm of about a thousand acres, and owned sixty or eighty slaves. Knowing these negroes as I did, during my childhood and youth, and those on the farms immediately adjoining, I became well acquainted with their peculiar characteristics, and can perfectly remember them. Subsequent observation convinced me that the darkeys who were, after a fashion, my companions at that day, were genuine types of their race. These negroes were well cared for and kindly treated, and were unquestionably the most contented and jolliest human beings I ever saw. They were kind-hearted, docile, and, in their way, quite honest. If they occasionally appropriated articles belonging to their masters it was upon the theory that it was "all in the family," and that they were entitled to a certain share of what was produced on the farm and by their labour. Unless the offence was unusually audacious the master generally regarded the matter in the same light, and was not inclined to punish the culprit.

The cabins in the negro quarters were rude but comfortable structures, usually built of logs, and affording substantial protection from the weather. The cottages provided for servants habitually engaged in household work, or for some who were especial favourites, often constituted, with their small but well-kept gardens, quite attractive abodes.

I am quite sure that, as an almost universal rule, the slaves were well housed, comfortably clothed, and bountifully fed. I do not remember to have ever heard one complain of short rations, and have more than once seen three or four of them eat more food at one meal than would have been furnished — at the latter part of the war — to a platoon of Confederate soldiers. Nor, so far as my observation extended, were they overtasked, or required to labour more than eight or ten hours a day. In Kentucky, and I believe it was the custom throughout the South, the "dinner horn" was blown at noon, and the negroes, however employed, came to the "quarters" for their mid-day meal. Upon the farm on which I was raised, a big couch shell was used for the dinner signal instead of a horn. A houseboy, who had been christened by his mother Peregrine Pickle — which she thought a very becoming name — was, for many years, in charge of this instrument. Punctually at twelve o'clock Perry would brace himself against the wall of the kitchen, place the shell to his lips, and send forth a sonorous summons which seemed to promise corn-bread, bacon, and cabbage to every hungry stomach in the county. Almost before the echoes died away a troop of jocund darkeys would flock in from the fields, some riding the farm horses or mules, which were also brought in to be fed, and all gabbling and guffawing, as if the quantity of victuals each would be permitted to consume depended on the volume of noise he could make.

On nearly every farm in the neighbourhood with which I was best acquainted, the negro men were allowed to cultivate small patches of ground for their own benefit, and the negro women raised poultry. The sale of the vegetables, chickens, and eggs so produced furnished them with money for their Sunday clothes and Christmas revelry.

The Kentucky farmers killed and cured the hogs, which supplied the greater part of their meat consumed during each year, when the first real cold weather set in. "Hog-killing time" was an important event, therefore, and it was not easy to determine whether the negroes or the small white boys most enjoyed it. Long before daybreak an immense fire of logs would be blazing near the hog-pen, on which large stones were placed. When these stones were heated red-hot they were thrown into big troughs filled with water, and as soon as the water was at boiling pitch the carcasses of the slaughtered hogs would be placed in the troughs and kept there until the hair, thoroughly scalded, could be readily scraped off. Then the carcasses would be hung up on stout cross poles and disembowelled, preparatory to being taken to the "meathouse" to be cut up into hams, chines, sides, and sausage meat. Much else, also, that was edible, did that useful animal provide. Even while the work was in progress, hogs' tails and livers were broiled on the big fire and eaten with a relish that only the small white boy and the adult darkey can experience. We were wont also on such occasions to procure our stock of "bladders," which, inflated and hung up in the garret to dry, were relied upon, in those comparatively primitive times, to produce the quantum of noise without which Christmas would have scarcely realized the bright expectations of boyhood.

But when Christmas came, all the black folk and all the small white fry fraternized in an acme of enjoyment. The frolics at the quarters usually began about midnight on Christmas eve, and continued throughout the night and until the next evening. On Christmas morning, before the eastern sky grew gray or the stars had lost their lustre, the revels were at their height. In addition to the good things the negroes themselves provided, a fair share of the cake and eggnog made for the white people was always supplied them, and master and overseer alike would wink at a negro drinking some whiskey on Christmas, although they might tolerate it at no other time.

To the white boys in the "big house," who had lain awake throughout the night in anticipation of the signal, the first obstreperous burst of African mirth was an irresistible call. Strict orders were usually given us upon the previous night not to visit the quarters in the morning, but obedience to such injunctions was impossible; indeed, I think it was not really expected, for we were never reprimanded when we disobeyed, which we invariably did. Snatching up our packs of firecrackers and everything else with which we could hope to swell the clamour, we would make a bee-line for the cabins. The big logs, glowing and roaring in the wide fireplaces, threw dazzling gleams from the open doors and windows far out into the night. Dancing, shouting, screaming with laughter, men, women, and "little niggers" were wild with joy. When occasionally a big firecracker exploded among the dancers, or a bladder stamped on by sturdy feet boomed like a small piece of artillery, the women would shriek in simulated fright, and the delight of the spectators was unbounded. Thus, without cessation, the merriment — this howling paradise — was continued until the morning sun smiled upon the scene.

It has been customary to describe the negro, when in slavery, as idle and shiftless. There has never existed a people, perhaps, which would not have been "shiftless" if maintained in a state of constant dependence; required to take no thought of the morrow, cared for like children, assured, no matter what change came to them, of food, shelter, and clothing, of all necessary provision when in health, and of medical attention when ill.

But many of them were not idle; and those who were placed in positions of trust and quasi-responsibility were not only themselves industrious, but were very exacting of proper attention to duty on the part of others. As I have said, I knew little of the conditions obtaining on the large Southern plantations, but have often heard that the black foremen — the "drivers" — were stricter in compelling labour from those under them than were the white overseers.

That the average negro — that much the greater number of them — vastly preferred leisure to labour is an undeniable fact. But the same thing may be said of very many, if not a majority, of every race. Many white men are indolent, although feeling an incentive to exertion which was not offered the black slave. It must be remembered, also, that the negroes, as a race, slightly appreciated and had scarcely yet learned to work. They were removed only five or six generations from the savage — from the native, naked African — who deemed work the direst affliction humanity could suffer. Emancipation has opened an immense opportunity to the negro, and I believe it will ultimately be improved. Slavery undoubtedly arrested his development at a certain point, but its discipline was of incalculable racial advantage. The number of vicious negroes among the slaves was not so large as is the criminal class of the freed blacks.

The negro of to-day may differ from the ante-bellum darkey very slightly in his love of fun and sense of humour, but he certainly fails to give it the same quaint and ludicrous expression. An experience of the harder realities of life seems to have dulled his capacity for finding enjoyment in the things which formerly amused him, and "book-learning" has made him strained and affected where he was formerly simple and natural. There was an essentially practical flavour in the dry witticisms of the plantation darkey, a subtle recognition of human nature in his sly satire, and a real and keen, although limited, perception of individual character.

The negro humour was most mirth-provoking when it was evidently unconscious, and he had a more than Irish faculty for blundering that was ludicrous indeed, but sometimes conveyed his meaning more perfectly than he could have expressed it in any other form. His aptitude for making excuses, frequently unsatisfactory, but almost always ingenious, was unrivalled. I once heard Mr. Davis tell a story that well illustrated the confidence with which an old-time darkey, who knew himself to be a favourite, would undertake to defend a manifest delinquency.

Mr. Davis was commenting on two curiously inconsistent reports upon the same matter, submitted to him by a certain official, and which seemed to amuse him greatly. He was reminded, he said, of how a negro who had been his especial attendant on his Mississippi plantation was accustomed to excuse the shortcomings of which he was often guilty. One of the duties of this servant, whose name, I believe, was Tom, had been to make the fire in his master's bedroom during cold weather. The fireplace, like all those in the old Southern mansions, was commodious and the only fuel used was wood. On some mornings Tom would bring in logs of very inconvenient length; so much so that while one end of a log was burning the other would extend out some distance on the hearth. When Tom's attention would be called to this misfit he would answer: "Marse Jeff, you oughtn't to blame me; it's dis fireplace. Dis fireplace is entirely too narrer." On the very next morning, perhaps, he would furnish logs too short to remain in position, and would fall between the irons. Mr. Davis would gravely point out this negligence, but Tom, with an air of injured innocence, would promptly respond: "Marse Jeff, dey ain't no use in blamin' me; de whole trouble is wid dis fireplace; dis fireplace is entirely too wide."

Judging by the relish with which Mr. Davis told this story, one might have been justified in believing that, much as he would have liked a properly constructed fire, he decidedly preferred Tom's attempted explanations.

I remember vividly an incident which occurred in my boyhood, when I was living in the Bluegrass country, and in which the more amusing traits of the negro character were brought out in distinct relief. An unusually audacious and extensive raid had been made upon the watermelon patch of one of my uncles, and a brief investigation disclosed the fact that it had been planned and executed by some of the younger negroes. The overseer, who was a rather harsh disciplinarian, wished, without further inquiry, to flog them all, but my uncle would not consent to this, and preferred to discover, if possible, who had been the most guilty and the leaders in the enterprise. A formal trial was therefore held, and all of the evidence, previously heard, recapitulated, with as much more, pro and con, as could be procured or suggested. I was then about sixteen years old, and with a cousin of the same age volunteered to act as counsel for the accused. We were each burning to acquire forensic experience and distinction, and entered into the case with great zeal. A number of footprints of different shapes and sizes had been discovered in the patch, some of shod and others of bare feet. The measurement of these tracks bore hard upon the prisoners at the bar, because closely corresponding with that of their shoes or bare feet. It became a matter, therefore, of prime importance with the defence to prove, when the measurement of a shod track fitted the shoes of one of the defendants, that he had not worn his shoes on that night; and, *per contra*, to prove that he had been shod at that time, if his bare feet resembled in conformation and dimension a measured track of that kind. It was very difficult to do this except by the testimony of the accused themselves, and, of course, no one would believe that. The most damaging evidence offered for the prosecution was that of two of the crowd, who had become, so to speak, state's witnesses, claiming that their connection with the offence was of an extremely slight and venial nature. One of them, named Toby, would have sworn away the life of his own grandmother if he could have escaped the cowhide in no other way. Upon cross-examination, while admitting that he was present when the melons were stolen, he denied all complicity in the theft. "Didn't you take one of the melons yourself?" I asked.

"No, suh, I nuvver tuk nothin' outen de patch. I nuvver went inside of de patch. De mos' I done wuz to ketch hol' of a watermillion when Dow handed it over de fence." The other informer's testimony — Sim was his name — sealed the fate of Dow, the one of all my clients I wished most to save. Sim, while positively declaring that he himself had no connection with the robbery, seemed cognizant of all Dow's movements on that occasion, from an early hour in the afternoon until late at night, and ingeniously related many apparently trivial incidents which, taken together, very strongly indicated Dow's guilt. I knew that there was bad blood between them, but when I tried to make Sim acknowledge this he swore that he loved Dow rather better than a brother. One of the tracks made by bare feet corresponded exactly with Dow's huge and ungainly hoof, and Sim swore that Dow had gone barefooted during the entire evening of the raid. At this point Dow's patience utterly gave way and he indignantly shouted, "I wish dat lyin' nigger had'er said I wuz wearin' my shoes. I'd'er proved I had 'em locked up in my chist."

A remark made by an elderly negro, after the trial was over, summed up all the philosophy of the subject. "When watermillions is ripe," he said, "you allus gwine to find niggers close to de patch."

All who served in the Confederate army will remember that, however much the soldiers might be straitened in other respects, almost every command was, for the two first years of the war at least, well supplied with negro servants. The Second Kentucky Cavalry, which I commanded for more than a year, was abundantly provided in this regard. The darkeys attached to this regiment were so numerous and so constantly scurrying about the country — leaving the column when it was on the march or running out of camp — in search of food for their masters more palatable than the ordinary ration, that I was compelled finally to take measures to stop a practice which had become a nuisance. I organized the negroes into a quasi-company and placed them under the command of a staid, reliable negro of about fifty years of age, who, on that account, acquired the sobriquet of "Captain" Jordan, I gave Jordan instructions to keep his "command" well in hand; to allow not more than four men to leave at one time, who should be absent not more than two hours; and to observe this rule, with certain others which were indicated, both in camp and on the march. Jordan strictly obeyed the instructions given him, enforced the sternest discipline in every respect, and became, indeed, a fearful martinet. Those under him used to say, "Ef you wuz burnin' in torment dat ole man wouldn't let you leave de ranks to git a drop of water."

When the soldiers, desiring to have their negroes go after a square meal, sought, as they often did, to have him relax the rules, he would answer grimly, "I gits my orders from de cunnel."

I remonstrated with him, on one occasion, for having punished, with what I thought undue severity, a young darkey who had been guilty of some breach of discipline. "What I gwine to do wid 'em?" he said. "Jess let 'em go long to suit deyselves?"

"Oh," I said, "report them to me and I'll have them tried by a court-martial."

"Now, cunnel," he replied with fine scorn, "what's de use of you talkin' like dat. Youse knowed niggers all yo' life. Dey doan' know nothin' 'bout no cote-marshal, and dey ain't skeered of it. But ef you warms dey hides wid a switch, dey 'preciates de 'tention."

When Bragg was retreating from Kentucky and Morgan was assisting to cover the rear of the army during the pursuit of the enemy, which was kept up for three or four days, we were constantly skirmishing during that period, and exposed at times to a brisk cannonading. Jordan's squad, on one such occasion, was drawn up on the pike, nearer to the enemy than they should have been and a smart shower of shells fell around them. The darkeys were ashen with fright, and begged piteously to be taken out of danger. But Jordan, who was as fearless as he was stern, stubbornly refused to move, because, as he said, he "hadn't no orders." I subsequently complimented him on his courage, but suggested that it would have been better if he had moved out of range.

"Dar' wan't no 'casion for it,"he replied. "Dem fool niggers wuz skeered mi'ty nigh to death; but mos' of de shells 'sploded way up in de a'r. Only three of 'em 'sploded on de pike, and dey didn't bust."

I may be pardoned for thinking that the best specimen of negro logic and irony that I can remember was one furnished by an old negro who did so in my defence. About ten years after the close of the war I was making a canvass in Louisville for the office of commonwealth's attorney for that judicial district. My opponent was also a Democrat, but at that date the party lines were not strictly drawn and nominations were not made, and he believed, with reason, that he could carry the negro vote against me because of my having been a Confederate soldier. Some of his more zealous and unscrupulous friends circulated a report among the negroes that I had, during the war, cut off the ears of unoffending coloured men — had perpetrated such mutilation upon a great number of them. They were, naturally, profoundly excited and angered by such a story, which there was little difficulty, at that time, in making them believe.

To the great disgust and irritation of the others, however, one old darkey declared his disbelief of the charge and his intention to vote for me. A large deputation of coloured brethren called upon him to protest against what they deemed a flagrant sin and infidelity to his race. He listened until they finished their remonstrance, and then quietly but firmly replied:

"You niggers," he said, "is all wrong about dis. Some of de white folks has fooled you. I doan' know Gin'rul Duke pussonally, but I was raised up whar he wuz born and brung up and knowed his people mi'ty well, and dey wan't de kind of people to cut off niggers' ears. But I'll make dis bargain wid you; ef you kin show me one nigger — jess one — who's done had one ear cut off — I won't ax for bofe — den I'll agree dat Gin'rul Duke cut it off, and I'll vote agin' him. But onless you fetch me dat nigger wid only one ear I ain't er gwine to b'leeve no sich tale."

The receptive nature of the negro and his fervid, emotional temperament made him peculiarly susceptible to religious impressions, and a great number of the elderly and more respectable negroes of both sexes professed some kind of religious belief. It would not have been easy, however, to define it. There were few Presbyterians among them. The doctrines of Calvin were not readily grasped by the African understanding, and the ascetism of such a creed was altogether distasteful. With many, of course, "getting religion" was a mere hysterical fancy, conceived under excitement, and as easily forgotten. Yet I remember some who, I believe, entertained sincere and intelligent religious convictions.

It is scarcely necessary to say that they were extremely superstitious. All ignorant people are so; and the vivid negro imagination conjured up a host of strange myths and fears. They talked much about the Devil, not only as a personage to whose custody they might be consigned in the future life, but as one whom they might at any time encounter in this world. But witches and ghosts — "sperits," the latter were termed in negro parlance — were the chief subjects of their superstitious faith and awe. I could never clearly comprehend the negro's idea of witches, whether he believed them to be human beings — men or women, who had in some strange fashion, by some illicit compact, become possessed of supernatural or preternatural powers — or believed them to be creatures alien to humanity, something like the fairies of European folk-lore and the genii of Eastern story.

I am inclined to think that they entertained both such beliefs, but without attempting to distinguish between them. The younger negroes frequently spoke of some very aged individual of their own race as a witch, but seemed not to ascribe any undue wickedness or malevolence to the persons so stigmatized, or to think him or her gifted with unusual capacity for either good or evil.

But they believed in another kind of witch — a sort of woodsprite — which performed strange and mischievous pranks. Horses running in pastures, partly marshy and containing brier patches, frequently appeared in the morning, splashed with mud and with curious tangles in their manes. The slow-witted, unimaginative white man supposed that the animal had been wallowing in the wet ground or wandering among the briers. But the intelligent and better-informed darkey discerned immediately that he had been ridden by a witch, and knew that the knots and tangles in his mane were "witches' stirrups."

They were not prone, however, to form or to express such opinion, when a horse which had been stabled over night showed on the next day signs of having been hard-ridden. If any darkey, especially one who was suspected of being addicted to such practices, ventured the suggestion that the horse had been witch ridden, the others would wag their heads and significantly remark, "I reckon dat nigger wuz de witch hisself."

I do not remember any trace of the voodou superstition, so common in the extreme South, among the Kentucky negroes of the ante-bellum period; but have been told that it has prevailed among them, to some extent, since the war.

The belief in ghosts, however, was universal and implicit. Every deserted house, almost every secluded and weird-looking corner of the forest or field, was supposed to be haunted by some spirit which jealously guarded its peculiar premises and resented nocturnal intrusion. This was an exceedingly disagreeable feature of the negro superstition, and made me, when as a boy I listened to their stories, feel very uncomfortable. "Doan you nuvver let a sperit see you," they would say. "Ef he once sees you, he gwine to allus ha'nt you." Near the place where I was born two duels were fought, in each of which one of the combatants was killed. There was a difference of opinion among the darkeys as to whether these spots were haunted — or should properly be haunted — for no one had ever seen a ghost at either. One side held to the opinion that every locality where a violent death had occurred was always and necessarily haunted by the spirit of the person who had so suffered. The other side contended that the spirit appeared only when foul murder had been done; and insisted that, "No white gen'elman what was killed in a fa'ar fight would 'sturb niggers what hadn't done him no harm."

A warm, reciprocal attachment almost invariably obtained

between the family negroes and the white people, more particularly in the case of those servants who were especially trusted by their masters. So much has been written about the fidelity and devotion of the old "black mammy," that I feel that little can be said on the subject, and I will only avouch that it cannot be exaggerated. The love of these old nurses for the children committed to their care, and their unremitting attention to their wants, could not have been exceeded even by parental feeling.

The most remarkable example of this kind that I ever knew was that of the nurse in the family of my mother-in-law, Mrs. Henrietta Hunt Morgan. Bouvette, or "Aunt Betty," as we usually called her, was a woman of strong sense and extraordinary character — amiable, sweet-tempered, yet very firm upon occasions, and imbued with a truly Christian spirit. She nursed all of Mrs. Morgan's children — my wife, Mrs. A. P. Hill, and Mrs. Morgan's six sons, including the general. To the day of her death, they regarded her as a monitress, and repaid her care with the warmest affection. Mrs. Morgan regarded her more as friend than servant, insisted that the other servants should show her every respect and attention, and relied very much upon her advice in all household matters. When Aunt Betty died the funeral services were held in the parlours of Mrs. Morgan's home, which were placed at the service of the pastor of the coloured church to which the old servant belonged. Many of the congregation attended, but Mrs. Morgan especially requested her surviving sons and myself to act as pallbearers, and we bore the good, faithful old woman to her grave.

These old nurses, although very indulgent in some respects, were autocratic and strict in all matters wherein they thought correction necessary, and would roundly scold the young ones under their charge for any serious misconduct. They sometimes asserted this privilege even after the children they had nursed had long outgrown their care and authority. But they resented such interference upon the part of others, were rather jealous sometimes of even the exercise of parental authority, and usually sought to screen the youngsters from punishment, although it might be richly deserved. On the contrary, the elderly male servitors who occupied responsible posts, the gardener or carriage driver, were as a rule offensively officious and arbitrary

— at least, we boys thought so — in the protection of everything about which they could possibly claim a right to be vigilant. If a boy trespassed on the strawberry or raspberry patches, loafed about the stables, threw a stone at a chicken, or chased a turkey until it took refuge in a tree, one of these argus-eyed detectives would almost certainly discover and report the offence, and magnify it in such a fashion that there was little chance of the offender escaping punishment.

During much of the Civil War, even after almost the entire South had been occupied by the invading armies, the slaves conducted themselves in a manner and with a remarkable docility, which can scarcely be understood except by those well acquainted with the negro character. Not only in Kentucky and Tennessee and other territory, the greater part of which was practically lost to the Confederacy at an early period of the struggle, but upon the more Southern plantations where slight protection was afforded the white people, the negroes, with few exceptions and nearly until the close of the war, remained at home, continued their accustomed vocations, were tractable, and gave little trouble.

Much the greater number of those — and there was a large number of them — who accompanied the Confederate armies and served in various menial capacities, were very faithful, the majority of them remaining with their masters until the final surrender. These negroes seemed to be as thoroughly imbued with the feeling which prevailed in the Confederate ranks as were the soldiers themselves, and spoke with as much pride of Confederate achievement.

Impressionable and so long as under salutary influences amiable, the negro of that generation readily accepted the sentiment of those — especially those above him — with whom he was associated, and just as readily reciprocated kindness and returned gratitude and affection for considerate treatment. He was essentially conservative, disposed to adhere to first opinions, or rather impressions, and maintaining in some measure, the respect he had been taught for certain things and certain families, even after he ceased to entertain any personal regard for them. But beyond all else he believed that absolute obedience was due to power — to might, whether with or without right — and when he saw, or thought he saw, the sceptre pass from the white people of the South, nothing seemed to him more natural or proper than that he should transfer his allegiance to the Freedman's Bureau and the Republican party, which, to him, then represented the authority he so revered.

The fierce atmosphere of the strife, the terrible apprehension felt by the white people, the unwonted privations and humiliation to which the whites were subjected, and the presence of the Federal troops seemed finally to bewilder and demoralize the negro, and when the proclamation of emancipation was issued they were like creatures deprived of reason. But the radical change in their feelings and conduct was more completely wrought by their enlistment as soldiers in the Federal army than by anything else. The simple fact that they were free, startling and attractive as it was to their imagination, might have been, at first, too abstract for their exact comprehension. But when they were clad in uniform, had guns placed in their hands, were made policemen where they had formerly been servants, and invested with, at least, apparent authority — all this was an object lesson they could perfectly understand, and which fired their blood. As a war measure their military enlistment may have been politic; in every other regard it was unwise and of vast injury. Long before the negro had acquired the discipline of the soldier he lost that which he had been taught as a slave.

If, previously, he had been ignorant and half savage, he had at any rate, been a "gentle savage." Given the bayonet and turned loose on those he had formerly served, it would have been a marvel if all of the insolence, ferocity, and evil passion that might have been latent in his nature had not been aroused. When he returned from military service to pose as a hero among those of his own colour he became a henchman of the white "scalawags" and "carpet-baggers," who incited the agitation and strife of the reconstruction period, and, abusing the confidence of the deluded blacks, robbed the whites, and well-nigh destroyed the already devastated South.

The Southern people were unquestionably the best friends the negro had in his years of slavery, and of all those concerned in or who profited by his servitude they had the least to do with its imposition. They resented his violent emancipation, and the untimely conferring of a suffrage for which he was not prepared. They were bitterly indignant when he was armed and employed in an effort made, they believed, for their subjugation. Since he has become a freeman, they have sometimes been compelled, in the defence of their civilization and protection of their homes, to deal with him in a manner which may not have seemed compatible with the rights of freemen, and in doing so they may sometimes have erred. But I am convinced that in the future, as in the past, the negro will find his real and intelligent friends among the people of the South.

And it is just as well and natural that this should be so. The Southern people know his better qualities as well as his weaknesses. They know that if he has sinned, others have sinned against him; and very often the wrong has been committed in the guise of benevolence. The South is the true habitat of the negro on this continent. He will always be needed there as an agricultural labourer, and in that capacity he has no superior. He will never find a congenial home in the North. Any hope he may entertain of "social equality" will prove as mythical there as in the land where he was recently a slave, and the people of the North will never understand him as thoroughly, nor be as lenient to his faults, as the people among whom he and his fathers were reared. The Northern white labourer will also always regard him jealously, as one who may some day become a competitor more or less formidable. In the South, among the descendants of his former masters, the old relations between the whites and blacks, but under better conditions and all compulsion removed, may be restored; and there, I hope and believe, he will receive the best incentive and the best help to attain the highest plane to which he may be destined.

CHAPTER XII

AMONG the innumerable stories told about the war, and of war times, one very seldom hears a ghost story. The old soldiers at least are not given to telling them; and wide as is the reminiscence of the veteran, various as are the experiences he relates, they seldom, if ever, deal with the supernatural. It would seem that the scenes he had witnessed might naturally suggest such thoughts, and his imagination call up apparitions to haunt every field and spot where men had fallen in conflict. The belief has always been prevalent among many good people that the spirit, reft from the body by violence, is unable to find rest and quiet in the grave, and decidedly prefers to revisit the locality where it suffered the last earthly agony. It may be, however, that this is the case only with those who have been the victims of assassination, and that the soldier slain in fair fight doesn't feel that he has been murdered. He doesn't, therefore, come back to earth by way of protest against the unjust manner in which he was sent out of it.

Sailors are proverbially superstitious, and are, it is said, firm believers, as a rule, in spectral appearances, visitants from another world. It might be expected that soldiers, leading an equally adventurous and hazardous life, should be quite as prone to such fancies. But such was not the case with the soldiers of our Civil War, so far as I know anything of the matter, on either side.

It may be that familiarity with the spectacle of death in strife and battle induces a skepticism regarding any subsequent appearance or return of the dead that might not otherwise be entertained; and that those who have seen a great many men killed, learn, unconsciously, to estimate conditions more practically and rationally, and to discard any idea that so great a host, having quitted the ranks of the living, is at all likely to parade as ghosts.

The superstition of the soldier, so far as he indulged in such speculations at all, seemed to be directed not to apparitions and spiritual manifestations, but to presentiments and signs of good luck or omens of disaster.

Some men believed in their "lucky days," of the week or month — days on which they might attempt any enterprise with good hope of success, or brave any danger with impunity. Others believed in the fortunate influence of some article of apparel or something carried about the person. Of course, this faith dwindled as the war wore on, until the man who had placed confidence in a lucky jacket, thought himself in "big luck" if he could get any sort of jacket. Some thought it brought better luck to ride a horse of a certain colour than of some other. I cannot remember, however, that such men ever hesitated to procure a horse of any colour whatever, when they were in need of a mount.

While a variety of suggestions might be heard during the war period, as in peaceful life, of what things were ominous of good or bad fortune, very few, so far as I can recall, were distinctly formulated or given much credit. I can remember only one such omen which was, so to speak, "classified" and definitely named. There was a notion prevalent in Morgan's command, and, perhaps, in some others of the Confederate army — I never heard of it in any other, however — that upon a man's face there was sometimes impressed unmistakable indication that he was about to die; that immediately or very soon before a man was killed in battle, or met with violent death of any kind, a premonition of his impending fate could be read in his face, discerned in a peculiar expression which was called the "death look." I myself know of three or four instances — in fact, witnessed them — in which the death in battle of certain men was predicted because they had this look, and they were killed very soon afterward.

I will not admit that I became a convert to this superstition, and doubtless the facial expression and the death speedily following were merely coincident. Yet I should not like to see the "death look" again. By the way, it was in no sense a ghastly look nor one of fright. It was not caused by apprehension of danger. On the contrary, the men who bore it exposed themselves at the time with habitual bravery, and, indeed, recklessly.

It was not an unpleasant expression, but one of bewilderment rather, as if the man's thoughts were intent on something else than that which was taking place about him.

Presentiments, of course, were very frequent; so common, indeed, that the man who never had one was regarded as being utterly destitute of imagination and almost of proper sentiment. The chief vice of the presentiment was that it rarely materialized, the expected accident or catastrophe scarcely ever occurred. Yet such disappointment seemed in nowise to affect the man with whom the habit of presentiment had become chronic, and he kept on predicting disaster as cheerfully as ever.

I am inclined to think that the presentiments were often the result of some suggestion, the effect of which, however, was not fully realized, as inducing the anticipation. Something might happen to a man which would cause him to apprehend serious injury, and the impression might remain after the incident itself had, perhaps, been forgotten. I knew of two or three instances in which men had presentiments that they would receive wounds in the head which might prove fatal. In every such case the man had narrowly escaped being wounded in that very way, and the presentiment was undoubtedly induced, I think, by that previous experience.

I cannot remember any presentiment of death in battle having been realized, but heard of one case in which very unpleasant consequences resulted. A man, so ran the story, believing that he would be killed at a certain time, distributed his personal effects among his comrades. The date passed by without his having been killed, and his donees positively refused to return the gifts. This man swore roundly that he would never again be such a d — d fool as to harbour a presentiment.

Those who have had no actual experience of warfare naturally consider only its picturesque or terrible features. They know, of course, that there must be minor incidents, humorous, prosaic, or pathetic; but it is the big events, the battles, sieges, and marches, "the pomp, pride, and circumstance," and the carnage of the stricken field of which they think in connection with the soldier's life. Yet every soldier who has seen much service, remembers more vividly perhaps than aught else many things which in the telling seem very trivial.

In the early summer of 1863, a part of Morgan's command encountered Colonel Jacob's cavalry regiment and some other Federal troops at a point on Greasy Creek, about twenty miles from Pulaski, Ky. Not more than eight or nine hundred men on each side were engaged and the fight was soon over; but it was quite hot while it lasted, and the percentage of killed, both Federal and Confederate, was large for a skirmish. The enemy had one piece of artillery, which was used pretty effectively. The fight opened by an attack on our line, in which the combatants came to close quarters. We repulsed our assailants, and charged in turn across a wide meadow enclosed on all sides by woodlands. During this advance I witnessed a sight which shocked me greatly. The enemy had withdrawn the piece of artillery to the edge of the farther woods and was endeavouring to protect his retiring line with its fire. When we were about half-way across the meadow a shell exploded on the right of Capt. James E. Cantrill's company, killing two or three men and literally tearing one poor little fellow into shreds. He was from my native county, and was not more than sixteen years of age. I had known him from his infancy.

Captain Cantrill, by whose side the boy was marching, was drenched with his blood. The spectacle was extremely painful; the more so because I had known the lad — who was exceedingly bright and attractive — so well. The Federals were driven into the woods and the gun was pulled off to a considerable distance, but still continued its fire. A small cabin stood about fifty yards from the edge of the woods through which the Yankees had retreated, and just as our line approached it a loud crash notified us that it had been stricken by a cannon-shot. Anxious to ascertain if it was tenanted, and, if so, whether the inmates had been injured, I entered the cabin. I can never forget the scene which met my eyes. It impressed me the more because I had not recovered from the shock which poor little Billy Graves's death had just given me. In front of and close to the empty fireplace a woman was seated as still as a statue, with her face buried in her lap. Three little children were around her clinging to her dress. An unexploded shell lay upon the hearth, almost touching her feet, and a gap in the stone chimney showed where it had entered. Mother and little ones were paralyzed with fright. I spoke to the woman and finally induced her to lift her head and look at me, but she would not speak a word. I never saw in human eyes such an expression of fear and horror.

In November, 1864, Gen. John C. Breckinridge, then in command of the department of South-western Virginia, moved into east Tennessee, and, attacking the Federal general, Gillem, at Bull's Gap, after sharp fighting drove him from that position, almost completely routed his command, and pressed him as for back as Strawberry Plains, not far distant from Knoxville. With the river between him and his pursuers, and having received reinforcements from Knoxville, Gillem succeeded in checking the Confederate advance. For several days the contending forces faced each other along the river banks, unable to come to close grapple, but constantly firing on each other with musketry and artillery. I was summoned on one occasion during this period, to General Breckinridge's quarters for some purpose, and, during my conference with the general, a woman brought a little child, some three years of age, into the room in search of surgical assistance. The child had been wounded by a shot from a Spencer rifle. Fortunately it had been at very long range, and, although the bullet was partially imbedded in the little one's leg, the bone was not badly shattered. The medical director immediately took charge of the case, and the general and I proffered such assistance as we could render.

The surgeon went to work with professional nonchalance, although in a very kindly manner, but General Breckinridge and I could not so well maintain our composure. The child had been very quiet until the surgeon began his work, but when he applied his forceps to extract the ball, the poor little thing struggled and wailed piteously. I had seen some dead and several wounded men that morning and while the sight was, of course, not a pleasant one, it had not much affected me. A soldier becomes accustomed to seeing men disposed of in that way. But that child's demonstration of suffering completely unnerved me. I became sick at the stomach and hurriedly left the room and the house. In a moment I heard some one else rush out of the house, and turning around discovered that it was General Breckinridge. He was affected just as I had been, and like me was seeking relief in flight and fresh air. Notwithstanding our sympathy for the baby we could not, as we looked at each other, refrain from laughter.

In August, 1862, Morgan's command, then consisting of the Second Kentucky Cavalry and Gano's squadron of two companies, was campaigning in Sumner County, Tenn., making its headquarters alternately at Gallatin and Hartsville. It was an exciting period in the history of the command. Its close proximity to Nashville, which was occupied by a large Federal force, and to the Louisville & Nashville railroad, on which stockades, well garrisoned, were erected for the protection of the necessary communication with Louisville, compelled the most alert vigilance and constant activity on Morgan's part, not only to harass and cripple the enemy, but to protect himself from frequent attempts at reprisal. In all his adventurous career he did no more incessant and successful service than during the three weeks that he was thus employed. His detachments and scouting parties were in conflict every day with the Federal expeditions sent out from Nashville. Not a night passed without some skirmish fought by the light of the moon or stars. The quiet farmer-folk who lived near any one of the broad white pikes or narrow country roads, fringed with forest or meadow, in which the combatants would meet, became accustomed to such encounters. The quick, ringing shots would awaken them to listen to the sudden clamour of the fight, followed by the wild hurrah and thunder of the chase; and then with the comment, "It's only our boys having some fun with the Yankees," they would fall asleep again. About the close of this period, after the country had been stripped clear of the outlying posts to the suburbs of Nashville, Boone's regiment had been captured, and General Johnson's brigade of picked Federal cavalry had been defeated and completely broken up, and just before we marched into Kentucky to assist in General

Bragg's grand raid, there occurred two incidents, both very painful and one extremely tragic, which I shall never forget.

Two deserters from Confederate regiments had fallen into our hands. One of them had been captured in arms and fighting in the Federal ranks. He was tried by court-martial and sentenced to the punishment prescribed for such offence by the regulations and the laws of war; *viz.*, to be shot to death. He was sent to me with orders that I should have the sentence executed, and I had twelve men detailed for that purpose. Of course, such a thing was extremely repugnant to the men of my regiment. They were willing to shed blood in battle, but, strongly as they abhorred desertion, they shrank from shooting a man in that cold-blooded way. The culprit was a very young man, not more than twenty years of age. He had been born and reared in the immediate vicinity of Gallatin. His neighbours believed that he had been induced to desert by his father, who was a bitter Union man. At any rate, grave as his fault was, we all felt sympathy for him, and I was greatly impressed by his demeanour. He was perfectly calm, showed no fear, and when I asked him if he had any wish that I could gratify before he was shot, if he desired to send any message to his family or see any of them, he answered that he had already bidden his mother good-bye and that he desired only to have some minister pray with him before he died. I sent instantly for the chaplain of the regiment, but could not find him. He said subsequently that he had absented himself purposely in order to avoid "a scene so painful." I responded that the "scene" was quite as painful to the rest of us as to him, and that he, more than any one else, should have been present on such an occasion, inasmuch as one of his holy calling might have given the poor wretch some comfort. The altercation resulted in my summary dismissal of the chaplain from office, for which I got into some trouble afterward myself.

However, after waiting two or three hours, which must have seemed ages of suspense and agony to the doomed man, I summoned old "Parson Ash" to my aid. Parson Ash was a Presbyterian minister, and one of his sons was a lieutenant, in company "B," of the Second Kentucky Cavalry. On this account the old gentleman, although far beyond the military age and not an enlisted man, always stayed closely with the regiment, went into every fight, and, notwithstanding all remonstrance to the contrary, insisted on strictly performing every duty and labour which fell to the lot of the private soldier. He was a very kindly and thoroughly earnest and courageous man, exceedingly intelligent and well informed, doubtless an excellent theologian, and certainly one of the coolest and best shots with a rifle I ever saw.

The parson came instantly after getting my message and when I explained to him the wish of the condemned man to receive the consolations of religion, expressed his earnest sympathy, and said he would remain with him to the last moment. No repugnance to a "painful scene" could prevent the old hero from peforming what he deemed a sacred duty. Parson Ash talked and prayed with the poor fellow in a way that impressed and affected all who heard him. I was not inclined to limit the time to be thus occupied, but in about fifteen minutes the condemned man declared his readiness to die. He thanked the parson for his ministration, saying that it had given him great comfort. He preferred only one other request, which was that his eyes should not be bandaged. The twelve men of the firing detail were drawn up in front of him, six with loaded, six with unloaded, rifles. Lieut. Samuel D. Morgan, a cousin of the general and a very fine young officer, was in command of the squad. Just before giving the order to fire he shook hands with the prisoner, and said to him:

"Die like a Tennesseean!"

"I will!" was the resolute response. Nothwithstanding the absolute sincerity of both the exhortation and the answer, under any other circumstances I should have been amused, but then this short colloquy added to the solemnity and pathos of the event.

Lieutenant Morgan gave the commands:

"Ready! Aim!" the rifles dropped to a level, and the prisoner looked unflinchingly into their muzzles. "Fire!" rang out the last order, and simultaneously came the crash and flame of the volley. Without a groan or the quiver of a muscle, the victim sank stone dead upon the ground.

On the day after the shooting of the unfortunate man, whose death has been described, the other fellow who had been sentenced to be flogged, was sent to me with the exceedingly disagreeable notification that I should have the punishment inflicted. This one had not deserted to the enemy, and consequently had not been taken in arms. Indeed, he was too cowardly to fight on either side. But he was infinitely the meaner of the two. Almost the entire able-bodied male population of Sumner County was then serving in the Confederate army. Only the women and children remained at home; and this scoundrel had been prowling about the unprotected farm houses, committing numerous depredations and terrorizing the inmates. His sentence to receive thirty-nine lashes on his bare back was richly deserved; no one felt for the wretch anything but contempt and disgust. Yet willing as all were that he should receive punishment, there was something revolting in its character. On the afternoon of the day preceding that on which the sentence was to be executed, a deputation of ten men, one from each company of the regiment, came to my headquarters and requested a conference with me. The one selected as spokesman asked if the report which had reached them, viz., that a man had been sent me to be flogged, was true. I answered, of course, in the affirmative.

"Well, colonel," was the response, "we are instructed by our comrades to say that no man in the regiment will consent to do such work. We feel no sympathy for the scoundrel. We think he ought to be hanged. We hated to shoot that man yesterday, but we would cheerfully shoot this fellow. Nevertheless none of us is willing to flog him, because we think such an act would be degrading to ourselves. It isn't on his account that we refuse, but on our own. We never expected to disobey any order you might give us, and we very reluctantly tell you that we will disobey this one if given. If you see fit to punish any of us for refusing, well and good; we'll make no complaint. But none of us will flog that hound, mean as he is."

I was somewhat disconcerted by this speech, but in my heart I was proud of the spirit the men exhibited, and thoroughly understood their feeling. I personally knew nearly every man in the regiment. They were of the pick and flower of Kentucky's best population. Many of them had been my schoolmates and ante-bellum friends and companions.

"Very well, gentlemen," I said, "I appreciate your frankness, whatever I may think of the determination you have expressed. As for punishing any one for disobedience, I have only to say that no order has yet been disobeyed. Go back and tell your comrades that I have received their message."

I knew that the men were in dead earnest and would never recede from the position they had taken. I was in a quandary. The prisoner had been sent to me with positive instructions that the sentence of the court-martial should be executed. But how was that to be done if no one would consent to be executioner?

While I was pondering this problem very seriously without being able to discover any solution, it was solved for me in a curious fashion. Shortly after the deputation had departed, an officer came with a proposition which amazed and disgusted me, but which in the end I accepted as the best that I could do. This man had been elected, a few days before, second-lieutenant of Capt. Joseph Desha's company, who was at that time serving in the Second Kentucky Cavalry. He was of dissolute, disreputable character, and his election had been a matter or regret not only to Captain Desha, but to every one in the regiment save the men who voted for him, and they eventually regretted it more than all else. He said that he had learned of the resolution taken by the men and announced to me, and that in order to help me "out of a difficulty," as he expressed it, he would himself flog the prisoner if I was willing that he should do so. I could not conceal the surprise, and could scarcely restrain the indignation this suggestion excited.

"Do you not understand, lieutenant," I said "that the private soldiers have expressed a disinclination to perform such service because they regard it as degrading and will you, an officer whom I cannot order to do such a thing, volunteer for duty so abhorrent?" He did not seem in the least abashed; he did not, I think, realize the sentiment that others entertained about the matter, and repeated his remark that he wished to help me "out of a difficulty." I assured him that I did not wish his aid; that no matter what might be the difficulty from which such action on his part might extricate me, I would not thank him or consider myself under obligations to him. Evidently failing to understand how I regarded his offer, and believing that he would earn my approval and gratitude he insisted, and I finally consented.

Sure enough, on the next day, when the appointed hour arrived, he was on hand, swaggering and flourishing a long, thick, leather strap, with which he proposed to inflict the punishment. The prisoner was bound by the wrists to a stake in front of the regiment, which was drawn upon parade, and stripped to the waist. The volunteer executioner plied his blows with vigour and apparent relish of the pain his victim was suffering. In a few seconds the back of the wretch was covered with bloody weals and bruises; he screamed and circled around the stake in his agony, but his tormentor continued to wield the lash with unrelenting energy. When the full tale of thirty-nine stripes had been given the executioner raised his arm with the evident intention of delivering another blow. A yell of execration arose from the men in the ranks, and Captain Desha, who was officer of the day, rode forward and threatened to shoot him if he struck again.

I sent for him that afternoon, and he came, still under the impression, I believe, that I would in some way reward him for the service he had rendered. When, however, I curtly informed him that I would permit him no longer to serve as an officer of the regiment, or even to remain with it, he was like a man thunderstruck.

After awhile he rallied, and declared that I had no right to dismiss him in that summary way. I admitted that his claim was in one sense true, but said that I had the right to protect the men under my command from the humiliation of serving under a man like him, and meant to do it.

"I believe," I said, "that if I preferred charges against you for conduct unbecoming an officer and a gentleman, a court-martial would convict you, and you would be regularly dismissed from the service. As it is, I simply tell you that you cannot serve as an officer of this regiment. You can go where you please."

Convinced that he could not placate me, and aware that he would get no sympathy, but perhaps very rough treatment from the men, he concluded to accept the situation. He left that night, and I never saw or heard of him again.

Much controversy has prevailed between the soldiers who served the Confederacy, whether in the infantry or cavalry, regarding the merits of their respective arms — a controversy which, of course, never was and never will be determined by the disputants themselves. Nor will they ever be able to agree in another matter which has been one of debate between them: that is, as to which branch of the service entailed the more arduous work and the greater amount of hardship. Each was, at times, abundantly trying, and tested endurance to its utmost limit; but the cavalry was decidedly better off in this respect, because shifting their encampments more frequently and traversing a much wider extent of territory, they were often enabled to procure food very superior to the ordinary ration, and enjoyed, too, in frequent and rapid movement, a comparative freedom from the routine and restriction of the usual camp life, which was highly agreeable. Gen. " Jeb" Stuart had this in mind, doubtless, when he hummed, as he so often did, his favourite song:

"If you want to have fun jest jine the cavalry."

The cavalry commands which were accustomed to make raiding expeditions, long incursions into regions not so constantly occupied by the large armies, and, therefore, less denuded of supplies, were especially favoured in this wise, and until the last year of the war might be said to have occasionally "lived upon the fat of the land." No memories of my life, indeed, are pleasanter than those of the service I saw in middle Tennessee and central Kentucky during the spring, summer, and autumn of 1862 when the abundant capacity of those fertile and lovely countries and the lavish hospitality of their people were very thoroughly tested and appreciated.

I am not sure, although it is saying a great deal when the almost insatiable appetite of a soldier is remembered, that the beauty of the landscapes amid which we made our bivouacs did not contribute as much to the enjoyment of such campaigning as the good cheer we found there, but we were duly grateful for all, receiving the æsthetic and material benefactions in the kindest spirit and with equal satisfaction. At any rate, these surroundings caused the most irksome duty to appear easy and cease to seem monotonous, and invested the most trivial circumstances with something of romantic interest.

On one occasion this was impressed upon me after a fashion which left a very vivid picture in my memory. Morgan's command, then less than one thousand strong, was taking a much-needed rest, and for that purpose was occupying a locality which not only provided every thing essential to the comfort of an encampment intended to be of several days' duration, but which exceeded in rustic beauty almost any spot I can remember.

It was in that Bluegrass region of Tennessee lying along the Cumberland, to which nature has been so generous, in an extensive woodland out of which the underbrush had all been cleared, and where the grass was thick and green — a perfect mat of verdure. The lofty and noble trees stood at wide intervals and seemed at once monuments to the fertility of the soil and guardians against wanton intrusion. A broad stream of cool, clear water, gushing from a large spring not far distant, wound through it, making the air more delicious in fancy, if not in reality, and every "balmy breeze" that was in business came and loved to linger there. It was a place which should have been dedicated to quiet and peace, and to men more inclined to poetic sentiment it might have seemed almost profanation to use it as an encampment.

We were there, as I have said, for rest, but it was hardly possible at that time to obtain uninterrupted rest, and more than once we had calls for assistance which could not be refused from our friends in communities which anticipated visits from the enemy. The people in all this region were intensely Southern in sentiment. Nearly all of the men capable of bearing arms were in the Confederate ranks, only the old men, women, and children remaining at home. These not only warmly sympathized with, but were always ready and anxious to furnish aid and comfort to the Confederate cause, and the boys, too young to serve as soldiers, but old enough to make active and useful agents for other purposes, were often employed as messengers to communicate with any rebel force which might be in the vicinage. A number of Federal garrisons were established at points best adapted to the military occupation and control of that county, and some strong Federal commands were constantly in long marching distance of our encampment.

Two or three of the requests for protection, of which I have spoken, necessitated only the sending of scouting parties or small detachments to the help of the supplicants, but at the expiration of eight or ten days an alarm came which demanded the prompt employment of our entire command and putting an end to recreation, summoned us again into hot and frequent service.

I was lying awake at a late hour one glorious August night, long after every one in the camp, not on duty, ought to have been asleep. The full moon was pouring down a brilliant flood of light; the glades of the wood were shining and the little stream gleaming with its rays, and they trickled through the foliage of the great tree under which I was stretched, in green and golden radiance. The air was fresh and elastic, although no breeze was stirring, and dim, misty shapes seemed to be gliding about in the shadows. While gazing on this scene a faint sound afar off fell softly upon my ear. I listened intently and it grew in volume, until I recognized unmistakably the quick hoof beats of a fleet horse pressed to a rapid gallop. Whoever it was was evidently approaching on the turnpike which ran past and not far from the encampment, and through the little hamlet nearby. Suddenly the sound ceased, and I knew that the rider had been halted by the pickets. Then it began again, fast and furious, and as continuous as the long roll of a drum. The iron shod hoofs clanged fiercely on the stony pike as the rider drew nearer, the cadence changing all at once to a duller rumble when he left the highway and turned into the trace which led directly to the camp. By this time nearly all the men were aroused and on their feet, awaiting in eager expectancy the news. With splintering crash and bang, the horse bounded in full stride upon the short bridge which spanned the brook and the next moment was in our midst.

A boy about twelve years of age was hanging on his back, exhausted and gasping, and scarce able to keep the saddle. So soon as he could speak he told us that a large Federal force had marched into the town, whence he had come, just at nightfall, making wholesale arrests, threatening dire punishment to those who were suspected of having most actively abetted the neighbouring rebel soldiery, and behaving altogether in a most offensive and "ridiculous" fashion. He had been smuggled out of town, mounted on the best horse that could be procured and despatched "hot-foot" to notify Morgan of the situation and beg him to come to the rescue.

He was taken at once to headquarters to repeat his message there. In five minutes the bugle rang out like the shrill challenge of a game-cock. Almost as soon the men were in the saddle, the column was formed and was in motion, and we were marching swiftly in response to the summons our friends had so hastily sent us.

CHAPTER XIII

MUCH has been said of Southern hospitality and it has at all times been justly famous, but I believe that no one who did not witness its exercise during the war, and when the South was subjected to all the hardships of hostile invasion, can form any accurate conception of how cordial and limitless it really was. Only personal experience and knowledge can enable one to understand the extent to which it was cheerfully rendered during that terrible trial.

I can now scarcely trust the fidelity of my memory when I recall the countless occasions on which I have seen it generously bestowed under circumstances which, it might be thought, would have made it absolutely impossible. And it was given without respect of persons, at least with very slight regard as to who might be the recipient. Not only was it never denied the stranger — that is to say, for the sole reason that he might be an utter stranger, or for any other cause than that which might compel its reluctant denial to the closest friend — but the fact that the applicant was a stranger seemed sometimes to be considered the strongest claim that could be preferred. It may be said that the practice of this particular virtue in an unusual degree might have been expected among a people of the character and living the life of the Southern people in the ante-bellum period, and it was not at all remarkable that the habit should have continued until the havoc and waste of war virtually destroyed the means of its indulgence.

The environment of the Southerner was unquestionably adapted to the cultivation of a liberal spirit in that direction. The country, in nearly every region of the South, was rich and productive, the soil yielding abundant crops without arduous tillage. It was comparatively sparsely settled, and the inhabitants of the towns lived very much as did those of the farms and were distinguished by very much the same characteristics. Hospitality has always been a trait more peculiar to rural than to urban communities, and has been more prevalent among scanty than dense populations. When a hearty, kindly, well-to-do man has plenty of room, he is ever inclined to have other people share it with him. The planter or farmer lacked in those old Southern days even more than he does now, facilities and opportunities for companionship and social enjoyment which the city man can find elsewhere than in his own domicile, and a guest was, for that reason, perhaps, more welcome.

The institution of slavery — whatever else may be said about it — was also a great aid to those who were by nature hospitably inclined. Nearly every householder in the South was a slaveholder, and the darkeys were not only better trained than they are now, but better cared for, inasmuch, as the average master took much better care of his slave than the average negro now takes care of himself: so that guests could be entertained with more convenience to the host, and more comfortably for themselves, than after the slave had become a voter and learned to visit the polls in "pursuit of happiness."

Therefore the liberal entertainment offered the soldiers, who were not at all diffident in asking it, and the warm reception accorded the unfortunate "sympathizer" who had fled from his home, where it was not safe freely to express rebellious opinions, to some more Southern and congenial clime, was not to be deemed extraordinary in the earlier period of the war. This, indeed, was only an extension, a rather more general observance of the rule which had always obtained, induced by the prevailing conditions and the additional incentive of patriotic sentiment.

But it was a matter of surprise that it endured so long; that this hospitality should have been still so generously furnished, even after every part of the South had been more or less devastated; when the necessaries of life had been in great measure taken or destroyed; when the food supply was nearly exhausted; and production had almost entirely ceased in many localities, because of the lack of men and facilities for adequate cultivation.

Nevertheless, although the host of "refugees" was constantly augmented in number, and the means of providing for them as steadily diminished, the disposition to welcome and share everything with them seemed in no wise abated. In the first months of the war they came from Missouri, Maryland, and Kentucky, Tennessee and northern Alabama, when those regions were later occupied by the enemy, then furnished their contingents; and the sorrowful procession was increased by fresh arrivals, as those unhappy populations felt more heavily the hand of oppression, until the whole South was filled with fugitives seeking an asylum.

All this was, of course, a very great burden on the people of the states not yet in Federal possession, but they bore it cheerfully. The care of these unbidden guests, regarded at first as a point of honour, became eventually to be deemed a patriotic duty, and every Southern family and household participated in more or less degree in the work of entertainment.

Of course many of these refugees, who were possessed of the means to do so, provided for themselves; maintained their own establishments, or paid board. But in many instances they were received by friends or relatives in the South who were already barely able to live without such additional strain upon the domestic menage, and kept as long as they chose to remain. And even when board was paid, it was usually ridiculously cheap when the high prices of all necessaries of life and the rapid and extreme depreciation of Confederate money is considered. Very often, too, when board was ostensibly charged, it was merely nominal and in the shape of some slight contribution to the maintenance of the household. I knew of one case in which the host positively refused any return for furnishing lodging and food to a lady, child, and nurse for several months, beyond the small sum required to provide candles, and of another in which he was induced, with difficulty, to accept as compensation the present of a horse. As, in this latter case, the officer who thus discharged his obligation was a raiding cavalry man, it may be inferred that he made payment for the board of his family in a kind of currency which he always had on hand.

But the most notable feature of it, perhaps, was the accommodation extended those who would now, in hotel parlance, be termed "transient guests," travellers seeking temporary entertainment. Houses sometimes were thronged with such visitors, all strangers, who would consume at one meal enough food to reduce the families to the verge of subsequent famine. When a railroad train would discharge, in some small town and in the dead of night, a crowd of passengers that was many times too large for the small and miserably furnished tavern, applicants for shelter would flock to every house in sight; it was asked with confidence and generally readily granted; to women and children, at least, it was rarely refused.

The generosity with which the Southern people then gave out of their scanty resources was even less remarkable than their entire willingness to incur any amount of trouble or annoyance. Such a spirit may be in a measure explained by the temper and conditions of the immediate period, but it was largely due to the character of a civilization which has passed away.

A great many stories have been told illustrative of the extraordinary and constant depreciation of Confederate money as the war progressed, and it is something which it would be almost impossible to exaggerate. Indeed, when we recall the extent to which it had proceeded long before the final disaster, it is difficult to realize how it could have in any degree performed the functions of money, or have been received as such at all.

The Richmond man who averred that he carried his money to market in a basket and brought the dinner back in his vest pocket, did not inaptly describe the cheapness of the currency, and the high prices of food.

Every old soldier and citizen of the Confederacy remembers how the value of all the necessaries of life went up, and how wofully that of the money went down. The citizens used money scarcely at all, but lived almost entirely upon what they produced. The soldiers were partially provided for by the government; but rations and clothing were inadequate, at every period of the war, to their real needs, and were so scantily issued toward the end as to become of little avail unless supplemented by their own provident efforts. After the second year of the war, the matter of pay cut very little figure, except that there seems to be something gratifying to human nature in the receipt of money even although it may be depreciated. But whatever theoretical advantage the officer who received one hundred and fifty to three hundred dollars a month had over the private, who got only thirteen dollars, there was little practical financial difference between them when a pair of boots cost two hundred and fifty or three hundred dollars and a jacket, shirt, or pair of trousers were sold at corresponding prices. In rural communities the soldier could pretty confidently rely on the hospitality of the householders, for in the direst straits the Southern people retained that characteristic. But if by any chance a man was enabled to visit a city, he found that the most indifferent meal was served for not less than forty or fifty dollars, and if he patronized the bar or the cigar stand, his money went as if he were literally burning it.

I remember that on one occasion, when riding alone at night in south-western Virginia I was compelled by the dense darkness and the difficulties of the road to stop at a small farm house a little after midnight. The proprietor gave me two bundles of oats for my horse and a glass of milk, and let me lie down on his bed until day-break. He made no charge, but as I happened to have a twenty-dollar Confederate bill, I gave him that. He took it without comment, as he doubtless would have done if it had been smaller, but evidently did not think it too much; nor did I. I thought the oats and milk much more valuable than the money.

One of the most notable features of the monetary depreciation was this indifference to face "values" and the total absence of anything like fixed or regular prices. No one seemed to think there was any material difference between five, ten, or twenty dollars, or at least to consider it; and articles of the same kind might be sold upon the same day and at the same place for widely variant prices.

But the most curious thing was that the soldiers were rarely without money; some of them seemed always to have, estimated in bulk, considerable sums of Confederate currency. A man whose pay was less than twenty dollars a month, and rarely drawn, would have about his person hundreds, sometimes thousands, of dollars. How he procured it was a mystery never solved, at least by me. Of course, good luck at the card table — or rather on the blanket which served in lieu of a table — accounted for the plethoric pockets of a certain number of these camp-fire plutocrats. But then how was it that so many were winners? and how did the losers get the money they parted with?

It need scarcely be said that the nominal amounts — that is to say in Confederate currency — which changed hands at cards, were quite large. One unacquainted with the true monetary conditions might have listened with amazement to the big bets made in the poker games, and have wondered how so many ragged millionaires could possibly have been gathered together.

I have heard of one such game, played during the last Christmas week of the Confederacy, which was remarkable not only for the reckless manner in which those engaged in it wagered their "wads," but also as exhibiting the generosity and self-abnegation of the Confederate soldier. There were two men who belonged to a certain cavalry command who had been associated during the entire war, and were warm friends and sworn comrades. They were very unlike in temperament, for Jim was sanguine and enterprising, while Billy was stolid and conservative; but in tastes and predilections they were much in unison, except that Billy was rather more addicted to the use of liquor than was Jim, and Jim was much fonder of gambling than was Billy.

One day Billy learned that at a certain small distillery not far from camp a very superior article of peach brandy was to be had if a man could pay for it, and he determined to procure some of it at any cost. He had on hand a small supply of "Pine-top," but what was that in comparison with peach brandy? So obtaining permission to leave camp for a few hours he started in hot haste after the brandy. He sampled it and found that it exceeded his expectations, was even better than it had been represented to be. But, as he had feared, the price at which the owner held it was "out of sight."

He offered a hundred, two hundred, two hundred and fifty dollars a gallon, but without avail; the distiller positively refused to sell it for Confederate money. Finally, with much reluctance, he offered a two dollar and half gold piece which he had brought from home when he enlisted, and had sacredly preserved during the many weary months of his army life; he proposed to give that cherished coin for three gallons of the coveted beverage. The distiller consented, of course, and Billy carried off the brandy in a small keg. He told no one but Jim of his good fortune and enjoined secrecy on him. That night, however, Jim invited four or five other comrades, who were accustomed to indulge together in such pastime, to come to the tent he and Billy occupied, and have a quiet game.

The game was soon in full blast, but Jim played in fearful luck. He had all sorts of hands beaten, and no expedient to which he resorted could propitiate the goddess of fortune. He lost all of his own money and borrowed all of Billy's. At length when he had only fifty dollars remaining, a sure opportunity of recuperating his depleted exchequer offered itself, provided he could secure the means with which to improve it. The dealer gave him four hearts and he drew another, making a straight flush. All of the players came in. Jim had gotten Billy's last dollar, but he suddenly remembered the three gallons of peach brandy, and felt sure that it would prove an available asset. The man "first to say" bet fifty dollars, the second man called; Jim, in turn, confident that one of the others would raise, also called. Sure enough, the next man raised it five hundred, and every one but Jim dropped out.

"Now, Billy," said Jim, "you must lend me that brandy."

Billy, for the first time since their long and devoted friendship had begun, evinced an indisposition to respond to Jim's wishes. He hesitated and burst into tears.

"I know it's a great sacrifice I'm demandin'," said Jim, "but this here's a crisis."

Billy slowly and sadly produced the brandy.

"Now, gentlemen," said Jim, "you'll all agree that this brandy is worth a thousand dollars more especially as I mean to give each man a drink if I win this pot."

The man who had bet five hundred made some demurrer, but the others, who wanted their drinks, overruled him. Moreover, Billy's declaration that "them three gallons cost two dollars and a half in gold" settled the matter. The brandy was rated at a thousand dollars in Confederate currency. Jim saw the bet of five hundred and raised the other fellow five hundred, who, inasmuch as he held four nines, called. Jim was rich once more, and, after deducting the promised drinks, returned the brandy to Billy.

But it was a great shock to Billy; he was never exactly the same man again.

In the long cold winter of 1863-64, when Longstreet occupied the upper portion of east Tennessee, his cavalry, watching Knoxville and vigilant to meet any Federal advance, was not only engaged in constant, arduous service, but was subjected to the severest privations. A certain Tennessee cavalry regiment, which was generally on the extreme front, adopted a camp regulation to the effect that whenever a horse broke loose and strayed from his own proper premises, the party upon whom he trespassed should have the right to confiscate the halter which the offending quadruped had on. Inasmuch as good, serviceable halters were scarce and in demand, the privilege was rigorously exercised.

One night "Mac" and "Ben," two young soldiers belonging to the same mess and sworn companions, had collected an extra quantity of excellent fodder. After giving an ample "feed" to each of their horses, they disposed the residue of the forage so as to make a snug, warm bed, and retired to enjoy, they hoped, an unusually luxurious repose.

Ben's horse, it should be remarked, was a veteran campaigner, known throughout the regiment as "Old Tige." He was by no means a beauty, but could go "all the gaits," gallop a week without rest, and for taking care of himself was smarter than a quartermaster. Ben loved him like a brother. In the dead hour of night Mac was awakened by a suspicious tugging at the mass of fodder in which they were embedded. He listened attentively, and there could be no mistake about it. There was a strange horse after the fodder, and quite probably he wore a halter. Here was a glorious chance for spoils. He shook off all drowsy feeling, awakened Ben, and communicated to him the important fact that a horse, perhaps having a halter on, was "stealin' our forage."

It was at once agreed that Mac should slip out, seize the horse, give him a good hiding, as a lesson for future behaviour, and of course, confiscate the halter. It was very dark, but Mac groped his way to the back of the shanty, and without difficulty captured the trespasser.

"Now tie him up and belt him good," said Ben. "Teach him how he comes foolin' round here, eatin' Old 'Tige's' feed." Mac, having procured a stout brush, proceeded to "belt" him. From the vigorous snorting and kicking of the previously docile animal it seemed that the monitory lesson both disgusted and amazed him. "Now, snake off his halter," said Ben, when the belting was over. "Old Tige's is gettin' mighty threadbare" Mac slipped off the halter and slipped it safely under the fodder, and the pair dropped off to sleep again. They were roused by the bugle. The face of each wore a broad smile at the recollection of what had occurred during the night. Ben triumphantly reached for the halter, but when it was produced a ghastly change came over his face. He gasped and said in a faint voice: "This is Old Tige's halter. It must have been him you was beltin'."

No Tennesseean who served in the Confederate cavalry is more worthy of remembrance, and few, perhaps, are more vividly remembered by those who knew him well than Maj. "Dick" McCann.

In the beginning of the war he enlisted in the infantry, but at an early date procured a transfer to Morgan's command, and was soon one of the noted men in it.

Recklessly brave and seeking every daring and hazardous adventure that cavalry service offered or suggested, he was, withal, shrewd, wary, and vigilant. Thoroughly trusted by his superiors in rank and possessing and deserving the confidence of his men, he was extremely active as well as efficient in every line of field duty. Although inordinately fond of scouting and fighting, he was, in camp, the most amiable and jovial companion imaginable, as famous and popular for his social gifts as for his soldierly qualities.

Upon the complete organization of Ward's fine regiment, the Ninth Tennessee cavalry, he became its major and was one of the best field officers in Morgan's division, but was better known, perhaps, because of his previous experiences. These were many and varied, and most of them quite thrilling, making his name a familiar one in the ears of his comrades. Seated about the camp fires whose gleams lighted up the glades of the

Tennessee woodlands or were reflected in the waters of the Cumberland, they had many a story to tell of Dick McCann and his exploits; some moving to admiration and some to mirth were duly chronicled among the stirring events so constantly ocurring in that region.

When Morgan entered Kentucky in his first important raid, McCann was left with a few men to scout and skirmish in the vicinity of Nashville, and produce the impression that a strong force of Confederate cavalry was still there. This could be done only by the most active and ceaseless work, but he was equal to the task, and the Federal pickets and outposts were given little rest, and he took none himself. In this sort of service he, of course, incurred a fair share of personal risk but on one occasion only, I believe, thought himself really in danger of death. A rifle ball struck the plate of his sabre belt, glancing and doing him no serious injury, but knocking him from his saddle and jarring him severely. "Bob," he shouted to a comrade, "Bob, I'm killed. Pass me the bottle before I die."

When General Breckinridge was holding Murfreesboro and Bragg was leaving Kentucky after his futile invasion of that state, McCann was placed in command of some three or four hundred cavalry which Breckinridge had collected. He was required to observe the enemy at Nashville and all intermediate points, and also keep Breckinridge informed of movements north of the Cumberland. It was no easy task, but Major McCann performed it thoroughly and successfully. He had numerous skirmishes, in which, fought as they were on his own terms, he generally came off with flying colours, and he made a great many prisoners. The greater part of these, of course, were Federal soldiers, but occasionally a non-combatant, for some reason, would fall into his net. One such unfortunate was a peddler, who, with a well-filled pack of portable articles, was bent on making a commercial tour through the Confederacy. Dick captured him, en route, a few miles from Murfreesboro and brought him in.

Among other things of light weight but considerable value which were in this party's assortment were a number of diamonds. Now, what this peddler expected to do with diamonds in Dixie at that date, or why he should be willing to part with them for Confederate money, will remain an unsolved mystery. Nevertheless he had them. It was Major McCann's duty to search the peddler's pack for any contraband goods he might be trying to smuggle in, or for any treasonable communication he might be conveying to Southern traitors. In making his examination the Major came across the diamonds and was exceedingly pleased. He at once informed the peddler that the jewels must be turned over to him for a day or two, but would then be returned. Inasmuch as the peddler could not help himself, he was obliged to consent. Major McCann fastened the diamonds — there were some ten or twelve of them — upon his breast, where, shining lustrously against the dark background of his somewhat rusty blue flannel shirt and gray jacket, they presented a very picturesque and pleasing spectacle.

In order to do full justice to himself, McCann took two days off and strutted around Murfreesboro and the camps in the environs with the diamonds in blazing evidence. The peddler stuck to him like a brother, always at his heels, eying him carefully and exhibiting a wonderful solicitude in his welfare. Finally the major announced that he must bring his holiday to a close and resume business.

"I'll start after the Yankees to-morrow," he said.

"For heaven's sake, don't do that," said the peddler. "Don't take any risk. You might be killed."

"Why," said the major, "I take that risk every day."

"But think awhile," responded the peddler. "You may be willing to lose your life, but I can't afford to lose the diamonds."

Major McCann served constantly and efficiently during the arduous campaigning of the autumn of 1862 and the winter of 1863, and on many occasions displayed more than ordinary gallantry. One instance in which his courage and presence of mind were conspicuous, and which earned him the warm and grateful commendation of General Morgan, is deserving of especial commemoration. During the months of March and April, 1863, when Rosecrans was massing and preparing for the campaign which culminated in the battle of Chickamauga, the Confederate cavalry, holding the country to the south and east of Murfreesboro, was incessantly occupied in repelling strong expeditions sent against them of Federal cavalry backed by formidable detachments of infantry. Having a long line to guard, outnumbered and harassed from every direction, we were sometimes taken at disadvantage and suffered disaster.

On April 20th, a general advance of this character having been made on our entire right flank, the enemy broke through our ward and dashed into McMinnville, where a considerable quantity of supplies was stored, protected by a very small garrison. Morgan's and Wharton's divisions were twenty-five or thirty miles distant and only a few companies of cavalry were picketing in front of McMinnville, which the enemy, coming in heavy force, easily drove before them. General Morgan, with his staff and three or four officers, happened to be in McMinnville at the time, and so sudden was the hostile advance they escaped with great difficulty. Two or more Federal columns dashed into the little town at a gallop, sweeping like a flood over the slight resistance which the few defenders could offer. Morgan, with Colonel Cluke, Lieut.-Col. Martin and Major McCann — fortunately all well mounted — barely gained the road to Sparta, the only avenue of safety, before the enemy turned into it, and a hot skirmish between these four and the leading files of the Yankee column immediately began. Morgan shot the officer leading the column; Cluke killed a man also, but Martin received a severe wound through the lungs, disabling him, and McCann's horse was killed.

McCann was not stunned by the fall, and, intent on doing something to aid General Morgan, instantly sprang to his feet and in front of the enemy, shouting, "I am Morgan. You have got the old chief at last."

He was at once ridden down and sabred, but the momentary check he occasioned gave the others a "good start," which they improved, and escaped.

Although badly bruised, as well as gashed, he managed to get away from his captors that night, and reached Sparta late the next evening. I saw him there, a day or two afterward, and his head and face were so covered with plasters and bandages that it was hardly possible to recognize him.

But the best story I ever heard of him, I think, was one told by a friend who knew him intimately in his ante-bellum days.

In his early youth, McCann, urged by the love of adventure which was always so strong in his nature, enlisted in one of the filibustering expeditions which invaded Nicarauga. He remained there some months, and when he returned brought back with him a considerable stock of experience, and a large and very intelligent monkey. This animal was much attached to his master and used to follow him like a dog. Dick reciprocated the ape's affection, and was very fond of making him exhibit the tricks he had learned. The monkey finally met with a sad fate, due to having unduly gratified the inquisitive curiosity which characterizes those creatures and a good many human beings, who seem closely related to them.

Dick was living with his father at the old McCann homestead, one of the handsomest places about Nashville. His mother, than whom no kinder or better old lady ever lived, was a notable housewife and manager, and felt especial pride in her poultry. She raised every spring a multitude of chickens, and would never suffer them to be molested. The chickens were allowed more privileges than the members of the family. They not only strolled and scratched everywhere on the premises, as pleased them, but entered the house, the doors of which were always open in warm weather, in flocks. No one was allowed to drive them out but the old lady herself, and she did so in a very gentle and considerate manner. She always kept some fire burning, at all seasons, in the dining-room. Over the mantel in this room hung a powder-horn full of powder, a reminiscence of the pioneer period, not uncommon at that date in Tennessee and Kentucky.

Not wishing to violently alarm her chickens, but only give them a gentle hint to leave, she would, when they gathered too thickly in this room, pour a little powder into the palm of one hand, throw it on the fire, and the consequent blare and splutter would effectually disperse the chickens. The monkey was often an interested spectator of this proceeding, and one day, when the chickens had invaded the room in unusual numbers and no one was present who would prevent him, he determined to perform the feat himself. But a monkey has, of course, little sense of proportion. Instead of throwing a small quantity of powder upon the fire, he dashed the entire contents of the horn to it. A tremendous explosion ensued. The room was wrecked, the air was filled with feathers, and the monkey completely disappeared.

Dick spoke of the catastrophe with deep feeling, "I made diligent search for his remains," he said, "to give them Christian burial in the family graveyard. But I could only find one of his back teeth on the garden fence."

CHAPTER XIV

A RECENT examination of the muster rolls of the regiments which composed the division of calvary commanded by Gen. John H. Morgan showed them to be in a condition very much to be regretted by the surviving members of that body and those interested in its history. On account of the constant and active service in which it was engaged, the rolls were imperfectly prepared at any date; after the Ohio raid little effort to keep them was attempted, and they can now be revised and partially completed only by data furnished by the recollection of the comparatively few survivors.

Especial effort should be made to record the names of the men who fell in battle. Unfortunately little attention seems to have been given this important matter by those who compiled the rolls now in existence. In the case even of well-known officers, who were killed or wounded, there is frequently no mention of such casualities; and in this regard the private soldiers had been almost totally overlooked.

The Second Kentucky Cavalry — the regiment commanded first by General Morgan, and subsequently by myself, Col. John B. Hutchinson, and Col. Jas. W Bowles — has suffered, apparently in this respect more than any other; or perhaps, because better acquainted with it, I have noticed the fact more particularly in the case of this regiment.

In going over its roll the memory of many incidents, almost forgotten, were vividly recalled by the names of men I had well known, but of whom I had lost all trace, and of whose record little could be learned from the rolls.

I found in many instances that the death of men, whom I knew had been killed in battle, was not recorded; and in several cases the names of men who had been killed were not upon the rolls. How such omissions, and some others nearly as remarkable, could have occurred, is inexplicable. With one name, that of Gideon Morgan Hazen, a peculiarly melancholy interest is connected. He had enlisted in the Second Kentucky cavalry at Knoxville, near which place he lived, in June, 1862. He was then a boy of about sixteen, and was a relative of General Morgan. I never knew a manlier or more amiable young fellow, nor a better soldier. He served very faithfully to nearly the close of the war, and was promoted for courage and good conduct. About the middle of December, 1864, a detachment of the small brigade I was then commanding was attacked by a heavy force of the enemy at Kingsport in east Tennessee. A number of my men were killed and made prisoners. Young Hazen was with this detachment. His comrades remembered his taking part in the fight, but he was never seen or heard of afterward. He was not among those who withdrew from the field, his body was not found among the slain, nor was he, so far as we could ever learn, among those captured. His father visited the Northern prisons, hoping to find him in some one of them, and after the close of the war the prison records were searched for his name but without finding it. He was probably cut off in the retreat from the ground on which the combat was fought, and killed in some wild corner of the mountains; but his fate is unknown, and the mystery in which it is involved attaches to that of many others.

I saw the name of another young and unusually gallant soldier of the Second Kentucky, whom I knew well and whose death I witnessed — James Cardwell, of Harrodsburg, Kentucky; yet there was no record that he had been killed. In fact, after three years of continuous and arduous service he was killed at Bull's Gap on November 24, 1864. On that day my brigade assaulted a strong position, crowned with entrenchments and defended by a force much stronger than my own. When within thirty or forty feet of the works my line was staggered and checked by a fire from which it received severe loss. Cardwell, calling to his comrades to follow, deliberately walked up to the entrenchments and was shot dead, a half dozen balls piercing his breast.

In the case of men whose deaths occurred in such wise as to attract peculiar or general notice, or who were slain in fights of some magnitude, the failure to record the facts on the rolls will, of course, almost invariably be corrected so soon as they are carefully inspected. But many men were killed in obscure skirmishes or minor combats, and it is to be feared that a proper record of their fate can never be made.

While going over the roll of company "C," of the Second Kentucky, with a former member of that company to assist me, I found that not only had a number of names been omitted, but among them were those of three very excellent soldiers who had been killed. Among the names missing was that of a man, than whom no one in the regiment was better known — Tom Boss. Tom was not killed, but it wasn't because he didn't give the Yankees numerous and favourable opportunities to get rid of him. He was an eccentric fellow, with strongly defined characteristics, among which a reckless daring was conspicuous. His physique was striking, although by no means comely, and he generally had his antagonist half whipped before the fight commenced. His shock of bristly black hair and big, bright, black eyes seemed to threaten disaster to any one who should tackle him. He was fully six feet six inches in height and, while slender and lathy in build, was exceedingly muscular and agile. He frequently, almost habitually, had an axe strapped at his back, and could wield that heavy implement with one hand as easily as an ordinary man would handle a hatchet.

In February, 1863, Lieutenant-colonel Bowles, with the greater part of the Second Kentucky, and supported by an Alabama battalion under Lieutenant-colonel Malone attacked a Federal force at Bradyville. For awhile the Confederates drove every thing before them. But the enemy was much stronger than they had supposed them to be, and consisted of both cavalry and infantry. The Federal regiments closed in on all sides until the Confederates were completely surrounded. They were compelled to fight their way back and out, and it was sharp and hot work to do so. In the mêlée a Federal captain rode up to Tom Boss and struck him on the head with his sabre. Tom had perhaps exhausted the loads in his rifle and pistol, or it may be, that he considered his foeman's conduct as a challenge to combat with the "white weapon." At any rate he snatched his axe from its sling, thrust out his long, sinewy left arm, catching his adversary's throat with a grip like that of a gorilla, and with his right dealt him a blow on the skull that drove the blade of the axe down to his eyes.

I was reminded of one incident which I had long forgotten, but which was immediately and vividly recalled when I heard it referred to. Just after Morgan's command had returned to Tennessee, at the conclusion of the First Kentucky raid, it was encamped near Sparta. General Morgan, for some reason, had gone to Knoxville, leaving me in command. The question of rations was just then, as it very often became, a serious and a very pressing one. We were unable to receive supplies from the Confederate commissariat because remote from and not often in touch with it, and were compelled to live off of the country; and the immediate region where we were, although fertile, was sparsely settled, and had already been drawn on for food supplies. It was not difficult to get a pretty good supply of meat and vegetables, but almost impossible to get even a small quantity of bread. Flour could be obtained, but we had few cooking utensils, and, although the people were quite willing to prepare it for us, we could not depend on their aid for an adequate or constant supply.

In this dilemma, it occurred to me to have a good-sized baking oven constructed out of some loose bricks that were lying around, relics of a deserted and tumbled down little house; so I caused the bugler to make proclamation that I wanted the services of two or three expert bricklayers — feeling sure that there must be some in the command — to build this oven, promising that they should be rewarded for their work. In response Tom Boss and a man named Jackson reported, went to work, and in a day or two constructed one which did very well, enabling us to make a fairly good apology for bread. I then asked Boss and Jackson what I should do to compensate them for their services. I should state that there were quite a number of small distilleries — "stills" they were called — within five or six miles, and the men had exhibited such propensity to visit them that I had been compelled to keep a strong detail on duty all the time as provost guard, and which was especially concerned in keeping the men away from the "stills."

Messrs. Boss and Jackson consulted apart for a few moments, when I put the question about compensation, and then returning announced that they would like to have three days' furlough, to go where they pleased, and particularly not to be interfered with "by that d — d provost guard."

I knew, of course, where they wished to go, and rather demurred; but they insisted it must be that or nothing. They came back, all right, at the expiration of the three days, and seeing Boss I asked him about the trip. "I hope, Tom," I said, "that you conducted yourselves properly."

"Yes, sir," he replied, with great dignity, "we did. Me and Jackson never does nothing wrong. We jest had a high old time."

Some one told me a story related to him by the pilot of one of the boats captured at Brandenburg on the Ohio raid and used to transport Morgan's command across the river. The pilot said that he was briefly informed of what he was to do; that the boat would be loaded with the troops and artillery to be ferried over to the Indiana shore and there disembarked, and this process was to be repeated until all were across. He stated that, with the officer who gave these directions, there was an extremely tall, dark, saturnine, and truculent looking soldier who was left in the pilot house evidently to watch him. This formidable looking individual announced curtly and rather sternly, "I'm here as a guard to see that you act right, and I don't want no nonsense." He then proceeded to make himself as comfortable as possible, selecting a convenient corner, but first placing his rifle where it would be handy, and hitching the holster of a big navy revolver within easy reach.

The pilot admitted that he was at first greatly alarmed. The appearance of this grim sentry boded every thing but good to any one who might give him offence, and he determined to strictly observe the warning "to act right" and indulge in "no nonsense."

The process of crossing, however, was slow, as it required some time to embark men and horses on the Kentucky side of the river and even more to put them off on the other, and after an hour or two his feeling of awe and apprehension passed away, and was succeeded by one of curiosity. He finally ventured to open conversation with his custodian.

"My name is Smith," he said. "Would you object to

letting me know your name, so I may remember the person to whom I owe the pleasure of this visit?"

"Oh, no," responded the big, fierce-visaged rebel, very affably; "I ain't at all partick'ler about who I makes acquaintance with. My name's Tom Boss."

Then the pilot inquired, "How long do you generally remain on your post when you are on guard?"

"Well," said Mr. Boss, "we cavalry stands four hours on and eight off. The web-feet, the infantry I mean, stands two on and four off. As we generally do twice as much work as they do, while we are about it, we need twice as long rest."

The conversation, having thus opened, continued very pleasantly; and finally, while they were lying at the Indiana shore, to allow a battalion to disembark, Mr. Boss remarked, casually, "Have you got anything on this boat to drink, stronger than water? I'm beginning to feel powerful dry."

"Why, certainly," said the pilot, "I'll get it for you;" and he skipped down the ladder, three steps at a jump, rushed into the bar-room and called to the bar-tender: "Here, make two real stiff toddies as quick as you can."

The drinks were prepared and the pilot returned with them to the hurricane deck and the society of his guard. It was his intention to drink one of the toddies himself, for he felt that he needed it; but when he came within reach of Mr. Boss, out shot both of that worthy's long arms, a glass was grasped in each hand and drained, one after the other with a scarcely perceptible interval of time.

Then Tom smacked his lips and said slowly and impressively:

"You needn't fetch any more until jest before I'm relieved. I don't like to drink too much while I'm on duty."

It can be readily understood, even by those who have had no such experience, that the rigid discipline and exact observance of military etiquette which obtains — or is supposed to obtain — in all regular armies and among professional soldiers, must be largely relaxed in the volunteer service. Such was the case during the Civil War, but more so, perhaps, in the Confederate than in the Federal army. The volunteer, as a rule, and especially in the early part of the war, before the rapidly depleting ranks were filled by the draft or the conscription, was of quite different material from that which was usually enlisted in the "old" or regular army of the United States. He entered the ranks not as a means of procuring a livelihood, but from a feeling of duty; wishing to serve his country in her need, yet regarding such service as temporary, accidental, so to speak, and to a certain extent a personal sacrifice. He readily acquired military habits and a quite thorough knowledge of what a soldier is expected to do. He became, in time, one of the most formidable "veterans" of modern warfare, but by instruction and experience, rather than by what is technically meant by "discipline." He was zealous, attentive, and obedient, not so much from fear of authority and punishment, as from feelings of pride and patriotism: more from a sense of what was due to himself than of what was due to any superior.

Indeed, the authority which could be exercised by officers of all ranks in the volunteer service was much in proportion to their individual strength of character and personal ascendency. The men obeyed much more implicitly those whom they admired and who could win their confidence.

Of course, this sort of feeling induced a relation between officers even of high rank and the private soldiers, out of which evolved many curious and amusing incidents, and occasioned many an exhibition of waggish "impudence"; which, however, savoured in nowise of insolence or lack of proper respect. Nearly every collector of such anecdotes will remember a story told on "Stonewall Jackson," which well illustrates my meaning. It was old "Stonewall's" habit not only sternly to issue and strictly to enforce orders against straggling and depredations of all kinds, but on one important march, so saith the chronicler in this instance, he gave instructions that no one, officer or private, should answer a question of any description, lest his (Jackson's) destination and objective might be disclosed.

It happened that during the march, having for some reason dropped to the rear, the general discovered a young fellow, evidently one of his soldiers, snugly ensconced in a cherry tree and making havoc with the fruit. "What are you doing there?" thundered the general.

"Can't tell you, sir," said the soldier.

"You can't, eh? What's your name, and what regiment do you belong to?"

"Don't know, sir."

"Why, you impudent rascal; what do you mean by talking that way to me?"

"Well, mister!" said the soldier, with an air of great candour, "I'd like to oblige you; but, you see, I belong to old Jack's foot cavalry, and he's issued orders that none of his men shall answer any questions, so I can't tell nothin' to nobody. But if you'll ask him, I reckon you can find out all you want to know."

This response was too much even for "Old Jack," and he rode off, his shoulders shaking with silent laughter. On account of their peculiar service this latitude of conduct and speech obtained more with the cavalry than with the infantry, and there were frequent instances of it in Morgan's command. General Morgan's peculiar sense of humour was always tickled by a really good specimen of this sort of thing, and I have known more than one offender escape punishment, more or less deserved, by adroitly "four flushing" at the right time.

During the winter of 1862–63, while Morgan's command was encamped along Stone River between Murfreesboro and Nashville, a detachment of the Seventh Kentucky Cavalry was one night on picket and stationed on the L'Auvergue Pike. An Irishman, Tom Murphy, well known throughout the command, was in this squad, and was posted as advance vidette in the fore part of the night. The night was cold and extremely dark. Shortly before midnight, and when he was anxiously expecting the arrival of the "relief," he heard a tremendous noise on the pike in front of him, the rapid trampling of many hoofs, a clatter and mad gallop, which made him think that the entire Yankee cavalry was coming, and coming "for business." Tom was a very daring fellow, and usually quite cool, but this noise in the dark was trying. He could see nothing, and he knew that the terrible din, drawing every instant nearer, would prevent any challenge from being heard, far less heeded. So blazing away at the approaching tempest, he turned and made at full speed for the picket base, consoling himself with the hope that he had reduced at least one Yankee to that condition in which only, according to Sheridan, Indians are "good."

"What's the matter?" queried Lieutenant Pickett, commanding the guard, as Tom dashed up.

"The whole d——d Yankee army is a' top of us," shouted Tom, "but I fixed one ov 'em, I know."

The lieutenant immediately despatched a courier to General Morgan, because the clatter, which by this time reached his ears, was alarmingly suggestive, and then mounting his squad, proceeded to reconnoitre and investigate. In a short time it was discovered that Tom hadn't been routed by the Yankee army, but by a large herd of cattle which had been feeding in a large field on the side of the road and frightened in some way, had stampeded, broken through the fence, and come rattling down the pike after a fashion that might have deceived any vidette.

But the whole command had been aroused and called to arms before this discovery was made, and General Morgan, seriously angry when he learned that it was a false alarm, ordered that the offender should be brought to him. A few questions, however, elicited the true state of the case and showed that Tom was not to blame; and when it transpired that an old bull which was in the herd had been the unfortunate recipient of Tom's bullet, the general's indignation entirely gave way to amusement.

"Why Tom," he said, "I'm surprised at you; to shoot an unoffending beast just as you would a Yankee! The bull wouldn't have hurt you. I'll guarantee that you don't even know whether or not he had horns."

Tom was quick to discern the general's change of mood and to take advantage of it.

"No, begorra!" he replied. "The night was so dark, and I was afther lavin' in sich a hurry that I cudn't see, sor, if he had horns or didn't. But, gin'ral"—this in an exceedingly insinuating tone—"owin' to the could and the skeer, I'd like mighty well to have a horn mesilf."

Tom was given a good, stiff "horn," and shortly afterward, by General Morgan's direction, was detailed for duty as courier at headquarters.

But the climax of impudence—of superlative, unparalleled "gall"—was reached by the famous Jeff Sterritt, the man most renowned among all the Kentucky Confederates for resourceful humour and audacity.

Jeff Steritt, Jack Trigg, and Tom Ballard were the all-licensed jesters, the "chartered libertines" of Morgan's command. Bright, good-humoured, and, despite their numerous escapades really good soldiers, they were always getting into scrapes which would have caused other men serious trouble, and always coming out with flying colours. General Morgan treated them with the greater leniency because they were among his earliest followers.

In the spring of 1863 the two brigades of Morgan's division were keeping watch on the upper Cumberland, the regiments stationed at convenient points for such purpose along the river. General Morgan's headquarters were at McMinnville, some thirty miles in the rear. General Wheeler's headquarters, were also there, and a detachment of infantry of the "Orphan" brigade, under Maj. J. C. Wickliffe, was at the same point guarding stores. A large crowd of staff officers, quartermasters and commissaries, with their clerks and attaches, were, therefore, quartered in the little town. Such a condition offered attractions to gentlemen who find profit in contributing to the amusement of their fellow men, and an enterprising faro dealer "opened up" at McMinnville and drove a thriving business. But the men on the front, finding out what was going on in the rear, contracted the habit of slipping away from camp in order to enjoy the game. They, of course, rode hard that they might lose as little time as possible, and, as a consequence, many horses were rendered unfit for service. The brigade commanders soon discovered why so many men were absent without leave and why so many horses were disabled, and, after unavailing efforts to check the evil, informed General Morgan of the cause and urged him to suppress the bank. General Morgan sent for the faro dealer and ordered him, under threat of condign punishment, to cease operations. The man promised, and, perhaps, sincerely, to quit, but some of the officers persuaded him to continue clandestinely for the benefit of a favoured few. It was impossible, however, to keep such a matter secret or to limit it, and in a short time things were as bad as before.

General Morgan got word of what was being done, and immediately ordered the provost guard to arrest the dealer and every man found in his place; and among others Sterritt, Ballard, and Trigg were caught. Each of the three had been given, by General Morgan's special direction, an easy berth at headquarters, and his wrath was great when he learned how they had requited his kindness. He ordered them to be brought before him, upbraided them with their ungrateful conduct, and promised to make an example, long to be remembered, of each one.

"Trigg," he asked finally, and rather unnecessarily, what were you doing there?"

Jack saw his chance, and, like the strategist that he was, at once availed himself of it. "General," he answered, "I went there to find Ballard."

"Well, Ballard," said the general, "what were you doing there?"

"I went there," said Ballard, "to find Sterritt."

This left Jeff last in say, and with no hope of evasion. He saw that his only safety was in candour. So that when the general sternly addressed the same question to him, he ingenuously responded, "Do you mean, general, what I was doing when I was arrested?"

"Yes," said the general, "what were you doing then?"

"Well, sir, to the best of my recollection, I was coppering the ace."

There was a long pause, Sterritt had returned a categorical answer to a direct question, and had answered truthfully. The tragedy was rapidly becoming a farce.

"You incorrigible wretch," said the general at last, "what ought I to do with you?"

"If you have any doubt about the matter, general," suggested Jeff, timidly, and as if honestly seeking to solve a difficulty, "you might give me a thirty days' furlough."

During the latter part of the war a certain tract of country lying along the border line of Kentucky and Tennessee and including a portion of the territory of each, was known as the "debatable ground." It doubtless received this appellation from some one who remembered that the same name was applied to the land adjoining the Scotch and English frontier before the two kingdoms were united. At any rate, it was given for a similar reason. It was territory never permanently occupied, but alternately and frequently visited by the combatants on both sides, and, of course, its inhabitants were unusually subject to the smaller annoyances, if not the direr evils, of the war, and were constantly compelled to furnish provender to roving cavalry squads of both armies.

There lived in this region one especially well-to-do old farmer. He owned a large, fertile, and productive farm and a good comfortable house, with a larder always fully stocked with nourishing food and excellent liquors. Consequently, the rambling cavalry men frequently called on him, and although he enjoyed their company much less than they did the entertainment, he could not well refuse. One day he had especial reason to deplore the popularity that he, or, rather his premises, had acquired. About that time, it will be remembered by many old soldiers, the Confederate cavalry men had gotten into the habit of dressing very much like the Yankees of the same branch of the service. The Confederacy did not issue clothing liberally, and it was difficult to obtain from domestic sources; so the Confederate army donned captured overcoats and trousers to an extent which sometimes made it difficult to distinguish a Confederate cavalry regiment from a Federal.

Upon the occasion on which this story hinges, a squad of mounted men rode up to the farmer's house early in the morning and demanded breakfast. Of course, it was prepared for them, and they ate heartily, consuming likewise a reasonable amount of peach brandy. When they had finished, one of the party asked the old gentleman about his political affiliations. He had been expecting such a question and had been earnestly endeavouring to "size up" the crowd accurately in order that he might give a safe answer. He had found it impossible to determine from their dress which side they belonged to, and they had dropped nothing in the course of conversation to enlighten him, so he was obliged to guess. He guessed that they were Confederates and answered accordingly.

"Most of the folks who live in this part of the country," he said, "are Union men. And I don't blame 'em much. They was raised old-line Whigs, and followed Mr. Clay in everything. So they've stood by the Union. But I can't see it that way. All of my kinspeople live in the South, and I've always owned niggers myself, therefore, gentlemen, I'm a rebel and stand by the South."

"The blazes you do," was the unexpected and appalling reply. "Well, then we'll just limb skin you," and they proceeded to carry out the threat.

At noon another gang arrived, and again the old man was involved in harassing doubt as to their identity. But as the other fellows had been Federal troops, he thought it highly probable that these were Federal, also, and when the time came he guessed that way. In response to the inquiry regarding his political status and sympathies, he said with much feeling:

"Gentlemen, I'll tell you straight, I don't know how you stand, but I've got nothing to conceal. The majority of the people who live around here is Southern in sentiment, and it isn't any fault of theirn. Most of 'em owns niggers and has kin in the South, and it's natural for 'em to feel that way. But I can't do it. I was brought up a Henry Clay Whig, and always taught to love the Union, and I'm fur the old flag and the enforcement of the laws."

Then the gang promptly and sternly informed him that his politics needed instant and serious correction and that he would be "jayhawked," which punishment they proceeded to inflict by confiscating the greater part of his peach brandy.

Late in the afternoon as the farmer was sitting on his veranda, mourning over the devastation of his household goods which the day had witnessed, another crowd put in an appearance and called for supper and drinks. The perplexity and incertitude which had assailed him in the two former cases, dwindled into insignificance compared with the bewilderment he now suffered. The very mothers of these soldiers couldn't have told from their garb and gait whether they were Yankee or rebel.

After eating and drinking their fill and making a tremendous gap in the old man's remaining store of provisions, the leader of the party propounded the usual question: "Well, old gentleman," he said, "what are your politics?"

"What am I?"

" Yes, that's what I said. What are you?"

"Well, mister, to tell you the God's truth, I'm nothing, and d — n little of that."

A better soldier than Bob McWilliams never shouldered a rifle. He was a member of that company of gallant Mississippians which contributed largely to the reputation of Gen. John H. Morgan's first regimental organization, the Second Kentucky Cavalry, C. S. A. But, although an excellent soldier, Bob was by no means deficient in a knowledge of those devices by means of which all sorts of Confederate soldiers contrived to add to the scanty rations usually issued them, and sometimes obtain even luxurious cheer. Indeed, he was remarkably successful in this kind of foraging, for he had "a face like an affidavit" and a tongue like a Jew's harp; and whenever and wherever persuasive eloquence was good for a "square meal" he got one.

When Morgan's command was in the Bluegrass region, on what was known as the "first Kentucky raid," the men sought to make up for previous deprivations by a voracious consumption of the tempting viands with which that country abounded. Every house had its throng of self-invited guests, and none was sent away unsatisfied. There was a certain mansion, however, to which these visitors resorted in numbers that would have alarmed, if not exhausted, ordinary hospitality. It was the dwelling of a beautiful and stately matron of the olden time, Mrs. David Castleman, whose dignity and grace were equalled only by her charity. She was an intense Southern sympathizer, and three of her sons were with Morgan; the eldest one of his best officers. This was the first place that Bob struck, in his irregular search for supplies. Two long tables were spread in the dining-room, covered with appetizing edibles, and a crowd of hungry rebs surrounded each. So soon as the dishes were emptied they were bountifully replenished, and as fast as one detachment filled up and fell back, another one, with craving stomachs, advanced to the attack. A bevy of lovely damsels waited on them, and pinned bouquets on their gray jackets as each concluded his repast.

Never in his life did Bob McWilliams show to better advantage than on this occasion. He ate as if an entire platoon was encircled by his belt; he discoursed in such wise that the young ladies believed him to be a weather-beaten, sunburned angel, and when at length he finished they unanimously bestowed on him the choicest bouquets. But then he suddenly remembered something which, in his rage of hunger, he had entirely forgotten, and the recollection made his hair bristle. He was not only ragged, but, from a certain point of view, absolutely unpresentable. The rear of his pantaloons, subjected to long and hard service, had given way in complete disorder. So long as he sat in the saddle this condition was not apparent but was almost impossible of concealment when he was on foot. Therefore, when he could eat no more, had stuffed his haversack with ham sandwiches, and had received more than his fair share of flowers, he directed all of his ingenuity to effecting an escape without exposure. With a profusion of thanks and compliments, he retired backward toward the door. But the girls followed him. Still bowing, smiling, and chatting, but in a perspiring agony of fear, he retreated through the hall and across the veranda, but his admirers still pursued him. Down the steps he backed and moved in the same fashion until he had gotten around the corner of the house. Then, as he turned about, devoutly thanking heaven that at last he was safe, he found himself face to face with his hostess. She held in her hand a stout pair of new jeans pants.

"My son," she said, "you had better take these. I think you need them more than you do a bouquet."

Doubtless many of the survivors of the Army of Tennessee remember the song "Lorena," and how, in the latter days of the war, its melodious but intensely melancholy strains used to sadden as well as soothe the bivouac. Just after the final surrender Gen. Frank Cheatham, of Tennessee, and Gen. John S. Williams — better known as "Cerro Gordo" Williams — of Kentucky, were wending their way northward in the hope of sometime regaining their ante-bellum homes. They were, of course, sore and dejected, and, notwithstanding the personal friendship which existed between them, found matter for acrimonious discussion in every topic which either broached.

Finally they got upon the causes of Confederate failure. Cheatham asserted that it was due entirely to the timidity and irresolution of Kentucky. Had Kentucky joined and assisted the Southern movement, he claimed, it would have been successful. This Williams stoutly denied. On the contrary, he contended, the reason why Kentucky did not cast her lot with the South was because she was prevented by the incertitude and hesitation of Tennessee. Moreover, there were, he insisted, other and serious objections to the Tennesseeans. "If I had nothing else against your people, Cheatham," he said, "I'd avoid them because they're always singing that infernal heartbreaking song, 'Lorena.'" Then Cheatham swore by all that he held holy that the song had never been heard in Tennessee, and that no Tennesseean ever had sung or ever would sing it. The dispute waxed hot and finally culminated in a bet, proposed by Williams, that the very first Tennesseean they met with would either be singing "Lorena" or would sing it before he got out of hearing. Cheatham promptly accepted. Each had about two dollars in silver and they put it up.

At that date the woods and the roads were full of disbanded Confederate soldiers, and they soon came upon one. He was a tall, stalwart young fellow, seated on a log and evidently resting after a long tramp. Williams at once accosted him.

"Where do you hail from, soldier?"

"Well," responded the soldier, "that's hard to say. For four years gone I've been in the Confederacy and belonged to the army. But now I feel as if I didn't hail from anywhar'. However, I came originally from Tennessee so I may say I hail from thar; but——

"'It matters little now Lo-ree-na.'"

"Cheatham!" said Williams, "hand over that money."

The most important consideration — the "burning question," indeed — with the Confederate cavalry during the latter part of the war was how to procure horses. The peculiar and very active work it was required to perform was extremely hard upon horse-flesh and depleted it very rapidly. In the last year of the war the South, that part of her territory, at least, which was still held by the Confederate armies, was almost entirely destitute of horses. The lack of them was severely felt by the farmers, and was one reason why food was so scantily produced during that period. At all times the men who enlisted in the Confederate cavalry regiments had furnished their own mounts, and even had the government been willing to provide them it would have found great difficulty in doing so; it was barely able, indeed, to procure horses in sufficient numbers to make the artillery efficient.

This was one and the chief reason why the Confederate cavalry did not, in the campaigns of 1864, so conspicuously hold its own against the mounted Federal regiments as it had previously done. But the Southern trooper, although he received little aid in any respect from his government and his military superiors, had early learned to take pretty good care of himself, and in this matter of prime necessity he always exhibited marked ingenuity and industry. If a horse was to be had anywhere or by any means, he usually managed to get it; acting very much in the spirit of the canny Johnstons of Annandale, that "Thou shalt want ere I want." The "pressing," or forcible taking of horses, a practice indulged in very extensively by the cavalry of both sides, was strictly inhibited and very seldom attempted by the Confederate within his own territory; and this, together with the constantly increasing scarcity of the article in the South, necessitated many incursions, which might not have been otherwise undertaken, into territory occupied by the enemy. It is related that on one occasion when Forrest entered Paducah, there was with him a gallant young Frenchman who had quite recently emigrated to this country and settled in Paducah, but at the outbreak of the war had joined a cavalry regiment which became part of Forrest's command. He had not, at the time of which I speak, acquired much English, but his vocabulary, while limited, was exceedingly clear and to the point. As he rode along one of the streets he was recognized and accosted by a former acquaintance.

"Hello, Charlie!" said the friend, "what did you fellows come into Kentucky for this time?"

"More horse," responded Charlie, briefly and doubtless accurately.

Central Kentucky, and more especially the Bluegrass

region, contained the pastures where the men of Morgan's command chiefly sought to exchange their exhausted horses for fresh stock, and sometimes, if it was a very pressing case, obtain new mounts without the ceremony of an exchange. Much of this, of course, occurred upon the raids and expeditions made into the state for strategic purposes; but in the autumn of '63 and the winter of '63 and '64, a good many men were given furloughs that they might go to Kentucky and procure horses. They frequently got them at their homes and from their relatives and friends, preferring to do so if possible, the donors cheerfully contributing in that way to the cause. But if the animal was not to be procured in that way, it was gotten otherwise. I cannot remember that any man who started upon such an errand and returned, came back without a horse.

In September, 1864, Frank Key Morgan, the general's youngest brother, then a boy of sixteen, accompanied a small scouting party into Kentucky and pushed on to the vicinity of Lexington. There Key exchanged his almost broken-down steed for a very fine mare, which he brought back to south-western Virginia and kept until very nearly the end of the war; until the incident I am about to tell occurred. She was one of the handsomest animals I ever saw; a rich blood, bay in colour, fully sixteen hands in height and beautifully shaped, having all the points of the thoroughbred; and quite probably she was, but as that matter was not discussed when the "swap" was made, it remained one of doubt. In two or three months, however, it developed that she was with foal, and in the following April, when, after General Lee's surrender, the remnant of Morgan's division under my command was marching through North Carolina with the view of reaching the army under Gen. Joseph E. Johnstone, it became apparent that the date of her accouchment was near at hand. It was therefore necessary that another exchange should be effected.

The mare was really such a fine one that neither her owner nor his comrades were willing to exchange her, except for something very superior; in fact, but that it was a matter of absolute necessity, they would not have been willing to part with her at all. It had to be done, however, and after much consultation it was determined that an effort should be made to swap her for a magnificent saddle horse, which belonged to a doctor living in a town we were approaching. The fame of this horse was widespread, and every one felt that it would be a credit to the command to have such an animal in the ranks. Some difficulty was anticipated about accomplishing the barter, for the doctor was in active practice and needed a good horse for his work; and, moreover, was attached to and proud of his saddler. But it was ascertained that he was not only an enthusiastic horseman, but had also a great fondness for thoroughbreds and had long wished to obtain some extra well-bred mares. This information at once suggested a successful programme. Two men, who were connoisseurs in horse-flesh and learned in pedigrees, undertook to make the trade. When we reached the town they took the mare to be inspected by the doctor, and stated their desire to exchange her for his horse. He at first received the proposition with derision. He was gravely assured, however, that she was not only thoroughbred but fashionably bred, by the Knight of St. George out of a Lexington mare, and that she was with foal by West Australian. Nothing, said the parties engineering the business, could have induced them to consent to give her up, but the fact that she could be carried no farther just then and the command was "in a hurry." Her appearance seemed to corroborate their declaration regarding her pedigree, and this, with the fact that she was carrying such a colt, overcame the doctor's reluctance to part with his horse and he consented to trade. The transaction occurred late in the afternoon, and what subsequently happened well illustrates that it is sometimes excellent policy for a cavalry command to march at night. Early the next morning the doctor came to the camp with blood in his eye and a shot-gun in hand, and fiercely demanded that the trade should be rescinded and his horse returned. During the night the mare had given birth to a mule colt.

General Morgan had, of course, at different periods during the war quite a number of horses, perhaps eight or ten; all very fine ones, two exceptionally so. These were "Black Bess," the famous mare with which he began his career, and another almost as spirited and hardy, a Glencoe gelding, which the men used to call the "high-crested bay."

I think that Black Bess was the handsomest and, all things

considered, the finest horse for saddle or cavalry purposes I ever saw. She was of a very peculiar and very rare type. While I have seen other horses of the same general conformation, I have never seen one that closely resembled her. She was scant fifteen hands in height and impressed one at first glance as being quite small, but closer inspection revealed the fact that she was not only compactly built, but had a frame of unusual, indeed extraordinary, power. Her pedigree, as I member Mr. Warren Vila, who bred her, giving it, was that she was by Drennon, one of the standard saddle horse stallions of Kentucky — and one of the most famous — and her dam thoroughbred. In form she was a curious but most beautiful blend between the handsomer specimens of the Canadian and the thoroughbred. She had the typical thoroughbred points in an almost exaggerated degree, especially the strong, tilted loins, thin, sloping withers, short back, and great length from brisket to whirlbone with also great depth in the girth and arched back rib. Her head was small and beautifully shaped, and there was an expression of intelligence in her eyes almost human. Her neck was not arched, as some equestrian theorists would have, perhaps, preferred, but was of the race-horse pattern, extending almost straight out from the shoulders and beautifully moulded. There was something deer-like in her shape, the same slender grace, yet suggestion of marvellous muscular strength and agility. Her colour was the deepest, glossiest black imaginable.

This mare was given Morgan by Mr. Vila when the former was leaving Lexington with his company, the Lexington Rifles, in September, 1861. Captain Morgan was riding her when I met him at Munfordville in the early part of October, and I saw her every day thereafter until the second day of the battle of Shiloh. I saw Morgan ride her on many scouts and in many skirmishes, and I think I retain not only a vivid but an accurate recollection of her. One of her peculiarities which I can well recall was the crouching, panther-like attitude she would assume when under fire. Having never been specially trained for the saddle, Black Bess had none of the artificial saddle gaits. A wonderfully smooth, rapid "flat-footed" walk, and an easy, graceful canter constituted the sum of her accomplishments.

This walk was so rapid that the other horses in the column, when trying to keep up with her, were always forced into a trot.

Black Bess was captured on May 6, 1862, at the "Lebanon races," as Morgan's men termed the first defeat which their leader sustained. Dumont attacked him at Lebanon, Tennessee, on that date with a greatly superior force, and a severe combat ensued. In the midst of the fight the curb of her bridle was in some way snapped, and the mare, always excitable and somewhat difficult to control, broke into a clean run and rushed down the pike like a whirlwind. Morgan, even with the assistance of one or two men who caught hold of the reins, was for some time unable to stop her. This accident prevented the men from being rallied, and the Federals pressed the retreat to the Cumberland river, which some of the fugitives crossed, but were compelled to leave their horses, Black Bess among them, on the southern side.

Mr. Vila, who wished to recover the mare for breeding purposes — indeed, he had stipulated that she should be returned to him if Morgan brought her back safely—made every effort, after the war, to ascertain what had become of her, but without success.

The bay Glencoe horse was given Morgan by Capt. Keene Richards in the summer of 1862. He was an altogether different animal from Black Bess, although nearly as fine a one. He stood sixteen hands, and perhaps half an inch in height, and was not only a strong, but a "big horse." He had the thoroughbred points in nearly as marked degree, but in more robust proportion, and in gait and action he was almost her equal. This fellow carried his head high, but not in the constrained fashion taught by "bitting" or tight reining, but with a natural, easy movement. Big as he was, he was yet extremely nimble and surefooted. I saw Morgan on one occasion, when we were in close and hot pursuit of a body of Federals, ride this horse over a steep "bluff" or eminence along a small watercourse, which was at least thirty feet in height and almost precipitous, yet he went down it as surely and landed at the bottom as lightly as a cat could have done.

Morgan rode this horse upon the Ohio raid, and was mounted on him at the time that he was so nearly over the river — after the disaster at Buffington — but turned back because he found that the gunboats had approached so near as to prevent those who were following him from crossing.

Many of the war lyrics which were familiar to the people of the South have been preserved, and will doubtless retain a place in poetic literature. It is hard for the present generation to understand the impression which some of them produced at the time when they were generally sung. They were the echoes of a highly-wrought sentiment, inspiring utterance and action equally intense, and were received as the natural and appropriate expression of the popular purpose and hope.

Certain representative songs were heard during the first two years of the war in every Southern household. "Maryland, My Maryland," "The Red, White, and Blue," "There's Life in the Old Land Yet," "The Bonnie Blue Flag," and "Stonewall Jackson's Way," like "Dixie," were to a certain extent *indicia*, if not exactly tests, of loyalty to the South. They were parts of the profession of faith.

But as the long conflict dragged on, losing much of its early illusion and becoming more bitter and productive of sorrow, these songs, so popular at a period of more sanguine expectation, were replaced in the household by others of a sadder tenor, and by the soldiers were tacitly voted rather too romantic for the camp and field. Young ladies still rendered them in compliment and, perhaps, as incentive, to military admirers; but the youth to whom battle and bivouac had become second nature, chanted in quite different strain on the march or at the camp fire. The veterans of the Confederacy will remember how unlike to those sung in the beginning of the struggle were the songs which became favourites with them after it had developed into its later phases of harsh, close, frequent grapple and almost constant privation. There was less of flourish, but more of meaning; not so much bravado, but a great deal more point. These songs, like the talk and the work of the veterans, were imbued with the grim earnestness of their experience and of the situation; when to phrase the thought in the vernacular of the camp, "a man was not inclined to bite off more than he could chaw, but mighty apt to chaw all he bit off."

There were some of these songs which breathed a fierce spirit and active resentment typical of the time, but now scarcely remembered; but the greater number of these rugged verses were good-humoured; quite full, it is true, of the soldier's disposition to exalt his own side and its heroes, but generally an accurate transcript in rude rhyme of current events, and often sappy with the homely satire of the camp, which stings foe and friend alike.

Every ex-Confederate must recall one such song, the most popular of all, which was raised in quaint, jingling tune whenever and wherever a half-dozen ragged rebels were gathered together.

The rollicking refrain, captivating in its very absurdity, ran as follows:

> "I'll lay ten dollars down,
> And count it up one by one.
> Oh, show me the man, so nigh as you can,
> Who struck Billy Patterson."

Innumerable verses were composed and sung to this refrain. The Army of Northern Virginia, the Army of Tennessee, and the Army of the trans-Mississippi had each its history rudely chronicled, as fast as made, in this rough minstrelsy. No one man knew, or could possibly have known, the whole of it, for new stanzas were constantly added. Every corps and command contributed some commemorative quatrain. The events of campaigns were told in this improvised verse as rapidly as they occurred, and thereafter were sung or recited by the rhapsodist who professed to know that much of the fragmentary epic. The wits and wags of the camp sought to make caustic criticism more effective by embodying in it lines which might be heard throughout the Confederacy.

The boundless, invincible confidence of his army in General Lee was simply but perfectly and, to one who shared the sentiment, pathetically expressed in language of cheer and assurance, assumed to have been spoken by the great commander himself:

> "Gen. Lee, he said, 'My soldiers,
> You've nothing now to fear,
> For Longstreet's on the right of them
> And Jackson's in their rear.'"

And also

> "You Yanks will never get across
> The Chickahominee,
> For you-uns fights mit Siegel,
> And wee-uns follow Lee."

The manner in which General Jackson habitually obtained supplies from a certain Federal commander was thus recorded:

> "Old Stonewall says, you hungry rebs,
> You'd better keep in ranks;
> For I'm goin' to draw some rations
> From Major-general Banks."

The dim, half-conscious recognition of the abnormal nature of the strife — of the ghastly folly of civil war — had its utterance:

> "I've shot at many a Mexikin,
> And many an Injun, too,
> But I never thought I'd have to shoot
> At Yankee-doodle-do."

A battle incident was thus preserved:

> "The Fourteenth Louisiana,
> They charged 'em with a yell;
> They bagged them 'Bucktail Rangers,'
> ———— ———— ———— ———— ————"

The profanity of the last line, if reproduced, would shock every well-regulated mind, and all feeling of admiration for the bravery of the Fourteenth Louisiana would be lost in one of compassion for the dreadful fate of the "Bucktail Rangers."

The explanation of how a soldier, who followed Morgan on his raid across the great river, became a prisoner is thoroughly clear:

> "Oh, Morgan crossed the river,
> And I went across with him;
> I was captured in Ohio
> Because I couldn't swim."

So also is the candid account given by another cavalry man of the manner in which he procured his outfit:

> "You see these boots I'm wearin'?
> I won 'em on a race;
> A store subscribed this suit of clothes,
> And I bought my hat on space."

The way in which fond hopes were sometimes disappointed is thus described:

> "My captain went a-scoutin'
> And took my brother Jim;
> He went to catch the Yankees,
> But the Yankees they catched him."

The ladies, of course, were remembered, and one minstrel declares that:

> "Georgia girls are handsome,
>   And Tennessee girls are sweet;
> But a girl in old Kentucky,
>   Is the one I want to meet."

Another, after a glowing tribute to his sweetheart, emphatically announces that:

> "When this here war is over,
>   She's a-goin' to be my wife;
> I'll settle down in Alabam'
>   And lead a quiet life."

No matter where this song was sung, whether on the Potomac or the Sabine, the Cumberland or the Gulf, nor which of the multitude of its stanzas were selected for rendition, this verse always concluded it:

> "But now my song is ended,
>   And I haven't got much time;
> I'm goin' to run the blockade
>   To see that girl of mine."

CHAPTER XV

OF ALL the officers of high rank who served in the Confederate army, the least kindly recollection is retained of Gen. Braxton Bragg. The conduct of more than one of them was, at sometime, criticized. But none other was criticized so generally and so bitterly. Some others inspired little affection and even a certain portion of enmity; but he was widely and intensely disliked. Many general officers, of less force and ability than he had, have been popular with their soldiers and those immediately under them, but if there was any such feeling for him it utterly lacked manifestation, and the very reverse was often shown. His friends and admirers were few in number, and not much in evidence; they were not often found among those who were required to obey his orders and execute his plans.

And yet this sentiment, so almost universally entertained for him, and the popular mistrust of his ability as an officer, was certainly, in large measure, unjust.

Mr. Davis was almost alone in his belief in General Bragg's capacity and in expecting good results from his efforts. But this is something decidedly in his favour.

Mr. Davis was accused of exhibiting undue favouritism in some instances and an unreasonable prejudice in others, and the charge may be true to a certain extent; the best and wisest men are not totally free from that fault, but he undoubtedly knew the officers of the old army, and the men from whom he was, in a manner, compelled to select his military chiefs, better than almost any one else knew them; and while he occasionally overrated some, and perhaps underrated others — while he expected of more than one of them things which that particular man was not competent to do—it will be difficult to indicate any one whom he placed in high and responsible station, who had not, in a marked degree, some of the qualities necessary to the performance of its duties. But Mr. Davis sometimes overlooked — a mistake easily made in the case of untried men — the lack of other qualities even more essential to success. He made this mistake in General Bragg's case, who, almost unrivalled as a subordinate and lieutenant, could never have become a great commander. He was lacking in the quick, fertile, and accurate conception and broad comprehension which makes the successful strategist; he was not an able tactician. So far from inspiring, as nearly all great captains have done, confidence and love in those who followed them, General Bragg aroused sentiments the very reverse. His temper was austere and even morose, his manner was repellant, his very look and bearing suggested in others distrust of his judgment, and doubt of successful achievement.

As time wears on, however, we often discover that resentments, once hotly felt, have been largely without proper provocation, and that opinions at one time firmly and honestly entertained have been induced by misconstruction. Such, I am sure, will be our ultimate estimate of General Bragg's character, although that of his capacity as a soldier may remain unchanged. Several years ago I expressed my opinion of General Bragg in the following language, and I am more than ever convinced that it is correct:

> It is generally conceded that he had no superior as a corps commander among the Confederate officers who had achieved distinction in that capacity, and an almost universal confidence obtained that he would be no less successful as chief of an army. He had demonstrated his possession in an eminent degree of the qualities necessary for the work of organization, discipline, and military administration. The improvement he immediately wrought in these respects confirmed the opinion induced by his labours at Pensacola; for out of the forces which were certainly much demoralized at Corinth, he had very soon made a disciplined army at Tupelo. His capacity as strategist and tactician — as field captain — was yet to be tested. His warmest friends will doubtless now admit that he did not, as army leader and departmental commander, sustain his previous fame or the expectations which had been formed of him. But the criticism which once so fiercely challenged his right to be estimated as a great soldier in any regard is now silent and must be held unjust. The severity, which was formerly believed to be the tendency of a harsh and unsympathetic nature to express itself in congenial acts of tyranny, is now better understood. We can discern that the strong, imperious, relentless will was executing, in a way which seemed to it best and most necessary, a sincere, unselfish, patriotic purpose. If, like some stern commander of the early legionaries, he sought to teach the discipline which makes the soldier fear his officer more than he does the enemy, he was as ready as the Roman to devote himself to "the gods of death and the grave," if it might win victory for his people.

I believe that such will ultimately be the verdict of history and the opinion of the Southern people, and that they will enroll his name among those which they wish remembered and honoured. At any rate, his record is so intimately connected with that of the Army of Tennessee and with the conduct of the war in the great department he so long commanded, that the historians of the Confederacy must give it ample consideration.

General Bragg's service in the regular army of the United States — the "old army," as it was frequently termed — was extremely creditable, and no officer stood in better repute for general soldierly conduct with his comrades and superiors. He was graduated from West Point in 1837, and was constantly employed in arduous service in the Seminole War and against the Indian tribes of the South-western plains, until the breaking out of the Mexican War. He earned an excellent, indeed brilliant, reputation in Mexico; serving with distinction at Fort Brown, Monterey, and other combats, and with exceptional gallantry and efficiency at Buena Vista, and was twice promoted, first to the rank of major and then to that of lieutenant-colonel.

After the Mexican War he resigned from the United States army, and became a planter in Louisiana. Immediately upon the establishment of the provisional government of the Confederate states, he was appointed a brigadier-general in the Confederate army, and placed in command at Pensacola, where he remained during the summer and fall of 1861. In February, 1862, he was appointed a major-general and given a very important command, with his headquarters at Mobile. It was at Pensacola and Mobile that he first evinced his extraordinary capacity as an organizer and disciplinarian; and all of the Confederate armies of the West owed much of their efficiency to his work in these respects. To this fact, and also because he was personally cognizant of Bragg's conduct in Mexico, is doubtless to be ascribed Mr. Davis's partiality for him.

When, after the disasters at Forts Henry and Donelson, Gen. Albert Sidney Johnston concentrated all of the forces available for such purpose at Corinth, to repel the threatened invasion of the Southern territory, along the lines of the Mobile & Ohio and Memphis & Charlestown railroads, General Bragg was called from his command upon the gulf, with the troops he had been training with such care and skill. In the organization of the Army of the Mississippi, composed of all the Confederate forces assembled at Corinth, he was appointed to the command of the Second Corps, and the men of that corps were conspicuous for superior equipment and soldierly bearing. It formed the second line of battle of General Johnston's army, when moving to the attack on the first day of Shiloh, and on that day Bragg commanded the Confederate centre.

So thoroughly well did all the officers and men of the Army of the Mississippi behave in that battle that it would be scarcely just to particularize any man or body of troops as having been distinguished more than the others; but it is undoubtedly true that the manner in which General Bragg manœuvred and fought his corps, and his general conduct in the battle, were universally and especially commended. So also his appointment soon afterward as full general, to fill the vacancy in that list occasioned by the death of General Johnston, was generally esteemed the fittest selection that could have been made.

Confederate reverses were numerous and came rapidly for some time after Shiloh. Island No. 10, on the Mississippi, fell on April 7th the same date as the second day of the battle. Fort Pillow was evacuated on June 1st, and Memphis on June 6th. Corinth, slowly approached, and invested by one hundred thousand men under Halleck, was evacuated on May 30th. The Army of the Mississippi, under Beauregard, retreated to Tupelo, a point on the Mobile & Ohio railroad, about sixty miles south of Corinth, where the greater part of it remained until the initial steps of the subsequent movement into Kentucky were taken.

With the exception of east Tennessee, all territory north of the Tennessee River, and even portions of Mississippi and Alabama, were temporarily abandoned to Federal occupation in the beginning of the summer of 1862.

The total effective strength of all the forces under the immediate command of General Beauregard at this date was something less than fifty thousand, including, of course, troops stationed at other points than Tupelo. There were twelve or fifteen thousand Confederate troops in east Tennessee, under command of Gen. E. Kirby Smith, occupying that territory from

Chattanooga to Cumberland Gap. There were also Confederate forces at Jackson, Vicksburg, and other points in Mississippi, and in Arkansas, but they were not available for operations to be attempted by the Army of the Mississippi.

Besides the Federal troops already mentioned as having been, at this date, with Halleck in front of Corinth, there was a division of Buell's army about seven thousand strong, under Mitchell, at Huntsville, Alabama holding the Mobile & Ohio railroad and threatening an advance on Chattanooga. Another division of Buell's army about ten thousand strong, under George W. Morgan, was in front of Cumberland Gap, and ten or twelve thousand men of the same army were at or in the vicinity of Nashville. Eight or ten thousand more, perhaps, were about the same time or soon after in the confines of east Tennessee and apparently ready to move toward Knoxville.

On June 3d, Halleck began such disposition — dispersal, indeed — of his troops as suggested an intention to relinquish the purpose of an active offensive during that summer. The divisions of Wallace and McClernand were sent to Bolivar, on the Mississippi Central railroad. Those of Sherman and Hurlbut were despatched in the direction of Memphis. Pope was ordered to suspend the pursuit of Beauregard and encamp at Corinth. Buell was instructed to press, with all his available force, along the line of the Memphis & Charleston railroad toward Chattanooga, the only thing in the nature of an aggressive movement that was attempted. Such was the situation when, about the middle of June, Beauregard relinquished command of the department, and Bragg was appointed to succeed him.

Soon afterward began a campaign based upon one of the grandest strategic conceptions of the war, but doomed to disappointment and failure because of the timidity and vacillation with which, just in its crisis — at the crucial moment — it was conducted. Almost immediately upon taking command, General Bragg prepared for the movement into Kentucky, which, had it been completely successful, would have done more than aught else to achieve final victory for the Confederacy, and which would have been successful if it had been prosecuted to its conclusion with the same boldness and vigour with which it was begun. The unfortunate result of this campaign did serious injury to General Bragg's reputation and prestige, for it was the almost universal conviction that he signally failed to utilize an opportunity pregnant with far reaching and valuable consequences to the Confederacy.

It was apparent to General Bragg, so soon as he took command at Tupelo, that a policy of inaction would be dangerous and perhaps speedily fatal to his army. Not only was aggressive action of some sort necessary to revive the spirits of the troops and of the people, greatly discouraged, as they were, by the recent disasters; but for strategic reasons, also, operations upon his part were requisite to prevent the enemy — when Halleck might become aroused from his lethargy — from closing the net around him, and using his superior numbers with crushing advantage.

Three alternatives were open to him, if he chose to assume the offensive. He might attack Corinth; he might advance against Grant in west Tennessee; or he might, heavily reinforcing Kirby Smith, move with the forces thus combined into middle Tennessee and Kentucky. The chances of victory in a pitched battle seemed very nearly equal, should he adopt either of these courses, but far richer results were possible if it should prove successful from the one last mentioned. Moreover, although apparently more daring, it was in reality the safer of the three. It would be easier for Grant to reinforce Corinth, or for the forces there to reinforce Grant, than for either to give aid to Buell. Indeed, it would be well-nigh impossible for Bragg to move against Grant without exposing his rear or flank to attack from the troops stationed at Corinth. It would be feasible for him — as he concluded to do — to engage the attention of the commander at Corinth, and prevent his interfering with the movement into Tennessee and Kentucky or reinforcing Buell, by having Generals Price and Van Dorn, whom he left at Tupelo and the vicinity with some twenty thousand men, inauguarate an active offensive. They did so with success, fighting the battles of Iuka and Corinth and arresting any attempt to interfere with Bragg's plan of campaign.

The immediate effect of the movement which General Bragg decided upon was to protect east Tennessee from the threatened invasion and occupation by Buell, which would have cut in twain the eastern and more important part of the Confederate territory rendering communication between Richmond and the Army of Northern Virginia with the armies further west very difficult if not impossible; as was abundantly shown by the disastrous effect so produced at a later period of the war. But it promised also the recovery of the greater and more fertile part of Tennessee, and the possession of the whole or nearly the whole of the territory of Kentucky. From these regions an inexhaustible store of food supplies and much other valuable material would be furnished the Confederacy, and thousands of recruits could be obtained for the Confederate armies. It would undoubtedly have also stimulated enlistment in the states farther south; for many young men who had resisted the incentives which first urged the youth of the South to enter the ranks, and who subsequently eluded the grasp of the conscription, might have been tempted into the Confederate service by successes so brilliant and the hope of a speedy termination of the war.

I have always believed that the complete success of this campaign would have had greater effect in inducing the people of the North to abandon the effort to coerce the South into submission, than Confederate victory, however decisive, at any other period of the struggle could have accomplished. At an earlier date the North scarcely believed that the South was really in earnest. At a later period — when Gettysburg was fought — the time had gone by when courage or fortune could have greatly availed the Confederacy. The people of the North had then ascertained the extent of their own resources and had accurately gauged those of their opponents. They had become convinced that persistent, relentless effort would ultimately break down the resistance of adversaries, who, lacking nothing in skill and bravery, were utterly destitute of the means and materials necessary to sustain prolonged and continuous warfare.

But at the date of which I write such perfect confidence of ultimate success — born of a thorough knowledge of the situation — did not yet obtain in the North. The South, rallying after her reverses in the spring of 1862, seemed more determined and defiant than before. The Confederate host, which had been driven southward, had turned and pressed forward, carrying its banners back again into Tennessee and Kentucky. At the same time the Army of Northern Virginia, having crippled the forces opposed to it in Virginia in a series of victorious battles, was marching into Maryland. The North still depended upon volunteering to fill her armies. The draft had not yet been suggested, and no one had thought of subsidizing the recruiting markets of Europe to replete the Federal ranks. If at that date, which may justly be deemed a crisis, the army under Bragg had won a great victory that would have placed Tennessee and Kentucky firmly in Confederate grasp; if the Confederate flag had been seen triumphant along the Potomac and Ohio both, and Northern territory had been threatened with invasion in the East and West alike, have we not reason to believe that Northern sentiment might have demanded peace?

I shall endeavour to show, without in the least disparaging the fine army commanded by Buell, or overrating the prowess of the troops commanded by Bragg, that the latter general had more than one opportunity, while in Kentucky, to deliver battle which should almost certainly have resulted in victory.

On June 27th, General Bragg despatched McCown's division to Chattanooga, as the advance guard of the force he intended to employ in his contemplated movement into Tennessee and Kentucky. The brigades of Cleburne and Preston Smith followed a little later. By the middle of August some twenty-five thousand infantry of the army, previously around Tupelo, had been transferred by rail via Mobile to Chattanooga, and crossing the Tennessee River a few days thereafter, General Bragg began his northward march on August 28th, moving across Waldron's Ridge toward middle Tennessee. Somewhat earlier than this date Kirby Smith, in pursuance of his part of the programme, commenced his advance through Big Creek Gap and Roger's Gap into Kentucky. He left Stevenson with eight thousand men in front of Cumberland Gap, to observe the enemy posted there. Stevenson was instructed — so soon as the Gap should be evacuated and his path was clear — to follow General Smith and join him at Lexington. In his own column General Smith had some ten thousand infantry and Scott's brigade of cavalry.

During July and August, Forrest and Morgan had been actively engaged in the territory which was now to be made the theatre of far more extensive military operations. Morgan had made a raid into central Kentucky as far north as Cynthiana, within fifty miles of Cincinnati, capturing nearly all of the garrisons and depots of supplies in that region. At the same time Forrest had entered middle Tennessee and performed similar work there. Both then settled down to the task which had been especially assigned them, which was to harass Buell in every conceivable way, and retard and if possible hinder his advance upon either Knoxville or Chattanooga. Morgan, returning from Kentucky, established himself on the north of the Cumberland in the country about Gallatin and Hartsville, and began a systematic interruption of Buell's communications with Louisville. Forrest was equally active on the southern side of the river, breaking all rail connection south and east of Nashville, and making foraging and the collection of supplies by the Federals in all the adjacent country both difficult and hazardous. Accurate and prompt information of Buell's movements and of the disposition of his troops was also furnished by these officers to their own commanders, while their activity in large measure masked the impending Confederate aggressive operations. On August 29th, Morgan, having received orders to that effect, marched to Lexington, Kentucky, which point he reached on September 4th. Forrest remained in Tennessee.

General Smith pressed on over very difficult roads through the mountains of south-eastern Kentucky and reached Richmond on August 30th. Here all of the Federal troops in central Kentucky immediately available for defense had been collected under Generals Manson and Nelson. General Manson states that this force was not more than six thousand five hundred strong. General Smith had marched so rapidly, and his men were so inadequately supplied that he had scarcely six thousand when he came in the presence of the enemy. He attacked without hesitation. The fight was waged hotly upon both sides, and resulted in a complete Confederate victory. More than a thousand of the Federals were killed and wounded, and four thousand three hundred and three made prisoners. General Manson was captured and Nelson wounded, nine pieces of artillery taken, and the Federal command utterly destroyed. The Confederate loss in killed and wounded was comparatively small.

General Smith instantly pressed on to Lexington, reaching that place on September 2d, and in a day or two had his entire command there.

Buell was, of course, in doubt at first of Bragg's purpose, and naturally supposed that he might be moving on Nashville. Some writers who have discussed this campaign seem to think that General Bragg was undecided whether to deliver battle in the vicinity of Nashville or to March into Kentucky. There can be no question that he had determined on the latter policy at the incipiency of the campaign and never wavered in such purpose. Success in Kentucky would have compelled the evacuation of middle Tennessee by the Federal forces, and the subsequent Confederate possession of Nashville without a struggle. The plan was clearly and wisely conceived, and contained no element of uncertainty. Had its later conduct been as prompt and vigorous as was its initiative, the results would have obviated all necessity of explanation.

Buell met the situation with alacrity and resolution, and skilfully disposed his army to deal with either emergency. Collecting the rolling stock of the railroads where it could be best used, whether he should have to fight Bragg in Tennessee or follow him into Kentucky, and getting his transportation ready for either alternative, he rapidly concentrated the bulk of his army at Murfreesboro, between September 2d and 5th. This point was judiciously selected. It was one where Buell could earliest discover Bragg's intention — if the latter meant to advance on Nashville — and fight him to the best advantage as he emerged from the mountains; or whence he could quickly and closely press him, if he continued his march northward.

Bragg pushed on, in pursuance of his original plan, through the Sequatchie Valley and across the plateau about Sparta. He made no demonstration in the direction where Buell was waiting to give him battle, but, heading his long column for the Cumberland, crossed it at the fords by which the Confederate cavalry were wont to pass when raiding into Kentucky, and on September 12th reached Glasgow. Buell receiving early information of his route, started, without hesitation and with all the speed he could make, for the same region. His first objective was Bowling Green, only a short distance from Glasgow. It was a large depot of supplies, and the only one he had between

Louisville and Nashville, and it was of extreme importance that he should reach it before Bragg could capture it. By expeditious marching he succeeded in doing so.

Chalmers, commanding the advance brigade of General Bragg's army, had been sent on to take position at Cave City on the Louisville & Nashville railroad, north of Bowling Green, to prevent communication between Louisville and that point. Chalmers, whose brigade was only sixteen hundred strong, conceived the idea, without orders, of attacking the garrison at Munfordsville on the north bank of the Green River at the point where the railroad crosses it. The position was one of considerable natural strength and was well, although not elaborately, fortified. The garrison, however numbered about four thousand men, nearly three times as strong as the attacking force; and Chalmers, after a sharp and gallant action, was repulsed with smart loss. General Bragg moved his entire army to Munfordsville, enveloped the place and compelled the surrender of the garrison. He now had his army between Buell and Louisville, held a formidable defensive position, and was in possession of the railroad and the line of the Green River.

It is almost impossible to reconcile General Bragg's conduct after he had taken Munfordsville with the idea and purpose on which it has been claimed and supposed, that his movement into Kentucky was predicated. If it was his intention, when he moved the greater part of his army from Corinth to Chattanooga, to simply relieve east Tennessee from the danger of Federal occupation, and compel Buell's army to evacuate middle Tennessee, without thought of any more decisive gain or success, we can understand why he marched so far north as Glasgow and then declined to give battle. But if that was his object it is difficult to understand why, when Buell marched toward Louisville, he did not immediately turn southward, move directly on Nashville, and, capturing that place, establish his army in middle Tennessee, occupying the whole of that territory with less of loss and labour than it cost him to regain only a part of it two months later.

I believe it was General Bragg's original plan and hope to force Buell to give battle somewhere in Kentucky, between Bowling Green and Louisville, utterly to defeat him, and to recover and firmly hold all of central and middle Kentucky up to the Ohio River. There can be no doubt that such was Kirby Smith's estimate of the results to be obtained from this campaign.

Why then, was a plan so sagaciously conceived and boldly and energetically inaugurated, apparently so completely abandoned? It is mild criticism to declare that it was marred by incertitude, vacillation, and timidity. General Bragg acted like one who had clearly foreseen and provided for what might happen up to the time when the serious and hazardous work of the campaign would begin, giving no thought to what might occur or what he might be required to do afterward. Strange as it may seem, I think this is the true explanation of his conduct during that period when so much was at stake, between September 17th and October 12th; and the reason for it is to be found in his mental and moral constitution. He could formulate the inception of an enterprise, but seemed incapable of thinking out a plan consistently to its conclusion. Exhibiting undaunted courage as a subordinate, he invariably evinced a lack of resolution and decision in emergencies after he was given independent command.

In charging that the real object of General Bragg's expedition into Kentucky was defeated by a lack of forecast upon his part, for which there can be no excuse, I am not unmindful of that element of chance and uncertainty which frequently determines, in great measure, the result of military operations. There are certain questions in the problems of warfare which can never be calculated with perfect accuracy, or positively ascertained in advance. No matter how sagacious, careful and skilful a captain may be, he must always be in doubt, to a certain extent, as to what his adversary will do, or how much that adversary may accomplish; nor can he always certainly foresee or avoid some accident which may derange his own plans or hinder his movements.

But General Bragg had no difficulties of this nature to contend with, and the failure for which he has been censured was lack of provision for contingencies which he must have anticipated, and, indeed, knew would happen. Moreover, there are sometimes circumstances under which the general who assumes and is able to retain the initiative can control the situation; if he can "keep the lead," he can win the game. This was General Bragg's attitude when he had gotten between Buell and Louisville, and could have called a considerable part of Kirby Smith's forces to his assistance, whenever he chose to fight.

General Bragg not only expected that Buell would follow him into Kentucky, but knew that he would be forced to do so, with all possible speed. He had been informed of the disposition and possible strength of the Federal forces in middle Tennessee by both Morgan and Forrest. Just before Morgan started to Lexington he had notified the officer in command at Chattanooga, who of course transmitted the information to General Bragg, that Buell was beginning his concentration at Murfreesboro. Bragg's movement, whether merely intended to clear Alabama and Tennessee of the enemy, or having a more important purpose, was based upon the supposition that Buell would be drawn as far north, perhaps, as Louisville. But if the ultimate object of the campaign was not only to compel the evacuation by the Federal armies of Alabama and Tennessee, but to obtain possession of Kentucky — and that such was its object is clearly disclosed, I think, by the correspondence between Generals Bragg and Smith of June and July, 1862 — then General Bragg not only wished and believed that Buell would follow him, but should have sought an opportunity to fight and crush him with the least possible delay. Under such conditions and with the prize contended for, prompt battle and decisive victory should have been sought at all hazards. Moreover, if General Bragg did not mean to fight to hold Kentucky, he should not have gone to Munfordsville, but should have remained in position to fall back rapidly on Nashville. After the capture of Munfordsville and the establishment of his army north of the Green River, a successful battle with Buell had become necessary to the accomplishment of either plan; and if he meant to fight he should have sought battle so soon as he was able to concentrate all of the troops available, for he could hope for no aid save from Kirby Smith; while Buell, if permitted to reach Louisville, might be reinforced to an indefinite extent.

Now, was General Bragg sufficiently in control of the military situation, after his success at Munfordsville, to have forced Buell to battle with the chances of victory decidedly in his own favour? I think it can be shown that he was.

General Bragg states in his report of this campaign, dated May 20, 1863, that he was able at no time "to put more than forty thousand men of all arms, and in all places, in battle." He certainly did not mean that there was in his own army that number; but if he meant to say that the troops under his immediate command aggregated, with those under Kirby Smith, only that number, there is every reason to believe that he greatly understated the total. In the two corps, of two divisions each, of the Army of Mississippi, which marched with General Bragg from Chattanooga, there were, according to the field returns of August 27th, 1862, an effective strength of 23,938 infantry, and a total effective of 27,320 men. The Federal writers who have discussed this campaign estimate his force at a much greater figure than this. None of the Confederate writers from whom I have seen any estimate of it computes it at less.

Buell had stationed at different points in middle Tennessee and Alabama, in the early part of August, perhaps thirty thousand men. General Gilbert estimates his total number at the date of concentration at Murfreesboro at thirty thousand. He left garrisons at Nashville and in the immediate vicinity of not less than eight thousand. He received no reinforcements from any quarter until he reached Louisville on September 25th, and could have gotten none. We are justified, therefore, in supposing that on September 17th, Bragg, at Munfordsville, with twenty-seven thousand men, was confronting Buell who was advancing with not more than thirty thousand, most probably a less number.

We are better informed in regard to the strength of General Smith's army — who, it must be remembered, had been reinforced by a division of the Army of Mississippi, McCown's. In his letter to General Bragg, of July 24, 1863, Smith states that the effective strength of Stevenson's division was nine thousand men; that of Heth, six thousand; that of McCown, three thousand. He subsequently stated that Marshall, who reported to him in Kentucky, had three thousand men. Marshall himself in his report to the Hon. George W. Randolph, dated August 19, 1862, just as he was starting to join General Smith, states that with one small battalion which was about to join him, he would have five thousand men.

General Smith as I have said, reached Lexington, September 2d. Within two or three days after, all of the troops at his disposal, with the exception of those under Stevenson and Marshall, were also there. General Bragg reached Glasgow September 12th. He had received information of General Smith's victory at Richmond and must have been thoroughly apprised of the situation. He knew that central and eastern Kentucky were denuded of Federal troops, except those at Cumberland Gap, under George W. Morgan, who would be forced to retreat and of whom Stevenson could take care. A swift message sent to General Smith on September 12th could have brought him with at least ten thousand men, to effect a junction with General Bragg's column at Munfordsville, or in that vicinity, before Buell could have forced a collision. Bragg, holding the line of the Green River, could have delayed Buell's crossing or his further progress until these troops came. Then he would have been able to deliver battle with nearly forty thousand men against not more than thirty thousand. The troops of the Army of Ohio were splendid soldiers, but they would have been confronted by men as seasoned and well disciplined as themselves. Bragg would have been not only numerically superior, but would have borne down on his adversary with the veterans of Shiloh and the combats around Corinth, flushed with recent successes at Richmond and Munfordsville, and inspired with a hope of success as ardent and more rational than they had ever felt before.

The distance General Smith would have been required to march in order to join Bragg in time for this battle would not have been more than one hundred and thirty miles. The roads were excellent; no obstruction would have been offered him, and he could easily have traversed it in six or seven days. It would not have been necessary for Bragg to go after Buell to compel battle. It was vitally necessary for Buell to get to Louisville. He would, at any hazard, have essayed to do so, and Bragg could have determined the time and place of their encounter.

Several explanations of General Bragg's failure to seek battle at this date and under the conditions described have been furnished by his apologists, but none of them seems adequate.

No one has succeeded in showing that he could not have received timely reinforcement from General Smith, and in such force as to assure him a decided numerical superiority. It is true that Smith, immediately upon his arrival at Lexington, had despatched Heth's division to threaten Cincinnati; but it was soon recalled, and, indeed, need not have been sent. All that it was necessary for it to do, and all that it attempted, could have been just as well accomplished without the employment of so large a force and one which could have rendered far more valuable service if sent to Bragg.

I was ordered to relieve Heth and observe the enemy in that quarter, and did so with six hundred of Morgan's cavalry. I was engaged in this work for ten or twelve days, frequently coming in collision with the Federal troops which moved out from Cincinnati, and found that the force under my command was quite sufficient to do all that was required.

It would have been a strategic blunder, at that time, to have made the capture of Cincinnati one of the principal objects of the campaign, or to have involved any considerable number of troops in operation north of the Ohio. It was of some importance so to threaten that city as to induce, for its defence, a diversion of a certain number of the troops which were being collected to reinforce Buell. But that could have been effected, as I have said, without employing a force anything like so strong as that under Heth, or, indeed, any of the Confederate infantry. Cincinnati so thoroughly shared the general consternation prevailing along the northern bank of the Ohio that her people could have been kept in a proper state of apprehension by a squad of cavalry.

Nor was Cincinnati in any sense a strategic point, or one whose acquisition then would have been of any value. On the contrary, its capture and occupation would have been a misdirected effort and a waste of opportunity. So long as Buell's army was unbeaten and intact, no Confederate gain would have been secure or permanent; and such separation of the Confederate forces then in Kentucky would not only have seriously endangered their communications, but have almost certainly resulted in their being defeated in detail.

But the capture of Cincinnati was of no great moment at any time. When this campaign was in progress, and until several years after the termination of the struggle, only one railroad ran southward from that city, and it extended no farther than Lexington, Kentucky. Consequently, all troops and supplies which were sent by rail from Cincinnati to the South, were necessarily forwarded via Lexington and Louisville, adding nearly two hundred miles to the entire distance of transportation. Cincinnati was also one hundred and fifty miles farther than Louisville from all points on the Mississippi, Cumberland, and Tennessee Rivers that could be reached by water transportation. It was not, therefore, a point of any great importance in the conduct of military operations at any time during the war. Louisville, on the other hand, was, during the entire war, a most important and indispensable base, whence supplies and reinforcement could be readily and speedily transmitted to the Federal armies operating in Tennessee, Alabama, and North Mississippi. The Louisville & Nashville railroad, of which it was the northern terminus, connected at Nashville with railroads extending to Memphis, into Alabama, and to Chattanooga. The loss of Louisville, therefore, would have been a far more serious blow to the Federal arms than the capture of Cincinnati, and its possession an infinitely more valuable gain to the Confederates.

But without considering these general features, and keeping in view only the then existing situation, the stratgeic importance of Louisville for the purposes of that campaign is apparent, when it is remembered that Buell knew — and his opponent must also have known — that the only hope of obtaining the reinforcements and supplies, without which the Federal army in Kentucky would, in a short time, be reduced to dire extremities, was in reaching that place with the least possible delay.

Another reason offered in support of the contention that it was not prudent to withdraw troops from Smith at this critical juncture was the alleged necessity of impeding the retreat of the force under the Federal general, George W. Morgan, when it had evacuated Cumberland Gap, and of protecting central Kentucky against a possible demonstration upon the part of that officer. It was sheer folly to suppose that George W. Morgan would have attempted such a movement. With a hostile command, as strong as his own, close on his rear, and other enemies, not so numerous, but actively harassing him, immediately in his front and ready to assail his flank should he deviate from his direct route to the Ohio, it was not probable that he would have turned aside to attempt questionable strategic experiments. There was never reason to suppose that he would do anything else than he did do; that is, march straight to some point where he might certainly find safety.

General Smith, holding Heth and McCown in readiness to be sent to Bragg, should he demand them, made every arrangement to obstruct the retreat of George W. Morgan; and had his instructions been followed with alacrity, and prompt coöperation been obtained between those charged with their execution, the surrender of that officer might have been compelled. Col. John H. Morgan, whose command had been increased by recent additions to nearly sixteen hundred men, was instructed to take a position in George W. Morgan's front, and make every effort to delay his march until Marshall, coming from eastern Kentucky, and Stevenson, following the enemy from Cumberland Gap, could strike him, respectively, in the flank and rear. As I have already stated, six hundred of John H. Morgan's cavalry were with me in the vicinity of Covington, so that Colonel Morgan, himself, had for the duty assigned him something more than nine hundred men.

George Morgan's first intention seems to have been to march from Manchester, via Booneville, to Mt. Sterling, and reach the Ohio River at Maysville; but on September 21st, he diverged to the right — perhaps, anticipating an effort to intercept his march — a movement which would bring him to the river farther to the east and higher up the stream. It indicated anything, however, rather than an intention to enter central Kentucky.

This deflection in the route of the Federal column made John H. Morgan's task more difficult, and only by continuous and very rapid marching for two or three days and nights in succession, was he enabled to get in its front on the 23d. Between that date and the 26th he succeeded, by incessant attacks upon the head and flanks of the column, in greatly retarding its march; and after that date a partial obstruction of the roads with felled timber, in addition to these attacks, so impeded the Federal advance, that the column progressed only thirty miles in six days. Neither Marshall nor Stevenson, however, came within striking distance, and on October 1st, Colonel Morgan received orders to rejoin General Smith.

General Bragg offers as the most cogent reason for withdrawing from Buell's front and permitting him to march unopposed to Louisville, the fact that his (Bragg's) army was lacking subsistence. He says: "Reduced at the end of fourteen days to three days' rations, and in a hostile country, utterly destitute of supplies, a serious engagement brought on anywhere in that direction could not fail (whatever its results) to materially cripple me. The loss of a battle would be eminently disastrous. I was well aware also that he (Buell) had a practicable route by way of Morgantown or Brownsville to the Ohio River and thence to Louisville. We were therefore compelled to give up the object (i. e., battle with Buell) before he reached Louisville, and send for some subsistence. Orders were sent for a supply train from our depot at Georgetown to meet us at Bardstown, and the march was commenced for the latter place."

The question of subsistence is, undoubtedly, very nearly the most important one that the commander of an army is required to consider. Nothing is more true than the maxim that "An army moves upon its belly." Without food it cannot fight. Nor would it be altogether fair criticism, perhaps, to say that General Bragg must have known that he would encounter this very difficulty when he decided to make his rapid dash into Kentucky. But the excuses he offers for his declination of battle in the language just quoted are contradicted by well known and incontrovertible facts. It is not altogether plain what he meant by the assertion that he was "in a hostile country." It is true that he was not in Confederate territory but in a state which had been entirely under the Federal control and authority; but it was not true that the population of that region was inimical to the Southern cause or indisposed to render assistance to his army. On the contrary, not only was Kentucky, generally, Southern in sympathy and sentiment, but a majority of the people living in that part of the state where he then was, and whence his immediate supplies were to be expected, were thoroughly imbued with the same feeling, and desirous of evincing it.

The statement that this country was "utterly destitute of

supplies" is even more inaccurate. The country immediately about where his army was then established — and it was to this region, it is to be presumed, General Bragg referred when using this language — is not so fertile, it is true, as that nearer Louisville nor as many parts of central Kentucky, but it is by no means sterile and unproductive, had at no time previously been occupied by, or required to sustain, large bodies of troops, and with proper effort could have been made to furnish all that was necessary to subsist an army for a few days at least. Supplies could have been obtained there in greater abundance than in much of the territory farther south in which Bragg's army had been quartered, or which it had traversed during the spring and summer.

But General Bragg had easy and unmolested access to a very wide territory from which, with a well organized commissariat, he could in a brief period have collected provisions which would have subsisted his army for months. All of the territory between Munfordville and Louisville, and that farther to the east, including the rich counties of the Bluegrass were in undisputed Confederate possession and control.

Bragg need not have held the crossings of the Green River any longer than the time required to enable the troops which might have been sent to reinforce him to get within supporting distance. We can agree with his apologists that it would have been a hazardous venture on his part to cross the river and assail Buell; but no one has ever contended that he should have done this. Nor will any well informed critic accept General Buell's statement that he could "have avoided the enemy (Bragg) by passing on either side of him." Bragg, directly between Buell and Louisville, and holding the interior lines, could have forced Buell to battle, had he so chosen, on any route by which the latter might have attempted to reach that city.

It would have been Bragg's wiser policy to withdraw from the river, permitting Buell to cross without hindrance, but always remaining between him and Louisville, and never relinquishing his chance to compel the fight so soon as he was prepared for it. With every mile he marched northward he would have gotten within closer communication with General Smith, and into territory where supplies could have been more readily procurred. His army might have suffered some inconvenience, but no real hardship, in the matter of rations. Certainly little, in comparison with the privations to which all of the Confederate armies were later subjected, without seriously impairing their efficiency.

General Bragg could have marched directly to Louisville, encountering no opposition on the way. The raw levies which were being hastily collected could have offered no effective resistance. Had Buell closely pursued him, it would have only been to invite the battle which Bragg should have desired.

In all the discussion this campaign has elicited, I have never heard any sufficient, or even plausible, reason presented why Bragg should not have kept constantly in Buell's front, barring his path to Louisville, and ready to fight him so soon as the troops which might be sent by General Smith should arrive. The situation was fully under his control, and offered the strongest assurance of victory; and while defeat might have crippled him, it would not necessarily or even probably have been disastrous. It can scarcely be doubted, however, that the defeat of Buell, under the conditions, would have meant the certain and utter destruction of his army.

When General Bragg marched to Bardstown and allowed Buell, without battle, to march to Louisville, he surrendered the initiative and lost an opporunity which could not be recovered. He failed to improve an advantage — temporary, but which could have been made decisive — over an opponent, then weaker, but who, if not then beaten, would soon be stronger than himself.

The grasp of the situation passed to Buell, who thenceforth shaped the course of the campaign.

It seems that Buell was also short of rations, not having been able to obtain what he required at Bowling Green; and so long as Bragg confronted and checked him he experienced yet greater difficulty in procuring them. That he perfectly appreciated the situation is shown by his statement before the commission which subsequently investigated his conduct in this campaign. Speaking of the military status at this date, and after Bragg had moved in the direction of Bardstown, he said: "Many considerations rendered it proper to direct my march on Louisville, instead of following his route. The want of supplies made it necessary, many of the troops being out before they reached the mouth of Salt River. This reason would have been insuperable, if, as was not improbable, the enemy should concentrate his force and throw himself rapidly between me and Louisville. The junction of Bragg and Kirby Smith was not only possible, but probable. It would have made their combined force greatly superior to me in strength, and such a disposition would have placed him between two inferior forces, which, from their position, could not have acted in concert against him, and which, therefore, were liable to be beaten in detail.

"One of these forces, then occupying Louisville, was composed of perfectly raw, undisciplined, and in a measure unarmed, troops, with but very little artillery and very few officers of rank or experience. It could not have withstood the veteran rebel army two hours, and the consequence of its defeat and the capture of Louisville would have been disastrous in the extreme. That force, however — judiciously mixed, could be made to render good service, as the result proved."

Bragg marched from Munfordsville on September 20th and reached Bardstown on the 23d. Buell immediately began his march to Louisville, and all of his army had gotten there by the 29th.

General Buell reached Louisville in person on the 25th, and employed the next four days with unusual diligence and energy in completing the equipment and armament of the new troops, refurnishing his veterans with all that they needed, and reorganizing his entire army in such wise that the recruits could be made most effective. This work was so rapidly and successfully done that he was ready, by the last of the month, to march from Louisville and assume the offensive.

On the 29th, however, an order came from Washington, which might, if it had been adhered to, have delayed and perhaps somewhat impaired the efficiency of the Federal operations. It was an order removing General Buell from command and appointing Gen. George H. Thomas in his stead. Thomas was one of the best officers then in the service of the United States, but it is not easy to believe that he would have proven as competent, under the existing circumstances, as Buell. He did not know either the army he was about to command or his adversary so well, nor was he as conversant with the situation. He generously, and doubtless very wisely, telegraphed a remonstrance against this action, representing that Buell had completed his preparations for an aggressive movement and was about to commence it, and urging that no change in the command be made. So soon as this protest was received Halleck suspended the order.

In the reorganization of the army, it was divided into three corps, the first commanded by Major-general McCook, the second by Major-general Crittenden, and the third by Brigadier-general Gilbert. Each corps was composed of three divisions; but one division — Dumont's — seems to have been, for a short time unattached. General Thomas was assigned to the position of second in command. General Buell reported in his ranks, present for duty, fifty-eight thousand men, of which, however, at least one half were raw and untried troops. He moved from Louisville on October 1st., the greater part of the first corps marching toward Taylorsville, but the divisions of Sill and Dumont took the Shelbyville pike in the direction of Frankfort. This was doubtless intended to produce the impression that Buell's objective was Lexington and the adjacent region, and the demonstration deceived General Bragg. The second and third corps marched directly toward Bardstown. Moving on excellent roads, the troops pressed forward rapidly and had made considerable progress before Bragg received intelligence of their advance.

So far from seeking or wishing battle in the vicinity of Lexington, Buell's object was to deliver it in a part of central Kentucky farther to the south, and was manœuvring to prevent Bragg, should he now wish to do so, from falling back on Nashville, and also to menace Bragg's line of retreat through south-eastern Kentucky and the gaps of the mountains.

General Bragg, as has been stated, withdrew to Bardstown on September 23d. He devoted several days thereafter, says one of his staff officers, "to a tour of inspection through Danville via Springfield and Perryville to Lexington." It is not easy to understand what it was that just then particularly demanded "inspection"; nor why, when he knew that a formidable foe, whom he had already declined and apparently feared to encounter, would soon turn upon him in strength nearly doubled, he might not have employed the time allowed him to better advantage. The only satisfactory explanation, perhaps, which can be given is that of the cynical Kentuckian, who declared that "Bragg inspected his army in order to find out how much it had that could be thrown away in a rapid retreat."

In the meantime, General Polk, who had been left in command of the Army of the Mississippi had established a depot at "Camp Dick Robinson," rechristened by the Confederates "Camp Breckinridge," a point nearly equidistant from Lexington and Danville, and betweeen the two. It was the intention that all the supplies which had been collected at Lexington should be transferred to this point, and the failure to do so may have had some effect on the result of the campaign. It has been asserted that General Bragg desired to give battle in this immediate vicinity.

On the 4th of October the Hon. Richard Hawes was inaugurated at Frankfort as provisional governor of Kentucky, succeeding in that station the heroic George W. Johnson, who had been killed at Shiloh, fighting in the ranks of one of the Kentucky regiments. The fact that General Bragg and General Smith were present and prominently assisted on this occasion, was construed as an indication that the Confederates would make every effort to hold the state. The inaugural ceremonies were very nearly interrupted by rumours of the approach of some of the Federal troops, who were moving in the direction of Frankfort; but no actual interference occurred, although the departure of some of the witnesses was greatly accelerated. The bulk of General Smith's forces was close at hand, and any real demonstration could have been promptly and successfully opposed.

General Bragg's strategic line at this date may be roughly described as extending from Bardstown on his right to Mt. Sterling on his left flank. It was an excellent one, as troops could move over good roads, by interior lines, to any point that might be threatened, and a concentration of both armies, his own and that of General Smith, could be promptly effected.

Now in what strength may we justly suppose that General

Bragg could have been able to concentrate, on or after October 4th? The total effective of his own army when he marched into Kentucky, was, as has been stated, 27,320 men. Stevenson and Humphrey Marshall had both joined Kirby Smith before this date. According to General Smith's estimate, heretofore quoted, his army — if Marshall had 3,000 men, and that command was probably more than 3,000 — numbered 21,000 effectives. Of this number nearly, if not quite, 17,000 were infantry; which, added to the 23,938 infantry Bragg reported in August, foots up for the combined forces over 40,000 in round numbers, of that army. From this estimate must be deducted, of course, the losses in killed and wounded at Richmond and Munfordsville, and by the ordinary wear and tear of a campaign. But it may be confidently asserted that such loss was more than compensated by recruits obtained in Kentucky. While no regiment or distinct Kentucky organization of infantry was formed during the Confederate occupation of the state, it has been computed, and I think correctly, that between two thousand and three thousand Kentuckians enlisted in infantry regiments from other states which served in this campaign. Not only did these men more than make up the loss occasioned by casualties of any nature, but they immediately became good soldiers; for it is a well recognized fact that, although time and diligent training are required to convert a considerable number of recruits collected in the same organization into efficient troops, they may, when distributed singly or in small groups among veterans, become in a few days as steady and effective as the veterans themselves. I speak, of course, of the average American volunteers; an intelligent man and one accustomed to the use of arms.

But in addition to the troops already mentioned there were at General Bragg's disposal nearly five thousand cavalry, not included in the enumeration just made, but which had been recently recruited, or had been operating independently and not regularly attached to either Bragg's or Smith's army. That is to say, Morgan's command fifteen hundred strong and five of six regiments of cavalry besides, which had been recently raised and were in the field. They were undisciplined, but composed of excellent material and imbued with a thoroughly martial spirit; were all well mounted and armed, and were skilful riders and good marksmen. A large proportion of their officers had seen service. These regiments were capable of performing and did perform valuable service, and fought well from the first hour of their organization. Morgan's command — like Wheeler's, Wharton's and Scott's, which had accompanied Generals Bragg and Smith upon the expedition — had been accustomed to fight infantry as well as cavalry.

We have good warrant, therefore, to estimate the entire number of troops subject to General Bragg's order — present for duty and effective — at little, if any, less than fifty thousand. We have General Buell's own statement that his army was fifty-eight thousand strong when he marched out from Louisville on October 1st. One half of this number, however, were perfectly raw troops. Nor were these recruits distributed in small squads among veteran regiments, as was the case with all those who then enlisted in the Confederate infantry, but they were organized and gathered together in separate regiments. The losses among these green soldiers, from sickness and straggling, during the first ten or twelve days of October, were heavy; far greater than were those of the Confederates from similar causes. Moreover, because of the superior numbers and audacity of the Confederate cavalry, the Federal army suffered a considerable loss in prisoners, picked up on the march. But even had there been no such depletion of Buell's numbers, between October 1st and October 15th, the great preponderance of veteranship in Bragg's ranks, should, it would seem, have made him stronger on the fighting line.

I have already said that General Bragg was deceived by the demonstration of Sill and Dumont in the direction of Frankfort, and induced to believe that Buell was moving in force either upon Lexington or to get between Smith and Polk, who was in command of the troops which were massed in the vicinity of Bardstown. It was undoubtedly a difficult matter to obtain prompt and accurate information of the exact routes taken by the several corps of Buell's army, all of which marched with celerity; and General Bragg should not be criticized perhaps, because he did not at once and definitely penetrate Buell's precise intention. But he certainly indicated a lack of strategic instinct himself, or greatly underrated Buell, when he supposed that the latter was about to attempt a manœuvre which would have given his adversary every advantage. Had Buell moved, as Bragg believed he was about to do, he would have been forced to traverse an exceedingly rugged country, unfavourable to the passage of troops and artillery, and to debouch thence at points where the Confederate forces could have been easily and rapidly concentrated to give him battle on ground of their own selection. Their communications and line of retreat would also have been absolutely secure.

On September 28th, General Bragg had instructed General Polk, in the event of an advance of the enemy, to retire from Bardstown in the direction of Danville, in order to protect Camp Breckinridge and the stores that would be collected there.

Under the erroneous impression, however, that Buell was marching directly eastward and toward Frankfort and Lexington, Bragg sent an order to Polk, dated 1 p. m., October 2d, directing him to march via Bloomfield toward Frankfort and endeavour to strike the enemy in flank and rear, while General Smith would attack him in front. Polk, however, was better advised of Buell's movements than was his chief, or guessed them more correctly. He wrote Bragg at 3 p. m., October 3d, acknowledging the receipt of the order, but gave his reasons for not obeying it, stating that under the conditions "compliance with it" would be "not only eminently inexpedient, but impracticable."

"I have called," he said, "a council of wing and division commanders, to whom I have submitted the matter, and find that they unanimously endorse my views.

"I shall, therefore, pursue a different course, assured that when the facts are submitted to you, you will justify my decision. I move on the route indicated by you toward Camp Breckinridge. The head of my column moves this afternoon."

When this despatch was written Crittenden's corps of Buell's army was not more than ten or twelve miles from Bardstown, and the greater part of Gilbert's corps was close to Crittenden. McCook's corps was in easy supporting distance, with two divisions at Taylorsville. The bulk of the Federal army could have been concentrated in front of Bardstown by the afternoon of the next day, the 4th; and had Polk moved toward Frankfort by the route indicated in General Bragg's order, he would have encountered all of these troops, without hope of assistance from General Smith.

On the afternoon of the 3d, General Polk fell back, as he had written Bragg he would do, in the direction indicated in his first instructions of September 28th, and took position first at Perryville, ten miles from Danville and about the same distance from Harrodsburg. Leaving Hardee there, with the left wing (second corps) of the Army of the Mississippi, he proceeded with his own corps to Harrodsburg.

In the meantime Sill, demonstrating in the direction of Lawrenceburg, continued to "amuse" and mystify General Bragg. So persistently did the latter cling to his delusion regarding Buell's real purpose, and insist upon believing that the Federal masses were projected against Lexington, that as late as the 7th he issued orders looking to concentration and battle at Versailles. His eyes were partially opened to the true situation by information received from Hardee that the enemy was in his immediate front at Perryville. Bragg had ordered both divisions of Polk's corps — Cheatham's and Withers's — to Versailles; but on receipt of this report he directed Polk to proceed with Cheatham's division to Hardee's support. That he was not yet entirely undeceived, however, is shown by his confident instructions given Polk to "give the enemy battle immediately, rout him, and then move to our support at Versailles."

Buell pressed on during the 5th and 6th, with the two corps of Crittenden and Gilbert, hard upon Polk's track as the latter fell back from Bardstown. On the night of the 6th both of these corps passed through Springfield and encamped on the road leading to Perryville; while two divisions of McCook's corps were on the road from Bloomfield to Harrodsburg, the other, Sill's, still being with Dumont's between Shelbyville and Frankfort.

Constant and heavy skirmishing occurred throughout both of these days, as also on the 4th, between the heads of the Federal columns and the Confederate cavalry, but the infantry were not yet close enough for battle. On the morning of the 7th Gilbert's corps continued its march on the direct road to Perryville, and Crittenden's was sent to the right, to move on the

Danville and Lebanon Road. McCook was ordered to proceed no farther in the direction of Harrodsburg, but to march straight toward Perryville. On that evening Gilbert's corps was in the immediate vicinity of Perryville, and McCook's not far off on the left. The sharp fighting, which began in the latter part of the afternoon and was continued until late into the night, for the scanty water supply the ground about the little village afforded, was a sure precursor of the next day's conflict.

One entire corps of the Federal army was on the ground where the battle was to be fought. One other and part of a third were near by.

General Polk, in pursuance of General Bragg's order to that effect, issued on the afternoon of that day, had sent Cheatham's division to Perryville to reinforce Hardee. It arrived, General Polk himself at its head, shortly before midnight, and was immediately placed in line.

The Federal army was approaching Perryville from the west. The Springfield Pike by which Gilbert's corps, already on the ground, had come, runs through the centre of the battle field, nearly due east and west. Farther to the south, the Danville and Lebanon Pike runs, skirting the battle field, in a southeasterly direction, until within about three quarters of a mile of Perryville, and then turning northward, enters the little town from the south. To the north of the Springfield Pike the Macksville Pike crosses the northern end of the battle field and enters the town from a north-westerly direction. McCook came upon this latter road and arrived upon the ground, where the Federal line of battle was established, between ten and eleven o'clock of the day of the battle. Crittenden's corps was advancing on the Danville and Lebanon Pike and was close enough to reach the field during the day. At the points where the Federal line of battle was formed the Springfield Pike is distant from the Danville and Lebanon Pike about two miles; from the Macksville Pike a little less than that distance.

Chaplin's Fork of Salt River, running through Perryville, flows here nearly due north and south until, about two miles from and north of the town, it makes a sharp bend to the west. To the west of Chaplin's Fork, a smaller stream, Doctor's Creek, flows through the battle field from the southwest and empties into the former about a mile from where it begins its western curve. The distance between the two streams varies from something less than a mile to perhaps two miles and a quarter, the shorter distance including that part of the field extending from their junction to the point where the Macksville Pike crosses Doctor's Creek. The ground between these water courses and along them is broken and rugged, a topographical feature which was of some advantage to the Confederates as affording them partial shelter from the fire of the superior hostile artillery. It was among the hills on both sides of the smaller stream that the struggle was most fiercely contested.

As has been stated, General Bragg, believing that only a fraction of the Federal army was advancing on Perryville, had ordered General Polk to attack at daylight and rout it. General Buell, on the other hand, thinking that the combined Confederate forces were in front of him, wished to delay battle until Crittenden corps had arrived and his army should be practically concentrated. Gilbert's corps was moved up and took position, early on the morning of the 8th, about three miles from Perryville, its left resting near the Springfield Pike and its right extending a little beyond and to the south of the Danville and Lebanon Pike. Col. Daniel McCook's brigade of Sheridan's division had been sent to Doctor's Creek at 3 a. m. to hold certain pools in the bed of the creek, the only water available. He encountered a strong Confederate outpost there, and a sharp fight ensued and was kept up until nearly seven o'clock and desultory skirmishing and cannonading continued during the greater part of the forenoon. Shortly after ten o'clock, the head of McCook's column reached the field, and that corps was formed upon the left of Gilbert's, with, however, an interval of some distance between them. McCook's line extended to the right a short distance beyond and to the south of the Macksville Pike, and stretched on the left in the direction of and nearly to the point of the junction of Proctor's Creek and Chaplin's Fork.

The number of Federal troops on the field when the real fighting began, and which were in line of battle, cannot be estimated at less than thirty-two or thirty-three thousand. It was probably greater than that. Gilbert's corps reported more than twenty thousand present for duty, and the two divisions of

Cook's corps on the field — Rousseau's and Jackson's — Sill's being still detached, must have mustered at least ten thousand, perhaps twelve thousand men. Moreover, Crittenden's corps arrived within supporting distance during the battle, although no part of it was engaged.

The total effective strength of the three Confederate infantry divisions engaged, *viz.*, Buckner's and Anderson's divisions of Hardee's corps, and Cheatham's division of Polk's corps was scarcely fifteen thousand; and the entire force under General Bragg's command on that day — infantry, cavalry, and artillery — was less than seventeen thousand men.

On the morning of the 8th — that of the battle — General Bragg, upon whom a better perception of the situation had finally forced itself, ceased to feel uneasiness about the enemy in front of General Smith, and became exceedingly and justly apprehensive regarding that part of his army which was at Perryville. He received no intimation that his order given General Polk on the previous evening, to attack the enemy "immediately" would not be obeyed; but ascertaining that the attack had not been delivered, he, instead of joining General Smith at Versailles, went to Perryville, arriving there at ten o'clock. General Polk explained his failure to obey the order by stating his belief that the entire Federal army, or much the greater part of it, was close at hand, and that the safety of the Confederate troops on the ground would be compromised if the offensive was assumed. General Bragg, however, thought differently, and, with a nerve and decision in strong contrast with his previous and subsequent vacillation, determined to deliver battle.

After a brief reconnoissance and obtaining as accurate information as was possible of the dispositions which had been made by the enemy, General Bragg formed for attack. He moved Cheatham's division from the left, where it had been stationed on the night before, to the right of his line, intending that it should open the battle. It was formed in column of brigades *en échelon*, and the expectation that, striking the Federal left in flank, it would thrust back and shatter all that part of the hostile array was fully verified. Buckner, on Cheatham's left, was expected to support Cheatham and strike a home blow at the

Federal centre. These preparations were not completed until after twelve o'clock. The Confederate cavalry was posted on the flanks. Wheeler on the left watching the Lebanon Pike, Wharton on the right. There was some previous fighting between Sheridan's division and a small Confederate detachment on the Confederate left, but the battle did not really open until two o'clock, when Cheatham, pressing forward, dashed across Doctor's Creek, and, falling first on McCook's extreme left, soon engaged all that part of his line. This spirited onslaught was ably seconded by a gallant charge made by Wharton. The attack seems to have been unexpected by the Federals, and, although bravely, was at no point successfully met. Indeed, Cheatham's division forced back everything it encountered, and its brigades coming successively into action, like waves lashing a beach, swept away after a fierce contest all opposition. Jackson's division of McCook's corps, exposed to the first fury of this onset, was broken to pieces. General Jackson and two of his brigadiers, Terrill and Webster, were killed.

Promptly following Cheatham's advance, Buckner made straight for the Federal centre, and struck it with an impact the more effective because it was already somewhat shaken by the vigorous blows delivered on its left. Although encountering from Rosseau's division a more stubborn resistance than Cheatham had received, his attack was finally quite as successful. The heaviest loss on both sides was at this point. As an example, that suffered by the Fifteenth Kentucky (Federal) infantry, one of the finest regiments in Buell's army, may be cited. Its colonel, Curran Pope, was wounded, Lieutenant-colonel Jouette and Major Campbell were killed, and its other loss, rank and file, was correspondent.

The Federal soldiers fought with unflinching resolution. Rosseau's division sustained Buckner's attack with fortitude for more than four hours, and the rest of McCook's line rallied repeatedly notwithstanding Cheatham's rapid and overwhelming rushes.

The battle was actually fought on that part of the field which lies north of the Springfield Pike. On this ground — the Federal left and centre — the greater number of the Confederate troops were massed, a comparatively small force sufficing to occupy the attention of Gilbert's corps, which did little serious fighting, although it gave some assistance to McCook, who certainly needed it sorely.

The combat between the lines of infantry continued without intermission from two until nearly seven o'clock, but constant artillery firing was maintained on both sides for an hour longer. Although not routed, the Federals were driven back in disorder along the entire line where the real fighting occurred, and at the close of the day, the Confederates were in possession of all that part of the field.

The severity of this conflict is attested by the loss in killed and wounded on both sides, which, when its comparatively brief duration and the numbers actually engaged are considered, was quite heavy. The Confederate loss, not including those reported missing, was three thousand one hundred and forty-five. The Federal loss was three thousand six hundred and ninety-six. Few prisoners were taken by either side.

It is a remarkable circumstance, but perfectly well attested, that General Buell was not aware, until half-past four of the afternoon, that a battle was in progress. For two hours and a half a furious combat had been waged, not much more than two miles from his headquarters, and yet he was ignorant of the fact. Even if as has been stated, the rugged conformation of the ground prevented his hearing the sounds of the strife, it is hard to understand why intelligence was not sent him from the fighting line, and still more so why he had not made the necessary provision to learn all that was going on.

When we consider what was accomplished at Perryville with little more than one third of the troops which General Bragg might just as easily have concentrated there, it is impossible to escape the conviction that, had he summoned and employed the entire force at his disposal, his victory would have been complete and decisive. Forty-five thousand Confederate soldiers upon that field, of the same mettle as those which won a partial but indubitable success over twice their number, and directed with the same vigour and tactical sagacity, would have borne down Buell's army in crushing, irretrievable defeat.

At midnight General Bragg withdrew from the battle field and from Perryville, unmolested by the enemy, marched to

Harrodsburg, reaching that place at noon the next day, October 9th. On the same day General Smith arrived at Harrodsburg with all the troops which had been assembled in the vicinity of Versailles and Lawrenceburg, and all of the Confederate forces in Kentucky were, for the first time, concentrated.

The belief was prevalent among the Confederate officers best informed about the situation, and it was universally hoped and expected by those in the ranks, that a decisive battle would be fought at Harrodsburg. Every thing in the attitude and management of the army — all the signs by which the soldier, who is not admitted to the councils of his commander, can yet sometimes understand his intentions — indicated that battle was imminent, and that General Bragg wished to fight.

I very distinctly remember a conversation I had with two or three officers of General Smith's staff on the night before the retreat and the consequent evacuation of Kentucky was begun, and, perhaps, just about the time it was determined upon. They spoke of the dispositions which had been made, unmistakably indicating that General Bragg was preparing to encounter the enemy with his entire force, and expressed strong confidence of a successful result. Aware, of course, that they had received this impression from General Smith and assuming that he knew General Bragg's plans, I entertained no doubt that within forty-eight hours, at the farthest, the final issue would be joined and the game decided.

There is every reason to believe that, when General Bragg concentrated at Harrodsburg, it was with the purpose of accepting the battle which he knew Buell would offer. He was as thoroughly ready as he could hope to be. His army was in better condition, in all respects, than at any time previously, and its morale was perfect; every man in his ranks was convinced that we were on the eve of victory.

If General Bragg had meant to fight at Versailles, in the event that the enemy had approached that point in force — and his friends assert that such was his intention — he should have been even more willing to fight at Harrodsburg.

The full strength of both armies was present or immediately at hand; but Bragg was relatively stronger at Harrodsburg than he would have been at Versailles. I have estimated, and I think correctly, that Buell, when he marched out of Louisville, outnumbered Bragg about eight thousand. The Federal army had suffered a heavier loss in killed and wounded at Perryville than had the Confederate, and its depletion on the march, by sickness and straggling — casualties of all kinds — had been much greater. The fighting at Perryville should have in nowise diminished, but might, indeed, have justly enhanced General Bragg's confidence in the prowess of his troops; and it would seem that his experience with Buell in that combat might have warranted the opinion that the Federal commander was not so alert and formidable as a tactician and battle leader as he had proven himself to be as a strategist. The two armies were more nearly matched in numbers at Harrodsburg than they would have been at any time previously, after Buell received his reinforcements; and the superiority of the Confederate veterans in the field over an army so largely composed of quite raw troops, had been clearly demonstrated. When, therefore, General Bragg, on October 10th, aligned his entire command on ground judiciously selected and adapted either to attack or defence — when every preparation for battle was completed, and he seemed to be awaiting with grim determination the arrival of his adversary — the feeling which prevaded the Confederate battalions that he would fight and ought to fight was certainly justified.

Yet, with a vacillation almost inconceivable and certainly unexampled among his compeers, he changed his mind again that evening — as certain of his despatches show — and resolved to fall back upon Bryantsville, probably to retreat to Knoxville. The sombre and unfriendly destiny which, from the beginning of the struggle had frowned upon Confederate effort, seeming to make success impossible or render victory fruitless, again intervened. It had stricken with death the valiant chieftain who led us at Shiloh; it now smote our commander in Kentucky with a panic, which no other man in his ardent and undaunted ranks shared or could understand.

On the same day the greater part of Buell's army took position south of the Confederate line and practically parallel with it. The two armies were bivouacked scarcely three miles from each other, both in line of battle and stretched out in semi-elliptical crescent formation. Although the night was cloudy and dark, a drizzling rain falling, the glare of innumerable camp fires, piercing the mist like the red-hot glow of a furnace, distinctly marked the positions of the contending hosts.

Late upon the afternoon of the 10th a demonstration by Buell toward Danville induced Bragg to believe that an attempt was about to be made to obstruct his line of retreat. It was nothing more than a strong reconnoissance, but it seems to have seriously alarmed the Confederate commander. Why so, however, it is hard to understand. Even had such been Buell's intention, it should have in nowise altered Bragg's purpose to give battle. Indeed, it improved his chances of success, for so great an extension of the Federal line would have correspondingly weakened its fighting force at the point and moment of actual collision; and a general who is reasonably assured of victory may be pardoned for giving small consideration to an academic question of retreat. But whenever that idea entered General Bragg's intellect it was impossible for any other to obtain ingress, and when the morning dawned which should have witnessed the Confederate army bearing down in resistless onset, it was, instead, retiring reluctantly and sullenly from the only field where victory might certainly have purchased ultimate Confederate success.

A council of war was held so soon as the army reached Bryantsville, and it was decided to evacuate Kentucky, and return to east Tennessee via Cumberland Gap "while the route was open and the roads were yet good." So upon the 13th, the movement began, Polk and Hardee marching through Lancaster, Crab Orchard, and Mt. Vernon, and the troops under General Smith's command proceeding by way of Big Hill to London. At the latter place the entire column was reunited and pushed on to and through Cumberland Gap to Knoxville. The cavalry of Wheeler, Morgan, and Ashby covered the retreat, which, for three or four days, was closely followed by a considerable part of Buell's army. During that time numerous skirmishes and partial engagements occurred, but, for the most part, bloodless and of small consequence. Marshall went back through eastern Kentucky and Pound Gap to western Virginia. Morgan, his services in the rear of the army being no longer needed, was permitted, on the 17th, to leave the column and make his way to Tennessee by any route he might choose. He dashed back upon

Lexington, defeating and capturing there the Federal garrison and a regiment of cavalry. Then traversing central Kentucky with a celerity unusual even for him, passing through the midst of the Federal masses which were pressing on to Nashville, burning wagon trains and picking up every straggling detachment in his path, he reached, after a week of rapid marching, Hopkinsville in western Kentucky.

On the 10th of October more than fifty thousand Confederate soldiers were upon the soil of Kentucky, eagerly expecting battle, confident and, I believe, invincible. Before the 1st of November they were all gone, and with them departed all hope, perhaps, of Southern independence. A victory won by these men at this time would have destroyed the only Federal army in the West which was then efficient or, indeed, available, and would have placed Kentucky and Tennessee firmly in the Confederate grasp. The South would have been, in large measure, cleared of invaders, and a host of recruits would have been brought into the Confederate ranks. The victories won in Virginia would have become fruitful of results, when their moral effect had been supplemented by similar successes in the west; and the people of the Northern states, however extreme may have been their reluctance, would have been compelled to consider the necessity of ending a bloody, ruinous, and apparently hopeless contest. But when Bragg refused to listen to the wish of his gallant army and consulted only his own fears, he threw away the best and last chance the Confederacy had to win.

General Bragg's army, subsequently entitled the Army of Tennessee, after a long and harassing march, reached Murfreesboro about the middle of November. The army which it had confronted in Kentucky — now commanded by Rosecrans, Buell having been removed — had, a few days previously, reached Nashville. Brief as had been their experience, the recruits received at Louisville had already become soldiers in spirit and discipline. Constantly augmented in numbers, this army was more formidable in each successive encounter; and the value of the Confederate opportunity lost at Harrodsburg was demonstrated on two great fields in Tennessee, and when Sherman, having pressed down from Dalton to Atlanta, marched from Atlanta to the sea.

It might be fortunate for General Bragg's memory if his career as a Confederate soldier should be fully told. No man has been more bitterly and in some respects, unjustly assailed. But a complete narration of his record would require that a great deal of Confederate history be recapitulated — especially that of the Army of Tennessee, with which, as I have said, no other officer was so closely identified.

But for more than aught else which he did, or with which he was connected, he will be remembered because of this campaign in Kentucky. The recollection of much really able and courageous conduct — with which he should be credited — will be overshadowed and forgotten when the weakness he then displayed is considered. Rightly or not, he will be responsible for the non-realization of the hopes which that campaign inspired.

He remained in command of the Army of Tennessee until after the disastrous affair at Missionary Ridge, November 25, 1863. The high state of efficiency in which that gallant host was maintained during that period must be accepted, in large measure, at least, as testimony to his capacity as a military administrator; but its unflinching morale in all adversity — the undaunted temper with which it sustained every reverse and disappointment — was inherent and taught by no commander. It furnished abundant proof of its readiness for combat and the effective style in which it always fought, in its first engagement after the retreat from Kentucky, the three days of stubborn and bloody conflict at Murfreesboro.

After reaching Nashville, Rosecrans had earnestly striven to prepare his army for offensive operations, but the injury previously done the Louisville & Nashville railroad greatly retarded him. Moreover, General Bragg used his cavalry with excellent effect during November and December. Morgan entered Kentucky and again, for a time, interrupted communication between Nashville and Louisville, while Forrest performed the same work in west Tennessee, shutting off all communication with Memphis. It was not until December 26, 1862, that the Federal advance began.

On that date Rosecrans moved out from Nashville, with the purpose of attacking Bragg at Murfreesboro. His march was so delayed by the energetic resistance which the Confederate cavalry under Wheeler and Wharton offered from the moment of its commencement that he did not arrive in the vicinity of Murfreesboro until the afternoon of the 30th. The Confederate army had in the meantime been concentrated, and formed for battle about a mile and a half west of the town. General Bragg's formation has been criticized, especially in that his line was established on both sides of Stone River and divided by that stream, but this objection seems to have been trivial, the river was fordable at all points; at any rate, his dispositions were such that his troops were brought promptly into action and could have readily supported one another at all points along the line.

There was some fighting on the afternoon of the 30th, although Rosecrans had not intended to give battle until the 31st. Bragg, however, whose troops had been in line for two days, chose to anticipate rather than await attack, and began the battle at daybreak on that morning, taking his adversary, whose dispositions were not entirely completed, partially by surprise.

The fighting opened in the stereotyped fashion in which Bragg was accustomed to commence action; the firing beginning upon one wing and being taken up successively by brigades extending toward the other, until the whole line was engaged. There may have been paucity of invention in this method, but it is certain that the Confederate attack, especially on this first day, was eminently successful.

Hardee on the Confederate left pushed vigorously against the enemy. The first shock of this onset fell, as at Perryville, upon McCook's corps, which was severly battered and driven for some distance. The remainder of Bragg's line came rapidly into action, and Rosecrans, although his centre held fast, was forced back upon both wings.

Notwithstanding the heavy punishment unexpectedly received, the Federal troops fought with a determination that could not have been excelled, and opposed stubborn and continuous resistance to every attack. They clung with especial tenacity to that part of the field where the cuts and embankments of the railroad furnished shelter equivalent to that of fortification. The fiercest struggle of the three days of actual combat, was on Friday, January 2d, when Breckinridge made the famous charge which will be remembered in Confederate military annals with that of Pickett at Gettysburg. The fighting in this desperate conflict lasted only one hour and twenty minutes, in which time Breckinridge's division lost seventeen hundred men out of forty-five hundred.

The battle of Murfreesboro, or Stone River, as it is generally termed by Northern writers, has been claimed as a Federal victory, because Bragg finally relinquished the ground on which it was fought. He withdrew at an early hour on the morning of the 4th. Nevertheless, it is indisputable that Rosecrans was on the defensive during the entire battle; that he was driven back upon almost every part of the field; and that there had been no fighting for more than twenty-four hours before the Confederate troops retired from the positions they had occupied at the termination of the fighting.

There can be no doubt that of the two armies the Federal suffered the more seriously. Rosecrans made no attempt at pursuit, nor did he do anything which might be construed into an effort to improve a victory. After occupying Murfreesboro, he remained inactive for nearly six months, and his advance, when he then began it, was cautious and dilatory.

General Bragg has been severly censured for retiring from the front of his enemy at Murfreesboro, but if it was a tactical mistake there is yet much to be said in excuse for it. The Federal army was at least ten thousand stronger numerically than the Confederate, and the efficiency of the latter was impaired by severe effort; not only had it been constantly and actively attacking during the battle, but its work for several days previously had been of an exceedingly exhausting nature. Some of General Bragg's best officers urged this course, and a council of war, convened on the evening of January 3d, advised it.

Bragg retreated no great distance and gave up really little territory, making his headquarters at Tullahoma, about forty miles from Murfreesboro. The greater part of his infantry was established much nearer the latter place, at Manchester and Shelbyville. His cavalry held the country in advance of these places and still farther to the west.

On May 10th, Gen. Joseph E. Johnston called two brigades from the Army of Tennessee to reinforce the forces in Mississippi, which were attempting the relief of Vicksburg, and on May

24th, Breckinridge's division was also sent to Jackson. These draughts so depleted the strength of Bragg's army that its retention of any territory in middle Tennessee became impossible. Nor was it any longer possible to replenish the decimated Confederate ranks. Voluntary enlistment was practically a thing of the past. Indeed, save when some high-spirited boy, barely old enough to shoulder a musket, offered fresh sacrifice, there was no longer material whence such recruits could be gotten. The conscription was at no time of much value in increasing the strength of the Southern armies, and at this date the area wherein it could be enforced was so restricted that it was virtually useless. So that when Rosecrans, who had been heavily reinforced, at length, on June 23d, advanced, Bragg was compelled to retire to the south of the Tennessee River, with the hope of obtaining aid from the Army of Northern Virginia, and of concentrating all forces available for further resistance in the neighbourhood of Chattanooga.

Rosecrans followed leisurely, and it was not until the 20th of September that the great battle of Chickamauga was fought. It is conceded that Bragg was the victor in this tremendous contest; that he in no wise utilized his victory is still less matter of debate. Failing to pursue and press that half of Rosecran's army which had fallen back, routed, into Chattanooga, and to capture, as he might have done, not only the fugitives but also Chattanooga, just then of supremely strategic importance, he threw away his advantage in unavailing attacks upon the unbeaten ranks of Thomas, which, posted amid the rugged hills of the Chickamauga, held him at bay.

After the battle he took position on the heights south of Chattanooga and began what has been termed a siege of that place, which was as futile as it was ill advised. Then came the disaster of Missionary Ridge, and no longer resisting the oft expressed wish of his army that he should cease to lead it, and either tardily recognizing that he was inadequate to successful leadership or that fate was against him, he voluntarily relinquished command.

In February, 1864, he was called to Richmond as military adviser of President Davis and made virtually inspector-general of all the Confederate armies, a position for which he was peculiarly well fitted. He commanded once again in the field, at the indecisive battle of Kinston, fought in North Carolina, March 8, 1865.

General Bragg was a good soldier, but in no respect a great captain. He could organize and adapt the means by which an end might be attained, but could not design or accomplish the end. He could plan to a certain extent, or partially execute a plan formulated by another, but seemed incapable of pursuing any plan to its consummation. He evinced undaunted and determined courage as a subordinate, but was subject, when in chief command and feeling entire responsibility, to sudden an apparently uncontrollable starts of timidity. As second in command to a leader like Lee or Albert Sidney Johnston, his assistance would have been invaluable; but it was a misfortune for the Confederacy, and for himself, that he was advanced from the position of lieutenant to that of leader.

CHAPTER XVI

THE third of June, the anniversary of the birth of Jefferson Davis, will be universally celebrated in the Southern states and remembered with more or less respectful observance wheresoever people of Southern blood reside. This date, and the 19th of January, the anniversary of the birth of Gen. Robert E. Lee, have been chosen by those who desire to preserve and honour the memories with which they are peculiarly connected, as the two days which all who served or sympathized with Confederate aspiration and effort should hold in especial reverence and regard as appropriate days of commemoration.

History shows nothing so distinctly, perhaps, as the popular tendency to accept the names of men who have been most conspicuous and representative in any cause or epoch, as symbolic of the ideas and sentiments which, at such time, have most strongly possessed the popular heart. Human nature is prone to typify in this wise. Principles may be imperfectly understood — at any rate, the masses may not be able to give them clear definition or articulate expression — events, however important or decisive, may be partially forgotten; but the men who have been foremost or most noted in seeking or striving after that which a people have loved or hoped for are remembered through the ages. Many others may have felt as earnestly and done nearly as much, many thousands may have suffered more, but the popular instinct, selects, and usually with unerring sagacity, those who have been chiefly instrumental in demand and action and makes their names immortal.

It is easy to understand why General Lee should be thus regarded. Amiable and conservative as was his nature, he yet represented more completely than any other leader — unless it was Jackson — the actual spirit and destiny of the Confederacy, which, begun in the face of threat and invasion, closing in desperate resistance to inevitable disaster, was militant always during the brief period of its struggle for separate national existence. Constantly in the field, constantly offering or accepting battle, the eyes of a people, who then thought of little else, were ever upon him. His name was associated with repeated and indisputable victory, and identified more than any other with Confederate glory. Before the end of the conflict he had become the idolized hero of the people of the South; and it is not to be expected that their love and admiration of him would be less after his fame had gone over the whole world.

But Mr. Davis was not so popular at the close of the war as when he had been elected President of the Confederacy. At that date he was the most prominent public man of the South, and generally esteemed the ablest. A well equipped and experienced statesman, a man of the highest personal integrity, perfect courage, and absolute conviction, and an eloquent and attractive orator, his influence with a people of whose social and political ideas he was a thorough exponent, was exceptionally potent. They looked to him as their advocate upon the floor of the senate, where he met few equals in debate, and as the champion of Southern views and interests in every public forum where such questions were discussed.

Yet intensely Southern as Mr. Davis was in feeling those who deemed him a secessionist, in that he desired the dissolution of the Union or that he would not have consented to any sacrifice compatible with what he believed to be the just rights of the South, in order to preserve it, did him gross injustice. He was in no sense a "fire-eater," and no man, probably, more profoundly deplored what he honestly considered a terrible necessity.

Mississippi having been one of the earliest states to secede, and Mr. Davis's commanding capacity and leadership receiving general recognition, he was logically chosen as President when the provisional Confederate government was formed, and subsequently continued in office by popular election.

Whether or not some other man might not have been more successful in that position has been a favourite theme of discussion. That Mr. Davis made some mistakes no one would, of course, think of denying. No man so tried, attempting a work so arduous with resources so scanty, and confronted with odds, both in men and material, so tremendous, could have avoided occasional error. The very magnitude of the task might sometimes induce over caution, or again tempt to undue rashness; and a temper less ardent than his might be urged beyond control in such an ordeal. But it is difficult to believe that any one whose name has been suggested in such connection could have done better or indeed so well.

Little opportunity was afforded him for exhibition of the capacity for civil administration which he undoubtedly possessed. The Confederacy, as I have said, was racked with war from its cradle to its grave — war which raged along its borders and burned in its vitals; there was no time nor chance then to cultivate the "arts of peace" or improve the teachings of political economy.

Mr. Davis has been accused of a short-sighted policy in not having made ample provision for the tremendous struggle in which the Confederacy became engaged. There can be no doubt that in common with many other public men of the South — indeed, the majority of them — he failed to realize the true nature and magnitude of the impending conflict; or, it may be he hoped that there would be no war. But in nowise could he in the then rapid progress of events have made such provision after his inauguration as President. To impute the lack of it to him and hold him individually or officially responsible is absurd. Such criticism would be juster and more pertinent if directed against those who hurried the South without preparation, into a movement certain to induce war.

It will always remain, indeed, a historical marvel that the Confederacy held out as long as it did; that the seceded states, lacking means, material, money, transportation, every thing, in short, supposed to be necessary to the successful conduct of warfare — having to improvise or capture arms and munitions — made such a fight. It is surely a high tribute not only to the spirit of the people, but to the ability and energy of those in authority.

Curiously and rather inconsistently, some of Mr. Davis's critics, who profess to believe that he should have employed his official opportunities in an arbitrary fashion altogether beyond the legal and constitutional restrictions imposed upon his conduct, also complain that he exercised in an autocratic spirit the authority which actually and rightfully belonged to him. It is not easy, of course, to understand that a government like that which the people of the Southern states were seeking to establish, "born in the throes of revolution" and fighting desperately for life, would scrupulously observe constitutional limitations and yield in matters of manifest and pressing expediency to the rigid requirements of law. Some confusion of ideas on this subject, therefore, may be expected; and it might have been more expedient to direct executive functions with less regard to theoretic propriety than with energetic and relentless purpose to achieve success. Better hope of success might have attended the effort if all that the territory of the Confederacy could produce or furnish had been utilized, even by compulsion, for the conduct of the war; if an earlier and more general enlistment had been enforced, and a sensitive regard for constitutional sanction or inhibition had been pretermitted until the Confederacy was firmly established.

But to expect Mr. Davis to do this, or to consent to it, would indicate a total misconception of his character. Imperious as was his will and fiery his temper, however wedded to certain ideas which may have been fallacious, and resolved upon policies perhaps inadequate, he was, nevertheless, in all things honest and devoted to principle, and above all intensely patriotic. Those who believed that ambition impelled him to countenance or aid in secession, and those who expected that, as President of the Confederacy, he would use unwarranted or even extraordinary means to accomplish the independence of the South, were mistaken. Ardent in temperament, his intellect was yet peculiarly conservative. No man adhered more faithfully to the traditions in which he had been reared and the tenets taught him in his youth and the novitiate of his political career. When he consented to secession it was because he religiously believed that the Union was a compact between equal and sovereign states, which, under certain conditions — conditions which he thought then existed — might properly be rescinded. He believed in and loved the form of government prescribed by the Federal Constitution, and the constitution of the Confederate States was in all relating to governmental form and powers a copy of that instrument. He thoroughly believed in the sovereignty of the people, in the strict subordination of people and magistracies alike to law, and in the duty of every one invested with official authority carefully to heed, in its exercise, every constitutional mandate. It is conceivable that in the clearly defined limits and well-recognized sphere of his authority he might have been arbitrary and obstinate, as was so frequently charged; but for no consideration would he have usurped power or over stepped or strained the law.

Mr. Davis was charged with favouritism both in his civil and military appointments. This is an accusation so generally preferred by disappointed applicants for office against every dispenser of patronage that little heed is or should be given it. In the more objectionable sense of the term — that he gave men positions merely because they were personally friendly to himself — there was little truth in the charge. He appointed some of his warmest friends to high office, but in every such case the appointees were men of unusual merit and repute. Two notable instances of such selections for militar preferment were Gen. S. S. Cooper and Gen. Albert Sidney Johnston. But surely the most captious critic would admit the propriety of heading the list of generals with officers of such eminent and acknowledged ability and previously excellent records.

Another ascription, as frequently and perhaps more justly, made, was that he was influenced to withhold preferment or promotion by his prejudices. He could never forget or divest himself, it was asserted, of his ante-bellum dislikes, having their origin chiefly in political difference.

Few men occupying such a station as he did, grave as are its responsibilities, can regard men or measures with purely impersonal feeling, and Mr. Davis may, in some instances and to some extent, have been controlled by hostile or antagonistic sentiment. But however much the personal equation may have influenced him, his nature was too frank and noble to cherish small resentments, and it is more probable that he refused what some men asked because he thought them unworthy or incompetent, than because he bore them malice.

It has been said that Mr. Davis thought he possessed more capacity and aptitude for military than for civil affairs. There is good reason to believe that, in this estimate of himself, he was mistaken. It is not probable that as field captain, personally directing military operations in the presence of the enemy, he would have been successful.

In that larger region of strategy, however, in which he was required to direct as ex officio commander-in-chief all the armies of the Confederacy, suggesting rather than planning or conducting campaigns, it will be conceded that he did display ability. If he had not the qualities which constitute sagacious leadership in the field or the tactical skill which wins battles, he was a wise adviser, and usually, in matters of dispute, a competent arbiter.

That he was mistaken in his estimate of certain men, overrating some and underrating others, as was so often charged, is unquestionably true; and it would be matter for wonder if it were not true. Nevertheless, the roster of his appointees, civil and military, exhibits the names of men certainly above, some far above the average in personal character and official capacity. This is especially true of his appointments in the army. No military service the world has ever seen, perhaps, could have shown a roll of officers superior to those who served the Confederacy. That he gave cordial and loyal support to those in command, even when he differed with them in opinion, will not be denied.

Whatever feeling of disappointment or bitterness any one entertained toward Mr. Davis in the latter days of the struggle was of brief duration, and was completely eliminated by his vicarious punishment and suffering. As the years roll on, his people understand him better and love and revere him more. The sentiment with which he was regarded when the effort for Southern independence was inaugurated, seems to have returned in greater volume. He is more than ever regarded as the best representative of the true meaning of that aspiration. He is, even more than when he lived and acted, identified in the popular mind with that thrilling and heroic episode of Southern history; and the day is far distant when his name shall no longer be venerated by the Southern people.

Almost anything that is written about Gen. N. B. Forrest will be interesting to a Southern reader, and some of my own recollections of him may prove so. I knew him very well, and the admiration which, in common with all who are familiar with his military career, I entertain for his extraordinary qualities and achievements as a soldier, is equalled by the warm regard his personal character inspired.

My acquaintance with General Forrest was much more intimate after than before the war. I did not meet him very often at that time, and to my great regret, never had an opportunity of seeing him in battle. My first recollection of him is when he made a brief visit to Bowling Green while the army was encamped about that place. It was just after his name had become widely known on account of his victory at Sacramento. Shortly afterward I saw him at Nashville during the exciting scenes of Gen. Albert Johnston's retreat and the evacuation of that city. He had just made his escape from Donelson, bringing off his regiment intact from that disaster. For two or three days he was busily employed in policing the city and in endeavouring to restore order, a very difficult task, in the panic and wild turmoil prevailing. As Morgan's squadron was engaged in the same duty, I had a good chance to observe how he performed it, and I rather think that a number of those with whom he came in contact did not soon forget it. I well remember how he looked, his resolute face seeming to subdue all he gazed on to his will and his tall powerful form towering above the mob which, in its most furious moments, gave way before him.

Some months later I was present at an interview between him and Morgan, when they were comparing notes of their respective expeditions made about the same date in the summer of 1862, the one into middle Tennessee and the other into Kentucky. Each seemed far more concerned to learn what the other had done and how he did it, than to relate his own performances; and it was interesting to note the brevity with which they answered each other's questions and the eagerness with which they asked their own. It was upon this occasion that Forrest used an expression which has been very often quoted. I was a good deal amused by it at the time, because of the terse way in which he rendered into the vernacular a proposition which General Beauregard had a few months previously clothed in very sonorous and academic terms.

Some of my readers may perhaps remember the letter which Beauregard wrote to Bragg shortly after the former relinquished and the latter assumed command of the army at Tupelo. Along with other excellent counsel, General Beauregard advised his successor to "be careful always to move by interior lines and strike the fragments of your enemy's forces with the masses of your own." This maxim was certainly not less worthy of suggestion, because Napoleon had previously commended it as comprising nearly all of the gospel of strategy. It was new, however, to the majority of the Confederate soldiers, and they read Beauregard's letter with profound admiration. I do not know, therefore, whether my surprise or amusement was the greater when I heard Forrest, in this conversation with Morgan, unconsciously paraphrase it in his own curt and peculiar way.

Morgan wanted particularly to know about his fight at Murfreesboro, where Forrest had accomplished a marked success, capturing garrison and stores and carrying off every thing, although the surrounding country was filled with Federal forces. Morgan asked how it was done.

"Oh," said Forrest, "I just took the short cut and got there first with the most men."

I did not meet him at any time during the period of his later and most brilliant achievement, but, immediately after the close of the war, saw him quite frequently and became well acquainted with him. After a fashion, he took much interest in politics, which was, I believe, purely impersonal. He had no thought, so far as I could discover in my talks with him, of any advancement or benefit for himself. Of course, during the reconstruction period, more especially the early part of it, there was little chance of an ex-Confederate obtaining office or political position; but I do not think Forrest at any time desired either the honours or emoluments of political office. His sole concern seemed to be to relieve his people from the terrible and oppressive conditions under which they so grievously suffered, and he went about that work with the same ardour and indifference to any personal hazard which characterized him in his military service. It was generally believed that he was the chief of "The Invisible Empire," that mysterious and dreaded association of the Ku Klux, created to counteract and hold in some sort of check the insolence of the Loyal League and other similar negro organizations, and the unscrupulous greed of the carpet-baggers. Secret associations of this character do not exist without some real and strong reason. They are always to be deplored, but they never trouble communities in which law is impartially administered and the rights of all citizens respected.

No candid man, who is familiar with the social and political conditions then obtaining in the Southern states will deny that the organization of the Ku Klux was perfectly justified, or that the evils such abnormal conditions were producing could be met or remedied in any other way. While the suddenly emancipated blacks were permitted every privilege and even invested with a certain authority, the Southern whites — with the exception of that renegade class which was more vicious and virulent than the carpet-baggers themselves — were deprived of all rights, civil and political, and subjected, with no means or hope of legal protection, to every outrage and oppression the malice of their opponents could devise. Such a people would never tamely submit to either the injuries or insults so constantly offered them, and in the absence of every other method of redress, naturally, indeed inevitably, employed force.

But situated as they were, force could not be openly attempted, and, as has always been the case under similar conditions, resort was also had to strategem and disguise. While it will not be denied that, under the very provocation of the situation itself, brutal violence and acts of cruelty were sometimes committed by the Southern whites against the blacks, and in some instances, perhaps, carried farther than either retaliation or example warranted, it has been always claimed, and I think justly, that such things were seldom, if ever, done by the Ku Klux proper. In this respect their methods seem to have been as astute as they were effective. Thoroughly understanding the character of the negro, they controlled him by exciting a vague apprehension of violence rather than by its actual commission, and especially by playing upon his superstitions. The carpet-bagger became impotent when his negro allies were frightened into docility and good behavior.

Whether Forrest was or was not at the head of "The Invisible Empire," it is certain that no man could have more ably and successfully conducted its operations. He had the skill to direct its deliberations and actions, although necessarily involved in the profoundest reticence and secrecy, and keep them strictly within the sphere of the prescribed purposes; he had as well the energy and force of character which could compel obedience even in such an association, although invested with no actual and legitimate authority.

Forrest was a delegate to the first Democratic Presidential convention which assembled after the war, that which nominated Seymour. I witnessed an incident on our way to New York which very well illustrated his capacity to intimidate men not supposed to be subject to such influences. A number of us from Tennessee and Kentucky were in the same coach. When the train reached some town, the name of which I have forgotten, it stopped before pulling up at the depot at a water tank a short distance below.

The train conductor, who had been a Federal soldier and was a very fine, manly young fellow, with whom we had all fraternized readily, came to me at this point and said that he apprehended some trouble when we reached the depot. He had just been informed, he said, that a crowd, having learned that Forrest was on the train, had collected there, and that the town bully, a very truculent fellow, was loudly proclaiming his intention to take him off the train and thrash him. The conductor did not believe that the crowd was disposed to back the bully in such attempt, but thought it had assembled merely out of curiosity. But he was apprehensive that in the excitement some of them, who had formed no such previous intention, might render him assistance, and then, as we would certainly stand by Forrest, a serious riot might occur.

"Now," he said, "if anything of the kind happens, I'm going to side with you men and give you all the help I can. I don't like this sort of thing, and, moreover, it's my duty to protect my passengers so far as I can. But let's have no trouble if it can be avoided. I want you therefore to advise General Forrest to remain in the coach, where, if it comes to a fight, we can make the best showing, anyhow, and not go out on the platform, no matter what that fellow says or does."

The conductor said further that he believed the man would seek a quarrel, inasmuch as he was a noted fighter and had never met his match.

I immediately communicated the information to Forrest, and advised that he act as the conductor suggested. He received the news very calmly, being too much accustomed to affairs of that kind to become excited, and agreed to the programme as indicated. But when the train stopped at the depot the bully immediately sprang upon the platform and entered our coach. He was a very powerful man in appearance, larger than Forrest, and I believe meant to execute his threat up to the time that he caught sight of the party he was looking for. As he entered the door he called out loudly: "Where's that d — d butcher, Forrest? I want him."

I never in my life witnessed such an instantaneous and marvellous transformation in any one's appearance as then occurred with Forrest. He bounded from his seat, his form erect and dilated, his face the colour of heated bronze, and his eyes flaming, blazing. He strode rapidly down the aisle toward the approaching champion, his gait and manner evincing perfect, invincible determination.

"I am Forrest," he said. "What do you want?"

The bully gave one look. His purpose evaporated, and when Forrest had gotten within three or four feet of him, he turned and rushed out of the coach faster than he had entered. Forrest followed him into the midst of the crowd outside, vainly shouting to him to stop, and several of us followed Forrest. But the man whose prowess that crowd had gathered to witness had no thought of holding his ground. He darted into and down the street with quarterhorse speed, losing his hat in his hurry, and vanished around a corner. Then the humour of the thing struck Forrest and he burst into a great shout of laughter. In a few moments the entire crowd joined in his merriment and seemed to be in complete sympathy with him, many of them pressing forward to shake hands with him. When the train five minutes later pulled out, Forrest was standing on the platform receiving the cheers and plaudits of the multitude and gracefully waving his thanks to his new friends and admirers.

Forrest attracted a great deal of attention at the Democratic convention of 1868, not only from the delegates but from the large crowd assembled to witness its deliberations. Having had no practice as a speaker and unfamiliar with parliamentary methods, he took little part, of course, in its more public proceedings; but his counsel, as one who knew the sentiment of the Southern people and perfectly possessed their confidence, was sought and heeded by the Democratic leaders. There was also a very lively curiosity entertained by people generally to see one whose career in the Civil War had been so remarkable and the remembrance of which was yet recent.

As I have already said he took much interest in politics at that time, and, so far as a man in his situation could do, tried to influence the course of political events. His efforts were at first directed, necessarily, almost solely to the restoration of the autonomy of his state, and, when that seemed impossible, he took the ground that any means of opposing grievous, immediate oppression were justifiable. His very active service in the latter part of the war had made his name familiar and peculiarly offensive to the Northern people, and when he became conspicuous in the reconstruction era he received a double share of criticism from the orators and editors who were then especially engaged in censure or vituperation of everything Southern.

In one such case the affair which at first seemed to threaten tragic consequences terminated almost in a comedy. Among those who reflected on Forrest most severely during the Presidential campaign of 1868, was the famous Federal cavalry officer, General Kilpatrick. Kilpatrick, who had been very busy as a lecturer after his service in the army was concluded, took the stump for the Republican ticket during that canvass and made stump speeches in all of the Eastern states. In some of these speeches he charged Forrest with the commission of many atrocities, and among other things said that Forrest had on one occasion tied a number of negroes to a plank fence and had then set fire to the fence. This remarkable accusation could hardly have been credited even by the most prejudiced, for even had Forrest been a cruel man, which — although very fierce when his wrath was excited — was not his temper, he would certainly never have wasted the time necessary to burn "niggers" in so elaborate a fashion. It is probable that Forrest would have given no notice to this charge, if it had not been especially brought to his attention in a way which he thought demanded that he resent it.

Another Federal general, of Connecticut if I remember correctly, a very gallant man, and one who gravely disapproved of such attacks upon his former opponents as Kilpatrick was making, not only remonstrated with the latter, but sent a copy of one of the speeches to Forrest with a letter expressing his disbelief in the story and his condemnation of its publication. Forrest, upon receipt of this communication, felt obliged to call Kilpatrick to account, and he accordingly wrote him an open letter, published in one of the Memphis papers. The letter was a long one, and in no degree less severe than the effusion which had provoked it. On the contrary, he explicitly set forth his opinion of General Kilpatrick's utterances and of that gentleman's general character and "style" in very vigorous English, and in terms which very nearly exhausted the retaliative possibilities of the language. This letter was of course very widely published, and I read it a day or two later in the Louisville *Courier-Journal*. I sympathized of course with Forrest, but was somewhat amused at the indignation he expressed, for I supposed that he had become so much accustomed to such attacks as to regard them with indifference. My admiration was also aroused by his eloquent and comprehensive treatment of the subject, and the forcible way in which he explained to Kilpatrick what he thought of him and of his conduct, and the many forms in which he impugned his veracity. The conclusion of the letter, however, struck me with consternation. Forrest wound up this communication by requesting General Kilpatrick to consider it a challenge to combat; the peculiar conditions then prevailing might excuse, he thought, a more regular and formal transmission of such a cartel, but he expressed the hope that Kilpatrick would waive all that and immediately communicate with his (Forrest's) friend, Gen. Basil W. Duke, at Louisville, who would be authorized to make, on Forrest's part, all necessary arrangements for the meeting.

I was flattered by Forrest's selection of me as his friend in this affair, and at one time would have acted with alacrity and even a certain degree of pleasure. But just then the thought of having to act as either second or principal in a duel was not at all agreeable. The laws of Kentucky against duelling were then, as now, extremely severe. The constitution provided that any citizen of Kentucky who participated in such an affair in any capacity within the borders of the state should be virtually disfranchised, and if he were a lawyer should be debarred from practising his profession until pardoned, and the governor was inhibited the exercise of the pardoning power in such cases until the expiration of five years after the commission of the offence. The statutes passed to execute the constitutional provision were very drastic.

I had come out of the war with a ready-made family and no visible means of support, and had begun the practice of law in Louisville. My prospects in that line were not brilliant, it is true, but were all that I had, and I was exceedingly loath to relinquish even a very small chance of making a living. The particular difficulty I contemplated might have been obviated by having the duel fought somewhere else than in Kentucky; but I was unwilling on Forrest's account that it should occur elsewhere. I feared that he would not get fair play anywhere north of the Ohio river. The entire South was still under military rule and occupied by Federal soldiers, and while I believed that the inclination of the soldiers — officers and men — would be in favour of a fair fight, I feared that those in authority would feel obliged to interfere and deal pretty harshly with all engaged in such an affair, which, on account of the prominence of the principals, would certainly excite interest and comment throughout the country. In Kentucky, however, both men would have friends and sympathizers, and the general sentiment would be that they should fight "in peace," without partisan or impertinent interference. The law would not take cognizance of such a matter between gentlemen until it was over, and then to deal only with citizens of Kentucky in the way I have indicated. I made up my mind, therefore, that while General Kilpatrick was undoubtedly entitled to designate the place of meeting, I would use every effort to have it come off in Kentucky.

On the same day I received a letter from Forrest in which he said that I would probably soon hear from Kilpatrick, and that he wished me to arrange a meeting as soon as possible. He went on to say that he recognized Kilpatrick's right to name "time, place, and weapons," and that he was prepared, of course, to accede to any terms the latter might designate; but, inasmuch as they had both been cavalry men, he thought it would be highly appropriate to fight mounted and with sabres.

I at once replied that any communication from General Kilpatrick should receive immediate and proper attention.

Although I was resolved to assist Forrest in every way I could in such an emergency, and to act in any way that he desired, I still hoped that, in some way, I might be relieved of direct participation in the duel, such participation as would subject me to the penalties of which I have spoken. I determined, therefore, to enlist some expert in such affairs, whose services might be agreeable to Forrest, and who might act in my stead when the period of actual hostilities should arrive. It was necessary, of course, to select some one who was not a citizen of Kentucky and who would be exempt from the consequences which I feared for myself. After due reflection, I concluded to ask the aid of Dr. James Keller, then living in St. Louis and a citizen of Missouri, who was an acknowledged authority on the duello and a warm friend of Forrest, as well as of myself. I accordingly wired the doctor, stating the case and asking his valuable assistance. It is difficult, of course, after the flight of so many years, to remember perfectly just how every thing occurred, but I think that the doctor was in Louisville and ready for business before the instrument ceased clicking.

In the meantime, mindful of the wish that Forrest had expressed to fight on horseback, I was desirous of providing him with a suitable mount, and with that view called on Capt. Bart Jenkins, formerly of the Fourth Kentucky Confederate cavalry, who then kept a livery stable in Louisville, and would, I was quite sure, have at his disposal a number of fine horses. Captain Jenkins was a thorough fighting man, as well as ardent Confederate, and I knew he would feel a profound interest in the matter in hand. When I reached the captain's place, I was informed that he was very ill but that I could see him. I was taken up stairs to a small room above his office, where he was lying on a lounge looking like an exceedingly sick man. In response to my inquiry regarding his condition, he responded in a voice scarcely louder than a whisper that he had pneumonia, was so weak that he could not rise from his couch, and would not be surprised if the attack terminated fatally. After expressing due sorrow and sympathy, I said that I had called to talk with him about the affair between Forrest and Kilpatrick, but, under the circumstances, could, of course, pretermit it.

"No, you won't," he said, his voice perceptibly stronger; "I want to hear about that."

"Oh, well, Forrest wants to fight on horseback with sabres—— "

"That's right," he interrupted, and rose to a sitting position, "that's right."

"So I have come around here to consult you and see if I couldn't get him a good horse."

"You just can," he declared in a perfectly normal tone. "I've got the very animal you want," and with that he got out of bed and began to put on his clothes.

"Don't do that, Bart," I said, "you've just told me that the doctor insists that you shall be very careful."

"The doctor be d—d," he replied. "Do you think I'll let a doctor interfere with important business of this kind. I want to show you my brown mare, the finest in the state and has taken the blue ribbon at every fair in central Kentucky. She's sixteen hands high, built just right for a man of Forrest's weight, and as quick on her feet as a cat. Place the men sixty yards apart, and tell Forrest that when you give the word he must drive in the spurs and ride straight at the other horse. She'll knock him off of his feet, and Forrest can cut off Kilpatrick's head before he touches the ground. But — I must see the fight."

Disregarding every remonstrance, he took me to the stable to inspect the mare, which was, indeed, a very fine one.

But the duel was not fought. I received no communication from General Kilpatrick, which was entirely to my satisfaction if not to Forrest's. General Kilpatrick, after some delay, published a statement in the Eastern papers to the effect that he could not afford to accept Forrest's challenge, inasmuch as a committee of congress appointed to investigate the alleged massacre of negroes at Fort Pillow, had declared him guilty, and he (Kilpatrick) could not therefore regard him as a gentleman.

General Shackelford, the officer who first called Forrest's attention to Kilpatrick's charges, published a letter in response to Kilpatrick's, in which he took the ground that while the report of a congressional committee might be pertinent and valuable for many purposes, no one could consider it conclusive of a man's standing as a gentleman; and he strongly urged Kilpatrick to meet Forrest after having wantonly assailed him. I have always thought that if Shackelford could by any possibility have been substituted for Kilpatrick, there would certainly have been a fight.

I met Forrest very infrequently in the latter part of his life. The last time I saw him he was so broken by illness and had aged so greatly that I scarcely recognized him. I have heard that he became deeply religious shortly before his death, but retained to the last the keen sagacity and indomitable spirit which had ever characterized him.

The enthusiasts who are convinced that the time is near at hand when war will no more plague the human race and the *ultima ratio regum* shall give place to a milder logic have had much encouragement recently, in so far as expressions of approval may be regarded as an aid in their work.

Undoubtedly, one of the noblest ideas humanity has ever cherished is this hope of universal and perpetual peace; a compact of amity which shall include all mankind, bidding "the war drum throb no longer" and binding the whole world in a federation obedient to canons of brotherhood and good will.

Nevertheless most of us are compelled, reluctantly, to believe that it is something humanity will find scarcely possible of attainment; at least until it is reconstructed, or developed and educated into conditions very different from those it knows and feels now. Indeed, even in quite modern history, and since peace congresses and courts of national arbitration have been in evidence, we have witnessed periods when the dream of universal empire accomplished by armed force, has seemed a more probable realization.

It is not at all likely, of course, that such danger will come, as of yore, from the fury of some insanely ambitious conqueror, although less than one hundred years ago Napoleon roused a very lively apprehension that he was about to emulate in this respect the record of his prototypes of antiquity. It is too late in the life of the world for the individual, the personal equation, to count for so much. But there does, at times, seem danger that some overweeningly strong and imperial people, selfish as the strong and the energetic usually are, may attempt something of the kind, urged on by greed of wide reaching dominion and consequent commercial supremacy.

The better spirit of each successive age is more averse to strife and bloodshed. A cosmopolitan opinion, constantly growing stronger, exalts the victories of peace above those of war. The profession of the soldier, although still honourable, is not held in so high esteem as in the past, and military glory loses something of its glamour. Yet we are frequently reminded that man — even civilized and educated man — is a pugnacious animal. To bear arms is no longer popular as a trade; conquests are not made merely that the conquered countries may be given over to plunder and oppression, or swell some already overgrown and arrogant power; nations are not so prone to "go to war for an idea," as the French formerly phrased it. But when their material interests are involved, or even when their pride is insulted or their passions really aroused, modern men seem to be nearly if not quite as ready to fight as were their ancestors.

Just before the French Revolution, notwithstanding quite recent and striking examples that might have taught a contrary opinion, the philosophers — and many believed them — were predicting that humanity had lost, or was in a way to lose, its lust for combat and carnage, and a millennial era of love and peace was about to dawn. While listening fondly to these promises, the world was astounded by the outburst of the great revolution, and those years of terror were immediately succeeded by the Napoleonic wars, devastating all Europe.

Then there was a lull in hostilities for the life of a generation; no great wars, at least, disturbed the earth during that period.

But it would seem that the race was only resting, like prize-fighters between rounds. The stock of pugnacity had been too heavily drawn on, and thirty years or more were required for recuperation. After some comparatively small affairs, like our war with Mexico, and some rather inocuous preliminaries on the other side of the water, the great events were rapidly brought on. The Crimean War, the Sepoy Rebellion, the war between France and Italy on the one side and Austria on the other, the tremendous conflict in this country, the war between Austria and Prussia, and the Franco-Prussian War followed in quick succession.

After this the hopes of the evangelists of peace were less sanguine, and their reputations as forecasters of coming conditions were considerably impaired; but, greatly to their credit, their purpose was in no wise daunted nor their zeal abated.

Among governments and people both, however, the effect of these conflicts, induced by no reasons which, judged by previous standards, would have been peculiarly serious, was to produce the impression that war, at all times probable, might often be imminent. An immense stimulus consequently was given to the preparation for war. Not only was every attention and effort given to improvement in arms, ordnance, and equipment, but standing armies, larger than any previously known, were maintained by every European power, and, to a certain extent, all over the world; while the reserves, the land wehr, the militia, as we call such forces here, and volunteers, as they are termed in England, were organized in vast numbers and provided with all the necessary equipment for field service. These reserve troops constitute in themselves formidable armies.

The status and relative strength of the European powers were greatly changed by these wars, and with each such change new complications arose, threatening fresh conflict. Italy, shaking off the grasp of Austria, became a united and independent country after centuries of division and subjection to both domestic and foreign despotism; and was counted a factor in the great game played with armies. France rose apparently to the first place as a military power, but met crushing defeat from Germany; and Germany and Russia became alternately the dread of the nations.

But a few years ago it seemed that England and Russia would inevitably fight for the possession of India, the dominion of Asia and its vast populations, the trade and wealth of the East. There was reason to fear that such a contest might involve Europe and ultimately the whole world; for when England, mistress of the seas and so powerful in the realm of commerce and finance, goes to war with an opponent which can match her power and really threaten her safety, the shock may unsettle the peace of the earth.

All mankind must feel it. Every people will, in some way, have brought home to them the realization that the great power which dictates the trade of the globe and governs values all over it is straining every nerve to maintain the domination so long and so widely exerted. More than two hundred millions of Asiatics who live under her rule, are subjects of her flag and make part of her immense empire, will feel when she arms for such a conflict that the fate of themselves and their posterity is at stake. From America, Canada, Australia, many millions more, some of whom owe her no allegiance, but are connected with her hardy race by blood and tradition, speaking her language and inheriting in some form her institutions — will look on the struggle with scarcely less of interest.

At the date when this conflict between England and Russia was imminent, it was believed by those most competent to judge accurately in such a matter that, upon the ground where it would be waged, Russia would prove a match for England. While much was reported, even at that time, of the corrupt practices and inefficiency of the Russian civil officials, few knew or suspected that a similar demoralization had extended throughout the huge armies of Russia, injuriously affecting the capacity and temperament of the officers and the discipline of the men. Nor was it understood how desperate and wide-spread was the feeling of political discontent, the spirit of revolt, in Russia, frequent and energetic as had been its demonstration. The war with Japan disclosed the dry rot which was sapping her military strength; the reverses in Manchuria encouraged the Nihilist to measures which really menaced official authority and paralyzed national effort. It may have been a premonition of these dangers that prevented Russia from striking the blow at England which she undoubtedly meditated, even when such an opportunity as the Boer War was offered her.

War between England and Russia, however, is only postponed, provided the latter shall be able to compose her domestic trouble and recover her prestige in Manchuria. It is the more probable, if the rumours of the almost universal disaffection of the native population in India be true.

And now Japan has bounded into the arena, a fully panoplied "world power," and one that has fairly earned the title. What

Japan holds she will keep, and perhaps go after more although she is scarcely so formidable nor so aggressive as some hysterical folk would have us believe. Her example has infected and aroused even sluggish China; and wise men who profess to understand the Orient are babbling about the "yellow peril."

All this bodes ill to the blessed and universal peace which good people preach and other people will not consent to practise.

The best chance for the peace so devoutly hoped for is to be found in the fact that modern ideas of economy, if not of morality, may be arrayed against war. Not only is the disturbance of commerce and destruction of values wrought by warfare more alarming than ever before, but the absolute cost of modern weapons, ordnance, and ammunition, the use of modern improved methods of attack and defence, is something appalling. The Roman legionary used a sword made by an ordinary blacksmith. The veteran spearman of Hannibal did good work with a strong lance, tipped with a few cents worth of iron. The English archers dealt death with bows of yew. The soldiers of Frederic fought with the clumsy musket and bayonet of their time, and the soldiers of Gustavus with weapons of earlier make and more awkward pattern.

Modern soldiery are furnished with weapons of a very different type, the arms of precision, the rifle whose range has scarcely a limit; but if the trajectory is fit the price of the implement is correspondingly high. The expense of modern ordnance, of all modern military material, is far greater than was that of such material formerly. The warship of to-day costs more than half a dozen squadrons of the old wooden frigates, and the cost of ammunition expended by two or three modern batteries in one battle will probably represent a sum that would have equipped an average mediæval army.

The progress of invention and improvement in the appliances of warfare will necessarily still further increase its cost and render military expenditures yet more extravagant. In this fact is to be found the best hope that war may some day cease; but judging the future by the past, even that hope is slender. Courts of arbitration and peace congresses are excellent in theory and purpose; but their decrees would have little more effect than treaties, and would avail little against superior and unscrupulous force. If, by some adequate device, the instinct and the energies which urge mankind to warfare, could be diverted into some other field of effort, affording like satisfaction to that craving for contest which war seems to furnish, actual bloodshed might be avoided. But how and by whom can such substitute be suggested or induced? I rather think it is best to be prepared for war.

CHAPTER XVII

A GREAT deal has been written about the treatment of the prisoners captured on both sides in our Civil War, and enough has been told to demonstrate that the lot of the prisoner was not a pleasant one; that, indeed, the hardships endured in captivity were harsher and harder to bear than those suffered by the soldier in the field. I have always believed that more fortitude was required of the Confederate soldier, subjected to a long term of imprisonment, to remain faithful to his cause than the severest strain of active service demanded.

It is not my purpose, and would, doubtless, now be inappropriate, to revive a discussion, once prevalent, regarding whose fault it was that so many brave men of both armies were compelled to endure an incarceration so tedious and painful, and apparently so unnecessary; nor shall I allude to the cruelties which each side accused the other of having inflicted. No one cares now, I presume, to listen to such recitals. But many things could be related of that prison life which need not arouse unpleasant memories; many of its traits and incidents which could, perhaps, interest and amuse the reader of to-day, especially the devices and expedients by which the unfortunates sought to forget or alleviate the terrible monotony and tedium of their condition.

The methods by which such diversion was obtained were as various as the tastes and temperaments of those who required it, and the multitude of recreations their ingenuity invented is amazing, when the limited opportunities their confinement permitted are considered. The more artistic betook themselves to carving a great number and variety of small ornaments out of cannel coal and vulcanized rubber; and the extremely imaginative devoted a great deal of time to writing poetry. Much of the carving was excellent, and many articles so produced were sold for fairly good prices. Quite probably the poetry also was of high grade, although there is not much testimony extant to that effect, and I never heard of a poem having been disposed of at any price. The poets, however, seemed to enjoy it very much, no matter how their work may have been appreciated by other people. Many prisoners devoted themselves to really serious and profitable study. It was quite common for men, previously entirely ignorant of those languages, to acquire in prison a tolerably good acquaintance with French and German, and, as the purchase of books was allowed in all the prisons, those who could afford to buy them might pursue almost any branch of knowledge they chose. Fortunately no one — at least, so far as I can remember or am informed — essayed to learn music. Nor do I believe that any one would have been suffered to procure musical instruments for such purpose. Even had the guards and jailers felt no concern for the comfort of the prisoners, who would have been compelled to listen to the efforts of the amateurs, they would, doubtless, have stoutly denied any such privilege on their own account.

In such prisons as Johnson's Island, Camp Chase, Fort Delaware, etc., where much open ground was contained within the enclosures, the prisoners frequently amused themselves with athletic games and sports. At Johnson's Island a favourite pastime in winter was a mock battle with snowballs. Parties would be told off for the contest and regularly organized, officers selected, and military usage observed as closely as possible. Snow forts and entrenchments would be erected, and the spectators were always greatly edified by the orthodox conduct of the "generals," who, with proper dignity and caution, carefully kept out of the way of the missiles, but sent in the "staff" and ordered forward the troops with commendable alacrity.

In the Ohio penitentiary, where a number of Morgan's officers were confined for several months, these open air recreations were of course impossible, and we were forced to resort to more sedentary methods. Chess was a very popular diversion. Even those who never learned to play the game with any skill, nevertheless bought books on chess and talked as wisely about the various gambits as the experts. When two skilful players became engaged a crowd was always collected to watch the game, and criticism and advice were freely offered. The knight, as was natural with cavalry men, was a favourite piece with the spectators; and when either player would make what seemed to be a dexterous flank movement with that agile combatant, he was sure to receive applause. Card playing was doubtless much resorted to in all the prisons, and was especially in vogue at Fort Delaware. One versatile officer ran a gambling establishment in the room of the barracks where he lodged, wherein all kinds of games were conducted during the week under his auspices. On Sunday religious services were held there at which he assisted with exemplary decorum and piety.

The nervous irritability which prolonged and close confinement induces was often exhibited in a manner that minds in a healthy condition could scarcely understand. In the Ohio penitentiary the most animated discussions would begin as soon as we were permitted to leave our cells, upon all sorts of topics, and would usually degenerate into clamorous and angry debate. The disputants became as earnest and excited over subjects on which they had, perhaps, never thought before, as if they were matters of vital and pressing importance. It was prudent, however, on the part of the prisoners to conduct these discussions entirely among themselves, and by no means to attempt them with the guards and turnkeys; indeed, it was a rather dangerous matter to address one of these officials at all, except on the most necessary occasions. If a remark made by a prisoner to one of them was construed, or misconstrued, as criticism, or even levity, the offender ran great danger of consignment to one of the punishment cells, or "dungeons," as they were termed, which were extremely disagreeable places to visit. On one occasion Major Elliott, quartermaster of Morgan's division, a gentleman very much accustomed to speaking his mind freely, got into trouble and was sent to one of these cells under circumstances which excited the sympathy of his comrades, but also, in a considerable degree, their amusement. A dish which was almost invariably served to us at breakfast was hominy. Getting it so constantly no one, of course, cared much for it unless it was very nicely prepared.

One morning the hominy was very dark in colour: it looked as if soot had fallen into it. When the meal was concluded Major Elliott called to Scott, one of the turnkeys, saying that he desired to speak with him. Scott came and asked what he wished.

"I wish to condole with you," said Elliott, "because of the death in the kitchen."

"What do you mean?" said Scott.

"I infer," Elliott replied, "that some one in the kitchen must have died because the hominy is in mourning."

This remark was esteemed sarcastic and therefore insolent, and the major was immediately escorted to the dungeon. He remained nearly twenty-four hours, and was released just before breakfast of the next day. During the meal he confided to those who sat near him that he had done a good deal of thinking in the dungeon, and had come to the conclusion that it was of little avail to a prisoner to be sulky and "kick against the pricks"; that he had made up his mind to be diplomatic and take matters amiably. In pursuance of this politic resolution he again notified Scott, when breakfast was finished, that he wanted a word with him. Scott approached, and Elliott said in a very gushing manner: "I desire to compliment and congratulate you on the excellent quality and condition of the hominy this morning. It almost reconciles a man to remain in prison to get such food."

"Very well," said Scott, "you just come along back to the dungeon."

"Back to the dungeon?" yelled Elliott; it had not occurred to him that his language might be deemed ironical and consequently impertinent. "What must I go back to the dungeon for?"

"Why," said Scott, "for what you've just said about the hominy."

"All right," said the major, very sadly; "but it's d — d hard for a man in this prison to know exactly what to say about the hominy."

Through all time, captivity has been regarded as a dire misfortune. It has been ranked in the category of evils with death itself, and considered often as one of not less magnitude. During the Civil War capture and confinement in the military prisons, where many thousands lay so long in painful durance, was more dreaded by the soldiers, Federal and Confederate, than any other hardship or hazard; and with good reasons, for it was more rigorous and almost as dangerous to life as service in the field.

If compelled the choice, I would far rather undergo all the peril and privation I knew while with the army than again endure, for even a brief period, the ordeal of the prison.

Nevertheless, inasmuch as kind providence permits some alleviation of the world's hardest lessons, even imprisonment was not altogether without it; and I can recall some personal experiences, while a prisoner, which I remember with interest and pleasure.

I was captured at Buffington's Island, at the conclusion of Morgan's raid through Indiana and Ohio, and after a short sojourn at Johnson's Island, was taken to the Ohio Penitentiary and lodged, with some sixty or seventy of my comrades, in that huge and gloomy den of malefactors — a probation which I could not esteem either reputable or agreeable. I spent several months there, subjected to treatment bad enough at best, but almost intolerable after General Morgan's escape had enhanced the suspicion, and apparently fomented the ill-will of our keepers; and then, upon the friendly intercession of some persons in the North, whose loyalty was unquestioned, I was removed to Camp Chase, one of the large prisons where a great number of Confederate soldiers were in confinement. I was paroled and allowed to go at large within the boundaries of the prison grounds; had comfortable quarters assigned me; and was treated with perfect respect by the officers of the guard stationed there, whose demeanour was very different from that of the penitentiary officials. I received, indeed, not only courtesy but kindness from Colonel Richardson, the commandant, and save for the partial restrictions upon my movements and my intense desire to get back to Dixie, was about as well off as any of my custodians.

These privileges, however, had been obtained for me without any request upon my own part, and indeed, without my knowledge that such request had been made by any one. So in two or three weeks, having become somewhat ashamed of enjoying favours and comforts denied my comrades, and finding that there was no hope of this condition leading to my exchange and return to the Confederacy, I made application that my parole should be revoked and that I should be sent back to the penitentiary. My wishes in each respect were promptly complied with.

For some reason, however, the Federal authorities decided

that I should be removed to Fort Delaware, and in two or three days an order was received by the warden of the penitentiary instructing him to turn me over to a military guard, which should proceed with me to that prison. So I was taken to the depot one frosty night in February and formally introduced to a tall, fine-looking young fellow, in a major's uniform, who informed me that he was Major Johnson, of General Heintzelman's staff, and that he was commissioned to conduct me to my intended domicile on the banks of the Delaware. He further notified me that while he would be very glad to talk with me, he had strict orders to forbid my holding any communication whatever with any other person on the journey. He had with him a guard of soldiers, whom he regarded apparently with little favour; and his manner, while perfectly courteous, was, I thought, rather "cold and distant" to me, as well as to the guard. It was not long before I ascertained the cause.

So soon as we boarded the train he peremptorily ordered the guard to go into another coach than that which we were about to occupy. He then produced a flask of excellent brandy, a package of sandwiches, and cigars, suggesting that as we would not be able to sleep comfortably, it was just as well that we should endeavour to enjoy ourselves otherwise. We proceeded, therefore, to eat, drink, and smoke together, like *bon camarades*, talking the while about various matters. The major's austere reserve, however, was maintained for some two or three hours, when it was completely dispelled by an incident which caused us both much amusement.

There were a number of Federal soldiers on the train, coming home on furlough from the Army of the Potomac. Quite a number of ministers, who had been in attendance upon a conference of their denomination held at Columbus, were also on board. Several of them were in the coach which we occupied. These gentlemen had been engaged in earnest, decorous, and, doubtless, edifying discourse, to which Johnson and I had paid little attention, until about ten o'clock, when there was an irruption from another coach of six or seven of the soldiers. They were in a hilarious mood, as soldiers on furlough usually are, but unfortunately, also about half drunk. As soon as they espied the preachers, whose dress, especially their white cravats, unmistakably identified them, the soldiers seemed smitten with an uncontrollable desire to converse with these reverend gentry, and without delay or hesitation indulged it.

One of the ministers, more elderly than the others, had taken a decided, indeed, dominant part in their previous discussions, expressing very positive opinions in rather pompous and pragmatic diction. To this gentleman a soldier, who seemed to be a leader among his comrades and was evidently a regimental wag, particularly addressed himself. He insisted on discussing theology, and boisterously demanded answers to the many grotesque religious propositions he propounded. To the intense delight of his companions, this elicited strenuous remonstrance from his victim and scathing rebuke because of his profane and flippant discourse, to all of which the unabashed persecutor responded with burlesque exhortation, and the not too delicate slang of the camp.

The preacher called for the conductor to protect him, but that functionary was either out of hearing or prudently preferred to abstain from interference, which might have induced unpleasant consequences to himself. He finally appealed to Major Johnson, and a few good-humoured but positive words from the latter obtained him relief.

Johnson and I had both been greatly amused by this episode — a feeling which the confrères of the distressed doctor of divinity had also unmistakably shared, although more within the bounds of decorum, and it served to completely break the ice between us. He then told me that he had been somewhat chagrined by the instructions he had received as to how he should deal with me. He was a very powerfully built man and in perfect physical training, and was quite proud of his prowess as an athlete, having found few peers in that respect in his native city of Boston. It seems that some of the loyal citizens of Columbus, learning of what he was about to do, had advised General Heintzelman that he should furnish the major with a strong guard, because, they represented, "this man Duke is one of Morgan's cut-throats and a very blood-thirsty desperado. If he gets a chance to do so he will cut Major Johnson's throat and make his escape, unless the major is provided with a sufficient escort."

General Heintzelman accordingly detailed half a dozen men

to accompany Johnson, much to his disgust, who declared his ability to take care of any one man single handed. When I was turned over to him at the depot, and he realized that all these precautions had been taken to enable him to safely handle a man little more than half his own size, he was ineffably humiliated, and, as L have said, virtually dismissed the guard. He expressed regret that he could not parole me, but said his orders on that score were imperative. I had no desire, however, to be paroled for the purposes of that trip, for Johnson treated me as a prisoner in nowise, further than keeping me closely by his side. I enjoyed every comfort that he had. I had no idea, either, of attempting to escape in that region and under the circumstances, no matter what opportunity might be offered. I had no overcoat and was not especially warmly clad, and would have soon frozen in the mountains unless I could have obtained shelter; and clad as I was in full Confederate uniform, and wearing a big slouched Southern hat, with a gold cord around it, I could not have escaped observation, but would certainly have been recaptured had I approached any habitation. My chance of concealment would have been even less in a town or city.

There happened to be on the train a lady whom I had known when I had lived in St. Louis, and with whose family I had been on exceedingly friendly terms. She was en route to New York with her daughter, a very pretty and attractive girl. This lady was an ardent Southern sympathizer, and learning that I was in the adjoining coach sent a gentleman who was of her party to request that she might be permitted to see me. I happened to know the envoy also quite well. He was a popular young lawyer of St. Louis, and an all-around good fellow. I was, of course, very glad to see him and receive his message, and Major Johnson quite readily consented that I should see the ladies. Just as we were about to start, my friend essayed surreptitiously to slip into my hand a roll of bank bills. As I was tolerably well provided with money at that time, and knew that I could procure more if I should need it, I declined the proffer with due thanks. I did so openly, for I felt assured that Johnson would appreciate the sentiment which dictated the intended gift and would never think of disciplining the donor. My friend, however, was terrified. He expected to be immediately arrested and thought he saw a worse fate than that which had befallen me staring him in the face. Neither Johnson nor I could help laughing at his evident dismay, but the major hastened to dispel his apprehension, saying that he was gratified to know that my friends were so kindly disposed toward me, and that he thought it was foolish in me to refuse the money which I could turn over to some other unfortunate rebel if I did not wish to use it myself.

On the next day our relations became yet more cordial, and he offered, notwithstanding his instructions, to accept my parole, which I declined to give, more on his own account than my own. When we reached Philadelphia he announced his intention of sending his guard to the barracks and of taking me with him to the hotel. I remonstrated against this, fearing that it might cause him trouble, but he was obdurate; so we went to the Continental Hotel, where, upon my suggestion, we occupied the same room, in order that if the matter should be investigated, it might appear that he had kept me under his eye.

As might have been expected, my appearance in Confederate uniform aroused a great deal of curiosity and excitement. A large crowd flocked into the office of the hotel to witness a sight so unusual, and I was subjected to many interviews.

The major, disposed apparently to go the limit of hospitality, suggested that something very interesting was on exhibition at one of the theatres, and proposed that he take me to see it. I reminded him of what had just before occurred in the hotel, and said I was averse to a similar experience at the theatre. I felt sure that he would incur, at least, a severe reprimand, and perhaps more serious punishment and was extremely unwilling that his kindness to me should bring such results.

We finally compromised by my agreeing to visit with him one of his friends in the city, to whom he was particularly attached. This gentleman, a Mr. Clement Barclay, was one of the most attractive men I ever met. I was informed that it was his habit to visit all of the great battle fields in Virginia immediately after the engagement, and institute a hospital of his own, where wounded men of both armies were cared for. I could well credit the story for benevolence and philanthropy were evinced in his look, speech, and manner.

Mr. Barclay received us with effusion, ordered supper, and straightway sent for two or three of his friends to meet us. In due time these gentlemen, who, by the way, were Federal officers, came in, and we proceeded to discuss a supper which to a man fresh from penitentiary fare, seemed like a feast fit for the gods. Our session was prolonged pleasantly until late in the night, and on the next morning Major Johnson proceeded to Fort Delaware, where he duly deposited and took a receipt for his prisoner.

In the course of two or three weeks he returned, this time with a number of prisoners, and demanded to see me. After very cordial greeting on both sides, I said: "Major, did you give these fellows as good a time as you gave me?"

"No," he answered, emphatically; "I did not, and I'm inclined to think that if it was to be gone over again, I would not treat you quite so well. Why, I've been under a hotter fire on your account than I ever saw in the field. Those newspaper fellows in Philadelphia tried to make people believe that you and I and Clem Barclay were hatching rebellion in the Quaker City. I have a stack of letters as high as my hat about the matter, and all red hot."

The major, however, got through all right, and I have always gratefully remembered his courtesy.

It may be readily understood, even by those who have had no personal experience in such wise, or have not listened to the stories told by those whose experience of prison life has left lasting recollections of it, that men will resort to every possible expedient to relieve the tedium and ennui of captivity. Such was the case in the military prisons during the war, as I have already said, the wiser and more prudent sought solace or oblivion of their unfortunate condition in healthy employment of some sort; in carving trinkets or in the yet saner and more absorbing enjoyments of literature. Some devoted themselves (thinking, or, at least, hoping, that it might prove useful in the future) to military study; others preferred the dime novel, or, looking forward to exile from their native country as the possible sequel of Confederate defeat, applied themselves assiduously to acquiring a knowledge of the languages they would be required to understand and speak in the lands where they might find refuge.

No man, perhaps, could enumerate the many devices, more or less ingenious and partially successful, which the Confederate prisoners invented to make tolerable their dreary days, weeks, and months of confinement, and bridge over the intervals when they were not planning escape or discussing the chances of exchange.

However painful or mortifying may be the admission, it must nevertheless be admitted — for the fact is entirely too well remembered and attested to be ignored — that a very considerable number of the sufferers succeeded in obtaining relief, more nearly than by aught else, in an almost exclusive devotion to the fickle goddess of fortune. The fascination of the "pictorial pasteboards," in their various and entrancing combinations, or other games of chance then current which yielded like excitement, afforded them the needed occupation and held them in hypnotic thraldom.

Confederate money, to be sure, was the only currency they could stake, but that, by a fond fiction of the fancy, passed with them as money. It had no purchasing power in the prisons, but its possession appealed to the imagination; even when a man had no money he was allowed to play on credit, and it was a point of honour with them to rate every comrade's credit as being quite up to the standard of Confederate money. So the game was open to all and every one could feel the gambler's fire and share the gambler's hope.

One of the largest Federal prisons was Fort Delaware, situated not far from the mouth of the river of that name. When I was a prisoner there, in the spring and early summer of 1864, its inmates numbered several thousand. I, with some thirty or forty others, was confined in the casemates of the fort, but was frequently permitted by the courtesy of the commanding officer, General Schoepf, a fine, stalwart, kindly old Hungarian, to visit the barracks, where there was a great multitude of captive Confederates, including quite a number of my own command captured upon the Ohio raid. Indeed, all the armies of the Confederacy were represented in this host. There were men from the Army of Northern Virginia, from the Army of Tennessee and from the Army of the trans-Mississippi, while every errant and unattached Confederate organization seemed to have sent delegates, who answered at the daily roll-call. There were representatives from every state in the South — from the Ohio River to the Rio Grande, from Kentucky, Maryland, and Missouri, and not a few of Northern birth, who yet wore the Confederate gray, and were as ardently Southern as any of those in whose veins coursed the blood of Virginia or South Carolina.

Among these latter was a captain in the Second Kentucky cavalry — the regiment which Gen. John H. Morgan had first commanded. He was a native of New Jersey, but had come to Kentucky in early life, and had entered the Confederate service when Morgan organized the squadron with which he commenced his career. A thoroughly courageous man, he was also exceedingly intelligent as an officer. No one was more skilled and successful at cards, and, in prison at least, he found such attraction irresistible. Before he had been at Fort Delaware a month he had demonstrated his superiority in this line over all competitors. But not content with individual excellence and victory, he aspired, with the instinct of a born organizer, to extend his operations and utilize the labour of others who should be his subordinates. So he converted the particular barrack in which he was quartered into an extensive gaming saloon, where games of short cards might be played by the more scholarly, who preferred the lucubrations of science to the mere outcome of luck, while a dozen or more faro and keno tables were exhibited for the delectation of those who were satisfied with a less intelligent gratification. Over each of these he appointed one of his room mates as dealer, and himself officiated as general manager.

Of course his "house" was crowded with visitors from reveille to taps; all ranks and arms — infantry, cavalry, and artillery, quartermasters and commissaries of subsistence — appeared upon the field and actively participated in the engagements.

But the captain, with all of his fondness for certain forms of relaxation, at the same time entertained an acute sense of propriety. He was not only inclined to strenuously inhibit upon the part of others any act which might "offend the most fastidious," but he liked to show decent respect to those opinions and customs by which social morality and order are preserved. He had also been piously brought up in a strictly religious family. He therefore never permitted gaming on his premises during the forenoon of the Sabbath. On the contrary, he invariably had the large room cleaned up and properly arranged on Sunday morning for religious services, and invited some pious and eloquent exhorter to conduct them. It was his wont on such occasions to act as usher and assist as far as he could; nothing could have been more edifying than his devout expression of countenance and decorous manner.

But accidents will happen sometimes, even though the most perfect system and best regulations are attempted. The captain learned one day that two ministers of the gospel were among a fresh batch of captured rebels, who had just arrived at the prison, and hastened to pay his respects to them. After offering all the assistance in his power, he warmly urged them to come to his barrack on the following Sunday and conduct divine service, saying that there would be an interested audience to hear them.

The gentlemen accepted the invitation, but unfortunately mistook the hour indicated and came in the afternoon instead of the morning. They found a crowd there, but it was apparently not animated by the kind of feeling they had expected, and it was engaged in the performance of, to them, strange and not seemly rites. It is to be regretted that the captain was not present, for his ingenuity and readiness might have suggested some sort of explanation. But he had been called away, and had left in his place a lieutenant, who, while thoroughly conversant with the regular business of the establishment, was totally unfitted to handle so delicate a situation. This party approached the strangers, so soon as they entered, begged them to make themselves at home and to "take a hand."

In considerable amazement, the reverend gentlemen explained that they had come in response to an invitation extended them by the captain to assist in the services which were in progress. The unexampled idiot at once conceived the idea that they were two new dealers whom the captain had employed, and affably remarked: "Oh, very well, thar's a faro and a keno table both idle; take charge of them."

The indignation of the ministers, when it finally dawned upon them what sort of place they had gotten into, was, of course, extreme, and they naturally felt that they had been insulted.

But their anger was mild and milky compared with that of the captain when he learned what had happened.

"You blamed wedge-headed ape," he said to the offending lieutenant, "with a hunk of mouldy limburger cheese where your brains ought to be, couldn't you see that those gentlemen were preachers?"

"No, I couldn't," answered the other, himself much aggrieved, "you didn't tell me anything about them, and I thought from their looks that they belonged to the profesh."

In the summer of 1864, a rumour reached Washington to the effect that fifty Federal officers of various grades, prisoners in the Confederate hands, had been placed at Charleston — then closely besieged and fiercely bombarded — in a situation which exposed them to the fire of the Federal fleet. Crediting this report, the Federal authorities at once issued orders that fifty Confederate prisoners of corresponding rank, should be taken to Charleston — or rather as near thereto as possible — and exposed, in retaliation, to the fire of the Confederate batteries.

Thus, by a novel turn of fortune, these soldiers of the South were selected — although, happily, not destined — to serve their flag, under the fire of their own comrades.

Intended, as I have said, to correspond officially with the reported Federal roster, four general officers headed the Confederate list: Maj.-Gen. Franklin Gardner, of Louisiana; Maj.-Gen. Edward Johnson, of Virginia; Brig.-Gen. George H. Stewart, of Maryland; and Brig.-Gen. M. Jeff. Thomson, of Missouri. The list of fifty was completed by the addition of a number of colonels, majors, and captains. It was made almost entirely from prisoners confined at Fort Delaware, and I was so lucky as matters turned out, to be on it.

It may seem somewhat strange to the reader born and reared in post-bellum times, when I say that all of these who were selected for this apparent holocaust were exceedingly gratified and deemed themselves fortunate. In the first place, wearied with the monotony of prison life, they were inclined to welcome anything in the nature of change and variety. Nor were they really alarmed by the prospect of getting within the range of heavy artillery. Some of them had learned from personal experience, many others from hearsay, that while the shells from the big guns can inflict terrible havoc when they burst where damage may be done, they do not often hit such spots; that at any rate the loss of life occasioned by them is comparatively trivial.

But our chief reason for regarding the matter with little or no apprehension was the fact that none of us believed the truth of the report that the Federal prisoners had been placed under fire. We, therefore, had no fear that we ourselves would be subjected to any such ordeal, but, on the contrary, hoped that, when the true state of affairs became known, an exchange of the members of the respective details would be arranged; and for the sake of such a result we would very gladly have encountered a much more serious risk. We, therefore, started upon this excursion in high spirits, and with most pleasant anticipations which were, for once, destined to be realized.

We were placed on board of a steamer which had previously been in the coasting trade, but which, at the time of which I write, was employed by the United States government as a transport. Steaming down the Delaware River and out into the ocean, we ran for two or three days down the Atlantic coast, during which nothing occurred to impress the voyage on our remembrance except a sharp squall of wind and rain, that struck the steamer just as she rounded Cape Hatteras. The sailors thought it a small affair, but the greater number of our party, who, if not exactly "honest farmers," had yet no experience of the sea, considered it quite a tempest. The waves seemed to us to be leaping to a very great height, and the vessel to be sinking to a dangerous depth; and many would have preferred the bombardment with which we were threatened to the watery grave that was apparently more imminent. Sea-sickness, however, soon quieted all such apprehension, and for several agonizing hours the sufferers cared very little whether the ship reached its destination or went to the bottom.

Instead of being taken on to Charleston we were stopped at Hilton Head, and there transferred to the brig *Dragoon*, a sailing vessel of about four hundred tons burthen, which was also in the service of the government. The reason for this change of programme, or at least delay in its execution, was, as we subsequently learned, that the Federal authorities had discovered that the information given them was erroneous, and the Federal prisoners had not been put where they would receive the fire of the fleet. Of course, when it was ascertained that there was no cause for retaliation, the order that we should be placed under the fire of the Confederate batteries was revoked, and it was decided that we should be detained at Hilton Head until a conclusion should be reached as to the final disposition to be made of us.

We remained here some two or three weeks, and the situation could scarcely be described as a pleasant one; for confinement between decks on a small vessel during the hot nights of that climate was not at all comfortable, especially as the ports were all kept closed, lest perhaps some of us might squeeze through them in an effort to escape. Nevertheless, taking all things into consideration, we were much better satisfied than we had been at Fort Delaware. The now reasonable expectation of exchange and bright hope of liberty and return to Dixie would have been ample compensation for any privation or discomfort.

Although kept below at night, we were permitted to remain on deck during the daytime from an early hour in the morning until after dark; but were always closely guarded. Soldiers were constantly on board the brig, and boats, with armed crews from the men-of-war lying in the harbour, surrounded her by night. The *Dragoon* was anchored immediately under the guns of the United States frigate *Wabash*, which seemed to watch the little prison ship as a bull-dog might eye a tramp. One night the *Dragoon* was driven from her moorings by a violent storm and drifted quite a mile away from her grim and jealous guardian. Early the next morning her captain received word from the *Wabash* that he must return without delay to his former anchorage, and that disobedience or any lack of diligence would be punished by a broadside from the big frigate. The guards were even more alarmed by this threat than were the prisoners, and the captain and crew made strenuous haste to execute the order.

Our favourite amusement was fishing, and especially catching sharks, which swarmed about the brig. In this the sailors aided and gave us lessons. Although we saw some of much greater size, the largest shark that we caught was only about five feet in length. This fellow, after taking the hook, plunged and fought with marvellous strength and tenacity, dashing through the waves in every direction. Two men were required to hold the line and prevent his escape, and when, after a pull of ten or fifteen minutes, he was finally drawn to the ship, it was only by the united efforts of half a dozen men that he could be hauled over the side. When on deck he lashed viciously with his tail and snapped at every thing in his vicinity, continuing to struggle even after the soldiers had riddled him with bullets and his back had been hammered with an axe. If any prisoner had previously contemplated attempting a swim for freedom he completely abandoned the idea after witnessing that exhibition.

The usual avidity for rumours and gossip which characterized prison life prevailed on the *Dragoon*, and the guards became as much infected by that spirit as we were. One day an absurd report was circulated that Mrs. Lincoln, having driven with an insufficient escort to a dangerous distance from Washington, had been captured by some of Mosby's cavalry and was a prisoner at Richmond. For a day or two speculation regarding how and for whom she would be exchanged was at fever heat. Finally, a certain Captain Wilson, a bright, inventive Irishman, who was of our party, announced that he had overheard a conversation held by the crew of one of the guard boats, which enabled him to furnish a solution of this question, and that it would be extremely gratifying to all of us. He said that arrangements had been made to exchange Mrs. Lincoln for our comrade and friend, Gen. M. Jeff. Thompson. General Thompson sternly demanded to know what he meant by such a statement. Wilson affably replied that he had gathered enough from the conversation to which he had listened to feel sure that the negotiations would be consummated without difficulty or delay. "We all know," he said, "that in exchange of prisoners, an effort is always made to effect it with as due regard as possible to equality of rank and condition of the parties to be exchanged. The Confederate government raised the point that Mrs. Lincoln is not a general — has not that titular rank at any rate. The Federal authorities admit that this is true, 'but,' they urge, 'General Thompson is such a lady.'" Somehow this explanation, instead of appeasing General Thompson's ire, seemed to aggravate it.

As we had hoped and believed, a special exchange of our party for the fifty Federal prisoners was at length arranged, and one bright morning we were removed to a fine steamer and borne away for Charleston. Comfortable berths were given us and we were practically unguarded. We passed through the great fleet lying in front of the city and noted, more curiously than any other craft, the "Monitors," of which there was then such frequent mention; of these there were some twenty-five or thirty that we could see and numerous indentations in their turrets, evidently made by shot from great guns, showed that they had seen service.

After the customary formalities had been gone through with and the exchange completed, a banquet was given the prisoners on both sides, in which the officers conducting the exchange and some of the officers of the fleet participated. To the Confederates and doubtless to the others so long accustomed to prison fare, this feast seemed ambrosial, almost incredible, and was done ample justice. We then went on board of a small Confederate boat and steamed down the harbour toward the city. It had been agreed that all real firing should be suspended for the day, both by the fleet and the Confederate batteries, but, in honour of the occasion, the big guns on both sides boomed out thunderous salutes when the exchange was concluded.

The generous, warm-hearted people of Charleston gave us a cordial, hospitable welcome, and their courage and ardour seemed in no whit abated by the bombardment and the other hazards of a siege. We were assigned to the houses of prominent citizens and delightfully entertained.

With five or six others I was quartered that night, at the residence of Major Huger. We were sitting, after supper, on the veranda, where quite a number of visitors were also collected, busily engaged in telling our prison experience or intently listening to narratives of the siege. About eight or nine o'clock, a tremendous roar came from the fleet, succeeded soon after by detonations almost as loud, as the shells dropped in the various parts of the town. The bombardment had been renewed, and immediately our guns began to answer. The thing was so unexpected to me — for I had forgotten that the firing was to be renewed at nightfall — that I was quite startled and sprang to my feet with an exclamation of surprise, and I rather think of alarm. "Sit down, colonel," said Major Huger, with a laugh, "we'll not let you be hurt; not one of those shells dropped within a half mile of us."

"Well, major," I replied, "I hope you are correct, but with all deference to your superior knowledge, I think at least one of those fellows burst within ten feet of my chair."

All feeling of disquiet, however, soon wore away, and the new comers were beginning to take matters as coolly as the more experienced, when suddenly a deafening, appalling explosion — as it seemed to me — rang out apparently in the very lawn. I again arose.

"Gentlemen," I said, "you must really excuse me this time. I want to take to the woods."

There was another laugh at my expense, and they explained that the sound which had so terrified me had been the bellow of the "Swamp Angel," the biggest of our own guns.

On the next day we were given transportation to our respective destinations, and after some hours, which in my impatient anxiety, however, seemed more like years, I was again with my wife and little boy, and found there another baby, a little girl I had never seen before, for she had been born while I was a prisoner.

CHAPTER XVIII

WHEN, in April, 1865, the Confederate troops in the department of south-western Virginia, under Gen. John C. Echols, then on their way to effect a junction with the army of General Lee, learned of the surrender at Appomattox, the surprise and consternation thus occasioned could scarcely have been greater had they seen the sun suddenly blotted out of the heavens. During the night following the reception of the dreadful news, officers and men rushed about wildly through the respective camps in a frenzy of excitement. No man slept; all were in eager but futile conference, and every conceivable plan of action which could in anywise fit the emergency was suggested and discussed.

On the next day General Echols convened a council of war, composed of his brigade commanders, and, after some consultation, issued an order furloughing for sixty days the men of the infantry regiments, with the understanding that if at the expiration of that time the Confederacy was still in existence, they should return to the ranks. He directed the commanders of the cavalry brigades to hold themselves prepared to march immediately to join the forces under Gen. Joseph E. Johnston.

General Vaughn's brigade, therefore, and mine commenced the march to North Carolina. The greater number of my horses had been sent thither during the previous winter on account of the scarcity of forage in south-western Virginia and had not yet returned; and having recently been joined by many of the Morgan men just out of prison, I was compelled to mount my command on mules taken from the wagon trains which General Echols was compelled to abandon. Six or seven hundred mules were turned over to me for that purpose. Notwithstanding this assistance I was unable to mount a considerable number of the men who had just reported for duty. These brave fellows having obtained rifles from the furloughed infantry-men, wished to follow the column on foot, and I had some difficulty to prevent them from doing so.

The troops, when this march began, were naturally dejected by the great disaster of which they had just learned, but after a few days of rapid and evidently purposeful movement their spirit and courage were perfectly restored, and they were not only willing, but anxious, to try conclusions with the Federal cavalry, which was reported to be between us and General Johnston and determined to bar our further progress. The point at which we expected, but least desired, to meet them, was at "Fancy Gap," a defile in the mountains which skirt the border line between Virginia and North Carolina in the region we were traversing, and through which ran the road on which we were marching.

While the scenery of this locality is unusually picturesque and impressive, the gap was the last place which we would have chosen as a battle ground. It is a sort of natural gateway between the two states, situated at the extremity of one of the most rugged spurs of the Alleghany range; and the country for many miles to the west of it, while so broken as to be difficult of access, can scarcely be termed mountainous. But the road through it, little wider at any point than is necessary to permit wagons approaching from different directions to pass, winds directly under a tall mountain whose bare, precipitous sides soar sheer upward to a very great height. On the other hand, the natural wall goes right down in dizzy descent to a depth which appalls the eye seeking to fathom it. The region immediately to the west of the road is an immense depression in the mountain range, seeming to have been by some convulsion of nature sunken to a level with the plain at the foot of the hills. If there are breaks in this shell they cannot be detected by one gazing from the road over the wide expanse. The view, comprising many miles in every direction, was, at the season of the year we saw it, extremely attractive. The low-lying valley was covered with a dense forest, but the trees, although doubtless large, were dwindled in the deep distance to the apparent dimensions of the smallest shrubs. The varied vegetation, just in the richest foliage of spring, waved beneath us in every shade of green. The western end of the valley was shrouded in a glimmering haze.

Col. J. Stoddard Johnston, General Echols's chief of staff,

after giving General Vaughn and myself, before we entered the pass, such instructions as might be necessary to govern our conduct if we encountered an enemy, supplemented them with a battle order of incomparable brevity and clearness:

> "Now, if the Yankees, d — n their eyes,
> Shall seek to take us by surprise,
> And hope to catch us in a nap
> As we file through this Fancy Gap;
> Wycher will skirmish to the front,
> While Duke and Vaughn abide the brunt,
> Meanwhile, the old Tycoon and staff
> Will mount a hill apart and laugh."

Very much to the satisfaction of all concerned, "Tycoon," staff, and troops, there were no Yankees in the gap when we reached it.

We crossed the Yadkin River on the second day after entering North Carolina, and on the next day reached Statesville. Here General Echols left us to report personally to General Johnston, who was supposed to be at Salisbury. Vaughn marched in the direction of Morgantown, and I pressed on toward Lincolnton, where I hoped to find the horses of my brigade and the detail in charge of them, under Colonel Napier, which had been sent during the winter to that point. We were compelled to cross the Catawba River by marching on the top of the covered railroad bridge, a tedious and somewhat hazardous undertaking, especially when attempted with mules.

I had by this time obtained credible information that the Federal cavalry, of whose proximity we had heard rumours, were now not far away, and were also marching in the direction of Lincolnton, which was about twenty miles distant. I was anxious to be first there, fearing that, if the enemy anticipated me, horses and detail guarding them might be captured or driven completely beyond my reach. In an hour or two I discovered that the Federal cavalry was marching upon another road leading to Lincolnton, parallel with that on which I was moving and some three miles to the west of it.

Our prospective scouts came in contact upon every by-road and trace connecting the two roads, and I soon found, to my great disgust, that my men were not holding their own as well as they had been accustomed to do in that style of fighting. When I inquired the reason, every fellow said it was the fault of his "infernal mule," which could not possibly be induced to behave reasonably in action or conduct himself creditably under fire.

I did not succeed in reaching Lincolnton before the enemy, who, however, did not succeed in capturing my horses. Colonel Napier, in command of the detail guarding them, got them all safely away and joined me the next day on the road to Charlotte.

We found one or two other brigades of cavalry at Charlotte and a great many paroled infantry soldiers and a host of small officials who had fled from Richmond. Mr. Davis shortly afterward arrived, escorted by the cavalry brigades of General Debrell and Col. W. C. P. Breckinridge. In the course of a speech made by Mr. Davis to the soldiers and citizens who assembled to greet him, he was handed a despatch announcing the assassination of Mr. Lincoln. He read it to the crowd, but, so far as I can remember, did not comment on it at all and, indeed, did not seem to credit its accuracy.

Gen. John C. Breckinridge, then secretary of war, was not with Mr. Davis when the latter reached Charlotte, although the other members of the cabinet accompanied him. General Breckinridge had been detained to assist Gen. Joseph E. Johnston in the conference held with General Sherman, which resulted in the armistice that was so promptly disavowed by the authorities at Washington.

Much to the joy of the Kentuckians General Breckinridge came to Charlotte about two days later. On the next morning he rode with me to my camp, and the men, who were warmly attached to him, gave him an enthusiastic welcome. He responded with one of those brief, felicitous speeches which no one else could make so well. At its conclusion he seated himself at the foot of a large tree and talked for more than an hour with the men who crowded around him, the majority of whom were personally known to him or were the sons of his old friends. Great curiosity was, of course, felt to learn something of the terms of the agreement with Sherman, and he answered all questions with perfect frankness. While this was going on an incident occurred which was the strangest combination of the ludicrous and the heroic I ever witnessed. A soldier of my command, who had not heard the general's speech or any part of his subsequent conversation, rode up on the sauciest-looking mule I ever saw, and, saluting and then tucking his ragged hat under his arm, begged leave to propound certain inquiries. He was a handsome, manly fellow, apparently about nineteen or twenty years of age.

"General Breckinridge," he said, "is it true that you have concluded negotiations which contemplate the surrender of all Confederate soldiers on this side of the Mississippi river?"

"It is true," was the response, "and I think the terms are such as all should accept."

"Do you think, general, that any terms of surrender are honourable and should be accepted?"

"I do, or I certainly should not have endorsed them."

"Well, I do not, and shall accept no terms," asserted the indomitable youth, drawing himself up yet more stiffly while the fire of a quenchless spirit flamed from his gray eye and lighted up every lineament. At the same time the mule, as if in full accord with his master, stuck out his forefeet, threw up his head, and snorted defiance. No man ever gazed on a more independent and irrepressible looking couple than this mule and his rider.

"I regret that," said the general, "and your comrades here, who are all good soldiers, do not agree with you."

"I can't help that," retorted the champion. "They may do as they please. But the sun shines as bright and the air is as pure on the other side of the Rio Grande as here, and I'll go there rather than surrender to any Yankee."

A hearty and general laugh, as much however of admiration as amusement, greeted this spirited declaration. The young knight was not abashed.

> "Round turned he, as not deigning
> Those craven ranks to see,"

and tossing his arm in the air while the mule tossed its tail, he cantered off as if determined to reach the Rio Grande before night.

In the course of a day or two information was received that

the Sherman-Johnston armistice and treaty would not be recognized by the Federal government, and we learned also that nearly every other Confederate force on the eastern side of the Mississippi, with the exception of those at Charlotte, had surrendered. Mr. Davis, therefore, and his cabinet, with the five brigades commanded respectively by General Debrell, General Ferguson, General Vaughn, Colonel Breckinridge and myself, as an escort all under command of Gen. John C. Breckinridge, left Charlotte and marched in the direction of Washington, Georgia.

I have never been able to form a positive opinion as to what Mr. Davis's real purpose was at that date. It was perfectly manifest to every one else that there was no hope of further successful resistance. Yet at Abbeville, S. C., he called together the commanders of the several brigades escorting him, and in a spirited and exceedingly eloquent speech urged a continued prosecution of the war. He seemed sorely disappointed when they declined to destroy all hope of procuring favourable terms of surrender for their men by consenting to such a policy, and informed him that they were still keeping the field only to enable him and the members of his cabinet to effect their escape.

There was much speculation among the men in regard to the chances of the president and the different cabinet officers to escape capture, and many guesses were made as to which of them would do so.

It was the general opinion that Mr. Davis could escape if he really wished to do so, but we feared that his pride would prevent his making the attempt. We all felt confident that Breckinridge would not be made prisoner if duty permitted him an effort to get away. As Judge Reagan had been a frontiersman and Texas ranger, the men thought his chance a good one. But all believed Benjamin would certainly be caught, and all deplored it, for he had made himself extremely popular. For some days he rode with us, always smiling, pleasant, and mixing and talking freely with the soldiers. Then he suddenly and unaccountably disappeared. No one seemed to know what had become of him. When we next heard of him he was practising law in London.

At the Savannah River, Mr. Davis ordered a portion of the

treasure which had been brought from Richmond to be paid to the troops composing his escort, and about one hundred and ten thousand dollars was thus distributed. The next day Mr. Davis, apparently yielding to the importunities of his followers, that he should attempt escape, set off from Washington with a select body of men, about twenty strong, commanded by Capt. Given Campbell, of Kentucky, one of the best officers in the cavalry service. I have no doubt that, had he really wished to escape, Mr. Davis with this guard, could easily have done so. But I have always believed that he regarded the thought with horror, deeming it a disgrace to one who had occupied his exalted position. His speech and manner, whenever the subject was mentioned in his presence, clearly indicated this feeling.

Immediately after Mr. Davis's departure the brigade commanders were notified that they should, as soon as possible, have their men surrender and be paroled. General Breckinridge, however, requested me to hold two hundred or three hundred of my men, and proceed with them on a two or three days' march in directions which might divert the attention of the numerous bodies of Federal cavalry, which were in the immediate vicinity, from that which Mr. Davis had taken. In pursuance of these instructions I marched with about two hundred of my men until I reached a little place called Woodstock.

Here I found myself directly confronted by a very superior force of Federal cavalry. I halted, having no wish, of course, to fight. In a short time a staff officer came, bearing a flag of truce and inquired for the officer commanding my detachment, and was immediately brought to me. He said that he had been sent by the officer commanding the Federal force in my front, whose name I have forgotten, to request that I would do nothing to bring on an engagement, for any further bloodshed was much to be regretted.

"My chief," said the staff officer, "instructs me to say that you can go in a northern, southern, or eastern direction, and that in such case he will give you a free path; but he says that if you attempt to march westwardly, he will be compelled, under his orders, to attack you."

"Lieutenant," I responded, "please say to Gen. ——, with my compliments, that I am obliged for his message, and agree with him that no more blood should be shed. Say that I may go south, north, or east, but I certainly shall not go west."

That afternoon Colonel Breckinridge joined me, bearing a message from the general to the effect that all had been done to assist Mr. Davis that was possible, and that he advised me to make immediate arrangements for surrender.

Perhaps there are few men besides myself still living who remember the distribution of specie at the Savannah River which I have mentioned.

I myself have a very vivid recollection of this event, and of all the circumstances attending the care and transportation of the fund of which this specie was part; for I was, very much against my will, made its chief custodian from Abbeville, S. C., to Washington, Ga., and in that capacity passed two or three days and nights of as unpleasant solicitude as ever befell me in the whole course of my life.

On the afternoon on which occurred that conference between Mr. Davis and the commanders of the five brigades which constituted the escort, which I have already described, and which those who attended it have been accustomed to term the "last Confederate council of war," Gen. John C. Breckinridge who was then secretary of war, and also actually commanding the troops in attendance upon Mr. Davis, gave instructions to the brigades to be prepared to resume our march in the direction of Washington at midnight. About ten o'clock I received a message from him to the effect that he desired to see me immediately about a very important matter. When I reported to him, he informed me that a considerable amount of treasure, which had been brought from Richmond, was at the railroad station, and said that it was necessary to provide for its removal and transportation along with the escort, and that he wished me to take charge of it. He instructed me to procure a sufficient number of wagons for the purpose and to detail a guard of fifty men under a field officer for its protection, but required me to personally supervise every thing that should be done. This was by no means an agreeable duty, especially as the general frankly stated that he did not know, and that perhaps no one knew, the exact amount of the fund, but that he believed it to be between five and six hundred thousand dollars in specie much the greater part in gold.

I represented that if no one knew what the sum was it was a very unpleasant responsibility to impose on an officer required to take charge of it. It would be impossible for me, in the limited time allowed, to count the money, or even approximately estimate its amount, nor could I be sure that the entire amount would be turned over to me. An exceedingly disagreeable question might arise, therefore, if a discrepancy should be subsequently asserted about the sum which so changed hands. He responded that all of this had been considered; that it was unfortunate, but unavoidable, and bade me immediately to proceed to execute the order.

I detailed fifty picked men as a guard and placed them under command of Col. Theophilus Steele and four of my best lieutenants, and, having obtained six wagons, began at once the work of loading them with the treasure. It was in charge, when I commenced the work, of some fifteen or twenty employés of the Confederate treasury department, and I could not, of course, exclude these men from the cars, because my men had to receive the treasure from them. While, therefore, guards posted at the open doors of the box cars, which contained the specie, prevented the entrance of all parties not engaged in handling it, there were so many of these, and they were so crowded in the narrow space that some of them might have appropriated a considerable sum and the others have not been aware of it.

I have never learned what was the exact amount of this treasure. It included, I believe, the Tennessee state school fund and some two hundred and seventy-five thousand dollars belonging to Richmond banks, and was all in gold and silver. It was packed in money belts, shot bags, a few small iron chests and wooden boxes, some of them of the frailest description. I searched through the cars by the light of a few tallow candles, and gathered up all that was shown me or that I could find. More than an hour was occupied in transferring the treasure from the cars to the wagons, and after the latter had been started off and had gotten perhaps half a mile away, Lieut. John B. Cole, one of the officers of the guard, rode up to me and handed over a pine box which apparently contained between two thousand and three thousand dollars in gold. After the rest of us had left the cars he had remained and continued the search, and in a car which we thought we had thoroughly examined he had discovered this box, stuck in a corner and covered up with a piece of brown sacking.

On the next day, at my urgent request, General Breckinridge directed that the guard should be increased to two hundred men, and he ordered me personally to command it. I suggested that, instead of composing it entirely of men of my brigade, it should be constituted of details from all five. I believed this would be the best method of preventing jealousy and suspicion among the men of the escort, as well as insure greater vigilance. I felt quite sure that these details would closely watch each other. This plan was adopted. Nearly the entire guard was kept constantly on duty, day and night, and at every halt a majority of the escort was generally collected about the wagons, closely watching the guards.

At the Savannah River Mr. Davis ordered that the silver coin, amounting to one hundred and eight or ten thousand dollars, should be paid to the troops in partial discharge of the arrears of pay due them. This was accordingly done. The quartermasters of the several brigades sat up during the night counting and dividing the money, and prorating it in proportion to the rosters of their respective commands. This procedure elicited a lively interest among the prospective beneficiaries of the distribution. A throng of men surrounded the little frame house where the money was being counted until after daybreak, and the windows were blocked with the eager faces of the interested expectants. The men had seen and received Confederate money in abundance for two or three years previously, but real money had been almost unknown to them. There is something gratifying to human nature in the receipt of even depreciated currency, and to get hard cash was inexpressibly agreeable. The men of my brigade received thirty-two dollars per capita, officers and men sharing alike. General Breckinridge was paid that sum, and was, for the purpose, borne on the roll of my brigade. At Washington, Ga., on the next day, I turned over what was left of the treasure to Mr. M. H. Clarke, acting treasurer of the Confederate states, and was very glad to get rid of it.

Mr. Clarke lived for many years after the war in Clarksville, Tenn., and was one of the most successful business men in that prosperous little city.

Mr. Davis, for some reason, gave orders that General Bragg and his staff should be paid each a month's pay in gold; a discrimination which occasioned some complaint among those who were not so fortunate. I was present when Mr. Clarke made this specific distribution, and listened to a homily from one of the staff officers, which was rather amusing because of the seemingly inconsistent demand with which it was concluded. General Bragg's ordnance officer was a major, or lieutenant-colonel — Olladowski — I am not sure of the exact rank, nor indeed that I have spelled the name correctly. He was an efficient officer, but not popular, because of his peppery disposition and his curt way of dealing with those who had business with him. The cavalry were especially "down on" him because of a story that had been current for some time among them. It was reported that when a certain cavalry command had sent in a requisition for ammunition for small-arms, he had returned it with the endorsement:

"Commanding General Say. No more issue of ammunition to de cavalry. De cavalry swap off de ammunition for de butter and de egg."

On this occasion, while Mr. Clarke was engaged in counting out the gold which was to be paid Major Olladowksi, the latter suddenly, and somewhat to the surprise of all his auditors, broke out into a fierce tirade against the precious metal. "Blank, blank de filthy stuff," he said; "I wish it had never been digged out of de bowels of de earth. It tempt a man to every evil. It make him false to his friend, to his brudder, to his fader. It make him do all mean and bad acts. I hate de sight of it." Just then Clarke pushed over to him one hundred and fifty dollars, thinking that to be the sum due him. But Olladowski was prompt to make correction. "Fifteen dollar more, eef you blease, Misser Clarke," he quickly suggested. "My pay is $165 per month."

Mr. Clarke did not retain possession and charge of the fund very long, for in two or three days afterward the entire Confederate government was dissolved and its former officials fugitives.

I never learned what ultimately became of the money, but for months afterward, I understand, there was a good deal of interest, if not excitement, in that part of the country about it. I believe that there were rumours current to the effect that it had been buried, and that parties were organizing to search for it. Perhaps some such legend will linger in that region for years to come.

The experience of the disbanded Confederate soldiers, who, after the final surrender, made their way back to their homes, or sought other destinations, was in some instances interesting and was varied by circumstances, depending a good deal upon the temper and disposition of the officials to whom they directly surrendered, and to some extent, doubtless, on their respective ability to take care of themselves. Some encountered very little trouble or inconvenience; others met with a large share of both. Nearly every man among them has a different story to tell about it, and, just as his own personal experience happened to be, remembers it with good humour or resentment. While the greater number in each department surrendered in a body, entire organizations being paroled together, there were many who did so individually or in small parties.

The terms conceded the soldiers of the Army of Northern Virginia were more favourable than those received by other Confederates, and General Grant insisted very positively upon their strict observance. The paroles issued to all were made out, I believe, in the same form, guaranteeing the recipient the right to return to his home and remain there unmolested so long as he obeyed the laws of the United States and of the state in which he resided. But other conditions than those specified in the printed form — some of them very galling — were occasionally imposed by the officers issuing the paroles; and this was done, probably, without authority either from the government or the military commanders, but dictated solely by the discretion or caprice of subordinates. There is the more reason for supposing this to have been the case, because the conditions were quite variant, some being reasonable and some absolutely harsh and unnecessarily offensive.

One of the requirements exacted in some instances was that, after giving his parole, the Confederate should also take the oath of allegiance to the government of the United States. It seems rather strange now, that any one should have objected to this additional test. Reason for the reluctance of some of the men to submit to it, however, was to be found, first, in the fact that the taking of such an oath during the continuance of the war had been held equivalent to desertion; and, secondly, they seemed to regard it as an abjuration of all they had formerly believed and professed. It was unreasonable, nevertheless, to require it, inasmuch as the obligations of the parole, if faithfully observed, imported the rendition of such allegiance. Many of those who obstinately refused to take the oath were confined in the stockades which had been erected at different points, and detained until released by order of officers of higher rank whose attention was called to the matter. A frequent condition imposed was that the paroled soldier should discard his uniform, or at least cover the buttons of his coat or jacket with cloth; when, as was usually the case, the doffing of his ragged uniform would have necessitated his appearing very nearly in the garb of nature. It was hard to understand how the uniform or the buttons could threaten serious detriment to constituted authority or the flag, when the man who wore them was unprovided with a weapon; but military reasoning, when exercised by the occupants of "bomb-proof" positions, is not always easy to follow. Of course there are men in every army who, lacking the more generous spirit of the soldier, are eager to display, at the expense of the vanquished and the prisoner, a zeal and prowess they never direct against an armed foe.

I was so fortunate as to avoid all such unpleasant complications, and got through with the procedure and formalities necessary to the abandonment of military and the resumption of civil life, without being subjected to any treatment which I could justly describe as being either humiliating or uncomfortable. After Mr. Davis had quitted the five brigades which had constituted his escort from Charlotte, N. C., to Washington, Ga., and General Breckinridge, commander of the escort and secretary of war, had instructed us all to surrender, I rode with the members of my staff, and a few others, across the country to Augusta, where I and my party surrendered and were paroled. We then proceeded, with quite a number of others, down the river by steam-boat to Savannah, where, despite the exhibition of our paroles, we were placed for some hours under a guard of negro soldiers, and threatened with a visit from the button inspector. We were finally released, however, with no serious loss or alteration of raiment. Four or five of us, who wished to return as soon as possible to Kentucky, thought that our best chance of getting there without trouble or detention would be to go via New York, believing that in that city, and clad in civilian dress, we would attract no more notice than if we had never attempted the life of the nation; that no one, at any rate, other than our friends and acquaintances, would be aware of our presence or feel at all concerned about our movements. We had determined upon this plan at Augusta, and in pursuance of it had gone to Savannah. But it was not without some difficulty and a good deal of negotiation that we succeeded in obtaining permission to go to New York, and there was then the further question of how we were to get there. We were scantily provided with greenbacks, and the transportation problem was a formidable one.

We learned that the steamship *Arago* was lying at Hilton Head, and that she would, in a day or two, sail for New York. She had brought down a party of Northern tourists, who, immediately after ascertaining that the surrender of the Confederate armies was general, had concluded to visit points along the Atlantic coast made interesting by the events of the war. We secured passage on this vessel, the officers stating that they would furnish us meals, but could not, on account of the crowded condition of the boat, give us berths or sleeping accommodations. We were quite satisfied with this arrangement, especially as we procured reduced rates, and never doubted that we could find some part of the deck soft enough to furnish a sufficiently comfortable couch for veteran cavalry men.

The tourists promenaded the upper deck all day and until a late hour of night, but we had no conversation with them as they seemed to regard us with some suspicion. Our attention was particularly attracted by a quartette of extremely dignified, opulent-looking gentlemen, who, we were told, were from Boston. They seemed to care only for the society of each other and kept as much aloof from the other tourists as the tourists did from us. But there was one of our party who, although he had not been in the cavalry, was a man of as alert intelligence as a mounted forager, and gifted with more assurance than a squadron of Buttermilk rangers. He was very nearly the brightest and most entertaining man I ever saw in a Confederate uniform, and one of the bravest and best officers. This was Col. Phil Lee, of the Second Kentucky Infantry. By some accident Phil became acquainted with the Bostonians and they conceived a strong fancy for him. They talked with him constantly, and he completely deserted our company for theirs. We guyed him about his sudden and violent affiliation with the Yankees, but he answered, that, having done his full duty to his country, he intended now to look out for himself and shake off all encumbering associations. His new friends seemed never tired of listening to him and laughing at his jokes, and I suppose he told them every Confederate chestnut current from the Potomac to the Rio Grande, besides much of immediate invention. Just before the *Arago* reached New York these gentlemen said to him:

"Colonel Lee, you have helped to make our voyage very pleasant, and have shown us a side of the Southern character that is new to us. Now, we would like to do something for you in return. We have no wish to pry into your affairs, but it's quite probable that after your long absence in the army they have fallen into confusion. We are men of some means and have some influence in Boston. If you will come there we will be glad to aid you in any sort of business you may prefer."

"Gentlemen," responded the colonel, "this is exceedingly kind upon your part, and I wouldn't for the world have you think that I don't gratefully appreciate it. I do, and thank you very much. But I can't accept your offer. It is true," he admitted, modestly, "that I am no longer the millionaire I once was, but I still have a few town lots in the city of Shepherdsville, Ky., a flourishing city of nearly two hundred and fifty inhabitants, and I may be able to practise law in Kentucky; while I am quite sure I couldn't anywhere else. I am obliged to decline your kind suggestion. I don't understand any sort of business that would pay in Boston, and am afraid I couldn't learn."

They heard this statement with impatience and some indignation. "Why, surely, Colonel Lee," said one of them, "a man of your intelligence could learn some business."

The colonel pondered deeply and at length asked:

"Have you a city government in Boston?"

"Why, you amaze me! Of course we have."

"Well, gentlemen," said the colonel, with great animation, "the matter looks better than I thought. For the past four years I have been engaged in the business of attempting to break up a government. I haven't been very successful, it's true, but I've rather learned the run of it, and if I should come to Boston and try to break up your government I might have better luck."

This proposition was at first received with grave displeasure, as if it were an unaccountable exhibition of treasonable impudence. But soon all four joined in a hearty burst of laughter, and admitted that perhaps the municipal government of Boston might be benefited by a little "breaking up."

Phil used frequently to declare in after years that if matters came to the worst he would be able to find an asylum in Boston.

Four or five young Federal officers were on the *Arago*, going north on furlough. They were jolly, spirited young fellows, were in funds, having just been paid off, and were disposed to enjoy their liberty and money. They passed a good deal of time playing *vingt et un*, a game not much in vogue nowadays, I believe, but of which some of my readers may have heard.

Col. Theophilus Steele, of our party, ex-commander of the Seventh Kentucky cavalry, C. S. A., and well known to all of Morgan's division, and, indeed, to all of the Kentucky Confederates, for dashing courage and fondness for every kind of adventure, entertained a strong desire to get into this game, but was handicapped by lack of funds. Our supply of money was very limited and after paying our passage none of us had much left. Steele, however, had fifteen or twenty dollars and I about as much. He proposed that we should pool our greenbacks and that he, with the joint amount, should try his luck at the table.

"If we lose," he said, "we'll be no worse off. We haven't money enough to take us home, far less keep us two or three days in New York; as it is we'll have to call on our friends:

while, if we win, we can make ourselves much more comfortable on the boat."

I agreed, and Steele, with the stake thus provided, asked leave to enter the game. The Federals, who had already manifested a disposition to treat us quite civilly, readily consented.

Any one who understands the game of *vingt et un* knows that the dealer has a great advantage over the other players, and that, according to a certain rule of the game, the deal is taken in turn. The Federal officers, either because ignorant of this fact, or from indifference, or in a spirit of liberality, relinquished their right to deal, and permitted Steele to deal continuously. Fortune also aided him. At the expiration of the first day he reported his success, and also that he has secured from the employés of the steamer two small rooms with comfortable sleeping accommodations — one for me and one for himself — by paying twenty dollars for each of them, good for two nights. This seemed homelike, as smacking somewhat of Confederate prices.

"But," I asked, "have you enough money left to keep on playing? Of course, you musn't 'jump the game.'"

"Oh, yes," he said; "I still have the original stake and nearly as much more, and so long as I'm dealer, I'm not likely to lose."

The second day was very nearly a repetition of the first. On the third luck changed, and Steele lost at that sitting. But at the conclusion of the game we were, in addition to the cost of the two nights' comfortable rest, still considerably ahead.

The young officers were "dead game sports" and congratulated Steele, saying they were glad "there was one game at which a Confederate could yet win."

We invested out winnings in wine for our party and the officers, and fraternized very pleasantly.

Colonel Lee, however, retaliated for our gibes about his intimacy with the Bostonians by expressing regret and disgust that an ex-Confederate brigadier and ex-Confederate colonel should begin their return to civil life by entering into a gambling partnership and robbing men who had been fighting for the old flag.

Although New York was not then nearly so large and populous as it is now, it seemed incredibly big and crowded to men accustomed to the little cities of the South. I had forgotten how the great metropolis looked, and its vast dimensions and roaring traffic, compared with what I had more recently seen of urban life, struck me with amazement and almost consternation. I could understand that the people living there had only known that a war had been raging in one part of their own country by the fluctuations of the Gold Board. We had every reason to appreciate the reception given us by our Southern friends there, who did everything for us that was possible, while even the most loyal New Yorker seemed to care very little about what the politics of any other man might be.

I have said that the treatment received by each Confederate, at the date of his surrender very largely influences his remembrance of that event. The character of his experience within a brief period after the close of the war doubtless had, in every individual case, much to do with the "acceptance of the situation." Those who had been the recipients in greater degree of kindness and courtesy were usually the earliest reconciled; while the "unreconstructed" were, as a rule, those who had felt or witnessed harsher dealing. Sometimes apparently quite trivial circumstances would serve to soften bitter and resentful feeling. My own memory furnishes more than one recollection of the truth of this.

About two months after I had returned home, I revisited the South, but this time on a peaceful and commercial mission. At the date at which I had been paroled in Augusta, Ga., cotton, of which there was a great deal in that region, was selling at a very low price. It occurred to me that the speculation so offered ought to prove profitable, so I went back to Augusta to buy cotton. After buying as much as my very limited capital would permit, I took a contract to raise and carry to Augusta a barge load of cotton which had been wrecked and sunk in the Savannah River, about ten miles below the city. I employed a gang of twenty or thirty negroes and remained with them, superintending their work, for ten days or two weeks, sleeping every night on low ground near the bank of the stream. As a consequence, I contracted the fever so common in that country, and which, if not fatal, is always pernicious and debilitating. After lying in bed at Augusta for two weeks and then winding up business as best I could, I started again for Kentucky in very bad shape.

Desiring to visit St. Louis on the way, where I had some antebellum affairs still unsettled, I took the most direct rail route for Memphis, and, as the roads were then in very bad condition, was several days in making the distance, travelling a considerable part of it in box cars. That sort of thing was not comfortable for a sick man, nor peculiarly conducive to an amiable temper.

One morning about nine o'clock, I was sitting on the platform of a station where I would have to change cars and waiting for my train, when my attention was attracted to a squad of Federal soldiers who had evidently been on guard during the night, but at the time I saw them were getting their breakfast. They were well supplied with rations and seemed in high spirits. Just then I caught sight of a lank, hungry-looking fellow who was unmistakably an ex-Confederate. He wore a ragged, faded, gray jacket with the buttons cut off, a pair of most dilapidated blue trousers and had an old canvas haversack, as empty as extra sidereal space, hung around his neck. If he had eaten a square meal within six months past his jaws and belly were villanous deceptions. He was partially hidden behind a cotton bale, whence he was watching the Yankee spread with eyes that threatened to protrude across the intervening distance.

Nearly about the time that I first saw him, the Yanks also caught sight of him. They held a short consultation, then one of them sprang up, started toward him, and shouted out, "Hello, reb! Come this way; we want you."

For some reason — perhaps because I was sick and peevish — I conceived the idea that they wanted to arrest him, and my blood boiled with indignation at what I considered so totally an unprovoked act of oppression.

The "Johnnie" evidently entertained the same opinion, for he began a rather rapid retreat. A fresh summons, however, reinforced by a volley of oaths, induced him to turn and approach the party, which he did with an attempted dignity of demeanour that appeared very ludicrous as compared with his previous hasty retrograde movement. But when he reached the spot where the grub was they seized him, made him sit down, and all exerted themselves to appease his manifest hunger.

I have known some extraordinary feeders, but I honestly believe that I have never seen any two other men eat as much as that fellow did. He kept at it steadily for not less than an hour, the Yanks aiding and encouraging him to the utmost. He drank six tin cups full of coffee. He swelled visibly, and I wondered how his frail garments stood the tension.

When he at length finished, his captors crammed his weather-beaten old haversack full of hardtack and bacon and sent him on his way rejoicing.

It is scarcely necessary to say that my own feelings in regard to the incident had very materially changed during its progress.

CHAPTER XIX

IT IS difficult for this generation to conceive, far more so to understand, the change wrought by the Civil War, not only in the states which had constituted the Southern Confederacy, but in the border states which had been slave-holding. No such metamorphosis, perhaps, has been produced in so brief a period — none like it, at any rate, has been recorded in modern history — unless it be that accomplished in France by the great revolution. The alterations in social and economic conditions, in political relations, in habits of thought, in the very mode of living, can scarcely be imagined by those who have no personal knowledge of the former status.

This change was perceptible so soon as the war was ended. It was apparent everywhere and in everything. The life of the post-bellum South no more resembled that of the other, than the life of the early settlers of this continent was like that they had left on the other side of the ocean. The material effects of multitudinous invasion and protracted warfare upon Virginia and the more southern states had been such as to reduce all of that territory to one vast wreckage. Tennessee had fared somewhat, but not much, better. Kentucky and Missouri had furnished fields for the conflict and suffered no small loss in its general havoc, and Maryland had not altogether escaped. The institution of slavery was gone. The negro was free, idle, unquiet, but far from contented. His imagination was excited to vague and impossible aspirations, and his soul troubled by a short harvest in his immediate expectations and a painful apprehension of future disappointment. A great triumph for humanity had been achieved, and a social conflict between the white and black races inaugurated. The labour system of the South was disorganized completely for the time being, and with little prospect of its early restoration.

The political situation was, if possible even more greatly changed. Shortly before the beginning of the war the South had been dominant in national affairs and the government of the country. For many years previously, no candidate for the Presidency who was not supposed to be amenable to Southern influence could hope to be successful; and even at the date of Mr. Lincoln's election, sympathy for Southern ideas and interests was so prevalent as to largely direct national legislation. In this, too, there had been a complete reversal. At the close of the war, the bare suspicion that it might meet the wishes of the Southern people or find Southern endorsement was enough to turn the overwhelming majority of the North and East against any policy or measure, however just and salutary it might be; and latitude became very nearly the only test of loyalty.

The people who had remained at their homes in the South during the continuance of hostilities, and after the occupation by the Federal armies of the territory in which they lived, had become gradually and in a measure accustomed to the new order; although it bore hard upon them and was not easy to realize. But upon the Confederate soldiers just returned from the ranks it broke with sudden and appalling revelation. They could no more recognize the old landmarks than could the sons of Noah have identified the old home farm after the subsidence of the deluge. There was, of what they had once known, scarcely anything left; and adaptation to the new conditions seemed at first impossible. Few of them had, at any time during the struggle, doubted of ultimate success. Accustomed during the two last years of the war to reverses, they had, nevertheless, never dreamed of the final disaster, but hoped and trusted to the last. Perhaps defeat was not so bitter and the actual results of subjugation scarcely so dreadful as they had imagined; but the reality was sufficiently harsh, and taxed their endurance to the utmost. They had known and been taught nothing in their military service — full of trial as it was — to tame their pride or subdue their native spirit. They had become veteran in resolution and knowledge of warfare, patient of physical privation, disciplined, in so far as attention to duty and obedience to command might be so termed, but had learned nothing of that unthinking automatic submission to authority which is supposed to characterize the professional soldier. On the contrary, their experience in the army had intensified the feeling with which their earlier education and associations had imbued them, and made them ever more strongly attached to and jealous of their personal rights. They had given their paroles in good faith; proposing perfectly to observe them and faithfully obey the laws and the authority of the United States government; few, if any of them, I believe, desired or expected to take part in politics. But they had totally misconceived, or rather had not anticipated, the nature of the obedience they would be expected to render. They had supposed that they would be subject to law as they had previously understood the meaning of the term; law administered according to statutes duly enacted, and by courts and magistrates formally and specially appointed for such purpose — courts in some measure trained to the dispensation of justice. They had not hoped for much share in the selection of such officials, nor that the official machinery, however selected, would be much in sympathy with them. But they had expected something like the impartiality which regularly constituted tribunals cannot easily refuse.

Such expectation, however, proved fallacious. Even in Kentucky the courts were well-nigh impotent, and martial law virtually prevailed at the close of hostilties. The military authority overshadowed all other until the election of 1866, when by a supreme effort the people resumed control. In Missouri these unfortunate conditions endured for a much longer period. In the states which had seceded, where the state governments had formally acknowledged the authority of the Confederacy and had enlisted troops in its defense, there was, for years after the termination of actual warfare, visually no semblance of law in its ordinary meaning or usage, no tribunal or procedure not recognized and controlled by the will of the military. The commandants of the troops still stationed in the South, after the main armies were removed, exercised for some months immediately afterward a curious jurisdiction which embraced nearly all matters and cases, civil and criminal. It is true that the Federal soldiery — many of them at least — felt a certain commiseration for their former opponents, and even for the citizens of the afflicted region, and evinced an irregular and capricious justice in dealing with them. But such rude methods were not adapted to either dispasssionate consideration or fair adjustment of disputes; and, by the parties who happened to be in political disfavour or under the ban of suspicion, were not held in much esteem. In all controversies between whites and blacks, the Freedman's Bureau claimed exclusive right to hear and determine; and as the negro was always fully and favourably heard and generally got the decision, he availed himself extensively of so valuable a privilege.

The most absurd complaints were entertained by this tribunal. At the time when it was most flourishing, Gen. Wade Hampton invited a friend from Kentucky to visit him at his Mississippi plantation, giving a number of reasons why the friend would enjoy the visit. "But," said the Kentuckian, after many items had been enumerated, "what about your whiskey?"

"Well," replied Hampton, "It's good enough for a white man, but if I should pass it off on a nigger, he'd have me before the Bureau."

Deplorable and anomalous as all this was, it was, perhaps, under the circumstances, in a measure inevitable. The courts and all magisterial officers, who had exercised any function during the brief continuance of the Confederacy were of course deposed — their commissions annulled — so soon as the Confederacy had fallen, and could not be immediately replaced. The sagacity, kindly feeling, and commanding influence of Mr. Lincoln might have solved the problem more promptly and humanely; but to reduce this weltering chaos to order was a task impossible for either Andrew Johnson or the Congress, and every thing attempted by either only seemed to make confusion worse confounded.

It soon became apparent that to hold and treat these states merely as conquered territory was a policy both too costly and too dangerous; nor would the most fanatical and implacable Northern sentiment consent to anything quite so drastic. But when the time came to begin the political "rehabilitation," to use a phrase much in vogue at that date, the trouble, instead of diminishing, increased. Incited by the hope of illicit gain — in modern parlance, "graft"— for which this new field of speculation offered abundant and inviting opportunity, greedy adventurers flocked in from the North and found colleagues, already in the South, as eager as themselves and even more unscrupulous. The negro having the sympathy of the party dominant in the

Nation and entitled, in some form, to recognition, became their blind and useful tool. Distrusting, not unnaturally, those who had opposed his enfranchisement, and inclined by nature to side with those who exhibited the symbols of authority, he allied himself at once with the carpet-bagger and the scallawag and implicitly did their bidding.

"Reconstruction" was attempted by similar methods and accompanied by similar acts in each of the states which had seceded. Its history in any one of them, with changes only in names, dates, and comparatively unimportant circumstances, may be safely accepted as true of all the others. It was, of course, inevitable and expected by every one that the people of these states would be required to undergo some kind of probation before they were accorded complete restoration to the rights they had formerly possessed as citizens of the United States. It was also expected, and was entirely logical and proper, that the "Union men" of those states should chiefly conduct this process of rehabilitation. But no intelligent man expected, and no patriotic or conservative man desired, no matter what may have been his previous political affiliation, any such condition as prevailed in the South for eleven years, crowded with mischief and disaster and which bequeathed evils scarcely yet cured. No one expected to see the suddenly emancipated slave raised to political equality with even the loyal white, and an attempt made to elevate him above his former master, if that master had been a "rebel."

No thoughtful or honest man imagined that the persons and property of millions of unfortunate people were to be virtually placed at the mercy of a horde of political banditti, whose only principle was lust and purpose of plunder and whose only political sentiment was malignant hatred of those whom they robbed and persecuted.

Had Mr. Lincoln lived to execute his hope and plan for the reëstablishment of harmony and Union, much, if not all, of this fearful experience would have been averted. In Andrew Johnson such reconstruction found its fit instrument. He was the very incarnation of its malign, remorseless, dastard spirit, and he began the congenial work with zeal and alacrity.

It is true that in the latter part of his Presidential term, when he had quarrelled with every leading man in his party, Johnson sought to obstruct some of the reconstructive legislation. But in so doing he was actuated by no feeling of justice or compassion, no desire to shield the stricken people of the South from further oppression, but solely by jealousy of men who had unexpectedly become his rivals. It is but just to say, however, that while much individual hardship was inflicted by the harsh conditions imposed immediately after the close of the war, upon all who had been prominently connected with the Confederate cause, the really serious, deadly menace to the peace and prosperity of the South was contained in the acts passed to compel the ratification of the Fourteenth Amendment to the Constitution, the effect of which was to give the negro suffrage. Inasmuch as the requisite number of the states, whose ratification was necessary to the final adoption of the Amendment, could not be procured unless some of the Southern states were made to vote for it, congress resolved to coërce such action. An absolutely essential preliminary to the accomplishment of this purpose was the disfranchisement of the majority of the white men of those states. Accordingly, by an act entitled, "An Act for the More Efficient Government of the States Recently in Rebellion," passed March 2, 1867, such states were divided into military districts, to each of which a military commander was assigned who was empowered to organize military commissions to try offences against his orders and regulations; and by an act passed July 19, 1867, the boards of registration, provided by legislation of March 23, 1867, were given authority and required, "before allowing the registration of any person, to ascertain upon such facts or information as they can obtain, whether such person is entitled to be registered under said act, and the oath required by such act shall not be conclusive on such question, and none shall be registered unless such board shall decide that he is entitled thereto."

Before he could vote a man must have registered, and, of course, these boards of registration had entire control over all elections; no man without their permission could become a qualified voter. If any were bold enough to take issue with them or resent their decrees, the authority of the military commission to try and punish such "offences" was promptly invoked and as promptly utilized. No form of tyranny more absolutely despotic could have been devised, and that the communities subjected to it escaped complete and degrading subjugation seems miraculous.

Primarily intended, as I have said, to compel the ratification of the Constitutional Amendment, this system was still further prostituted and applied to yet baser uses. It furnished the class of politicians of which I have spoken the means of obtaining control of the state governments and legislatures, and of inaugurating an era of extravagance and speculation which threatened each state with bankruptcy and the whole region with hopeless impoverishment. Fortunately the lust of plunder was so fierce, and even that sort of honour which is said to obtain among thieves so lacking in the vile adventurers who attempted this policy, that they invariably fell to quarrelling among themselves whenever the booty would not well bear sharing. At every such division and the contests necessarily resulting for possession of the state offices, by manipulation of which the plunder was gotten, opportunity was afforded those for whose oppression this infamous machinery had been invented, to better their conditions.

Taking part sometimes with one side, sometimes with the other — and as a rule each was equally bad and corrupt — the Southern whites whose disfranchisement had been intended gradually acquired the mastery. The Fourteenth Amendment was ratified and the negro became a voter; but even the negro vote became, in large measure, influenced by the white element whose political domination, whose political existence, indeed, it had been expected to destroy.

The whites were also largely aided in their efforts by the friendly sentiment of the United States soldiers stationed in Southern garrisons. The military commission, composed usually of fanatical partisans, meant mischief and gave much trouble but, as a rule, the military otherwise, officers and men alike, were reluctant to interfere in political controversy, and not only sympathized with the whites against the blacks, but usually with the "rebels" against the "carpet-baggers."

But that which above all else served to rescue these people was their own indomitable spirit. Nor can it be denied that their courage and resolute perseverance was assisted by an astute intelligence such as has seldom been manifested in an ordeal so trying. For a time congress seemed disposed to abandon all other business in the effort to legislate the South into submission to the corrupt rule of the tramp politician and acquiescence in negro equality. To all else that the victors dictated she yielded silent assent, but these things she would not have. Her determined resistance preserved her own civilization, and averted a great shame and evil from the whole country and its history.

Had the condition to which a band of audacious and unscrupulous men in the South sought to subject that section been successfully and permanently imposed; had the backing those men for a time received from a misinformed Northern sentiment been one whit more general and persistent; had the Northern people remained undeceived as to the true purpose and character of those men; or had the masses of the Southern whites wearied or relaxed, in the least, in their stubborn opposition — remediless ruin would have overwhelmed the South, and we may reasonably believe that the evil would not have been confined entirely to her territory.

At no time during the Civil War were the people of the South required to display a fortitude greater than that which they exhibited during those memorable years. Never upon any of the bloody fields where Southern valour was so conspicuous, was braver conduct inspired by patriotic devotion than in that long, dreary struggle against fanatical hate and brutal cupidity.

Kentucky escaped the evil effects of reconstruction, chiefly because its methods could not be consistently employed within her borders. Legislation intended "for the more efficient government of the states recently in rebellion," could not logically, or by any stretch of construction, be applied to a state which had never actually been in rebellion. While the greater part of the population of Kentucky was in sentiment strongly with the South, she had never formally, or by any legislative or executive action, taken part with the Confederacy. The state government had been during the entire war in the hands of men who had professed and rendered allegiance to the government of the United States, and notwithstanding that her people were more than suspected of disloyal feeling, and punishment had been freely inflicted for every act which could in anywise be regarded as inimical to the Federal authority, Kentucky was counted among the states loyal to the Union.

A convention of her citizens held at Russellville on the 18th of November, 1861, in which sixty-five counties of the state were represented, had, indeed, passed an ordinance of secession and adopted a provisional form of government. But although the validity of this action was recognized by the Confederate government, it was denied by the government of the United States. The latter could, therefore, on no pretext, hold or treat Kentucky as a seceded state. Fortunately, also, the large majority of the Union men of Kentucky and those who were in control at the close of the war of the state government were exceedingly conservative and immovably opposed to the extreme measures which the more fanatical desired to inaugurate. They promptly repealed the statutes disfranchising the Kentuckians who had served in the Confederate army and restored them their former rights as citizens. The result was that, notwithstanding the effort of the radicals and some military interference at the polls, the conservatives and returned Confederates conbined, won a decisive victory in the elections of August, 1866, and all danger like that with which the South was threatened, was avoided.

One of the most remarkable and at the same time natural outgrowths of the immediate post-bellum social and political conditions in the South was the sudden existence and wide extension of the secret organization known as the Ku Klux Klan. It seems to be well established that this organization which became so famous and certainly exerted a very potent influence originated in Tennessee sometime in the latter part of the year 1866. It has been claimed, and probably correctly, that it began as a small social club or society of young men in the little town of Pulaski, and was formed merely as a means of amusement. The high sounding and fantastic nomenclature of its officers, "Cyclops," "Grand Wizard," etc., and the grotesque ceremonial with which it was reported its members were initiated, induces credence of this statement. However that may be, the circumstances of the period and locality soon caused it to be used for quite other purposes, and it became an agency by which quite serious and important results were accomplished.

The intolerate rule of the military commissions, acting at the instigation and governed by the advice of men as bad as any civilized community has ever produced, the arbitrary and sometimes oppressive orders of the commanders of districts, the general state of affairs, indeed, in the South, which I have attempted to describe, had wrought the temper of the people so treated to an extreme and dangerous tension. Denied all other relief, they sought it by methods which, under similar conditions, the oppressed have so often employed. Refused all proper remedy, they resolved to find some kind of remedy. Remonstrance and peaceful opposition had proven futile; there was no legal tribunal to which an appeal could be made; open resistance was impossible. Whatever might be done, must, of necessity, be done secretly or in such wise as to prevent discovery of the instrumentality by which it was done. The organization of the Ku Klux, whatever may have been its origin, furnished just the machinery requisite for the policy they meant to pursue.

While many things combined, as I have said, to demand such action, its immediate inducement seems to have been the origination of the Union League. This organization was composed chiefly of negroes, nearly all of whom were herded into it, but was officered and directed by white men who advocated the most objectionable features of the scheme of reconstruction and especially such as promised lucrative returns. Some of these — and perhaps the worst — were men, natives and residents of the South, who had previously affected the strongest Southern sentiment, but had become apostate in every sense.

The object of the Ku Klux Klan was to combat the efforts of this organization, to weaken its hold upon the negroes, and, undoubtedly, to prevent the latter, so far as possible, from voting. It proposed also to effect this purpose by intimidation — not intimidation, however, accomplished by physical violence, but adroitly addressed to the negro's superstitious beliefs. Little that was cruel or brutal was at any time done, I believe, by the real Ku Klux; although certain organizations of much later date and which assumed the same title did perpetrate many dastardly deeds. A story was told me by one, who was perhaps a witness of the incident he related, which very well illustrates, no doubt, the nature of the Ku Klux procedure. An elderly negro preacher, very influential with the coloured people of his vicinage, had attained considerable prominence in the Union League, and was the principal medium of communication between its white leaders and their black retainers in that locality. He lived in a whistewashed, double log-cabin near Lauvergne, between Nashville and Murfreesboro. The cabin was situated in a small yard and about forty yards from the pike. I, myself, remember the spot quite well, and had often passed it during the war.

This place was the headquarters of all the negro politicians in that part of the county. The preacher would hold meetings on Tuesday and Friday evenings, reciting the instructions issued by the "bosses" for their guidance, and sweetening his discourse with the customary promise of "forty acres and a mule" to each loyal member of the league when final success had been achieved. One night, when these exercises had been prolonged to a late hour, they were suddenly interrupted by a deep tone, "Hello to the house," coming from the road. The startled inmates of the cabin looked out and saw a quaint and ghostly sight. At the stile block was a horse and a rider, both apparently of colossal size. The horse was covered from head to tail with a white sheet which fell almost to his hoofs. The rider was enveloped in what seemed a shroud, with a hood on his head and a large cape falling over his shoulders. All this the darkies saw with amazement and consternation; but what they failed to detect was a rubber tube fitted with a large mouthpiece, which descended underneath hood and shroud to the ground. The preacher opened the door and responded to the hail.

"Bring a bucket of water and a dipper out here," commanded the same appalling voice. "I don't wish to enter your cabin because I might set it on fire. Bring the water here quick."

The old man procured the bucket and dipper, and with trembling limbs approached the stile and offered his fearful visitor the water. The spectre seized the dipper, twice emptied it, then threw it away, and, taking the bucket, drained, or seemed to drain, it.

"Good Lord, Boss!" said the horror stricken preacher, "you 'pears to be dry."

"Dry!" echoed the thirsty goblin, with a groan of anguish,

"If you had been in h — ll as I have been, since the battle of Murfreesboro, you'd be dry too."

With a yell that rang to the skies, the minister fled back to his flock: but ere he had turned in his tracks, an answering yell from the other darkeys who had seen and heard all that had happened, and a smashing of doors and windows in the rear of the cabin, gave evidence that he would find the premises vacated.

The power of the "invisible empire"— as it was grandiloquently styled — was more due to the mystery with which it was surrounded and the vague fear it inspired, than to any strength of numbers or coherence of organization. Although it was extended into every state which was being subjected to the process of reconstruction, comparatively a small proportion of the population of each, perhaps, was enrolled in its ranks or took active part in its proceedings. It is to be doubted, also, whether there was any regular gradation of rank among its members, or any supreme authority entitled to direct them all, although such was generally believed to be the case. It was so alert and seemed so ubiquitous that every one thought it must be numerous, and a common purpose induced the unity of action usually effected by a common head.

If the organization of the Klan was productive of harm, it was so, I believe, solely in that it may have furnished example and stimulus for the formation of other secret associations of later date, which were controlled by ignobler motives and directed to less legitimate ends. It certainly accomplished a great deal that was of ultimate benefit to the Southern people in the desperate contest in which they were then engaged; and accomplished it by little, if any, actual violence. Its establishment in Kentucky was attempted, and had the same conditions then prevailed in Kentucky as in the South the attempt would have been successful. But after the conservative Union men and the Southern sympathizers had obtained control in that state, anything of the kind there would have been not only unnecessary, but culpable and inconceivably foolish. The Klan was disbanded, or, at least, ceased active operations, sometime in 1869.

Much of the lawlessness which has prevailed in the South has been due to this habit of meeting force and fraud by methods as drastic, which the reconstruction policies compelled. Her people claim — and, if there be anything in statistical proof, with good reason — that violations of the public peace and order have been quite as frequent and flagrant in other sections of the country and with less excuse.

The accusation of peculiar injustice to the negro, so often brought against the Southern people, is perhaps the least founded in truth of all. Every instance which may be cited as proof of it, which cannot in some measure be justified by the provocation, is, in its last analysis, only a manifestation of that racial antagonism which is as strong and incorrigible in the North as in the South — which urges the white race everywhere to assert supremacy. It has been shown, indeed, in more unreasonable and remorseless degree in Northern than in Southern communities. There has been less excuse for the race riots which have occurred in some of the Northern states than for the lynching — the swift, irregular punishment inflicted in the South upon black men guilty of that crime which arouses the most ungovernable resentment.

It is a waste of time to discuss the question of so-called race prejudice and the sentiment of caste. Whatever lack of equity there may be in this feeling, howsoever erroneous the white man's conviction of his natural superiority to the black man may be, it is inherent and ineradicable, and time and experience only strengthen it. The writers who choose to describe this feeling as the "tyranny of colour," may be in one sense right; but the fact will remain that, with every concession of civil and political equality, the black people must occupy an inferior social plane to the white.

All that can be defined by law and formulated in statutes for the protection of the negro may be and should be done; yet will he remain the servant of Japhet so long as he dwells in his tents. No class of white men feel that more instinctively and act on it more rigidly than do those of Northern birth when brought into contact with negroes. They develop very often a repugnance to all association with the blacks, which the native Southerner does not entertain and can hardly understand.

Many of the Northern people have condemned the conduct of the Southern people toward the black race, simply because they have not understood it. Ignorant of the negro character, they have received a totally false idea of it; sometimes from sources whence they had a right to expect an accurate delineation.

The average Northern man and the Englishman believe that the negro is merely a white man with a black skin. Placed in similar positions, surrounded by similar circumstances, subject to like influences, they would expect him to feel and act just as a white man of about the same degree of intelligence and information would feel and act.

Perceiving in the negro little intellectual inferiority to the white man in those standards by which intellectual ability is commonly measured, recognizing in him excellent capacity for much that is supposed to, and doubtless does, evince a high order of mentality, they cannot understand in what his alleged inferiority consists. In imaginative fervour, in those qualities wherein emotion and intellect are blended, he is certainly equal to the white man. It will not surprise those who know the negro race best, if in another generation it produces orators, poets, and artists who shall rival their contemporaries of white blood. But in the art of government; in the knowledge of and capacity for the conduct of political and social affairs; in self-control; in an acute perception of what ought to be done and what should not be attempted; in the organizing instinct which detects how best to adapt the means to an end, and the ability to subordinate passion to judgment; in those qualities, in short, which it has been asserted make the Aryan race capable of self-government and the Anglo-Saxon preëminent in that great faculty — the negro is vastly and unmistakably beneath the level of the white man. His distinguishing characteristics are a worship of power, an adoration of might, and a ductile susceptibility to the influence of any one stronger than himself who is immediately in contact with him.

As a rule he is good or bad, just as he is under good or bad influences. He is naturally docile and amiable, but can be incited to acts of savagery and frenzied folly which even ignorant white men would not commit, unless drunken or insane. The absolute, unqualified veneration which the negro feels for power in its every form and symbol — of power as might, and without regard to the principle or right — is the strongest feeling of his nature and the instinct by which his conduct is chiefly governed.

Nature formed him for obedience, and even when he is riotous and apparently insubordinate, it is often but his expression of contempt for what he deems weakness, and an indirect tribute to that which he deems the representative of superior and controlling force. The same instinct which induces him to yield to the strong and serve without remonstrance, is manifest upon occasion in fierce resentment of any assertion upon the part of the weak. During the war, so long as the invaders had not made their appearance, the negroes on even the most populous plantations were submissive and tractable. In communities whence the greater number of the white males had departed for service in the army, on plantations where no white persons remained save women and children, or sometimes an overseer, the blacks remained quietly and obediently at work. Under conditions which the fierce Anglo-Saxon, had he been the slave, would have instantly welcomed as the signal and utilized as the means of his deliverance, the negro was docile as in all his former years of servitude. He still saw in the overseer, the white woman, even the white child, the type of power, the representatives of authority. But when the blue-coated soldier came, he at once perceived that the terms were reversed, and in the uniform and epaulet, as subsequently in the Freedman's Bureau, he recognized the dominant force in which his soul delighted, and to which he instinctively and completely acknowledged allegiance. When the war ended and the horrible era set in, when the rule of the carpet-bagger and the scalawag was well-nigh absolute, and the Southern white who refused to stultify his every conviction, abjure all manly impulse, sacrifice all self-respect, was threatened with lasting disfranchisement and punished with every insult and oppression possible to inflict, then it was that the real trouble with the negro began, and it continued through all the years of reconstruction.

The negro realized that the old order of things was gone, that a new régime was inaugurated. He could not understand how any man identified with the old system and not in accord with the new could have any right of speech or action. Nor did he regard it, as an equally ignorant or very prejudiced white man might have regarded it, as a fitting punishment of rebellion; he looked upon it merely as the logical and proper consequence of the Southern white man's loss of ascendency. He knelt in implicit submission before the representatives of Federal authority and the agents of the bureau, followed with blind fidelity the counsels and guidance of the white leaders of the "league." But to obey those in authority was not enough. His zeal also urged him to assail those under the ban. His loyalty seemed to him incomplete without earnest and frequent manifestation of the opprobrium which he felt ought to be visited on the "rebel trash," who presumed to encumber the land they could no longer govern. He resented every attempt of the Southern white population to maintain or assert any control over property, or exercise even the most necessary police regulation; and not so much because he deemed it an infringement on his own rights, as because he honestly considered such conduct as inexcusable impudence on the part of a deposed class, holding only a shattered sceptre.

This trait of the negro character, and another almost as marked, *viz.*, his curious propensity to become unduly elated by trivial circumstances which would not at all have impressed a white man — an elation often arising to presumption and arrogance — have contributed quite as much as any difference in colour to induce trouble between the two races.

The dissimilarity, moral and intellectual, between them, due perhaps to heredity, racial education — the white man having three thousand years of some sort of civilization in his past, the negro only seven or eight generations removed from the savage — has made it impossible for them to live together amicably unless the white race rule. The question was presented in a shape that could not be avoided: it was white rule or black. The Southern white resolved that the negro should *not* rule; that it should be proven that, though beaten in war and broken in fortune, he was yet more than a match for carpet-baggers and blacks combined. The question was settled, we have reason to believe, finally, and there need be little apprehension that the friction and sometimes collision, so frequent in that period when the white man realized that he must maintain his ascendency or give up all that made life worth living, will ever recur.

CHAPTER XX

IT WOULD unquestionably be well if religious feeling and strict piety were always characteristics of the soldier, more especially of soldiers called on to perform real service. Men who are required to constantly risk their lives and are frequently near to death should be prepared to meet it, and the more conscientious a man is — the stronger his sense of obligation — the better soldier he ought to be.

The "Christian soldier," Gustavus, Havelock, or Stonewall Jackson, always commands admiration in an unusual degree, and it is accorded sometimes to fanatics. We feel a certain interest — even because of their fanaticism — in the grim militant sectarians of the Cromwellian army of 1650, and their prototypes of Scotland, who strove for a "broken covenant" against the tyranny and perfidy of the Stuarts.

But, unfortunately, it is a fact that the training of the soldier is not usually conducive to piety and religious feeling. The monotonous life of the camp is apt to breed a restless craving for excitement and recreation, and a reckless disposition to gratify such desire whenever occasion is offered. I met with few examples of Christian resignation in my army experience, although I often found a peculiar crude philosophy which inclined a man, while he "swore at" his bad luck, to make the most of it.

Nor was a devout assurance of divine protection or providential assistance a prominent article of the soldier's creed. As a rule, he took that more practical, more mundane view of the matter which is expressed in Napoleon's famous maxim, that "Providence is on the side of the heaviest battalions."

Even the most orthodox could not altogether free themselves from this habit of thought. It was General Pendleton, I believe, chief of artillery of the Army of Northern Virginia, who, on some occasion after the war, said, in fervent prayer: "Oh,

Lord, when in Thy divine wisdom Thou had'st determined that the Confederacy should not succeed, before Thou could'st execute that purpose Thou wast obliged to remove Stonewall Jackson."

The suggestion that he meant to say that if Stonewall Jackson had remained on earth this particular purpose of Providence would have been frustrated, would doubtless have greatly shocked the brave, good, and devout man who uttered these words; but they sound mightily that way.

The conviction that, in the game of war, he who "held the best hand" would most probably succeed, was very general; and while the aid of a power superior to human intelligence and effort, was often desired it was seldom invoked save, indeed, by those especially commissioned for such duty.

The lesson of Æsop's old fable of the teamster who prayed Hercules to extricate his cart from the mire was always in the mind of the veteran; he relied largely on his own exertions, or if he expected assistance, it was from some quarter whence his experience taught him it would probably come. It is reported that in one of the great battles fought in Virginia, a Federal chaplain found himself out on the firing line at a point where a red-hot artillery duel was in progress between a New York battery and a Confederate battery of the same number of guns, both being handled in excellent style.

One of the sergeants of the Federal battery, in the excitement of the combat, had lost his grip on simple and seemly English, and was pouring out a startling flood of profanity.

"My friend," said the chaplain, "are you not ashamed — indeed, afraid — to use such language at such a time? Can you expect the support of Providence if you utter such horrid and blasphemous language?"

"We ain't calkerlatin' on that, parson," responded the sergeant. "The Ninth Pennsylvania has orders to support this battery."

While the sergeant was altogether to blame in the matter of swearing, I am inclined to think he was right in his unformulated logic. He was merely disavowing his belief in a Special Providence that would take cognizance, in a big battle, of so small a detail as a battery; and he justly concluded, therefore, that the battery would have to depend on more proximate and visible means of support.

It is scarcely necessary to say that men who were thus skeptical of Providential interference with the battle field had little faith in its influence in other matters. It was difficult to convince them that it could be evoked by solicitation or ceremony. So, with whatever sincerity the good people at home might observe the days on which the respective governments, during the Civil War, prescribed religious services, either to avert the divine wrath or win the blessing of heaven, the soldier was incredulous on that score. He gave no more credence to the supposititious effect of a day of thanksgiving or a day of humiliation, than an austere Protestant believes in the efficacy of a Catholic holiday.

I remember that very nearly at the close of the war, and when our rations were at the lowest ebb — when the slightest further reduction in that regard almost meant starvation — Mr. Davis issued one of his many proclamations appointing a day of fasting and prayer. I heard a number of officers on that occasion discuss the subject in all of its aspects. None of them, save one, hoped that divine help could be thus obtained, but expressed the opinion that the moral effect of such a document might be good, as evincing a decent and proper respect for the sentiment of many excellent people. One gentleman, however, stoutly maintained it was good *per se;* that it was the way to win the aid of the Almighty to our cause. He finally appealed to Capt. Calvin Morgan, who had up to that time been silent, to know what he thought about it.

Captain Morgan said that he had no doubt, of course, that it was proper for an individual to ask divine guidance and support, and that benefit might come of it; he said, further that what was good for an individual might also be good for a community. "But," he went on to say, "I think that, under the circumstances, Mr. Davis makes a mistake in relying on "fasting and prayer," and in officially committing the Confederacy to such methods. The Yankees are stronger than we are on both those counts. We fast every day as it is: we are compelled to do so because we have scarcely anything to eat, and I don't think we will get much credit above for doing something we can't help doing, with or without an executive order. As for the matter of prayer, the Yankees can beat us hands down on that. They have twenty preachers to our one, and outnumber us more formidably in the pulpit than they do in the field. If Mr. Davis risks the fate of the Confederacy on such policies we will be whipped, in my opinion, before another week."

But making every proper concession to the intelligence that willing to believe much, yet refuses to accept anything for which it cannot discover a reason, it must be admitted that religious sentiment largely contributes to make good soldiers as well as good citizens. History furnishes abundantly such examples. Leaving out of consideration the fact that among Christian peoples, the armies which have been composed of material in great measure imbued with this sentiment have, all else being comparatively equal, been generally successful in protracted struggles, the extent and rapidity of Mohammedan conquest illustrated what it may be made to accomplish, even when we are compelled to term it fanaticism. The religious conviction is deeper and more controlling than any other known to human nature, and its usual concomitant, a strong sense of duty, often supplies the lack of discipline, and always helps to establish and strengthen discipline.

The old saying of '76 — I forget which one of the revolutionary heroes was its author — "Trust in God and keep your powder dry," seems to be a judicious compromise between superstition on the one side and skepticism on the other.

That which a learned judge has recently denominated "exaggerated ego" is an infliction common to humanity, and cases of it are to be found everywhere. It does not, however, manifest itself everywhere in the same form, and its type seems to be largely influenced by the idiosyncrasies and racial temperament of the people among whom it prevails. We have examples of its various symptoms afforded by the different nationalities of which the great, conglomerate American population is composed. The man who "takes himself too seriously" exhibits this overestimate after a different fashion, accordingly as he happens to be native American, German, Irish, or Hebrew.

In the majority of instances, of course, it is a purely personal trait — plain, unadulterated self-conceit. It may be excused when it is due to inexperience or lack of the information, only to be acquired by association with other men; in one who has led a secluded life, or has been partially isolated from his fellows. But when this self-conceit remains or grows worse, notwithstanding what should be the corrective effect of metropolitan experience, the patient, if sane, should be promptly taken out and assassinated, after the summary method of the Mississippi sheriff, "without bail, mainprise, recaption, or benefit of clergy."

But this inclination to undue self-estimate does not always proceed from the personal and complacent vanity which indulges the belief of individual superiority. Very often the feeling is one of class or association — a certain *esprit de corps* — rather than an entirely personal one. It is frequently something like the state pride which induces every patriotic citizen to exalt his own "grand old commonwealth" without meaning to glorify himself.

The most impecunious New Yorker can speak with an air, and, doubtless, with a real sense of self-gratulation, about the vast wealth and financial power of his great city. A Bostonian who himself may be barely over the border of illiteracy may yet feel that he reflects and modestly shines in the scholarly radiance of his cultured townsmen. No just man would attribute personal vanity to the Virginian who boasted that he was born within two miles of Culpeper Court House, and could have been born at the Court House had he so chosen; nor would he urge such charge against the old-time Tennessee orator because he declared that "Down here, we folks — men like me and Gin'ral Jackson and Col. Davy Crockett — always demands our rights; and if we don't git 'em somebody else is mighty liable to git hell."

Our Northern brethren, at the date when they were accustomed to criticize the South, speak slightingly of "plantation manners," and condemn our predilection for the duel and street fight, did not suggest that we were normally a vain and conceited generation, but laid the blame of the "exaggerated ego" with which they charged us upon our civilization — on a mistaken social education and sentiment which induced an undue idea of personal consequence. Some of them were even so generous as to intimate that if we would get rid of these and all other faults we might become almost as good as themselves.

This quality of exceeding self-esteem — or over self valuation — is, perhaps, more common, at least more widely diffused, in America than in any other country, and naturally so. Every American has been told from his infancy that he is a "sovereign," and a good opinion of himself, therefore, is his birthright and a part of his constitutional inheritance.

With men in public station, more particularly if they have been especially the recipients of popular favour and applause, the personal equation is naturally more pronounced and an exalted self estimate more thoroughly developed. This was more frequently the case, if tradition is to be credited, with the distinguished men of two or three generations ago than of this day. A certain *hauteur* and exaction seemed to be expected then of the great leaders, and was readily pardoned. Few critics blamed Mr. Clay's lordly and magnificent arrogance or General Jackson's imperious dictation, and the masses seemed rather to like and admire it.

A large share of pride — or of that self-confidence which is akin to vanity — seems to be always an ingredient in the make-up of men of this calibre. Many stories are yet told in Tennessee illustrative of this quality in General Jackson. One of them relates to his political protégé, Mr. Van Buren. General Jackson was extremely fond of thoroughbred horses, and always bred and raced them until he had reached a devout old age. Mr. Van Buren, when a Presidential candidate, visited "Old Hickory," and the latter took him out one morning to witness the exercise gallops of some fine youngsters which the old man had in training. Among them was a three-year-old stallion — the pet and pride of his master — and which he expected every one else to admire as much as he did himself. He had particularly impressed Mr. Van Buren with an idea of his excellence.

The two gentlemen took position on the side of the "track" waiting, expectantly, to see the colts "brush." "Old Hickory" stood just on the edge of the course, perilously near to where the horses would pass; Mr. Van Buren was cautioned not to stand so close. In a little while the pet colt and a stable companion almost as fleet as himself, came rushing like tornadoes down the home stretch toward the post. In his anxiety to see the horse the general had so highly vaunted, Mr. Van Buren pressed even beyond General Jackson and stepped out upon the track. It never occurred, perhaps, to General Jackson in all his life, that any horse would attempt to run over him, or could do so if he tried, but he was concerned for his friend. He seized the New York statesman by the collar and dragged him forcibly back. "Get behind me, Mr. Van Buren," he shouted in a tone that drowned the rattling thunder of the rapid feet. "Keep behind me, sir! Then you will always be safe."

Senator Benton, of Missouri, who in the beginning of his public career was a violent personal enemy of General Jackson, but afterward one of his most potent political supporters, evinced the same characteristic in even greater degree, but in a less pardonable way, for Benton's self-assertion always savoured of insolence. It was said of him that he so resented opposition that he could not tolerate the ordinary courtesies of life from any one who did not absolutely agree with him. On one occasion a St. Louis editor, who had somewhat freely and, as the old statesman thought, offensively criticized his action upon some important measures, happening to meet him in the statehouse at Jefferson City, formally but politely saluted him.

"Don't bow to me," roared 'Old Bullion'; "if you lift your hat to me again, I'll break your neck. I make no objection to your criticism. It simply shows that I'm right. I rather like your abuse, but I'll be hanged if I submit for one moment to your civility."

It would be difficult to imagine a more arrogant temper than that which could inspire and deliver such an utterance.

After such specimens of extraordinary, extravagant egotism, it is refreshing to recall the milder and more amiable effusions of humbler men. We find something like a sense of consolation in the lament of the honest old Kentuckian, who, many years since, deplored the departure from this world of so many of his eminent contemporaries. "Yes," he said pathetically, "they are mighty nigh all gone. I have attended Mr. Clay's funeral; I have seen the clods dropped on Crittenden's grave. John

Morgan and Rodger Hanson was killed endurin' of the war. John Brackenridge and Humphrey Marshall has passed away since, and John Carlisle is lookin' mighty feeble. And worst of all, I ain't feelin' at all well myself."

It has been a common opinion that the Southern people are rather too quick to take offence and prone to resentment; and we cannot successfully deny that such opinion is correct. It may be justly claimed, however, that, as a rule, they are placable and willing to make reparation when they have been in the wrong. Indeed, a readiness to render proper apology for either unwarranted affront or injury has always been a Southern attribute, and in the olden time the Southern gentleman prided himself quite as much upon knowing how to make a graceful *amende* when in fault himself, as upon his perfect acquaintance with the most efficient and speediest method of obtaining satisfaction when himself offended.

They also entertained a chivalrous feeling and sense of fair play, which required that the apology should not be made clandestinely, but should always be as public as had been the offence for which it was given. Much good, and real reformation of much that is censurable, may be expected from a people whose conduct is directed by such a sentiment.

Innumerable examples of what has just been said might be furnished, but one will suffice to demonstrate its correctness.

Many years ago two well-known citizens of Louisville, Judge Burnett and Colonel Jacobs, were visiting a neighbouring town while the annual agricultural fair was in progress. They were cordially welcomed, of course, and treated with great hospitality; and as a demonstration of the respect which every one desired to testify, were requested to serve among the "judges" of a number of the important "horse rings."

In one ring — for the best pair of light carriage horses — a close contest occurred, which elicited much excitement; every person on the grounds took sides, either for a very fine pair of bays, or for an exceedingly showy, high-stepping pair of browns. The judges themselves were long in doubt, but ultimately by a divided vote, three to two, gave the premium to the "browns" and the red ribbon to the "bays." Whereupon, the driver and owner of the bays stood up in his vehicle and solemnly swore at the judges as a "passell of blamed idiots who didn't know the points of a horse from the bark on a buckeye tree, and instead of judging a horse ring ought to be attending a normal school."

The profoundest feeling was at once aroused. The majority of those present might have been willing not only to pardon but to a certain extent sympathize with a man who, really feeling himself aggrieved, had shot a man in fair fight, even for mistaken provocation; but this sort of thing was unprecedented, and not only ungentlemanly, but a reflection on the community wherein it occurred. The managers and authorities of the fair association and the people generally — even those who had been the strongest partisans of the "bays" — were scandalized and indignant, and there was a general demand that the offender should be expelled from the ring and the grounds. Some even went so far as to say that his behaviour was so extremely disgraceful and "ridiculous," that, if a shot-gun was handy, he ought to receive the benefit of it.

The managers held an immediate session, and in a few minutes adopted a resolution, pronouncing sentence on the offender, condemning him to everlasting banishment from those premises and all the privileges thereunto belonging, never to be permitted to show another horse there, bay, brown, sorrel, gray, or black. This sentence was unanimously approved by all present.

The friends of the erring horseman took him aside and strove to impress upon him the enormity of his action. They told him frankly that he had behaved badly. They laid proper stress upon the sanctity which should always attach to the "bench," and pointed out that judicial decisions should be treated with respect, even if erroneous.

"How are we going to get along," they urged; "how are we to maintain our fair associations, so necessary to the maintenance and encouragement of our horse-breeding and other important interests, if every man who fails to take a blue ribbon denounces and insults the judges? It will be impossible," they said, "to procure the proper sort of men to officiate, to accept those exalted positions."

One of the offender's most intimate friends declared with

emphasis that he had "No self-respect for a d — n fellow who couldn't lose a premium without cussin' like a drunken nigger at a cornshuckin'."

It finally dawned upon the defendant that he was really greatly to blame, and had committed a gross breach of etiquette, and under this conviction he expressed himself as willing and anxious to apologize.

The Kentuckians, although hot-tempered, are in most matters of a forgiving disposition, and so, when it was announced that the gentleman sincerely regretted his offence, it was decided that he should be permitted to acknowledge and ask pardon for the "mistake" he had committed, and should be reinstated. Judge Burnett was especially earnest and eloquent in his plea for such action, inasmuch as he had been strongly in favour of awarding the blue ribbon to the "bays."

When this decision was reached it was announced to the crowd, and the same people who had previously clamoured for the culprit's expulsion, on learning that he was contrite and willing to say as much, agreed that his improper language ought to be condoned. On that afternoon, at the hour when it was understood that the apology was to be offered, a much larger crowd was assembled than had been on the grounds in the morning, for many who had learned what had happened came to hear the apology.

When the hour arrived the judges assembled and stood with official dignity in the centre of the ring, and the penitent, escorted by the gentleman who acted as ring master and grand marshal of the ceremonies, entered the arena. Amid profound silence, and unfaltering, notwithstanding the somewhat unfriendly gaze of the multitude, he walked forward with a firm step and composed demeanour to within a few paces of the spot where the judges were awaiting him, and, lifting his hat, said in a clear voice heard by every one in the listening and deeply interested audience: "Gentlemen, I am greatly mortified by what has occurred, and I cannot adequately express my regret that your conduct was such as to compel me to employ the strong language which I uttered."

The silence of the multitude remained unbroken and intense, but there came a look resembling astonishment and incredulity on every face. Then Judge Burnett stepped forward, grasped the hand of that contrite and candid man, and said: "My dear sir, in behalf of myself and colleagues, I accept the handsome acknowledgment you have just made, in the same spirit in which it is offered, and trust that it will never have to be repeated."

For some reason, the audience thought both speeches a trifle ambiguous. A few hours later the reinstated horseman reappeared in the ring and drove a spanking pair of chestnuts to victory. When returning thanks for the blue ribbon, no man's speech or manner could have been more refined or appropriate, and everybody said that he had received a lesson which had been of great service.

Kentucky has always been more or less renowned as the home of men of large stature. There was better reason for it, perhaps, in the earlier days of the commonwealth than now, because of the hardier and doubtless healthier life of the pioneers. Byron, writing of "Colonel Boone, Backwoodsman, of Kentucky," seems to be of this opinion, for when he describes the Kentucky hunters and their children, declaring that

> "Tall and strong and swift of foot were they,
> Beyond the dwarfing city's pale abortions,"

he evidently believed that the air of the woods is better adapted to the rearing of a stalwart progeny than that of the streets.

Nevertheless, the Bluegrass State has produced some rather striking specimens of ample physical development even since the period when the "bar, the buffler, and the Injun" were to be found within her borders, and when it was consequently necessary that human beings should be built upon a corresponding scale in order to successfully compete with them. Whether the average Kentuckian has been compelled to earn his livelihood by his rifle or more modern implements of industry — whether he has fed on venison or "hog and hominy" — he has attained rather unusual proportions of height and girth, and every generation has exhibited an abundance of robust physical manhood.

The fame of some of the tallest of these Kentuckians survives in legends, which, if not authentic are yet impressive.

Tradition fails to preserve the name but relates the exploits of a certain native of Nelson county, in the days before Nelson county was subdivided into many others. This veritable son of Anak, it is said, preferred to pluck fruit from the very top of an apple tree, while himself standing at its foot, and could easily nail shingles on the roof of an ordinary log cabin without having to mount either stump or ladder. No one now living, however, has ever talked with any one who had seen him perform either of these feats. Wonderful stories have been told about Jim Porter, the hack driver, the "Portland giant," as he was called by residents of Louisville, and the "Kentucky giant" by those who lived elsewhere. His length of arm and reach was so great that his admirers claimed he could not only open the door of his hack without descending from his seat, but that he could, with one hand, yank off any fellow who might try to steal a ride behind, while still managing his reins and team with the other. Dickens thought Porter worthy of mention as one of the curiosities he saw during his stay in America.

The ranks of the professional "giants," who travel with the great shows and delight and amaze the eyes of sight-seers, have been recruited from this peculiar growth of Kentucky's prolific soil. The best known of these were "Captain," or, as he was sometimes — with a fine humour — termed "Baby" Bates, and Smith Cook, his scarcely less famous and colossal compatriot. Bates was said to be more than eight feet in height. I have often seen him, and had I been asked to hazard a guess at his vertical dimensions, I should have said he was fully nine. Nor was he of a lank and meager frame, by any means. He weighed nearly four hundred pounds, was well made and powerful, and quite a "well-favoured" man. He served, when a very young man, in one of the Kentucky cavalry regiments, and his comrades used to say that when the road was very bad he would sometimes dismount and carry his horse over the worst places. I do not vouch for this story, because soldiers, in their moments of leisure, will occasionally lie, and it is well to receive much that they say with caution. Bates had none of that heavy stupidity and dullness of intellect which history and fiction seem agreed in ascribing to those who have exceeded the usual stature of humanity. He was a man of good and alert intelligence, relishing a joke exceedingly and always willing to take part in any pleasantry. Once on a steamboat trip down the Ohio with Col. Dick Wintersmith he aided that merry gentleman in mystifying an acquaintance of the latter in a way that highly delighted both himself and the colonel. As the boat rounded in at Owensboro, Colonel Wintersmith recognized a man standing upon the wharf and evidently about to come on board, as an old and very intimate friend of his own and a relative of his wife, but whom he had not seen for years. Wintersmith at once turned to Bates, pointed out his friend and said: "When that man comes aboard I'm going to introduce you to him as my son. Do you catch on?" "I do," said the giant, and the plot between them was perfectly understood. The meeting between the colonel and his friend was very cordial, and after a number of mutual inquiries usual on such occasions, the latter asked where the colonel was going and upon what business. "Ah," sighed Dick, in melancholy cadence, "I have an unpleasant matter in hand. My eldest boy, who has been at school in Memphis, ran away the other day. I caught him in Louisville and am taking him back. But," he added, with apparently sudden indignation, "I'll make him sorry for what he has done. I'll thrash him within an inch of his life."

"Now, Dick," said the friend, with the consideration we invariably entertain in such cases for other people's children, "don't be too hard on him. Boys will be boys." "It's well to say that," replied Dick, "but you never saw such a boy as this fellow is. But I'll show him to you. Come here, Jimmy."

Bates, who had remained out of sight but within hearing, immediately responded to the call. "This is my boy Jimmy," said Colonel Wintersmith. "Shake hands with Mr. Brown, Jimmy."

Mr. Brown fell back into a chair and almost fainted. "Dick Wintersmith," he exclaimed in a sepulchral voice, "you say that's your son?"

"Oh, yes," said Dick, "but he's a very bad boy. What made you run away from school, you little rascal?"

"Well, pa," said the giant, grinning sheepishly, "they treated me so bad I couldn't stay."

"My God, Dick!" said Mr. Brown, oblivious to the ordinary courtesies incumbent upon an introduction, "you don't mean to tell me that's Lizzie's child!"

"Of course I do. What's the matter with you?"

Mr. Brown was still paralyzed with amazement. The smooth, beardless, rosy, boyish face of "Baby" Bates, in contrast with his enormous frame, bewildered him. Then, in well-enacted confusion, Bates simpered and with an easy gesture took down his pipe from where he had previously deposited it on the hurricane deck ten feet above where they stood. It was a huge meerschaum, as big for a pipe as Bates was for a man. He loaded it with a full handful of tobacco and began to smoke.

"For the love of heaven!" ejaculated Mr. Brown. "Do you permit that boy to use tobacco?"

"I can't prevent him," said Dick. "He both smokes and chews. I'm afraid it's going to injure his growth. But he don't take a bit after his mother. He has all my vices. You would hardly believe it, but he drinks and swears."

"Well," said Mr. Brown, apparently at last resigned to the situation, "if the habits of drinking and smoking become confirmed, in two years from this date there won't be a barrel of whiskey or a hogshead of tobacco left in Kentucky."

Smith Cook was neither so tall nor so bulky as Bates. His height, I think, was seven feet and eight inches, and his weight about two hundred and seventy-five pounds. He had a good, although rather excessive figure, and a handsome countenance with a somewhat sad expression; the expression of one, who, from a superior eminence, looks down upon the follies of mankind. He exhibited a good deal of the intellectual slowness and simplicity which, from time immemorial, have been imputed to the giant. But he was gentle and amiable, and while always ready and consistent in his defence of the showmen and circus people with whom he has long been associated, was austere and uncompromising in condemnation of the numerous "fakirs" who follow a big show, and of whose malpractices he ever spoke with abhorrence.

When Cook finally quitted the show business and the road,

he became smitten with that passion which has fascinated and impaired the usefulness of so many Kentuckians who would otherwise have been valuable citizens. His soul was fired with the desire for political distinction and a longing for office and public preferment. He was doing quite well on his little farm in his native county of Henry. He was, in some respects, peculiarly fitted for the successful prosecution of agricultural pursuits. His length of arm was so great that when he swung a scythe or wielded a cradle, no mowing or harvesting machine ever invented could accomplish more, in a given length of time, than could his unaided strength; and no scarecrow was more effective to frighten away marauding birds from the corn field. His tall form stalking once a day in the vicinity would cause the boldest crow to keep aloof for a week.

But in an evil hour, he allowed himself to be elected doorkeeper of the lower house of the legislature. Like Cincinnatus he was persuaded to abandon the plow, although I believe that he required rather less persuasion than was exerted in the case of Cincinnatus. He performed the onerous and responsible duties of this position with ability and fidelity, until he struck the rock on which so many promising statesmen have been wrecked. He permitted his private feelings to unduly influence his official duty. The personal equation asserted itself so strongly, that not only did he fail on one important occasion to observe the impersonal conduct which is justly expected of every public servant, but he violated that salutary rule which inhibits interference by one coördinate branch of government with another, and permitted himself, although merely a doorkeeper, to offer advice to legislators.

It must be admitted, however, that the temptation was unusually strong, and it can also be said in his excuse that he acted not so much for his own interest as in behalf of his friends and former associates.

At that date, the idea of regulation by legislative enactment was taking strong hold of the popular mind and inflaming the imaginations of aspiring politicians. A certain member of the Kentucky senate was exceedingly anxious to do something in that line; but, having been dilatory, ascertained, when he finally determined to introduce some such measure that the field of corporate regulation was already fully occupied. Thorough attention had been paid to railroads, banks, and insurance companies, and he could discover nothing of that nature at which he could shoot an enactment. After much thought, however, a bright idea occurred to him. He reflected how basely a long-suffering people had been — and were being — deceived and disappointed by those whose business it was to furnish them amusement. So he carefully prepared and introduced a bill requiring all shows, circuses, and theatrical companies of every kind, to conform in all respects to their advertisements, and have their performances come thoroughly up to the expectations excited by their bill posters.

Cook had quitted the show business many years previously, and had no intention of reëntering it, but his blood boiled at what he deemed a rank injustice, and he felt keenly for his old friends, threatened with such oppression. He forgot his customary caution and reticence, and utilized every occasion to denounce a measure so iniquitous.

When the wags of both houses — and a majority of the names on each roll-call might have been included in such category — learned how profoundly he was interested, they determined to make the best possible use of such opportunity for amusement. Some came to notify him, kindly but firmly, that they felt compelled to vote for the bill, as one sorely needed for the protection of a fraud-ridden community. Others pledged him unreservedly that they would vote against it, believing it to be the extremest expression of legislative imbecility. This declaration gave him much comfort. But the greater number claimed to be undecided. They said that they wished to avail themselves of his superior practical knowledge of the subject; that if he could state substantial reasons why it should be defeated they would vote accordingly; but that, with their then understanding of the matter, they didn't see how they would be able to satisfy their excited constituencies unless they helped to pass the bill.

Cook had never, perhaps, in all of his life attempted to give a reason for anything; but in this grave emergency he made the best effort he could, and even essayed an argument before the committee. The committee listened to him with profound respect and attention, but seemed hopelessly divided. Then he resorted to more practical methods. He wrote to all of the big shows which habitually traversed Kentucky, and received assurances from their proprietors that to every legislator, who voted or in good faith worked against the bill, a ticket of admission should be issued to be good if the show visited Frankfort during the continuance of the session, or if presented at any time during the year at any other point. He did not feel entirely easy, however, until, after many long and earnest conferences with Judge Mulligan, of Lexington, who was then a member of the senate, he had secured that gentleman's apparently reluctant consent to oppose the bill upon the floor. Yet somehow or another, Judge Mulligan, usually quicker of apprehension than any one, seemed strangely unable to understand Cook's presentation of the case; and more than once, after he had appeared to be entirely satisfied, came back with startling objections which cost Cook many wakeful nocturnal hours to successfully combat. At length, however, he announced that he was convinced.

When the day arrived upon which the bill was to be considered, Cook was white and tremulous with suppressed emotion. At first its advocates had decidedly the advantage of the discussion, and its opponents seemed to be half-hearted and afraid to extend themselves. But Cook said to the friends who were commiserating:

"You jest wait — wait till Mulligan gits up. He won't leave enough of them fellers to feed a snipe — he'll make 'em look like thirty cents. You jest wait!"

Finally Mulligan got up. He said that, at first, he had been greatly impressed with this bill. To him it had seemed to have merit, and to be intended to correct an unmistakable evil.

"I, myself," he said, with that candour which adds so much to the effect of oratory, "have more than once suffered the pang of disappointment which assails the man who carefully studies the bill and afterward sees the circus. When I was a boy I read glowing accounts of the equatorial African hen, to which crushed ice had to be given three times a day to prevent her from laying boiled eggs, and in whose cage no straw could be placed because her fiery breath would ignite it. In the simple, pathetic confidence of youth, I hastened to see this highly attractive bird; and what did I witness? Only, so far as I could discover, a plain, motherly yellow hen. Afterwards I saw a picture of the hippopotamus hunted in his native river by the black savages who lived upon its banks. The infuriated animal had rushed, with a mouth stretched wider than a railroad tunnel, upon his foes, had crushed the boat with his mighty teeth, had swallowed one of the Africans, blood raw, and had tossed the others fifty feet into the air. I went to the circus. Consumed with anxiety and curiosity, I rushed to the tank where the hippopotamus had his habitat, and I saw, what? Merely the nose of the creature an inch or two above the water, and there wasn't a canoe or a nigger anywhere around.

"On one occasion, when I was visiting New York, I was taken by a friend over to Jersey City to visit an extensive menagerie which was wintering there. When we were in the very acme of enjoyment — admiring the many interesting animals we saw — the black rhinoceros was suddenly smitten with one of those unaccountable fits of rage which sometimes drives that beast to distraction, and makes him so disagreeable to both man and beast. Suddenly and without any ascertainable provocation, he began to attack every thing in sight. He spread destruction and terror all about him. He slew the musk-ox and crippled the giraffe. The camels humped themselves for flight, and the elephants packed their trunks to leave. In the wild disorder everybody and every animal was seeking refuge as best he might. Five or six of the employés climbed the centre pole of the tent, hoping to find safety at its top; but one of the elephants, now insane himself with rage and fear, wrapped his trunk around the pole and shook it as a boy shakes a fruit tree. All of these unfortunate men were shaken down and tramped to death by the monster — all save one; he was highest on the pole, and he succeeded in gnawing his way through the canvas, and escaped by sliding down on the outside like a man going down a fire-escape.

"I was so paralyzed with fear, that I stood still — thinking that I was lost. But fortunately the attention of the rhinoceros was attracted to the gorilla. That formidable and ferocious ape, excited by the tumult, was conducting himself as he is said to do in his native forest when something occurs to arouse his fury. He had erected his horrent crest, was beating his hairy chest with his huge hands, and was emitting those blood-curdling, thunderous growls which shake and appal the jungles of the Gaboon. The rhinoceros made a dash straight for the den of the gorilla. He struck it quartering and ripped out the bars as easily as a monkey would tear away the wires of a canary bird's cage; and then the gorilla dropped upon his knees, and wailed out, "Oh, Holy Moses! oh! all yez blessed saints in heaven! help me out of this scrape; and if iver I thravel as a gorilla agin, I'll go to hell by consint."

"Just think of that! Here was a poor exile from Erin, caught on the beach — picked up as soon as he landed on these shores, and induced to travel as a gorilla — think of this outrage inflicted on him, and of the imposition upon the public.

"I mention these things senators, to show you that I have experienced, more than any of you, perhaps, that deception which so arouses your indignation. But let us try to be just. Upon reflection, I am satisfied that something — perhaps much — may be said in palliation, if not in excuse, of this practice we are seeking to correct. We must remember that every man, woman, and child cannot go to the circus. Thousands are prevented by poverty, and yet their eyes are delighted by these beautiful show bills which have elicited so much criticism. We had best pause, lest we be suspected of legislating in the interests of the wealthy — the bloated bond holder who can pay to enter the tent — while we deprive the common people, the children of the poor, of the only part of the entertainment which is furnished without cost.

"I say nothing of other criticism to which we might subject ourselves, if we pass this bill — that it might be claimed that we have interfered with the free control of private property, and have discouraged the development of art. But these are trivial objections. The reflection, which to my mind is most seriously disquieting, is that such legislation will deprive the poor of the only solace which, for them, is associated with a circus. It will take from their eyes those radiant pictures which are things of beauty, and — until patent advertisements are pasted over them — joys forever.

"I therefore, move you, Mr. Speaker, that this bill be recommitted to the Committee on General Statutes, with instructions that that committee shall consult with the Committee on Claims and Grievances, and that no further report shall be made until both committees shall unanimously agree."

In vain the author of the bill strongly protested against this action, which he justly declared would stifle his measure, and which he also alleged to be unprecedented. Every senator said that he had always entertained exactly the same opinion expressed by Mulligan; only he hadn't known just how to formulate it. So the motion was carried by acclamation.

But then Cook's real trouble began. Every senator claimed the reward he had offered those who should vote against the bill.

"You didn't vote against it," he said, "it wasn't put upon its passage."

"That's a vile subterfuge," they asserted. "We voted for a motion which was equivalent to an indefinite postponement, and that amounted to voting against it."

Next came eighty or ninety members of the house demanding, in return for what they had done, certificates which would obtain them free admission to all the shows.

"But," said Cook, "you fellers didn't vote at all. The bill didn't reach the house."

"That wasn't our fault. We were ready to vote against it; and we gave you our moral support, we used our influence with senators and we want the recognition that is our due."

Cook never was able to settle. The claims and the claimants multiplied, and the show people ungratefully went back on him. His political career was ruined. His life was blighted. He became so bent and stooped with care as to lose twelve inches of his height and he fell off nearly one hundred and twenty pounds in flesh; so that the couldn't have gone back to the show business had he wished. He died a lofty but melancholy example of misdirected zeal.

CHAPTER XXI

GEN. JOHN C. BRECKINRIDGE used to tell a story of ante-bellum politics, which he enjoyed none the less because the joke was on himself. On one occasion, during his second canvass for congress, he was advertised to speak in a certain county where political sentiment was pretty equally divided, and the partisan prejudice against him about offset the strong personal devotion he generally inspired. He therefore felt unusual interest in the result of this meeting, and determined to exert to the utmost his powers of eloquence and persuasion. He was staying on the night preceding at the house of Mr. Cohen, a warm personal friend and the most influential Democrat of the county.

They were engaged in consultation for many hours, discussing momentous strategical questions connected with the canvass and the attitude of numerous precinct leaders not yet positively committed. Soon after breakfast, "Major" Breckinridge, as he was then styled, and Mr. Cohen got into the latter's buggy and drove to the place of the meeting. It was known that the crowd would assemble at an early hour, and deemed important that the major should employ two or three hours in "mixing."

When they reached the ground, Major Breckinridge did "mix," and to good effect, if the earnest approbation accorded his remarks about the crops and the live stock and the open-mouthed laughter with which his jests and anecdotes were received was evidence thereof. His friend was, in the meantime, doubtless also well employed, but the major lost sight of him until the hour for speaking was announced and he mounted the stand together with the other prominent citizens.

It is scarcely necessary to say that at that time John C. Breckinridge had no peer as a stump speaker in Kentucky — it is a matter of history. But those who never saw or heard him can form no conception of his wonderful magnetism. It resided as much in his look and gesture as in his voice. Often a mere glance over the crowd, while he remained seated and silent, would elicit wild cheers and a tumult that could with difficulty be stilled. On this occasion he surpassed himself and seemed resolved to capture every auditor and conquer all prejudice.

The crowd soon yielded to the spell of his eloquence with one exception. A tall, burly, hard-featured, sarcastic-looking "cuss" had posted himself in the front rank of the closely packed audience, and it became immediately apparent that he was not a "Brackenridge man," but on the contrary, very hostile to the Democratic champion. Indeed, before the speaker had well opened his argument, this individual had interrupted him half a dozen times in an exceedingly offensive manner.

The crowd became indignant and Mr. Cohen arose, and, in a voice almost inarticulate with wrath, threatened the noisy ruffian with expulsion and punishment if he did not desist.

"You shet your damn head, Jim Cohen," responded the offender. "I reckon this air a free country and I've got a right to talk."

Then a universal rush was about to be made upon him, but Major Breckinridge intervened. He deprecated the popular fury and begged that the man should be allowed to remain, modestly announcing the belief that if he would listen he would be converted. The crowd was pacified, the defiant disturber of the peace grunted that he would be quiet and listen, but added, "You'll have a hell of a time convertin' of me," and the orator proceeded.

The speech was now addressed particularly to this man, who still maintained a belligerent demeanour. No longer noisy and boisterous, he was yet sufficiently demonstrative in look and gesture, and intimated his dissent by derisive glances and half-muttered ejaculations of contempt. Gradually, however, his manner changed as the voice whose "mellifluous thunder" was used to sway all hearts, poured upon him the tide of its winning, resistless eloquence. His corrugated brow relaxed, the smile of scorn faded from his lip, he shifted from one foot to the other, like a bear on hot plates, and turned once or twice as if seeking to escape, but the dense crowd held him in his place. Tears at length began to steal down his cheeks, and, finally bursting into sobs, he exclaimed, "By hell, Brackenridge! You kin beat 'em all. I'm fer you agin' the worl'."

The effect was electrical. All opposition was destroyed, and in one grand cheer the crowd declared itself unanimous "for Breckinridge."

As the major and Mr. Cohen were driving home in the cool of the evening, the former, still aglow with his triumph, alluded to the incident just described with pardonable pride:

"I must have been making a pretty good speech," he said, "to affect that fellow the way I did."

"You think you did it, do you?" said Cohen dryly, with a quizzical glance out of the corner of his eye.

An indescribable dismay smote the major; an awful feeling that some cherished conviction was about to be dissipated.

"Why," he stammered, "what do you mean?"

"Well, I'll tell you. While you were mixing I caught sight of that fellow, who is the rankest bummer unhung, but as smart as an old fox. I knew that the people about here didn't know much of him, for he don't live in this precinct. Thinks I, I'll put him to work. I called him to one side and said, 'Bill, how do you stand in this race?' He answered, 'I ain't in it. Neither side ain't showed cause yet.' 'Well,' I said, 'I'll give you ten dollars if you will go to work for Breckinridge.' He reflected for a moment. 'Jim Cohen,' he said, 'if you'll make it twenty-five dollars, I'll act a piece afore that crowd to-day which 'ull fetch every dad-burned son of a gun in it; git 'em all. I'll jes' have a whoopin' fer Brackenridge.' With that he sketched the programme you saw him carry out. Before he got half through I closed the bargain. I felt sure that you would show up well — do the magnanimous, and all that, and I believed we had the work done.

"Now, don't you think I did pretty well?" General Breckinridge always declared that, after hearing this, for a moment he felt stunned, and then, as it all dawned upon him in its full significance, as he realized the dramatic perfection and histrionic success of the incident, he forgot all chagrin and disappointment in admiration of the chief performer's ingenuity and cheek.

The "joint" political discussion wherein the candidates, or representatives of contending parties, or rival aspirants for political preferment, met on the rostrum in actual debate, once so popular and frequent, has now gone almost entirely out of fashion in Kentucky and is, I believe, equally as obsolete in other communities where it was formerly as prevalent.

The lists are now almost closed against such forensic contests and oratorical gladiators must meet and exhibit themselves before courts and juries only, or furnish the public no opportunity of determining their respective merits by immediate comparison. The champion who was once spurred to emulation by the presence of his competitor, or warned to caution by risk of prompt retort or successful contradiction before the same audience he had just exhorted, no longer feels the same incentive or the necessity of such discretion. He not only addresses a crowd composed in large measures of those who already agree with him, but has the field to himself, a clear track, and trots, as it were, "against time." It is not surprising, therefore, that the old time stump oratory is almost a lost art.

While less interesting than when the speakers were directly pitted against each other, in that the partisan feeling elicited is not so keen, and the excitement of contest under better control, the modern method is for those very reasons, perhaps, preferable. Political debate, however conducted, is apt to evoke bad feeling; and it is certainly better that it should not cause bloodshed, as in the old times it sometimes did not only with the principals, but among their friends and supporters. It is true that the sudden and violent extinction occasionally of some hot-blooded citizen, who was unable to conclude an argument without producing a weapon, was not regarded as an irreparable loss to the community. I have read a story somewhere in which it is related that two war vessels, English and Dutch respectively, met upon the high seas shortly after peace had been concluded between the two nations. Each commander, anxious to do the civil thing and evince good form, fired a salute. Unfortunately the shot had not been withdrawn from one of the English guns, and the big bullet, fulfilling the billet for which it was originally intended, killed a Dutchman. The English captain despatched a boat in great haste, bearing an officer commissioned to make profuse apology, and explain that "it was entirely accidental." The Dutch captain received the explanation in admirably good temper.

"It is all right," he said, "Dere is blenty more Dutchmens in Holland, blenty more."

When, in the old days, debate transcended the limit of parliamentary order and decorum, resulting in an accident of like nature, people with a philosophy akin to that of the Dutchman reflected that there was an abundance of similar material to supply the place of the gentleman who had fallen.

Many such joint discussions were duly reported and are therefore accurately preserved; many others survive only in tradition. One of the most interesting and spirited of the latter, doubtless well remembered yet by a number of men still living, occurred at Lexington two or three years after the close of the war. I heard it, and its salient features are almost as fresh in my memory as if it were a matter of yesterday.

The election of a commonwealth's attorney for that judicial district was approaching, and was eliciting unusual interest because of the personnel of the candidates.

The two first who entered the field, Col. W. C. P. Breckinridge and Capt. Lawrence Jones, were extremely popular and very highly regarded. Colonel Breckinridge became afterward so well known that it is scarcely necessary to more than allude to his marvellous gift of oratory, not fully developed then, but already making him famous. Captain Jones was a man of high character and strong sense and a clear and forcible speaker. Soon afterward the Hon. Edward Marshall announced himself. He was in the meridian of his intellectual powers, brilliant, eloquent, witty, and the most consummate actor that ever trod the rostrum. He had served with distinction in congress, and his reputation as an orator and politician was national. He was, however, extremely erratic, and his sarcastic tongue had made him many enemies. He was accustomed to say of himself that "the people would rather hear me speak than anybody, and would rather vote for anybody than me."

The latest to appear in the ring, but by no means the less confident of success on that account, or indisposed to compensate for delay by especial activity and effort, was Gen. John S. Williams.

In this quadrilateral contest, Marshall laboured under one decided disadvantage. At that date the people of Kentucky were greatly in love with Confederate soldiers; and although Marshall had been an avowed and intense Southern sympathizer — had, indeed, been sent to prison because of his Southern proclivities — he had not served in the Southern army. The other three had well known records as Confederate soldiers — Williams and Breckinridge had won real distinction, and all three were as ready to assert and improve that claim as the people were to recognize it.

Williams was also a veteran of the Mexican war; had gone in as a captain and been promoted to a colonelcy, and had acquired by a display of exceptional gallantry in that battle, the soubriquet of "Cerro Gordo" Williams. He was an extremely handsome man, tall, large, and splendidly proportioned, with a manner and bearing which clearly indicated that he believed himself entitled to a large share of popular approbation and was fully determined to claim his rights. He had a large following and a host of devoted personal friends, for he possessed many generous and manly qualities. He was withal an adroit poiltician and one of the best stump speakers in Kentucky.

As brigadier-general in the Confederate army he had rendered excellent service and had won and deserved a high reputation for courage and efficiency. He had many enviable exploits to his credit, but the most conspicuous was his repulse of the first attempt by the Federals to capture the salt works in southwestern Virginia, when he defeated Burbridge at Saltville in a hotly contested combat, fought against great odds. Full justice has never been done General Williams for his conduct in that battle, and for the really important victory which he gained. But the reason, perhaps, why other people did not comment upon it more frequently was because he mentioned it so often himself. It was a favourite topic of discourse with him, and any one who ventured a suggestion which detracted in any degree from his full credit for the success achieved there incurred his dire and everlasting displeasure.

Before the war Williams had been a resident and citizen of the judicial district in which he was seeking office, but for nearly a year after the close of the war had resided in New Orleans, and for another year thereafter had lived in Logan County,

Kentucky. Grave doubts, therefore, of his eligibility were entertained, and, by those who were opposed to him, fully expressed; inasmuch as he had returned to the district only two or three months previously to the announcement of his candidacy.

He was not the sort of man, however, to permit a little thing like that to hinder his attainment of an important object. Sophisticated distinctions of that nature troubled him very little, and mere geographical lines or ill considered statutory limitations could not prevent him rendering useful public service. He stated, in a way that obviated all negation, that he had been absent from Clark County for the past four years by the cruelest compulsion, and all the time *animo revertendi;* and now that he was back again, he intended to claim all of his rights and privileges as a citizen, and hold any office the people might choose to give him.

At that time Breckinridge, whose law practice was not so lucrative as it subsequently became, was editing the Lexington *Observer and Reporter.* During the heat of the canvass, an article appeared in this paper severely criticizing General Williams's attitude in the race, roundly asserting that he was not eligible to the office he sought, and, in utter defiance of historic truth, declaring that his claim to be the hero of Saltville was altogether unfounded.

Williams, of course, supposed that Breckinridge was the author of this article — it appeared as an editorial — and was naturally exceedingly indignant. In fact, Breckinridge had not written the article, and was in no wise responsible for it, except in that it was published in the paper of which he was editor.

It was one of those unfortunate journalistic accidents which have more than once caused trouble. While actively engaged in his canvass, Breckinridge had been compelled to invoke assistance in his editorial work, and had requested a friend to conduct that department when he himself should be absent; and this gentleman, more zealous than discreet, had conceived the idea of eliminating from the contest, by one trenchant editorial stroke, the colonel's most formidable antagonist. Breckinridge promptly sent word to Williams, explaining how the matter had happened, disclaiming any endorsement of the offensive statements, and offering to make any *amende* which mutual friends might deem proper.

But the general's ire was too thoroughly aroused to permit of his consenting to any amicable adjustment. He might possibly have overlooked other objectionable matter, but the impugnment of his Saltville record was unpardonable. He discerned also, he thought, an opportunity of making good political capital out of the manifest injustice which had been done him, and sternly rejected all overtures. He preferred a grievance to an apology.

He accordingly gave formal notice that on a certain evening he would speak in Lexington and answer seriatim and fully the statements contained in the said article, all of which he pledged himself to prove conclusively to be false and injurious. He invited his competitors to be present, and requested the largest possible attendance of his fellow-citizens, especially those who were entitled to vote, in order that he might establish fairly and fully the justice of every claim he had ever asserted.

Of course, when the appointed date arrived a large and interested crowd was in attendance, and public expectation was on the alert to hear speeches in which the personal equation would be largely represented.

When the audience, composed not only of citizens of Lexington and the immediate vicinity but of many others from neighbouring counties, was assembled, General Williams mounted the rostrum. The other candidates, except Breckinridge, were present. Breckinridge was compelled to attend a meeting at a neighbouring town that afternoon, where he was booked to speak, but had notified his friends that he would return in time to hear and answer anything which the general might say about him.

If there had been any previous doubt that General Williams was disposed to make matters warm and interesting, it was dispelled by the first sentences which he uttered.

He announced with impressive solemnity that a double obligation was imposed upon him; that he felt it just and proper to make a statement due his own reputation, and necessary, also, to vindicate the truth of history! It might become his painful duty, he said, in the course of his remarks, to comment severely upon the conduct of one of his opponents, but, however unpleasant that duty might be, he would not shrink from its performance; no consideration should restrain him from dealing fairly and candidly with the people whose suffrages he asked.

Then, with a voice constantly increasing in volume and unmistakable symptoms of a rapidly rising temperature, he read the article from the *Observer and Reporter*, in which his right to be styled the "hero of Saltville" was questioned, and fiercely and unequivocally charged Breckinridge with its responsibility. By way of establishing the claim, which skeptical and sarcastic criticism was now assailing, he gave the history, not only of the battle, but of the campaign immediately preceding it. He recited the conditions which rendered it absolutely necessary to repel the threatened Federal attack and to conserve to the Confederacy the department of South-western Virginia — more especially the salt works — and in glowing and picturesque language described the consternation with which the approach of the Yankees had stricken the inhabitants of that region, and the concern so dire a threat occasioned the authorities at Richmond. With a modesty equalled only by the candid and convincing way in which it was stated, he related the judicious dispositions which were made — under his operation, although not by his sole direction — to meet and roll back this formidable invasion; and having thus wrought his hearers up to the highest pitch of expectation, he entered upon a description of the combat itself.

Seated near the stand was a well known and gallant ex-Confederate officer — Capt. Orville West — who had served on General Williams' staff at Saltville; and in the course of his speech, more particularly when narrating some peculiarly striking and interesting incident, the general would turn to the captain and say, "Isn't that so, Captain West?" or, "Do you not remember this, Captain West?" and the captain would bow and smile assent.

But as the speech progressed in a fervid flow of mingled imagination and invective, when the torrent of ardent and angry eloquence broke over the boundaries not only of memory, but of a reasonable credulity, and threatened to scorch like a stream of lava any one rash enough to hint dissent, Captain West became restless and apprehensive. A pained and startled expression replaced the original smile upon his face, and he looked like a man who wished to plead a pressing engagement and leave. But when General Williams reached the climax of his recital Captain West utterly succumbed.

"Finally," said the general, "the Yankees, anticipated in every movement which they attempted, and foiled in every onslaught they made, essayed as a last resort to break through the left of my position by a determined charge of cavalry. I had expected something of the kind and had prepared to receive and defeat any such effort. The few troops at my disposal had been imperatively needed at other points of my line, and I could not strengthen this point without endangering others; but I had stationed there a battery of four pieces of artillery under an excellent and thoroughly reliable young officer. I warned him that the Yankees at some time during the battle would charge him with cavalry, and directed him what to do. 'When they come,' I said, 'reserve your fire until they are right upon you. Double-shot your guns with grape, and when the forefeet of the hostile horses are clanging upon their muzzles, pull your lanyards.' He implicitly obeyed my instructions. The Yankee cavalry charged gallantly. They rushed upon that battery with sabres whirling, and at such speed that the foam from the mouths of the horses shot back into the faces of the riders. Nothing, it seemed, would be able to withstand their onset. But just as the horses were rearing in front of the battery and about to plunge upon the cannon, the lanyards were pulled and the red and deadly glut rushed forth. Fellow-citizens, I shudder even now when I remember the effect of that terrible volley. That cavalry went down before it as the half-ripened wheat goes down before a storm of wind and hail. Those who were near enough could hear the bones crash in that ill-fated column, as, in the bleak December, you have heard the sleet dash against your windows."

The entire audience was immensely impressed by this vivid picture. The old farmers, especially, realized its horror. Their hair stood on end and their flesh crept, notwithstanding the victims were Yankees. Then General Williams turned and in a voice like thunder asked, "Isn't that so, Captain West?"

Captain West was a loyal staff officer; no one was ever more so. He desired to do his full duty and stand by his chief; but there are limits to human endurance. He essayed to furnish the usual tokens of corroboration; but he was over taxed, his nerve was flanked and, after an ineffectual effort to bow and smile, he dropped from his chair in a limp and fainting condition.

Some time before General Williams had concluded his speech, Breckinridge entered the house and heard the greater part of the criticism bestowed upon himself. Even had he not been inclined to answer it, his friends would have insisted that he should do so; and he needed little urging. As soon, therefore, as Williams sat down, Breckinridge began to speak.

He had little difficulty in convincing the audience that he was guiltless of the most serious charge the general had preferred, that of having used his editorial position to aid his own canvass and injure that of an opponent, but, smarting under Williams's caustic censure, he unfortunately, although quite naturally, retorted in kind, and with a severity that in his cooler moments he regretted. He not only successfully defended his own military record but attacked that of General Williams, and thus the Confederates witnessed, to their scandal and sorrow, two of their favourite representatives assailing each other, and doing more serious detriment to the Confederate prestige than many score of civilian politicians could have accomplished.

The most lamentable, not to say ludicrous, feature of the matter, was that neither was sincere in his attack upon the other, for each was on record — and honestly so — as having testified to the other's merit as a soldier. But here were two comrades, who had "fought, bled," and nearly "died together," denouncing each other like scullions in the effort to obtain an office that neither would have sought had he known in advance that such altercation would have resulted.

Breckinridge, excited by frequent interruption, finally became so warm in rejoinder that a personal encounter between the two was barely averted. The discussion was brought to a sudden termination by a declaration from Williams that he thought the time for words had passed and that for action had arrived, and, as Breckinridge manifestly entertained the same opinion, a clash seemed inevitable. Their partisans, having become thoroughly heated, loudly announced a willingness to participate in this sort of debate, and for a while "blood" was thick "upon the face of the moon." Luckily some ingenious and quick-witted individual hit upon an expedient which diverted the thoughts of all into a safer channel and prevented the collision of which there had been imminent danger.

A voice called loudly for Marshall, and the cry was immediately taken up and shouted from all parts of the hall. Marshall mounted the stand. He was pale, and seemed to be greatly agitated; but this was only a part of the consummate acting of which he was capable. He said that he responded to the call made upon him with extreme reluctance. He had hoped, it was true, to address his fellow-citizens on that evening, but under quite different circumstances. He deeply regretted, he said, the altercation which they had just witnessed, and felt that, perhaps, he ought to be silent. This was a family quarrel between the Confederates, with which other candidates had nothing to do and had better not meddle with. Nevertheless, as it seemed that the crowd wished to hear him, he would try what he could do as a pacificator.

He professed, however, an utter inability to understand the reason for so much excitement. He picked up the paper containing the article which had given so much offence, examined it carefully, held it on the further side of the gas jet in order that he might discern more clearly what there was in it so obnoxious, but declared that he could discover nothing "of a mortal or even dangerous character."

"But," he said, "I find to my great mortification, after what I have heard this evening, that while I prided myself upon knowing a great deal about the Civil War, I have really been very ignorant. I had heard the names of Robert E. Lee, Albert Sidney Johnston and Stonewall Jackson, of Forrest and Morgan and Stuart, and I fondly believed that they had taken some part in the conflict. It seems that I was mistaken; that the information I have been at such pains to acquire is altogether fallacious, and that the only two leaders of real note and merit in the Confederate army were Gen. John S. Cerro Gordo Saltville Williams, and my cousin, Col. William Cabell Preston Breckinridge; and as the classic god of war sometimes ruled the battle under the name of Mars and then again as Enyalyon, so Williams and Breckinridge, under various appellations, dealt death and destruction to the enemies of the South. It was difficult, fellow-citizens, to shake my confidence in the ultimate success of the Confederacy; I believed and hoped to the last, but if I had known what these two gentlemen had done, were doing, and would do if opportunity permitted, I should not have credited the news of Confederate surrender even when announced by Lee."

He said that he also had burned with a desire for military glory at the very time that Colonel Breckinridge had joined the Confederate army, and the real reason why Colonel Breckinridge and not he had become a hero, was to be found in a difference in horse-flesh. "We started for the Confederacy," he said, "at the same date. He was mounted on a superb thoroughbred mare and distanced all pursuit. I was riding a wind-galled, frost-bitten pony. A big Michigan infantry man met me in the pike. I was foolish enough to think the pony could outrun him and tried to escape. In three strides he overtook me, caught the pony by the tail and me by the collar and I was sent to Camp Chase. Had I been on the mare and Colonel Breckinridge on the pony, how unlike would be now our respective political fortunes: it might even, indeed, have wrought some difference in the fate of the Confederacy. As it is, he stands here the peer of Cerro Gordo Saltville Williams; if he doesn't get the office he now seeks, he will get some other, while I shall be lucky if I can pick up a few crumbs after all the Confederates have eaten."

Marshall proceeded in this strain for more than an hour, and if his real object was "pacification" he certainly accomplished it. There was never a crowd, perhaps, so absolutely converted from a temper in which bloodshed had seemed almost inevitable to perfect good humour.

At one time the people of the Northern as well as those of the Southern states were wont to say and, perhaps, inclined to believe that they little resembled one another, each ascribing to themselves peculiar and supposedly superior virtues claimed to be inherent or hereditary. They spoke of the matter as if they had come of widely different stocks, and seemed to think

"Cavalier" and "Puritan" as little akin as Caucasian and Mongol. Very few of them, even of the well informed, chose to remember or cared to consider whether a residence of some two hundred and fifty years in localities not greatly distant from each other, and exhibiting no great dissimilarity in climatic conditions, could have wrought any decided change in the natures of men who came orginally of the same breed and from the same lands.

A bitter quarrel had prevailed long enough to cause them temporarily to forget their earlier history, their pioneer struggles with the wilderness and the savage, the toils and dangers they had shared in the Revolution, and the more recent years of fraternal effort and glory. They were angry with each other and found it distasteful to admit or believe that they were of the same family.

That they are fundamentally the same people, notwithstanding any variant influence of environment, has been abundantly shown by the numerous examples, in peace and war, in which the Northern and the Southern man has each, under similar circumstances, acted in the same fashion, evidently urged by like impulse, and as might have been expected of an American descended from staunch British or Teutonic stock. There were notable instances of this during the Civil War. "Blue-blooded" Southerners, following their convictions, fought for the Union and adhered to "Yankee" ideas with a tenacity equal to that of the grimmest Puritan. There were men of Northern birth, who, by long residence in the South, had become thoroughly imbued with Southern sentiment and thought, and had developed what are generally considered the salient traits of the Southern character. I knew men from New England who became inveterate "rebels" and, as Confederate soldiers, displayed that reckless dash and daring, once thought to be essentially Southern, in such degree as to win them notice among the boldest of their comrades.

Yet while in all material respects, in blood, in traditions, in ideas of how conduct, social and political, should be regulated, and in their general mode of life, almost the entire native population of this country, fifty years ago and previously was as nearly homogeneous as any people, so numerous and spread over so wide an area, could well be, there were minor differences in habits, manner, and speech that were noticeable — far more so, at least, than now. These mere provincial peculiarities — their effect exaggerated by mutual jealously and distrust — served fifty years ago to enhance antagonism and furnish illustrations for those who preached the creed that the peoples of the two sections were alien in race.

These differences, especially of speech, were not nearly so marked, perhaps, as those to be found elsewhere among many peoples of the same nationality — as the various patois of Continental Europe, or the dialects of the English shires. It is possible that the shrewdest foreign observer would not have detected them, but they were quite apparent to the native. An American would discover, in almost every case, what part of the country a stranger with whom he talked hailed from, by his voice and mode of speech. Certain idiomatic forms of expression were unmistakable, and no very acute ear was required to identify the nasal intonation of the New Englander, the quick, sharp inflection of those reared in other Eastern states, the broad Doric of Viriginia, and the softer recitative of the man from the farther South. Culture and travel, or a more extended intercourse with people of both sections, so modified all such peculiarities in those of a certain class and station that, with them, they became scarcely discernible; but with the masses of each section they remained, for many years, distinctive badges.

Even between the natives of the different Southern states, some similar distinguishing indicia, although in less degree, could be detected. Unquestionably a prevailing social tone and general habit of thought were apparent among the entire people of the South, exhibited, of course, in such external expression as was consonant with individual intelligence and rearing. But while the types were practically the same, while one "Southern gentleman" was much like another, and one Southern yeoman — if I may use the term — closely resembled his every other compatriot in Virginia or South Carolina, Kentucky or Georgia, nevertheless there was a more or less marked but perceptible differentiation of manner and speech among nearly all — sufficient, at least, to indicate from what state or region each came.

Many of the mannerisms and colloquial forms peculiar to the South have been greatly exaggerated by recent writers of fiction both Northern and native; and it may be said, also, that in some instances the Southern character has been unfairly as in many others it has been erroneously portrayed. Perhaps, however, no great fault should be found with that. The Northern writers have the excuse that they are attempting to describe something to which they are not only unaccustomed, but which seems contradictory of previous experience; and the unusual, whether tragic or ludicrous, is apt to strike the oberver as being eccentric, if not bizarre.

More than one Southern writer seems impressed with the idea that, in order to perfectly vindicate his birthland from unjust aspersion or gain her just appreciation, he must surround everything Southern with an exceptionally glowing halo of romance.

It is difficult to resist the temptation to either caricature or idealize; and if exercised with due discretion and in proper temper, the one is no more to be censured than the other. We would so on lose interest in the drama and the novel, if each were confined to bare, rigid realism, and the caricaturist can often convey a lively and pretty accurate idea of a matter of which serious description might fail to furnish any conception.

But the disposition to caricature the Southerner, whether in a good-humoured or in a caustic spirit, has, I think, been unduly indulged. I cannot remember ever having met with any Southerner in fiction whom I recognized, although his face may have been slightly familiar and his voice have awakened some dim recollection. He was usually an impossible paragon, an abnormal ruffian, or an attractive incompetent, half darling and half devil. Think of how the high-spirited, chivalric, scholarly, capable Virginian, the man of historic virtues and genial habits, who, if he is somewhat given to high prancing is withal as full of good sense and human nature as an Old Dominion decanter is of consolation — think of how he has been treated. Why, his own grandmother wouldn't know him if she met him in a novel. When we are introduced to a Virginian in fiction, we see either an elderly, landed gentleman, equipped with much ornate and useless knowledge and a ruffled shirt, and who is an authority on good liquors, states' rights, Democratic platforms, and the code of honour; or we watch the progress of some scion of a first family, riding on horseback from the paternal mansion to Kentucky, Tennessee, or Missouri, stopping at the first county seat where he finds a Democratic convention in session, hitching his steed, entering the court house without taking off his spurs, and announcing himself as a candidate for the office of county attorney. Shades of Jefferson and Patrick Henry, of Fitz Lee and Magruder — was ever such sacrilege!

And has not such unjust measure been meted out to all other denizens of the sacred soil? I enter no plea for the Kentuckian; they seem to think he deserves, and he certainly receives, no more quarter than an Irishman.

But then the Texan! What they do to him might make a mustang shed tears. Ninety-nine men out of every hundred, who know him only in literature, imagine that his vast and soon to become imperial state is peopled only by rangers and cowboys, wearing the beaded effigy of a snake around their hats, and notching the stocks of their revolvers *in memoriam*.

I believed at one time that I could distinguish — if only by some slight evidence which I couldn't have explained — the native inhabitants of most of the Southern states. But I was never able to tell a Kentuckian from a Tennesseean — although they were the people whom I knew most intimately. The resemblance, for me at least, exists between the people of the corresponding portions of each state. A Kentucky mountaineer is the exact counterpart of a Tennessee mountaineer; the man of central Kentucky is as much like the man of middle Tennessee as one chip cut out of a white oak or a hickory is like another; and if the entire population of any one of the counties of Western Tennessee should move bodily into any one of the counties of Western Kentucky — like some ancient barbarian immigration into the territory of a kindred tribe — I am sure that the sheriff would never ascertain what had occurred because of any perceptible difference in appearance, speech, and demeanour between the old residents and the new comers.

The conditions of the pioneer period induced a connection and understanding between the people who occupied the territory out of which the two states were subsequently created, which has been maintained ever since. Separated by the almost pathless Appalachian range from the colonies on the seaboard, having no neighbours of their own race save each other, the settlers of Kentucky and Tennessee — and both were settled nearly about the same time — experienced an identity of situation and fortune which seemed to indicate the same destiny for both. Occupying a country alike in climate, soil, and productions and reared under influences so similar, a close sympathy in thought and feeling has always characterized their relations.

This community of interest and close and frequent social intercourse between the people of the two states — encouraged by geographical propinquity and easy means of communication — necessarily had an effect upon both. But whatever may have been the cause, the Kentuckian and Tennesseean — to use an illustration which each will understand — are as like as twin colts "in form and action," and "go the same gaits" in the same style.

I saw a great deal of the Tennessee soldiery during the Civil War, of both the cavalry and infantry. There was one regiment in Morgan's division composed entirely of Tennesseeans — the Ninth Tennessee Cavalry — and it was one of the best I ever knew. In the regiment I first commanded — Morgan's original regiment, the Second Kentucky Cavalry. C. S. A.— there were, probably, one hundred and fifty Tennesseeans. They were in every respect, in combat, scout, and march, in general deportment and occasional lack of deportment, exactly like their Kentucky confreres; they gave no more trouble in camp than did the Kentuckians and in candour, it must be admitted, no less. I would and can claim no superiority for Kentuckians and Tennesseeans over their Confederate comrades. It is a great and sufficient honour to them to affirm that they were equal to the best. Nor, as one who has made up his mind to preach the gospel of reconciliation, would I boastfully speak of successes they may have achieved. I will not even declare that every enemy who encountered them found out that " he had had a fight." With that caution and modesty of statement becoming a man born in Kentucky, and who once almost became an adopted citizen of Tennessee, I shall merely remark that, after every such affair, however it terminated, the said party of the first part was quite sure that he had provoked a serious breach of the peace. I am the more content to be reticent, for the reason that I, somehow, feel that those of whom I speak will not permit the record to suffer.

I feel confident that no intelligent and careful observer could remain for any length of time in these states, mingling with the people of each, and noting those things in which they showed most interest, without being impressed with the fact of how nearly they think and feel alike on all essential matters; of how nearly identical they are in every thing idiosyncratic. If he should attend their public meetings he would be struck with the extreme similarity, in aspect, utterance, and bearing, of those who frequented them. If he witnessed a political convention in Kentucky and afterward one in Tennessee, he might doubt whether there was any actual change of personnel, and if he were not looking upon the same body. He might discern some slight variation occasioned by purely local causes, some changes of name and issue, but in methods and management, in atmosphere and colour, in the general character of the topics discussed, he would see little that would distinguish the one from the other. He would find no guide, certainly, in the delicate blending of sentimental politics with machine manipulation, which would be much in evidence in both.

Possibly, however, this latter feature should not be mentioned as being peculiar to Kentucky and Tennessee, although surely very rife there. Nor also, the fervid and picturesque eloquence which resounds in the political assemblies and legislative halls of those two commonwealths — "an eloquence which," in the language of an enthusiastic critic, "gleams about its subject like the forked lightning, and don't care a continental where it strikes." That is common to all the South and West, and sometimes illuminates even more conservative territory.

I can remember only one instance in which I heard it suggested that there was any material difference between the two peoples, and I by no means agreed with that. About a year after the close of the war, when the people of Tennessee, no longer harassed by the presence of large bodies of hostile troops, had begun partially to realize that it was over, and had plucked up heart to attempt something like their former pleasant social life, I attended the annual fair at Clarksville, held for the first time since Tennessee had passed the ordinance of secession. I had received a special invitation, gladly accepted, because I knew whom I would meet the brave, warm-hearted people of middle Tennessee, whose truth and steadfast constancy I had seen so often manifested in every form of trial, and whose loyal friendship to my own immediate comrades I had such reason to remember with affection and gratitude.

A large crowd was assembled from the adjoining counties of both Tennessee and Kentucky, in which I found quite a number of young fellows, ex-Confederates from the latter state, many of whom had served under my command. Everybody was given generous welcome, and as cordially received it. The cup that cheers and sometimes inebriates was accepted as freely as it was offered. The older people glowed with recollections of that former time so fondly remembered, when the "annual harvest was housed," and the fine stock exhibited amid general festivity and in keen but friendly competition, and hoped that this occasion crowd was the signal of its return. The young people were like a of boys and girls who had been cooped up during a long, hard winter, and just turned loose for a spring holiday. During the week that the fair lasted there was a universal indemnification for all past deprivation of such pleasures, and the partially disfranchised white felt as free as the emancipated darkey.

But toward its close something occurred which threatened to mar its enjoyment, for me at least, and caused me no slight uneasiness. I had more than once noticed that the Kentucky boys had been figuring more conspicuously in the limelight than was actually required of them, and that their conduct, in some trifling particulars, was not altogether such as an unusually austere taste might have approved. Yet I couldn't see that they were doing anything really wrong, and apprehending no serious consequences thought little about the matter.

One afternoon, however, a young Tennesseean whom I knew quite well, came to me with information of grave character. He had served for two years in the Army of Northern Virginia, and was then transferred to one of Morgan's regiments, and had remained with that command until the close of the war. He was well acquainted with most of these erring Kentuckians, and felt in them the interest of immediate comradeship.

"General," he said, "there's a matter I want to talk to you about, and yet I hesitate to do so. But I know you will understand me. Some of the Kentucky boys are acting in a way that

I'm afraid will cause trouble. They've done nothing ungentlemanly, but they're putting on entirely too much style and assuming an air of superiority which the boys who live here find very offensive. The fact that these Kentuckians are a good deal with you, and that you are here by special invitation, has held the others in check so far, but some fellow may break loose at any time."

He told me that he was chiefly concerned lest the trouble should be started by a youngster who for the last eight or ten months of the war had been a guerilla, and had made quite a gory record. I knew something of this man myself. He was as mild and pleasant as a May morning when unmolested, but as bloody as a young tiger when rubbed the wrong way. "Now," he said, "whatever happens, I shall stand by the Kentucky boys, as my guests and former comrades, but I think you can stop any unpleasantness. The Tennesseans have the kindest feeling for you, and I think you have influence enough with the Kentuckians to induce them to correct what has been found objectionable."

I assured him, of course, that I would at once act as he suggested, and make every effort to prevent the unseemly quarrel he feared. I felt, however, that it was a matter in which I must proceed with a good deal of discretion, for I knew that the Kentuckians would be greatly shocked at learning that such a charge had been preferred against them, and, in their indignation, might precipitate the very thing we wished to avoid. So I concluded to advise with one of them whom I knew to be the shrewdest and most reasonable, and, for that purpose, had him come as soon as possible to my room. I told him what I had heard, and that I wished to consult with him about what was best to be done.

In view of what he said I should explain that the Northern newspapers were accustomed to say a good deal about that time regarding the alleged superiority of the civilization of the North to that of the South, and the South was becoming very sore over it, especially as some recent lessons in civilization the Yankees had given us were neither palatable nor we thought canonical.

When I had finished my statement my young friend responded promptly that there was reason for apprehension.

"I had intended to speak to you about it myself," he said, "for our boys ought not to behave that way. It is an offence against good breeding, and they should remember that these men were our comrades, and that we have never received aught but kind treatment from this people. "But," he went on, with an air of ineffable complacency, "there is some slight excuse for it. Our boys feel that we have a higher civilization in Kentucky than obtains in Tennessee."

"For God's sake, Frank," I exclaimed in trembling haste, "don't talk that way. If there be any difference in the respective heights of the two civilizations, no instrument has yet been invented delicate enough to determine it. But don't say that outside of this room, unless you want that blamed guerilla to kill us all."

I am glad to record that matters were happily adjusted without the introduction of any disturbing question of civilization.

I have already spoken of the similitude of parliamentary methods in Kentucky and Tennessee. In this connection I may be permitted to relate two legislative incidents which happened under my own observation, taking care to remark, however, that, while alike, they were unusual. Each, too, happened with immature and inexperienced politicians, in whom the impulse of the individual had not yet been subdued by the self-restraint of the statesman.

I was once a spectator of a legislative session at Nashville, when a vote was being taken on some motion which had aroused a good deal of feeling. The speaker had temporarily quitted his chair for some reason and it was occupied, at the moment of the vote, by a member of the house who was an extreme partisan of the measure under consideration. He was manifestly and grossly unfair in his rulings, and refused a call for the ayes and noes. A storm of protest at once arose and the house was in an uproar. I saw the member from a county on the confines of east Tennessee rush toward the chair, evidently meaning business. He was a gray-eyed, resolute-looking party in appearance, just the sort of gentleman who, in the mountaineer's phrase, "When he sees fitten' to shoot is goin' to shoot." An older and less excited colleague caught hold of him and begged him to do nothing "out of order." "I'm goin' to do nothing out of order," he replied, "I'm only goin' to fling that d — d special speaker out of the window."

Some twenty or twenty-five years ago a very similar scene occurred in the Kentucky legislature. An earnest and impassioned orator was repeatedly warned by the speaker that he was out of order. Instead of conforming his declamation to the suggestion, the orator wandered yet more wildly beyond the proper boundaries of debate, and the speaker threatened him with arrest by the sergeant-at-arms. "No official of this house shall arrest me," shouted the offender in tempestuous wrath. "I should be sorry to sully a hitherto spotless legislative record by slaying a sergeant-at-arms, but the rash man who places a profaning hand upon my person dies in his tracks."

The speaker seemed disposed to be obdurate, but fortunately the sergeant-at-arms happened, just then, to have important business outside of the chamber; so finding his executive arm out of place the speaker permitted the orator to blow, like a fierce wind, until his bellows were exhausted.

I cannot abandon hope that the salient features of the resemblance I have endeavoured to trace — even in those things which a colder critic might term their "eccentricities"— will continue to characterize the people of Kentucky and of Tennessee. Mellowed by time, and, in a measure, corrected by adaptation to milder models, they may become very beautiful.

CHAPTER XXII

THE years which passed between the fall of the Confederacy — the final close of the slave-holding epoch — and such time as the people of the states south of the Ohio had become appreciably in touch with the new order, were filled with minor events and silent influences, not easy to specify and more difficult to describe, yet each of which not only indicated, but served, in its measure, to induce the change that was going on.

Even in the dire throes of reconstruction and during the desperate efforts to retain that which the people of the South felt to be essential to their very existence, other and better feelings than those evoked by the fierce struggle were at work; and the experience and discipline learned in that struggle were of benefit.

Much — and that which was of most value — was retained. The Southern people preserved their self-respect, and, although compelled to surrender the hope of separate political existence and the dream of a "new nation under a new flag," maintained control of their own communities and the direction of their own affairs. Nevertheless, this period of transition is more remarkable because of what was relinquished than because of what was kept.

By this I do not mean to call attention, at least as matters of immediate discussion, to the emancipation of the slaves and the immense destruction of tangible property from which the South suffered such vast material loss. These topics are naturally suggested by any reference to the Civil War and its consequences, and I have partially treated them in a previous chapter. The positive injury, the havoc and disturbance so occasioned were incidents of the war period, not of that of which I am now writing, and require mention in this connection only in so far as, in conjunction with other causes, they affected the future life of the people and gave it another impulse and direction.

In a country where there had been many wealthy men,

according to the standards by which wealth was then estimated, but where, also, wealth had been pretty equally distributed, a sudden and almost total ruin of all upon which that prosperity was founded wrought, of course, a corresponding alteration in the mode of living, and made it much harder for very many to obtain a living. The general distress and impoverishment of all classes left no hope nor scope for a distinctly idle class. The gentleman of elegant leisure might continue to pursue his vocation if he so chose. There was no danger that he would die in the poor-house, because there were no funds available for the maintenance of poor-houses, but there was great danger that he might die of inanition. The gentleman who only a few years previously had been wont to boast that he "had never earned a cent in his life and had never tried" found the outlook extremely discouraging.

But there were not many who were really and incorrigibly idlers; much the larger number were more than anxious to be employed. For the great multitude, however, of the youth and men of middle age in the South who had been reared in ease and the expectation of comparative affluence, and yet were capable, energetic, and desirious of doing good work for themselves and the communities in which they lived, there was an almost entire lack of opportunity. In nearly every instance, the young man reared to be a planter was unable to refit and restock his devastated plantation or find means to work it. It was practically impossible to get a job as an assistant or overseer with some friend or kinsman, who might be better provided, because, when the negroes were freed, the overseers were virtually put out of commission. It was not especially easy to get work, at one time, even as a farm labourer. To procure industrial employment was even more difficult. As little encouragement was offered in the learned professions; for, when nobody had money, lawyers and doctors could scarcely expect remunerative fees.

The conditions were better and more promising in the cities and larger towns of the South, where a certain commercial prosperity still obtained, and to these many of the younger men resorted in hope to find profitable occupation or at least a livelihood. A host from all parts of the South flocked to New Orleans. There were living in that city, between the years of 1865 and 1870, almost as many ex-Southern soldiers bearing the title of "general" as there are to-day in the ranks of the "United Confederate Veterans."

A multitude, also, went upon the same mission to the cities of the border, St. Louis, Louisville, and Cincinnati, and not a few continued their flight as far north as New York. Quite a number remained permanently and were successful in their adopted abodes, but the majority returned, with the returning prosperity of the South, to their early homes.

Not only was there a general decline in values, disorganization of business, and stagnation of industry throughout all the subjugated region, but the lack of competent labour, as well as of money, intensified all else that was unfortunate and made the situation almost desperate. The South, before the war, had been distinctly an agricultural country; that interest greatly predominated all others in every community. For many years after the war, much the larger proportion of the population depended upon agriculture as a means of support. The labour employed for the cultivation of the cereals, as well as the cotton, sugar, and tobacco crops, was chiefly negro labour. It was not habitual for white men, with the exception of the small farmers who tilled comparatively scanty acreage, to work in the fields. But the demoralization of the negro as a labourer began with his enfranchisement, and was completed by his introduction into politics. It is to be doubted whether, even if the negroes had remained in slavery and could have been compelled to stay upon the plantations, they could for many years at least have been employed as profitably and as numerously as in the ante bellum days, for the reason that the planters were otherwise so straightened, so lacking in facilities, that it might not have been possible to keep them all employed. It must also be considered that men — white or black — who have been trained under one system do not readily adapt themselves to another.

But at this date, the negro, intoxicated with sudden freedom and excited by strange hopes, had little desire to do any work at all, even the most necessary, and his labour was no longer reliable.

During all this period and until the beginning of the administration of Mr. Hayes, the Southern people were treated as if still in rebellion, and, however honestly inclined they might be to obey the National authority, were made to appear in the attitude of resisting it. Emphatic and resolute protest against acts of glaring maladministration and injustice was regarded as convincing evidence of a disloyal spirit. Opposition to appropriations made by legislatures filled with ignorant negroes and white thieves — made for manifestly dishonest purposes and to be provided for by ruinous taxation — was denounced as the recalcitrance of men not yet reconciled to the Union and the flag. How the people who put forth such heroic effort to preserve the Union and defend that flag, could have permitted such a "Walpurgis dance of political witches," is one of the mysteries of history which remains for Northern writers to explain.

It is a matter for wonder that the Southern people were not driven by such an experience, coming in the hour of sore material distress and before the passions aroused by the war had time to cool, into inveterate resentment and rancour — something like that which the Irish have felt toward the English. It is fortunate that the good sense, for which they have not always been credited, preserved them from such error.

But, in real truth, the people of the South, although determined to maintain the autonomy of their states, had utterly abandoned the hopes and purposes with which they had attempted secession. They had in no sense "repented" of such action. They did not believe that their effort to establish the Confederacy had been culpable, but they fully realized their failure and the futility of any such attempt for the future. While there was, of course, bitter disappointment, they were willing, in the phrase of the time, to accept the situation in good faith and without reservation. I am firmly convinced that all the time the South was being so harassed there were not five hundred men living within her borders who entertained any real desire to renew the contest, or who, in their saner moments, would not have deemed such a wish criminal as well as absurd. Even then the Southern people did not for an instant contemplate resistance to the Federal authority. They were trying to get back into the Union, and while they may not, just then, have loved it very dearly, they recognized the obligations it imposed, and were inclined to return to their former allegiance. I do not mean to say that it was a matter of sentiment, for, of course, it was not. They wished to do the best thing they could under the circumstances, to accommodate themselves to the new and inevitable régime and make the best of a bad situation. But they were open, honest, and sincere in their action.

There was one feature of the situation which ought not to be overlooked because it unquestionably exerted a very considerable influence for good. With the influx into the South of the carpet-baggers and political adventurers, there had also come a considerable number of Northern born men of very different character — many of them former Federal soldiers — who migrated there with another purpose. These men came to locate permanently and cast in their lot with the native population. Without in anywise surrendering their political opinions, they manfully stood by the Southern whites. The assistance which they had rendered in the reconstruction controversies cannot be overestimated; and the example they gave, and the work done by them in the social and industrial transformation which was later in progress, were of scarcely less value.

The general effect of all the various forces, busy in the South from the date of the fall of the Confederacy until the virtual cessation of the political troubles, was, it might be said, to make of the people of the South another and a different people.

The altered social and material conditions necessarily produced a certain change in the people themselves, in their habits, and in their thought. Clinging still to their traditions, they largely gave up old customs, adopted new methods, and entertained other views and aspirations.

The old plantation life, with its numerous retinue and profuse management, had passed away. The previous commercial and mercantile modes of transacting business, chiefly in conformity with the plantation demands, had undergone a corresponding change. All the avenues to success or promotion were either painfully blocked or ran in other directions than they had formerly pointed. The Southern cadet, of distinguished family, who could once have confidently relied upon public preferment, found himself no longer a political pet to be always supplied from the public patronage, but a political pariah denied all official recognition.

All around the circle the old order was giving place unto the new, and something had to be done. To compare great things with small, the situation was like the case of Capt. John Daviess, of Harrodsburg, Ky., brother of the famous Joe Daviess, who prosecuted Aaron Burr. The captain had been a successful candidate many times, but after a signal defeat abandoned the political field.

"Captain," asked a friend, who was curious to know the reason of it, "why have you quit politics?" "I have quit," responded the captain, "because, although I was a popular favourite for many years, I have recently discovered that I have become not only unpopular but positively d — d odious, so I think it better to turn my attention to something else."

Some years elapsed before this substantially new direction in Southern thought and purpose was apparent in external or superficial evidence. Notwithstanding the resolute efforts to repair the terrible devastation of the war, there was little in the aspect of either rural or urban community to indicate its success until the era of industrial activity set in — until the resources of the South began to be developed in earnest and by her own people. Then indeed, it seemed as if a "new nation," although in another sense than that in which the term had been meant in 1861, had been born into the world.

It should be borne in mind when considering any period of Southern history that her people have been in large measure more distinctly homogeneous, composed, at least, more largely of the white stocks which originally settled this country, and with less admixture of purely foreign element, than the population of any other territory of equal extent included at any time within the limits of the United States. They have consequently been more thoroughly and continuously than any other under the influence of — what I may designate for lack of some more appropriate term — a native sentiment and habit of thought, more closely attached to the soil and its associations, cherishing a stronger sympathy with the past. While it has been the fashion, in some quarters, to speak of a certain feeling they have sometimes displayed and somethings they have done as "un-American," they have been in many respects more "American". than all the rest of the people on the continent together.

Although this feeling, unduly stimulated by a mistaken view of sectional interest, had impelled them to strife, it had also much to do with causing them to endure defeat less sullenly and more hopefully. I think it was this feeling, unconsciously operating, which more than anything else helped them to deal successfully with the novel conditions, at first as irksome as they were unfamiliar.

It will be remembered by those who "were there," that immediately after the general and final surrender there was much talk of expatriation. A multitude of Confederate soldiers spoke of seeking in some other country the liberty they believed would be denied them in their own. I think that those who talked that way really meant at the time what they said. Gen. Jubal A. Early told me that he had greatly desired to head a considerable exodus of Confederate families to New Zealand. I suppose that the indomitable old fighter, when he could no longer live under the Southern flag, wished, as the next best thing, to die under the Southern cross. A great number wished to go to Mexico. Unwilling to remain under Yankee rule, they preferred the beneficent government of Maximilian. Of course, they could not then know that Maximilian would be able to retain neither his government nor his life.

General Early encountered one insuperable difficulty in the way of his scheme. No one was willing to go so far, and not a colonist enlisted. A good many did go to Mexico, but, in a brief time, nearly every one came back. There was quite an interchange of population within Southern territory, but comparatively few left the South except to settle somewhere else in the United States.

Whether the Southern women had or had not much to do with keeping the Southern men at home, I do not know. I think they had. I am quite sure, at any rate, that if the women had wished to leave they would have done so, and that the men would have followed. But it is certain that they had a great deal to do — and for good — with all that transpired in the South in those days of trial and tribulation; and that the men of the South gained from them strength, as well as comfort and consolation.

So much has been said and written about the conduct of the Southern women during the war that any mention of it, especially any laudation, now seems trite and superfluous; yet it is a theme on which it is impossible to be silent and difficult not to enlarge.

The battles of the South were fought by soldiers furnished almost entirely from her own population. At any rate, there were so few others that, save for their courage and generous devotion, they need not be considered. There was scarcely a family in the South which had not its representative in the Confederate army; many had more than one; some sent its every male member into the ranks. There was not a woman in the South, therefore, who did not have a father, husband, son or brother, or some relative in the field. It has been said that regard for the opinion of the women compelled many men to enlist who would have preferred not to do so. However that may be, it cannot be denied that, like Bedford Forrest, the Southern women had "No self-respect for an able-bodied young man who wasn't in the army."

Moreover, these women were themselves in the thick of the strife, and personally witnessed and suffered its calamities. They were constantly reminded by what they saw every day of the danger which threatened those they loved most dearly. The full, horrible realization was always with them, with never any actual relief from its monotonous misery.

I have seen, amid the hottest street fighting, one of the ghastliest forms of combat, women come out of the houses to succour the wounded. I have seen women tenderly nursing dying strangers with all the solicitude they could have given their nearest and dearest, when they knew that in some distant spot a son or husband needed like care. I have seen them in their lonely homes, whence the husband had gone to battle along the Cumberland or Potomac, striving patiently to keep privation from the door and provide clothing for the children; and I have often seen them offer from their meagre stores food to the hungry soldier, when they knew that the gift meant a yet shorter ration for themselves and the children. They bore with equally heroic fortitude the tests of the later ordeal, when it seemed as if worse horrors than those of the war might be their portion; and the best hope, the wisest counsel the men received was at the domestic hearth.

The Federal soldiers have often declared that after they had succeeded by a considerable expenditure of blood, time, and treasure in overcoming the men of the South, they found the women still unconquered; and the Southern man — especially the Southern husband — realizes with pride, and a certain wholesome, almost timid, respect, that the Southern woman never has been and never can be subdued.

Nor are the hearts of these women even now less warm, nor has their labour relaxed in patriotic endeavour. The work done by the Daughters of the Confederacy in recent years is one scarcely as yet to be fully appreciated, and, perhaps, never to be rivalled. They have inaugurated and conducted to successful termination, or largely aided in so doing, every enterprise in which sympathy has been enlisted to render relief and charity to suffering incurred by service to the South or to commemorate the Confederate cause. They have done much to preserve the true history of the struggle and induce a just understanding of Southern motives and action; but in any such memorial record the best and brightest chapter must be given them.

The South evinced an inclination, shortly after the close of the war, to follow the example of the North and the rest of the civilized world in suppressing, or, at least, in discountenancing, duelling; and it is somewhat remarkable that it should have become manifest just when it did. There were few duels fought during the war, and I can recall only one which resulted fatally. Only three I believe have been fought in Kentucky in post bellum times, all between the years of 1865-70. They were much less frequent elsewhere in the South after the war than previously, for then duelling had been almost universally prevalent there. It is not a matter of wonder that few duels occurred during the war time, for when so much other fighting — entirely "legitimate" — was going on, this mode of combat was regarded as irregular and not in "good form." But it may well create some surprise to note that just afterward, when such strong feeling was rife and there were so many animosities yet unallayed, it should have so suddenly gone out of vogue.

Duelling, I believe, still prevails in some parts of Europe, but rather as a pastime or game of skill, although not so dangerous as football, than with any idea of fatal termination. It would seem that care and pains are always taken to eliminate from the European duel any chance of homicide. But the Southern duel, and, indeed, the American duel, wherever and whenever fought, was conducted upon a totally different theory — and, it seems to me, the correct one. For if men have real reason to fight, and deliberately go out to fight, it is surely logical that each should try to kill. While often, of course, a matter of congratulation, it is hard to conceive of a more absurd anomaly than the "bloodless" duel.

Even so far back as 1852 an effort was made to put a stop to duelling in Kentucky by constitutional provision, to be enforced by appropriate legislation. It was provided that any citizen of Kentucky, who, after the adoption of that constitution, should fight a duel with deadly weapons within the limits of the state, or send or receive a challenge to fight a duel, should, upon conviction, be disqualified from voting and holding office in the commonwealth, and, if a lawyer, should be disqualified from practising his profession. It was further provided that the governor should have no power to pardon in such cases, until five years had elapsed after the commission of the offence. If the duel should be fought with, or the challenge sent to or received from, another citizen of Kentucky, the penalty for the offence was the same, although it might be committed outside of the state.

When it is understood that the chiefest pleasure and most inestimable privilege of the average Kentuckian is to seek and hold office, and that, when he cannot find anything else to do, he likes to try to practise law, the ingenuity, the refined cruelty — worthy of a Torquemada — of such punishment will be appreciated. Furthermore, inasmuch as a Kentuckian after committing the offence might yet escape indictment, he was required, before being inducted into office or admitted to practice at any bar of the state, to take an oath that, since the adoption of this constitution, he had committed no such offence. The diabolical cunning of such a contrivance, intended to catch a man "coming or going," is shocking to every humane mind.

Notwithstanding all this, however, duelling was not entirely stopped in Kentucky, and a number were subsequently fought. It has been enacted, in a constitution adopted later, that the penalty shall apply whether the duel occurring beyond the limits of the state be fought with a citizen of Kentucky or with some one from the world outside. Consequently the only terms on which a Kentuckian can now constitutionally enjoy a duel is by temporarily renouncing citizenship and ceasing to be a Kentuckian until the affair is concluded.

By a strange partiality, the doctors — doctors of medicine, I mean— although a much more belligerent class than the lawyers, were relieved of that part of the penalty, inflicted upon the lawyers, which inhibited practise of their profession. Such a distinction seems strangely to resemble class legislation, but, being, constitutional instead of statutory, the question, unfortunately could never be raised. It has been suggested with some force — although I admit the suggestion seems a little strained — that this omission in favour of members of the medical fraternity was done advisedly, and with the hope that it might induce them to indulge their homicidal inclinations at the expense of other doctors, rather than of their patients.

I have always doubted the wisdom of these drastic provisions against duelling — at any rate, of visiting it with exceptional penalties at a time when the population for which they were intended was so generally pugnacious, and the disposition for personal combat, if prohibited in one way, was apt to find another. Had the habitual carrying of concealed deadly weapons, street fights, and sudden affrays in which weapons are used been also and equally penalized, the effect I think would have been more wholesome. If men must engage in personal combat, the duel is unquestionably the most preferable method.

It is certainly the fairest. It has often been said, and with some justice, that if duelling be tacitly permitted, certain men will make themselves skilful in the use of weapons and pick quarrels with others who are not in such respect their equals. But the same thing may be said with greater force of the "street fight." The coward, the bully, and the would-be murderer can find infinitely more advantage and impunity in that method than in the duel. In the duel the parties face each other with similar weapons and fire at a given signal. The best shot may fail of his aim; the combatant of inferior skill has, at least, a chance. Sometimes men meet in a street fight by appointment and equally armed. Then it is, in all save formalities, a duel;

but with the indecency of being a public performance, and the danger to the "innocent by-stander." In the majority of cases, however, the street fight is only a covert form of assassination, in which the assailant has in advance planned how to kill his victim with no peril to himself, and has already formulated his plea of "self-defence."

There is, also, always excellent opportunity in quarrels, which the principals wish to settle by a duel, to compose them amicably. The seconds almost invariably strive to do this, and if the hostile feeling has arisen only out of a misunderstanding, or unless the principals are incorrigibly unreasonable, usually succeed. When the other method is contemplated there is little opportunity for peaceable adjustment, because the parties seldom declare their intentions and cannot be advised.

I shall never forget the last occasion when I was consulted in what might have become "an affair of honour," because of its extremely amusing features. It reminded me, but in a ludicrous fashion, of the preliminary correspondence between the belligerents, of the fine points raised and nice distinctions taken in the "good old times" when the duel was earnest and real, and still in order even in the days of its "innocuous desuetude."

It occurred at the Capitol Hotel in Frankfort, some twenty or more years ago. A number of the citizens of the town were assembled one evening to discuss some matter of local interest. The debate became quite warm, especially between two of the disputants. One of these gentlemen, a tall, dignified official — a man of undoubted courage, but amiable and usually discreet — finally, in a moment of unaccustomed asperity, said in response to an exceedingly emphatic statement made by the other: "Sir, you are egregiously mistaken."

The other was a champion of small stature but colossal spirit — a Tydeus, "whose little body held a mighty soul." The very pink of chivalry and courtesy in his ordinary mood, his temper, when excited, was of a fiery flavour compared with which tobasco sauce is as mild as mother's milk. He immediately sprang to his feet and rushed at his opponent to strike him. He was with difficulty and only by superior force prevented from doing so.

He promptly came to my room, narrated what had occurred,

and requested me to carry his challenge to the offender. For many reasons I was averse to taking any part in an affair of that nature; and even when the duel had been most popular, an adviser who would not have counselled his friend that the provocation in a case like this was too slight to justify a challenge, would have been strongly censured. I told him so but he answered hotly, "I have a right to challenge any man who calls me a liar."

"Why," I said, "according to your own story, he simply told you that you were mistaken."

"That is the language he used, but considering the circumstances and the manner in which he said it, it was equivalent to giving me the lie."

In the meantime four or five other gentlemen had dropped in, and with that easy freedom and total absence of formality which is nowhere so charming as in Kentucky, took part in the discussion; but all agreed with me and counselled peace.

The aggrieved party, however, was not convinced and stoutly maintained his position. But fortunately one of the gentlemen who had joined us was, in addition to extensive and useful information on other topics, an authority on the code. He had participated in more than one duel, both as principal and second, and what he didn't know about the subject could have been written on a postage stamp. At length he spoke, and all turned to him as to an oracle. We all knew that what he said would "go," but we could no more divine in the impenetrable gravity of his visage, what he was about to say, than you can see the sugar which has been dissolved in your julep.

"I disagree with General Duke," he said. "I think Louis is right in holding that when, under the circumstances, he was accused of being mistaken it was tantamount to calling him a liar."

Louis glowed with satisfaction; one might have supposed that he thought no happiness in life was equal to that of being called a liar.

"But," the oracle proceeded, "he has put it out of his power to challenge in this affair."

"What," shouted the irate little game-cock, "can't I challenge a man who calls me a liar?"

"Not in this case after what you have already done. The Irish code and the Virginia code — the best authorities — while they vary in some small particulars, agree upon all material points, and each specifically declares that there are two modes of procedure open to a gentleman when he has received the lie. He may respond to the insult promptly with a blow, or he may send a challenge. But having elected to take either course, he is estopped from pursuing the other. You elected to strike, therefore you may not challenge."

"But I didn't strike him. I was prevented from striking."

"Louis, I regret to see you take refuge in a sophism unworthy of you. A gentleman is always considered to have done that which he has meant and tried to do. He constructively gave you the lie; you constructively struck him. He may challenge; you cannot."

"But, d — n it, Sam, he *won't* challenge."

"Very well then" said Sam, "that's the end of the matter."

I was for a moment almost stricken dumb with admiration by this amazingly able and absolutely conclusive exposition. So soon as I recovered my breath, I declared that I had been endeavouring to say that very thing all the time; and so said all the others. So it went at that.

The charge, once made so freely and often heard now, that there is less respect for law in the South than elsewhere in the United States, is I think, based upon shallow observation and very partial, if not imperfect, reasoning. I might, perhaps, appeal successfully to the statistics of crime committed in this country to refute it and show its fallacy; but that is not the sort of evidence which should be considered in a discussion of this nature. Criminal classes exist everywhere, and a certain demonstration from them is to be everywhere expected. More is to be reasonably expected in a densely than a sparsely populated community; and it is scarcely possible to determine to what extent a latent criminal tendency may be developed, in the former, into active operation by suggestion and opportunity.

Nor do I claim that a people should be exonerated from this accusation because they may be able to offer more in the way of excuse and provocation — valid or plausible — for the particular violations of law with which they stand charged. The justest method, perhaps, by which such a question may be determined, is to ascertain, as well as can be done, how far each community honestly desires and tries to suppress and punish, upon procurable proof, the special, the particular offences against law which its population is most prone to commit.

Yet, making the concession, which is, perhaps, hardly fair to the South, that crime, in its general sense, the crimes common to human nature and perpetrated the world over, and the terrible degradation and vice of the great cities induced by grinding poverty — a curse we trust God may long spare the South — shall not be considered in such discussion, what proof can be adduced or reason given for the assertion that "lawlessness" is exceptionally prevalent in the South? By that term, as it is usually employed, is meant either organized and violent defiance of law, open or secret, or systematic, dishonest evasion of the law, although it may be done under some colour of legal form. In neither acceptation of the term, can it be justly applied as descriptive of a condition obtaining more generally in the South than elsewhere in the United States.

I am not attempting a *tuquoque* argument, but wish to avoid anything of that nature. In sober truth, if we wish to find the cause of the lawlessness that, in some shape, is the bane of the whole country, we must consider the influence of a feeling which can be discovered everywhere, and would seem to be an outgrowth of our free institutions. The individual liberty, which is our proudest boast and best possession, does not make, absolutely and in all respects, for righteousness. The intense individualism bred here has stimulated the more selfish and arrogant instincts of humanity to greater and wider activity than would have been possible under more rigorous discipline. America has been aptly termed "the land of opportunity," but much of it has been the opportunity of the crank and promoter to try every kind of experiment, whether brutal, visionary, or sordid. We live in an atmosphere of self-seeking and self-assertion. Our national education has always been to "get there," and having done so, at any cost, to stay there. The average man believes that a "square deal" is one in which he will get all the four sides.

In this almost universal habit of regarding each class,

business, or corporate interest as of manifest and paramount importance; this general disposition to claim and assert some special privilege or immunity, no matter whether or not it contravene the law; and in the utter intolerance each and all entertain of any opinion, public or private, not in accordance with their own, or which would restrain them from infringement on the rights of other people — in these heresies are to be found, I think, the seeds of all the lawlessness, of that kind about which we talk so much, and which crops up throughout the whole land.

In every locality and instance in which the lawless spirit has been notably manifested, it has proceeded upon the idea entertained by those who exhibit it, that under certain conditions they may properly get what they wish by means which the law does not provide or sometimes inhibits — get it in spite of the law. They persuade themselves that a number of men having a common interest, or animated by a common feeling, can by association acquire the right to do that which no one of them can rightfully do singly. The same explanation applies to all. The dynamiters of the Colorado mining districts, the "Molly Maguires" of Pennsylvania, the union men of the great cities who knock non-union men in the head because they want to work and not to strike, the "white cappers" of Indiana, the "night riders," of Kentucky and Tennessee, indeed, the men who anywhere proclaim and act upon the dogma that anything that they may see fit to do to serve their own special interests is something with which the law should have no concern and not interfere, are all exponents of the same selfish and destructive creed. These are the violent types; but the plutocratic monopoly and corporate aggression sometimes attempted, although not to the extent generally believed, are productive of even more evil, in that they are not only harmful *per se*, but furnish apology for disorder and arouse sympathy, natural, however mistaken, for violence.

Unquestionably a supreme effort to correct all this general tendency to lawlessness must at some time and in some way be made; but the surest method of correction, by a better national understanding of justice and the substitution of a higher standard of social duty and obligation for the unreasonable and brutal code now prevalent, will be accomplished none the sooner by criticism of special lawless manifestation in some particular community.

At some time, the people of the whole country will be compelled to practically realize as well as theoretically acknowledge that if the public peace and order cannot be maintained by local, it must be by national authority. It will be universally recognized that a government — state or national — must possess and exercise powers commensurate with its duties and responsibilities, and be able to enforce all that it may be justly expected to perform. There is little reason to apprehend that so long as the institutions we have inherited shall continue to exist, any authority will fail to respect the general popular will or to consult the best interests and real welfare of the people. There is far greater danger, as experience has amply demonstrated, that the public welfare will be injuriously affected by requiring only partial obedience to law and relaxing its universal application. The special statutory privileges which Jefferson deprecated are less frequent and threaten the "equal rights to all" not nearly so much as does the privilege to defy the law usurped by men who band together under high-sounding titles or, secretly associated, accomplish unlawful ends by wrong and oppression wrought upon the peaceful community. A rigid suppression of these practices has become the most imperative governmental duty. The day is not distant when a long-suffering majority will insist that the minority shall be restrained from acts as insolent as they are harmful.

This much needed reform may be more difficult and come more slowly in the South, for the reason that men there are inclined, I think, to adhere more strongly to misconceptions as well as convictions. I have never been able to discover that there is much real, substantial difference between the people of the two sections, although environment has made some.

If I were required to designate any particular quality or characteristic in which the average Northern or Eastern man is most unlike the Southern man, I should say that it consists in the ability of the one to avoid and readiness of the other to accept a certain form of self-deception.

The Northern man has, I think, in many matters a keener

perception of the practical facts which underlie and ultimately control human conduct — of what Carlyle calls the "verities." The Yankee rarely lies to himself, the Southern man frequently does so. A Yankee might sell a wooden ham, but he would never try to eat one. On the other hand, a Southern man might fabricate a "gold brick," with a definite intention of putting it upon the market, and yet — if he kept it a few months — finally persuade himself that it was really the precious metal.

The various influences I have endeavoured briefly to indicate, and many others which may be surmised, at length wrought their effect, not only in reconciliation but in restoration. With industrial development in the South, and the growth of a commercialism unlike anything known in its former history, that phase of sectional feeling which had once been esteemed a menace to the peace of the country entirely disappeared. Community of interest, similitude of occupation, and the general and extended intercourse which modern commerce has demanded and modern facilities of transportation made possible, have welded together all parts of the country and united many populations into really one people.

The spectacle so gratifying and so often commented on, of the Northern and Southern boys in the Spanish-American war, marching to battle under the same flag and with a common sentiment of patriotism, was merely an evidence, a demonstration of the change of feeling that had already taken place. The youth of the South, the men of middle age, all who had grown to manhood since the close of the Civil War, felt full fellowship in the existing civic order and were above all else American.

History is constantly repeating the shrewd saying of the old Ommeyad Caliph that, "Men are more like unto the times in which they live than they are to their fathers."

A few "unreconstructed rebels" yet survive; ancient stumps of gnarled and stubborn oak which "may break but cannot bend." They have their counterparts among the aged federal veterans; and the growls the former emit, sometimes on slight provocation, are occasionally echoed by a roar from some Grand Army post when a Confederate flag is returned, or it is proposed to honour some typical Confederate hero with marks of national respect. When this feeling is genuine, when it is exhibited by men who really fought and not by some one merely simulating it with the hope of obtaining a certain éclat, it is impossible not to respect it, and it elicits a kind of sympathy. We recognize it as the crude, half-articulate expression of long-cherished conviction.

An old veteran of the Army of Northern Virginia is credited with having declared that what he anticipated with most interest in the next world, was hearing "What Jubal Early would say when he met Fitz Lee wearing a Yankee uniform." Now that was wrong; such curiosity is reprehensible in either Christian or patriot; yet we cannot avoid being impressed with its quaint candour and apposite, even if untimely, suggestiveness. Justly understood, the caustic speech of the unreconstructed Confederate — which sometimes creates amusement and occasionally incurs censure — is no more than his unconscious protest against the destiny which has torn him away from surroundings which he loved and to which he was adapted, and stranded him in a region to which he can never become accustomed. But he is rapidly passing; he is not often encountered even at Confederate reunions, and it is not at all probable that we shall ever look upon his like again.

Should any one, however, desire to see him painted as he really was, it is only necessary to read a sketch written long before the "unreconstructed rebel" appeared *in propria persona*, but which is as faithful a portraiture of him, in its distinctive features, as if taken from life. Read Washington Irving's description of the closing days of Governor Stuyvesant, "Peter the Headstrong," a man with a great soul, which important fact the somewhat undue levity of the historian makes only the more conspicuous.

After long and valiant effort to defend the people of his province against crafty foes who looked with covetous eyes on the fair fields of the New Netherlands — meeting, with equal resolution, war without and sedition within — he was at last confronted with a situation that even his courage and constancy could not overcome. The English came in overwhelming force, and wrested from the Dutch republic the territory over which Peter had exercised arbitrary but beneficent sway. Deposed, yet with a spirit unsubdued, he retired forever from the city whose name had been changed from New Amsterdam to

New York, and would not even gaze upon it for fear that his eyes might be offended by the hated English flag.

He lived at his country seat, dispensing hospitality and charity, kindly in act but rough in speech, and maintaining still over all around him strict and salutary discipline. His only solace was in the remembrance of the successes his Dutch countrymen had achieved over the English; of how Van Tromp, with a broom at his mast-head, had swept the channel clear of their cruisers; and to read of some victory even yet won by De Ruyter. But one day the news came that De Ruyter had met with crushing defeat. The shock was too much for him; all hope seemed gone, and he took to his bed and died.

But for many years the old Dutch burghers who remembered him in the prime and pride of his stalwart manhood, as they sat pensively smoking under the shade trees in front of their dwellings, would say with moist eyes to sympathetic vrows, "Well den! Hard-koppig Peter ben gone at last."

Kentucky, as I have said, although many of her citizens had served in the Southern armies and much of her territory had been included within the zone of actual warfare, had sustained less injury from it than had been inflicted on the seceding states, and had altogether escaped the subsequent evils from which they had suffered so severely in the years immediately succeeding. Because of this, and because also of the fact that so many near relatives had fought in opposing ranks — in many instances, brother having stood against brother, and even father against son — less rancour characterized the division of political sentiment in Kentucky, and a stronger disposition for reconciliation prevailed.

Moreover, the emancipation of the slaves and the horrible atrocities perpetrated by two federal generals — Burbridge and Paine, the former a native Kentuckian — who, under guise of military execution, murdered nearly two hundred citizens and Confederate prisoners, had caused a great revulsion of feeling in that element of the population which had originally staunchly adhered to the Union. Reinforced by these recruits, those who had always entertained Southern proclivities suddenly found themselves overwhelmingly in control, and the post-bellum democracy of Kentucky began its career with a majority that could scarcely be counted.

The gubernatorial term of John S. Helm, who was elected in 1867, was the first of a succession of Democratic administrations which continued until 1895.

Governor Helm had long been distinguished in both state and national politics. Himself an ardent Southern sympathizer, the support of that element was given him all the more warmly out of respect for the memory of his son, Gen. Ben Hardin Helm, a gallant and much loved Confederate officer, who fell at Chickamauga. Governor Helm, dying soon after his inauguration, was succeeded by Lieut.-Gov. John W. Stevenson, also a politician and lawyer of considerable repute, and an exceptionally able man.

The most noted Kentucky politician of that day, the one who certainly exercised most influence in the national councils, was James B. Beck. A native of Scotland, he had been a resident of Fayette County and afterward of Lexington from his eighteenth year. Studying law while a farm labourer, he was, at still an early age, admitted to the bar and rapidly attained success and prominence in his profession.

Although Beck's intense and uncompromising Southern sentiment was well known, inasmuch as he made no attempt to conceal it and was assiduous and liberal in rendering aid to Confederate prisoners and his fellow "sympathizers" when in distress, the "Canny Scot" managed to avoid serious personal trouble at a time when others of his way of thinking and feeling became dangerously involved. He was cautious in act and discreet of speech, had strong friends among those in authority on the dominant side, and could be extremely useful to a friend no matter on which side he might happen to be. So that, while he was watched closely and jealously, he escaped both exile and imprisonment, one or the other of which fate befell nearly every other prominent Southern suspect.

He was elected to the lower house of congress from the Ashland district, in 1868, and immediately became a conspicuous figure, taking rank with the ablest men in the house, and, notwithstanding the then hopeless Democratic minority in that body, assisting in some directions to shape legislation. As was expected of him, and was his chief purpose when he began his congressional career, he especially devoted his efforts to combating the hostile legislation directed against the South, and succeeded in modifying much which could not be altogether defeated. During the years in which the Southern people were virtually denied representation in congress, they looked to Beck as their spokesman and advocate.

He displayed when sent to the senate, to which body he was thrice elected, dying in the harness, the same shrewd perception and strong sagacity which had characterized his service in the house, and the same extraordinary capacity and willingness for hard work.

Perhaps one of the most remarkable instances — from the standpoint of purely practical politics — of how the people will sometimes capsize the best laid plans of the politicians, was the nomination as a gubernatorial candidate of Luke P. Blackburn in 1879. His subsequent election was not at all so, for a Democratic nomination at that date in Kentucky was equivalent to election, and because the same sentiment which gave him the nomination was irresistible at the polls.

He was a native of Woodford County, perhaps the most fertile and beautiful part of the Bluegrass region. His father was one of the wealthiest and most prominent farmers of that country, and his younger brother, Joseph C. S. Blackburn was afterward United States senator from Kentucky. He was educated as a physician, and began his professional life at the age of twenty-one, during an epidemic of cholera which wrought terrible havoc in central Kentucky. Every physician, save himself, in the little town of Versailles where he was living, and in the vicinage, had died or fled, and Blackburn alone remained to care for the many victims.

That was the commencement of an extraordinary and heroic medical career. In the course of his long professional life, he served through a number of other epidemics of cholera and seventeen of yellow fever. The news that one of these dread plagues was prevailing would call him at once to the scene of danger and death. He felt the same impulse to encounter these dire enemies that some men have to seek battle, but with a nobler motive.

That Doctor Blackburn had a better understanding of these two diseases than any other physician of the period when he was practising cannot, I think, be disputed. He was not so learned nor so well trained as some of his professional contemporaries, but he possessed that faculty of acute and intelligent observation which, I take it, is indispensable and most valuable to all scientific discovery and knowledge. He had a theory that if any one during the prevalence of a cholera epidemic would drink only cistern water from a cistern into which there could be no seepage, that person would be immune. He claimed that there had been no exception to this rule in his experience. He was much ridiculed for this by many of his learned confrères; but, if I am not mistaken, Koch, who years afterward discovered the cholera microbe, announced that this mischievous creature finds its way into the human system by means of some liquid, most generally water. If this be true, water from a well protected cistern should be the safest.

He believed that yellow fever had been originally brought from Africa and naturalized in the tropical and sub-tropical zones of America. He believed it to be, as he termed it, a "heat disease"; that is to say, the material for its existence having been furnished by the presence of an infected patient, it could be propagated in any locality by severe and long continued heat and would continue its ravages until freezing weather checked it. I often heard him declare his belief that, if yellow fever should at any time be introduced into any of the Southern states as early as the first part of June, it might spread over the entire country. This, it must be remembered, was years before the germ theory of disease had been propounded, or the agency of the mosquito in disseminating yellow fever was even suspected. The therapeutic fraternity laughed at this also, and at his suggestion of quarantine precautions. I do not mean to contend that they were not correct; I, of course, know even less about such matters than do many highly intelligent men who have received medical diplomas. Some of them went so far as to say that for certain reasons, explicable, perhaps, but never fully explained, yellow fever could not prevail in Kentucky. I am sure, however, that they were wrong in that, because it did come, and its path was marked by many graves.

Doctor Blackburn's announcement of his candidacy was at first received with amusement. His best friends thought it an indiscreet and hopeless venture. He was widely known and extremely popular but had never had experience in office seeking and was thought, quite justly, to know as little about the game as a boy. Moreover, he had two or three opponents who were veteran and astute politicians, and almost as popular as himself. For some weeks his aspirations were a matter of jest with the multitude and of distress to those who felt compelled to support him.

But just then his oft-repeated prediction was verified. The yellow fever suddenly appeared along the gulf early in June, broke out almost immediately afterward at Grenada and other points in Mississippi, and, rushing up the great river with the velocity of an arrow fell with fearful virulence on the little village of Hickman in south-western Kentucky. In an appallingly brief time more than eighty deaths occurred there out of a population of less than one hundred and fifty.

Doctor Blackburn at once gave up his canvass and proceeded to offer his services to the sufferers in this obscure community. His friends sought to influence him not to go. Although much older than myself, we had long been close and devoted friends, and I earnestly strove to dissuade him. I had little hope that his political aspirations would prove successful, but, thinking the suggestion might be of some avail, urged him not to abandon his canvass at a time when his every effort was necessary to success. He answered that he ardently desired the preferment he was asking, but that his duty was plain and imperative, and he must go to those stricken with the pestilence.

The work which he did at Hickman was not only dangerous but exceedingly arduous. He had little assistance. Two other physicians, animated by the same heroic spirit, had hastened to the town, but one of them had been prostrated with the fever and died in a few days. The little place could furnish few nurses for the sick, and all of these were killed or driven away by the plague. At one time, Blackburn, in addition to the attention paid his other patients, was compelled for several days personally to nurse a negro woman and her five children, who were lying helpless in the clutches of the terrible sickness. He remained at Hickman until the disease had disappeared, and, with the good fortune which had attended him in many similar experiences, passed through with immunity.

When he returned to the political field he found a canvass no longer necessary; all opposition had vanished. Those who had regarded his former services of like nature performed at places and dates more remote, with only languid admiration, now seeing them done close at hand and when the danger was near and menacing, were enthused with desire to reward him. His competitors gracefully and wisely retired, and he was nominated by acclamation.

As governor, while evincing no marked ability in the general details of administration and sometimes making the mistakes usual to inexperience, he accomplished great good in one direction. He inaugurated prison reforms greatly needed, and, against formidable opposition, courageously carried them to completion. He was an unusually brave, true, earnest, and generous man, and altogether worthy of the affection and esteem he inspired.

J. Proctor Knott, who succeeded Blackburn as governor, was in many respects — as a lawyer, forensic debater, and writer — one of the ablest men Kentucky or the South has produced. In congress, he did very much the same sort of work as that which was so persistently and successfully accomplished by Beck. His indulgence of a vein of humour, unusually keen and racy, and a certain satiric propensity, to some extent diverted appreciation from stronger and more substantial qualities; but he will always be ranked high on the roll of statesmen Kentucky has given the nation.

It is impossible, I believe, for any intelligent and sincere man who has known Gen. Simon B. Buckner, either personally or by repute, not to regard him with respect and admiration; and with those who have known him best, who are intimately acquainted with the record of both his public and private life, these feelings are enhanced nearly to that of reverence.

Esteemed by his comrades of the "old" army one of its best officers, he fully vindicated that opinion by his military conduct during the Civil War and his services to the South. The rank of lieutenant-general, given him after more than three years of service, was a testimonial of the confidence reposed in him by the President and congress of the Confederacy; and, in the estimation of competent judges, he was one of the most deserving on whom the grade was conferred.

He was elected governor in 1887. During his administrations one of the most important and salutary political reforms ever effected in the state was inaugurated, and afterward, largely by his agency and example, was completed and made permanent. The vice of "special legislation," prevalent and bad enough in many other states, had become, in Kentucky, an intolerable evil. At every session of the legislature numerous private acts were passed for the benefit of individuals or in aid of certain corporations. "Charter peddling," as the practice was well named, had become almost a recognized profession. Men would procure legislative acts of incorporation with no thought of applying them to any useful or legitimate purpose; with no intention at least of themselves utilizing such grants.

Acts authorizing the construction of railroads constituted the principal stock in trade of the "charter peddler." He would procure one which, judiciously employed, might menace the interests of some established and "going" railroad company, with the hope, frequently realized, of selling out to the company threatened. Charters would be obtained for the construction of railroads through parts of the state where none had been built, but where they were much needed, with no purpose, however, of actual construction, but in order to control the situation until parties entertaining a *bona fide* desire to build should be ready to buy them out. The facilities this afforded for blackmail and harmful obstruction will readily be seen. There were at one time to be found in the Session acts of Kentucky more than one hundred such inutilized acts of incorporation.

But very often, even when the parties obtaining them honestly intended to utilize these charters, the effect of such reckless legislation was pernicious. Almost always the right was given the incorporators to submit propositions for county and municipal subscriptions in aid of such enterprises, to be provided by taxation. In the anxious desire felt at one time to obtain railroads, the people would vote almost any aid asked, and, as a consequence, more than one county was made bankrupt.

Of course, this had occasioned criticism, and strenuous but unavailing efforts had been made to stop it. When Buckner became governor he adopted a very simple method which effectually put an end to the evil during his term. He vetoed every bill passed by the two houses, containing any such objectionable provision, or savouring in any degree of the practice; and in each veto message pointed out with minute particularity what he deemed objectionable. It was useless to attempt to pass one of these bills over his veto and a rather amusing as well as unusual legislative custom resulted, and for awhile prevailed. Almost every morning, during a session, a score or more of solons could be seen repairing to the executive office, reminding one of the matutinal visits of congressmen to the President in search of patronage. The Kentucky lawmakers, however, came to submit their bills to the governor, to have them overhauled in advance, to find out, as some wag expressed it, "Just how much he would stand." Although this imposed upon Governor Buckner that task of reading many bills twice — reading them before they were passed as well as after — he cheerfully performed the work; counselling freely with all, and always frankly indicating "what he would stand."

The convention which framed the present Constitution of Kentucky met during his term of office. He was one of its most prominent members, and aided materially in the best work it performed, that of requiring the legislature to enact general acts of incorporation and in other ways making special legislation well-nigh impossible.

His administration as governor — and his entire political life — was marked by clear, wise judgment, perfect dignity and firmness, and unswerving rectitude and consistency of purpose.

There were three men in public life from Kentucky, at the time of which I write, who, I have always thought, were superior intellectually to their contemporaries, and equal in that respect to any who had preceded them. These were John G. Carlisle, William Lindsay, and William C. P. Breckinridge. Of the three, Breckinridge excelled in general culture, but they were all well and widely informed.

Carlisle and Lindsay were each gifted with a mental trenchancy, a power of incisive penetration that was marvellous. Their minds sought out and found the salient, material points of any subject of discussion, as unerringly as the lightning searches for iron. Carlisle's extraordinary capacity for clear and cogent statement won the admiration of all who ever heard him. His presentation of his case was so lucid, so comprehensive, and yet so terse, that it seemed to render contradiction impossible and dispense with the necessity of argument.

Lindsay, although himself strong in statement, was Carlisle's inferior in that regard; but he possessed a greater faculty of logical illustration, and could present his contentions in more varied form. Neither was a rhetorician nor an orator, although each was a ready, impressive, and entertaining speaker.

I have sometimes thought Breckinridge was the most gifted and attractive orator I ever heard. He was very brilliant, but there was nothing of grandiose declamation or ostentatious ornament in his speech, and it was replete with reason and argument. His eloquence, even when most impassioned, flowed like a river, bank-full but limpid, and bearing a rich and abundant freight.

Buckner, Lindsay, Carlisle, and Breckinridge, with thousands of others, were read out of the Democratic party when a new gospel was expounded and their souls, like the lion heart of Grover Cleveland, still clung to the old. They could neither sanction nor condone what they deemed heresy — the adoption of financial fallacies which had time and again been exposed, but which the national Democratic convention sought to impose as Democratic articles of faith. They refused to accept Mr. Bryan's amazing conclusion that "Sixteen to one is the *natural* ratio" between the precious metals, and found his "quantitative theory" of monetary circulation quite as shallow.

All such men condemned also the political manipulation which, conceived in fraud, is often achieved by violence, and totally rejected the political morality which holds that an election stolen for partisan benefit is pardonable theft.

While the Republican party has increased little in actual numerical strength in Kentucky since 1896, the differences upon the money question and revolt against the objectionable "machine" management and methods, which seem to be invariably developed in any party long remaining in power, have so shorn the regular Democracy of much of its strength, and induced so large an independent vote, that Kentucky can almost be reckoned among the doubtful states.

If an abolition of the intolerant spirit engendered by partisan passion could be accomplished by the total obliteration of party lines and distinctions, and a more patriotic and fraternal spirit be substituted, it would be well to try the experiment not only in Kentucky, but elsewhere. Practical men, however, will be deterred from attempting it by patent considerations. In the first place, they must realize how extremely difficult it will be to supersede a form of contention so perfectly in touch with modern ideas; and if they should succeed in diverting human attention from this prolific and now favourite theme of dispute, what then? Mankind must have something to wrangle about outside of and more general than their ordinary and every-day affairs. It must be of a kind, too, to enable every fire-eyed disputant to believe that he is rending his nether garment for a "principle." The Byzantine mob, in the days of the Eastern Roman Empire, were satisfied to cut throats about the colours of the circus, the green and blue badges of the charioteers. But that sort of thing is scarcely refined and sublimated enough for modern civilization. Religion — that is to say, in its dogmatic expressions — long furnished an extensive quarry of extremely satisfactory controversial material, more gratifying, perhaps, than any other, for the reason that where proof is impossible or evidence hopelessly perplexing, belief is always more ardent and assertion more confident.

It is probable that, for a long time yet, this peculiar excitement which human nature seems to demand, will be found in political controversy and partisan debate. Many men crave it as a sort of dissipation, expecting no reward and not always perfectly understanding, or caring to understand, the platforms and party cries about which they become so aroused. Almost every interest, every question affecting society, is dragged into the political forum, not always because actually requiring legislative attention, but to supply topics for partisan discussion and to provide, as Mr. Bryan phrases it, "paramount issues."

In this agitation which furnishes agreeable entertainment for the people, the practical politician finds serious employment and profit. An industry is created from which the multitude derives amusement, and substantial benefit accrues to the professionals of high and low degree who deal the cards and run the game.

But it is greatly to be deplored that this partisan spirit is so prone to engender a bigotry and bitterness of feeling which often disturbs the social relations of those whom nature meant to be friends. It is something, however, which will always be difficult of correction. The combative inclination and pride of opinion out of which it proceeds, are deeply implanted in humanity and manifest themselves in protean shapes. It is strange how even the best of the race sometimes cling, with exceptional pertinacity, to ideas which promise the least of happiness and solace, and which reason would most readily reject. There have been many orthodox Christians and excellent men who I am convinced, would, if compelled to make the choice, relinquish their trust in the Deity rather than their belief in the devil. I am quite sure that I have known men to whom it would afford greater satisfaction to think that those they disliked were going to hell, than that they, themselves, were going to heaven.

CHAPTER XXIII

I CAME to Louisville in March, 1868, with the intention of making it my residence, have lived here ever since, and am very glad to believe that I will never live anywhere else. My experience in such regard has been neither extensive nor varied, but I am convinced that no opportunity nor care in selection could have enabled me to find a home more agreeable, certainly none more congenial.

Having no wish to indulge the common and, doubtless, pardonable American habit of sounding the praises of one's own city, I shall leave to abler and less diffident exploiters the duty of proving Louisville's superiority in all urban particulars; of indicating its extraordinary claims to commercial and industrial attention; and the many reasons why intelligent financiers should favourably consider the opportunities always open within her hospitable domain for profitable investment. It is just as well, perhaps after all, that other people shall not recognize these advantages so thoroughly as we ourselves do, for Louisville would lose much of its charm if it became an overgrown city.

I like better to remember and think of the people I have known here; to recall the characteristic traits I have so often known them exhibit — which, good or bad, have been genuine and very decided — but more especially the warm, generous sympathy, the kindliness they have always been so ready to bestow.

We feel sometimes indefinable impressions which, while they may coincide with recognized facts, yet seem independent of them. Such are often our likes or dislikes of people or things. It may be that the love of locality, the preference for well known haunts and familiar scenes which the child feels, is revived in advanced age; or that the old man instinctively clings to his accustomed habitat as an old dog hugs his peculiar chimney corner. But without seeking any occult explanation, it is enough to say that for many reasons my present place of residence has always been to me a pleasant one, and becomes more so as the years roll by.

Louisville has always been essentially Southern in its social spirit and in its customs, and an epitome of Kentucky, in that every part of the state — almost every county — has been at all times represented in its population. Whatever is typical of the Kentuckian has been abundantly exhibited in the Louisvillian, and especially his genial desire to entertain and be entertained. A numerous array of Civil War veterans, of both sides and of creditable records, has provided material for those reunions in which the reminiscent old soldier delights, and at which, for many years past, Federals and Confederates have met as comrades. Among its people have ever been found thousands of brave and true men and good and noble women, of whose friendly regard the most exalted might be proud; and *per contra*— that we may avoid the appearance of perfection — it must be admitted that the "undesirable" citizen has been constantly, actively, and sufficiently in evidence to quicken the consciences of those who require a visible warning against unrighteousness, and furnish the reformer with suitable employment.

I have esteemed myself fortunate in my choice of an abode; and now, at an age when a man can reasonably expect little if anything more than he can find in his friendships and affections, I should earnestly regret a separation from old and long associations, and would deem it in some sense a pleasure to die among those whom I have known so long.

Louisville was formerly often described as "a city with village ways." While this was said to a certain extent in a spirit of depreciation — in criticism of business methods supposed to be not quite so alert and up to date as those of some of her commercial rivals — it might just as truly have been said, and was doubtless partly intended, as indicative of a social trait which can scarcely be thought a just matter of criticism. A hearty and cordial fellowship was characteristic of the people. Everybody felt a lively and usually good-humoured interest in the affairs of every one else; and if much gossip was thereby occasioned it was not often malicious.

Founded in the first years of the pioneer period, in 1778, and incorporated by act of the Legislature of Virginia in 1780,

Louisville's original population was composed of the hunters and backwoodsmen who formed the advance guard of that great army of emigration which crossed the Alleghanies to ultimately occupy and people the West. The immediate successors of the pioneers were a class of men much like them, when the keel-boats, and soon afterward the big steam-boats, began to ply the broad, inland waters from the falls of the Ohio to New Orleans.

A refining influence may have been exerted upon this ruder element by the French colony which at an early date located at Louisville, making its headquarters at Shippingport, that part of the community situated at the Falls. Its most conspicuous member was Audubon, who came to Louisville in 1808 and lived there until 1820. But the Tarascons, Berthouds, Honorés, and DeGallons were almost as well known.

These Gallic settlers were, as a rule, enterprising and excellent citizens; they became widely known and their names are well remembered. Many of their descendants remain in Kentucky and the neighbouring border states.

The growth of Louisville keeping pace with the increasing population of the state — very considerable for that day — the little pioneer post soon became a city, as cities were then rated. A host of more civilized immigration, heralding increase and multiplication, rolled in from the Atlantic States. In its van and constituting its main strength came the ubiquitous and ever welcome, the polished and prolific, Virginian. Inasmuch as I might probably not be here now had he not come then, I regard his advent, from a personal as well as historic point of view, with a glad and pious feeling.

Intimate and advantageous commercial relations with rapidly developing communities of the Mississippi Valley had contributed largely to the prosperity of Louisville in the ante-bellum period, but it was materially, although temporarily, impaired by the war. She shared the fate of some other flourishing cities of the South and the border which were permanently occupied by Federal troops at an early stage of hostilities. Escaping the more evident havoc of warfare, these cities, nevertheless, suffered seriously by the diversion or lack of their accustomed trade. Their former customers were either denied access to them or bereft of the means of patronage. Louisville was, perhaps, more injured in this way than any other place with the exception of New Orleans. Although for four years it was an important base of operations and supplies for the Federal armies operating in Tennessee, Georgia, Alabama, and part of Mississippi, the city derived no advantage from these strategic dispositions. The government purchased little material and expended scarcely any money there. Military occupation was of no help to the local business, but rather a handicap upon it. The troops in garrison or in transit bought whatever they needed beyond their rations from the sutlers, and of every conceivable floating population a nomadic soldiery, at least in time of war, is the most undesirable. The merchants had little opportunity to do business at all; but what there was of it was hampered by the system of issuing "permits to trade," which, granted by the commanding military officers, were generally refused to those who were unable to present a clean bill of loyalty and not always given to those who could. This method of restraint was very effective in diminishing the general commercial prosperity, but was quite valuable to certain favourites.

Evidences of the detrimental effects of thus converting a city into a garrisoned town and depot were yet visible in 1868 and even later. Quite a number of troops were still stationed there; many of the best residences were occupied by officers and chiefs of supply departments, each with a numerous clerical array; and in certain parts of the city long lines of plank structures, used as barracks, stretched as far as the eye could see. It seemed well-nigh impossible to dispense with the tokens and clear away the debris of war.

I have hitherto spoken in these reminiscences, with few exceptions, only of the dead; and, for obvious reasons, will observe the same rule with little deviation in speaking of those whom I have known in Louisville.

Should I allude to all of those yet living, who are entitled to grateful recognition and kindly and admiring mention at my hands, the list would swell into something like the dimensions of a directory; and some of them, inasmuch as the greater part of what I have written relates to the past, might feel as if they were reading their own obituary notices unaccountably delayed. Moreover it is never altogether safe to speak of the living, even in what might be regarded by third parties as very flattering terms. We are a sensitive generation and some of my compatriots, excellent and reasonable people in many respects, are yet critical to the last degree of any mention made of themselves. I have known well meaning men get into trouble, even when they thought they were paying a compliment, simply because it wasn't exactly the compliment, or didn't stretch quite so far as, the other fellow would have liked.

"D — n it, sir," said an indignant member of the legislature to the correspondent of a daily newspaper, "you say in your report this morning that my speech on yesterday was the best delivered during the debate."

"Well! wasn't it?" queried the astonished reporter.

"Suppose it was! Couldn't you just as easy have said it was the best of the session?"

It is to be borne in mind, also, that, at this present writing, opinion fluctuates readily and with surprising rapidity. Some men do not entertain the same opinion to-day that they held on yesterday; some of them entertain two or three sets of opinions upon the same subject, at very nearly the same time. Commenting on this type of thinker, George M. Davie once remarked: "There must of course be two sides to every question, but Major ———always takes the third."

Now, if in writing about one of these gentlemen with whom it is so difficult to agree, I should inadvertently represent him as having entertained the right opinion at the wrong time, or *vice versa* — that is to say, if I should write in ignorance that he had quite recently changed his opinions, complications unpleasant to myself might ensue.

One of the men, for many years prominent and useful in the community, with whom I was well acquainted before I came to Louisville, was the veteran journalist, Walter N. Haldeman, the founder of the *Courier-Journal*. In 1861, Mr. Haldeman, was, and had been for some years previously, the proprietor and editor of the Louisville *Courier*. An intense and ardent "Southern rights" man, openly declaring his sentiments, both personally and in his paper, and in terms which could be neither misunderstood nor forgiven, he found it impossible — inasmuch as he was not a man either to recant or be silent — to remain in Louisville after it became apparent that the city would soon be and probably long continue in Federal possession. Early in the war, therefore, he moved with his family and his paper to Dixie, publishing the *Courier* first at Bowling Green, afterward at Nashville, and ultimately wherever the nomadic course and varying fortunes of the Army of Tennessee permitted. It was always in close attendance upon that army and as near the front as was compatible with safe and convenient publication, and always retained its title of the Louisville *Courier*. Mr. Haldeman and his wife—an example of every sweet and womanly virtue—were earnest and faithful friends of the Confederate soldiers, but especially of the Kentuckians; and there was scarcely one of these who was not, at some time and in some manner, a recipient of their kindness.

He returned to Louisville shortly after the close of the war and two or three years subsequently the *Courier* was consolidated with the *Journal*, the paper so long and brilliantly edited by George D. Prentice. Under Mr. Haldeman's able control the paper, with its double title, was eminently successful and became a very valuable property.

Mr. Prentice was one of the editorial writers of the *Courier-Journal* until he died. I shall never forget one interview I had with him, because of its strange mixture of the pathetic and the amusing. His two sons had been in the Confederate army. The elder, Courtland, belonged to the Second Kentucky Cavalry, the regiment I at one time commanded, and was killed at Augusta, Ky., in 1862. I wrote his father about his death, and succeeded in sending some of his personal effects, which I thought she would value, through the lines to his mother. The younger son, Clarence, was like his brother in that he was a brave soldier, but totally unlike him in all other respects. He was an uncommonly bright man, but as wild and reckless a creature as I ever knew, and an inveterate spendthrift. After Clarence got back from the army the old man never had a dollar which he might with confidence regard as his own.

Two or three months after my return to Kentucky, I was walking one day along one of the streets of Frankfort, when Clarence came hastily out of a house and accosted me.

"General," he said, "the old man is in there and wants to talk to you about Courtland. Will you go in and see him?"

I, of course, readily assented, and found myself in the presence of a man apparently broken in health and very aged; he looked, indeed, much older than he really was. He immediately began to talk about his dead son and showed great emotion; his voice was almost inarticulate, and tears streamed down his cheeks.

I was, naturally, much affected by his sorrow and could scarcely utter my sympathy.

When this had continued for a few minutes, however, Clarence, who seemed to think the affair was becoming too lugubrious, interposed in a manner that, I confess, at first greatly shocked me.

"Father," he broke in, "you have no right to distress General Duke with your personal griefs. We all deeply regret Courtland's death, but no amount of lamentation can bring him to life again."

Then turning to me, he went on, "General Duke, you must excuse the old man. He isn't now what he once was. He's old and feeble and pretty well played out, but he shall never suffer while I have got a cent."

To my surprise, the old gentleman instead of resenting this ill-timed pleasantry of Clarence, seemed greatly to enjoy it. He grinned broadly and said in a thin, quavering voice:

"That's very filial, my son! It's a very proper sentiment, indeed. But it's no more than fair, for you know I suffer like hell when you haven't got a cent."

I was admitted to practice at the Louisville bar in 1869. I think I risk nothing in saying that it would have compared favourably in legal ability and attainment, forensic talent and devotion to professional duty, with any similar body of men in the United States.

Among its veterans were James S. Speed, attorney-general during Mr. Lincoln's administration; Joshua A. Bullitt, previously a member of the appellate bench of Kentucky; Isaac Caldwell, William F. Bullock, Thomas W. Gibson, Humphrey Marshall, Edward P. Worthington, Robert W. Woolley, Peter B. Muir, John W. Barr, afterward judge of the United States District Court for the district of Kentucky; Kemp Goodloe, Martin Bijur, A. M. Gazlay, James Harrison, and others of perhaps equal ability, although not so successful or well known. Just coming into full practice, although not yet risen to the eminence they subsequently attained, were John M. Harlan, since and for many years associate justice of the Supreme Court; Benjamin D. Bristow, afterward secretary of the treasury; Byron Bacon, W. R. Thompson, John Mason Brown, D. W. Sanders and genial, eloquent Phil Lee, whose oratory charmed susceptible juries and whose humour delighted his colleagues of the bar.

There were many younger men, then in their professional apprenticeship, who in due time won merited distinction, and quite a number of these are yet living. Of those who have passed away, and whose names are held in especial honour and affection by their associates, may be particularly mentioned Albert S. Willis, George B. Eastin, Alex. Booth, St. John Boyle, Thomas S. Speed, George M. Davie, Thomas W. Bullitt, and James P. Helm.

Bullitt was my college mate and one of my closest comrades in the army. At the date of his death, our friendship had endured for more than half a century, becoming, if possible, constantly more cordial. For many years a warm friendship had existed also between Helm and myself. I have never known men purer, nobler, and braver than they were, or who more deserved and more generally commanded respect and admiration.

At that date the elevation of comparatively young men to the bench was not so frequent as it is now, and the judges who presided over the courts sitting in Louisville, at the time of which I write, were men of mature age and ripe professional experience. Horatio W. Bruce, who not a great while before, had served in the Confederate congress, was judge of the Circuit Court of the judicial district in which Jefferson County was then included; he was afterward chancellor, and then became chief counsel of the Louisville & Nashville Railroad Company. Henry S. Stites, judge of the Court of Common Pleas, was already distinguished for previous and long service on the bench, in the course of which he had served a term on the appellate bench. Thomas B. Cochran, a strong man and excellent lawyer, was chancellor.

Bland Ballard, then judge of the United States District Court for Kentucky, was a remarkably able man. His intellect was clear, vigorous, and unusually fertile and acute, his character positive and unyielding, and in temper he was somewhat cynical, a disposition much modified, however, by his keen appreciation of the humorous.

While his knowledge of law was profound and extensive, he seemed as little influenced by precedent or controlled by mere technicalities as was possible in one of his professional education and instincts. Apparently his main difficulty on the bench was to overcome a natural inclination to become the advocate. He discerned with quick apprehension every point in a case, but could be urged by imprudent insistency into undue consideration of something quite opposite to the pleader's contention, and whoever was so incautious as to enter into argument with him was almost sure to be worsted.

He was extremely partisan in his political opinions, but I never thought him so influenced on the bench. He was certainly no respecter of persons, and the younger members of the bar generally fared better before him than the older and more established practitioners. Some of the lawyers who had been Confederate soldiers hesitated, for a time, to practise in his court because of his very decided hostility to "disloyal" sentiment; but it soon became evident that the ex-Confederates would receive from him their full share of favourable countenance, and that his political bias in nowise controlled his personal feelings or official relations.

Gabriel C. Wharton and Eli Murray were at that time serving respectively as United States district attorney and United States marshal for the district of Kentucky; both were extremely popular and capable. Each had served during the entire war with the Kentucky Federal troops and Murray was, perhaps, the youngest brigadier-general in either army. At the age of twenty-one, he commanded a division of cavalry in Sherman's march to the sea, with exceptional gallantry and efficiency.

Two of the lawyers whom I have mentioned, Byron Bacon and George M. Davie, were, in addition to excellence in their profession, possessed of more than ordinary talent in other ways. Had either devoted his attention exclusively to literature, he would, I believe, have achieved marked success in that line; for each wrote with unusual wit and vigour and in a singularly lucid and pleasing style. Very little written by either has received even limited publication. Both were extremely reluctant to appear in print, entertaining a nervous and rather amusing apprehension that notoriety so gotten, might discourage their clients and injuriously affect their practice. But as such harm cannot now be done them, and as I naturally desire to sustain a claim in which I feel full confidence, by actual proof, I may be pardoned if I reproduce a brief specimen from the pen of each.

Some thirty or more years ago, Bacon at a meeting of the Kentucky Bar Association, responded to the toast, "How to Explain to Your Client Why You Lost His Case." This address appeared in the papers at the time and was subsequently republished in the *Southern Bivouac*. It is something that does not lose its flavour with age.

> I deprecate any thought that I respond because, from a more extended experience than my legal brethren, I bring to the solution of this question the exhaustive learning and skill of the specialist. The characteristic modesty of our profession forbids that I should arrogate to myself to instruct the eminent lawyers around me, wherein they doubtless have attained that perfection which only long practice can give.
>
> I assume, therefore, that the subject was proposed for the edification of novitiates — those "young gentlemen" to whom Blackstone so often and so feelingly alludes, who, after a long and laborious course of study, have been found, upon an examination by the sages of the law, not to have "fought a duel with deadly weapons since the adoption of the present constitution," and have been admitted to our ranks.*
>
> To them, then, I shall offer briefly some suggestions upon this point hoping that they may not find them of practical value upon the termination of their first case.
>
> The question, as framed, is not unlike that with which Charles II long puzzled the Royal Society. He demanded the cause of certain phenomena, the existence of which he falsely assumed. The answer was simply the denial of the existence of the phenomena. What lawyer ever attempted to explain the failure of a case upon the hypothesis that *he* had lost it? That a lawyer cannot lose a case is as well established a maxim as that the king can do no wrong, or, that the tenant cannot deny his landlord's title. Eliminate this error, and our question is of easy solution.
>
> Coke tells us that law is the "perfection of human reason"; Burke that it is "the pride of the human intellect"; "the collected reason of ages, combining the principles of eternal justice with the infinite variety of human concerns"; "the most excellent, yea, the exactest of the sciences"; and the eloquent Hooker, that "her seat is the bosom of God, her voice the harmony of the spheres; all things in heaven and on earth do her homage — the least as feeling her care, the greatest as not exempt from her power." But we know that, if it be the purest of reason, the exactest of the sciences, its administra-

---

*Before admission to the practice of law in Kentucky, the applicant is required to make oath that, since the adoption of the present Constitution of that State he, being a citizen thereof, has not fought a duel with deadly weapons with another citizen of the State.

tion is not always entrusted to the severest of logicians or the exactest of scientists. We know that the great, the crowning glory of "our noble English common law" is its uncertainty, and therein lies the emolument and pleasurable excitement of its practice.

If, oblivious of this, you shall have assured your client of success in the simplest case, the hour of his disappointment will be that of your tribulation, and professional experience can extend to you no solace or aid.

But your client's cause has resulted unfavourably. You, of course, are never to blame; the fault is that of the judge, the jury, or your client himself, and it may be of all three. It becomes your duty to divert the tide of his wrath into those channels where it can do the least possible harm. If he be a crank and shoots the judge or cripples a juror, they fall as blessed martyrs, and their places and their mantles are easily filled; but not so readily your place or your mantle. As one of America's sweetest poets, Mr. George M. Davie, has expressed it in a touching tribute to our professional and social worth, unequalled for delicacy of sentiment, boldness of imagery, and beauty of diction in the whole range of English poetry:

> "Judges and juries may flourish or may fade,
> A vote can make them as a vote has made;
> But the bold barrister, a country's pride,
> When once destroyed can never be supplied."

The selection then of a target for your client (I use the word "target" metaphorically) must rest upon the peculiar facts and circumstances of the case and the "sound discretion," as the venerated Story has it, of the counsel. But avoid, if possible, imputing the blame to your client; for although this has been attended with very happy results, yet his mood at such times is apt to be homicidal; and, moreover, you should bear in mind that there your aim is to conciliate.

"Who wrote that note?" demanded the Indiana lawyer who, under the old system of procedure, had declared in covenant as on a writing obligatory, and gone out of court on a variance.

"I got Squire Brown to write it," answered his sorely perplexed and discomfited client.

"I thought so," sneered the learned counsel. "Didn't you know that no d—n magistrate could write a promissory note that would fit a declaration?"

First, as to the jury: Upon this head I need not enlarge, only remind you that you are not held by the profession as committed or estopped by any eulogium, however glowing, which you may have pronounced during the progress of the trial on their intelligence and integrity. It is only in the capacity of a scape-goat that the American juror attains the full measure of his utility, and as such he will ever be regarded by our profession with gratitude not unmingled with affection.

But it is to the judge that we turn in this extremity with unwavering confidence. The serenity and grandmotherly benignity enthroned upon his visage is to the layman that placidity of surface which indicates fathomless depths of legal lore; to the lawyer it bespeaks the phlegmatic temperament of one whose mission is to bear unmurmuringly the burdens of others.

It comes upon you like a revelation that your weeks of study, your elaborate preparation, your voluminous brief, are all for naught; that the impetuous torrent of your eloquence has dashed itself against his skull, only to envelop it in fog and mist, and more "in sorrow than in anger" you confess that the presumption that every man knows the law cannot be indulged in his favour. Even your luminous exposition has failed to enlighten him.

You need not spare him. He thrives on abuse. Year in and year out he bears the anathemas of disappointed lawyers and litigants with the stolid indifference of Sancho Panza's ass in the valley of the pack-staves, or beneath the missiles of the galley-slaves, and society comes finally to regard him pretty much as did Sancho his ass. It berates him, overtasks him, half starves him, and loves him.

But, seriously considered, our question is only a long-standing and harmless jest of the bar, meaningless in actual practice.

The lawyer is untiring in his client's behalf, and the client knows, be the result what it may, that he has had the full measure of his lawyer's industry, zeal, and ability, and requires no explanation.

Lord Erskine said that in his maiden speech "he felt his children, tugging at his gown and heard them cry, 'Now, father, is the time for bread.'" The British bar applauded the sentiment. The American lawyer throughout the case feels his client tugging at his gown, and if unsuccessful, is sustained by the consciousness that he has done his whole duty as God has given him to see and perform it; and, should he want further consolation, he can open that oldest of all the books of the law and there read these words, which may soothe his wounded spirit, and possibly best answer the question of to-night:

"I returned and saw under the sun that the race is not to the swift, nor the battle to the strong; neither yet bread to the wise, nor yet riches to men of understanding, nor yet favour to men of skill, but time and chance happeneth to them all."

I might choose at random from Davie's productions, prose and verse, with the assurance of selecting something that would meet with favour. His translations of the Horatian odes have been esteemed by competent critics as among the best attempted of these graceful, versatile, and fascinating poems. and it was the work in which he took most pleasure.

"There is scarcely a man of letters," it has been said, "who has not at one time or other versified or imitated some of the odes of Horace"; and "Horatian scholars feel an interest in examining how each succeeding translator grapples with the difficulties of interpretation."

My own judgment in such a matter is of little value, but no translations I have ever seen seem to have rendered more perfectly the meaning and spirit or caught more accurately the rythmic measure and cadence of the original. I append his translation of the ode "Eheu Fugaces," which I think was his own favourite, in which the usually jovial poet, forgetting something of his merry badinage and careless philosophy, suggests sadder yet grander reflections in more exalted strain:

"Posthumus, O Posthumus! how swift the years are flying!
　Alas! no piety can bring delay to wrinkling brows
Nor stay the step of Age that's pressing closer on us,
　Nor check, but for a moment, unconquerable Death!

"Not even, O my comrade! if, as the days are passing,
　You should appease with sacrifice of hecatombs of kine
The unrelenting Pluto — whom Tityus imprisons,
　And triply huge Geryon, within his sombre waves.

"Those waves, ah! well we know, must some day be sailed over
　By all of us who've tasted the bounties of this earth;
Whether the time allotted, in regal wealth we're living,
　Or struggling on through penury, poor tenants of the field.

"For, all in vain we guard us from bloody fields of battle,
　And from the broken billows of Hadria's shrieking wave;
In vain we shun the hot winds, that blast the fields of autumn
　And bring the deadly pestilence to blight the frames of men;

"Still are we doomed, hereafter, to see the black Cocytus,
　That wanders on forever with always languid stream;
To watch the foul Danaids, and Sisyphus, Æolid,
　As hopelessly he labours on at his eternal toil.

"Your lands must be relinquished; the house that you inhabit,
　And the dear wife, so pleasing, must all be left behind,
And, of the groves you cherish — a little while the master —
　Shall not a leaf go with you, but cypress wreaths accurst!

"Then will your heir — more worthy! — bring forth that old Cæcuban
　That you have kept so charily beneath an hundred keys;
And, splashing with profusion the very floors, be drinking
　Your wines, more rare than those that crown the feasts of Pontiff kings!"

The medical profession was also well represented in Louisville, when I first knew the city, as, indeed, it has been at all times. There were in its ranks many bright and talented men, reputed to be of excellent ability, and who certainly strove honestly to be useful in their vocation.

The patriarch and Nestor of these disciples of the healing art was Dr. Theodore F. Bell, a sincere, well-meaning, but rather visionary man. While there is much of wisdom apparent in medical science, as we see it in practice, there is so much more concealed from vision behind the veil of faith that we rarely know just how to rate its exponents. It was generally believed that Doctor Bell was exceedingly learned, and universally conceded that he was extremely theoretical. He had an abundance of the sort of erudition which can furnish quotations, seemingly conclusive, in support of any conceivable contention, and no amount of practical contradiction, no opposing fact, could shake his confidence in a theory once adopted. His record of cures effected was not, I believe, remarkable; but he could talk and write in a fashion which might have consoled the afflicted visiting the pool of Siloam, or excited hope in the bosom of Lazarus.

During the yellow fever epidemic of 1878, he won the admiration and regard of the merchants of Louisville — who deprecated the unbusinesslike reluctance of customers to come to the city for fear they might be plague stricken and die — by proving so far as it could be done by scholastic argumentation, that, because of certain mysterious hygenic conditions, the yellow fever could not possibly visit Louisville. The commercial gratitude for service so conservative was expressed at a large public meeting, attended by the best citizens, the majority of whom were qualified voters; and a gold medal intended to be commerative of the victory of speculative science over vulgar prejudice, was presented to the doctor. It might have been supposed that such an endorsement would settle the matter, even against the laws of nature. But the perversity of a malignant disease sometimes baffles all human calculation, and that same night fifty indigenous cases of the fever, resulting in nearly as many deaths, appeared in Louisville.

The three members of the medical fraternity with whom I was most intimately acquainted, and they were certainly among the brightest, were Drs. David W. and Lundsford P. Yandell, and Dr. Richard O. Cowling. Each ranked high in his profession, and was cultured, witty, and exceptionally agreeable. They were all, of course, social favourites.

I knew Dr. David Yandell very well during the Civil War, in which he acquired enviable reputation as a surgeon. I shall never forget an episode in which he figured at Murfreesboro, shortly before the battle of Stone River. It occurred on the occasion of Gen. John H. Morgan's marriage to Miss Ready, of that place, which was attended by General Bragg, commander-in-chief of the Army of Tennessee, all of the corps and division commanders and a large concourse of officers of minor rank.

At a late hour of the evening, Generals Bragg, Polk, Hardee, and Cheatham, with three or four subordinates, all of whom except myself were staff officers, were assembled by special invitation in one room of the mansion to discuss some particularly good wine, which the host had jealously reserved out of his ante-bellum supply.

Doctor Yandell, of course, was present, much in evidence, and, as it might be said, " in a class by himself." He was a symmetrically formed and quite handsome man, and showed up well even when beside the tall, soldierly figures and impressive bearing of the three senior generals, which were in striking contrast with the shorter, sturdier frame and almost boyishly jovial manner of Cheatham.

The conversation soon became animated and informal between the chiefs, the younger officers maintaining a discreet and respectful reticence while manifesting a due and proper appreciation of what was said by their superiors. A number of excellent stories were told; even General Bragg, I remember, told one on Cheatham at which, of course, everybody laughed very heartily, especially as Cheatham, who was disposed to laugh at anything, set the pace.

At length Yandell was requested to furnish an exhibition which was always immensely popular with his comrades of all grades. His power of mimicry was almost unrivalled, and he could on the spur of the movement invent situations and put speeches into the mouths of those he impersonated as *vraisemblant* as the look, tone, and gesture he reproduced.

On this occasion he represented first General Polk, then General Hardee, as *dramatis personæ* in some imaginary scene and dialogue, in a manner which greatly delighted his auditors. Stately and dignified as were these distinguished officers, than whom none were more admired and loved by all who served under or with them, they were yet extremely good-humoured, and, in their hours of relaxation, disposed even to be on familiar terms with their subordinates. Moreover, they not only liked Yandell but they liked to be amused; so they made no protest, General

Polk only occasionally interpolating a good-natured criticism when he thought the delineation a trifle strained.

Just as the doctor was finishing with Hardee, General Bragg was called out of the room and there was at once a general demand that Yandell should imitate him. This, indeed, was one of Yandell's favourite rôles and he could render it to perfection; but he did not like to attempt it except when at safe range from the original. Nearly every one stood in some awe of the fierce old miliatary autocrat, and, of course, those of lesser rank especially so.

The doctor, therefore, for a while positively declined. He was not borrowing trouble, he said, and had no wish that Bragg, suddenly returning, should surprise him. One of the staff officers, however, said that he knew that the general was occupied with business — the examination of important despatches — which would detain him at least an hour; so the doctor yielded to importunity and began his star piece.

Every one present was a competent judge of it — that is to say, all had at some time witnessed the real thing — and all realized that nothing could be more true to life than his representation of Bragg when in one of his paroxysms of tigerish ire and expatiating on his favourite themes, of the too prevalent use of whiskey and lack of discipline in the army; striding to and fro, rasping his hands savagely, scowling like an Afrite, and jerking out brief sentences in abrupt, raucous utterance.

At the very climax of the performance, but when the doctor's back was turned, unfortunately, toward the door, so that he could see no one enter, Bragg unexpectedly came in. He seemed immediately to take in the situation, and halted just within the room, clasping his hands behind his back and drawing his tall, gaunt form to its full height. His head was dropped slightly forward, and a grin of malicious amusement flitted over his stern features, partially obscuring the gleam of habitual menace in his fierce eyes.

Of course, this greatly enhanced the interest previously felt in the rendition. Polk and Hardee gave way to unrestrained laughter, and Cheatham fairly roared his enjoyment.

The doctor, encouraged by the redoubled merriment which he construed to be a tribute to the excellence of his performance, exerted himself all the more strenuously; but suddenly turning found himself confronted with the grim old martinet. He stopped as if he had been shot through the heart and staggered back to the wall.

"Go on, doctor," said Bragg, "don't let me interrupt you. It is certainly entertaining and doubtless quite accurate."

But the doctor wouldn't go on; and never, I have reason to believe, repeated the performance.

Of the ministers of all sects and denominations whom I have known in Louisville it is impossible to speak too highly. Among them were several eminent divines, and all of them excellent, devout and earnest men, striving to conform their own lives to the religious tenets they taught and zealous in the work of charity and humanity.

The names of some of them have been widely known and are held in reverence by thousands who never saw them. Drs. Stuart Robinson and John A. Broaddus were the most famous of these divines as preachers and writers; but Edward P. Humphrey, Samuel R. Wilson, Wm. H. Whitsett, James P. Boyce, Basil Manly, and Charles Craik were scarcely less distinguished and as greatly loved.

For many years the Presbyterians of Kentucky were sorely perturbed in spirit by the controversies, ever waxing warmer, between Dr. Stuart Robinson and Dr. Robert J. Breckinridge. Each was an ecclesiastical Titan, with the ability and spirit of a pontiff, and neither could well brook a divided sovereignty. In the extremity of polemical fervour, Dr. Breckinridge finally declared:

"There can be no harmony in the Presbyterian church until the Almighty in his mercy has taken me to Heaven, or, in His wisdom, has sent Stuart Robinson back to Ireland."

They were also antagonistic in political sentiment; Doctor Breckinridge was an intense Union man; Doctor Robinson an ardent Southern man. During the war the latter was compelled to leave Kentucky. He would probably have preferred to go South and fight in the Confederate ranks; but as this, however consonant with his inclination, was scarcely compatible with his sacred calling and advanced age, he went to Canada; but never lowered his colours or suffered his controversial batteries to be silenced.

I cannot forbear especial mention of one of these pious and estimable men, not only because in eloquence and in every exalted quality, he was among the foremost, but also because he was the first playmate and friend of my earliest boyhood. I made Thomas U. Dudley's acquaintance at Richmond, Va., so long ago that the memory of man runneth hardly to the contrary; that is to say, it is nearly threescore and ten years since we were at school together when neither was quite five years old. Neither, I think, made much progress in academic study at that time, but we learned to like each other very much and the warm friendship then formed continued until his death.

As bishop of the Episcopal diocese of Kentucky, he evinced the same brave and zealous spirit he had shown as a soldier, and was no less loved and regarded as gentleman than as divine.

If I were attempting to write a history of Louisville, rather than making only brief mention of certain individuals of whom my personal recollections are especially distinct, I might say a great deal about the merchants, bankers, and leading business men who were prominent in all affairs when I became a citizen of the place, and for years afterward. Very many of them were as well known and held in as high repute throughout the South as at home. Those best remembered, perhaps, by the people of Louisville, are James Guthrie, Virgil McKnight, H. D. Newcomb, James W. Henning, H. A. Griswold, Joshua F. Speed, William Garvin, John P. Morton, Archibald A. Gordon, Samuel L. Avery, Abram D. Hunt, Grandison Spratt, Richard Knott, Thomas L. Barrett, James S. Bridgeford, James S. Lithgow, John T. Barbee, Nathan Bloom, R. A. and John M. Robinson, Wm. B. and Samuel S. Hamilton and Albert Fink.

They were all men of exceptional intelligence, business capacity, and integrity, and of strong, positive character, and each left his impress upon the community. Joshua F. Speed was probably Mr. Lincoln's closest and most trusted personal friend; James Guthrie's reputation was national; Albert Fink's writings upon railway economics have been accepted as authority in Europe as well as in America.

One of the contemporaries of those I have just named yet lives to enjoy the esteem and affection of his fellow-citizens. In his eighty-sixth year, Col. Reuben T. Durrett maintains the mental vigour of his earlier manhood, and still pursues, with undiminished interest, the studious and intelligent inquiry which has made his contributions to the history of the Ohio Valley so valuable and has furnished much of the material successfully and judiciously used by other writers. The Filson Club —so named in honour of John Filson, the first historian of Kentucky and friend and companion of Boone — was founded in 1884 by Colonel Durrett, and under his direction has done excellent and widely recognized work.

If I should fail to speak of another club of somewhat like kind — the Salmagundi — established in Louisville nearly forty years since and still in existence, I might justly be deemed ungrateful and inappreciative, because of the unusual pleasure so frequently afforded me by its sessions and its suppers.

The Salmagundi Club could — and can — be scarcely termed an historical society, inasmuch as its members have always been averse to the constraint imposed by canons of accuracy, even although so liberally construed as those of history are sometimes asserted to be. It was even hinted that in its graver discussions more than one disputant was accustomed to invent history in such fashion and quantity as the exigencies of his contention demanded. That sort of thing, however, is so common that it should not greatly impair the credit of even a professedly scientific association, far less of one intended chiefly for amusement.

Nor was it any more entitled to be called a literary club, for the reason that it permitted the same liberties to be taken with literature. While characterized to some extent by both historical and literary features, it was more distinctively social; and although some special question for discussion was always selected for each night that its members assembled, the topics most frequently chosen were of current interest, and interpolation, therefore, of much local gossip was in order.

In short, debate in the Salmagundi has always been conducted with much the same latitude that renders it so pertinent in the Senate of the United States, no one being required to confine his remarks strictly to the subject matter of discussion. It can be readily understood how much of variety and occasional pungency can be thus secured.

Of course there are a number of other such clubs. Every city I suppose has a similar one; but I doubt if any has mustered a more congenial and entertaining membership; and when I recall the names of many — the brightest on the roll — who have passed over the river, I am comforted with the thought that age knows a saner pleasure in its memories than youth enjoys in its aspirations.

Two of these, Jouett Menifee and Prof. Jason W. Chenault, were especially esteemed while living and are especially remembered by their surviving confrères. The former was the son of a Kentuckian, who, dying in early manhood, had yet achieved success so distinguished as lawyer and politician that the Whigs of Kentucky looked to him as the successor, in party leadership, of Mr. Clay. He was the grandson of the eminent and gifted painter, Matthew Jouett. Inheriting the artistic temperament of his grandsire, and much of the talent, although nothing of the professional inclinations, of his father, he possessed, in uncommon degree, those qualities which attract love and confidence in private life, and had the nature which seems to make friends without effort and never to excite envy or enmity.

Although never in public life, Professor Chenault was widely known and no one was more highly esteemed. He was a man of strong, although not particularly active mind, of useful attainments and recognized scholarship, and an exceedingly entertaining and instructive companion. Earnest, faithful, and capable, no man in Kentucky or the South, perhaps, did better educational work.

Every man, I suppose, who contrasts his habit of thought in age with that which characterized him in youth, will realize what a change he has undergone in his general views of life. The different light in which we regarded events when we were in their midst and striving to influence them, from that in which we view them now that they are accomplished, may be likened to the changed aspect in which, after the sun has risen, a traveller sees the landscape through which he has made his way by the dimmer rays of the moon.

My own life has been comparatively uneventful — at any rate from the point of view of more ambitious compatriots—inasmuch as I have rarely held public office, nor, personally, been much in the political "swim." Nevertheless I have witnessed many events which have appeared to me remarkable and which, if not important, have yet been significant of the strange progress, the blended incertitude and, if I may use such term, logic, of human affairs. Unlike the Psalmist, I have more than once seen "the seed of the righteous," if not exactly begging his bread, at least sadly in lack of it. But in almost every such instance there was reason to believe that it was because the fault or incapacity of the son was greater than the merit of the father. While never inclined to fatalism, for the reason that the least intelligence or independence of spirit should require a man to reject a creed which induces blind submission to events, rather than constant opposition to what seems wrong and consistent struggle for that which seems right, I have learned to believe in a Providence which, while it may not always direct, often overrules human effort and shapes events to far better effect than human intelligence or human purpose, unaided, can accomplish. I have become convinced that there is something which, in some way, ever "worketh for righteousness," and that, when human passion and selfishness have wrought their utmost, there intervenes a power which usually in unexpected fashion furnishes a corrective.

There seems to be a force latent in the moral constitution of mankind, like that which, we are told, exists in the physical nature of the individual man, that tends to throw off disease. We seldom see what we may consider complete retribution for evil inflicted in individual cases, but we often see it visited by society on classes of offenders; and while not nearly so many of the malefactors are disposed of as we might wish, the evil itself is often destroyed.

Experience is proverbially the best school for a certain class of individuals, and my experience during the latter years of a rather long life has taught me, I trust, a certain practical philosophy; enough to afford in some degree the sort of consolation one needs in declining age. It has taught me, at least, to believe that the old man who will look back upon the past with vision as clear as human passion will permit human judgment, can, unless his life has been clouded with more than the common share of sorrow and misfortune, see much more that it is pleasant to remember than it is necessary to regret. Grief for those he has loved and lost is his sorest trial; but time dulls the sting of distant bereavement, and he learns to regard the more recent as inevitable, and knows that it can only for a brief period afflict him. The disappointments of life should seem trivial to one whose own life is nearly over, and his hope remains for those who are to succeed him when it is no longer a personal incentive.

Unless a man has been very unlucky or cursed with an extremely unhappy disposition, he can reckon, among the people he has known, more of those he once esteemed his enemies, but with whom he has been reconciled, than of former friends from whom he has become estranged. I have always found the Christian forgiveness which requires us to love those who really despitefully use us exceedingly rare in all Christian communities; but the common-sense and good temper which suggest a condonation of offence hastily offered, or injury not serious, perhaps even unintentional, should be expected of every man of ordinary brain and not abnormal conceit.

It is extremely trying to be obliged to relinquish opinions long tenaciously held or surrender even a cherished prejudice, but circumstances sometimes compel such sacrifices.

Indeed the perversity of a majority may occasionally force us to an entire change of base in order to escape some incredible and some unstomachable heresy. Nevertheless it is well to bear in mind that even those who disagree with us may possibly be right and, at any rate, in the absence of convincing reasons to the contrary, are entitled to think so.

It is always a sad day for the elderly citizen when he must abandon, as no longer tenable or tolerated, that belief in his own personal infallibility which the average man at some time entertains, secretly perhaps, but as absolutely as does His Holiness Himself; when he realizes that he, also, has been an object of commiseration because of that very self-confidence he deplores in others; but it must come. If he be wise, he may find in this change of mental life a mental regeneration and even learn to love adopted ideas and opinions almost as well as he formerly did his own.

The longer a man lives, the more thoroughly he becomes convinced that the great majority of his fellow-men would prefer to do what is right although — paradoxical as it may sound — they are not particularly concerned whether or not they think what is right; and a great deal of noisy utterance of very fantastic theory may be given slight contradiction, so long as it finds no expression in dangerous conduct.

But the hardest lesson that age has to learn is to acknowledge, with becoming modesty, the superiority of all that is modern; to abandon querulous and unavailing protest, and listen in seemly deference to the inspired *dicta* of youth. It is a severe strain on the feeble senile comprehension, but sooner or later we must realize that experience, wheresoever gathered and however valuable, *per se*, to the septuagenarian who has it, possesses no negotiable quality or exchangeable value, and will not pass current translated into advice or admonition.

All things have moved so rapidly and so far in the last half century that experience of the oracular brand seems to have been left out of sight. Brief time is required to render any idea, in a measure, obsolete. The first battle of the Civil War is farther removed from us by lapse of time than is Waterloo from that battle; yet the men of the Civil War and the men who fought at Waterloo were, probably, more like in thought and sentiment to those who dwelt in medieval Europe than to the men of this generation.

The world rushes along the path of progress with greater velocity than the earth whirls in its annual orbit, and innovations come quicker than the years. The invention which surprised us yesterday seems simple compared with the one which startles us to-day. The most elaborate scientific work, written a year ago, is regarded as stale and of slight authority if it conflicts with the latest magazine article on the same subject; and that will, in turn, be superseded by another to appear next month.

Why then should youth listen to age? How can the ancients instruct the moderns? Especially when modern information is supplemented by modern intuition. How can one who grew to manhood at a time when people yet rode to church on horseback, possibly hope to teach the ethereal intelligence which soars seven thousand feet nearer to Heaven in an aeroplane?

No! Let age gracefully recognize its limitations and try to be happy. Content with the past and its recollections, and with no pretense that we can enlighten our juniors, we will admit as candidly, if as sadly, as did the Knight of La Mancha when cured of his illusions, that, "The birds of this year are not found in last year's nests."

OTHER
COOPER SQUARE PRESS
TITLES OF INTEREST

ON CAMPAIGN WITH
THE ARMY OF THE POTOMAC
The Civil War Journal
of Theodore Ayrault Dodge
Edited by Stephen W. Sears
304 pp., 11 b/w illustrations
0-8154-1030-1
$29.95 cloth

THE FINAL INVASION
Plattsburgh, the War of 1812's
Most Decisive Battle
Colonel David G. Fitz-Enz
320 pp., 50 b/w illustrations
0-8154-1139-1
$28.95 cloth

THE SELECTED LETTERS OF
THEODORE ROOSEVELT
Edited by H. W. Brands
464 pp., 20 b/w photos &
illustrations
0-8154-1126-X
$29.95 cloth

WOLFE AT QUEBEC
The Man Who Won the French
and Indian War
Christopher Hibbert
208 pp., 1 b/w illustration,
4 b/w maps
0-8154-1016-6
$15.95

THE WAR OF 1812
Henry Adams
New introduction by
Col. John R. Elting
377 pp., 27 b/w maps & sketches
0-8154-1013-1
$18.95

MEMOIRS OF MY LIFE AND TIMES
John Charles Fremont
New introduction by
Charles M. Robinson III
696 pp., 89 b/w illustrations
0-8154-1164-2
$24.95

THE STORY OF THE OUTLAW
A Study of the Western Desperado
Emerson Hough
New introduction by
Larry D. Underwood
400 pp., 18 b/w illustrations
0-8154-1168-5
$18.95

HISTORY OF THE CONQUEST OF MEXICO &
HISTORY OF THE CONQUEST OF PERU
William H. Prescott
1,330 pp., 2 maps
0-8154-1004-2
$32.00

Available at bookstores
or call 1-800-462-6420

150 Fifth Avenue ♦ Suite 817 ♦ New York, NY 10011